*This Is Enlightenment*

# THIS IS ENLIGHTENMENT

EDITED BY CLIFFORD SISKIN
& WILLIAM WARNER

The University of Chicago Press   Chicago and London

CLIFFORD SISKIN is the Henry W. and Alfred A. Berg Professor of English and American Literature at New York University and the director of The Re:Enlightenment Project at New York University and the New York Public Library.
WILLIAM WARNER is professor of English at the University of California, Santa Barbara.

The University of Chicago Press, Chicago 60637
The University of Chicago Press, Ltd., London
© 2010 by The University of Chicago
All rights reserved. Published 2010
Printed in the United States of America

19 18 17 16 15 14 13 12 11 10    1 2 3 4 5

ISBN-13: 978-0-226-76147-3 (cloth)
ISBN-13: 978-0-226-76148-0 (paper)
ISBN-10: 0-226-76147-9 (cloth)
ISBN-10: 0-226-76148-7 (paper)

Part of Ian Baucom's essay appeared in *States of Emergency: The Object of American Studies*, edited by Russ Castronovo and Susan Gillman. Copyright © 2009 by the University of North Carolina Press. Used by permission of the publisher. http://www.uncpress.unc.edu.

A version of Michael McKeon's essay originally appeared in *Eighteenth-Century Novel 6–7* (2009): 197–259. Reprinted with permission of AMS Press, Inc. Copyright © 2009 AMS Press, Inc. All rights reserved.

The University of Chicago Press gratefully acknowledges the generous support of the Faculty of the Humanities at the Norwegian University of Science and Technology and The Abraham and Rebecca Stein Faculty Publications Fund of the Department of English of New York University toward the publication of this book.

Library of Congress Cataloging-in-Publication Data

This is enlightenment / edited by Clifford Siskin and William Warner.
    p. cm.
Includes bibliographical references and index.
ISBN-13: 978-0-226-76147-3 (cloth : alk. paper)
ISBN-13: 978-0-226-76148-0 (pbk. : alk. paper)
ISBN-10: 0-226-76147-9 (cloth : alk. paper)
ISBN-10: 0-226-76148-7 (pbk.)
 1. Enlightenment—Congresses. 2. Communication—History—18th century—Congresses. 3. Communication in learning and scholarship—History—18th century—Congresses. 4. Mass media—History—18th century—Congresses. I. Siskin, Clifford. II. Warner, William, 1954–
B802.T468 2010
190.9′033—dc22
2010000873

♾ The paper used in this publication meets the minimum requirements of the American National Standard for Information Sciences—Permanence of Paper for Printed Library Materials, ANSI Z39.48-1992.

We dedicate this book to the memory of

YNGVE SANDHEI JACOBSEN

who disappeared on a hike in the Sunndal Mountains of Norway in August 2008. Yngve was a talented young scholar, a true friend, a creative and stimulating colleague, and one of the instigators of *This Is Enlightenment*. We, as friends and colleagues, mourn his loss. We are glad to be able to keep something of him within the covers of this book.

CONTENTS

Acknowledgments                                                          xi

This Is Enlightenment: An Invitation in the Form of an Argument           1
CLIFFORD SISKIN AND WILLIAM WARNER

· · · · ·

MEDIATION: A CONCEPT IN HISTORY

Enlightening Mediation                                                   37
JOHN GUILLORY

Where Were the Media before the Media?
Mediating the World at the Time of Condillac and Linnaeus                64
KNUT OVE ELIASSEN AND YNGVE SANDHEI JACOBSEN

Mediation and the Division of Labor                                      87
PETER DE BOLLA

Transmitting Liberty: The Boston Committee of Correspondence's
Revolutionary Experiments in Enlightenment Mediation                    102
WILLIAM WARNER

Modes and Codes: Samuel F.B. Morse and
the Question of Electronic Writing                                      120
LISA GITELMAN

## ENLIGHTENMENT: EVIDENCE AND EVENTS

Mediating Information, 1450–1800     139
ANN BLAIR AND PETER STALLYBRASS

Mediated Enlightenment: The System of the World     164
CLIFFORD SISKIN

Romanticism, Enlightenment, and Mediation:
The Case of the Inner Stranger     173
ROBERT MILES

The Present of Enlightenment: Temporality and Mediation
in Kant, Foucault, and Jean Paul     189
HELGE JORDHEIM

The Strange Light of Postcolonial Enlightenment:
Mediatic Form and Publicity in India     209
ARVIND RAJAGOPAL

## PROLIFERATION: MEDIATION AND PRINT

Mediating Media Past and Present: Toward a Genealogy
of "Print Culture" and "Oral Tradition"     229
PAULA MCDOWELL

Mediating Antiquarians in Britain, 1760–1830:
The Invention of Oral Tradition, or, Close Reading before Coleridge     247
MAUREEN MCLANE

Mediating *le philosophe*: Diderot's Strategic Self-Representations     265
ANNE FASTRUP

Novel Knowledge: Judgment, Experience, Experiment     284
JOHN BENDER

The Piratical Enlightenment     301
ADRIAN JOHNS

## EFFECTS: EMERGENT PRACTICES

Financing Enlightenment, Part One: Money Matters     323
MARY POOVEY

Financing Enlightenment, Part Two: Extraordinary Expenditure     336
IAN BAUCOM

"The Horrifying Ties, from which the Public Order Originates":
The Police in Schiller and Mercier     357
BERNHARD SIEGERT

The Preacher's Footing     368
MICHAEL WARNER

Mediation as Primal Word: The Arts, the Sciences,
and the Origins of the Aesthetic     384
MICHAEL MCKEON

· · · · ·

Notes     413

References     439

List of Contributors     475

Index     479

ACKNOWLEDGMENTS

This book is the product of years of collaboration across two continents. A host of conferences—in Santa Barbara, under the aegis of the University of California Digital Cultures Project, on "Interfacing Knowledge," "Copyright and the Networked Computer," and "Digital Retroaction"; in Sheffield, England, on "Scenes of Writing"; in Trondheim, Norway, on "Literature, Technology, Imagination"; and in Stirling, Scotland, on "Textual Cultures"—led in 2007 to the event that generated this volume and its argument: a conference at New York University (NYU) entitled "Mediating Enlightenment Past and Present." As we go to press, our ventures together continue in the form of The Re:Enlightenment Project—an effort both to pursue our inquiries into Enlightenment and the history of mediation—and to put what we have learned to work in the world. The publication of *This Is Enlightenment* in spring 2010 will coincide with the Project's first public "Exchange," "Futures for Knowledge and Institutions" at the New York Public Library.

Conceptual and material support for the 2007 conference came from our Norwegian colleagues. Knut Ove Eliassen not only suggested that we focus on the notion of "mediating Enlightenment," he also became cosponsor of the event. We would like to express our deep gratitude to the Faculty of the Humanities at the Norwegian University of Science and Technology for their generous contributions at two key stages of our work. Their financial support played a crucial role in the success of the conference and in the publication of this volume.

We are grateful as well for the intellectual and financial support of Richard Foley, dean of the School of Arts and Science at NYU. Together with President John Sexton, he has transformed the university through a creative burst of hiring and the encouragement of new disciplinary constellations. Thanks as well to former NYU trustee Kevin R. Brine for his role in that transformation. Financial support for the conference came from across NYU, including Jane Tylus, director of the Humanities Initiative, and Deans Catharine R. Stimpson, George W. Downs, Edward J. Sullivan, and Matthew S. Santirocco. Eileen Bowman, on loan from the Institute for the History of the Production of Knowledge, was a superb conference coordinator. Professors Mary Poovey, Paula McDowell, and John Guillory of NYU's English department constituted the local organizing committee. The department provided valuable support for both the conference and, through its Abraham and Rebecca Stein Faculty Publications Fund, the publication of this volume.

Yohei Igarashi and Seth Rudy, doctoral students in English, were our editorial assistants for this volume. From bibliographic and proofreading work to their insights into essays to their courage in facing the logistical nightmare of coordinating multiple files from so many authors, their efforts were extraordinary. Our gratitude is correspondingly deep.

Alan Thomas's ideas regarding the role of the polemical in contemporary scholarship put the argument of *This Is Enlightenment* on track, and his later critiques kept it there. Thanks also to Chicago's Randy Petilos for helping us to navigate the complexities of illustrations and copyrights and to Maia Rigas for her copyediting skills and patience.

Finally, Cliff would like to thank Leslie Santee Siskin for mediating when and where it counts—in the world of ideas we share professionally and in private moments of loss and cheer. Bill would like to thank Elizabeth MacArthur, a joyful intellectual companion and a scholar of the French Enlightenment in her own right, for exacting, but always invaluable, criticism of this project.

*Clifford Siskin and William Warner*
*New York and Santa Barbara, 2009*

# THIS IS ENLIGHTENMENT

## AN INVITATION IN THE FORM OF AN ARGUMENT

CLIFFORD SISKIN AND WILLIAM WARNER

"What is Enlightenment?"

*Sometimes, Francis Bacon observed, "a question remains a mere question" for "centuries."*[1] *"Mediating Enlightenment Past and Present," an international conference organized by Clifford Siskin at New York University, with William Warner in California and Knut Ove Eliassen in Norway, sought answers to many questions about Enlightenment. We now invite you to find them—in abundance—in the individual essays in this volume. However, to our surprise, the conference as a whole also yielded a collective answer to the big question— the centuries-old question quoted above. We suspect that many of you assume that there cannot be a single answer to such a query, except, perhaps, the self-reflexive one: Enlightenment is what asks itself what it is. And we recognize that others have argued that there are many Enlightenments or none at all. But, in the spirit of Enlightenment conversation, we offer the collected efforts of our colleagues, as well as our own framing introduction, as evidence for a very different answer:*

Enlightenment is an event in the history of mediation.

*We will begin by recovering that history, for our place in it is the reason that the time for this answer has, we think, finally come.*

## Part One: This Is Enlightenment

The first step to a timely answer is to establish the timeliness of the question—and that does appear, at first glance, to be a very straightforward matter. "What is Enlightenment?" first came to the fore as the eighteenth century drew to a close. In 1783, that query echoed in the meeting halls of secret societies and in the periodical press in Germany.[2] Posed in a footnote to an essay published in December in the *Berlinische Monatsschrift*, it elicited responses the next year from Moses Mendelssohn and Immanuel Kant. With that exchange a conversation started that has now dominated inquiries into Enlightenment for over two hundred years. Their characteristic feature is a two-step movement back to Kant's moment and then forward into discussions of Enlightenment's purchase on the present. But is the moment a question was first posed still the best place to look for an answer? This is a particularly pressing issue in regard to Enlightenment, since the decade of the 1780s is a black hole for our standard periodizations of European history—the moment that elicited Kant's claim that it was an "*age of enlightenment*"[3] and our subsequent consensus that this same moment marked the end of the historical Enlightenment and the onset of another (Romantic) age.

Our first step, then, is to step back. We turn to the more distant past to gain some perspective on Kant's claims. Four hundred years ago, in 1605, Francis Bacon performed for an earlier age what Kant did for his: he polemically addressed the current state of knowledge. Bacon's call for a "Great Renewal" put knowledge under pressure—the pressure to "advance." When Kant gave his own report less than two centuries later, however, he changed the subject, putting "man" under pressure to do the same thing: it was time now, Kant announced in 1784, for men to advance from "self-incurred tutelage" into "general enlightenment." The label "enlightenment" has stuck with us in part because Kant gave "us" such a central role in it. From its opening paragraph, Kant's "Answer to the Question: What Is Enlightenment?" is user-friendly, offering a "motto" rather than a formal definition. Instead of a mystery to be dispelled—"What is it?"—Enlightenment became a practice to be followed: "Do this!" The motto tells us how—subliming Baconian pressure on knowledge into a direct challenge to the self adapted from Horace: "*Sapere aude!*" (Dare to know!).

Since self-help manuals target the future and not the past—they point us forward rather than back—it is not surprising that generations of readers have ignored Kant's differences with Bacon. The focus in "What is Enlightenment" on what to do next, from the politics of living under Frederick II to the imperative to develop, has from the start kept its audience facing in the same direction. Whether with regret or admiration, readers to the present day have seen Kant's motto as a signpost to modernity, turning Enlightenment into a precursor to be blamed or celebrated.

Foucault, for example, turned to Kant's essay again and again as a touchstone for defining his own project. Although he stressed the historical specificity of Kant's response—"The Prussian newspaper was basically asking, 'What just happened to us?'" (Foucault 2007, 121)—Foucault, too, did not hesitate to treat Kant's "us" and his arguments as preludes to the present. Our modern habit of self-reflexivity, he declared, dates from Kant's strategy of "deporting the question of the *Aufklärung* into critique": the "critical project whose intent was to allow knowledge to acquire an adequate idea of itself" (67).[4]

In what we might call, then, a long revolution of knowledge under pressure—of efforts to renew and advance from Bacon to Foucault—Kant's 1784 user manual for Enlightenment falls, precisely, in the middle. But can it tell us about the past as well as the present—about Enlightenment not as anticipating us but as the historical event that precipitated the very question Kant was supposed to answer? The motto itself was, in fact, a turn to the past, not just to Horace, but to Germany earlier in the century. "Sapere aude!" had been foregrounded in German philosophical discussion since the Society for the Friends of Truth adopted it as their motto in 1736 (Kant 2007, 37). What is most telling about Kant's use of the phrase, then, is not that he chose it but how he translated it into German: "Habe Muth dich deines *eigenen* Verstandes zu bedienen!" (Have courage to use your own reason!). The translation is an elaboration that raises issues that are not a necessary part of the original. Kant recasts "Daring to know" as a problem of having the courage to use one's own understanding. When first printed, "eigenen" (own) was in bold, an emphasis that anticipated the essay's later turn to the *political* matter of obeying Frederick. That is one reason that Horace's "dare" became, in Kant, a matter of individual courage.

But was politics—"managing freedom" (Kant 2007, 37)—the only danger raised by man's *Verstand*, his "understanding"? Or was there a more fundamental concern? Did the very act of using it pose a risk—not necessarily to the user but to the desired result—to "knowing?" Here is where a turn to the past, rather than to our present, can illuminate what was at stake in Kant's formulation. The opening words of Bacon's *Great Instauration* provide the startling counterpoint: he writes because he "believ[es] that the human understanding creates difficulties for itself" (Bacon 1994, 3). This is the premise of Bacon's entire project: you should *not* depend on your own understanding. Such dependence is not a courageous act but an irresponsible one, a willful decision to ignore the track record of "stak[ing] everything on the mind's endless and aimless activity" (Bacon 2000, 27). It is for this reason, Bacon argues, that we need "a complete *Instauration* of the arts and sciences and all the learning of mankind" (Bacon 1994, 3–4). In the enterprise of knowing nature, sticking to your "own" is the problem, not the solution: "[F]rom the very start, the mind should not be left to itself, but be constantly controlled; and the business done (if I may put it this way) by machines" (Bacon 2000, 28).

What changed between Bacon and Kant is nowhere more evident than in the ways they used the word "machine." To push his readers into taking the dare, Kant ends *What Is Enlightenment?* with a before and after of what they will become: if they use their own reason, "men" will be "more than machines" (Kant 2007, 37). This binary—man versus machine—became, of course, a staple of modernity and thus another barrier to our thinking of Enlightenment in terms that precede Kant's courageous selves. In Bacon, those terms are radically different: machines are not what we don't want to *be*; they are the means for men to *do* what they should be doing—making "advances worthy of mankind" (Bacon 1994, 8).

"Machine" is one word in a cluster of terms that reappears again and again in Bacon: "aids," "assistance," "means," "instruments," and "tools"—the last two words being the most common translations of the term enshrined in the title of the second part of the *Great Instauration: The New Organon*. Bacon describes that part as the "digested" version of what renewal requires, since it consists largely of aphorisms, but, for our present purposes, it can be digested even further: "Men need tools."

Without tools, Bacon argued, "we would have the situation we have had for many centuries, that the sciences are almost stopped in their tracks, and show no developments worthy of the human race" (Bacon 2000, 7). Knowledge has stalled—and for an "utterly obvious" reason:

> If men had tackled mechanical tasks with their bare hands and without the help and power of tools, as they have not hesitated to handle intellectual tasks with little but the bare force of their intellects, there would surely be very few things indeed which they could move and overcome, no matter how strenuous and united their efforts.

Whether moving a "heavy obelisk" or "advancing" knowledge, daring to depend on one's own strength or one's own understanding was not courageous, but an "act of utter lunacy" (Bacon 2000, 28–29).

Sanity, for Bacon, then, is accepting the necessity of tools—tools that work. The "Organon" must be "New" because the "errors which have grown powerful with age" resist correction by the "native force of the understanding," even when that force is reinforced by the "help and assistance of logic." In fact, Bacon asserts, the old Organon—the collective title traditionally given to Aristotle's works on logic—only "keeps and accumulates" "faulty" things. The syllogisms and dialectic of Scholasticism produce "a kind of giddiness, a perpetual agitation and going in a circle" (Bacon 2000, 2).

Bacon's new instruments, in contrast, are about control and "restraint" as a means of "open[ing] and construct[ing] a new and certain road for the mind from the actual perceptions of the senses." Some of those instruments were what we would now consider the equipment of the "actual"— of observation and demonstration—objects such as bottles, bladders, bells, scales (Bacon 2000, xiv–xvii). But the new instrument of "control" was not a physical thing but rules for the "road": a "method" to supplant Aristotelian logic. For Bacon, method was a "machine" for getting the mind's "business done" (Bacon 2000, 28).

His particular method, induction, has won Bacon a prominent place in the history of science. But we should not forget that it was only part of the solution to a larger problem: how to renew all knowledge. Induction itself was but one kind of method, and method was but one kind of tool, and tools were important because knowledge could never be direct: knowing required tooling. The problem of renewal—of why knowledge stalled and what to do about it—was thus fundamentally for Bacon a problem of "mediation." We use "mediation" here in its broadest sense[5] as shorthand for the work done by tools, by what we would now call "media" of every kind—everything that intervenes, enables, supplements, or is simply in between—emphasizing the Baconian stipulation that media of some kind are always at work.

Yes, Bacon is famous for pairing knowledge and power, not knowledge and mediation. And, yes, the link to power does explain why knowledge is useful—"ignorance of cause frustrates effect" (Bacon 2000, 33)—and induction does tell us how to get our hands on it. But the "renewal" was not a static problem in logic and method; it was a problem in history, and by casting knowledge as necessarily mediated, Bacon found a way to identify and articulate change: mediation was always necessary but the forms of mediation differ over time. There is a history of mediation.

The differences illuminated in that history allowed Bacon to plot a new relationship to the past. Rather than rehearsing yet again the already tortured classical distinction between *episteme* and *technê*, the imperative of mediation mixed knowledge and tools, theory and practice. And since retooling produced historically different ways of knowing, Bacon could choose the "happy" option of "carry[ing] out our design without touching or diminishing the honour and reverence due to the ancients." New tools, he argued, opened for him a "way to the intellect" that the ancients simply did not have. Ancient versus modern was thus not a "contest" but history—a history that told of Bacon's good fortune in living in a moment of different "resources" than they did (Bacon 2000, 29).

The renewal, then, was historically specific. Since knowledge always required mediation and the forms of mediation were mutable, every historical moment was potentially a moment of change. But Bacon's project insisted on a hierarchy of change: there were moments of renewal, and there was an opportunity for a "Great Renewal"—the magnitude generated by the temporal conjunction of more new resources and more frustration with the old ones. In his time, Bacon observed, the "mechanical arts grow and improve every day" while the "received kinds of learning" are "barren of results, full of questions; slow and feeble in improvement" (Bacon 2000, 7–8).

What made this particular conjunction special—high up, that is, in the hierarchy of change—were what Bacon called three "mechanical things" with recent origins. Together, Bacon argued, they "have changed the face and condition of things all over the globe": "the art of printing, gunpowder and the nautical compass." More than "soil, climate or bodily qualities," these things, Bacon believed, made the difference he perceived between "civilized" Europe and "barbarous" New India. In his history, the most powerful "empire" had less purchase on the present than this trio of mechanical mediations; they set the stage for the new intellectual mediations of the *Instauration* (Bacon 2000, 100).

Bacon used the word "mediation" repeatedly throughout his oeuvre, usually in reference to divine and human intercession. In their invaluable prehistory of the term "media" in this volume, Knut Ove Eliassen and Yngve Jacobsen point as well to his frequent use of "medium" as a term for a generating or connecting substance or milieu (e.g., water is a "medium" for sound). Their essay tracks the changes in this cluster of words between past and present—between Bacon's moment of "renewal" and our current experience of change. Faced with a similarly disruptive mix of new tools and new frustrations with old ones, we have been expanding the cluster. Certain tools have become known as "media," "mass media," and "the media," and we now have a term, "remediation," that describes what they do to each other.

With a venerable past and expanding purchase on the present, "mediation" can bring a new history to bear on our efforts to understand Enlightenment. More are needed, for every kind of history foregrounds certain things and obscures others. The history of science, for example, has spotlighted "induction," and "power" has itself been empowered within the progress narratives of the nation-state. In similar fashion, Kant's siren call of the "self" continues to be amplified by the "historical" and "critical" "ontolog[ies]" described by Foucault. We have used "mediation" here to steer us past that call to Bacon's call for renewal, opening up a new perspective on what happened in between. Enlightenment, we argue, was an event in the history of mediation.

Pursuing this claim is not just a matter of locating Enlightenment against a static backdrop of mediation(s), for "mediation" is itself a moving target—from Bacon's centering of tools to our expanding semantic cluster. How did it become what Peter de Bolla calls in this volume a "load-bearing concept?" In John Guillory's formulation, this entailed a crucial "convergence" of "medium" and "communication." His essay blocks out with great care the movements of the supporting actors in this play of concepts: the intimacies of speech and persuasion yielding center stage to the distance technologies of writing and print.

Taking the "distance" of communication as the "indispensable condition" of our modern concept of mediation, Guillory offers it as an alternative to "the dominance of representation in Western thought." Unlike representation, mediation can "capture" the "hidden complexity of the process" it has for so long purported to describe—particularly the issue of "'in what' form a representation is transmitted." This is where we should hear Bacon leading the way: on what besides our "own" selves should we rely? What do our tools do to what we do?[6] Unfortunately, as Guillory points out, these concerns have been lost yet again in the many versions of "media theory" that habitually "collapse the mediations performed by the media back into representations" in order "more easily to sustain the project of ideology critique."

To break that habit, cold turkey, we must start the moment we first repeat Kant's question, for asking What is Enlightenment? again, and yet again, turns Enlightenment into a problem of representation—into something that is guilty from the get-go of being hard to find and easy to judge. And the more times we pose the question, the more the mystery deepens: When did Enlightenment occur? Where did it occur? Did it really occur at all? On the slippery slope of Enlightenment studies, the turn to what Guillory calls "complexity" is more like simplicity itself: just juggle a few words and ask, "Occurred *in* what?"

Now that is a question with some answers. For Kant, Mendelssohn, and others in the 1780s, for example, Enlightenment was *in* the newspapers and magazines; it was, as Foucault slyly put it, "a current event," something "familiar and diffused which was in the process of happening and of going away" (Foucault 2007, 80, 121). But as the immediacy of the event faded, so too did knowledge of the forms of mediation that were central to it—the "in what" gave way to an interpretative focus on philosophical content. In that mirror, Kant's "motto" has taken on monumental proportions. We no longer see "Aufklärung" as the subject of a local debate about life under Frederick II—the essay containing the footnote to which Mendelssohn and Kant responded was about the presence of clergy at marriage ceremonies (Schmidt 2007, 2)—but, in Foucault's words, as both "a singular event inaugurating European modernity" and "the permanent process which manifests itself in the history of reason" (93). Neither of these historic, rather than historical, Enlightenments speak directly to what had happened and in what. If we want to know, that is, how Enlightenment "manifest[ed]" itself as an "event," we need to know what other forms and practices—in addition to writing in periodicals—were involved.

Foucault's re-posing of Kant's question begins with a reference to periodicals and ends with an injunction to put "reflection to the test of concrete practices," but Enlightenment for him here and elsewhere remains primarily and crucially "a philosophical question" (97, 118–119, 93). To shift not only from the philosophical but to an actual answer to the question requires a history other than our Whig history of modernity, the history of Reason, or Foucault's governing rubric for his genealogies of practices, the "ontology of ourselves." We are indebted, of course, to those genealogies as themselves experiments—innovative efforts whose importance can be grasped anew within the rubric we are mounting here, the "history of mediation."

The practical advantages of this strategy can be clarified by comparing it to the two primary ways in which "Enlightenment" has been understood: as a period and as a thematic designation. The former too often begs the question of context: a period *of* what? If, for example, the period following Enlightenment is Romanticism—as it is in the developmental narratives of many nations—and Romanticism is most frequently understood as a literary/philosophical period, then is Enlightenment such a period, and in what nations? Thematic tagging, on the other hand, constructs context as a layering of "ideas," offering up Enlightenment as some kind of intellectual, or more broadly "cultural," movement. Among the many notorious problems with this approach[7] are the chronological problems generated by animating ideas with the requisite agency to change history on their own. Good historiographic intentions then fall victim to the Frankenstein syndrome: once you start them you can't stop them. They run amuck across national and other kind of boundaries, foraging in all directions across the history they were supposed to organize.

The Frankfurt school carried this hunter-gatherer style of intellectual history to its logical and absurd limit by starting with Bacon but then leaping all the way back to Homer's cunning Odysseus as the initial embodiment of the "instrumental reason" they used to identify Enlightenment—an idea that just as easily scurried forward in their horror movie to haunt modernity from Hitler to Hollywood to the present (Horkheimer and Adorno 1947). For those uncomfortable with such chronological excess, thematizing also stretches in the other direction. Instead of using one idea to extend a single Enlightenment across thousands of years, for example, it has also turned different ideas, within more conventional timeframes, into multiple Enlightenments.

Our primary purpose here, however, is not critique. These strategies have produced valuable knowledge and will produce more. We are seeking instead to take advantage of what could *not* be done before now. In Bacon's terms, we enjoy the historical good "fortune" of writing at a moment of new and powerful mechanical and intellectual mediations. Thanks to networked computers and expanding semantic clusters—such as "medium" into "media" and "remediation"—we think it is time to take two steps in a different direction. First, we have specified what our history is a history "of." Second, we will try to locate Enlightenment as an "event" in it.[8]

To engage something as an event is to direct attention to the possibility of its singularity—of an Enlightenment that doesn't dissolve into too many years, too many things, or too many versions of itself. And that singularity, by emphasizing contingency of time and place, links an event to the elements of which it is not the product but rather the effect (Foucault 2007, 64). The relationship of "effect," that is, allows us to establish the multiplicity *and* specificity of that contingency without sacrificing both to the reductive linearity of causality.

"Event" can thus give us the traction we need to avoid slip-sliding through history; it helps us to think more clearly about practical matters such as dates. When, for example, does Enlightenment begin and end? Since that particular label was applied more or less *retroactively* in different locations, its ongoing usefulness lies in improving the ways that we have already applied it. Better dating thus lies not in inventing new dates for Enlightenment but in coming to newly useful terms with old ones. Here is where turning back past Kant to Bacon pays off: it gives us room to work on those established markers. What may at first appear to be a puzzling gap between Bacon in the early seventeenth century and Enlightenment in its conventional home in the eighteenth is for us an opportunity to see what a history of mediation can do.[9]

The first thing it tells us is that we shouldn't be surprised. Our own experience with computing suggests that it takes time for tools and technologies to take hold—to mediate, that is, in the particular ways that we come to expect. But they do so only after assuming forms and functions that were not obvious, or even possible, when first introduced. To the now familiar timeline of the computer's long metamorphosis from Charles Babbage's programmed gears of the 1830s to the ENIAC's missile-targeting tubes of the 1940s to the iPhone, this volume adds Lisa Gitelman's often hilarious case study of how telegraphy morphed from a visual and writerly tool that used electricity to record messages on paper tape to an aural and speechlike medium for electronic communication.

*This Is Enlightenment* as a whole frames a long history of mediation—one that reaches back to 1450, in the arresting images and analysis of Ann Blair and Peter Stallybrass, and forward to twentieth-century India, in Arvind Rajagopal's turn to the modern mediations we know as advertising. Within that history, at its chronological core between Bacon and Kant, print took center stage. Its proliferation, through new forms and networks of mediation, is also a story of apparent delay in which the fifteenth-century technology of inscription—printing through the use of moveable type—took hundreds of years to implicate and modify an already existing media ecology of voice, sound, image, and manuscript writing. Bacon, as we have seen, recognized print's growing power and tried to capitalize on it.[10] However, his critique of Scholasticism, like his positive program, arrived linked to and dependent upon developments in the history of mediation that took almost a century to resolve.[11]

Print became central to that history not only because there was more of it, but also because it insinuated itself into other forms of mediation. To assert its prominence in these terms is thus not to downplay other forms of mediation, such as the visual. Instead, a history of mediation highlights the ways that the interrelated practices of writing, reading, and print informed those other forms—as when viewers began to "read" paintings and, increasingly, "write" about them.[12] And it helps us to avoid as well the debate that derails so many efforts to engage the power of print: since "mediation" embraces both the technological and the human—it does not discriminate, that is, against any particular form of agency—discussing print *in* its history points us past the increasingly unproductive binary of technodeterminism.

Where we can go instead is into more detail about how mediations of *all* kinds interact over time. A history of those interactions offers two other strategic differences from related modes of inquiry. First, we emphasize "all," because "mediation" is the inclusive term for the history we propose; it can include what we now call "media," but as our examples below demonstrate, it is not restricted to them. The history of mediation can thus engage "media history" and "media theory," but its wide range of objects, forms, technologies, agency, and interactions—and thus its chronological scope—differentiates it from both of those established enterprises.[13]

Second, since mediations can be more easily pinned down to specific times and places than "ideas,"[14] we can track more of them more accurately—and thus more readily identify patterns in those interactions. A history of mediation thus provides new—and newly useful—ways of thinking about change. We propose the following framework for locating Enlightenment in that history. For each of the three critical chronological markers we engage a particular kind of change:

1. To map the *"delay"* between Bacon and the conventional start of Enlightenment in the 1730s–1740s we project a historical hierarchy of mediations. It is historical in that it highlights certain forms of mediation as not inherently "better" but as enabling—in particular times and particular places—of others. In our elaboration below, we call those mediations *cardinal mediations.*
2. To identify Enlightenment as an *"event"*—one that conventionally occupies roughly a half century between the 1730s–1740s and the 1780s—we take a quantitative turn, focusing on the number as well as the kinds of mediation enabled by the early eighteenth century. Enlightenment emerged, we argue, as an effect of these *proliferating mediations.*
3. To understand how that event came to an *end*—and why it was at that same moment retroactively labeled by Kant's subject—we couple the concept of *saturation* to proliferation. Enlightenment, we argue, can be best understood not as failed, or interrupted by revolution or Romanticism, but as an event that was "successful" in two ways.[15] First, it performed as our label for it advertises: Enlightenment mediations produced change. Second, in detailing the effects of saturation on key mediations, we will show how Enlightenment contained the formal conditions for its own demise: in a strange way, it succeeded in ending itself.

Histories have their perks, and this one spares us more intellect-wasting custody battles over Enlightenment: "It's French, of course." "No, it's actually British." Grounded in specific mediations and yet yielding regularities, the history of mediation can clarify both the singularity of each local event *and* what those events have in common. Here we must settle for a very preliminary sketch, but one that does do double duty—mixing enough detail from one place (Britain) to convey local contours with sufficient specifics from elsewhere to suggest the shared features of a larger-scale event.

CARDINAL MEDIATIONS

When we focus on the historically specific ways in which mediations can enable each other, the "gap" between Bacon and the onset of Enlightenment becomes a window that frames four interconnected changes. All involve mediations that were new, or newly important, in the seventeenth and early eighteenth centuries. Taken together, these four changes—in infrastructure, genres and formats, associational practices, and protocols—establish the conditions for the possibility of Enlightenment.

- A *new infrastructure* formed to enable the transmission and communication of information. In 1600, Cardinal Duke Albrecht VII, viceroy of the Netherlands, granted the official postal system of the Holy Roman Empire, Taxis, permission to charge postage for private letters. Over the course of the seventeenth century a public postal system for private letters developed in efficiency and scope. The Royal Mail service was first made available to the public by Charles I in 1635 and the General Post Office (GPO) was officially established by Charles II in 1660. The British Postal Bill of 1710 established uniform postal rates throughout the British Empire. Postal transport was facilitated by the development of fixed mail routes, as well as the formation of private trusts to fund and administer the turnpikes (Laguero 1995). In addition to new tools for mediating motion, the second half of the seventeenth century also saw new forms for gathering in one place. Most prominently, the social lives of the generations after Bacon were altered by a steady increase in the number and kinds of public houses (coffeehouses, taverns, inns) where individuals could meet, read, discuss, and otherwise act out new forms of sociability and publicity. The first coffeehouse in Britain, for example, was started in 1652, with the number rising dramatically until by 1700 it is estimated that London had from several hundred to over 1,000 coffeehouses (Cowan 2005, 154).
- In this same period, *new genres and formats* were developed that extended the reach of print and speech and enabled more of both. Regularly published public newspapers began with the *London Gazette* (first published in 1665 as the *Oxford Gazette*). This was the first of a steadily increasing number of newspapers in Britain, Europe, and their colo-

nies. The newspapers not only provided much of the content that circulated through the new infrastructure of the post and turnpike, they also became a new interface for mediating the users' knowledge of events, opinions, and even the speech of public figures. Right at the turn into the eighteenth century, a raft of additional periodic genres appear and flourish, including the wildly popular periodical essays of Joseph Addison and Richard Steele's *The Spectator* (1711–1713) and the proliferation of party political papers (e.g., Daniel Defoe's *Review of the State of the British Nation* [1704–1713] and John Trenchard and Thomas Gordon's *Cato's Letters* [1720–1723]. We see these as cardinal mediations because they were enabling in a fundamental way. Increasing numbers of their readers became writers, their flow of contributions inducing the flow of capital, for this was the appropriation of surplus value in its purest form: almost all of this material was provided (and could be reprinted) for free. New periodicals could thus be launched and sustained with very little capital, making them a primary engine for the takeoff in overall publication levels in the latter part of the century. Writing in these forms mediated a fundamental change in readers—leading them to behave as writers—that, in turn, induced more writing and print (Siskin 1998, 155–171). Other kinds of writing and print played roles in inducing other flows, including the new genres of financial instruments discussed below.

- New infrastructure and new genres and formats became crucial to the promotion of new *associational practices*. The Enlightenment emerged in part from the creation of a remarkable number and variety of voluntary associations, each promoting a distinctive discourse: political parties (like the Whig Kit Kat club), secret societies (like the Freemasons), scientific corresponding societies, gendered intellectual clubs, and group formations of many other kinds. Historians of science, for example, have argued that Bacon's prospectus for the reform of knowledge only begins to be realized after the founding (out of informal and secret societies) of the Royal Society in 1660 (charters come from the Crown in 1662 and 1663). The society rapidly became a node for relationships of correspondence with similar groups. The resulting network initially took shape as a European Republic of Letters, and then, in the second half of the eighteenth century, it spread throughout the newly forming empire (e.g., William Jones's Asiatic Society). The scientific breakthroughs of Isaac Newton (the *Optics*, 1671 and the *Principia*, 1687) benefited from the resulting reorganization of the discourse of natural philosophy. Like the Royal Society, with its periodic meetings, its varied interest groups, and its printed journal, many of the clubs and voluntary associations enabled distinctive ways of harnessing to their purposes oral and aural communication, manuscript writing, and print.

- Finally, *new protocols* emerged to underwrite the infrastructure, genres, formats, and associational practices we have described. Protocols are enabling constraints: the rules, codes, and habitual practices that help to secure the channels, spaces, and means of communication. Many transmission protocols could be named, but we will focus briefly on three that were particularly enabling: the postal principle, public credit, and the regime of copyright. The *postal principle*—by which "any one can address any one"[16]—gains currency with the increasingly efficient operation of the postal system. Its protocols—consistency of address, periodicity, dispatch, and privacy—assure that groups and individuals can communicate regularly and securely by manuscript, letter, and printed matter. *Public credit* is in a sense the postal principle for money—that is, value formatted for transmission. Its enabling constraints clear and secure paths for the flow of wealth through a society. That flow took its distinctively modern turn with institutional innovations in what became the banking system, as in the founding, in 1694, of the Bank of England. Serving as a vehicle for borrowing by the government, public credit had the important secondary effect of greatly expanding the financial instruments that underpinned the growth of global commercial markets (see the essays in this volume by Poovey and Baucom). In his description of the Royal Exchange published in 1711, Mr. Spectator, the fictional narrator often employed in Addison and Steele's periodical, offered a rousing appreciation of the wealth that a free global trade had brought to England (no. 69). The late seventeenth and early eighteenth centuries also saw the instituting of a new set of protocols enabling and constraining ownership and circulation of printed matter: the *regime of copyright*. John Locke's 1684 "Memorandum on Licensing" attacked both the legal printing monopoly extended by the government to the Stationer's Company as well as the official licensing of printed books, which continued even after the political settlement of 1688. Locke's critique, which blends an argument for free trade with an argument for open access to knowledge, offered a conceptual groundwork for Parliament's decision to allow the expiration of the Licensing Act (in 1695) and, during the reign of Queen Anne, for the passage of the first modern copyright law. The limited-term copyright first formulated by the Statute of Anne (1710) balanced two opposing ideas: on the one hand, the author's ownership of his or her creation is supposed to provide incentives for the expansion of knowledge. But, on the other, a term limit for copyright assumes the general benefits to the public from the robust and unencumbered access to knowledge. For knowledge to be renewed on the scale envisioned by Bacon, it had to change hands; as the essay below by Adrian Johns demonstrates, hotly contested protocols regarding ownership, use, and punishment were negotiated as a way to enable this exchange.

PROLIFERATING MEDIATIONS

The "magazines" that first proliferated in Britain during the 1730s, such as the *Gentleman's Magazine* founded by Edward Cave in 1731, exemplify how cardinal mediations enabled mediations of other kinds. As "storehouses" of previously printed materials, they were literally filled with the output of the mediations described above, including the newspaper and the periodical and the new clubs and coffeehouses in which they circulated. They joined a plethora of new forms for mediating expanding outputs that appeared during the second quarter of the eighteenth century. These included efforts to manage the twin flows of print and knowledge by steering print into the newly idealized back formation of the "oral" (see Paula McDowell's essay in this volume) and squeezing knowledge into newly comprehensive forms of classification and condensation. The year 1728, for example, saw the publication of both John Henley's *Oratory Transactions* and Ephraim Chamber's *Cyclopedia*. Henley harnessed print to make his case for instituting a new range of forms and practices grounded in speech, from "conferences" and "disputations" to a "Week-Days Academy." "This Scheme will bring Home to any Person," he argued, "all the Benefit of Schools, Universities, Tutors, Academies and Professors, with more than can be reap'd from them." Chambers's similarly high and practical ambitions for his effort to mediate knowledge—encircling it in a single work—are evident in his subtitle, "An Universal Dictionary of Arts and Sciences ... the Whole Intended as a Course of Antient and Modern Learning."

By the end of the second quarter of the eighteenth century, another wave of proliferating mediations—in kind, in number, and in scale—swelled from the presses. Variations on the magazine replaced repackaging with more actively critical strategies such as the combination of summary and evaluation that became the trademark genre of the *Monthly Review* (1749) and the *Critical Review* (1755). At that same midcentury moment, Thomas Sheridan raised the stakes for Henley's "elocution" movement. As part of the inclusive undertaking Sheridan called *British Education* (1756), the "revival of the Art of Speaking" was now tipped to be a cure for "the Disorders of Great Britain."

And imitators of Chambers were similarly emboldened, most famously in France, where efforts to translate the *Cyclopedia* into French in the 1740s led to the *Encyclopédie* project (1751–1772).

That project has remained the most visible single artifact of the historical phenomenon of proliferation we are describing. When numbers are invoked, the usual suspects are 71,818 articles, 3,129 illustrations, and Louis de Jacourt authoring an average of eight articles per day over six years. But in a history of mediation what counts as well as numbers is how they perform a proliferation of another kind: the expanding array of mediations geared to the goal of "Universal" encirclement: access to all knowledge for all people. These range from the practical (cross-referencing the alphabetic arrangement for ease of use) to the political (including the secrets of technique and craft so as to bring general human improvement through the sharing of knowledge). Diderot mocked those who would sequester the encyclopedia by giving it "the form of an enormous manuscript that would be carefully locked up in the king's library, inaccessible to all other eyes but his, an official document of the state, not meant to be consulted by the people" (Kramnick 1995, 18, 19). Authorship was similarly dispersed by the associational practice credited on the title page: "Par Une Société De Gens De Lettres" (By a Society of Men of Letters).[17]

What the scope and gathering intensity of all of these proliferations demonstrate is that the cardinal mediations we have described had not only enabled many new forms of mediation; they had also added a new dimension to the very act of mediation itself. With new channels and stopping places for new genres and formats to circulate through new social matrices sustained by new protocols, possibilities and expectations for what mediation could accomplish changed. The very medium of mediation—its architecture of forms and tools, people and practices—became load-bearing. On this new platform, each individual act came to be understood—and the result deployed—as working not only on its own terms but also as a part of a cumulative, collaborative, and ongoing enterprise.

That sense of enterprise was initially communicated through a cluster of terms that took on new meanings and force during the first half of the eighteenth century. In Britain, "improvement" and "progress" became rubrics within which vectors of comparison across more and more fields of endeavor changed direction. Comparisons that had pushed off from the past, as in "ancient versus modern," now invoked a future as something that could be accomplished: a better and more perfect whole made collectively out of more and more parts. Thus Chambers presented his *Cyclopedia* as "a Work so disproportionate to a single Person's Experience" that the reader must "suspect something of Disingenuity" in his claim to sole authorship. The work of the preface, then, was to recast his work in different terms—as a matter of what we have been calling "mediation." The job did not require an "Academy," Chambers argued, because "superior" access to earlier efforts to mediate knowledge, including "Dictionaries" and "Lexicons," had made him "Heir to a large Patrimony, gradually rais'd by the Industry, and Endeavours of a long Race of Ancestors" (Chambers 1728, 1).

The point of Chambers's encircling, however, was to make a better circle—not just to collect and repackage but to point knowledge forward, to enable proliferation. He thus "augmented"—that is, remediated—the earlier mediations in two ways. First, he updated by adding "Extracts and Accounts" of "a Multitude of Improvements . . . made in these last Years." Second, he sought to integrate "Patrimony" and "Improvement" through a "thing" that he claimed could not be found in previous works—"structure." "See[ing] nothing like a Whole"—his goal—"in what they have done," he drew a line between himself and his ancestors. Their "Materials," he declared, "needed further Preparation, ere they became fit for our Purpose; which was as different from theirs, as a System from a Cento." By his own description, then, "the chief Difficulty" of the *Cyclopedia* lay not in authorship and content but in "Preparation" and "Form"—in figuring out how to mediate the patchwork of the past.

It was those experiments in "Connexion," such as the "Course of References" between entries adopted by the French, that proliferated across what Chambers called the "Commonwealth of Learning." And as this traffic in new mediations increased, so, too, did a collective sense of difference from the past and of shared enterprise in the present. Since this was a matter, as Chambers emphasized, of being *formally* different from one's predecessors, ideas were not the primary issue—and histories of them can thus easily miss the point. To borrow Chambers's word, the issue was "structure" and the point was mediation—forms of mediation that he saw as "nothing like" those that came before. And the world in which those mediations proliferated—"so many Parts of some greater Whole"—also came to be experienced as different—as something that could *now* be known.

Right then, as if on cue, Francis Bacon appeared anew. A century after their first publication, his *Philosophical Works* were reissued in a new edition and translation, "Methodized, and made *English*" (Bacon 1733, title page). Although not forgotten—Bacon himself had remained a revered figure, especially within the Royal Society—the "renewal" had remained, in the words of the new editor, "unexecuted in most of its Articles." But by 1733, the "delay" was over. Within a few years of Chambers, Henley, and the *Gentlemen's*

*Magazine*, Bacon's "PLANS" for knowing the world became a part of the proliferation we have been describing.

Like the other parts, this was not a reprinting but a mediation of the original texts. Dedicated to Horatio Walpole, as the *Novum Organon* was to King James, Peter Shaw's edition sought to reverse James's judgment of the *Organon* as "past all Mens Understanding." A more "intelligible" version of Bacon's "whole Plan," accessible to "the wiser and better Part of the Nation," would, Shaw hoped, secure support from Walpole, a person who had already executed "very important Designs for the Publick Good" (Bacon 1733, v). The strategy for improvement was to methodize the methodizer; it was now time to remediate Bacon's mediations.

Like Chambers, Shaw[18] identified as his first step the goal of a new "Whole": in this case, a whole that would rectify the failure of earlier translations to publish together the "Pieces" that "entirely depend upon" each other (Bacon and Shaw 1773, vi–vii). He then added, along the lines of Chambers's cross-references, new tools for forming that whole, including an "Index" and a "Glossary" (viii). The purpose of this retooling was not to preserve Bacon's oeuvre as it had originally appeared but to allow the texts to become different—and thus participate in the kind of "renewal" that was now understood to be possible. The glossary, therefore, does not "give exact Definitions" but ones that "facilitate" (lxiv). And the translation is not "direct" but "a kind of open Version, which endeavours to express, in modern English, the Sense of the Author, clear, full, and strong" (vii).

Shaw opened up Bacon—augmented him—so that the mid-eighteenth century could, finally, make more out of him. And more at that moment, as we have been arguing, became different.[19] This new Bacon was new on paper—and thus would have qualified as a candidate for the very Society that long considered the old Bacon its father. In 1731, however, as Shaw was remediating Bacon, the Royal Society was remediating itself: new members now had to be proposed in writing and the written certificates signed by those who supported them.

New associational practices thus underwrote the sense that something different was happening. Although the cluster of words, formulations, and practices that we have been noting did not precipitate the term "Enlightenment" until later, our retrospective use of that term does not mean that we are imposing a coherence on the past that was not experienced then. That timing is, in fact, precisely what we should expect when an event emerges out of proliferating effects. France and Germany experienced the same clustering articulation of difference that we have identified in Britain, and at roughly the same time. The combination of "esprit philosophique" (philosophic mind), and "lumière" (light), for example, as Dan Edelstein has noted, were closely linked in texts by Fontenelle and Dubos in 1732–1733 (see Fontenelle 1732, 8; Dubos 1733, 487).[20] "And Sapere aude," as noted earlier, surfaced as a motto for the Friends of Truth in Germany in 1736.

### SATURATION

If we understand the roughly half century that follows this clustering sense of difference as a period in the history of ideas, then we are left with only one way to explain the paradox of labeling cited earlier: why did Kant turn that motto into a motto of Enlightenment-in-process at the very moment that we think the historical Enlightenment ended? The answer must be that the ideas changed—changed in a way that made the process fail. Enlightenment must thus have been cut short or somehow interrupted by revolution or Romanticism—with, in some versions, its ghost returning to haunt modernity with nightmare versions of itself. These tales do have their insights and uses, but the history of mediation can direct our attention to other kinds of evidence and thus different explanations.

Having linked Enlightenment as an event in that history to proliferation, for example, we can track that event by looking for the consequences: when does proliferation turn into saturation? In Britain, we find that the proliferating print mediations of the second quarter of the century set the stage for the even more startling takeoff in overall print production in the 1780s (Siskin 2005, 818–820). At the level of the pervasiveness of the technology itself, the term "saturation" can point to the moment when the sense of difference generated by initial proliferation becomes more of the same. In that sense, saturation is signaled by the paradox of access. On the one hand, saturation means that more people have more access to the technology; on the other, it indicates that, strangely enough, direct access is not required—that even those lacking or refusing access are transformed by the ubiquitous presence of the technology.

This is the tale now being retold by the early twenty-first-century advent of electronic and digital media. Whether individuals have the technology or try to avoid it, everyone now has the sense that there is nowhere to hide from its mediating powers; in fact, the desire to hide is itself an index to saturation and confirmation of difference becoming a new norm. As Clifford Siskin argues in his solo contribution to this volume, certain genres and procedures identified with Enlightenment did not disappear but changed and mixed, performing new functions in newly normal roles.

Siskin's example is the genre of "system," which he describes as the vehicle for Adam Smith's effort to secure Scotland's place in the sense of shared enterprise we have described. As with Chambers and Shaw, Smith's strategy was improvement through mediation: by methodizing the English, he thought he could secure a future for the Scottish as British. But saturation here played a genre-specific role. What Siskin calls Smith's "master systems" always included specific sections for comprehending the competition within a larger whole. Thus, within a few decades of their start at midcentury, the genre and the project became victims of their own success: more writing of more systems made reconciliation into a single system less and less likely — there was simply too much system for system to master. The genre had saturated itself.

The encyclopedic system-making taking place in France during the same decades met a similar fate. The startling numbers of Diderot's project indicated both success and a limit. Even before the first version was completed, *Britannica* had appeared across the Channel (1768) proclaiming its rival's obsolescence Its editors saw saturation in the very image of the *Encyclopédie*'s ambition — its master diagram of knowledge — and in its "repugnant" organization. They abandoned the diagram and replaced alphabetization of technical terms with a new mediation: knowledge was "digested" into a different kind of system — "distinct treatises" devoted to what we can now see as the prototypes of the narrow-but-deep divisions of the modern organization of knowledge. By the completion of the second edition in the year of Kant's essay, 1784, *Britannica* included 150 of these treatises. When we understand Enlightenment as the mediation of knowledge — and not just the bits and pieces of knowledge we call ideas — then the evidence that it *happened* includes the new protocol for knowledge that it established: the enabling constraints of disciplinarity.

Tracking saturation thus shows Enlightenment to have been successful in its own terms; it was, in these concrete ways, an event that ended itself. Kant's role in that end, however, was not what it may have first appeared to be. In the history of mediation, he did not *change* Bacon's subject from "knowledge" to "man." Rather, Bacon's plan for renewing knowledge *produced* Kant's daring subject. After the many mediations we have detailed, man became a new kind of tool — a tool whose power now lay in its insistence on using its "own" understanding to change itself. And since change for this new, modern self was now always ongoing — we still define ourselves by our need and capacity to develop — Kant *had* to insist that we are not yet "*enlightened*," just living in an (ongoing) "*age of enlightenment*." His claim was philosophical, not historical. The event in history that we call Enlightenment, however, was coming to an end — an end signaled by the kinds of saturation that characterize our own moment in the history of mediation. We hope that this introduction and the essays that follow will prove to be useful efforts to mediate that experience.

## Part Two: The Distinctness and Organization of This Collection

In the past twenty years a remarkable number of books have attempted to rethink Enlightenment.[21] Rather than trying to subordinate all of them to our own effort through summary and critique, we will instead clarify what we consider this collection's distinctive contribution to this vigorous conversation. Most important, this book should not be read as a study of Enlightenment *and* media/mediation. Many scholarly collections strategically pair "Enlightenment" with more specific topics for study, whether through the use of the conjunction "and" (as in *Women, Gender and the Enlightenment*, [Knott and Taylor 2005]), or by using a preposition that locates something "in" Enlightenment (*The Sciences in Enlightened Europe* [Clark, Golinski, and Shaffer 1999]), or by specifying a scholarly contact zone for the encounter of Enlightenment and the colonized other (*Postcolonial Enlightenment* [Carey and Festa 2009]). Each of these collections, all published within the past decade, presents a relation between two terms that are separated before their complex and manifold interrelations are specified: Enlightenment and gender, Enlightenment and the sciences, Enlightenment and the postcolonial. In every case, recent developments in the disciplines have encouraged a new critical practice, so Enlightenment and its discursive "other" can codevelop and cast each other in a new light.

The scholars of gender who have contributed to *Women, Gender and the Enlightenment* come to their study with a theoretically inflected sense of the plasticity of gender. This enables them to develop new ways to examine "the gender dimension of Enlightenment thought and practice" (Knott and Taylor 2005, xvi). Because contemporary historians of science have accepted a "post-positivist" concept of science, one that sees science as embedded in culture and history rather than apart from them, the scholars who contribute to *The Sciences in Enlightened Europe* bring a new range of Enlightenment scientific practices into view, which acquire a new critical salience (Clark, Golinski, Shaffer 1999, ix). Finally, those postcolonial scholars who contribute to *Postcolonial Enlightenment* have fully assimilated a critique of the Enlightenment's expansive colonizing projects. However, by rejecting the Enlightenment as a "monolithic bogeyman," their studies give us access to Enlightenment's plurality, including its anticolonialism (Carey and Festa 2009, 10). In each of these studies there is a valuable expansion of our understanding of Enlightenment as well as a historically inflected renewal of a term paired with Enlightenment: "women," "science," and "postcolonialism."

Although we acknowledge the cogency of this contrapuntal strategy, this collection pursues a different approach. By apprehending Enlightenment as an event in the history of mediation, we are arguing that one cannot disentangle the phenomenon called Enlightenment from the history of mediation as it unfolds in the particular forms and genres, the associational practices, and the protocols first developed in the long eighteenth century. Therefore, our use of the copula—Enlightenment *is* an event in the history of mediation—radicalizes the intimacy of Enlightenment and mediation, so as to catch their mobius-strip-like co-implication. If Enlightenment and mediation are understood in this way, then mediation is the condition of possibility for Enlightenment—and Enlightenment mediations become the condition of possibility for the many other discursive, material, and intellectual transformations that often become the focus of Enlightenment studies, including, in the collections we have just discussed, those falling under the rubrics of gender, the sciences, and postcolonial politics. Thus, without a complex historical mutation *in* mediation—that is, without postal communication, the newspaper, the pamphlet, voluntary associations, and generic inventions (like the system or the popular declaration)—there could not be the sort of reorganization of knowledge that was sponsored by the Royal Society or the *Encyclopédie* project, or the sort of distributed communication and associational practices that lie behind the revolutions in America, France, and Haiti. Without a media sphere that is open, public, and (relatively) cheap, there could not have been the highly coherent and widely disseminated Anglophone "debate about the French Revolution" as it was developed by Dr. Richard Price, Edmund Burke, Mary Wollstonecraft, and Thomas Paine. This debate reacts to and builds upon the comprehensive style of address to "mankind" found in the popular declarations of 1776 and 1789, and all of this universalizing public discourse about the rights of man and women emerges out of and presupposes the mutations and proliferations of mediation that generate the event we call Enlightenment.[22]

Our account of Enlightenment mediation assumes a debt to Jürgen Habermas, and those many prominent scholars who have extended, critiqued, or revised him (Baker 1990; Goodman 1994; Warner 1990, 2002). Habermas was one of the first scholars to shift the study of the Enlightenment from intellectual history, whether elite or popular, to a much more capacious and heterogeneous set of terms as they operate together: places, like coffee shops and *salons;* voluntary associations of every kind; media, like letter writing and print; as well as the ideas they circulate (see also Darnton 1970; Chartier 1991).

However, understanding Enlightenment as an event in the history of mediation differs in fundamental ways from the public sphere approach. First, studies of the public sphere invariably downplay the mechanics of mediation, the role of technologies, the influence of genres, the dynamic of association, and the aggregate effect of elemental protocols. By separating the human from the tool and the group from its informing structures, public sphere studies makes the business of mediating meaning something that rests with strictly human agency, appearing in the collective guise of "the public." The abstractness of the term "public" explains both the allure and the liability of Habermas's terminology. Scholars have used this terminology to demonstrate that numberless nations and epochs engaged in "making publics," "publicity," and addresses to the public. Habermas's analysis depends, as Keith Baker has pointed out, upon a blurring of the boundary between using the "public sphere" as a descriptive term, as denoting the communication practices that emerged in the eighteenth century, and a normative term, which offers a model for rational negotiation through communication that we moderns have fallen away from (through the modern "decay" of the public sphere) but to which we should return. By contrast, the studies of Enlightenment mediation collected in this volume are not constrained by this nostalgia. They comprehend a broader and more capacious set of phenomena than that opened by the study of the public sphere. By understanding those mediations as themselves constituting a history, this volume saves the enormous variety of Enlightenment mediations from being relegated to supporting roles in Habermas's political master plot: the liberal-Marxist story of the bourgeois critique of and resistance to political absolutism.

While the essays in this collection might have been gathered under many different rubrics, we have arranged these essays to foreground one aspect of Enlightenment considered as an event in the history of mediation: in part 1, the concept of mediation and its operation within particular historical itineraries (natural history, the American Revolution, and the invention of the telegraph); in part 2, the diverse genres of Enlightenment (files, systems, the spiritualized inner dialogue of soul and self, and advertising); in part 3, the novel effects of the proliferation of the numbers and kinds of print (ballads, art criticism, novels, and piracy/copyright); and, in part 4, the emergent practices of Enlightenment (finance, policing/policy, preaching and aesthetic knowing). Here is a brief overview of the essays of the collection.

## MEDIATION: A CONCEPT IN HISTORY

Part 1 of this collection, "Mediation: A Concept in History," suggests various ways in which mediation can be said to have a history. In "Enlightening Mediation," John Guillory offers a philological genealogy of related terms—persuasion, communication, medium, media, mediation—in order to excavate a struggle that works through the whole (hidden) history of mediation: the tension, on the one hand, between the supposed purpose of communication (whether it be the use of rhetoric to persuade or the later ideal of transparent representation that overcomes the opacity of language) and, on the other, the diverse means by which information has been transmitted between sender and receiver by a medium, the media, or (most generally) mediations. In our second essay, Knut Ove Eliassen and Yngve Jacobsen caution against the anachronism of applying the modern concept of "the media" to Enlightenment in their essay, "Where were the media before the media? Mediating the world at the time of Condillac and Linnaeus." For them the cleavage between Enlightenment and post-Enlightenment media arrives when new early nineteenth-century technologies—the telegraph, the photograph, Babbage's analytical engine—separate information processing from the eye, the hand, and the interiority of the individual, which during the Enlightenment still sustained the vital middle position in the transmission of information. For example, in order to fashion Carl Linnaeus's traveling body into a medium through which data about the natural history of Lapland can flow back to the Royal Society of Sweden, the young naturalist prepared for his journey by assembling his instruments: the notebook, the magnifying glass, the measuring rod, and so on. In their account of Enlightenment epistemology, Eliassen and Jacobsen show that these tools are presumed to function in the same way as the human senses that they extend.

Peter de Bolla, in "Mediation and the Division of Labor," traces the steps by which Adam Smith developed a new concept, the division of labor, out of a chain of terms that depended upon and followed from one another: the division of the manufacturing process, worker specialization, machines, productivity gains that are (mathematically) sublime, time as speed as a coefficient of the cost of labor that "saves time," among other things. De Bolla's analysis shows that what held this chain of terms together and gave Smith's interpretation of political economy its coherence was Smith's invention of a new load-bearing concept, the concept of "the division of labor." How, then, might the concept of "mediation" bear the weight sufficient to support a new concept of Enlightenment? Taken together, the first three essays of the collection suggest the analytical power of a general concept of "mediation," that is, one that can be applied across different historical periods.

In "Transmitting Liberty: The Boston Committee of Correspondence's Revolutionary Experiments in Enlightenment Mediation," William Warner argues that we can counteract the unreadable familiarity of one of the paradigmatic historical episodes of the Enlightenment—the American Revolution—by situating it within the history of mediation. By Warner's argument, the Boston Committee of Correspondence came to play its decisive role in the British imperial crisis through a series of consequential mediations: the institution by the Town of Boston of the committee as an interface for political mobilization; the rewriting of the ancient petition to authority as a popular declaration addressed to fellow citizens; and the interlinking of the towns of Massachusetts, and then the thirteen colonies, into a network that could declare independence from Britain and fight the war to uphold that declaration. It is these particular mediations that give form and historical force to the "ideas" that dominate most histories of both the American and French Revolutions: liberty, equality, the imperative to critique authority, and popular sovereignty, as well as what we assume to be a distinctly modern experimental and optimistic orientation toward the future.

Since the new American republic is born out of media innovation, it is especially well positioned to experiment with new forms of mediation (Starr 2004, 3–5). In "Modes and Codes: Morse and the Question of Electronic Writing," Lisa Gitelman's genealogy of Morse telegraphy zooms into the complex mediations necessary to produce one of the most consequential events of the modern era: the invention of a new media technology. Instead of the flash of divine genius—encoded into telegraph history with the supposed first message, "What hath God wrought?"—Gitelman tells the story of a chain of mediations, from Morse's first schemes for telegraphic writing, the several patents he registers and then defends, to the final decision of the Supreme Court. Gitelman's account leaves us with a story that links successful implementation of the new medium with the notion of "delay" discussed in our argument above. In this case, the delay involves simplification and paring down. Thus, Morse's initial scheme, which is visual, writerly, print-heavy, and recording-capable, is transformed into a faster, aural, speechlike one, by the bodies of telegraph operators, who can take the written messages and translate them into clicks, which can then be heard and transcribed on the fly by the receiving operators. As with Warner's discussion of the aggregation and prosthesis made possible by political committees of correspondence, Lisa Gitelman's analysis of the Morse telegraph suggests a feedback loop by which human bodies mediate the new technologies they become mediated by.

### ENLIGHTENMENT: EVIDENCE AND EVENTS

The essays in our second group offer evidence for understanding Enlightenment as an "event." In "Mediating Information, 1450–1800," Ann Blair and Peter Stallybrass argue that the Enlightenment involved not so much a radical break with, but an inheritance of, established technologies for storing, organizing, and retrieving information. Thus, for example, heroic narratives of the Enlightenment *Encyclopédie* conveniently forget that it was in the first age of print (1450–1650) that technologies of information were developed. These include ways to stockpile information (for example, by collecting notes taken on books, using blank forms, the development of shorthand); finding aids (alphabetic indexes, running heads, the use of a thread to file loose papers); and methods for collaborating to edit huge compilations of knowledge (hidden editorial assistants; "slips" to update indexes; and literal "cut and paste" of previous books into new books). But even if one accepts their idea of the strong continuity between the early modern (Renaissance) and the Enlightenment is correct, and if one agrees that the "info lust" that so characterizes the modern period was transmitted from the earlier to the later period, how are we to account for the distinct contributions of Enlightenment?

In "Mediated Enlightenment: The System of the World," Clifford Siskin argues that we should look to the late seventeenth-century upsurge in the number and ambition of the new genre of the system: "System was the formal means to Enlightenment's end: comprehensive knowledge of a world that *could* be known—of parts that formed a whole." Newton demonstrated the "system of the world" that *is* nature through the use of induction, simplicity, and mathematical proof. Adam Smith then capitalized on Newton's success by launching the project we now call the Scottish Enlightenment as a remediation: the systematizing of "English philosophy," including Newton. But Siskin shows that as systems proliferate and efforts to produce "master systems" that incorporate all systems founder, the genre is increasingly embedded into other forms. The result was a turn toward more specialized and localized knowledges and practices in writers such as William Wordsworth and Walter Scott. These new practices issue in the narrow but deep knowledge strategies of the modern disciplines. In "Romanticism, Enlightenment and Mediation: the case of the inner stranger," Robert Miles zeros in on the knowledge strategies of the self. Miles shows that the popular poet Edward

Young and the author and critic Anna Letitia Barbauld use the figure of the "inner stranger" to reconcile a transcendental soul with a mundane self. Through a reading of the way Samuel Taylor Coleridge takes up the same figure (in "Frost at Midnight"), Miles traces a secularizing movement from a "porous" to a "buffered" self (cf. Charles Taylor), so the enigmatic equivocations of this "inner stranger" mediates the appearance of a distinctively modern concept of the unconscious it (or Id) within the self.

In "The Present of Enlightenment: Temporality and Mediation in Kant, Foucault, and Jean Paul," Helge Jordheim analyzes how these three writers negotiate what he sees as a central contradiction of Enlightenment. On the one hand, each insists, within their distinct discursive itinerary, that the value and promise of Enlightenment consists in the way it allows us to think the present, the distinctness of the present age, and build a "now" that requires a certain ethos: "a voluntary choice made by certain people; in the end, a way of thinking and feeling; a way, too, of acting and behaving that at one and the same time marks a relation of belonging and presents itself as a task" (Foucault). Without this sense of a present, Jordheim asks, how could a task like political revolution be attempted? On the other hand, Jordheim's analysis demonstrates that each of these writers, in their different ways, runs up against the inevitability that the "present" of Enlightenment not only entails temporal deferrals and spatial differences; crucially, Enlightenment can only materialize within the various mediations of speech, writing, print, and image.

The heteronomy of Enlightenment mediations becomes more still acute when a state seeks to transmit aspects of Enlightenment modernity to non-European nations and peoples. In "The Strange Light of Postcolonial Enlightenment," Arvind Rajagopal interrogates the contradictions that befell the Congress Party in the wake of Indian independence in 1947. What happens when concepts and practices associated with Enlightenment—suffrage, freedoms of various kinds, political economy—are not homegrown but imports? When they do not develop gradually but are instituted in one year? Are not expressions of popular sovereignty but the explicitly pursued policy of a state seeking to discipline a people into modernity? Rajagopal describes the special privilege the Nehru government gives to modern communications, and most especially television and advertising, as channels through which to reach the nonliterate members of the nation and reorganize the sensorium of India. Rajagopal's reading of one television ad for the *Times of India*, entitled "A Day in the Life of India," demonstrates the complex mediations entailed in the co-mingling of the promises of Enlightenment, advanced capitalism, and alluring visual displays of wealth, with the knowing skepticism of an indigenous oral Hindu culture.

## PROLIFERATION: MEDIATION AND PRINT

The essays in this section offer new ways of engaging a phenomenon that was widely remarked upon during the eighteenth century: the proliferation in the quantity and kinds of print media. The proliferation of print helped create new disciplines of knowledge and new understandings of print's relation to its others. In "Mediating Media Past and Present: Toward a Genealogy of 'Print Culture' and Oral Tradition," Paula McDowell develops a striking historical analogy around the perception of what she calls "media shift." Just as twentieth-century studies of oral (as opposed to scribal and print) culture took off in the wake of new twentieth-century oral technologies like telephony, the phonograph, and the radio, so too did the eighteenth-century conceptualization of oral tradition emerge in a complex dialectical relationship with an emerging sense of the sometimes reviled and sometimes improving effects of the steady proliferation of print. While McDowell is finally skeptical of those eighteenth-century theorists who postulated an original oral tradition, one that is then supplanted by a print one, McDowell documents the eighteenth century's first draft of the comparative media analysis later conducted in the twentieth century. In her exploration of the practices of "Mediating Antiquarians in Britain, 1760–1830," Maureen McLane offers a case history to support McDowell's media analysis. McLane's account of what antiquarians do to transmit ballads—gathering, citation, forensic editing, authentication, and quarrels over value—allows us to see the antiquarians as mediators and inventors of an oral tradition that can then be used retroactively to legitimize literary and national claims. Both McDowell and McLane enable us to identify the procedural, technical, and conceptual debts that the scholars in the present must assume from these pioneering Enlightenment mediators of oral and print culture.

Anne Fastrup puts the question of the positive or negative valuation of print media at the center of her discussion of the encyclopedists' project of Enlightenment. In "Mediating *le philosophe*—Diderot's Strategic Self-representations," Fastrup describes the diverse strategies pursued by Diderot to guard the exalted aims of the *Encyclopédie* project: an idealization of the figure of the truth-loving "philosophe," the excoriation of the journalist, and finally a recourse to art criticism, where the critical detachment of the critic can be secured against the competitive din of journalism. Fastrup's essay lays bare the contradiction that challenges Diderot at each turn: to transmit knowledge to the public they would uplift, the *philosophes* must rely upon the unruly print market that sustains journalistic critics—even though the attacks on the "Encyclopedists" are often ill-informed, mean-spirited, or patently self-interested.

In spite of its commercial entanglements, part of the potential prestige of print came from the belief that it could offer unprecedented access to the new systematic knowledge of eighteenth-century science. In "Novel Knowledge: Judgment, Experience, Experiment," John Bender argues that the British novelists of the early eighteenth century adopted three elements of natural philosophy in fashioning their narratives: surrogate witnessing, the contrived experiment, and the induction-based reasoning that could translate the findings of a single experiment into truths of general validity. In an essay that resonates with Michael McKeon's contribution to this volume, Bender shows how early novelists fashioned printed texts into experiments that mediated different kinds of knowledge as a means of mediating the fictional and the real. The tools he describes both confer experience to the fictional characters and advance the judgment of both characters and readers.

The overall proliferation of print during the eighteenth century foregrounded the problem of who owns and controls the products of that technology. In "The Piratical Enlightenment," Adrian Johns shows how eighteenth-century German states, as net importers of intellectual property, found that piracy, the free reproduction of books first published by others, could support the Enlightenment ideal of free and open access to knowledge. However, in the story that Johns unfolds, the ensuing debate about the comparative value of a restricted copyright (the English system) and liberal reprinting (German piracy) not only implicates the mediation of Enlightenment (where piracy offers robust circulation of knowledge) but also bears upon what became the most important positive rational for seeing writing as an expression of the self: the idea that the writer is a genius, whose distinct form of thought emerges from a unique self. Ownership in the form of copyright became the primary way of instituting this connection between writing and genius.

### EFFECTS: EMERGENT PRACTICES

The event in the history of mediation that was Enlightenment, as well as the proliferation of print media that helped to give distinct shape to that event, carried diverse effects. The five essays in this section offer ways to understand the economic, political, social, and religious practices that emerged from Enlightenment: financing, policing, preaching, and aesthetic criticism. In "Financing Enlightenment," Mary Poovey highlights a paradox concerning the relationship between money and memory, the practices of Enlightenment and power. Enlightenment economic projects require money, but the effective power of money (to hold and transmit value) depends upon transforming an earlier medium for transmitting value (like gold) into new genres of money (such as bills of exchange, letters of credit, Bank of England notes), but—and here is the paradox—the efficacy of these proliferating money genres depends upon an abstraction that effaces the memory of any relation to original forms of value. Poovey, echoing earlier critiques of Enlightenment rationalization like the Frankfurt school, further suggests that her analysis of "how money lost its own history" suggests that "erasure is intrinsic to Enlightenment . . . as one of the conditions of its possibility" (p. 323 below).

In the companion piece to Poovey's essay, "Financing Enlightenment, Part Two: Extraordinary Expenditure," Ian Baucom offers one example of the not so "enlightened" payoff from the abstraction and forgetting Poovey describes: money carries law, and law sanctions violence. Baucom's critique pivots on the 1653–1660 account ledgers of Jan Van Riebeeck, the founding commander of the Dutch East India Company's fort and provisioning settlement at the Cape of Good Hope. Alongside the routine expenditure for cows, food, and supplies, there is an "extraordinary expenditure" in the year 1659 to suppress a rebellion of "Caapmen and Hottentoos," who had suddenly attacked the Dutch trading post. Baucom shows that Van Riebeeck's legal rationale for this "just war" against an indigenous people depends upon the political theory of Hobbes's *Leviathan* (1651), as well as Zouch's *Exposition of Fecial Law and Procedure, or of Law between Nations* (1651) and Hugo Grotius's *Rights of War and Peace* (1625). These texts conceptualize a law that extends outside the state and justifies violence not merely against pirates and brigands but other "inimici," those who are inimical by virtue of failing to possess a state, a senate, and a treasury, by failing to commit themselves to commerce and commonwealth, and are therefore incapable of entering into treaties with others. According to Baucom, this nexus of law/money/violence, in which each mediates the others, wins formal philosophical sanction as a global imperative or universal rule during the Enlightenment, through Kant's *Metaphysics of Morals* and his concept of cosmopolitan universalism and "perpetual peace." Baucom further argues that this same conceptual machinery has been revived by the post 9/11 U.S. national security agencies on behalf of "an unabashedly conjoined theory and practice of international law, global war, and speculative capital" (p. 337 below).

In "'The Horrifying Ties, from which the Public Order Originates': The Police in Schiller and Mercier," Bernhard Siegert offers a very different way to raise the question of Enlightenment mediations of power. Siegert begins by contesting the "two-hundred-year-old myth" that understands the Enlightenment as the epoch when media mediates the private citizen's self-realization as the Public, enabling, in Habermas's influential account, bourgeois society's successful confrontation with the absolutist state. As an alternative to this familiar narrative, Siegert describes an Enlightenment project that gives the state an intimate role in policing, forming policy for, and shaping the communications media that link together the network of people and things, all in the name of securing the welfare of modern state and society. Drawing on Friedrich Schiller's plays, historical writings, and translations, as well as Louis-Sébastien Mercier's *Tableau de Paris* and Kant, Siegert develops a counter-image of the police as the medium through which the unity of a complex urbanizing society can be grasped as a transcendental unity. Siegert argues the salience of the police chief, who, as the new "father confessor," uses his many agents to mingle with the public, making police and public unthinkable apart from one another.

In "The Preacher's Footing," Michael Warner locates Enlightenment mediations in early American religious practice. Challenging the tendency of critics to align religion with orality and Enlightenment with print, Warner makes use of Erving Goffman's concept of the "footing" of a speaker and a listener to analyze the debates triggered by the religious revivals of the 1730s about the proper role of preacher and listener. Warner shows that the sermons of the reformed tradition set themselves against both the Anglican reading of preprinted sermons and the essayistic literary sermons being developed in London. Within the reformed sermon, a preacher's speech might be authorized, delivered with feeling, ironic, or quoting the words of another, while the listener might be figured as an eavesdropping bystander, a fellow Christian, or speaking with special authority because they are in "extraordinary circumstances" of conversion or death. The revivals, by bringing large bodies of strangers before preachers, removed preaching from a pastoral relationship, helping to encourage an Enlightenment remediation of religion. In his reading of Edward's *Some Thoughts concerning the Present Revival of Religion in New-England*, Warner shows how difficult it had become for Edwards to secure a distinction between traditional concepts of ministerial authority and what Warner calls "the existential urgency of conversionistic preaching." Warner's account allows us to see that the evangelical preacher's success in addressing "a world of strangers prophetically" helped, ironically, to produce a "social imaginary of denominationalism," where secularism could appear as one of many denominations.

In "Mediation as Primal Word: The Arts, the Sciences, and the Origins of the Aesthetic," Michael McKeon argues for the importance of "mediation" by highlighting its antithetical senses—"mediation" can connote both "connection/communication" as well as "intervene/separate." His historically grounded case history of mediation details the rather intricate process by which the concept of the aesthetic emerged from an explicit project: the effort (pursued in different ways by a very broad group of Enlightenment thinkers from John Locke to Joseph Addison to David Hume) to transport the epistemological posture developed by natural philosophy—one based in empirical observation, induction, and experiment—to the mediating work of the imagination in plays and novels. Thus McKeon confirms what Bender finds in his essay contribution to this volume: the centrality to eighteenth-century writing of experimental testing through experience. For McKeon what is crucial is the emergence of the aesthetic, a way of knowing that leans up against the prestige of empirical epistemology but produces a new kind of sensuous knowledge. McKeon finds that knowledge in a wide range of Enlightenment aesthetic and generic mediations: in the early debates about the two unities of time and place in the drama; in the way Daniel Defoe's most famous novel is organized around an experiment that tracks the progress of Robinson Crusoe from a "state of nature" to a civil society; in the way Samuel Richardson "tests" the young virgin Pamela through the death of her mistress and the temptation by Mr. B; in the way Samuel Johnson appeals in his criticism to an empirical "test of time" to uphold the objective aesthetic value of Shakespeare's plays. To recover the aesthetic from these instances as both a somatic and sensuous mode of knowing, McKeon recalls the double valence of mediation. While in the modern era we remember, and live with the effects of, the *separation* of the aesthetic from the scientific, we forget in doing so that this differentiation is grounded in an original *connection and linkage* between the knowledge projects of natural philosophy and the knowledge projects of the arts. Both, he argues, were grounded in the experiential and experimental bias of Enlightenment mediations of knowledge.

THE LOGICAL AND TEMPORAL PRIORITY OF MEDIATION

At the 2007 New York University conference "Mediating Enlightenment" from which this volume evolved, Geoffrey Bowker led a plenary discussion. His disciplinary appointment, in communications and the history and philosophy of science, gave him a unique perspective on the importance of positing a "history of mediation." Both then and after the conference, Bowker made a strong case for the generative power of mediations or, to use his own words, "the ontological priority of mediation." Bowker argued that, since mediations subtend and generate the dualities through which we think (e.g., human/nature, self/other), it is an error to understand mediations as emerging from the dualities. For example, in Anglo-Saxon England, it is the mediation of the new written contract that produces the fraught duality, the before and after, of "orality" and "writing" (M. T. Clanchy). Or, to take another example, it is the mediation of the European empires that produces the modern duality of the human (who are capable of discovering the limits of the world) and nature (which must be now cataloged, stored up, and known as other than human).

Our primary purpose in this volume is to intervene productively in the ongoing discussion of Enlightenment. In Bowker's terms, however, our local efforts can be understood as an experiment that may speak to a broader constituency: what happens to what we know when we act on the premise of the ontological priority of mediation? The work that follows may thus carry implications for other kinds and areas of inquiry, and thus contribute to a conversation that extends across the disciplines that Enlightenment itself first configured.

# *MEDIATION*
A CONCEPT IN HISTORY

# *ENLIGHTENING MEDIATION*

## JOHN GUILLORY

### Persuasion and Communication

The essays in this volume engage the event of Enlightenment on the terrain of its *mediation*, a term closely allied to notions of *transmission* or *dissemination* but invoking the material forms of these processes, especially print. The concept of mediation also implies a certain challenge to the figure of speech enshrined in the concept of Enlightenment insofar as any medium can diffuse or darken what it is intended to transmit. For twentieth-century physics, light apparently travels without benefit of a medium, but it was not so for the natural philosophers of early modernity, who supposed that light needed a medium, however imperceptible. If that "ethereal" element was not the air itself, it was like air, a substance more attenuated than glass or water, but like them dispersing and dimming what it also propagates. Inasmuch as the figure of enlightenment brings in the notion of medium, it perhaps also risks the dual effect of mediation. In this essay I propose to consider moments in the philological history of the terms *medium* and *mediation*, but not in order to batter the advocates of Enlightenment once again into a state of abject deconstruction. These figures were on the whole very aware of what was to be gained by strategic use of the print medium, and they tended to regard the new means of disseminating knowledge as an unqualified good.

Condorcet. In his *L'Esquisse d'un tableau historique des progrès de l'esprit humain* (*Sketch for a Historical Picture of the Progress of the Human Mind*) of 1795, Nicolas de Condorcet celebrates the advent of print above all other inventions of the modern world, destined to "unmask and dethrone" the tyranny of priests and kings:

> Men found themselves possessed of the means of communicating with people all over the world. A new sort of tribunal had come into existence in which less lively but deeper impressions were communicated; which no longer allowed the same tyrannical empire to be exercised over men's passions but ensured a more certain and more durable power over their minds; a situation in which the advantages are all on the side of truth, since what the art of communication loses in the power to seduce it gains in the power to enlighten. (Condorcet 1955a, 100)

Condorcet seems here to be thinking of printing by contrast to the immemorial art of face-to-face communication, *rhetoric*. He sees the medium of print as undermining the "power to seduce," that art of persuasion upon which the hierarchy of persons often depended. By contrast the art of printing spreads the light of knowledge "all over the world," magnifying its brilliance and subversive effects. Condorcet goes on to praise these mediations in their multiple material forms: "[E]lementary books, dictionaries, works of reference containing a host of facts, observations and experiments in which all proofs are developed and all doubts discussed" (Condorcet 1955, 101). The absence of the modern sense of *medium* in his framing account of the revolutionary effects of printing scarcely limits the scope of the claims he makes. Condorcet settles upon the term *art*: the "art of communication." The waffling between "means" and "art" is transitional, perhaps even a little belated. If printing is an art of communication, it is very unlike the art of rhetoric. Printing was, to be sure, still an art in Condorcet's time, in the sense of being a highly skilled craft, but printing disseminates what is already written. It constitutes an art of communication only if we assert with Condorcet that precisely the *technology* of print somehow makes the art of the orator unnecessary, presumably because writers who compose for the medium of print will be compelled to argue (or write) *differently*. The medium itself ensures that "all proofs are developed and all doubts are discussed," and hence that no cause prevails through the old techniques of verbal seduction. The decline of formal rhetoric that results (in part) from writing for print is an event to which Condorcet is here a witness and a prophet; the high-water mark of the dominant art of Western education was already visible to him.

It will be helpful to recall that rhetoric entailed an ancient assumption about the primacy of *speech*, as the substance upon which this art was first and longest practiced. Even though rhetoric had long incorporated writing into its art, the concept of speech retained preeminence as the ground of practice until the final demise of rhetoric in the curricular revolutions of the later nineteenth century. The demise was the result of an evolutionary change in language proceeding too slowly at first to be noticed for its epochal consequences; this tendency was nothing less than a rearrangement of the relations between speech and writing, in which writing would come increasingly to dominate the most important social venues. This reordering of language practice was unquestionably related to the pressure of the print medium on the conceptualization of writing; but I do not argue in this paper for an outcome simply determined by this new technology. Rather, I propose to index the deep shift by annotating several responses to the pressure of the "medium." These responses (of which Condorcet's is one) adumbrate a narrative with four phases, both successive and overlapping:

1. A new conception of language use emerges that is oriented toward the goal of *communication* rather than *persuasion*.[1]
2. The uses of *medium* converge with the concept of communication to yield the concept of a *medium of communication*.
3. The concept of medium is *pluralized* in the grammatical form of "media," which are recognized as a dominant feature of modernity.
4. The concept of *mediation*—implicit in the concept of medium but autonomously developed in social theory as a high-order abstraction for understanding relations among social domains—comes to be understood as a process arising from the proliferation of media.

This is the narrative, in brief, I propose to relate, by way of offering philological annotations for a linked series of evolving terms: *persuasion, communication, means, medium, media,* and *mediation*.

The first of these terms—persuasion—has an inaugural role to play by *dropping out* of the subsequent networks and their permutations. We feel today that the concept of communication is somehow implied by the concept of persuasion, just as conversely our neorhetoricians believe that the motive of persuasion is hidden in every act of communication. But it would be more accurate to say with regard to the first hypothesis that the communication concept exists in the art of persuasion only as a semantic possibility. As to the latter hypothesis, I will assume (without arguing this point further here) that rhetoricism is a totalizing and highly suspect theory of language use. It will be necessary to reject this totalization in order to set out accurately the genealogy of the communication concept, which emerges in early modernity as a challenge to the motive of rhetoric. In the premodern world, language theory needed no concept of communication, and speech was regarded most importantly as a *means* to the end of persuasion, what Condorcet tendentiously called "seduction." This end lay at a tangent to that of communication, which posited the transfer of the speaker's thoughts and feelings accurately to the mind of the auditor. By contrast, rhetoric supposed that the speaker typically occupied a "forensic" position, in which his own thoughts and feelings were best kept to himself. According to rhetoric's detractors, every rhetorical utterance possibly concealed a lie; in the absence of an elaborated theory of communication, the desire for a pure transfer of thought can best be heard in antiquity in the anti-Sophistic chorus that descends from Plato down to the recession of formal rhetoric in the nineteenth century.[2] That chorus became very loud in the seventeenth century, resulting in an urgent attempt to advance another term for the goal of speech.

## Means and Medium

*Bacon.* In order to understand this transition in philological terms, I would like to call Francis Bacon to the bar as the first witness to the missing term. In this passage from *Of the Proficiencie and Advancement of Learning*, in which Bacon considers the art of "transferring or expressing our knowledge to others," he skirts very near to the continent of communication, without quite deciding whether he has come upon an Indies or an America:

> For the organ of tradition, it is either Speech or Writing: for Aristotle saith well, "Words are the images of cogitations, and letters are the images of words"; but yet it is not of necessity that cogitations be expressed by the medium of words. For whatsoever is capable of sufficient differences, and those perceptible by the sense, is in nature competent to express cogitations. And therefore we see in the commerce of barbarous people that understand not one another's language, and in the practice of divers that are dumb and deaf, that men's minds are expressed in gestures, though not exactly, yet to serve the turn. And we understand further that it is the use of China and the kingdoms of the high Levant to write in Characters Real, which express neither letters nor words in gross, but Things or Notions; insomuch as countries and provinces, which understand not one another's language, can nevertheless read one another's writings, because the characters are accepted more generally than the languages do extend; and therefore they have a vast multitude of characters; as many, I suppose, as radical words. (Bacon 1996, 230)

The phrase "organ of tradition" can be translated approximately into modern English as "instrument of transmission." Bacon is still thinking within the framework of "arts" (like Condorcet after him), the subjects that constituted the curriculum of the premodern university. The "organ of tradition" does not refer here to an ordinary speech situation but to the formality of school techniques. Yet Bacon's elaboration of the phrase lurches suddenly into a more general reflection on the relation between language and thought (cogitation) than is warranted by the Scholastic context of transmitting knowledge. Bacon may appear to have crossed a certain threshold of conceptual innovation by offering the "medium of words" as an equivalent for "organ of tradition"; but the word *medium* here falls just short of that crossing; it should properly be understood in Bacon's sentence as an *instrument* or *means* (a hammer is an instrument or means for building, but it is not in the sense we are inquiring after a medium). The antecedent term *image* points away from our concept of medium to another semantic complex, wherein the submerged conceptual cognate for "image" would be *imitation* rather than communication (the sense here is also close to *representation*, which has a role to play later in this story). The word *medium* circulates in Bacon's day as a common variant of *means*. But drawing the term *medium* into the context of "transferring thoughts" puzzles the difference between means and medium. *Medium* hesitates at the threshold of that other familiar sense by virtue of Bacon's assertion of a commonality of function between words and gestures as two different means of expressing thoughts. This difference is rather like the difference between poetry and painting, two "arts" in Bacon's time but not yet two "media."

The further invocation of Chinese characters suggests that if Bacon is moving toward a conceptualization of the communicative function, it is precisely by moving *away* from the element of speech in order to affirm the greater utility of writing for transferring thoughts, writing as a means of "communication"—the quotation marks here indicate anachronism—that seems to transcend (spoken) words. The "Characters Real" break free of speech while remaining a form of writing. Because these ideograms are intended to connect directly with thoughts, transcending differences between languages, they suggest that the communicative function of writing is perhaps best accomplished in nonalphabetic script. Because such writing does not represent speech, it might be said to constitute a wholly different (and possibly more effective) *medium* for transferring thoughts. But Bacon is not there yet.

*Hobbes*. In *Leviathan*, Bacon's disciple takes a very different approach to theorizing speech, reflecting his intention to develop an a priori psychology of human passions and entailing the thought experiment of imagining a bare humanity. Hobbes does not, like Bacon, generalize the purpose of speech on the basis of its practice as an art of rhetoric. Nor does he, like Bacon, celebrate the technical medium of print. On the contrary, he opens his discussion of speech in chapter 4 of *Leviathan* with an abrupt demotion of Printing, which "though ingenious, compared with the invention of Letters, is no great matter." Neither is Hobbes so impressed by "letters"; he goes on to declare that speech is "the most noble and profitable invention of all other." This double derogation of print and letters inaugurates a remarkable repression of what Bacon so nearly uncovered:

> The general use of Speech, is to transferre our Mentall Discourse, into Verbal; or the Trayne of our Thoughts, into a Trayne of Words; and that for two commodities; whereof one is, the Registring of the Consequences of our Thoughts; which being apt to slip out of our memory, and put us to a new labour, may again be recalled, by such words as they were marked by. So that the first use of names, is to serve for Markes, or Notes of remembrance. Another is when many use the same words, to signifie (by their connexion and order,) one to another, what they conceive, or think of each matter; and also what they desire, feare, or have any other passion for. (Hobbes 1991, 25)

For Hobbes, the primary use of language is for "remembrance," and for reasoning upon those observations we call to mind by means of words. What we recognize as the "communicative" function of speech is allowed, but almost as an afterthought. Hobbes is determined to bend speech to the service of his geometric method of argument, which proceeds by establishing fixed definitions and requires immense control over the chaos of language, with its inherited ambiguities and plurisignifications. The fantasized scene of Hobbesian definition takes place at a site withdrawn from social discourse, for the purpose of preserving cogitation from any admixture of "desire" and "feare." And yet the result of this withdrawal from the social scene of communication is oddly that writing reappears as the *trope* of speech; the "names" that serve as "Markes" and "Notes" gesture toward the diary or the commonplace book, even the ledger—but in the artificially asocial world of the single human speaking to himself.

When writing returns as literal fact, as it does in part 3, "Of a Christian Commonwealth," it returns as the problem of interpreting the bible, the infinitely contested and mischievous book that Hobbes remands to the custody of the sovereign. So it will be in the Hobbesian commonwealth with all books, with all print. Writing and print are instruments (mediums) too dangerous to rest in private hands. Hobbes imagines a monopolization of the medium of writing correspondent to the state monopoly of violence. The control that Hobbes exercises over speech in theory, mastering words in Humpty-Dumpty fashion, can be figured in the commonwealth of letters by the sovereign's control over those letters; in this way Hobbes pays a powerful backhand tribute to print. But Hobbes does not name his adversary as the very thing the reader holds in her hands. Once again, we make a note here, a philological annotation, on a network of words in shifting interrelation, unsettled and unsettling themselves in advance of some later moment of explicitation.

*Locke.* If Bacon moves briskly in his text from speech to writing, Hobbes moves just as quickly in the opposite direction, narrowing his focus to speech only. And yet both Bacon and Hobbes are pressured into theorizing by the same unnamed idea looming over their conceptual struggles. This idea is not speech or even language, but something else: the idea of communication. Having no recourse to this concept, Bacon was unable to assign speech, writing, gesture, or the "real Character" to one larger category or genus to which all belonged. Hobbes acknowledges communication, but implicitly, by relegating the "transfer" of ideas to a secondary purpose of speech, conceived primarily (and defensively) as rational discourse with oneself. In the later seventeenth century, however, the term *communication* began to appear more frequently in theoretical discourse, as the name for the main purpose or end of speech. Unfortunately there is no way to capture this transition as a moment; we can only observe that the word's range of meaning changed during this period. On the evidence of the *Oxford English Dictionary* (*OED*), its former common senses invoked at base a scene of physical contact, the scenario in which a person hands over to another person some object such as a gift or a parcel, a usage that survives (ironically) in our notion of a "communicable" disease (the root derives from L. *munus*, exchange, and is the radical for "remuneration"). In premodern English the base meaning of *communication* is exemplified with particular vividness by the liturgical rite of Holy Communion. The sense of physical contact is reinforced by an emphasis on presence, which survives in certain exceptional current uses, as when we say that one room "communicates" with another. Speech, discourse, or conversation was only *one* example of this close (face-to-face) mode of presence or exchange, but by the later seventeenth century the sense of communication as speech or discourse was selected out as the *primary* sense, which ceased thereafter to imply the scene of immediate contact or presence and came contrarily to be associated with an action often involving distance in time and space.

The *OED* records the first use of the term *communication* in the primary sense of the "imparting, conveying, or exchange of ideas, knowledge, information, etc. (whether by speech, writing, or signs)" as 1690. The plural noun *communications* is defined as "the science or process of conveying information, esp. by means of electronic or mechanical techniques"—but this is obviously later. The plural invokes the fact of "media" (though not the word) and hence imputes distance to the modern scene of communication. The first example of the singular noun is cited from Locke, *An Essay concerning Human Understanding*, from one of many instances in that work. Although this is not in fact the first such use, Locke registers in his monumental text an important qualifier of the term *communication*, its inherent link to sociability. He does not, like Hobbes, imagine speech as kind of private language for reasoning upon things; the "Comfort, and Advantage of Society," he writes, is "not to be had without Communication of Thoughts" (Locke 1990, 405).

Located in a social rather than a physical matrix, communication for Locke defines the end of speech but also the precise instrumentality of words: "[T]hey [words] being immediately the Signs of Mens *Ideas*; and, by that means, the Instruments whereby Men communicate their Conceptions, and express to one another those Thoughts and Imaginations, they have within their Breasts" (Locke 1990, 407). This definition labors to connect words on the one hand "immediately" with ideas, and on the other hand mediately (as "means") with the aim of communication. Locke carefully maneuvers around the problem of the relation between speech and words by simply conflating speech with words (a questionable assumption for later linguistics). Everywhere in his discussion of words, Locke insists upon the "immediate" signifying relation between words and ideas, even as he allows the intermediacy of words as means to communicative ends. The *Essay* up to this point has been concerned wholly with ideas; when Locke turns to words in book 3 (from which I have been quoting), he does so only because he feels that he has established his principles of human understanding on the basis of ideas and *not* words.

We need not venture into the scholarship on the subject of the Lockean idea to advance the present argument. Suffice it to say that just as ideas for Locke, "being nothing but bare Appearances or Perceptions in our Minds," are absolutely distinct from things, so are words. Locke's conventionalist "semiotics" (the term he invents in book 3, chapter 21), means that the chief mistake people make about words is to take them as signifying things.[3] Words are related not to things but to ideas; these ideas are plunged in books 1 and 2 into a kind of cleansing bath of analysis, a thoroughgoing clarification. For words there is no such definitive clarification, and Locke's analysis of them is consequently oriented to explaining their irremediable defects, the historical result of which, he writes, was that "the greatest part of Disputes were more about the signification of Words, than a real difference in the Conception of Things" (Locke 1990, 485). Notoriously, Locke says that he would have preferred to omit consideration of words altogether from the *Essay*, but such a demurral would have reduced his book to an idealizing fragment. In the same paragraph in which he offers his rueful confession, Locke also offers a conception of words that exposes the fundamental reason for their "imperfection" and vulnerability to "abuse":

> I must confess then, that when I first began this Discourse of the Understanding, and a good while after, I had not the least Thought, that any Consideration of Words was at all necessary to it. But having passed over the Original and Composition of our Ideas, I began to examine the Extent and Certainty of our Knowledge, I found it had so near a connexion with Words, that unless their force and manner of Signification were first well observed, there could be very little said clearly and pertinently concerning Knowledge: which being conversant about Truth, had constantly to do with Propositions, And though it terminated in Things, yet it was for the most part so much by the intervention of Words, that they seem'd scarce separable from our general Knowledge. At least they interpose themselves so much between our Understandings, and the Truth, which it would contemplate and apprehend, that like the *Medium* through which visible Objects pass, their Obscurity and Disorder does not seldom cast a mist before our Eyes, and impose upon our Understandings.... But I am apt to imagine, that were the imperfections of Language, as the Instrument of Knowledge, more thoroughly weighed, a great many of the Controversies that make such a noise in the World, would of themselves cease; and the way to Knowledge, and perhaps, Peace too, lie a great deal opener than it does. (Locke 1990, 489)

Locke's desire not to deal with words in the *Essay* yields to an even stronger counterfactual wish, wholly to remove the "imperfections of language" that lie between us and a world in which knowledge and peace can prevail. Today we are long past crediting the realism of either wish, however impressive this resounding chord of Enlightenment remains. But for Locke, the wish fathers an interesting thought: the means also lie *in the way*, the medium makes communication possible and makes it fail. The convergence of means and medium closes a circle. If in the *Leviathan* Hobbes repressed the material medium, the book itself, Locke expresses in the *Essay* a more radical antipathy toward language, the "cheat" of words; at the deepest level, then, Locke is expressing a desire to communicate without words, by means of an immediate transfer of ideas. This desire for the direct transfer of thoughts and feelings, inasmuch as it is counterfactual, is the evidence of a recurrent anxiety that troubles the development of communication theory; we shall see it again. For Locke, signs exist by a kind of default condition, the inaccessible immediacy of ideas to the mind:

> For since the Things, the Mind contemplates, are none of them, besides it self, present to the Understanding 'tis necessary that something else, as a Sign or Representation of the thing it considers, should be present to it: And these are *Ideas*. And because the Scene of *Ideas* that makes one Man's Thoughts, cannot be laid open to the immediate view of another, nor laid up any where but in the Memory, a no very sure Repository: Therefore to communicate our Thoughts to one another, as well as record them for our own use, Signs of our Ideas are also necessary. (Locke 1990, 721)

Communication by signs (words) compensates for the absolute (because unmeasurable) distance between one mind and another. That distance, which is not exactly physical, is nonetheless conflated in the history of communication theory with the physical distance between bodies in space. Every communication can be seen as a telecommunication, and conversely long-distance communication as a figure for the inherent difficulty of communication.

*Wilkins.* In the assertion that words function "like a *Medium*," Locke gives a reason for his meliorist view of language, his inability to offer more than a modest set of remedies for the abuse of words, based on the principle that we should adhere as closely as possible to common significations. The recourse to the standard of common usage is like an anchor holding signification to the smallest range of drift, but at the cost of conceding the inaccessible depth at which the anchor contacts its ground. Locke's resignation to these limits explains why he rejected the attempts of the universal language theorists to fix signification permanently by orienting it to the axis of words and things, so many words for so many things.[4] I propose now temporarily to reverse the chronology of my exposition in order to consider several moments in the work of John Wilkins, the most notable of the universal language theorists in England. Looking back from the perspective of Locke, it is evident that Wilkins's work belongs to a Baconian milieu of speculative optimism. Yet it is also, I will suggest, prescient, more forward-looking than Locke, and needs to be situated on a different historical time line than the monumental philosophical texts touched upon thus far. That other time line charts the history of technology, or more precisely, *communications technology*. These two time lines are noncoincident.

Decades before Locke's *Essay*, Wilkins employed the communication concept in a surprisingly modern sense, most famously in the *Essay towards a Real Character and Philosophical Language*, published in 1668. To say this is not so much to credit Wilkins with originary distinction but rather to acknowledge that the universal language projects were nothing other than attempts to grasp the idea of communication; these projects already approached language as a medium of communication, while symptomatically falling short of formulating a coherent conceptual object. In the *Real Character*, Wilkins takes as his point of departure the perception that distinctions between kinds of communication are based in distinctions between the sensory organs: "The *External Expression* of these Mental notions, whereby men communicate their thoughts to one another, is either to the *Ear*, or to the *Eye*" (Wilkins 2002, 20). The real character, though it can be spoken, is chiefly a written language, for the eye. The conspicuous visual appearance of the ideographic script effectively foregrounds writing as a material medium. If spoken words can also be said to constitute such a medium, recognition of this fact does not have quite the same effect of foregrounding the material. The difference here may be rendered null, perhaps, by insisting that air is the physical medium of speech—this would be correct, but the visibility of writing and its technical paraphernalia account for the perception of its materiality, its translation of speech into visible signs, ink, and paper. This difference is what we mean by "technology." Writing is a technology, but speech is not. This difference is muddled, as linguists tell us, by alphabetic script, which permits us sometimes to forget that writing is a technology. But Wilkins's real character famously bypasses alphabetic script; his ideographic writing was intended to free writing from the purpose of representing spoken words and so enable the real character to establish an unambiguous and permanently fixed relation between symbols and ideas on the one side, and things on the other. Locke saw that this was an error, but it is worth specifying what kind of error. Today we would say that Wilkins hoped to correct the communicative deficiency of language by means of a "technological fix." This recourse, which has the same sort of charm as much science fiction, also has something of that genre's capacity to leap beyond conceptual safe ground for something new and strange.

Granting the *Essay towards a Real Character* its moment of fame and conceding its philosophical failure—its logical failings and inconsistencies are legion—I will pursue here the link between medium and technology by annotating an earlier fabulation of Wilkins, entitled *Mercury, the Secret and Swift Messenger*, published in 1641. This work is even closer than the *Real Character* to Bacon in its interest in technology and in its science-fictional resonance. The subject of *Mercury* is announced in the subtitle: *Shewing, How a man may with Privacy and Speed communicate his Thoughts to a Friend at any distance*—the subject, in other words, is communications technology (Wilkins 1694, 2). Wilkins of course did not have this compound term at hand; instead, he gives his subject the name of a god, Mercury, who will be remembered thereafter in just this connection. The treatise purports to describe current and possible means of secret and speedy communications at a distance, with the first half of the book devoted to secrecy, the latter half to speed. The question of the connection between secrecy and speed is puzzling, but partially illumined by the third term, *distance.* The premise of secret communication is that a message transmitted to an absent party must be made unreadable in the event of interception along the way. The context here is manifestly political, and the aims of espionage as statecraft are invoked throughout the treatise. The subject of speed also responds (more obviously) to the problem of communication at a distance, which again can have urgent political contexts, but not exclusively. Wilkins remarks that the "invention of Letters" allows us to "discourse with them that are remote from us, not only by the distance of many miles, but also of many Ages" (Wilkins 1694, 4). He understands writing as a technology for overcoming distance, both spatial and temporal, but a technology that might be improved in the former instance especially. It remains for us to explain why such improvement is premised in all circumstances, political or otherwise, on the *fusion* of secrecy and speed, which Wilkins insists throughout his treatise "may be joined together in the conveyance of any message" (Wilkins 1694, 131).

Interest in the "art of secret information" or *code* among Renaissance writers is common—Bacon gave this subject an important moment in *The Advancement of Learning*—but Wilkins sees a much wider use for code in the context of communication. Inasmuch as coded writing sets out to frustrate legibility, it produces intentionally the very effect that for Locke inheres in the "cheat" of words, their imperfection. Locke's theory reveals a defect in language itself, whether spoken or written; but Wilkins is in a way not interested in words at all—that is, in what they *mean*. He is interested rather in what technical devices exist or might be invented to frustrate immediate legibility without failing ultimately to communicate to a select addressee. The effect of his technologism is to isolate the material medium itself—pen, ink, and paper—dissevered from the message. The most basic coding effect is thus one in which the words disappear and only the medium appears: "A man may likewise write secretly with a raw Egg, the letters of which being thoroughly dried, let the whole paper be blacked over with Ink, that it may appear without any inscription, and when this Ink is also well dried, if you do afterward gently scrape it over with a Knife, it will fall off from those places, where before the words were written" (Wilkins 1694, 42). Now Locke is surely the more sophisticated theorist in suggesting that all language is in a way "blacked over" by reason of its inherent inadequacy to the mind's ideas. But does this more sophisticated conception of language as medium not gain its insight by reducing the medium to a metaphor?

At the hinge of *Mercury*, between the chapters on secrecy and the chapters on speed, Wilkins offers a prospect of his later treatise on the real character, suggesting that the same code that frustrates communication might also be used to universalize it. In the *Essay towards a Real Character*, the principle of code is employed to rectify the innate deficiency of languages, the ambiguity of words in the natural languages; and it would not be inaccurate to say that the vast apparatus of the real character is in fact a code, whose key is happily supplied to everyone. The real character is a universal language, transcending the differences of natural languages. But the unfortunate reality of the real character is that it does just what code does, namely, translate natural language into artificial language. The code, once decoded, sends us back not to things but to some version of a natural language, with all its imperfections, as Locke understood.

If the real character was a dead end, the resolute technologism of *Mercury* opens onto a more hopeful scenario. After his brief excursus on the real character in chapter 13 of *Mercury*, Wilkins goes on to take up the subject of speed. He insists as always that secrecy and speed "may be joined together in the conveyance of the message," but again, why should that be? The first clue is that, as with secrecy, the aim of speed brackets the content of the message and asks only that we consider the medium. Wilkins rehearses some improbable technologies—the communication of sound through pipes, for example—but settles on two more plausible technical possibilities: the first is the transmission of very loud sounds over long distances, the second is the transmission of messages by the use of bright light. Unfortunately, in both cases the material means is ill suited for the transmission of natural language and even for the transmission of alphabetic script. Wilkins proposes, however, that the reliability of transmission can be ensured by the use of coding, which relies on the most minimal differences between sounds or between flashes of light to produce the effect of articulation; finally, only two marks of difference are necessary to send any message. Wilkins devises here something like a precursor to Morse code, or what we would call "digitization": "It is more convenient indeed, that these differences should be of as great variety as the letters of the Alphabet; but it is sufficient if they be but twofold, because two alone may, with somewhat more labour and time, be well enough contrived to express all the rest" (Wilkins 1694, 132). With two different sounds or light flashes, every letter can be assigned a digital code, and communication at great distance and speed can be accomplished.

The point here is not so much to note the anticipation of the digital principle but to observe that Wilkins's communication at great distance is possible only by recourse to the same device—code—that is otherwise the means to *frustrate* communication. Putting Locke and Wilkins together, we see that whether communication fails (Locke) or is deliberately frustrated (Wilkins), the effect is to bring the medium into greater visibility. The difference between Locke and Wilkins, however, is reinstated at another theoretical level, because it does make a difference precisely where one locates the operation of the medium. For Locke, it would be correct to say that *words are the medium of thought*, whereas for Wilkins, one must say that *writing is the medium of speech*. Wilkins locates the operation of the medium in the *technical means*, making us see that we might even write with sound or with light. The "medium" is located in the middle position, wherever that happens to be. The difference between language as medium (of thought) and writing as medium (of speech) produces a certain philosophical confusion, which turns around the conceptualization of the medium in relation to a physical instrument.

*Campbell and Mill.* The confusion is evident in what follows historically from these two versions of communication. The Lockean version—language as medium of thought—provides a philosophical basis for a canon of language use, a *stylistic* norm applicable both to speech and writing. This is the familiar notion of "clarity," which seeks to make language as transparent as possible. The stylistic norm is the nervous tribute of communication theory to the medium concept, still hovering between a metaphor and a literal nomination. Here is an exemplary passage from George Campbell's *The Philosophy of Rhetoric* (1776), which claims to recycle the classical ideal of perspicuity drawn from Quintilian but is really concerned to establish a post-Lockean stylistic norm:

> Perspicuity originally and properly implies transparency, such as may be ascribed to air, glass, water, or any other medium, through which material objects are viewed. From this original and proper sense it hath been metaphorically applied to language, this being, as it were, the medium, through which we perceive the notions and sentiments of a speaker.

> Now, in corporeal things, if the medium through which we look at any object be perfectly transparent, our whole attention is fixed on the object; we are scarcely sensible that there is a medium which intervenes, and can hardly be said to perceive it. But if there be any flaw in the medium, if we see through it dimly, if the object be imperfectly represented, or if we know it to be misrepresented, our attention is immediately taken off the object to the medium.

Perspicuity as the chief rule of style is everywhere asserted in the rhetorical and belletristic handbooks of the period. The norm of clarity is extraordinarily important as a literary historical event and leaves virtually nothing in the realm of literary culture untouched. Because Campbell's presentation of perspicuity brings in a little more theory than is requisite for the purpose of recycling Quintilian, it permits us to appreciate the true complexity of this concept. By asserting once again the metaphoric status of the medium, Campbell rehearses Locke's desire for words that are simply transparent to ideas. Any failure of communication brings the medium into an unwanted visibility, or in Campbell's terms draws our "attention" to it. But let us imagine, for the sake of argument, a hypothetically converse (or perverse) desire, the desire *not* to communicate. We know that this desire is what motivates code, as in Wilkins's account of communication; can it also motivate literary composition or *writing*? The fact that we already know the answer to this question will allow me to accelerate my account at this point, and to allow a rather unlikely figure, John Stuart Mill, to conclude this line of inquiry into the medium concept.

Mill's attempt to define poetry in "Thoughts on Poetry and Its Varieties," first published in the *Monthly Repository* of 1833, is famous for a certain aphorism loosely identified with the period concept of Romanticism. Mill sets out to define poetry initially by comparing it with oratory on the basis of their common identity as forms of expression operating "through an impassioned medium," or language marked by a "colouring of joy, or grief, or pity, or affection, or admiration," among other strong emotions. But this assertion demands a more strenuous effort to distinguish between poetry and eloquence:

> Poetry and eloquence are both alike the expression or utterance of feeling. But if we may be excused the antithesis, we should say that eloquence is *heard*, poetry is *over*heard. Eloquence supposes an audience; the peculiarity of poetry appears to us to lie in the poet's utter unconsciousness of a listener. Poetry is feeling confessing itself to itself, in moments of solitude.... All poetry is of the nature of soliloquy. (Mill 1973, 70–71)

These familiar words have since floated free of their context, and circulate as a topos of literary culture, a notion of poetry that can scarcely be found much before Mill's time but dominates criticism after it. The poet here is granted the license to ignore the injunction to communicate, and this must have consequences for the *stylistic* norms governing the poetic mode of discourse. Most important, the rule of clarity is implicitly abrogated if Mill's characterization has any accuracy. We may then regard the language of poetry as like a code, a technique of writing that deliberately confounds the reader, that retards comprehension by provoking a hermeneutic exercise of no small complexity or duration. But it would be premature to impute anything more than this, if even this, to Mill, who only wants to establish the principle that true poetry must be written in a state of mind in which communication is disregarded. But the disregard for communication makes possible what we might call a "thickening" of the medium, a darkening of its material substance even as attention is drawn to it. This counter-principle to Locke is familiar to us now in many versions—including those of critical hermeneutics and communications theory.

## Medium and Mediation

Looking back over these glosses on the term *medium*, the reader will have noted that the concept of mediation makes as yet no significant appearance. The process of mediation would seem to be everywhere implied by the function of the medium, and yet there are few instances before the twentieth century in which a process of *mediation* is extrapolated from the term *medium*. On the evidence of the *OED*, the word *mediation* was for the most part used with reference to agents or actions involving intercession between alienated parties, as in—the grandest example—the "mediation" of Christ as Redeemer. The most common use of the term *mediation* today is not unrelated to this theological sense, referring largely to the area of dispute resolution. The most common use of the term gives us an important clue about the social investment underlying the more abstract sense we find in communication theory. If we think of mediation as a process whereby two different realms, persons, objects, or terms are brought into relation, the very necessity for this process implies that these realms, persons, objects or terms resist a direct relation and perhaps have come into conflict.

The sense of mediation as an abstract process is given in the *OED*, definition 2.a: "Agency or action as an intermediary; the state or fact of serving as an intermediate agent, a means of action, or a medium of transmission; instrumentality." The basis for abstraction in this definition is the shift of focus from "agent" to "agency," that is, to an impersonal process. This allows for any number of objects or actions to occupy the "third" position of mediation. Two of the examples cited by the editors give the range of possibilities: The first, from Chaucer's *Treatise on the Astrolabe* (1391): "By mediacioun of this litel tretys, I purpose to teche the a certain nombre of conclusions"; and the second, from H[enry] Lawrence, *Of Communion & Warre with Angels* (1646): "The understanding receives things by the mediation, first of externall sences, then of the fancy."[5] It might seem evident from our current "media" perspective that the use of the word *mediation* in the example from Chaucer must have been the more seminal; yet that was not the case. (This would confirm, however, our earlier observation, that the idea of communication is very late.) The sentence from the work by Lawrence reflects the more common usage until well into the twentieth century, suggesting that the *mediation* concept was most useful in constructing a picture of the mind in its relation to the world. This range of meaning points to psychology, to which the editors of the dictionary devote subsection b: "The interposition of stages or process between stimulus and result, or intention and realization." The philological evidence thus turns up an anomaly: the idea of a medium seems to require a process of mediation; yet this process was rarely associated with the sort of medium instanced by Chaucer's "litel tretys."

Hegel and Peirce. We have been tracking the uses of *medium* and *mediation* by annotating appearances of these terms mainly in philosophical texts, because the concepts in question are highly abstract and tend to be employed and elaborated in complex philosophical arguments. This is especially so with the concept of mediation, which names a process rather than an object. In the philosophy of Hegel, mediation debuts as a concept of the first order of importance, but without reference necessarily to communication. The term *mediation* and the problem of communication do not seem to have been brought together in any systematic way until the later nineteenth century, with the work of Charles Sanders Peirce, and then only intermittently thereafter. Communications theory is disposed now to extrapolate a process of mediation from the operation of particular media, but the older philosophical tradition put the term for process *first*; if the medium of communication appears at all in this tradition, it appears as one instance of a more universal process of mediation supposed to govern relations among different terms of thought or domains of reality. This formulation would describe the use of mediation in Hegel.

The English word *mediation* has a near equivalent in the German word *Vermittlung*, which is a key term for Hegel. In his corpus, mediation belongs to a logic or dialectic of relations, by which concepts such as subject and object, or mind and world, are assigned roles in his system. In the most general sense, the principle of mediation denies the possibility of an "immediate" (*unmittelbar*) relation between subject and object, or the immediacy of any knowledge whatsoever.[6] It will be possible within the limits of this essay to improve only slightly upon this description by acknowledging that Hegel's use of *Vermittlung* is subtly inclusive of the other senses noted above, theological and disputational, which belong to both the English term and its German cognate. Hegel's dialectic of mediated relations thus points toward reconciliatory moments along the trajectory of Hegel's peculiar self-generating dialectic.[7] We may set aside at this point the goals of Hegel's idealist system in order to aim at another target: the concept of mediation expresses an evolving understanding of the world (or human society) as too complex to be grasped or perceived whole (that is, immediately), even if such a totality is theoretically conceivable. It becomes possible then to present mediatory agencies as *necessarily* characteristic of society—a generative thought that enables later social theory to develop the idea of mediated relations by contrast to simpler notions of causality.

I will return to Raymond Williams's reservations about the concept of mediation at the end of my essay, but for the present it will be necessary to press further with a consideration of the anomaly noted above, the apparent lack of relation between *medium* and *mediation* in the philological record.[8] This problem, in my view, is crucial to our understanding of the way in which the concept of mediation as a process seems to come in and out of philosophical and social theory, without establishing a home in a field of communication. The philological evidence suggests that concern with communication continues to be expressed, often still metaphorically, by use of the term *medium*. On the other hand, the concept of mediation, as it appears in Hegel and is taken up in the tradition of Marxist and sociological theory, posits this concept in connection with more universal contexts than those of communication. For Hegel, mediation concerns nothing less than the question of *being*; for Marx the question of *labor* (as the mediation of mankind and nature). The communicative relation seems to lie below the radar of thinking about mediation until later. As we shall see, the extrapolation of a process of mediation from the fact of a particular communicative medium (language or writing) depended not on the incorporation of the concept of medium into a more general conceptual framework but the reverse, a reduction of the social totality to communication as its representative instance.

A version of that reduction characterizes the work of Charles Sanders Peirce, who elaborates the first full-scale theory of a specifically *semiotic* mediation. Peirce's typology of signs is notoriously complex, but I will emphasize only one small feature of that typology, setting out first a typical definition of the sign given in Peirce's oeuvre: "A sign, or *representamen*, is something which stands to somebody for something in some respect or capacity. It addresses somebody, that is, creates in the mind of that person an equivalent sign, or perhaps a more developed sign. That sign which it creates I call the *interpretant* of the first sign. The sign stands for something, its *object*. It stands for that object, not in all respects, but in reference to a sort of idea" (Peirce 1931-1935, 1958, 2, para. 228). What Peirce calls the interpretant is actually another sign (not a signified), the function of which is to interpret the first sign; the interpretant then becomes a representamen for another interpretant. Umberto Eco observes in his discussion of Peirce that this formulation inaugurates an endless series or "endless semiosis" (Eco 1979, 68). The infinitude of the structure of the sign permits the model to incorporate virtually all other discourses of knowledge by way of translation into semiotic terms: "The entire universe is perfused with signs, if it is not composed exclusively of signs" (Peirce 1931-1935; 1958, 5: 448). Peirce's ambitious claim for a concept with formerly so narrow a role to play in philosophical reflection interrupts the conversation in philosophy by violently displacing traditional philosophical questions into the domain of the semiotic (a displacement that is without precursor but is paralleled in the work of Frege). Peirce's implicit reduction of philosophical system or notions of totality—the world or human society—to the instance of symbolic exchange is a strategic gambit of considerable symptomatic importance and quite outweighs the actual influence of Peirce in the twentieth century.[9] The desire to generalize social theory from the instance of communication, language, or writing is recurrently a feature of twentieth-century thought, propelling the development of structuralism (Jakobson, Lévi-Strauss et al.), poststructuralism (Derrida), systems theory (Bateson, Luhman, and Habermas), communication studies (Innis, McLuhan, Ong), and information theory (Weiner, Wolfram et al).

In this context, Peirce's conception of mediation is of undoubted historical importance. The use of the term *representamen* for the manifestation of the sign confirms that Peirce is thinking of the sign primarily as a certain kind of representation. But it is not sufficient merely to say that an object is "represented" by the representamen. Peirce speaks of the object in two senses: in a formulation that sounds reminiscent of Locke, he posits first an "immediate" object as what is given in the sign, in much the same way that ideas are immediately present to the mind in Locke's system. In the second place, however, when he speaks of the object as a thing in the world, he describes it as *mediate* (we would say *mediated*). To say that representation is a means by which objects in the world are *mediated* indicates that the concept of representation is inadequate of itself to describe the effect of its own operation. When Peirce brings the process of semiotic mediation forward in his work, he complicates the concept of representation, including his own invocation of it.

The emergence of this complication testifies to the dominance of representation in Western thought. From Aristotle onward, representation names the process of signification but also a species of prestigious cultural works. If it always seemed proper to say that the sign "represents" thought, the sense in which the *Iliad* (for example) represents heroic action discovers the insufficiency of that concept from a Peircean perspective. The notion of mediation points to a hidden complexity of the representational process. Whatever is mediated by Homer's poem may not be only or primarily heroic action, but other, myriad aspects of Greek culture the representational status of which is not equivalent to that of the figure of Achilles or the event of the Trojan War. These other elements of "context" raise a question about the adequacy of the concept of representation to capture the complexity of the very process for which its name stood for so long.

## Mediation and Representation

This complexity is at once apparent if we were to consider the difference between the depiction of the same subject in an epic poem and in a painting. The difference is first of all a matter of the medium, in which scholars of course have always been interested, even if they do not always bear this difference in mind *comparatively*. It has always been easier to settle comfortably within the horizon of a single medium and to direct one's attention thence to what the work represents. The preference for the representational schema, which in the Western tradition extends to works of art generally, can be traced all the way back to Aristotle, who identified his subject in the *Poetics* as the "art of representation" (mimesis), setting aside in the same passage the question of "in what" form a representation is transmitted. The Greek phrase here is translated as "means," or sometimes "medium," even though there is no equivalent term in the Greek text.[10] *The question of medium was set aside for two millennia*. We can hypothesize that it was only the proliferation of *mediums* in the twentieth century, and the fierce competition among them, that forced the fact of medium into full visibility and solicited a new conceptual analysis of medium in the form of communication theory.

The claim that the proliferation of new media is the context for the development of communication theory is large enough to require a separate essay, though the argument is certainly familiar. It will have to suffice here to recollect some of the philological evidence that attests to a mutation in the medium concept. The *OED* is especially rich in its citations, which suddenly multiply from the later nineteenth century on. These include *medium* as (1): "Any of the varieties of painting or drawing as determined by the material or technique used," and (2): "A channel of mass communication, as newspapers, radio, television etc." Increasingly the term *media* is used to name what were formerly called *arts*; in addition, new information or communication media are identified that do not rise to the status of arts.[11]

To carry this enumeration forward into the twentieth century, I would cite finally the emergence of the new profession of public relations or advertising, which completes the modernization of the media concept. For obvious reasons, the pioneers in this field were highly sensitive to the diversity and specificity of media, and one must look to these figures for the first analyses of subjects later taken up by communications studies. We can do no better than to cite here the figure of Edward L. Bernays, who baptized the new field in his seminal study, *Crystallizing Public Opinion*, and described its arena of operation: "His [the public relations advisor's] advice is given not only on actions which take place, but also on the use of the mediums which bring these actions to the public it is desired to reach, no matter whether these mediums be the printed, the spoken or the visualized word—that is, advertising, lectures, the stage, the pulpit, the newspaper, the photograph, the wireless, the mail or any other form of thought communication" (Bernays 1923, 14). It was only necessary thereafter to standardize the plural form of medium with the Latinizing *media* in order to disembark on the new continent Bacon glimpsed in his *Advancement of Learning*.

*Saussure and Jakobson.* The proliferation of new meanings and professional fields provides a context for understanding the twentieth-century project of reconceiving the process of signification within a model of communication. The drive to produce such a model was in part the result of the immanent development of linguistics as a discipline; but that discipline also gestured toward a discourse—semiotics—whose scope was greater than that of linguistics and included potentially the study of all forms of communication. Still, Saussure and most twentieth-century linguists continued to insist that the model of communication should be grounded in the scenario of one person speaking to another. Predictably, the exclusion of writing and of new, "mediated" forms of speech—telegraphic, phonographic, and so on—undermined the model over the long term, with the manifold results much later twentieth-century theory has given itself to analyzing. The clamor of mass communications was already too great to be successfully contained by linguistic theory. Two brief annotations of Saussure and Jakobson will suggest the failure of theory to exclude these modes of communication even in the process of conceptualizing communication.

It has not escaped anyone's notice that linguistics turned increasingly in the twentieth century to the scene of communication and to the task of modeling this scene. Saussure's inaugural *Course in General Linguistics* depicts communication in its starkest form, as two talking heads whose mouths, ears, and brains are linked together by two dotted lines. However firmly this picture insists on the speech scenario, its slackly suspended lines hint at the telegraph or the telephone, a visual pun that Saussure surely did not intend. Does this picture acknowledge, if only unwittingly, the fact of new mediums? Saussure is of course openly worried about that old medium, writing, which he firmly grasps and just as firmly excludes under the category of representation: "The sole reason for the existence of the latter [writing] is to represent the former [speech]" (Saussure 1973, 24). This entirely conventional description spells trouble of the sort with which we are all too familiar from the later critique of Derrida; but that is not the problem to which I am pointing.[12] The question raised by Saussure's exclusion is rather why signification requires more than just representational tokens in order to operate.

Elsewhere Saussure tells us, "The value of a word is mainly or primarily thought of in terms of its capacity for representing a certain idea" (Saussure 1973, 112). This sentence states the proposition to be refuted, namely, the most familiar model of signification: "language represents thought." Saussure is unhappy with such an *antithetical* distinction between language and thought, however, and his theory of the signifier and signified as a composite "articulation" asserts an indissoluble or constitutive "link" between these two elements of the sign. The articulating function is different from representation and is expressed in Saussure's analysis by a series of figures: the action of wind producing waves on water, cutting the recto and verso of a folio, and the coin as medium of exchange. Without attempting to explicate these figures individually, we can register the extent to which an unstated concept of the *medium* governs the figures, a small troop of medial metaphors conscripted to fend off the model of representation: "If words had the job of representing concepts fixed in advance, one would be able to find exact equivalents for them as between one language and another. But this is not the case" (Saussure 1973, 114–115). Representation is happily relegated to writing, as the medium that is supposed to do *no more* than give us tokens for spoken words.

We need not draw any philosophical conclusions from this analysis, which attempts only to describe the philological context for modeling linguistic communication. In context, two very different formulations are contending for dominance: (1) "Language represents thought"; and (2) "Language mediates thought"—the second, however, only tacit in Saussure. His theory of signification rejects a *representational* relation between words and concepts in favor of a looser relational concept, one that is closer in the end to mediation, though this concept never comes out from behind the figures Saussure uses. In the following half century, the conceptual architecture built on the higher ground of mediation reaches a great height; we need only ascend a few stories to get a view of the surrounding terrain, which brings the arguments of Whorf, Sapir, Vygotsky, and Wittgenstein into view. Reality itself can be described for these theorists as mediated by language. The hypothesis of language as medium is no longer just a way of pointing to the distorting effect of words, in Locke's sense, but of evoking the world making of semiotic mediation. This thesis goes far beyond what can be inferred from the scenario of the talking heads. The proliferation of communication media in the social environment suggests that communication can no longer be modeled as the representation of silent thought by spoken word.

The more rigorous the analysis of communication, the more likely it is that a process of mediation will come to the fore. Jakobson's much later model is exemplary in this respect. In his extremely well-known and influential essay, "Linguistics and Poetics," Jakobson analyzes the scene of communication into six constituents, the two poles of *addresser* and *addressee* and four intermediate terms: *context, message, contact*, and *code*. Of these, the "contact" isolates the medium as such, without apology, and possibly with some awareness of the new information theory of Claude Shannon and others who disseminated the notion of "channel" that Jacobson invokes in his definition of contact: "a physical channel and psychological connection between the addresser and the addressee, enabling both of them to enter and stay in communication" (Jakobson 1981, 27–29).[13] Although this physical channel of course includes the medium of speech in face-to-face exchange, the physicality of the channel is best evinced by technological devices of communication, which are prone to obvious physical (mechanical or electronic) failure. When Jakobson describes the communication "function" specific to contact, which he calls "phatic," he evokes the vicissitudes of telephonic communication: "Hello, do you hear me?" It is difficult to know what other *content* phatic utterance can have than a query about the failure of the channel; but behind the apparent semantic poverty of this utterance lies the entire problematic of mediation as the extrapolation of a social/communicative process from the physical medium.

The purpose of Jakobson's model is ultimately to give an account of the poetic function, which he defines as a "set toward the MESSAGE as such."

The "message" does not name a content so much as the words of which the message is composed; the "set toward the message" is thus a use of language that "promotes the palpability of signs, deepens the fundamental dichotomy of signs and objects" (Jakobson 1981, 25). By directing attention to the words of the message, as opposed to its "meaning," poetic function implies the special quality of poetic language, although this quality is not restricted to poetry. Jakobson immediately attributes the quality of the poetic to many other uses of language, most famously the campaign slogan, "I like Ike." The slide here from poem to advertising suggests that a concern with media was more than implicit in the structure of Jakobson's model. The poetic function introduces a kind of melodious noise into the channel of communication, which heightens consciousness of the channel as such, and so distances the message from the "object" or referent. In the case of the slogan cited, the pleasant concatenation of syllables allows us to admire the words without endorsing the candidate.

It would be hard to deny that the "set toward the message" effectively fuses contact and message; the same words constitute both the channel and the self-reflexive message. Jakobson is typically drawn to the phonemic manifestation of such self-reflexivity, but his preference for sound pattern allows him to overlook the mediation of poetic speech by writing as a channel of communication overlaying (or remediating) the medium of speech. Whatever Jakobson asserts with regard to the possibility of making the verbal channel "palpable," the same is true of writing; and much poetry depends on that fact. Despite the emphasis on sound, Jakobson's model of communication does not theoretically exclude levels of mediation, such as the mediation of speech by writing, the mediation of writing by print, and so on. At any of these levels, the medium can be disturbed or manipulated in such a way as to heighten its self-reflexivity, resulting either in noise or poetry. The semantic poverty of the phatic utterance is thus the converse of the semantic fullness of the poetic.

In other scenes of theory, the archaistic term *poetic* is replaced by *literariness*, or even *writing*. In all of these venues, the "referential" or representational function is interrupted by something that theory likes to say belongs essentially to *language*. But the language paradigm, to which Jakobson made so crucial a contribution and which still dominates the cultural disciplines, fails to grasp communication as an underlying problematic, and so loses the opportunity to see the poetic, the literary, or writing, as media. This thesis, unfortunately, can only be offered as an assertion, awaiting demonstration in some other context. It remains for us to consider in this essay some implications of the challenge posed to representation by the notion of mediation—if it is indeed the case that what was set aside by Aristotle millennia ago has now thrust itself into the foreground of culture.

## Mediation and Media

The fact of media proliferation suffers from no lack of interest among scholars. As with much theory concerned with technological change, early efforts tend to be written in the manner of prophecy, and worse, exhibit a tendency to ratify technological determinism.[14] A more sober reflection on the question of mediation will resist imputing determinism to the mere fact of a technical means. There is no question, however, that a process of mediation can be extrapolated from the operation of media, and that this extrapolation has deepened the theory of media and of society. The work of John B. Thompson can be cited in this context, specifically his mapping of the types of "mediated interaction" in modernity.[15] This work dovetails at a higher level with that of Anthony Giddens, Manuel Castells, and others working in the general fields of media and information theory. Granted the distinction of this work, it is a puzzling fact that the concept of mediation remains undertheorized, especially within the cultural disciplines.

*Williams.* In his invaluable account of the mediation concept, Raymond Williams observes that its emergence responded to uneasiness with the relegation of culture to mere "reflection" of the economic or political domains. I shall consider "reflection" in this context to be a version of the ancient topos of representation, in certain respects both simpler and more complex than classical mimesis (simpler because the metaphor of reflection reduces the cultural work to a passive role implied by the metaphor of reflection, more complex because the object of reflection is potentially the social totality). Williams argues that the "social and material character of artistic activity" was "suppressed" in reflection theory, and that "[i]t was at this point that the idea of reflection was challenged by the idea of mediation" (Williams 1977, 97). This account seems plausible, although it is difficult to pin names and dates to it. Although Williams credits mediation theory with a less "alienated" grasp of culture, he is reluctant in the end to see mediation as a successful remedy for the deficiency of the reflection concept, largely because mediation assumes "separate and preexistent areas or orders of reality, between which the mediating process occurs whether independently or as determined by their prior natures" (Williams 1977, 99). Putting the problem in this way, a mediation can be hard to distinguish from the kind of reflection critical theory likes to expose as ideological distortion. Indeed, representation has been easily incorporated into many versions of media theory in preference to mediation, in order more easily to sustain the project of ideology critique.[16] For Williams, if mediation cannot be shown to operate *positively* to draw social divisions together, as opposed to merely confirming their separation, then he is inclined to conclude that mediation "seems little more than a sophisticated notion of reflection."

It is not too difficult to see what diminishes the usefulness of the mediation concept, even in the context of studying the "media." It is always possible to collapse the mediations performed by the media back into representations, which become vulnerable at once to exposure as ideological distortions. This has been the perennial strategy of cultural critique, and its reassertion in recent years has in effect *set aside* mediation once again even as the study of media has intensified. But what is mediation anyway, if it is something more or other than a species of representation, as Williams feared? Let us refrain from the temptation to make this question disappear by resorting to the High Theoretical move of dropping down to the process of signification, conceived as the undoing of representation (or reference). Grasping the nature of mediation depends in my view rather on affirming the communicative function in social relations, that is, the *possibility* of communication. The indispensable condition of mediation is the interposition of *distance* (spatial or temporal) between the terminal poles of the communication process (these are persons but also now machines). This distanciation is another way of looking at the operation of *transmission* (what Bacon called "tradition," but meaning now something much more inclusive than he imagined). The notion of distance should not be mistaken, then, as an equivalent term for *absence*, or as a pole in the philosophical antinomy of presence and absence. Distance creates the possibility of media, which become desirable for themselves and not as the default substitute for an absent object. If this were not the case, we would not be able to explain the pleasure of reading novels, seeing films, or for that matter, accumulating money, the medium of exchange. This pleasure may have been produced at first as the byproduct of the sense of urgency driving the formation of media in response to the real differentiation and dispersion of social locations, but arguably this pleasure has become an end in itself, spurring the creation of new media where there is no compelling social necessity for their existence.

The introduction of the theme of pleasure at the end of this essay will perhaps seem surprising, but the point I am making can be confirmed fairly simply by noting that certain "mediated" interactions—e-mailing or text-messaging, for example—have come to seem preferable to face-to-face encounters (as in the notorious occurrence of e-mailing the coworker in the next room). These examples of mediated communication are far less grand than the grandest works of culture but operate on the same basis. At another level of abstraction, the question of culture as a "mediation" for the economic and political domains of society poses the same question. The tactical problem that emerges from the multiple levels and forms of *media* operating in the process of mediation is how to join the theory of mediation to the fact of media, without reduction of the former to the latter or displacement of the latter by the former. The more layers of mediation, the more tempting it is either to overleap them, to make links of a "representational" sort, or to attend only to those connected with *technical* media, as opposed to, say, genres or discourses that are just as much mediations as print or film. It has been difficult, that is, to grasp the fact of mediation in light of habitual turns to representation and without the help provided by the presence of a technical medium. As a result, the question of mediation and its relation to media remains to be resolved.

# WHERE WERE THE MEDIA BEFORE THE MEDIA?

## MEDIATING THE WORLD AT THE TIME OF CONDILLAC AND LINNAEUS

KNUT OVE ELIASSEN
AND YNGVE SANDHEI JACOBSEN

### 1. Theoretical Ambitions

One of the chapters in Bruno Latour's *Pandora's Hope*, "The Historicity of Things," comes with the challenging subtitle, "Where were the microbes before Pasteur?" And to drive the point home, Latour opens his argument with a provocative question: "Were the microbes made up by Pasteur?" (Latour 1999, 145). Those familiar with the author's rhetorical style will identify the key words "made up by." Pasteur's microbes, Latour argues, should not be thought of as given, "objective" natural phenomena, silently and invisibly awaiting their discovery and naming by the French chemist, and therefore ready to become a "breakthrough" in biochemistry. "Microbes" is rather the name of an event, the constitution of a new field of knowledge and an institutional framework that allowed nature, institutions, scientists, textbooks, politicians, and money, to meet and circulate in a novel and different discourse network. Our title indicates an ambition to transpose the epistemological insights from *Pandora's Hope* to the issues of the historicity of media and the relationships between modernity, Enlightenment, and media. If the term "media" can be said to be subject to a historicity comparable to Pasteur's concept of microbes, the field of media studies might be treated to a similar exercise in historical reflexivity as that of biology. Duly aware of

Latour's aversion to the epochal category of the modern (Latour 1993, 10), we are, nevertheless, of the opinion that his particular take on science studies permits a fresh approach to the question of the historicity of the media and their relation to the issues of modernity and Enlightenment. The philosophical monism underpinning Latour's critical analysis of the modern dichotomy of nature and culture has a striking affinity to important currents in Enlightenment philosophy.

Extending Latour's historicizing perspective to the notion of *media* in an analytical strategy that also draws on impulses from media archaeology, we would like to ask the following question: Is "media" an adequate term for analyzing and describing the transmission of information in the period before the first half of the nineteenth century? Particularly as the term's modern signification—"a channel of mass communication"—did not appear in the English language before 1850, "media" might arguably be an anachronism with respect to the study of earlier centuries (cf. *OED*; Peters 1999). Up until the nineteenth century the content of the term appears to have been organized chiefly in two semantic clusters, and it was used primarily in the singular; a medium was either a material means of expression or it was the milieu in which a communication took place. The first signification can be illustrated by a quote from Francis Bacon: "Cogitations bee expressed by the Medium of Wordes." The second sense of the term is exemplified by the scientific notion of the *aether*, a substance that in the physics of the seventeenth century allowed for the transmission of light waves and in the eighteenth century permitted natural forces like electricity or magnetism to work at a distance. The chief difference is that "medium" did not signify technology, invention, or even *technê*. Rather, a medium was either a *representation* (both separating and joining) or a *milieu* that created contact between separate entities (cf. Foucault's analyses of the classical episteme's notion of representation in *The Order of Things*). It appears that the plural form did not come into common usage until the nineteenth century and then significantly in relation to technologies and cultural phenomena that in the early twentieth century would be referred to as the "mass media."

In his study on the history of the visuality of the eighteenth and nineteenth centuries, *Techniques of the Observer*, Jonathan Crary (Crary 1990) shows how the development within physics and the advent of such new sciences as biology and psychology entailed a new understanding of the nature of human perception. Contrary to eighteenth-century notions of the sensory apparatus, the physiology of the nineteenth century no longer conceived of the senses as open receivers to a materially given outside world, Crary argues, but instead as productive faculties. One of the many consequences of this modern anthropology is that the Aristotelian conception of the senses as the "windows of the soul" is once and for all relegated to the history of philosophy. Henceforth, perception is essentially defined by its limits or flaws. From now on the human sensorium was a possible source of impure representation due to noise produced by the sense organs themselves (cf. the interest in the visual afterimage). Moreover, perceptions were essentially marked by the limited "bandwidth" of the sensory channels (cf. the discovery of "invisible light," infrared and ultraviolet). Crary's version of the shift from a classical to a modern model of perception is not restricted to the discourses set forth by science and philosophy. Human perception was reconceptualized and, according to Crary, regulated and organized according to different patterns. Articles and books were important parts of the process, but so too were instruments, experimental practices, institutions, works of art, and numerous optical instruments. The nineteenth-century stereoscope challenged, as much as any philosophical treatise, the commonly accepted idea of the human subject as a stable center of perception organizing sensorial data of a spontaneous and literally "immediate" nature. It is the shortcomings of human perception that are exploited by stereoscopy. Our eyes show us a three-dimensional and continuous room even though what we in fact are looking at are two flat and separate surfaces. In this perspective later inventions like that of photography and cinematography can be considered both a way of demonstrating the limits of human vision and an attempt to overcome these restrictions by means of technology.

What the telegraph shares with photography and the analog computer is not only that the information processes are automated, but also that their mode of operation eludes human perception. A central concern in Friedrich Kittler's *Optische Medien* (Kittler 2002) is to show that the removal of the human agent from the communication loop is a decisive feature of the communication technologies of the first half of the nineteenth century. In these new information circuits, such as the telegraph, photography, or Babbage's analytical engine, the dominant forms of information processing were no longer mediated by eye and hand, passing through the interiority of an individual occupying the middle position in the chain of transmission—as was the case with such older communications systems as painting, text copying, and optical telegraphs. This new cluster of technologies made the procedures of registering, storing, and distributing information take a decisive step in the direction of the automation of the communication situation. In modern discourse networks human operators, as James Beniger so convincingly has shown, are sources of noise and error, and thus beyond the control mechanisms of the system (cf. Beniger 1986).

Following up the leads left by Kittler and Crary as well as those that can be gathered from the semantic history of the term, a formula like "modern media" has the ring of a pleonasm. Media is an inherent part of modernity; it is one of its constituents. Hence the question of whether a term like "modern media" should be considered a "false friend," to borrow a formula from French "mediologist" Régis Debray. "In *mediology*, 'medio-' signifies neither 'media' nor 'medium' but *mediations*, that is, the dynamic assemblage of procedures and intermediary bodies that insert themselves between a production of signs and a production of events. These in betweens belong to the hybrids (Bruno Latour), mediations that are at the same time technological, cultural, and social" (Debray 1994, 29). Thus the questions: What are the costs of analyzing the communication structures of the eighteenth century with the concept of media? What can be gained by structuring the analysis of the flows of information with other conceptual tools?

The historicity of words like "medium" and "media" neither should nor can be separated from the historicity of the things they denote. There is a historicity of things and technologies just as there is a historicity of concepts and discourses. Furthermore, their respective modes of functioning interact. Thus, the history of the development of the various technologies and techniques of communication is not independent of the history of the notion of "media." What Latour calls a semantic "abyss" opens up between words and the world. The problem can to a large degree be considered the consequence of a particular and familiar philosophical preconception, namely, that the nature of the nonhuman world of things is conceived of as stable and solid, substantial and objective, while discursive orders are of a transient nature (saturated with subjectivity and human interest). The issue of conceptual referentiality may be dealt with in a more adequate or productive manner by considering both the material world of technological objects and the discursive world of concepts as elements that interact, thereby avoiding the strict ontological division between the human and the nonhuman.

Such an approach would permit a double perspective that includes both the history of the various technologies and apparatuses that make up the materiality—the *hardware*—of the history of the media and the various discourses on the media. We hope that this analytical strategy will facilitate a perspective on the history of media technologies that does not understand technology as the material precondition or grounding of culture, formatting, and even determining history's political and social spaces but instead highlights its contingent character. The typewriter, the telegraph, Braille, and the gramophone are all examples of technologies originally developed for purposes different from those they ended up serving. Our "media archaeology" of the historical nature of information flows in the time period before the advent of the notion of "media" highlights the ruptures and discontinuities rather than the opposite. A term like "media ecology" neatly sums up how the technologies of information produce a particular life world, providing the forms of experience that make up, give shape to, and regulate the interiority of the socially constituted individual.

## 2. Pre-media Mediations?

It has been noted that neither the seventeenth nor the eighteenth century thematized its channels of propagation of information in any explicit way, be they oral, written, or pictorial (Raymond 2006; Schulte-Sasse 2001). Despite such seventeenth-century neologisms as "propaganda" (from the Counter Reformation institution Sacra Congregatio de propaganda fide), or the use of terms like "communication," there have been, to the best of our knowledge, no attempts at establishing overreaching conceptual elaborations determining the common aspects of such various "media" as books, pamphlets, newsletters, posters, engravings, coins, and magic lanterns. However, if the demarcation between the flaws of the sensory apparatus and the automated signal flows plays such an important role in the establishment of the notion of "modern" media, as the arguments of Crary and Kittler imply, it might be worthwhile to look at the idea of information flows from a different angle. If we accept Crary's (Foucault-inspired) claim that the eighteenth century did not perceive the human senses as epistemological obstacles in any absolute sense, and if we, furthermore, concede that the technologies, which the parlance of a subsequent era was to refer to as "media," were not defined essentially as a means of representation and distribution external to the mind or the body (but also of a completely different nature), but rather were conceived along the line of the human sensorium, the possibility of a different configuration of the nature of the flows and processes of information emerges.

Schulte-Sasse (2001) claims that the first instance of a modern use of the word "medium" in German is to be found in Johann Gottfried Herder's *Vom Erkennen und Empfinden der menschlichen Seele* (On the Cognition and Sensation of the Human Soul) from 1778. Schulte-Sasse quotes the following passage: "Then my mind uses all the acquired skills and finesse of a blind man with his rod, to grope, to feel, to learn about distance, difference, measures; and in the end, without this medium we do not know anything, we must trust it." And Herder continues: "For a thousand other sensing individuals through a thousand other media, the object may also appear as something quite different, even if itself might be a complete abyss, of which I sense or suspect nothing; for me it is only that which my mind and its medium ... present to me" (Herder 1994, 348). Schulte-Sasse employs this passage to advocate Herder's status as a precursor to later media theory. The media discussed by Herder, however, has little in common with contemporary revolutions in book printing or with new technologies such as optical telegraphy. Rather, he is out to discuss a very simple tool, the rod, and the analogy between this tool and the physiology of the human senses. The rod is somewhere in the middle between man and world, it is a medium, and as such it operates across the same border (or abyss) between mind and matter, between subject and object, as the senses. Man's perception of the world is the main concern of the argument, and Herder's concept of medium is thus embedded in his epistemology.

Although the appearance of the word "Medien" might suggest that this passage in Herder can be seen as an early meditation of the nature of media and their transformative powers, we are inclined to emphasize the elements in the quotation that connect it to an earlier "pre-media" reflection upon the nature of man and the faculties of perception and communication. Most striking in this respect is the nature of Herder's example, the blind man. This is in fact a reference to a recurrent topos in seventeenth- and eighteenth-century epistemology and the philosophical debates of the nature of sense impressions; a topos that with the anthropological turn of the new medical paradigms of the early nineteenth century migrated from philosophy to physiology and psychology.

One of the origins of the topos of the blind man is René Descartes' *Dioptrics* (1637). The philosopher suggests that someone deprived of sight could triangulate distances using crossed handheld rods by sensing hand separation and wrist angles. The suggestion was most likely inspired by John Napier's invention of logarithms (1614), and the contemporary growth of trigonometry from a subfield of geometry to a mathematical discipline in its own right with practical applications in fields such as map making, surveying, and artillery range finding. Descartes only adds one more discipline to the list of such applied sciences when he suggests that a blind person might familiarize himself with his surroundings by tapping the objects around him with a rod. In an interesting move, he goes on to argue that the perceptual operations of those with normal vision resemble the blind man in the way he probingly explores and maps the world with the aid of his rod. Thus the French philosopher combines analytic geometry with the epistemology of perception and cognition. For Descartes, as Peter Dear formulates it, "human behaviour was part of human physiology, and that physiology, like the rest of the physical universe, was mechanistic" (Dear 1998, 53).

The similarities between visual and tactile perception of the world, between the eye and the rod, are also discussed by Descartes in one of his early works, *Le Monde, ou Traité de la lumière* (1629–1633). The treatise suggests that light rays passing from luminous bodies to human eyes are material entities traveling instantaneously and in straight lines through space. The comparison of light rays and rods is thus not a didactic metaphor. In principle the light rays are just like wooden rods. But because the particles that pass in straight and unbroken lines between an outer world and the human eye are so exceedingly small, because this rod is thinner than all other rods at our disposal, we are unable to grasp the light rays as easily as we grasp the wooden rod in our hand.

In the narratives of the history of philosophy, Descartes' mechanical explanation of vision is often introduced as the beginning of "Molyneux's problem." Named after the Irish natural philosopher William Molyneux, this problem remained for a long time a crucial point and a matter of contention in empiricist and sensualist philosophy. It was famously articulated by John Locke in 1690 in his *Essay concerning Human Understanding* (where Locke in fact is paraphrasing Molyneux): "Suppose a man born blind, and now adult, and taught by his touch to distinguish between a cube and a sphere of the same metal. Suppose then the cube and sphere were placed on a table, and the blind man made to see: query, whether by his sight, before he touched them, could he distinguish and tell which was the globe and which the cube?" (Locke 1995, 94). Descartes' rod-wielding man and Molyneux's problem will in the following converge into a series of questions: What are the functions of the sensory apparatus in the mapping and recognition of the world? How does it mediate between the mute outside of things and the sensitive inside of the body? What are its relations to the talkative and denominating mind? And last but not least, how are the shortcomings of the human senses improved upon (by making use of technologies of mediation that a later era would call media)? This set of problems was a recurrent topic in the epistemology of the eighteenth century, discussed by virtually every philosopher who had an opinion on epistemological issues; to name a few, G. W. Leibniz, George Berkeley, Voltaire, Christian Wolff, Denis Diderot, David Hume and Julien Offray de La Mettrie. We will follow another and perhaps not so obvious a lead, Etienne Bonnot de Condillac's *Traité des Sensations*.

## 3. From Condillac's Statue . . .

Etienne Bonnot de Condillac's *Traité des Sensations*, originally published in 1754, is generally considered his most important work. Both an analysis of perception and a work of epistemology, its main thesis can be condensed to one question: How does the mind gather information from the world that surrounds it?

Condillac's argument starts with an analogy between the human body and an imagined statue. The statue has the same mental potential as a person who has never experienced any sense impressions. As the author unlocks one sense channel after another, the statue gradually becomes sentient, an awakening that is conceived as a parallel to the processes of human cognition, or more precisely, as a psychogenesis. Organized inwardly like any individual, it is, however, devoid not only of experience but also of innate ideas or intuitive knowledge.

As we are dealing with nothing less than an experiment in materialist psychology, this requires as with every experiment, an observer, and furthermore that this observer is placed in a specific position. Initially, Condillac invites the reader to assume the point of view of the statue, a rhetorical device that strongly suggests that the following will be about the reader: "I would therefore like to underline that it is very important to put oneself exactly in the place of the statue we are going to observe. It is necessary that we begin to exist when it begins to exist, to have only one sense when it only has one; to acquire but the ideas that it acquires, to acquire nothing but the habits that it acquires, in one word, it is necessary to be nothing but what it is. It will not judge things like we do until it has all our senses and all our experience; and we will not judge like it unless we conceive ourselves deprived of all that it lacks"(Condillac, 1984, 9).

One of the polemical purposes of Condillac's treatise is to challenge Locke's notion of how the senses provide intuitive knowledge of objects, an ambition realized by studying the senses separately and analyzing the particular nature of the information each of them provides (becoming manifest in the mind as ideas). Although perception is famously understood by Locke to be "the first faculty of the mind," it is still a property of the mind, not a property in and of itself. Condillac's thought experiment suggests that consciousness is an aftereffect of perception rather than a stable center registering and processing what is seen, heard, smelled, tasted, and felt. Hence the central issues of his treatise are formulated from the beginning: How do we discover and map cognitively the space that surrounds us and the objects that fill it? What is the nature of the process from which this faculty emerges? How does each sense mediate in its own specific way between us and our surroundings? The last question is particularly important as each sense, according to Condillac, produces its own particular sensations, and, as ideas are but transformed sensations, generates its particular ideas. Human knowledge is thus essentially nothing but transformed perception.

Following a commonplace in philosophical anthropology, at least since Aristotle's *De Anima*, Condillac's analysis begins with the basest of the senses, smell. This first sensation, the first conscious moment, has no other specific qualities than the presence of an undefined sensation, of a diffuse but intense quality. The statue's mind is not yet a consciousness in the sense of a center of reflexivity or a container of knowledge; the statue is completely absorbed by the single presence of smell, creating its first and basic psychological response, attention. From this simple stimuli model, the experience of sensation deepens as experience broadens and diversifies: some smells are pleasant, others less so, even unpleasant or painful. On and off, presence or absence, pleasure or pain, are the basic principles for the statue's knowledge and such binary oppositions continue to determine the operations of its mind even as these operations grow in complexity. Complexity follows from memory, the ability to recall sense impressions and compare new ones with older ones. Recollections permit comparisons and lay the ground for judgment; memories of earlier sense impressions lead the statue to the discovery of its own temporal existence, generating self-consciousness. By comparisons and judgments, series of impressions are established, habits are formed, and general ideas born.

Condillac follows the same line of argument through his analyses of the senses that make up the three subsequent levels of his perceptual hierarchy: hearing, taste, and sight. In the initial analyses of the first four senses, the statue's contact with the exterior world is strictly limited to the nature of its sensations. The existence of an exterior world has certainly been taken for granted, but only from the point of view of the reader. The statue is pure receptivity, solipsistically limited to its own sensual interior. Nothing but a receptacle, it is but an interior surface wherein the sense impressions of the things of its world, transformed through the channels of the senses and simple binary oppositions, are turned into increasingly complex series, based on repetition and difference, all due to the increased training and fine-tuning of the sensorial apparatus. Consequently, even though its mental interior gains in complexity, the statue is still without any sense of space; it remains folded in on itself.

The second part of *Traité des Sensations* introduces touch, and thereby the statue to the world that surrounds it. Tactition confronts the statue with the external world of things (and, by the same token, Condillac with Berkeley's idealism from *An Essay towards a New Theory of Vision*). Surprisingly, considering the conventional system of philosophical anthropologies, touch thus crowns the hierarchy of the five senses. Condillac's initial definition of touch is the self-perception of breath: "I will call this the *fundamental sentiment* as it is by this machinal function [*jeu*] that animated life commences" (Je l'appelerai *sentiment fondamental*, parce que c'est à ce jeu de la machine que commence la vie de l'animal; Condillac 1984, 89). Touch is fundamental, and life is regarded from the point of view of mechanics. However, there is no life before there is *animation*, movement. And there is no proper self-consciousness, no *anima*, before the statue registers its own movement, and simultaneously the mechanical and sensual fact of its own breathing.

If the first tactile impressions are passive self-perceptions, they are nevertheless crucial for the process of becoming sentient. The decisive moment arrives when the statue is set in motion, when it literally reaches out for and confronts its environment. As the statue's hand meets an obstacle, it is halted, generating the double impression of touching and being touched. From this elementary fact it deduces the reality of external objects, acknowledging that there are at least two objects in this world, itself and the obstacle. Any notion of extension requires that the statue is set in motion. By venturing out into the world, groping (*tâtonnant*) its way from one obstacle to the next, the statue charts the material world of things and the distances between them; space being the experience of that which does not offer resistance (a procedure analogous to Descartes' account of the blind man's tatterings in *Dioptrics*). Touch is the condition of possibility for experiencing the limits of the body, things, and spaces, and teaches the other senses to recognize objects as external. Most important, touch transforms perception from a passive receptivity to an activity; seeing is turned into gazing.

We will not dwell on Condillac's analysis of the forces and desires that stimulate the statue to venture out into the world. Let it suffice to say that such initiatives follow from the psychological model based on stimuli and response, in short, the theory of needs introduced in his initial analysis of the basic functioning modes of perception. More interesting is a remark the philosopher makes in passing at the end of part 2, chapter 7, about how the statue, by chance, may discover how to use a rod, not only to help it maintain its balance, but also to measure the objects it encounters on its way "By the same chance that made it grasp for a rod, it learns little by little how to maintain its balance, how to judge bodies into which it might crash, and to recognize the places where it might safely place its feet" (Le même hasard, qui lui fera saisir un bâton, lui apprendra peu-à-peu qu'il peut l'aider à se soutenir, à juger des corps contre lesquels elle pourroit se heurter, et à connoître les endroits où elle peut porter le pied en toute assurance; Condillac 1984, 117). The passage appears somewhat out of the blue, and the example of the rod does not reappear until a few chapters later, where Condillac explicitly addresses Descartes' discussion of the rod-wielding and sightless blind. Molyneux's problem is discussed briefly in passing (chap. 8, pt. 2), interestingly enough, in connection with the rod: "In gripping a pebble, our statue makes itself an idea of a body different from that of a rod that it has touched in all its length; it senses in a cube angles that it cannot find in a globe" (Condillac 1984, 121). The analogy between sight and touch is explicit and vision is repeatedly defined as tactile: "The way in which the hands judge objects with the aid of a rod, of two rods, or even a larger number, resembles so strongly the way in which the eyes judge, aided by rays, that since Descartes, one usually explains the one problem by the other" (Condillac 1984, 137).

An important event in the psychogenesis of the statue is the birth of reflexion that is, for Condillac, the faculty of comparing complex ideas. It has already learned how to abstract by separating parts from a whole; likewise, it has acquired the skill of analyzing by examining the constitutive parts of a given object. Analysis precedes synthesis as simple ideas precede the more complex ones. But due to touch, to the tactile grounding of the things of the world, the statue develops the ability to perform the mental operation of joining into well-ordered and meaningful ensembles that which the initial analysis took apart. Touch allows the statue to compare the different aspects of any given object, thus it *reflects*. "The number of ideas that might be created by touch (*tact*) is infinite, as it comprises all relations of size, thus a knowledge that the greatest mathematicians will never exhaust" (Condillac 1984, 126). The basic qualities are numbers and extensions, so through them the world is fundamentally experienced as measurable. Size is not of an absolute nature; measures are always relational, established by comparing previous sense experiences.

After having analyzed the particular nature of the various senses and the particular character of touch, Condillac's next step is to discuss the combination of sensations. Step by step he follows the initial hierarchy and, thus, the first mixed sensual experience is that of touch combined with smell. Interestingly, the example chosen is that of flowers; Condillac brings the statue out into a field of flowers. Like many philosophers and natural historians of the eighteenth century, the statue appears to have a natural penchant for botany, not only enjoying the flowers for the olfactory pleasures they provide, but also finding gratification in categorizing them by linking tactile form to smell and thus imposing the geometrical order of tactility on the less tangible nature of olfactory impressions: "That a certain odor is, for instance, always in a triangle, another one in a square. . . . It believes sensing a figure in an odor, and touching an odor in a triangle"; "The rose differs from the carnation, because it has this form, this tissue" (Condillac 1984, 161). The passage quoted is significant for at least two reasons: it conceives of the statue in the model of the natural historian, the botanist, as the exemplary figure of the activity of mapping the objects of the world and the system of their internal order. Furthermore, it links sensation to representation. What we are witnessing bears a striking resemblance to taxonomy, the organizing of the world into tableaux, a central epistemological procedure of the seventeenth and eighteenth centuries, that, according to Foucault, spans from the grammatical treatise of Port-Royal and the mathematical world systems of Leibniz, by way of the geographical maps of the explorers and the tabulations of the new statistical sciences, to the *tableaux économiques* of Quesnay and the botanical systems of Linnaeus. And finally, as Foucault points out in his analysis of the tableau in *The Order of Things:* taxonomy does not preclude communication; it orders the world, thus providing the medium through which the transfer of representations of the world may take place. These representations are, in Condillac's analogy, neither linguistic nor geometrical in a strict mathematical sense (the question of language is not dealt with in the treatise), but are nevertheless of a general character and have the nature of signs: Sensations are turned into objects that can be represented, organized, and in the end, transferred and set into circulation.

Information is thus the result of a series of operations beginning with sensation. The first step consists of sensations that are, with respect to the individual form of perception, differentiated, systematized, and ordered into series. "Single-channel" information is juxtaposed to and compared with information stemming from other channels, thus through the act of reflection producing abstract ideas, mental representations: "To abstract is to separate one idea from several others that enter with it in a composite whole" (Condillac 1984, 41). Knowledge is the product of repeated abstractions leading to habits and general ideas. The repetition or serial nature of sense impressions is the condition of the possibility of turning perception into cognition. Cognition is thus based on habits, in other words automated cognitive processes: "Seeing and judging are done simultaneously and are confused" (Voir et juger se font à la fois, et se confondent; Condillac 1984, 178).

Condillac's emphasis on the automation of cognition is worth dwelling upon as he expressly considers it one of philosophy's callings to analyze notions where experienced phenomena tend to be confused with its causes.

Philosophy thus runs contrary to the nature of common experience, which Condillac in fact considers a by-product of the way our sensation-based mind works. However, another facet of this argument is more pertinent in this context. As we have seen, the increasing lucidity of the statue is conceived as the result of a series of binary processes as its memory functions by establishing a series of categories. This analytical and systematic nature of the statue's mental processes does in fact point toward an obvious analogy; the statue is analogous to an automaton, an android, set into movement by its maker, a complex machine for registering, recording, and even, in principle, distributing information about the world. What we are dealing with is an entity that is receptive and *programmable* at the same time; an organic mechanism controlled by external stimuli and with responses. Although qualitatively changing, it is regulated by a given systematic matrix and thus lays the foundation of a vision of Man that is nothing less than mechanistic.

### 4. . . . By Way of the Android . . .

The analytical approach of Condillac's treatise, the systematic nature of his procedure, and the underlying mechanistic ontology, is a classic example of what has been called the eighteenth century's *esprit de système*. Nowhere was this strong belief in the systematicity of the mind and world more clearly expressed than in the metaphor of the clock, "the emblematic figure of the 'machines of machines'" (Mattelart 1996, 22). The clock mechanism was visible proof of the notions of regular motion and the discrete nature of time, and the rising prestige of the art of building timepieces also made its impact on the issues of philosophical anthropology. "The body is but a watch, whose watchmaker is the new chyle," La Mettrie states in his radical, and immediately forbidden and indexed, work *L'Homme-machine*. The utopian rationalism of the thought of La Mettrie—whose first philosophical work was aptly called *The Natural History of the Soul* (*L'Histoire naturelle de l'âme* [1745])—and Condillac (and others) found a remarkable illustration and parallel in one of the recurring figure of the eighteenth century, the anthropomorph automaton, or *android*.

The interest evident during the seventeenth and, even more so, the eighteenth century in the automaton borders occasionally on obsession. From Cervantes and Descartes to Kant and E. T. A. Hoffmann, automata were a recurring philosophical and literary topos. In the words of Foucault, the first pages of the anatomico-metaphysical register of the Classical age were written by Descartes, and continued by physicians and philosophers (Foucault 1977, 138), and, we would like to add, by craftsmen. Among these are not only the famous and brilliant works of engineers and watchmakers like Jacques de Vaucanson, Pierre and Henri-Louis Jacquet-Droz, Vargas Kempelen, and others, but also a large number of lesser-known makers of automated puppets and figures of various quality. From the courts to the marketplaces, from royal societies to church spires, these mechanized humanoids are found throughout the eighteenth century, providing ample material both for literature and philosophy (cf. Chapuis and Droz 1958; Mayr 1986). The android plays a particularly important role for the era's defenders of the notion of the mechanic nature of living organisms. As Cassirer remarks, the materialism of the eighteenth century no longer considers the relation between body and soul from the viewpoint of substance, "but almost exclusively from the viewpoint of causality" (Cassirer 1979, 68). However, a mechanistic, mathematical universe need not be specifically mechanical; the machine is a model of intelligibility, the material in which its principles unfold might just as well be organic as inorganic.

The history of the android's relation to philosophy goes back a century to a remark in the *Discourse on the Method*, where Descartes notes that animals must be considered "automates" as the two cannot be distinguished from each other. Descartes elaborates his ideas on "the animal machine" (*la bête machine*) when he stresses that in principle it would be possible that automata might be so cleverly designed that they could not be discriminated from a living organism. Animals are complex organic machines, thus susceptible to mechanistic explanation. From a Cartesian point of view, there is no absolute criterion separating the animate subject from the animated object with respect to physical activities.

The mechanized puppets of the eighteenth century surpassed those of the previous century with skills that were not only astonishing but in fact quite convincing. The three famous androids made by father and son Droz—the Piano Player, the Draughtsman, and the Scribe—were able to play, draw, and write. The Scribe, the rumor went, even took dictation. Vaucanson's famous flutist combined mechanics and pneumatics with such sophistication that his flute could be exchanged with any other flute and the puppet would still produce the most beautiful music. Also well known is Vaucanson's duck that not only flapped its wings and quacked, but also ate and defecated. However, the most famous automaton is probably Vargas Kempelen's Chess Player—known from Walter Benjamin's "Theses on the Philosophy of History"—that toured the courts of Europe for decades, virtually a counterpart to the modern media event, and, like Vaucanson's and Droz's dolls, an element in the propaganda of the new rationality heralded by the spokesmen of the Enlightenment. The importance of these puppets lies not in the tensions between the rationalism of the mechanistic worldview they illustrated and the elements of trickery or illusionism involved in the successful presentation and staging of the dolls, but rather in their phantasmagorical or even utopian dimensions. Vaucanson was reputed for his ambition to build a moving and talking mechanical man. The representatives of what Jonathan Israel recently called "Radical Enlightenment" subscribed more or less wholly to Spinoza's famous definition of man as a spiritual automaton (*automata spirituale*). And even the more moderate Leibniz states in paragraph 64 of the *Monadology* that "any living being's organic body is a kind of divine machine or natural automaton."

Vaucanson — who is one of the inventors of the punch card and who thus helped to clear the way for Babbage — was not the only one playing with the idea of making a genuine automated individual. However, to a modern observer, there is a remarkable absence of any uncanny dimensions in the eighteenth century's androids. They are a far cry from Hoffman's or Shelley's Romantic troubling and troubled monsters. "What finesse in the details! What grace does not its mechanism have in all its details!" Denis Diderot exclaims in admiration of Vaucanson's mechanical miracles in the *Encyclopédie* article "Androïde." And in Diderot's novel *Jacques le fataliste et son maître*, the idea of the natural automaton is explicitly celebrated as an emblem for the causal relationships that govern organic and psychological life. The narrator and the novel's two central characters are referred to as automatons throughout the text, the former complaining that the reader treats him like an automaton, while both the master and his servant Jacques act as if preprogrammed on numerous occasions. Their automated behaviour is in line with the materialistic philosophy of the time as it is formulated, for instance, in Diderot's own *Philosophical Thoughts*, paragraph 18, in terms that clearly demonstrate his affinity to La Mettrie: "The world is quite simply a machine, with wheels, ropes, blocks and tackles, springs and weights" (Diderot 1975, 17).

Condillac's humanoid statue is closely related to one of the eighteenth century's most popular mythological figures, Pygmalion. Like its more famous mythological predecessor, Condillac's statue is set into movement and its animation is a function of its anima. The crucial moment in Condillac's psychology occurs, as we have seen, when the statue reaches out and gropes for its rod. However, the significance of the gesture is not limited to the fact that in doing so the statue proves to be animated. The gesture also implies another ambition, the desire or need to map the world as the rod is turned into a measuring tool, a piece of technology that allows the statue to discover, analyze, and format its surroundings. It is the urge to know and to interact with the world that sets in motion the processes that spawns the genesis of its existence as a self-reflective and experiencing being. The measuring rod is a prerequisite for the necessary ordering of the sensual impressions; it mediates between senses and objects, providing a scale that allows for the representation of the world. Thus, armed with its rod, it is ready to make its first foray into the world of natural wonders, initially, as we have seen, driven by its passion for flowers.

## 5. . . . to Linnaeus Preparing for His Journey to Lapland

In his older days, the then famous botanist Carl Linnaeus liked to praise himself for his unparalleled gifts of observation. Showing few signs of false modesty, he thought of himself as "one of the mightiest observers ever," and he regarded it his special responsibility "to write down everything God ever let my eyes see in this world" (Linnaeus 2003, 1). An early example of how Linnaeus goes about his duty of perceiving, registering, and annotating the world is his diary from the journey to Lapland in 1732, *Iter Lapponicum*. Here, the ideals of seeing and writing are combined with the notion of being mobile. In his correspondence with the Royal Scientific Society in Uppsala in which he solicits funding for the journey, Linnaeus had already singled himself out as a man particularly fit for such an undertaking. Not only well-educated in the three realms of nature and endowed with an incomparable talent in representing the world in writings and drawings, he also had the advantage of being in his best years, unbound by family commitments, a man in good health capable of "running up and down" every mountain he might come across during the expedition. The travel diary confirms this image of Linnaeus as a highly mobile observer of the world. From the very first paragraphs of *Iter Lapponicum*, the author seems keen to depict himself, or should we say his body, as particularly well-equipped for the three scientific purposes of observation, representation, and mobility:

> As I had been assigned by the Royal Scientific Society [of Uppsala] to travel to Lapland with the aim of illustrating the three Regna naturae of the same region, I thereupon ordered my things and dressed up in the following equipment. My clothes consisted of a small frock of simple Swedish wool; it had no pleats but small lapels and a collar of shag. Neat leather trousers. Tie-wig. Bast-green carpus [a cap with ear flaps], boots with no heels on my feet. A small leather bag, one foot long, somewhat shorter in width, made of tanned leather, with hooks on one side so you could tie it together and hang it onto yourself; in this bag I placed one shirt, two pairs of half sleeves, two nightshirts, inkhorn, pen case, magnifying glass, perspective. Head-net to protect me from mosquitoes.

> This protocol. A pile of paper to preserve herbs in folio. A comb. My *Ornithology, Flora Uplandica,* and *Characteres generici.* The hunting knife hung at my side, and a small flintlock musket between my thigh and the saddle. An eight-cornered rod marked with mensurae. A notebook in my pocket with a passport from the Chancellor of Uppsala and the Society's recommendation. With this I travelled from Uppsala town, May 12, 1732, which was a Friday, at 11 o'clock, 25 years old, give or take half a day. (Linnaeus 2003, 1)

This seemingly disordered list of heterogeneous items, wig, pen, pajamas, comb, handgun, and so on is not without a certain affinity to Borges's famous apocryphal Chinese encyclopedia. It presents us with a jumble of mixed and unrelated objects with no obvious connecting link. Some of the items are clothing meant to shelter and comfort the body of the traveler (for example, the trousers), others are scientific tools. But like its Borgesian counterpart, the list leaves us with the feeling of a strange will to order, a system of the world that we might not fully apprehend but that we nevertheless can appreciate.

A salient feature of Linnaeus's account of himself as the observing and writing subject fully prepared for travel is the rod. It establishes a common link between Descartes' blind man in geometrical space, Condillac's statue in the flower field, and Linnaeus's body as the scientist embarks upon his journey from Uppsala to Lapland. Like his philosophical predecessors and counterparts, Linnaeus uses his rod as an instrument; it is not merely the wanderer's support or a prosthesis helping him attain balance and speed, but it is also a scientific instrument ready to be employed in the measurement of quantities and distances in the regions through which he will travel through. The small leather bag, one foot long, is only the first in a long series of objects that the travel report describes by the measuring standards supplied by the rod. Soon we are to be informed about the height of the rye, the length of the road, and numerous other measurements. Depending on the object described, Linnaeus can apply any of the rod's eight measuring standards—one on each side of the rod—to transform the things of nature into the names and numbers of the book. The distances are either found by direct comparisons, the rod employed as a measuring stick, or by trigonometric calculations, the rod used as a surveyor instrument.

As remarked by Foucault in *The Order of Things*, Linnaeus introduces us to a world of visible and measurable quantities. However, its basic visibility does not prevent some objects from being perhaps too far away or too small to be discriminated and studied properly with the naked eye. As one would suspect, the natural scientist is equipped for such eventualities. The magnifying glass and its perspective give Linnaeus the opportunity to continue observation where unaided vision proves insufficient. It might be tempting to conclude that Linnaeus's scientific vision of the world is brought about with the aid of eighteenth-century media technologies. The rod aids the eye in passing judgments by establishing scales, points of reference, and internal relations. The magnifying glass and its perspective help the scientist see otherwise indiscernible details, and human memory is enhanced by the notebook, the portable herbarium, and the protocol we are reading, *Iter Lapponicum*.

Contrary to Crary's and Kittler's analyses of how nineteenth-century media tend to suspend the human agent from the information circuit, in the case of Linnaeus the function of the body is to be a junction for flows of information. The body of the natural historian is the medium through which data have to pass in order to be collected (registered), represented (processed), and set into circulation (distributed). No information is brought back from Lapland to Uppsala without having first passed through the scientist's eyes and ears and then found a representation by means of his hands. These steps in the processing of information are, in turn, understood in an analogy to optical and mechanical devices. Modern (or Romantic) demarcations (dichotomies), like those drawn between technology and nature, organic limbs and mechanical devices, sense impressions and analog registration technologies, seem anachronistic when applied to eighteenth-century theories of perception. The eye is a lens, the lens is an eye; the chiasm illustrates how there is no principal difference between the state-of-the art representation technologies of the camera obscura and the physiological processes involved in vision. The light rays whereby the human body orientates itself are analog in form and function with the rods whereby a blind man charts the space that surrounds him. Because the differences between bodies and machines are not crucial ontological demarcation lines, Linnaeus can draw a picture of himself where he is—simultaneously the scientific subject exercising its function as a supreme observer of nature and an assemblage of organs and perceptual prostheses of all sorts—a surface where optical devices, metering instruments, and different registers of perception converge.

Although the human body is situated at the intersection between different faculties of perception, and although technologies of scaling and representation are connected to this junction, this is not to say that elements of noise, filtering, or imperceptibility are allowed to enter the circuit. Such an understanding would imply elements of opacity, noise and hidden depths, or abysses, in the relation between nature and man. The world observed by

Linnaeus is, however, open to the senses; it is a world where things and words may converge in proposition (cf. Foucault, *The Order of Things*, on articulation and proposition as the two central procedures of classical epistemology). Nature exists as if to be counted, measured, analyzed, combined, set up in a list or laid out on a table, presented in a veritable tableau.

Inserted between the reference to the comb and the hunting knife, Linnaeus makes note of the portable library he brought with him on his journey. The classification tables of the ornithology, the flora, and the *Characters Generici* (an early draft of Linnaeus's later main work, *Systema Naturae*) gave the young scientist a powerful instrument for naming the known and the unknown in the world through which he traveled. The sexual system of classification worked out by Linnaeus in his *Flora Uplandica* (1728–1732) gave him the basic framework for the later *Flora Lapponica* (1737). The tableaux from these books, in turn, gave ideas for new journeys and an intensified search for species still unknown, but with a predetermined position in the botanic system. Just like Pasteur's microbes one and a half centuries later, the Linnaean sexual system is also the name of an event, an event that allowed nature, scientists, textbooks, politicians, and money to meet and circulate within new discourses, institutions, and channels of transportation and communication.

Measuring and classifying are two of the most central procedures in Linnaeus's analysis of the world. In the first case, the scientist proceeds by wielding his measuring rod, in the other, by the aid of systematic tables. An important part of Linnaeus's journey to Lapland will, however, remain unnoticed if we limit our study to the inventory list of his tools. Knowledge only becomes science when it is distributed; measuring and ordering are only the first, albeit necessary steps. To set up a successful distribution of knowledge, mobility is a requirement. Linnaeus cannot remain within the borders of his study chamber. Like Condillac's statue he must be confronted with the uncharted world of objects. He has to move through the world, gather information on his way through Lapland, and communicate this information to the archives of Uppsala and the printing presses on the continent.

Thus regarded, the instruments of representation that Linnaeus brought with him on his journey to Lapland were important, not only for realizing the ambition to map and understand these regions, but also to transform the world into what Bruno Latour has called "immutable mobiles" (Latour 1987, 1990). The work of the scientist is described by Latour as a way of "drawing things together" (Latour 1990, 19). With this expression Latour neatly captures how science, on the one hand, might proceed by actually transferring physical objects from one place to another and how, on the other hand, it often makes this work more efficient when aided by representations (for instance, drawings). The world is mobilized by changes of scale and material. It is split up into exemplary bits and pieces that may easily be transported back and forth between the periphery—where the confrontation with nature takes place, sense impressions are registered, and objects collected (Lapland)—and a center of science (Uppsala) where the information is analyzed, stored, and redistributed to wider circles of the scientific society (the Republic of Letters). The inventory we are reading gives an illustrative example of how data compression is at work in Linnaeus's travel account. As the list makes it possible to store a maximum of things in a minimum of space, it is a perfect genre for this kind of traveling account.

That mobility is an absolute requirement is of consequence not only for the scientific instruments Linnaeus carries with him but also for his choice of clothing and equipment. Contrary to earlier explorations of northern Sweden, Linnaeus set out alone. Rather than moving through the Swedish mountains with a band of colleagues and servants, Linnaeus turned himself into a minimal mobile entity. As his luggage is limited to what he can carry with him, he is free to choose the fastest means of transportation in any given situation, be it by horse, boat, or on foot. Speed is the decisive factor when choosing equipment. If a simple Swedish frock is more appropriate for the practical needs of the journey than a more elegant outfit, in itself more appropriate considering Linnaeus's social standing, simplicity is to be preferred. Even clothing used by the "primitive" Sámi population that Linnaeus is out to investigate is employed by the scientist in his attempt to acquire the necessary speed. The Sámi were known throughout Sweden as fast runners, and since Linnaeus believed their light footwear with no heels to be a partial cause of this swiftness, he set out on his journey with similar boots.

The passport mentioned toward the end of Linnaeus's inventory draws our attention to the fact that mobility also is a question of politics and law. From 1555 until 1860 passports were compulsory not only for crossing national borders, but also for domestic journeys in Sweden. A lot of effort went into the control of the movement of the country's inhabitants. If someone wanted to be ferried across a river, for instance, a passport or other appropriate travel documents were mandatory. Linnaeus had, of course, no problem in obtaining the necessary permission.

The institutional and economic context of Linnaeus's journey is quite explicitly referred to in the inventory. Linnaeus starts his list with a gesture of gratitude to the institution that sent him out on the road (Sweden's Royal Scientific Society), and he ends the list by referring to the institution that finally will receive the information he is about to gather (the very same Royal

Scientific Society). In a catalog otherwise characterized by how the similar and the dissimilar are placed side by side, this institutional framing is worth noting. Far from propagating a view of himself as an autonomous scientist free to move wherever he wants, Linnaeus makes it clear that the institution with the money also sets up the limits for the adventure he is about to embark upon. In this perspective *Iter Lapponicum* can be regarded as a travel account even in the economic meaning of the concept. It has been suggested, for instance, that Linnaeus's obvious exaggerations as to the distances covered were not only supposed to impress the society members but also to explain why he overextended his budget. Travel grants from the society were namely given from an estimation of the capital required, not per day, but per mile.

One of the items Linnaeus brought with him on the journey, but which remains unmentioned in the inventory list, was the *Qwærenda*, a list of ninety questions that the members of the society wanted the young scientist to examine when traveling up north. The questionnaire contained topics that we today would consider proper aims of investigation for such sciences as geology, botany, and anthropology, just to mention a few of the disciplines that the document touches upon. An example is question number nine: How thick are the glaciers in the mountains? Other questions, however, seem to mix rumors, mythology, classical literature, and scientific studies in a fashion that is not so easily recognizable for the modern reader. Linnaeus was not only supposed to measure and organize the world but also to investigate the possibility that remnants of Noah's ark could be found on a mountain top in Jämtland, to examine an eight-foot-long sea serpent described in the Italian manuscript *Iter septentrionale* (Northern Journey), and to find out more about a Sámi girl who had reportedly turned into stone near the town of Piteå in northern Sweden. The questionnaire was in fact a guide or even a checklist for Linnaeus's investigations. With this instrument in hand, he knew what to look for in Lapland and thereby what to write down in his travel journal. In the final manuscript of *Iter Lapponicum*, Linnaeus returns repeatedly to topics that the *Qwærenda* had pointed out in advance. The fabulous gift of observation that Linnaeus prided himself on was therefore not as unmediated as the author tries to suggest when he describes himself as "one of the mightiest observers the world has ever seen." Whereas Linnaeus seems to describe a system where perception comes first and writing follows, the *Qwærenda* makes us aware of how writing might be involved already in the act of observation, prefiguring and formatting what we see.

In his autobiographical sketches, Linnaus describes his scientific activity as a double enterprise of seeing and writing, where sensual impressions constantly are transformed into physical representations. One activity leads seamlessly into the other, and little attention is given to the gaps or noises between the respective acts of perception and notation, between what is seen and what is said, between things and words. They all come together in the protocols and activities of the scientists. In accordance with this, his self-portrait is that of a man constantly taking note (and notes) of the world, in incessant interaction with nature or with books. His "media" are everywhere as Linnaeus's books abound with instruments of observation, accumulation, and communication. The common trait of the various technologies deployed are their basic nature; they can all be thought of as simple extensions or representations of the human body's own capacities of travelling and observing the world.

## 6. Two Images of the World: The Seventeenth and the Eighteenth Centuries

At the turn of the century the android was no longer a model of intelligibility. Anthropology, what Foucault called the "invention of Man," turned the automaton into a monster and the body of the scientist into a problem, a change that can find no better illustration than E. T. A. Hoffman's tale "Der Sandmann." The happy positivism of Linnaeus's days gave way to new forms of reflection and self-reflection. The android was no longer a mirror, but rather an abyss, a mechanic other that threatened the ideal of man's powers of self-legislation, in short, his dignity, as Kant remarks at the very end of his essay "Was ist Aufklärung?" In fact, an abyss also occurred in the quote from Herder at the start of our investigations. Considering the possibility that we all have different senses at our disposal and that the objects of an outer world only can come to mind through these senses, Herder is suddenly struck by the fear that the outer world is empty and groundless. The objects that we see and touch might not be there at all, maybe they are nothing but an abyss [*vollends in sich selbst ein Abgrund*] that we never can know anything about. All we can know, Herder, concludes, is the mind and the media. With this statement, the processes of modern self-reflection and media reflection can begin. *Errare humanum est* is the order of the day, when with the dawning of the nineteenth century, as Kittler, Crary, and Foucault have insisted, an anthropological opacity is inserted in what was once a circuit for the transmission of data. The takeoff in modern media technologies and the advent of modern anthropology both require that the transmission of information be separated from its human substratum. The world has become invisible; what you see is no longer what you get.

In February 1967 in an interview with the French public radio station France Culture, Michel Foucault gives a succinct résumé of the central historical argument of *The Order of Things:* "That which characterizes the culture of the seventeenth and eighteenth centuries is a kind of relation, it is the attempt to establish a direct, immediate, and controllable relation between discourse and truth. How may a discourse be so that it is susceptible to arrive at the truth? That what the nineteenth century, from its very start, invented for this question, is, precisely, a third term. The nineteenth century substituted the truth-discourse line, the bipolar axis of truth and discourse, with a triangle, a triangle on the summit of which there is Man" (quoted in Chartier 2006, 153). Things, words, and bodies come together in quite different ways in the seventeenth and eighteenth centuries. The sensualist of the mid-eighteenth century was no stranger to the idea that the senses could deceive, that there was a singularity in the impression of each sense so that the information it conveyed was not necessarily comparable to that stemming from another channel. However, these insights did not in principle challenge the idea that the world as such was open to a cognitive mapping based on the sense impressions; it is a system of thought that is a stranger to the idea that there should be an element that is counterproductive, that in the very act of perception it generated rather than filtered noise. Such an epistemology allows for a quite different logic of mediating between words, things, and bodies, or for that matter, mediating in the sense of communicating words, things, and bodies. This logic was brought to an end with the advent of media. "Media" is the name of an event that helped close the epistemology of mediation of the eighteenth century and replace it with a media anthropology. The concept of media, as the Western world has known it since the nineteenth century, is thus inextricably linked to the phenomenological premises of modern anthropology. The best way to escape from the immanentism of media-formatted epistemology and phenomenology, and the abysses that surround it, can only be realized by a radical historicizing of the notion of media.

# MEDIATION AND THE
# DIVISION OF LABOR

PETER DE BOLLA

1

This brief essay sets out to make some headway into two related areas of speculation: the historicity of concepts and the history of conceptual formation. Both, in their different ways, ask the question of mediation—in the sense of the travel between two points—and of history. In the case of the first we can legitimately ask whether concepts are susceptible of being parsed historically. Which is to say, are concepts historical forms? In the case of the second the question of history appears in a different locale: whether different periods develop concepts at different rates, or if historical conditions determine the rate of change of concepts, or the rate of their production. Change, of course, in the sense of mutation or *mediation*, might not be the same thing as the invention or production of new concepts. This brings up questions about the nature of conceptual formation and its relations to social and cultural practices, about the rules that relate concepts in any one conceptual array, and about the mediation of concepts from within an array and across arrays. History, then, rears its head in all of these interrelated questions. We might inquire, therefore, if certain periods expose the need for the invention of new concepts, while others block or prevent new conceptual formation; if certain concepts have limited half-lives while others have extremely long duration. And of course behind all this is the unanswered question as to whether it makes sense at all to talk about concepts in a temporalizingly contingent fashion.

Perhaps the most pressing issue—as to what, precisely, a concept *is*—will be my point of entry into the topic at hand, the formation of the concept of the division of labor. This question immediately raises the distinctions or distinctiveness of the disciplines. It poses the question of mediation between and across disciplines in a particularly stark fashion. It might, perhaps, be said to pose the question of disciplinarity itself.

If one goes to what some might imagine the most obvious place for a definition of the word "concept"—say, philosophy as that term designates a history of Western thinking around ideas that have, by consensus, been understood to be foundational—the matter is far from settled. This is not the place to present a tour d'horizon of the arguments that have flowed back and forth between philosophers of only the last three centuries—some proper names will have to stand as placeholders here: David Hume, Immanuel Kant, Ludwig Wittgenstein, Gottlob Frege—but it is useful to call to mind the fact that even within this tradition the word "concept" is used in a variety of ways. It is sometimes distinguished from, among a number of other terms, belief, mental representation, or idea. The analytic tradition often seeks to make further distinctions from within the term itself—thus perceptual concepts are to be distinguished from logical concepts—and to differentiate properly philosophical questions about concepts from psychological questions. And then, of course, the moment one introduces another discipline—psychology as it has become (it could be argued that for some philosophers in this long tradition, psychology was not thought of as distinct from philosophy)—and then another, and so on, the range of distinctions between the uses of the word "concept" and its others (meaning, representation, notion, thought, sensation, norm, knowledge, episteme, theory) becomes unwieldy.

Another approach might be to look at those places where particular pressure has been brought to bear on the usefulness of thinking about concepts historically. Once again I am not going to provide a conspectus but the work of, among others, Reinhart Koselleck, Michel Foucault, Lorraine Daston, Ian Hacking, Donald Davidson, and Quentin Skinner could all usefully help one take the measure of the difficulties in answering the question, What *is* a concept? once one opens it up to interdisciplinary contamination.

The use of the word *concept* is ubiquitous within the humanities, and most especially within those terrains that either constitute themselves as specifically *historical* disciplines or accept the contingency of historical formation. Much of the time its definitional indistinctness does not seem to worry us, and on those occasions (by far the greatest) the term "concept" merely means "the use of a word." I say "merely" here to indicate that when one begins to forensically analyze these occurrences it becomes immediately clear that a certain freighting to the selection of the term "concept" rather than "meaning" or "word" is implied. As if in saying "the concept of power" rather than "the word power" some special emphasis or weight is given to the usage by dint of the selection of "concept." But if we are to follow Skinner here, we are unlikely to ascertain much about how, say, an individual negotiates social linguistic acts and social reality if we do not hold fast to a distinction between the words the individual uses and the concepts that individual possesses. Words, on this account, are not identical to concepts.

This brings me back to my initial question. From this angle, does it make sense at all to talk of concepts as being subject to history, to the vagaries of historical formation and transformation? Or, rather, is the conceptual apparatus we inhabit a given? Time or space, for example, might be understood as concepts determining how humankind has sought to think about "relation"—to the world and others, between points or locations on a map or within a terrain, between the present and the past, and so forth—since humankind itself was identifiable. Thinking about the problem this way suggests that there may be a difference in kind to concepts. Some are, let us say, load-bearing, while others are decorative. In introducing a deliberate architectural metaphor here I mean to press on what I shall call the epistemological architecture of a concept. Load-bearing concepts are those that enable us to think (or conceptualize) something else. They provide a support for the uses of other concepts whose relations to the field of other decorative motifs are governed by rules. I take it that the task of sorting out my initial questions would be to describe these rules of relation—let's call this a grammar—and to give a sketch of the overall architecture of any specific conceptual array. A third task would be to investigate something like the genetic code of a particular concept or array of concepts in order to understand the organic processes by which it might produce new or dependent conceptual forms.

In so far as this is a method, I think of these three metaphorical ligatures—architecture, grammar, and genetic code—as each providing different accounts of a concept's definition. In other words, it helps us identify the contexts in which the use of a particular named concept (a word or phrase) is or might become intelligible. This brings to the foreground the notion that any mediation—between disciplines or subdisciplines, between interests within a field, and certainly between historical moments—can only be the result of the construction of a shared discourse within which a consensus must be sought for the use of specific words (hence, concepts). And that will tell us how concepts are formed in a purely functional sense. This may be all we can do. But that might well be more than enough. In order to make this rather more concrete, let me now move on to an example.

2

*The Wealth of Nations*, Adam Smith's great treatise on the economic rationale for modern society, opens with a discussion of the division of labor. But how did Smith come up with this idea, where did he get the term "division of labour" from? Since there is no use of the precise term in any of the literature pre–*Wealth of Nations* does it make sense to conclude that he invented it? Let me introduce a qualifier here: although in the literature on Smith another view is often put forward—that the phrase was not original to Smith—in fact this is not, technically, correct. I will begin with the claim that Smith invented the concept of the division of labor. Implicit in this statement is the claim that the concept as we use it—which essentially understands value as a consequence of labor—was not available pre–*Wealth of Nations* and that postpublication was "naturally" or unproblematically taken to be a load-bearing concept. Thus the category "value" is thinkable under the concept "division of labour." And in relation to this invention it is important to note that value, for Smith, does not only appear in the sphere of the economic. It also, simultaneously, appears in the sphere of the aesthetic–this is what I mean by a "conceptual array"—but for the sake of brevity I am going to leave that aside. Consequently throughout the body of this discussion I am going to keep fairly close to the economic dimensions of Smith's argument.

Let us start at the beginning, with the very opening of *The Wealth of Nations*:

> The greatest improvement in the productive powers of labour, and the greater part of the skill, dexterity, and judgment with which it is any where directed, or applied, seem to have been the effect of the division of labour. (Smith 1976a, 7)

Smith goes on to present the famous example of the manufacture of pins—an enterprise that in the scheme of things is really only very "trifling"—which he has observed being done by many hands:

> To take an example, therefore, from a very trifling manufacture; but one in which the division of labour has been very often taken notice of, the trade of the pin-maker; a workman not educated to this business (which the division of labour has rendered a distinct trade), nor acquainted with the use of the machinery employed in it (to the invention of which

the same division of labour has probably been given occasion), could scarce, perhaps, with this utmost industry, make one pin in a day, and certainly could not make twenty. (Smith 1976a, 8)

As we see here, Smith's first observation concerns the benefit of the introduction of mechanical means of production—where a sole laborer may take hours to produce just one pin, the division of the manufacturing process into separate tasks, procedures, or *stages* allows for a far more efficient means of production. The division of the manufacturing process requires mediation between discrete parts of it. Here technology—however understood (and the division of manufacture is itself a technology quite apart from the invention of machinery qua machinery)—necessarily introduces the requirement that different segments of a larger entity be negotiated or subject to mediation. There is, however, a cost to this invention. This atomization of the making process alienates the laborer from ownership of the thing made—since under this organization of the manufacturing process, one laborer might only get to perform one task, may only see or handle one element of the finished product:

> But in the way in which this business is now carried on, not only the whole work is a peculiar trade, but it is divided into a number of branches, of which the greater part are likewise peculiar trades. (Smith 1976a, 8)

It is important to dwell a moment on the use of the word "peculiar" here. A casual reading takes this word to signify something like "singular," belonging exclusively to a single person. But the word may also, of course, mean "strange," "odd," or "queer" (all meanings available at the time of Smith's writing). This brings to the surface of the discourse some of the tensions that need to be resolved in Smith's attempts to conceptualize what the effects of the division of labor will be. And here the alienation of work, or more properly the alienation of the laborer's relation to what he produces, is going to be fundamental in the subsequent fortunes of the division of labor. As a load-bearing concept it is going, a hundred or so years later, to enable the construction of another set of concepts that articulate property relations under capital.

Smith goes on to detail the various subdivided processes or procedures that are required: "One man draws out the wire, another straights it, a third cuts it, a fourth points it, a fifth grinds it at the tops for receiving the head." In this way the division of labor is not, essentially, a division of the energy, as it were, needed to produce the object but a parceling out of the tasks required in a particular process of manufacture. In this sense, what Smith is noticing is the *division of manufacture*, the atomization of the manufacturing process. It is not *labor* that is being divided up into segments but a set of making processes. From here, however, it is possible to trace how, starting from this observation, Smith goes on to invent a new concept, one that enables us to think labor *as itself capable of being divided*. It is important to my overall methodology to sort out what kind of conceptual form this invention might be—to give it a shape or form, to type it as well as subject it to a forensic analysis. In essence I shall be attempting to elaborate the epistemological architecture of the invented concept, the division of labor *as such*. And here it seems important to notice that as a concept it does not name something that might fall within the domain of empirical observation. In other words, Smith may be able to observe the *division of manufacture* but not the division of labor. Why this is so brings me to my next section.

### 3

What I have said so far might seem to fly in the face of accuracy: surely, it may be objected, Smith begins with his empirical method. It is completely uncontentious to claim that he starts with an observation of a manufacturing process that is capable of being atomized, and equally uncontentious to note accurately that he calls this the division of labor. The phrase itself is, one might reasonably opine, intended to simply describe this atomization. As I have pointed out, something like this is the aim or objective of the first chapter of his treatise. This is how he continues:

> Those ten persons, therefore, could make among them upwards of forty-eight thousand pins in a day. Each person, therefore, making a tenth part of forty-eight thousand pins, might be considered as making four thousand eight hundred pins in a day. But if they had all wrought separately and independently, and without any of them having been educated to this peculiar business, they certainly could not each of them have made twenty, perhaps not one pin in a day; that is, certainly, not the two hundred and fortieth, perhaps not the four thousand eight hundredth part of what they are at present capable of performing, in consequence of a proper division and combination of their different operations. (Smith 1976a, 9)

The point here is that *manufacture* is prey to the logic of arithmetic. Taken in another register, what Smith is identifying and then using to build his concept is what Kant called the mathematical sublime. The empirical observation that one person working on his own can only produce—perhaps—one pin in a day, while working in a team of ten he can contribute to the manufacture of forty-eight thousand pins requires a conceptual framework in order to render the observation intelligible. Here that load-bearing concept is the sublime.

This then enables Smith to extend the observation from the peculiar or singular to the more general—thereby beginning to build a concept capable of providing the architecture necessary to understand each instance under a general rule. So he is at pains to demonstrate that this effect is not only a feature of the manufacture of exclusively trifling items. Or of only those goods susceptible of improvements in technology relating to their manufacture. The wonder of division, of the multiplier *as such*, is capable of being applied to any number of cases: "The division of labour, however, so far as it can be introduced, occasions, in every art, a proportionable increase of the productive powers of labour" (Smith 1976a, 9). And, in an important step in the argument, such benefit accrues not only from the manufacture of a single item but, when extended to the business and commerce of society, plays out its magical effects throughout the entire productive system: "The separation of different trades and employments from one another, seems to have taken place, in consequence of this advantage" (Smith 1976a, 9). In this way the performance of the engine of society may itself be improved by dividing the totality of actions. And, given the multiplier, this naturally leads to the increase of total wealth.

But it is not at all immediately clear how this outcome comes about. How can the process of *division* lead to the multiple effects Smith describes? How can division into constituent parts lead to a manifold increase in the whole? If the commonsensical view holds that division merely breaks into smaller segments an unchanging quantity that is the whole, why would this process of the division of manufacture get started in the first place? At first it looks as if the answer to this lies in the same mystified analysis of the making process—just as manufacture is enhanced by the atomization of the tasks required so any whole that may be broken into parts will benefit from the same mysterious logic and plenty will result. The answer here *lies in the machine.* But Smith is too much of a confirmed empiricist to be satisfied by this. Starting once again from empirical observation, he identifies three quite different causes for the benefit of the division of labor. The first, perhaps obviously enough, concerns the skills needed in any particular process. And, again commonsensically, the last is derived from the amenability of manufacture to machines. He writes:

> This great increase of the quantity of work which, in consequence of the division of labour, the same number of people are capable of performing, is owing to three different circumstances; first to the increase of dexterity in every particular workman; secondly, to the saving of the time which is commonly lost in passing from one species of work to another; and lastly, to the invention of a great number of machines which facilitate and abridge labour, and enable one man to do the work of many. (Smith 1976a, 11)

I think it is pretty clear that the first and last are *conceptually* determined by the division of manufacture—labor here is merely a set of tasks that, when grouped together, comprise an entire manufacturing process. According to this description the improvement of dexterity has obvious and tangible effects at the level of craft. And the invention of machines is itself a consequence of the recognition of the benefits of the division of manufacture:

> [E]very body must be sensible how much labour is facilitated and abridged by the application of proper machinery ... I shall only observe ... that the invention of all those machines by which labour is so much facilitated and abridged, seems to have been originally owing to the division of labour. (Smith 1976a, 13)

But the second, "the saving of time," is conceptually very different. This is the key to understanding how the division of manufacture is going to mutate into the division of labor itself, the creation of a concept of labor that is itself divisible (the sharing out of labor). Here—although I can only signal this in a very cryptic form—what philosopher Jacques Rancière has to say about the aesthetic and its formulation in terms of the division of the tangible seems to me to be of the utmost moment in understanding how a load-bearing concept plays out in both the aesthetic and economic realms.

But let us keep with the observation above, that "the saving of time" introduces a very different conceptual architecture into the analysis. In Smith's account it is the time saved by having to travel from place to place in the production of goods that leads to increased productivity:

> A country weaver, who cultivates a small farm, must lose a good deal of time in passing from his loom to the field, and from the field to his loom. When the two trades can be carried on in the same workhouse, the loss of time is no doubt much less. (Smith 1976a, 12)

But why should the conservation of time be one of the causes of the division of labor? How, in fact, does one *save time*? As if it were a quantity that might be conserved, or banked, even traded? This is far from a simple idea, as we shall see, but for the moment let us keep with the easier notion that duration in the manufacturing process has a cost. If it takes a day to make a pin then the cost of the labor as a function of the time taken is higher than if forty thousand pins can be made in the same time. That much seems to be obvious to us since we have naturalized the concept that Smith is here inventing. For, of course, this observation is only conceptually intelligible once labor itself, labor in the abstract, can be valued. Thus what might be called the "time of labor" can now be understood as an abstraction that is both measurable and divisible. Within this epistemological architecture it becomes possible to see how one might "save time" in the sense of using it to different ends. The concept of speed now becomes a coefficient of cost.

Smith himself found the origin of this notion of the division of labor mysterious and worth pondering. He notes, for example, that it does not arise from a process of intellection and cannot, therefore, be understood to be a product of man's wisdom. In this sense, one might say that for Smith, at least at this point in the treatise, the division of labor is *preconceptual*:

> This division of labour, from which so many advantages are derived, is not originally the effect of any human wisdom, which foresees and intends that general opulence to which it gives occasion. It is the necessary, though very slow and gradual, consequences of a certain propensity in human nature which has in view no such extensive utility; the propensity to truck, barter, and exchange one thing for another. (Smith 1976a, 17)

So, far from being the fruit of man's ingenuity, it is in fact hardwired, as it were, in human nature, and, on this account, is not susceptible to further analysis. It cannot be parsed any further, remaining simply a function of our humanity, like speech or reason. He notes:

> Whether this propensity be one of those original principles in human nature, of which no further account can be given; or whether, as seems more probable, it be the necessary consequence of the faculties of reason and speech, it belongs not to our present subject to enquire. (Smith 1976a, 17)

This analogy to speech seems a little forced. Why should the propensity for exchange be a consequence of reason and speech? If by this Smith means communication then, I suppose, exchange can be seen as a function of conversation or communication. Note here that Smith is almost certainly picking up on an analogy—really a tropological maneuver—made by his friend David Hume who explicitly likens conversation to trade:

> The balance of trade we need not be jealous of, nor will there be any difficulty to preserve it on both sides. The materials of this commerce must chiefly be furnish'd by conversation and common life: the manufacturing of them alone belongs to learning. (Hume 1985, 535)

This then gets developed into the theory of exchange, which underpins the entire wealth of nations. So the architecture of this array is now pretty evident: speech connects to reason, which then connects to exchange. And this then connects to the principle of division observed empirically, that is, the division of labor understood as manufacture. It is important to note that in this scheme we have yet to uncover the load-bearing concept which will stabilize the entire structure of the speech–reason–exchange–division of labor complex. In order to get to that we need another link in the array: competition. Thus Smith next observes that the principle of exchange must be regulated by the competition of self-interest. As he says:

> It is not from the benevolence of the butcher, the brewer, or the baker, that we expect our dinner, but from their regard to their own interest. We address ourselves, not to their humanity but to their self-love, and never talk to them of our own necessities but of their advantages. (Smith 1976a, 18)

And the origin of the division of labor (understood here as the division of manufacture) can be found in this propensity to exchange: "[I]t is this same trucking disposition which originally gives occasion to the division of labour" (Smith 1976a, 19). From here Smith outlines how some people make bows and arrows, others farm cattle or venison, and then trade with each other. Trade, then, is in effect founded upon the concept of exchange: "[I]t is the power of exchanging that gives occasion to the division of labour" (Smith 1976a, 21). But how does Smith get from here to the new concept that allows one to think labor as, in itself, divided? To the load-bearing concept that will take the weight of the edifice he has built? The answer lies in the introduction of the notion of excess or surplus. Once labor can itself be thought of as a quantity, as something that can be measured, then it becomes possible to think of it as something that can be divided. Chapter 4 begins:

> When the division of labour has been once thoroughly established, it is but a very small part of a man's wants which the produce of his own labour can supply. He supplies the far greater part of them by exchanging that surplus part of the produce of his own labour, which is over and above his own consumption, for such parts of the produce of other men's labour as he has occasion for. (Smith 1976a, 26)

So here Smith has begun to articulate a very different grammar for the concept of labor. Now, it appears, labor itself may be understood as a quantity, not as a process. From here it is evident that within this grammar it makes sense to see labor as something that might be portioned out. It is but a small step further to realize that another grammatical function is required in order to gauge the efficiency of such portioning. This, then, introduces the necessity for the concept of value, since without value one cannot begin to judge one division as more or less efficient than another. And then, in the furthest link in this conceptual array, value itself must also be subject to a form of counting or measurement.

Lest this seem an overly speculative or abstract way of following the steps in Smith's own analysis, let me backtrack a little to the text. Once Smith has noted that labor itself may be divided, he goes on to ponder what the consequence of this might be for commercial society. How, he asks, does one share out goods and services under such a dispensation? It does so, he says, by using a means for measuring value. In some countries, Smith remarks, they use salt, in others sugar or shells. But none of these are particularly convenient—you need sacks of salt to exchange for an ox—so it comes about that metal provides the basis for coin. And the primary reason for its superiority over other materials is its capacity for division *without loss*: "[M]etals can . . . without any loss, be divided into any number of parts" (Smith 1976a, 27). Hence money becomes "in all civilized nations the universal instrument of commerce" (Smith 1976a, 32). And now we get to the theory of exchange value, and from here we are in the orbit of the market and the logic of capital. And the rest, as they say, is history.

But something remains obscure in my account so far. The mechanism by which one arrives at the market is clear enough—and has, of course, been used throughout the subsequent two hundred–plus years to justify all manner of political and economic initiatives (many of which would have been distasteful, to say the very least, to Smith). But how did Smith get to this concept of the division of labor *as such*? How did he invent this load-bearing concept? The route toward an answer lies, I think, in Bernard de Mandeville.

It is often claimed in the literature that Smith borrowed the term "division of labour" from Mandeville's *Fable of the Bees*. This, it seems to me, is not quite the case. Let me rehearse the main claim made by Mandeville in this text, which has been more cited than read (at least its full title seems to have stood in for a thorough reading of what was contained within its boards). Mandeville's main claim was that human beings are primarily motivated by self-interest, and their deeds, when taken in isolation and individually, do not have any of the attributes we commonly associate with virtue. He thought that our acts are often motivated out of self-indulgence and the desire for personal gain. To him the notion that one might act on behalf of a disinterested concern for the welfare of others is ridiculous. However, and this is the crucial point for his treatise, although this is so, although egoism is the primary motor and justification—the means and end—of all human action, there is nevertheless an unintended social consequence, namely, the prosperity of all. Our greed and rapaciousness, according to Mandeville, lend the impetus for the creation of the market, which is increasingly dependent upon the division of labor as manufacture, and this in turn leads to the creation of ever increasing quantities of goods and services.

Again, according to Mandeville, production and commerce were not aided by frugality but by prodigality and luxury—both of which were customarily understood to be morally repugnant. And, in order to maximize this, he recommended that government take a leading role in promoting such vice. Although he has often been understood as proposing the opposite—of recommending a freewheeling deregulated market, the politics of laissez faire —this is a misperception. Mandeville in fact is keen to point out how, from within a set of rules determined by government, "Private vices by the dextrous management of a skillful politician may be turned into Publick Benefits" (Mandeville 1988, 1: 369). Smith's own understanding and promotion of the "invisible hand" should also be seen in the context of his reading of Mandeville.

I think it would be a mistake to claim that the idea of the division of labor in the sense of the division of manufacture was first minted in the eighteenth century. Throughout antiquity the benefit of atomizing complex processes of production were noted, although this did not lead to a concept of the market for regulating surplus production as it did in Smith. But it was perhaps William Petty, in his *Political Arithmetic*, who first began to think about the full economic implications of this idea. Some twenty or so years later, Mandeville is using the expression in ways that are going to reverberate in Smith's attempt to systematize a theory of commercial society and lead toward the invention of the concept of the divisibility of labor in the abstract. In the third dialogue of *The Fable of the Bees*, we find Cleomenes musing on the accomplishments of human ingenuity:

> [I]t certainly is almost inconceivable to what prodigious height, from next to nothing, some arts may be and have been raised by human industry and application, by the uninterrupted labour, and joint experience of many ages, tho' none but men of ordinary capacity should ever be employ'd in them. What a noble as well as beautiful, what a glorious

machine is a first rate man of war, when she is under sail, well rigg'd and well mann'd. As in bulk and weight it is vastly superior to any other moveable body of human invention, so there is no other that has an equal variety of differently surprising contrivances to boast of. There are many setts of hands in the nation, that, not wanting proper materials, would be able in less than half a year to produce, fit out, and navigate a first rate: yet it is certain, that this task would be impracticable, if it was not divided and subdivided into a great variety of different labours. (Mandeville 1988, 2: 141–42)

So here, as per Smith, we find the notion of the division of manufacture. Many hands are able to produce by a multiplier what the mere addition of this labor could not produce. But the second time Mandeville uses the term the context is very different. In the sixth dialogue, Cleomenes and Horatio are talking about the divine laws and how good in society is generated. And then Cleomenes notes:

Of all the difficulties, that mankind have labour'd under in completing society, nothing has been more puzzling or perplexing than the division of time. Our annual course round the sun, not answering exactly any number of compleat days or hours, has been the occasion of immense study and labour; and nothing has more rack'd the brain of man, than the adjusting the year, to prevent confusion of seasons. (Mandeville 1988, 2: 282)

Once again the empirical is crucial—one cannot get to the system or theory by observation alone. And this study, intellectual work, is called by Mandeville "labour." He then goes on to sketch out how society is established, this time Horatio remarking:

I am satisfied that the third step towards it is the invention of letters; that without them no laws can be long effectual, and that the principal laws of all countries are remedies against human frailties. (Mandeville 1988, 2: 283)

To which Cleomenes replies:

[W]hen once men come to be govern'd by written laws, all the rest comes on a-pace. Now property, and safety of life and limb, may be secured: this naturally will forward the love of peace and make it spread. No number of men, when once they enjoy quiet, and no man needs to fear his neighbour, will be long without learning to divide and subdivide their labour. (Mandeville 1988, 2: 283–284)

What is crucial to my parsing of the concept of the division of labor in Smith—crucial to his invention—is the proximity of what Mandeville refers to as the division of time with the division of labor. "Nothing," Mandeville has Cleomenes remark, "is more perplexing than the division of time." It is this, I think, that will trigger in Smith the need to invent the concept of the divisibility of labor *as such*, that is, the concept as we have come to know it. Since if time is conceivable as divisible it is so only in the abstract—you cannot observe time to be portioned out (even if you can observe its measurement being portioned out). Furthermore, time, once understood as divisible, is only so insofar as one might *count*. Here then we find the concept under which the division of labor itself falls, a concept of counting that does not rely upon the evidence of the *material counted*. By this means, what one counts in the division of time—say, duration—may be grammatically accidental to what one counts in labor, that is, value. Put another way, counting, in respect to time, registers the total amount of time there might be in the world; counting, in respect of labor, registers the total value that might be produced by the totality of labor. Both of these things are, of course, uncountable. One could never count all time or all the value of labor. In this way the market can only ever be a temporary reconciliation of production and consumption, demand and supply. Thus, although the total value of labor is incalculable at any one moment, that same labor, in the abstract, may be divided and its value ascertained. And it is this concept—the division of labor as we have come to understand it—that provides the architecture for the modern concept of economy. This concept that allows Smith to describe the logic of capital and the mechanism of the market. And it is an abstraction, not an observable phenomenon—hence conceptual in its very core—that allows it to be applied *to any market*. Unlike the division of manufacture, which is specific to a particular process of making, the division of labor is applicable to anything.

Smith claims that this idea is consonant with human nature itself—it is brought into existence on account of the impulse to barter or trade—and is, according to his own description, not susceptible of further analysis. Yet I think this is merely the blind side of his own invention. For the confluence of Mandeville's phrase with the abstraction that is the division of time, effected through counting, leads Smith to invent the load-bearing concept that we know as the division of labor, one of the founding concepts of modernity. Here I mean to make a glancing reference to the concept's genetic code or imprint. For, without the division of labor, would we be able to think capital?

Does this mean that concepts have history? It does, I think, tell us that *some* concepts are temporally contingent—they are formed at very precise historical junctures, under precise circumstances, though it is not always very easy to follow through the distinctive grammar and architecture that allows us to sketch the rules of integration that lie behind the uses of specific concepts. Here mediation once again comes back into the frame since we might now want to know how, and to what extent, those rules become visible and then fall from sight. How, over time, do we maintain our competence in particular grammars of use? How do we rewrite them?

# TRANSMITTING LIBERTY

## THE BOSTON COMMITTEE OF CORRESPONDENCE'S REVOLUTIONARY EXPERIMENTS IN ENLIGHTENMENT MEDIATION

### WILLIAM WARNER

As the event that founds the United States, the American Revolution is often thought to carry the secret kernel of what America is. However, the overfamiliarity of the American Revolution makes it most difficult to transmit. It is remembered in civic celebrations, through ritual readings of the Declaration of Independence, in American elementary school and high school pedagogy, through required trips to Washington, D.C., in commemorational battle reenactments, through visits to colonial theme parks like Williamsburg, and so on. At times the American Revolution moves from history to a lethal myth. The American Revolution, by grounding a distinctly American culture of war, also has had significant consequences for the rest of the world. In both foreign policy and entertainment, Americans repeatedly seek to understand their wars as a moral struggle between tyranny and liberty, between an evil empire and a young but bold republic, so every national struggle may acquire the purity, selflessness, and idealism that we often attribute to the American Revolution. Whether it is a war from the last 60 years—World War II, the cold war, the war in Iraq, or the so-called War on Terror—or it is one of the wars we consume as entertainment—as in George Lucas's *Star Wars* cycle or the Wachowski Brothers' film *The Matrix*—we wish to return to and repeat the American Revolution. Within this pleasing Ur-narrative, the American

Revolution is understood as an extraordinary time when aroused individuals united to fight a stifling system, and when our recourse to violence could be characterized as defensive, necessary, and (therefore) morally justifiable.

However, over the course of the long political history of the United States, the American Revolution and the Declaration of 1776 have been remembered, taken as models, and applied so as to do political work that most now value: in 1842, with the Seneca Falls Declaration of Women's Rights, in 1852, with Fredrick Douglass's lecture on the question, "what for a slave is the Fourth of July?" in 1863, at Gettysburg, when Abraham Lincoln meditates the survival of a nation "conceived in liberty," in 1971, when the Black Panthers write their ten-point plan, and in 1996, when John Perry Barlow offers his own "Declaration of the Independence of Cyberspace." On these occasions, the American Revolution appears more as a scriptural resource and political lexicon than as a distinct historical event. In every day's newspaper, commentators from every position on the political spectrum have recourse to an appropriate passage from a favorite founder to bolster whatever political proposition they advance. In short, for Americans at least, there is a sense in which the American Revolution has never ended. This has disorienting effects. On the one hand, it produces a strong sense of the Revolution's inevitability, the "rightness" of history becoming nature, as it seems to "speak" the clichés of national progress developed by Whig historiography in the nineteenth century (for example, in George Bancroft histories). On the other hand, the American Revolution may simply appear banal, unreadable, hopelessly worn-out, and thus, that which can no longer be transmitted.

The American Revolution is not merely a historical event that has been well or poorly transmitted; it is also an event that was itself centrally concerned with transmitting liberty. For American Whigs, there was little difficulty *communicating what liberty was*; it was embedded in English history from the Magna Carta to the present; it had been masterfully described in the classics of English political writing, from John Milton and John Locke, to John Trenchard and Thomas Gordon. The political crisis concerned transmitting a liberty that they became convinced was endangered by British imperial designs developed in the wake of the Peace of Paris in 1763. Here it is useful to use a distinction between communication and transmission developed by Regis Debray. While communication aspires to overcome differences of space and time, transmission assumes that distance and deferral, and the "noise" they introduce, become part of the transmission. While communication dreams of transparency (so that one person shares a meaning with another that is complete but carries nothing extra) and unity (as when communicants become the corporate body of Christ, out of many there will be one, *e pluribus unum*), transmission assumes that what is transmitted requires intricate media work of humans, material supports, channels, protocols, and genres, which inevitably transform what they transport. Transmission is a kind of communication that cannot elude the dialectic of selection and erasure, remembrance and forgetting. Transmission is intrinsically collective and political. While one person can communicate ideas, it takes a group of persons acting together to transmit ideas, objects, and values through time. Finally, while what we communicate can be trivial and (like the latest media event) last only for a moment, we transmit what we most value, those precious things that we believe we cannot live without: schools transmit knowledge; churches and temples transmit religious faith; parents transmit a family's distinct way of life to their children; and, in the modern epoch, at least since the Enlightenment revolutions in America, France and Haiti, politics transmits liberty (Debray 2004).

Understanding the Whig project as one of transmitting liberty helps to clarify their approach to naming their revolution. In Britain, the war that broke out in 1775 between Britain and the Whigs of British America was called "the American War"; it was condemned as a "rebellion," or lamented as a tragic civil or "brother's war." After the war was over, it was dubbed "the American War for Independence," as if that protracted struggle was always motivated by its outcome. But for the Whigs of British America, the preferred name was the "American Revolution." This mode of denomination makes its project explicit: the modifier "American" helps to distinguish it from that other, much admired revolution, "the Glorious Revolution" of 1688 that the American Revolution explicitly repeats. In doing so, the makers of the American Revolution seek to transmit the ancient English liberties, protected nearly a century before in that earlier revolution and given legal form by the Bill of Rights (1689). Scholars have noted that the "re-" in "revolution" gives emphasis to revolution as a rotation, like the periodic revolution of the planets, as a turning that returns to some more valued earlier moment (Baker 1990; Wills 1979). Such a return is supposed to transmit the past into the present, so, with an endangered liberty recovered, it can be transmitted into the future.

If, in the colonies' protracted political crisis with British administration, the American Whigs were motivated by the wish to transmit English liberties, then the war that results from that crisis, as well as the independence that results from that war, cannot be seen as the preconceived scheme of a group of American Whig radicals.[1] As contemporary commentators noted, and subsequent histories have suggested, the crisis of 1765–1775 might have ended not with independence, but with a political arrangement that limited the sovereignty of Parliament in America. Such an outcome would have been modeled upon the settlement negotiated by Parliament with William and Mary in 1688, which seriously limited the sovereignty of the British sovereign. Although the American Whigs seek to repeat that earlier English history with a difference, what results is a singular event that may be said to begin with an open-ended but generative sentiment, one that Foucault has used to describe what unites a very broad range of Enlightenment political and knowledge projects, which might be paraphrased this way: We will not be governed in this way any longer. What happens when that sentiment is turned into political projects, like the formation of the Boston Committee of Correspondence, surprises both Whigs and Tories and those participant-observers like Mercy Otis Warren and Peter Oliver, who were caught up in the political crisis, but only later reconstruct the event in their divergent histories, Warren's *History of the Rise and Progress and Termination of the American Revolution* and Oliver's *Origin and Progress of the American Rebellion*. The open-endedness of events that come to be designated the American Revolution/ the American War has another implication. What is transmitted does not preexist the transmission; it exists in and through the transmission; American liberty is created retroactively, by the words, actions, and new institutions that carry the transmission (cf. Arendt, "What is Freedom?").

## The Institutional Agency for Conducting Revolution: The Boston Committee of Correspondence

If we understand the American Revolution as centrally concerned with transmitting liberty, the next step is to ask who first instituted themselves into a group, a collective agency that set about transmitting liberty, when and where they emerged, and how they sustained themselves over time at the center of the imperial crisis until it developed into a revolution. If one goes backward through a chain of events from the traditional, point-of-no-return flashpoint, the Battle of Lexington and Concord (April 1775) and look to locate a coherent site for institutional agency, one's first resting place must be the meeting of the First Continental Congress (Sept.–Oct. 1774). The congress was called to forge a united colonial response to the Boston Port Bill (May 1774), which was passed, along with other acts of Parliament, to punish Boston for the destruction of the tea on December 16, 1773. But if one continues back in time, one must go back thirteen more months to the decisive organizational project undertaken by the Boston Whigs in November 1772, the institutionalization by the Town of Boston of the Boston Committee of Correspondence. It is there that we see the emergence of an agency—a gathering of persons, communication practices, genres, and networking activity—with the purpose of transmitting liberty. The Boston Committee of Correspondence met weekly (and sometimes a good deal more) in the selectmen's room in Faneuil Hall throughout this critical medial period (1772–1774), where it coordinated various forms of resistance to British sovereignty in America.

Space does not permit a detailed account of the emergence and effective agency of the Boston Committee of Correspondence (Brown 1970). Instead, this essay will focus on the distinct innovations of the Boston Committee of Correspondence, innovations that became useful throughout the colonies in the struggle against British sovereignty in the years before and directly following the convening of the Continental Congress (1772–1774): 1) the canny exploitation of the eighteenth-century media infrastructure, most crucially the Anglophone newspapers circulating throughout the Empire by the Royal Post; 2) the invention of the standing committee of correspondence as a new interface for political action; 3) the development of the genre of the declaration, which is addressed to fellow citizens, so as to incorporate and overwrite the traditional petition to authority; 4) the interlinking of the towns of Massachusetts and the emulative adoption of the committee system in most of the thirteen colonies, which develops the political unity essential for convening as a "congress," declaring independence, and fighting a war to uphold that declaration. Each one of these activities—media work, committee formation, making declarations, and networking—should be understood as a distinct way of transmitting liberty. These four rather distinct mediations of Enlightenment expand the effective political power of those Whig committees assuming authority in the name of "the people."[2]

## An Infrastructure for a British American Discourse That Is Open, Public, and Free

It was crucial to the success of the Whig committees of correspondence that they had easy access to the broadcasting medium of the newspapers of British America. This access depended upon an information architecture that was decentralized and resistant to government control. The forty-two papers of British America were locally owned and run by printer-editors. Several used this slogan to assert their independence and general appeal: "Open to all parties, but influenced by none." These papers were loosely connected with each other by the practice of "franking" free copies through the post to each other. This gave them some of the properties of the wire services (like Reuters, UPI, and AP) later developed in the nineteenth century. Since newspapers were regarded as ephemera and there was no copyright on a paper's content, the content was free to other newspapers in both senses of the word—it costs nothing, and it is available for recopying. In fact most of the documents, news items, and opinion pieces set in type by colonial newspaper printers are copied right out of the seventy or so papers printed in Britain. The habitual use of anonymous and pseudonymous publication in both pamphlets and newspapers helped to protect the sort of provocative, wide-open, ironically inflected political debate that had prevailed in Britain for over a century. Because of the failure of earlier prosecutions for seditious libel in both Britain and America, the colonial press of the 1770s was remarkably "censorship-resistant" (Warner 2005, 343–355).

### Inventing the Committee of Correspondence as an Interface Technology for Distributed Politics

The importance of the invention of the committee of correspondence, as a technology of political mobilization was recognized by John Adams toward the end of the American Revolution in a letter dated February 23, 1780, that he wrote from England to his remote second cousin Samuel Adams:

> You will see by the public papers that your committee of correspondence is making greater progress in the world and doing greater things in the political world than the electrical rod ever did in the physical; England and Ireland have adopted it, but, mean plagiaries as they are, they do not acknowledge who was the inventor of it. (Adams 1989, 9: 353)

Days later, in a letter to Thomas Digges, a delegate to the Continental Congress, John Adams gives still more explicit credit to Samuel Adams as the inventor of the committee form: "The Committee of Correspondence is purely an American Invention. It is an Invention of Mr. Sam. Adams, who first conceived the thought, and made the first motion in a Boston Town Meeting" (John Adams to Thomas Digges, March 14, 1780; Adams 1996, 10: 14). By using the word "invention" to describe the standing committee of correspondence, John Adams acknowledges its role in American mobilization. By comparing the committee to Franklin's lightning rod, Adams confers upon it the central traits of an invention: appearing at one time, it is new; but, after its invention it is open to imitation by others. But John's conferral of credit upon Samuel Adams for this invention, by putting the inventor before the "invention," the human before technology, recuperates the alterity and unintended effects of technology by emphasizing the priority of the designing, intending human inventor. While most historians acknowledge Samuel Adams's role as the prime mover in the formation of the Boston Committee of Correspondence, John Adams downplays (and may not have understood) the collaborative emergence of the Boston Committee of Correspondence. Finally, committees were of course hardly "new": they were a well-established feature of provincial and town government, and even the idea of a network of committees had been used by Presbyterian ministers in the colonies of British America (Brown 1970, 45; Bridenbaugh 1962, 203–204).

A committee's claim to legitimacy—resting upon its always contestable claim to represent "the people"—is dependent upon the circumstances of its formation and the procedures through which it operates. On November 2, 1772, the Boston town meeting, boycotted by the Tories, appointed a committee composed of twenty-one prominent Whigs. Over the next seventeen days the committee is divided into three drafting subcommittees (one each for each subsection of the document) and it repeatedly meets to read drafts of each subsection and develop a draft of the forty-three-page pamphlet that was acceptable to the whole committee. On November 20, 1772, the letter-pamphlet was formally submitted for consideration at the town meeting, where it was read aloud twice, modified according to suggestions during the meeting, and formally adopted (in a unanimous vote). The pamphlet was published as *The Votes and Proceedings of the Town of Boston* by Benjamin Edes and Thomas Gill, the Whig publishers of the *Boston Gazette*, as well as by Thomas and John Fleet, publishers of the *Boston Evening Post*. Copies were sent to each of the 260 towns and districts of the Colony of Massachusetts, as well as to selected Whig leaders throughout the thirteen colonies and in London.

The anodyne title page of the Boston pamphlet—the name it soon received—offers no indication of the fiery arguments against British tyranny contained in the text. Instead, the title page of *The Votes and Proceedings* emphasizes the town of Boston's strict observation of correct procedure ("in town meeting assembled," "according to law," "Published by Order of the Town," "An attested copy . . ."). The pamphlet has none of the intellectual coherence, legal rigor, or elegance of expression found in Whig pamphlets by Otis, Dickinson, or Jefferson. Instead, this is a piece of vernacular political theory where verbal form reflects the intended function. It is best understood as a script to be read at the town meetings, with a very clear line of argument, based upon familiar natural rights arguments from Locke, avoiding difficult or unfamiliar concepts, graced with repetitions to aid the inattentive listener, and concluding with a rousing, emotionally piquant call to action.

THE

## VOTES and PROCEEDINGS

OF THE

FREEHOLDERS and other INHABITANTS

OF THE

Town of BOSTON,

In Town Meeting aſſembled,

ACCORDING TO LAW.

[ *Publiſhed by Order of the Town.* ]

To which is prefixed, as Introductory,

An atteſted Copy of a Vote of the Town at a preceeding Meeting.

BOSTON:
PRINTED BY EDES AND GILL, IN QUEEN-STREET,
AND T. AND J. FLEET, IN CORNHILL.

*The Votes and Proceedings of the Town of Boston* (pamphlet, 1772). Reproduced by permission of The Huntington Library, San Marino, California.

However, *The Votes and Proceedings* does not just develop arguments against British policy. It is the first product of the standing committee of correspondence that also models the way for other towns to form their own standing committees. Because the committee form is simple, flexible, and extendable, it greatly expands the scope and effective agency of American Whig opposition to British measures. To understand the effects of Boston's institutionalization of the standing committee of correspondence, it is useful to engage in strategic anachronism. The twentieth-century development of the computer has given us new concepts to understand Boston's innovative technology: they can be understood through the concepts of the *interface*, the *communication protocol*, and the *network*.

My use of these terms in an eighteenth-century historical context may open me to various charges (anachronism, "presentism," over-loose expansion of terms, among others); nonetheless, I join a large and expanding group of historians, critics, and communications theorists in making a retroactive application of concepts from the networked computer to early epochs in the history of communication media.[3] In taking up the question of media and communication technology, this wide spectrum of scholarship seems to be shaped by four key ideas. First, the transformative effects of developments like the Internet and personal computing have produced a retroactive reinterpretation of media history. Thus, after surveying the many kinds of technologies embraced since the earliest days of American settlement, Chandler and Cortada (2000, v) insist, "In short, Americans have been preparing for the Information Age for more than 300 years. It did not start with the introduction of the World Wide Web in the early 1990s." Second, for scholars of contemporary media policy, the introduction of a historical perspective allows policy makers to invoke time-honored American values and practices (public libraries, limited copyright, the public domain) to negotiate the thicket of issues opened up by the networked computer for copyright, privacy, surveillance, and access (St. Clair 2004; Lessig 2000; Starr 2004; Warner 2007). Third, this historical perspective on media technology has led to a revival of interest in the media studies of Marshall McLuhan, the first thinker to develop a systematic approach to a comparative and historically informed study of media technology. Finally, science studies has demonstrated the critical leverage that arises from putting into question the categorical distinction between human and nonhuman (Haraway 1991; Latour 1987; Latour 1991).

This analytical procedure—what Clifford Siskin and I have elsewhere called "digital retroaction"—allows scholars to grasp the general traits of communication across different historical epochs and very different media forms and practices. Computer scientists developed the term "interface" to describe "a point of interaction or communication between a computer and any other entity."[4] Computer culture has occasioned a rich and diverse elaboration of this term because computer design makes the interface the crucial boundary, or zone of articulation and translation, whenever a computer needs to communicate with devices (such as printers, networks, monitors, machines) or human users. Between the computer, where algorithms are encoded and data stored within unintelligibly vast and fast flows of 0s and 1s, and the human, is the interface; the interface, as the surface of inscription and representation placed before the user, as screen and as control panel, is a source of information and an inscribing device. The interface—in the expanded sense in which I am using the term—does not just consist in the "look and feel" of a book, a film, or a computer running software; it is also the placement of the body; the habitual actions and activities built into the interface; the inventive (and often unintended) uses to which users put a new technology; it is the range of communicative actions into which social humans take the technology. Because of the way an interface can become a zone of social possibility, it stimulates utopian desires in its designers.[5]

Considered as a communications technology, the Boston committee functions as an interface, adheres to certain communication protocols, and (after its success) becomes the central hub of a network. As a communications interface, the Boston committee is composed of the minds and bodies of twenty-one members acting together. The official "user" of the interface is the Town of Boston; the twenty-one members are selected to represent it, and if the committee fails in this representative function, it could be dissolved. The purpose of this communications device is to conduct two-way communication between Boston and the other towns of Massachusetts. Certain features of the interface are crucial to its operation. The Boston committee is autonomous (it is a standing committee of the town that does not need permission from any other authority to hold its meetings); it conducts its weekly business in secret; the committee secretary, William Cooper, keeps a log of its official actions and its correspondence but not of its discussions; and, periodically, the committee has recourse to one of several forms of written "output": the manuscript document (like the original manuscript of *The Votes*, which is read to the Boston town meeting), the printed pamphlet (like the copies of *The Votes* that are sent to the other towns), the manuscript letter (written to and from the Boston committee), and the broadside (for distribution to all the towns of Massachusetts).

## Overwriting the Petition with a Declaration

Because *The Votes* is written by a committee, and because it aspires to speak for all the freeholders and inhabitants of Massachusetts, its statement of grievances and its appeal to the other towns begins small and local but aspires to grow large and continental. To initiate communication with the other towns, the Boston committee observes certain protocols. By protocols I mean the constraints voluntarily adopted by the Boston committee to facilitate felicitous two-way communication with the other towns of Massachusetts.[6] We can see these protocols at work in the third part of *The Votes and*

*Proceedings*, the most innovative and operationally consequential section of the pamphlet, "the letter of correspondence to the other towns." This letter directly addresses the towns in an urgent and personal tone and invites the other towns, either through their town meeting or through their own appointed committees of correspondence, to engage in a new species of multimedia public communication.

> The affair [of judicial salaries] being of public concernment, the town of Boston thought it necessary to consult with their Brethren throughout the province; and for this purpose appointed a committee, to communicate with our fellow sufferers, respecting this recent instance of oppression, . . . [In this document] this committee [has] briefly recapitulated the sense we have of our invaluable rights as men, as Christians, and as Subjects; and wherein we conceive those rights to have been violated, which we are desirous may be laid before your town, that the subject may be weighted as its importance requires, and the collected wisdom of the whole people, as far as possible, be obtained, on a deliberation of such great and lasting moment as to involve in it the fate of all our posterity. (Boston Committee of Correspondence 1772, 32–33)

*The Votes and Proceedings* repurpose two elements of the traditional petition to monarch, Parliament, or governor: 1) it states the rights of the subjects, and 2) it lists the violations of those rights. However, the document is defective as a petition, because it does not address any higher authority. Instead it addresses "fellow sufferers" as a part of an open-ended conversation in writing about what should be done, as if to say: if "we," in this declaration, don't speak for "you," then please write and tell us so; but if "we" do speak for "you," write so as to extend our claim to speak for the "people." The change of the direction of address in the rewriting of the petition as a declaration— from vertical to horizontal, from up to out—carries revolutionary potential. It is also cast in a strange new idiom that we might call "committee speak." The speakers and writers of *The Votes and Proceedings* show they are embedded within the new committee interface by the communications protocols they observe. By speaking in the collective first-person plural "we," the committee strives to be representative: the words that the committee members circulate are supposed to represent those for whom they speak (the Town of Boston, whose meeting commissions and then accepts the pamphlet in a formal vote). At the same time, they also aspire to be accepted as representative of those whom they address. In order to win over the largest possible number of their auditors and readers, the committee adopts a style that is simple and direct and a tone that is sincere and earnest. Irony, double entendre, ornamental language, and abstruse allusions are alien to the committee's writing. Finally, the committee shows deference to the opinions of those they address as presumptive equals.

The passage quoted above is immediately followed by the pamphlet's most crucial performative: a request that each town will reply to the Boston committee.

> A free Communication of your Sentiments, to this Town, of our common Danger, is earnestly solicited and will be gratefully received. (33)

Every word in the phrase, "a free communication of your sentiments," is important: these communications are *free* because they are not constrained by the protocols of the petition (deference and patience) or by mediation through the town's officially elected delegates to the provincial assembly; following eighteenth-century usage, these "sentiments" imply a mix of idea and feeling, and they are important because they are *yours*; and finally, by circulating them freely among the towns of Massachusetts they are a communication that has the potential to become communally shared. By hailing the citizens of all the towns of Massachusetts into a public exchange of writing, forms of print such as *The Votes and Proceedings* open a space for not just the expression, but the performance, of political opinion. Words like "I do" (in a marriage ceremony) or "I declare war," as J. L. Austin (1976) argues, have the potential to move beyond description to action. The London edition of *The Votes and Proceedings*, written in February 1773 and published in London, June 1773, features a new preface written by Benjamin Franklin entitled "Preface to the Declaration of the Boston Town Meeting" (Franklin 1976, 82). Here Franklin gives emphasis to the performative agency of this text by noting that this "piece" is "not the production of a private writer, but the unanimous *act* of a large American city lately printed in New-England" (Franklin 1976, 84–85, emphasis added). The arguments and form of address of *The Votes* anticipate the decisive act of American rebellion against British authority, the Declaration of 1776.

Governor Thomas Hutchinson soon grasped and condemned the "dangerous tendency" of the "unwarranted" address to the towns in *The Votes* (*Boston Gazette*, 22 February 1773). By submerging their individual identities in the identity of the committee, by presuming the equality of all committee members, by striving to represent the people's sentiments, by speaking as "we," the committees of correspondence embodied an alternative to Britain's constitutional monarchy: the republicanism so despised by the Tories. Thus, after the news of the closing of the port of Boston (on June 1, 1774), and after the Philadelphia Committee of Correspondence joined other Pennsylvania county committees to organize a "convention" to recommend delegates to the Continental Congress in 1774, the conservative speaker of the Pennsylvania Assembly, Joseph Galloway, writing as "Freeman," challenged the committees as "setting up anarchy above order—IT IS THE BEGINNING OF REPUBLICANISM" (Ryerson 1978, 61). This warning proved correct.

## The Ideological Articulation of Liberty with Popular Sovereignty

Space does not permit a full discussion of the content of *The Votes and Proceedings*. So a brief look at the rhetorical and ideological work done by the text must suffice. At the emotional high point of the plea for a response from the towns, the threat to American liberty by ministerial tyranny is given this striking expression:

> We are sure your Wisdom, your Regard for yourselves and the rising Generation, cannot suffer you to doze, or set supinely indifferent, on the brink of Destruction, while the Iron Hand of Oppression is daily tearing the choicest Fruit from the fair Tree of Liberty, planted by our worthy Predecessors, at the Expense of their Treasure, and abundantly water'd with their Blood. (Boston Committee of Correspondence 1772, 3)

In this sentence, part of a longer excerpt from *The Votes and Proceedings* that was published in newspapers throughout the colonies, what is finally at stake in this struggle, the Town of Boston insists, is "the fair Tree of Liberty, planted by our worthy Predecessors, at the Expense of their Treasure, and abundantly water'd with their Blood." The threat to Liberty, here figured as a tree, is rendered as a rape—a theft and a ravishment—by the "Iron Hand of Oppression," which is "daily tearing the choicest fruit from the fair tree." This "hand of oppression" figures the British ministry as "iron," that is "firm, inflexible; stubborn, obstinate, unyielding" (*OED*, s.v. "iron"), in the determination to engage in a machinelike imperial system that would destroy American liberty. Here arboreal liberty is put at risk by imperial machinations. Why does "the Tree of Liberty" become the figure favored to secure a consensus as to the threat to American liberty?

The idea of a tree of liberty developed in this passage builds upon a familiar analogy of colonial settlement to horticultural planting. The "plantation" of European colonies translates European humans, animals, and horticulture so they both enrich and benefit from the new world into which they are planted. Because New England liberty needed to be defended from encroaching enemies—especially Native Americans and French Catholics—it not only required treasure (money and labor), but it must also must be "watered" with blood (sacrificial love). This mythos of New England settlement is gradually elaborated in Samuel Adams's private letters and anonymous public writings between the years 1765-1769. Adams's argument for the special flourishing of liberty in New England develops along this line: because they carried the ancient rights and liberties of Englishmen with them, because the earliest New England settlers were not sent or sponsored by the British state, because they received no direct or indirect subsidy from others (and this was very different from both the failed and successful Virginia settlements), because they had no grand proprietor-investors behind them (the way Pennsylvania and Maryland did), because they emigrated to preserve their religious freedom from encroachment, because of the bitter privation upon their arrival (arriving in December, they only survived by eating clams from the sea), for all these overdetermined and rather differently grounded reasons, *the first English settlers of New England knew freedom as their original and natural condition* (Adams 1904-1908, 1: 7-297).

This mythos of the organic growth of liberty in New England is condensed in the passage's climactic invocation of the "fair Tree of Liberty." This figurative tree also offers an oblique reference to one very literal tree. If the British associated the survival of the Stuart monarch with the mighty Royal Oak that saved Charles II from capture at the Battle of Worcester in 1651, the Whigs of Boston honored their liberty under one particular huge and ancient elm. It was planted in 1646 soon after the founding of Boston (in 1630) near the intersection of Essex and Orange streets. Located in the front yard of Deacon Jacob Elliott, it was made available by its Whig owner to the Whigs for public use as a site protected for oppositional political speech. Paradoxically, its status as private property helped to protect it from the legal manipulation of public agencies (like the Governor or His Majesty's Army) to which it might have been vulnerable if it were located on the Boston Common.

If we link this figural tree (in *The Votes*) and the literal elm (in Boston), a cluster of related ideas are subsumed under "the fair Tree of Liberty." The fact that the liberty tree is old, tough, and ancient suggests the antiquity of English rights; its vast size connotes the greatness of liberty; and its longevity suggests that liberty may (or *should*) survive from the dim past into the distant future. Yet, because the tree is alive, it is vulnerable to disease, fire, and cutting, just as liberty itself is vulnerable to sudden destruction or gradual decay. The thought of the loss of this ancient and precious living endowment—once it is destroyed, it is lost forever—produces the sentimental solicitude, anxiety, and dread that suffuse this climactic passage from *The Votes*.

In 1772, the recent uses of the "Tree of Liberty" by Boston Whigs gave it particular salience in forming committees of correspondence throughout Massachusetts. Because Boston's liberty tree was a place of voluntary assembly, political speech, and symbolic protest, the tree also becomes a metonym for the voluntary association of the Boston Whigs throughout the last eight years of protest (1765–1772). To destroy the tree would be to disable the liberty practiced in Whig gathering, speaking, protesting, but also that associated with the crucial first free act, the settlement of New England. The figural "fair Tree of Liberty" not only naturalizes the human desire for liberty. By publishing *The Votes and Proceedings*, the Boston Whigs have recourse to the media prosthesis of print so as to invite all the towns of Massachusetts to assume a place beneath the(ir) "fair Tree of Liberty." In this way all the towns of Massachusetts can achieve a new unity by joining their "brethren" in a freely communicated consensus, under Boston's liberty tree. The sheer numbers gathered around this figural tree, and the intensity of their shared sentiments, will then enable each of them, through a free communication of sentiments, to "stand firm as one man" against that firm, or "Iron[,] Hand of Oppression." By associating their own technology of uniting with the organic-natural-arboreal "Tree of Liberty," and opposing it to the oppressive iron machines of British power, the Boston committee conceals by sublimating what is machinelike, repetitive, and protocol-controlled about their own technology, the committee of correspondence and the communication network it initiates.

## The Emergence of a Colonial Actor-Network

The development of a network for bidirectional communication is intended to solve a problem inherent in any claim of popular sovereignty: the people may be sovereign but who speaks for the people—the monarch (or sovereign), the parliament, the governor, the colonial assembly, the town Meeting...? The Boston committee responded to this problem with a communications experiment: if none or few respond in kind to our letter-pamphlet-declaration, we don't speak for the people; but if many do, we do. In the event, *The Votes and Proceedings* succeeded beyond the most ardent hopes of the Boston Whigs. In the months between December 1772 and September 1773, over 110 towns held meetings to discuss the pamphlet and frame their own supportive resolutions. By December 1773, the time of the destruction of the tea, 140 towns had responded. Approximately half of the responding towns established their own committee of correspondence. The letters and resolutions of the other towns were sent to the Boston committee, which wrote individualized replies to each, but the committee also published the letters and resolutions of selected towns in the *Boston Gazette* and other papers of Boston and New England. To the modern reader, the responses of the towns to the Boston pamphlet may appear mind-numbingly redundant: but their sameness, sometimes even down to the level of the phrase, suggests that the writers did not aspire to novelty. Instead, these transmissions of liberty confirm, through a kind of symbolic exchange most familiar from gift-giving economies, the common subscription to a shared political idea. American Whigs who retransmitted liberty found themselves in a large and highly visible imagined community. The Boston committee gradually extended its periodic communication to include committees of correspondence in New York, Philadelphia, Annapolis, Williamsburg, and Charleston. Publications of the Boston committee are reprinted throughout the colonies and in London. In March 1773, the Virginia committee is formed and proposes intercolonial communication through committees attached to the assemblies of all the colonies. By the middle of 1773 an intercolonial network of committees is available for conferring upon and organizing opposition to the Tea Act in the fall and winter of that year.

Only after the destruction of the tea in Boston Harbor (December 16, 1773) does the robustness and flexibility of this intercolonial network become evident. For the British Ministry, the destruction of the tea was the "last straw": Lord North, addressing Parliament on March 14, 1774, announces that it was now time to exercise a "firm hand" with Massachusetts and to punish Boston for being the habitual "ringleader" in the "American troubles" by passing a series of bills that will once and for all settle the question "whether or not we have any authority" in that country (Simmons 1985, 72, 79). The four bills passed over the next months, which American Whigs labeled the "Intolerable Acts," closed Boston Harbor to all trade and traffic; changed the charter of Massachusetts so the council was appointed by the governor rather than elected; required towns to ask permission of the governor to meet; enabled those accused of crimes against British authority to be transported to Britain for trial; and extended the borders of Quebec so as to prevent westward settlement from New York, Pennsylvania, and Virginia. Britain's sudden and resolute extension of its sovereignty over Massachusetts offers an instance of what Carl Schmitt theorizes as a state of emergency and what Giorgio Agamben has analyzed as a state of exception: the paradoxical moment when the sovereign sets aside the normal rule of law so as to rule outside of the law but with the "force of law."

Writing to his brother Arthur Lee in London, Richard Henry Lee characterizes the response of the Virginia House of Burgesses to the news flash provided by the arrival of what he calls "the Tyrannic Boston Port Bill":

"[N]o shock of electricity could more suddenly and universally move—Astonishment, indignation, and concern seized on all. The shallow Ministerial device was seen thro instantly, and every one declared it the commencement of the most wicked System for destroying the liberty of America, and that it demanded a firm and determined union of all the Colonies to repel the common danger" (Lee, Richard Henry 1970, 114). What enables Lee to go from "shock" to a "firm and determined union" is the network of committees of correspondence; the "electric shock" does not electrocute but it instead "electrifies" the network. These committees register an uncanny recognition—"this can not be; but, oh yes, we now see, empire *is* finally based on violence"—but then channel rage into methodical planning with other committees and assemblies for the meeting of the First Continental Congress (on September 5, 1774). By the time of Lee's letter in late June 1774, the American secretary at Whitehall, Lord Dartmouth, began to receive reports from colonial governors of North America, confirming a catastrophic unraveling of British authority in America: colonial legislatures were meeting without the permission, or the presiding presence, of the governor; royal courts were prevented from convening; and local militia were openly preparing for war. Remarkably similar acts of resistance to British authority, justified by very similar words, were happening thousands of miles apart at virtually the same time. What may have looked to the ministry in Whitehall like a well-concerted conspiracy were in fact self-organizing and decentralized acts of resistance directed by standing committees of correspondence. The Pennsylvania Whig Joseph Reed, writing in 1778, reflected on what happened this way: "[In 1774] the Convention [of Pennsylvania] established the government of Committees in conformity with other Provinces. Thus the public Machine was at length organized & put in motion" (Thomson 1878, 273). By choosing to embed themselves in the new communications technology of the committee, by embracing and communicating the shared sentiments of a new community, Whigs throughout the American colonies became a new "public machine" that could then convincingly speak the collective "we" so crucial to the performatives that would institute American self-government in 1776 and 1789.

## Conclusion

Michel Foucault justifies his turn to the Enlightenment by arguing that it is during the Enlightenment that "the relations among power, truth, and the subject that it is concerned with analyzing appear in some way, raw and at the surface of visible transformations" (Schmidt 1996, 392). The American,

French, and Haitian revolutions are the "raw" and highly "visible" instances of Enlightenment "transformations." Both scholarship on the eighteenth century and on popular political culture see these revolutions as the wellspring of ideas—of the modern value of critiquing authority; of liberty, equality, and popular sovereignty; and of a distinctly modern experimental and optimistic orientation toward the future. By putting the study of Enlightenment mediation in the foreground of its account of the Boston Committee of Correspondence, this essay offers a fundamental revision of this picture. I am suggesting that these ideas can only *do* something, and indeed, they only achieve their modern salience, within Enlightenment mediations. So, it is the open media-communication system of British America that is the condition of the possibility of the public resistance to British rule in America; it is the committee of correspondence that launches the decisive critique of instituted systems of authority; it is the new genre of the popular declaration that gives the ideas of liberty, equality, and popular sovereignty articulate force; and, it is the intercolonial Whig network of committees that pulls off an experimental and optimistic orientation toward the future by forming a committee of committees, the Continental Congress, which can organize the colonies in its struggle with Britain, and eventually, evolve into the United States of America.

# MODES AND CODES
## SAMUEL F. B. MORSE AND THE QUESTION OF ELECTRONIC WRITING

LISA GITELMAN

As historian Robert Friedel explains, "The question, 'Who invented the telegraph?' does not make much sense," so many were the contributors and so broad the field (Friedel 2007, 300).[1] Scientists, mechanics, and amateurs across Europe and North America proposed multiple versions and myriad components, before and after the first commercial system, developed by Samuel F. B. Morse and associates in the United States succeeded. If the singularity of "the inventor" is thus impossible to establish, so admittedly is "the telegraph." Not only did telegraph devices and telegraph circuits take many forms, telegraphic communication—in which "symbols could now move quickly and independently of bodies," as John Durham Peters puts it—was variously and broadly understood (Peters 2006, 147). The electric telegraph worked like human nerves, it was early decided,[2] yet it introduced an unnerving imperceptibility and immateriality into human communication. Electronic signals were instantaneous and invisible, available to the senses only by instrumental proxy, whether the sound of a mechanical click, the sight of a needle moving on a dial, or—as with Samuel Morse's telegraph—the sight of a trace made automatically on paper. Telegraphic communication was actuated and registered by operators and instruments; it displaced human communication even as it facilitated communication among humans at a distance.

While electrical telegraphy thus aligns in some respects with the newly destabilized and observing modern subject (see the essay by Eliassen and Jacobsen in this volume), the instrumentalism of the telegraphic regime also worked to restabilize and hyperrationalize the modern subject by bracketing perception, reducing it to a question of yes or no. Coincident with modern "techniques of the observer," that is, the telegraph ironically made the senses fully adequate to observation by reducing its relevant parameters to the binary on/off of a circuit. *Switching* became crucial to media and modernity, even as instantaneous electronic communication aided in the reorganization of markets and the maturation of finance capitalism.[3] Telephone switchboards and Internet switch hotels were still decades in the future, however, so telegraphic switching should be understood first on its own terms and according to the contexts of its invention. Samuel Morse, his associates, and his competitors struggled for priority, for recognition, and for more mundane rewards. It was only in the process of development that telegraphic communication—what we now denominate "the electronic"—came to be understood as such. Because of his early and celebrated success, the case of Morse's telegraph is particularly revealing in this regard.

1

The Library of Congress in Washington, D.C., houses the Samuel F. B. Morse Papers, a collection of some 10,000 items documenting Morse's life and work.[4] The library's Web site includes an archival finding aid that describes the scope and content of the collection and offers an inventory, which gives reel and frame numbers as well as box numbers, since researchers who visit the library are asked to use a microfilm copy instead of the documents themselves. But many of the Morse Papers have also been digitized, so researchers at home can click right to digital images, scanned for the most part from microfilm.[5] The library's digitized documents help vouch for the nineteenth-century origins of electronic information and electronic writing. As the Morse Papers home page puts it, "The collection includes the original paper tape containing the *first telegraph message*, 'What hath God wrought?'" which the inventor so famously sent on May 24, 1844. The underlined words signify a hyperlink that leads users to images of the paper tape wherein the message—the semiotic entity that was electronically conveyed—is embodied.

But the *first telegraph message* is also part of a second digital collection on the Library's Web site, "Words and Deeds in American History: Selected Documents Celebrating the Manuscript Division's First 100 Years."[6] The digital documents in Words and Deeds are all selected from "parent collections," where the archival source documents are organized and preserved. The resulting distinction between indexical digital collections and recombinant ones remains moot for researchers on-line: the Morse Papers and Words and Deeds each point to different images—different digital image *files*—of the same thing. One might say that digital images contain the paper tape the same way that the tape contains its electronic message, with the notable exception that digital images proliferate—they themselves are hard to contain—while the paper tape presumably, at least, remains a single material object, made singular in the circumstances of Morse's priority. The tape has been indented so that it contains three rows of dots and dashes, which appear as so many bumps in the surface of the paper. Morse's holograph translation of the bumps is spelled out below, and his penciled letters have been overwritten in ink by Annie Ellsworth, the friend who suggested this quotation from Numbers 23: 23.

What is "first" about this telegraph message that users can glimpse on computer screens today, on microfilm, in the archive, and on paper tape? Morse himself annotated the original tape in ink, "This sentence was written from Washington by me at the Baltimore Terminal at 8:45 A.M. on Friday May 24, 1844, being the first ever transmitted from Washington to Baltimore by Telegraph." So this message is first at least because it was the first sent from Washington to Baltimore. But the *first telegraph message* is first in other ways, too. As John McDonough of the Manuscript Division explains for Words and Deeds, "Four tapes of the message sent that day were produced": one outgoing in Washington, one incoming in Baltimore, and then the same message in reply as confirmation, outgoing in Baltimore and incoming in Washington. Which of these should be considered the original? Is that a fair question in this, the electronic age? The Library of Congress possesses the tape produced from Washington *at* Washington, making it "first" geographically if not chronologically, since the same message was received at Baltimore instantaneously: Telegraph signals travel at the speed of light. This means that the first message was registered in triplicate (three rows of bumps) four times (four paper tapes) all while still being "first," at least in America.[7] Like today's digital images, Morse's paper tapes propagate the message that they represent in the circumstances of its electronic transmission. Digital images exist at once on my screen, in my browser's cache, across the Internet, and on Library of Congress servers, just as this message existed

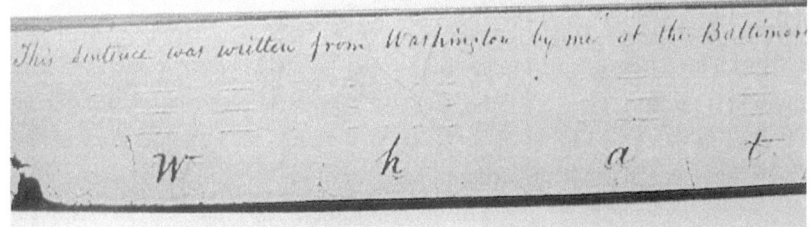

Samuel F. B. Morse's first telegram (excerpt, nineteenth century). Library of Congress.

at once in Washington and in Baltimore. Amid the confusion, the message–as–semiotic entity exerts a controlling logic, pulling tapes, microfilm, GIFs, and JPEGs into a concerted priority: There was one first message, for all of the accompanying clutter. "Intelligence," as Morse usually called it, had been transmitted. "Information," as it is styled today, had arrived, incumbent from the first with its own potential surplus.

Even still, the *first* telegraph message is most significantly first in the portentousness of its production, preservation, and display. Morse had struggled for years to perfect his apparatus and had finally received a $30,000 appropriation from Congress to construct the line between Baltimore and Washington. Here was the initial public test of that publicly funded circuit. Congress paid the bill, and now its Library authenticates and preserves the result. Never mind that the unfinished line, reaching a railroad junction within fifteen miles of Baltimore, had been used to report the results of the Whig national convention on May 1, 1844.[8] The event resulted in newspaper acclamations and several souvenir tapes that spelled out the vice-presidential nominee, F-r-e-l-i-n-g-h-u-y-s-e-n, in dots and dashes. "The reason I asked you to repeat so often Frelinghuysen," Morse explained the next morning to his partner Alfred Vail, "was that there were a great many who wanted the name as written from the junction. I understood you the first time."[9] Even before then, Morse made successful demonstrations of his technology using long spools of wire. In February 1838 he had been in Washington to solicit government support (test message: "The enemy is near!"). Still earlier demonstrations were made publicly and semipublicly in Philadelphia ("Steamboat Caroline burnt!") and New York ("Attention the Universe!") (Silverman 2003, 166–167), while the first official message Morse *imagined* he would send appears in his 1837 application for a U.S. patent caveat ("Send 56 copies").[10] Amid all of these other "first" messages, "What hath God wrought?" stands out as self-consciously grandiose, a government-sponsored appeal toward a higher purpose. It was an optimistic moment, Perry Miller noted, when the "happy conjunction of religion and technology in a free society" briefly seemed assured (Miller 1965, 52).

If the first-ness of this message is at once so vital and so vexed, the same must be said for its written-ness. The message as semiotic entity has a syntactical character—Morse calls it "this sentence"—and a semantic valence (viz., Protestant republicanism), but its other qualities remain a puzzle: "This sentence was written from Washington by me at the Baltimore Terminal." Writing from Washington at Baltimore, like the name Frelinghuysen "as written from the junction," neatly expresses the etymological "tele-" (distance) and "-graph" (writer) of "telegraph," but the graphology of Morse's invention is far from transparent. Before Morse's American Electro Magnetic Telegraph, the terms "telegraph" and "telegraphy" applied primarily to optical or semaphore messaging systems, which were neither inscriptive nor instantaneous. These "ordinary telegraphs"—as they would be called in 1837—could only be used in daylight and in clear weather, and any writing associated with them was done by hand (Anon. 1873, 323). Was Morse taking the metaphorical writing of optical telegraphy and making it literal? Or was he revising a metaphorical writing by making it American and Electro Magnetic? What does it suggest that indented dots and dashes caused by the on/off of an electrical current were so self-evidently "writing"? Further, what was the relationship being assumed or suggested between electronic information and the material trace?

Questions like these have broad implications for the history of electronic communication and, relatedly, for the history of what might be called the "textual interface" of words and/as images, where the ugly "and/as" forms a persistent if variable component of the experience of texts as written and of writing as visually perceived. As John Durham Peters has noted in his insightful appreciation of James Carey, "Telegraphy helped inaugurate a new kind of writing" and new attention to writing as "the tracing of fleeting processes" and invisible forces. Telegraphs and related innovations contributed to a radical diversification in "writing" during the nineteenth century (Peters 2006, 143, 144). Writing made visible and was made visible in new ways, according to newly modern perceptual regimes. In what follows I seek first to unpack the written-ness of Morse's putative first telegram by examining some of its contexts, starting with his initial creative impulses in 1832 and extending to the U.S. patent he was granted in 1840. I turn then to the modern writing subject produced in the earliest telegraphic practices, both the labor practices that continued to articulate "writing" in relation to electronic communication and the site or subject of legal practice, particularly regarding Morse's patent claims. Intense litigation in state and federal courts revolved in part around the "writing" that telegraphy might somehow entail. Together the contexts of Morse's invention and the legal contests it initially provoked offer a neglected window on the possibility and the experience of writing electronically and of "the electronic" as such.

2

Morse's interest in textual interface or the visual perceptibility of writing was neither self-conscious nor systematic, but the circumstances of his invention reveal a striking engagement with relevant concerns. When he built his first prototype in 1837, he used both a frame—on which a painter might stretch a canvas—and a composing stick—on which a printer might set type. In this first instance and in successive, improved versions, the telegraph modeled relations between writing and the visual field. Despite its extraordinary ambition, the initial model was based in part on "practical experience" (Israel 1992, 30). Morse was an accomplished painter and his brother Sydney published the evangelical weekly *Observer* (N.Y.), so sibling logic suggests the artist's canvas and the printer's craft as contexts for the imagination of telegraphy. One of Morse's paintings in particular offers a frame of reference for his prototype.

The idea of an electromagnetic telegraph occurred to Morse while he was making a return voyage from Europe to the United States in 1832. The novelty of his inspiration would be hotly contested in years to come, but at least one circumstance was and remains certain: Morse was returning to New York City with a huge, (6' × 9') partially finished canvas among his luggage. Completed the next year, *The Gallery of the Louvre* is a "jigsaw puzzle" of a painting (Staiti 1989, 191).[11] It represents in miniature thirty-seven paintings from the Louvre collection that are imagined together as an exhibition.[12] The result forms an art lesson for the young republic: Morse published a descriptive catalog containing a "Key to the Pictures" and organized public exhibitions in several cities. It is an example of the sort of improvement of knowledge through reorganization so typical of the Enlightenment. The "Key" identifies the works pictured in *The Gallery* by their location in the painting, using numbers between 74 and 1256 that refer to a catalog or plan of the museum that Morse must have used on site. (A notebook sketch Morse made in 1830 contains the same kind of reference number.[13]) Appearing in the "Key" these numbers underscore both his discerning selectivity and the daunting magnificence of the collection, while they ask readers to navigate

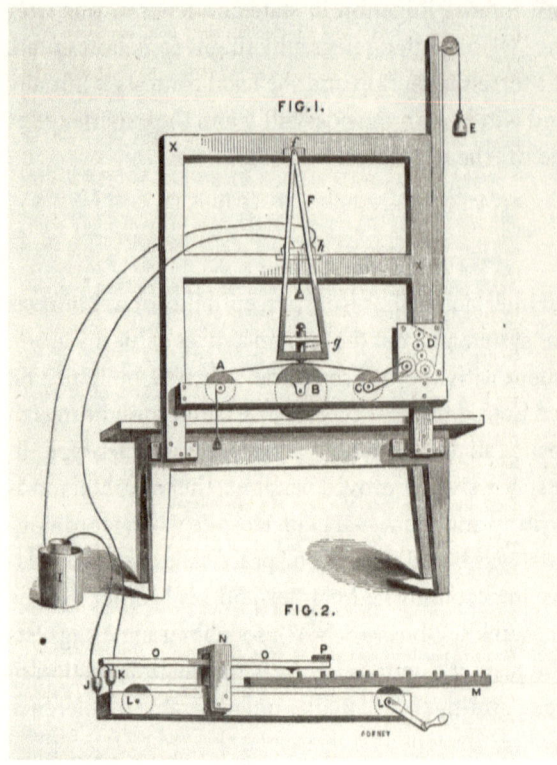

Samuel F. B. Morse's prototype of a telegram machine. From *Samuel I. Prime's Life of Samuel F. B. Morse* (1875). Courtesy, American Antiquarian Society.

from reference numbers to names and thence to the painting of paintings. Though press notices were generally good, exhibitions of *The Gallery* disappointed Morse financially, as did its later sale for the cut-rate of $1,200 plus $100 for the frame (Morse 1973, 2: 24).

As an enlightening art lesson for Americans, Morse's painting is not without complexities. Paul Staiti notes that the painting is at once "a grand national homage to and quest for a usable European past." The figures in the foreground help make it an image of "bourgeois education," with Morse himself at the center of the painting, instructing a young woman copyist. Copying stands as both method—of tuition and connoisseurship—and subject of the painting. Copying with a twist: Morse offers both Old Masters and his mastery of them. Great works are literally and figuratively belittled, de- and then recontextualized for a republican context.[14] And, as Patricia Johnston argues, a significant element of the painting's recontextualizing is its reaction to the Catholic content of its subject paintings and their Continental origins. Morse, a strident and paranoid anti-Catholic, was somehow processing and reinterpreting religious subjects by Correggio, Veronese, and Raphael as he copied them (Johnston 2006, 42–65). He flattered himself in a letter to his brother, "Everyone says I have caught the style of each of the masters." He had finished copies of all but one of the paintings at the museum itself before he sailed, leaving only one Rembrandt, "the frames of the pictures, the figures &c" to be finished at home.[15]

In capturing style while reinterpreting content and adjusting size and context, Morse relied upon Enlightenment aesthetic theory, which drew a decisive distinction between "mechanical" and "intellectual" imitation. As Morse himself explained in public lectures on the arts, "There are two kinds of imitation which should not be confused." He was pirating wholesale from Joshua Reynolds's second discourse on art (1769) when he explained that mechanical imitation involves "copying exactly any object just as it is, with every beauty and defect," whereas intellectual imitation involves discerning "the rules and methods according to which that object is constructed to serve a particular purpose."[16] A painting like *The Gallery of the Louvre* would seem to offer a superb example of intellectual imitation, but in illustrating his point Morse's lectures swerve instead to consider an example by then

KEY TO THE PICTURES.

"Key to the Pictures" from Samuel F.B. Morse's pamphlet (nineteenth century). Item Y1834, Morse Non-Circulating "Descriptive Catalogue," Special Collections, The New York Historical Society.

hackneyed and—in light of future litigation—oddly perspicacious. James Watt, inventor of the steam engine, produced a "masterpiece of mechanism," Morse notes, such that

> Mr. Watt's engine may be imitated in two ways: another engine may be made exactly like it, or the principles on which it was made may be variously modified and applied to the construction of other ingenious instruments. To the first kind of imitation the ordinary illiterate mechanic, as is well known, is perfectly competent, while the latter requires genius and mental cultivation similar to those of the inventor himself. (Morse 1983, 59)

In appealing to the steam engine, Morse's lecture joins "countless descants upon [this] majestic theme" in contemporary American arts and letters (Miller 1965, 293). He also raises the matter of "principles" in relation to invention, precisely the issue, as it happens, which would later take him and his telegraph to the U.S. Supreme Court.

Paul Staiti and Patricia Johnston both confirm the intellectual imitation of Morse's great painting by imagining him with his easel on wheels, hauling the gigantic canvas around the hallways of the museum to reinterpret first one masterpiece and then another.[17] No doubt there was some of that, but Morse appears to have worked on smaller canvases too as a means toward the same end. When he had finished all but the one Rembrandt, he wrote with satisfaction to James Fenimore Cooper about his penultimate copy, "When I put it in the gallery by pinning it to the large canvas, you cannot conceive what a difference it makes." This suggests that Morse made his intellectual imitations first on smaller canvases and later repainted these studies onto the larger canvas. According to Morse's own aesthetics, repainting might have been fairly rote, less interpretive, at least because it happened away from the presence of the original artwork. This means that each Old Master in the finished *Gallery* may be a more mechanical copy made in the studio of a more intellectual copy made at the museum. The remaining Rembrandt proved an exception to this method, as Morse regrets in the same letter, "I shall have to finish the Rembrandt when I get home temporarily from the print, but when your copy that I made shall arrive it can easily be corrected."[18] This time he would make the more mechanical copy first, copying from an existing print, but he might later freshen it against an intellectual copy that he had made for Cooper the year before.[19]

What these details of production suggest is that Morse's more mechanical imitations survive, while his more intellectual imitations do not, except to the extent that intellection persists within mechanics, each proof of and proven by the other.[20] Whatever he may have said, Morse's work exhausts Reynolds's intellectual/mechanical dichotomy. If the painter's method varied in the course of painting *The Gallery*, then the intellectual copies he made and the mechanical copies he made (of intellectual ones) are impossible to distinguish from one another in the final painting. Their distinction—a question of labor—has been lost in transmission, no matter Morse's warning that "there are two kinds of imitation which should not be confused."

### 3

Morse's original idea for the telegraph involved specially designed type used to communicate numbers and specially enumerated dictionaries to translate words into numbers and numbers back into words. The type sorts consisted of ten numerals, 0–9, and four special characters: a space, a rest, a stop, and "the cypher [*sic*]." Each piece of type had a unique pattern of notches on top. To send a message you had to set up type, selecting the right pieces and placing them onto a modified composing stick or type rule. Then, rather than emptying the composing stick into a printer's form, you placed it with its type into a "port rule," a device that Morse contrived in several shapes to move the type under a lever. The lever, "somewhat like the levers to the keys of a hand organ," passed up and down across the notches in the type as the port rule moved the type rule. Up-and-down motion of the lever completed and broke an electrical circuit, which caused the action of an electromagnet in a separate "register" device, moving a pencil back and forth across the surface of a paper tape. Morse proposed that his "system of signs" could be rendered in one of several "modes": the register and pencil could be modified to produce a sequence of Vs, a sequence of dots, or a sequence of lines. Using a sequence of dots and dashes to represent letters was an innovation of early 1838. As Morse moved from his 1837 patent caveat (a legal instrument indicating intent to patent) to his 1838 patent application, his eventually eponymous code appears as a late addition, the third and last example of his fourth and final mode.[21]

If copies of copies haunt Morse's *Gallery*, here signs of signs complicate his telegraph messages. His system worked by mapping type notches indexically onto numbers and thence onto words, where "every word in the language has a Telegraphic number." But for numbers to represent themselves, the cipher could be used to arrest that chain of signification. The cipher character was needed to indicate when a number should be understood as a number, not the "representative of a word," for example, in the message, "Send 56 copies." It is an odd use of the word "cipher," uniquely Morse's,

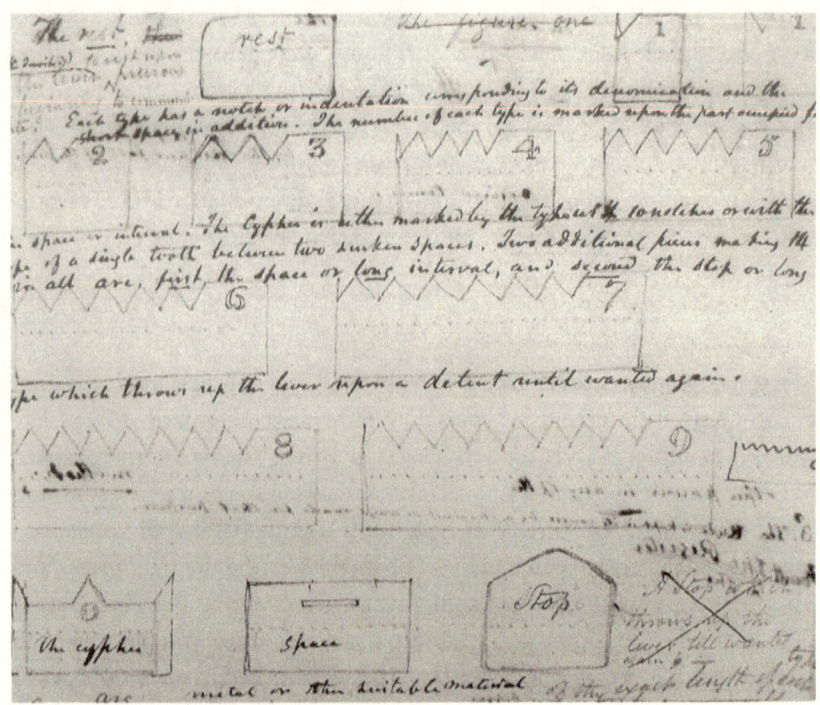

"Draft Patent Caveat" (excerpt, 1837). Library of Congress.

since Webster had lately defined a cipher in four different ways, as a zero; as "a character in general"; as an "intertexture of letters" in a monogram; or as "a secret or disguised manner of writing; certain characters arbitrarily invented and agreed upon by two or more persons" (Webster 1828, s.v. "cipher"). Morse triangulates the first and second definition with the fourth; his draft patent caveat squeezes in a zero, ten notches along its top, but also includes the zero-shaped cipher. It is a code, his first, an arbitrary and agreed upon signal, which happens to signify numerical signification.

Indeed, numerical signification suggests a telling resemblance to Morse's "Key to the Pictures." As in the "Key," numbers in empty frames refer intertextually, but whereas the numbers of the "Key" point doubly to the copied copies of Morse's creation and to the museum guide he used to navigate the original paintings and the museum, the numbers of the telegraph point (except when they don't) toward his dictionary, navigable by means of alphabetical order. He slaved at the dictionary during October 1837, after sending the patent caveat off to Washington. "I am up early and late," he wrote to Vail, "yet its progress is slow." Curiously, he suggested that he had a "plan of bringing the whole Dictionary of 30,000 words within the compass of about *six* square feet," as if it were a painting, "and this too without diminishing the size of the letter[s]." Two weeks later he was finally finished. "You cannot conceive how much labor there has been on it," he wrote, "but it is now accomplished and we can now talk or write anything by numbers."²² If using the "Key" meant the coordination of numbers and spatial relations among canvases, using the dictionary meant coordinating alphabetical and numerical order. In an unfinished trial page that survives, letters A–Z are numbered 1–26, followed by "27 abaft"; "28 abandon"; and so on.²³

Despite the convergence of alphabetical and numerical order evinced by Morse's dictionary, his system of signs at this point depended upon an unstated distinction between letters and numbers, since only the self-reference of the latter needed to be signaled. Letters as letters would be readily comprehensible without the cipher character, but would be reserved for words that were not in the dictionary. Only proper nouns are properly spelled in Morse's initial system. Other words are alphabetically ordered even though their alphabetical character was never spelled out: they were sent whole across the circuit by means of a numerical representative.

In 1837 and 1838 Morse clearly had printing in mind, specifying his type, cases to keep it in, and rules in which to set it up. But his telegraphic register more properly wrote than printed, and his typesetting formed a curious initial step in the production of what was actually a manuscript, first penciled on tape, later inked, and eventually "impressed" by steel points, once Alfred

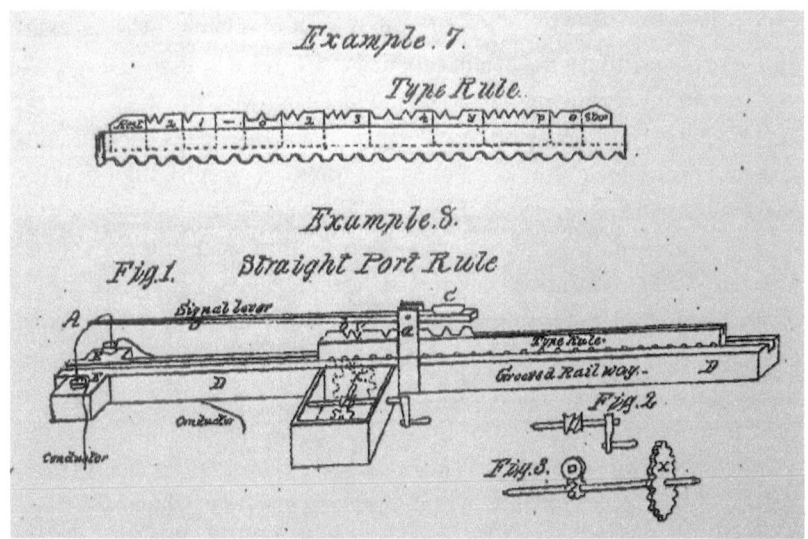

Patent 1,647 (excerpt, nineteenth century). United States Patent and Trademark Office.

Vail had helped him work out the kinks in his apparatus.[24] He adapted printer's type but disregarded the typeface, changing the relevant plane or surface of the sorts. He set up lines of type but left them unjustified. His "rest" type hints at an analogy to musical play, just as the telegraph key or lever recalls a hand organ. The composition of messages might involve its appeals to the print shop, but sending was a serial performance. The signal lever passed in and out of the indentations on the type as the port rule advanced the composing stick along a "grooved railway."[25] Though telegraphy may have severed transportation and communication, Morse's initial version more particularly internalized transportation in its port rule apparatus. "Words and Deeds" makes an apt title for the Library of Congress, but the unnecessary complexities of Morse's prototype evince his struggle to produce words *as* deeds, the serial and incremental results of electromagnetic process.

4

By the time he sent that putative first message in 1844, most of the patent Morse had received in 1840 had become ridiculous, because it specified so much that had already dropped out of telegraphy: gone were the type, the port rule, and the dictionaries. What remained in use was his "system of signs," which could be registered at a distance by the action of an electromagnet. So it reflects no idle crotchet that, as Morse's biographer notes, "Hundreds of manuscript pages survive in which [Morse] repeatedly tried to narrate the history of his invention and define its essential originality" (Silverman 2003, 312).[26] This wasn't just vanity or self-obsession; it was necessity. Morse managed to get his patent reissued twice, once in 1846 and again in 1848, extending its life but also tweaking its claims. After that, lawyers and judges took turns identifying Morse's invention, parsing his patent against potential infringements by competing telegraphs in an epic tangle of litigation that came to be known as the Great Telegraph Case.

The central holding in the Supreme Court's ultimate decision of the case was that principles could not be patented. Morse could no more own the use of electromagnetism for sending messages than Robert Fulton could own the use of steam for moving vessels.[27] Patents were for specific means, not abstract means aimed at specific ends. The court's reasoning sounds a lot like Morse's own celebration of intellectual imitation years before: someone with a "genius" like James Watt's could adapt Watt's principles to make "other ingenious instruments" without making a mere mechanical (that is, infringing) copy of Watt's steam engine. Likewise, Morse's competitors could adopt the use of electromagnetism, if their devices for doing so were demonstrably different than his. Morse was lucky, then, that the court reached for an element of his circuitry, implied in his patent, to affirm the validity of the patent at the same time that it rejected his broadest claim. The Supreme Court affirmed the Morse-friendly verdict of the lower court, even though it spurned that court's patent-a-principle reasoning. Morse has been called "the inventor" of electrical telegraphy ever since—in the United States, that is—and he was soon a wealthy man.

In the lengthy opinion, Justice Taney felt obliged to underscore that Morse's "patent is not for the invention of a new alphabet," as if owning the use of electromagnetism and owning an alphabet somehow caused like imposture. Questions about writing and about alphabets had vexed earlier hearings of the case. Judge Monroe in Kentucky had enjoined the Morse's competitors from "the transmission of intelligence" from one place to another by making a record in "the alphabetical characters" that Morse had specified, or even by making "with the action of the instrument" the concomitant "alphabetical sounds," which could then be written out.[28] The lower court, in short, bundled the use of electromagnetism and dots and dashes into a single principle that it then granted Morse the right to monopolize for the life of his patent. More, the court broadly construed the Morse alphabet as *both* the marks indented on paper tape *and* the sounds of their indentation, because both were caused electromagnetically. It was largesse based upon current telegraphic practice: by the time Judge Monroe heard the case in 1849, skilled telegraph operators had learned to receive messages by listening to the clicking of the register device, rather than by waiting to read indented tape.

So how was the Morse telegraph "alphabetic"? How, that is, did telegraphy tap and reconfigure this most basic visual component of text? What sort of "writing" was this? Everyone involved with the telegraph—Morse, Vail, their partisans and competitors—seemed to have different answers to these questions.

Alfred Vail, for example, understood that telegraphic dots and dashes formed an alphabet of "new, but intelligible characters" that were "as much at the pleasure of the telegraphic manipulator, as the English alphabet is with the letter writer." If Morse's 1837 prototype had embraced type without typeface, in 1844 the telegraph involved letters without the usual letterforms.[29] An "oh" can be written "o" in different sizes and a (small) range of shapes, but it can also be written ".." once you learn the knack. ("Oh" later became three dots, not two.) The equivalence was part literacy and part labor: just as Roman letters required learning to identify letters and then learning to form them (writing) and form them well (penmanship), telegraphy required learning to identify letters and practice with the key: "Strike your *dots firmer* and do not separate the two dots of the *O* so far apart," Morse chided Vail annoyingly from Washington, in a handwritten note.[30] The Morse alphabet in this respect formed a strikingly modern account of what alphabets consist of: arbitrary letterforms mapped to arbitrary names and arbitrary phonetic values.[31] For Vail and Morse, dots and dashes kept the names of Roman letters and kept their phonetic values, but changed their graphical shapes, handily replacing ABC with marks of duration, the binary on and off used to make dots, dashes, and spaces, that could be combined and recombined into distinct, agreed upon letterforms.

What telegraphic practice (and thus Judge Monroe) added to the Morse alphabet was the second-order arbitrariness of nonphonetic sounds. Morse's letters had old names, old phonetic values, and new letterforms, but in practice those letterforms themselves had come to have sounds, the established patterns of "dit" and "dah" that telegraphers now recognized. In a certain sense, "dit dit" formed a new and arbitrary *name* for the letter "oh." In another sense, however, "dit dit" was less an arbitrary nomination than the non-arbitrary, machine noise of the ".." letterform being indented onto paper tape. The writing (noun) of the telegraph was its writing (verb) with a stunning directness: No wonder, then, that electromagnetism and alphabets came to American courtrooms so closely bundled in these years.

Morse assembled a dream team of lawyers to make his case when it reached the Supreme Court. Their arguments, the arguments of their opponents at the bar, as well as the arguments and the decisions from the lower courts, all tangle the question of electronic writing. Despite the warnings of one attorney who pleaded, "We must not lose ourselves in the use of terms," lose themselves they did, until the Supreme Court justices groaned that it was hard "to make a fair report of this case without writing a book."[32] On Morse's side, St. George T. Campbell, Esq., argued prosaically that Morse had made electromagnetism into "the obedient penman of man." But his associate, George Gifford, Esq., urged that Morse's success was "a new, complete, and perfect art" of telegraphing, which must be distinguished from "the art of writing" and "the art of printing." (This was an argument aimed at the competing House telegraph, which printed Roman letters instead of dots and dashes and used a pianolike keyboard.)[33] Telegraphing, Gifford continued, depended upon an ingenious, functional, "new vehicle of thought," the "system of signs" of Morse's patent. Though "men for centuries" had invented new alphabets, exhausting themselves with "angles, curves, and circles" so that "geometry has been rebuked for its meager supply of forms to meet the demand," nonetheless Morse applied his "genius" to the task. He was limited to a "single material," "a single element, a continuous line." Gifford celebrated switching and binary code, the line broken into dots, dashes, and spaces: so "the simplest form known is wrought into a capacious store house of thought, to be employed as a receptacle for telegraphic messages, but with a capacity ample for the reception and dispersion of all human knowledge." Gifford spoke eloquently, but contradicted himself in the next breath when he defended Morse against competing systems based on dits and dahs. These sounds were so integral, "so strictly allied to" the telegraphic record being made, "that each may be employed as an interpreter of the other; in short, the one is the written and the other is the spoken language" of Morse's "messenger of thought" (Gifford 1853, 32). Telegraphy wasn't writing, and it was.

Gifford's contradiction remained ascendant in telegraphic practice and in scattered state court hearings. For one, the Morse alphabet quickly achieved an almost vestigial status, important for learning telegraphy and then wireless, but rarely in evidence on paper. It was the sound of these new letterforms that mattered, as paper tape dropped out of telegraphic practice, too, except in specialized devices. The "register" of 1844—Alfred Vail wanted everyone to call it the "writing desk"—was soon replaced by a "sounder." Customers wrote down the messages they wanted to send. An operator sent them as dits and dahs to an operator at another office who wrote them down in Roman letters for delivery to the indicated recipient. The Morse letterforms were never visible as such in this communication. They show up only in reference books, manuals, and specifications. In one final twist, the courts were left to decide whether it was the customer's written version or the recipient's that offered the best evidence of the message as semiotic entity. Which one was more self-evidently the information in question? In 1856 a Vermont court noted that if the "original message ordered to be sent is preserved, that should be produced, although this were not strictly the original in the case, *the letter delivered [is] the original.*" By contrast, in 1861 an Illinois court was sure that "[t]he paper filed at the office, from which the message is sent, *is of course the original*, and that which is received by the person to whom the message is sent, purports to be a copy."[34] Like "the first" then, "the original" remains an open question.

# *ENLIGHTENMENT*
## EVIDENCE AND EVENTS

# MEDIATING INFORMATION, 1450-1800

ANN BLAIR AND PETER STALLYBRASS

From about 1450 information began to be stockpiled in Europe on a radically new scale. This stockpiling depended upon material conditions including the displacement of parchment by paper, the decreasing cost of paper, and the increased use of blank notebooks and paper slips, which coincided with a proliferation of printed matter.[1] The stockpiling also depended on new cultural attitudes that valued expansive collections of many kinds for long-term storage. We call this new cultural attitude "info lust." The accumulations of textual matter it drove prompted experimentation with new methods for storing, retrieving, and disseminating information. These built on medieval inventions such as the alphabetical index and ordinated layout, but also involved innovations such as filing systems that began to be widely adopted in the late fourteenth and early fifteenth centuries, by which letters and other documents were strung together on a piece of string. ("File" is derived from the Latin *filum*, meaning a thread.) Printing also facilitated new kinds of finding devices, starting with page numbers. Probably less than 10 percent of manuscript books had folio or page numbers in 1450. By the end of the fifteenth century, the great majority of new printed books were either foliated or paginated. The development of folio and page numbers coincided with the standardized organization of the Bible by chapter and verse.[2]

Many of the new collections of information depended upon collaborative authorship. Collaborative work was crucial to the composition of large reference works both diachronically and synchronically. For example, the largest printed florilegium, the *Polyanthea* first published in 1503 by Domenico Nani Mirabelli, grew sixfold through additions made in successive editions down to 1620 (then remained stable in a dozen more editions to 1681). Some editions of the *Polyanthea* named those responsible for large additions, but many of the hands that contributed to the text remained anonymous. In an example of synchronic collaboration, Diderot and d'Alembert made explicit their reliance on articles from some 250 contributors in the *Encyclopédie*, published in 1751–1772. Collaborative "authorship" was also involved in the production of documents (printed, manuscript, or hybrids of the two), which were generated by mercantile, ecclesiastical, and government records. Our suggestion is that the literary categories of authorship that still dominate our understanding of "texts" are inadequate for many kinds of books and manuscripts, notably those cut and pasted from other works, and are even less adequate for the great bulk of printed matter such as blank forms, bills of lading, printed slips, commonplace books, accounts, and paper money.

The broadening of the "history of the book" to include all textual forms is counterproductive to the extent that it is still held in thrall to the concept of the book. The book was only one of a wide range of material forms in which information was stored. In this essay, we want to examine methods of information management in the varied media of the early modern period by looking at the makers and users of Latin reference works on the one hand, and at methods of mercantile and vernacular note taking on the other hand. Fragments and slips were central to both areas of knowledge; the book was only *one* way of storing, organizing, and disseminating those fragments.

## 1. Stockpiling Information

Storing knowledge or information on a large scale was not new to the Enlightenment.[3] Pliny's *Natural History* is the principal large work to have survived from antiquity, but there were others in circulation that were not recorded on parchment and transmitted to later periods. Some large Byzantine collections, for example, offer indirect evidence of the existence of earlier Greek compilations now lost. Starting in the thirteenth century, new habits of textual layout (including running heads and divisions into sections and subsections) and new finding devices such as the alphabetical index accompanied the considerable growth in the number and size of Scholastic and

Mendicant works. Vincent of Beauvais's *Speculum maius* of 1255 was by far the largest medieval compilation totaling more than four million words, which filled a hefty folio in its last printed edition of 1624.[4] What was exceptional in the Middle Ages became the norm in the Renaissance as the *Polyanthea* of Domenico Nani Mirabelli, which started at about 400,000 words in its first edition of 1503 grew to about 2.5 million words in editions after 1620.[5] The largest printed compilations were considerably larger: the *Theatrum humanae vitae* of Theodor Zwinger started at some 1.8 million words in 1565 and more than tripled in size by 1586, before its sequel, Laurentius Beyerlinck's *Magnum theatrum humanae vitae* (1631), reached some 10 million words in seven folio volumes of about a thousand pages each.[6] Before the *Encyclopédie* a further record for bulk in reference works was set by Johann Zedler's *Universal-Lexicon* published between 1732 and 1750 in 64 volumes and over 67 million words.[7] With its 17 folio volumes of text and 11 of plates, the *Encyclopédie* (at about 25 million words) fell within the norms of the very large reference book in the eighteenth century, though the plates constituted an innovative and exceptional expense.[8]

Within this trajectory of reference books becoming progressively larger in size both at the norm and at the outer limits, the Renaissance figures as a significant moment of change, with the spread of a new practice of accumulating large collections of personal notes. On the one hand, these personal reading notes formed the material from which large printed compilations and successive additions to them were made; on the other hand, the new value placed on stockpiling notes created a demand for printed compilations on the part of those who did not have the diligence, access to books or time to accumulate collections of notes of their own. Many Renaissance reference works offered readymade the kind of notes that Renaissance pedagogues recommended taking and that readers probably wished they had taken themselves—namely, by collecting quotations, examples, and anecdotes from classical literature and history, sorted by topical headings that were either alphabetically arranged or, if thematically, then also accessible by alphabetical index. The explosion of printed reference works in the sixteenth century (one author has estimated at one million the number of printed florilegia in circulation by 1600[9]) certainly correlates chronologically with the survival of many large collections of personal notes.

Medieval notes were temporary rather than stockpiled for the long term. We know about notes on oral events like sermons or lectures called *reportationes* because from them clean copies of these texts were drawn up for circulation; the notes themselves were taken on wax tablets or cheap scraps of parchment that were erased or used for other purposes after the finished copy was produced.[10] Florilegia and encyclopedias turned what began as personal notes into shared resources designed for circulation. But we almost never have a stockpile of personal notes that survive qua personal notes from the Middle Ages. Even for a very abundant and prominent author like Thomas Aquinas, whose autograph manuscripts were saved and treated with the status of relics in his own day and since, we have no surviving personal notes. Instead the reconstruction of his working methods by Antoine Dondaine suggests that Aquinas consulted books as needed while composing and composed by dictation to one or more secretaries. (He reportedly could dictate simultaneously on different topics to three or four secretaries at a time). Aquinas composed whenever he was ready, including in the middle of the night, in one instance waking up his companion Reginald in order to do so (Dondaine 1956, 10–11, 17).

By contrast starting in the Renaissance we have many, often very large, collections of personal notes that have come down to us thanks to the care with which they were saved by the note takers themselves, then by their heirs, and in many cases by continuously surviving institutions such as the Royal Society or various libraries. Humanists like Angelo Poliziano (1454–1494), left many volumes of notes and papers that are now are dispersed among various European libraries (Maïer 1965). From the fifteenth century we also have the first large collections of letters.[11] A recent volume edited by Michael Hunter offers careful studies of the transmission of a number of collections of papers by the "new scientists" of seventeenth-century England (Hunter 1998). Other large stockpiles of personal notes include the twenty-odd volumes of William Drake's reading notes studied by Kevin Sharpe and the 45,000 pages of notes by a German professor Joachim Jungius, which are estimated to be only a third of the notes he took in his life (Sharpe 2000; Meinel 1995). Some but not all of these abundant note takers were also published authors.

The stockpiling of abundant reading notes required specific material and cultural preconditions. One was a medium that was cheaper than parchment and larger than wax tablets. Paper was manufactured in Italy starting in the thirteenth century and spread north in the fourteenth century. But the production of paper was vastly increased and its price lowered once printing created a regular and heavy demand for it.[12] It is striking that large-scale note taking, always on paper, emerged around the same time as printing. Another possible connection between the stockpiling of reading notes and printing is that some note takers became newly aware of the possibility of profiting in reputation or financial gain by printing their notes or selections from them.

While printing may have facilitated the stockpiling of notes, equally important was a new cultural conception of scholarly method prevalent in the Renaissance—what one might call "info lust." This attitude is evident notably in Drexel's assumption that it is useful to accumulate notes throughout one's reading simply for the purpose of forming a treasury of material to have on hand for any writerly or conversational need (Drexel 1638). This kind of stockpiling is distinct from taking notes with a specific compositional purpose in mind; instead, it looks like a textual manifestation of contemporary practices of collecting objects, medals, and paintings in cabinets of curiosities.

One of the presuppositions of info lust, sometimes made explicit, was that, in the words of the expert on Joachim Jungius, "no field was too remote, no author too obscure that it would not yield some knowledge or other" (Meinel 1995, 166). Similarly Gabriel Naudé observed, in his advice on forming a library, that it was "necessary to pose as a maxim that there is no book, however bad or decried, which will not be sought after by someone over time" (Naudé 1963, 33). Naudé was echoing here the tag attributed to Pliny by his nephew that there is no book so bad that some good cannot be gotten from it.[13] This desire to trawl all sources in search of items worth selecting and storing for safekeeping was an important motivation driving the stockpiling of notes on unprecedented scales in the early modern period.

Other motivations have been suggested too. Some scholars have argued that note taking among gentlemen without publishing ambitions (like William Drake or the younger Robert Sidney) served as a kind of "therapy" during the tensions of the English Civil War, or as a place in which to work out one's personal values and positions (Warkentin 2005, 238–239, 244; Sharpe 2000, 192).[14] For somewhat different reasons, Adrien Turnèbe associated his collection of commonplaces on classical literature with the French civil wars, because "the unpleasantnesses of the time and the country's fall into decline" made it impossible for him to focus on "serious studies" (Turnèbe 1581, sig. 2r–v).

Others emphasized the role of note taking in working toward the common good for an international Republic of Letters. Conrad Gesner, for example, acknowledged in print the contributions of scores of people all over Europe who had sent him their observations and specimens. Pierre Gassendi comments of Nicolas Fabri Peiresc (1580–1637) that he was most diligent in writing down "any notable thing that came into his mind, or was suggested by some other or observed in reading" because he could "never endure that the least invention or observation of any man should be lost, being always in hopes that either himself, or some other, would be advantaged thereby" (Gassendi 1657, 200). Therefore "he wrote things down in his memorials because he then judged they were out of danger of being forgotten" (Gassendi 1657, 191–192). Although he never published anything, Peiresc would share material from his abundant collection of notes with his many correspondents across Europe. The value of a collection of notes for readers beyond the original note taker is evident from attempts to buy the notes of famous scholars (rarely successful) and the careful arrangements made to save and bequeath them.[15]

Scholarship, though, was only one of the areas in which note taking developed in new ways. The increasingly organized state institutions in early modern Europe were crucial agents in the gathering and storing of information, and they increasingly drew upon the resources of the printing press. In the 1580s, Philip II ordered *relaciones geográficas o topográficas* (geographical or topographical reports) to be sent out to every town council in Spain. The printed forms required that a series of questions be answered in a prescribed sequence so as to facilitate the tabulation of the answers received. And in 1622, Philip IV sent out printed questionnaires on a massive scale to elicit opinions on his new proposals "for the Well-Being, Preservation, and Security of These Kingdoms." Spanish inquisitorial trials were also recorded on printed blanks such as the following:

> In the town of Valladolid, the _____th day of the month of _____ of one thousand, five hundred and _____, in the presence of the Lord Inquisitors _____; _____, resident of _____, having been called to appear in the court at _____, . . . (Bouza 1999, 33–34)

The printed forms that Fernando Bouza describes proliferated throughout Europe and the New World. When William Bradford proclaimed the arrival of "that great Art and Mystery of Printing" in Philadelphia in 1685, he was not thinking of publishing books but rather of printing the necessary blank forms for the business of the colony. Similarly, William Goddard advertised that he printed "Blanks, Policies of Insurance, Portage Bills, Bills of Lading and Sale, Letters of Attorney, Administration Bonds, common Bonds, Deeds, Writs, and Executions, and all Kinds of Blank. . . either Wholesale or Retail" (Wroth 1965, 225). Printed forms, to be completed by hand, were necessary for government and commerce alike.

Such forms were not the only new system of note taking. As Chris Kyle and Jason Peacey have shown, the *arcana imperii* or state secrets of the English Parliament were opened up in an extraordinary way during the 1620s and 1630s. For the first time, members of the House of Commons and the House of Lords openly took notes during parliamentary sessions. As they exited the chambers, professional scribes copied their notes and circulated them all over Britain. A gentleman in Cornwall recorded in his diary receiving transcriptions of the main debates in Parliament a week after they had taken place—the week being the time it took for the postal service to deliver the news. And the desire for accurate parliamentary news was a driving force behind the development of shorthand in the seventeenth century.[16] While shorthand was at first mainly employed for taking down sermons, it was professionalized in the later seventeenth century by state functionaries like Samuel Pepys.

Pepys's diary was famously written in shorthand but an overemphasis upon the diary has misled commentators as to the significance of Pepys's shorthand—as if he only developed it to protect his sexual secrets from the eyes of his wife. The diary itself is written in such a fine and careful script that it cannot have saved Pepys very much in terms of time. But it helped him to perfect the shorthand that he used on a regular basis for his work. On November 17, 1666, Pepys records writing his "great letter" to the Duke of York on the state of the Navy, which he had "writ foule in short hand" (Pepys 1972). He then read it aloud to Will Hewer, who was acting as Pepys's secretary, while Hewer took down Pepys's dictation "fair in short hand." Hewer then read his "fair" shorthand version of the letter back to Pepys, while Pepys took it down in long hand "which saves me much time." It is this long-hand version that Pepys read aloud the next day to his patrons, Lord Bruncker and Sir William Coventry: "I read over my great letter, and they approved it." But the approval must have clearly come with suggested revisions, since Pepys records: "Back home in my Lord Bruncker's coach, and there W. Hewer and I to write it over fair; dined at noon, and Mercer with us, and mighty merry, and then to finish my letter." It was this *fourth* copy—a longhand revision of an earlier longhand revision that was a dictated copy of Hewer's fair shorthand that was in turn a dictated copy of Pepys's rough shorthand—which was finally delivered to the Duke of York.

If shorthand played an increasingly important role in the practical business of the Navy Office, it was also useful for scholarly note taking. On March 15, 1669, Pepys went to the Office of the Rolls to find material for his work on English history. He recorded:

> Up, and by water with W. Hewer to the Temple; and thence to the Rolls... : and so spent the whole morning with W. Hewer, he *taking little notes in short-hand*, while I hired a clerk there to read to me about twelve or more several rolls which I did call for: and it was great plea-

sure to me to see the method wherein their rolls are kept; that when the Master of the Office, one Mr. Case, do call for them. . . he did most readily turn to them.

Relying upon Hewer's shorthand and the clerk's reading aloud, Pepys himself had the leisure to note and admire the filing system that enabled the speedy identification and retrieval of the required rolls.

For our final example of new techniques of note taking, we turn to the sea. Surprisingly from a modern perspective, ships were one of the main schools for the development of note taking. When the English East India Company was founded at the beginning of the seventeenth century, it was decided that four different people on every ship should keep a daily journal: the captain, the master, the master's mate, and the purser. Their journals were handed in to the central office in London when they returned, where they were transcribed into notebooks, which were in turn given to the captains of the next outgoing fleet. These records of the previous voyage were checked against the prevailing conditions so as to compile constantly revised accounts of currents, winds, and other relevant navigational information.

Of the notebooks that survive, one is by Thomas Bonner, who was engaged as master's mate on the merchant ship, *Expedition*, in 1614:

> The neat, compact writing of the first two or three pages [of his notebook] deteriorates in the later pages and at times becomes loose and scrawling. . . The variations in the handwriting and the use of different pen points, despite the over-all unity of presentation, are consistent with the transfer at convenient times, but under varying climactic conditions, of several days' entries from an original rough journal which would have been written up daily. (Strachan et al. 1971, 13–14)

Before he sailed, Bonner bought "six pair of gilded table books" in which to keep notes.[17] It was probably in these table books that Bonner made the rough notes that later, "at convenient times," he transferred into his journal. "Table books," or "writing tables" as they were also called, were first commercially produced for the use of merchants in the late fifteenth century. They were usually composed of printed material, including a "perpetual almanac" with the dates of relevant fairs and a variety of useful tables, bound together with leaves of erasable paper or parchment on which one could write with a stylus made of soft metal.[18]

Jan Gossart's *Portrait of a Merchant* (c. 1530) depicts a merchant with all the accoutrements of writing. In the bottom right corner of the portrait is a notebook, about half the size of the merchant's hand. The tables are rather difficult to make out because a scale for weighing the gold coins has been

Jan Gossart, *Portrait of a Merchant* (ca. 1530). Oil on panel, 63.6 × 47.5 cm, Ailsa Mellon Bruce Fund 1967.4.1, The National Gallery of Art, Washington, D.C. Gossart's merchant is using the latest technologies of notebook (the erasable writing tables, bottom right) and of filing (Alrehande Missiven, miscellaneous letters received, left, and Alrehande Minuten, miscellaneous copies of letters sent, right).

put on top of them. They have a wallet binding with metal clasps on the flap, and the clasps are secured by a brass stylus.[19] By an extraordinary coincidence, the earliest tables that we have seen were made at the same time, in the same city, and by the same man as the tables in Gossart's painting. The title page of the printed almanac at the front of these tables, which are now in the New York Public Library, gives cleaning instructions and calls attention to the significance of the stylus:

Calendar: ¶Item you may write here with a stylus of gold, silver, tin, copper, or brass, and you may erase [what you have written] with a wet finger. ¶And when you have worn out [the erasable surface], so that you cannot write on it any more, you can get it repaired by Jan Severszoon, parchment maker, for a little money, and you can then write on it as if it was new. ¶ Sold for your benefit in the famous mercantile city of Antwerp, on the Lombaerde veste: wholesale by Jan Severszoon, at the house of Jan Gasten, bookbinder.
¶Item if you get grease on it by erasing with your finger, you should use a clay sponge [*cleyspongie*] with a little flour, and the grease will come off.
¶In the year of our Lord, 1527. (New York Public Library, Spencer Coll. Neth. 1527 94-143)

Erasable notebooks like this combined printed information with blank leaves in which to take notes even when the use of pen and ink would have been difficult or impossible.

There is a further, practical point to be drawn from Gossart's painting. As we noted above, the writing tables in the picture are partly obscured by a pair of scales for weighing the gold coins that are also depicted. If you could open Gossart's tables, as you can the tables in the New York Public Library, you would find a table giving the appropriate weights for the different kinds of gold coins in circulation. Such tables were, in fact, a standard feature of these erasable notebooks. When they were mass-produced in London in the later sixteenth century, they contained not only similar tables giving the appropriate weights but also six pages of woodcuts of gold coins to help in identifying the different currencies in circulation. An additional feature of these English tables helps to account for the curious "backwardness" of English merchants in the adoption of arabic numerals, which were in standard use in France at the same time. They contained convenient multiplication tables—but these tables were still in roman numerals.[20]

From the fifteenth century on, scholars, state bureaucrats, and merchants developed and shared new technologies of note taking that played a crucial role in forms of information management that we associate with modernity, including the encyclopedia and more systematic record-keeping in many areas, from science to government and commerce.

## 2. Finding Devices and the Decline of Memory

Abundant stockpiles of notes posed new problems of information management. Drexel complained of the weakness of memory and assumed that note takers would forget the notes they had taken and the headings they had used.

He therefore recommended keeping not only three different notebooks—one for quotations, one for historical examples and one for bibliographical references—but also an index to each notebook to facilitate recovery of the material stored there. In practice, few abundant note takers seem to have devised such systematic methods for retrieving items from their notes (Drexel 1638, chap. 3, 85ff).

Indeed, many scholars commented on the messiness with which abundant note takers kept their personal papers. Some were able to manage the mess themselves, like Peiresc of whom Gassendi reports: "though he would frequently excuse himself that all in his House was nothing but a confused and indigested Masse, or heap, yet was he never long in seeking anything in so great an heap, provided that none meddled with his Rarities, Books or Papers but himself; and that some body else, being commanded to fetch this or that, had not put them out of order" (Gassendi 1657, 197). Others were less successful. Although he devised many an organizational scheme in the abstract, G. W. Leibniz apparently reported being unable to find things among his mass of unsorted notes: "After having done something I forget it almost entirely within a few months and rather than searching for it amid a chaos of jottings that I do not have the leisure to arrange and mark with headings I am obliged to do the work all over again" (Leibniz 1962, 2: 227–232, as cited in O'Hara 1998, 160).

Robert Boyle, too, was notoriously messy with his papers. Scholars working through Boyle's papers after his death did not have the advantage of personal memory of the work on which Boyle himself must have relied; one called them a "chaos, rude and indigested."[21] Boyle often composed on loose sheets, which could be rearranged within and between the various treatises that he worked on simultaneously and which facilitated using the same passage in more than one place. But the sheets were "often lost or mislaid, by himself or his amanuenses," and the order between them was indicated only by catchwords to the next sheet (Hunter and Davis 1996, 204–271; Hall 1987, 111–116, esp. 111, 115).[22] As a result Boyle had to apologize in print for one instance in which parts of a work were published in the wrong order because of a "transposition of loose sheets where the copy was sent to the press."[23]

If some individual stockpilers of reading notes could rely on their memories to find their way through their papers even when minimally sorted, the users of reference works needed formalized finding devices to navigate materials they had not had a hand in preparing. Compilers of printed reference works were responsible for a number of innovations in finding tools and page layout which became standard trappings of various genres aimed at organizing information, including many still in use today. The oldest paratext to accompany compilations was probably the list of authorities. Such lists had ancient antecedents and were transmitted to the Middle Ages through legal genres (Skydsgaard 1968, 101–116). These lists were not finding devices but a kind of advertisement for the quality of the work by displaying the range of authorities mentioned, often only through intermediate sources that were only occasionally acknowledged.

Alongside the list of authors the other list commonly found in early modern compilations was a list of headings in the order in which they appeared in the book. These lists were often called indexes, though they would not be considered indexes in modern parlance. The list of headings offered a browsable overview of the categories under which the material was sorted. The most elaborate of these also listed the sections and subsections in each heading with appropriate indentations and page numbers referring to the main text. Such outlines provided a powerful visualization of the hierarchical structure of the work, as well as an effective way to access specific parts of the text.

The most powerful tool was the alphabetical index, first devised in the thirteenth century for biblical concordances. With printing, indexes routinely referenced page and folio numbers even though this meant that they had to be redone with each new edition of the text. Explanatory blurbs indicate that contemporaries considered the consultation of indexes to be slow and burdensome—they were well aware of the multiple terms under which something of interest might be entered.[24] Drexel recommended taking one's own notes rather than relying on printed reference works precisely because it was so hard to find what one was looking for in them.[25] The first attempts at standardizing subject headings date from the professionalization of library science in the late nineteenth century, but printed reference works served as a source of conventional headings often imitated in manuscript notebooks. In Renaissance florilegia, many of these headings had been borrowed from medieval antecedents and were focused on the Christian vices and virtues. By the eighteenth century the headings used in both personal notes and printed reference works ranged much more widely and idiosyncratically (Décultot 2003, intro.). The *Encyclopédie* offered no browsable list of headings or standard of systematic coverage but a vast number of articles of varying lengths, depending on the contributions received and Diderot's own willingness to supplement them.

One Jesuit advice book of 1614 still in print in 1785 (but now for the use of Calvinists) called for note takers to recopy and reread their notes in order to master them from memory.[26] This advice, if it was ever followed by schoolboys, was certainly not widely heeded in the eighteenth century, when note collections were larger and more idiosyncratically arranged than ever. Whereas humanists reported and boasted of feats of memory, by the late seventeenth century memory was perceived by some as a drag on the more important faculties of reason and wit.[27] By making so much available without prior mnemonic contact with the material, Renaissance reference books may have contributed to the downgrading of memory as something merely mechanical.

If the significance of memory diminished in posthumanist scholarship, both government and commerce required new solutions to an "information overload" that could not possibly be stored in human memories alone. As we noted above, Pepys in his role as amateur historian was able to admire the efficiency with which the Office of the Rolls stored their records for rapid retrieval. A variety of new forms of shelving, cabinets, pigeonholes, and bags were employed to make the scholarly trope of the beehive a material reality in everyday practice. In the first century of the common era, the Greek historian Plutarch had elaborated what was already an ancient conceit, comparing the good reader to a bee:

> [L]ike as Bees have this propertie by nature to finde and and sucke the mildest and best honie, out of the sharpest and most eager flowers; yea and from among the roughest and most prickly thornes: even so children and yoong men if they be well nourtured and orderly inured in the reading of Poemes, will learne after a sort to draw alwaies some holesome and profitable doctrine or other, even out of those places which moove suspition of lewd and absurd sense. (Plutarch 1657, 43)

The Protestant humanist Philip Melanchthon elaborated Plutarch's conceit into an organized program by drawing parallels between the work of the bee, the material properties of different kinds of notebooks, and differentiated techniques of note taking.[28] One can schematize Melanchthon's program as follows:

| The Bee's Work | Material Support | Form of Writing |
| --- | --- | --- |
| 1. Finding the nectar in the flowers | Books and their margins | Underlining, marginal marks, and notes |
| 2. Gathering nectar from flowers | Small erasable tablet or waste book | "Promiscuous" notes |
| 3. Putting the pollen in the correct cell of the honeycomb | Large commonplace book | Notes under proper alphabetical headings |
| 4. Making honey | Sheets or a gathering | Composing, writing |

A hundred and fifty years later, in a small town in North America, the German Quaker Francis Pastorius was still working out the details of Melanchthon's program in his massive manuscript compilation, *Francis Daniel Pastorious, His Alphabetical Hive of More than two thousand Honey-combs Begun in the year 1696*. Pastorius's "Paper-Hive," as he called it, was the final alphabetical "digestion" of a series of smaller notebooks on diverse subjects, ranging from the laws of Pennsylvania to land-sales to gardening. Pastorius wrote on one of the several title pages of his massive compilation: "From *Bees* returning to their hive learn in collecting how to thrive." And he added below:

> For as much as our Memory is not Capable to retain all remarkable Words, Phrases, Sentences, or Matters of Moment, which we do hear and read, it becomes every good Scholar to have a *Common Place Book*, & therein to Treasure up what ever deserves his Notice &c. And to the end that he may readily know, both wither to dispose and insert each particular, as also where upon Occasion to find the same again &c. he ought to make himself an Alphabetical Index, like that *of this Bee Hive*. (Pastorius 1696, first title page)[29]

What is striking about Pastorius's compilation is the range of practical purposes to which he put it. While he was steeped in European scholarship, he was committed to using that learning for the founding and governing of Germantown. Moreover, although he was himself German, and knowledgeable in seven languages, including Hebrew, Greek, and Latin, he decided to write in the vernacular of the dominantly English province. By that act, he self-consciously cut himself off from transatlantic Humanist scholarship so as to create a book that he made available to anyone who could read English in his new homeland.

While Pastorius employed a technique that had been developed by scholars for the practical sorting, storing, and retrieval of information, merchants developed their own methods of filing information. If we return again to Jan Gossart's *Portrait of a Merchant*, we can see not only the depiction of a new kind of erasable notebook but also one of the earliest representations of a simple but practical filing system. Like many of the most radical inventions, this system seems too simple to *have* a history. Yet we know of no earlier example of this use of pieces of string to file letters, hanging up on a wall, upside down and back to front.[30] The two files are identified as *Alrehande Missiven* (miscellaneous letters) on the left and *Alrehande Minuten* (miscellaneous drafts) on the right. So hung, not only were the contents of the letters preserved from the observation of casual intruders, but also they could be read by the merchant by the simple expedient of turning the letters up. It was only after understanding the significance of Gossart's representation of this filing system that Heather Wolfe discovered that Cambridge University routinely kept its archives in this way into the seventeenth century. Just as in Gossart's painting, the filed documents at Cambridge are protected by a piece of vellum at the back, in which they can be rolled up when they are transported about. Indeed, one crucial aspect of the new organization of information was the combination of permanent depositories with portable units of notes.[31]

One can trace the spread of such filing systems throughout Europe in dictionary entries:

> *File, filacium,* is a threed or weier whereon Writs or other exhibits in Courts are fastned for the more safe keeping of them. (Minsheu et al. 1617)

> To File up a letter *Eenen brief aan een snoer rygen.* "Snoer, *a String, Cord.*" (Sewel 1708)

Increasingly, inventories of large-scale purchases of stationery include the simple but necessary equipment for filing. A 1643 Parliamentary bill recorded not only the purchase of parchment, paper, quills, and ink but also two shillings spent on "Needle thred and Lases." On a larger scale, a 1699 "Accompt of what hath been deliver'd for His Majestys Service, To the Clerk of the Hon.ble House of Commons," recorded not only a thousand quills and ten thousand wafers (for sealing letters) but also two kinds of bags for storing documents and "6 large Needles, ½ lb of Thread" for filing documents.[32] As with new methods of note taking, new methods of organizing information moved with increasing ease and rapidity between the scholar's study, the merchant's store and the government office.[33]

## 3. Methods of Collaborative Composition

Large-scale scholarly reference works were always collective undertakings, dependent on the contributions of many both diachronically and synchronically. Reference works routinely drew heavily on preexisting sources, though these were not often acknowledged, and each new edition involved the work not only of the author listed on the title page, but also of usually unnamed others (indexers, amanuenses, and copyists, for example).

We know very little about how medieval compilers worked, but the large compilations like Vincent of Beauvais's were surely collaborative. Religious orders, the Dominicans in particular, offered a good source of manpower for major undertakings like the biblical concordances of the thirteenth century or the *Speculum maius* (Congar 1980). Most monks were literate, some even learned; all would carry out assignments, usually without expecting remuneration or recognition. A few remaining working papers from biblical concordances, only surviving because they were used in the bindings of early modern books, indicate that the monks were each assigned a different letter of the alphabet and entered the words in the Bible beginning with that letter onto large sheets. In this medieval method of indexing, however, the results were only partially alphabetized (Rouse and Rouse 1974).

From the sixteenth century we find authors recommending the use of slips for notes and, indeed, some surviving manuscripts from the period have slips glued into place in alphabetical order. The Italian naturalist Ulisse Aldrovandi (1522–1605) compiled many manuscript indexes and collections of notes by gluing slips into notebooks, generally in alphabetical order.[34] Slips survive also in the working papers of Theodor Zwinger of Basel (1533–1588), a professor at the University of Basel and the author of the largest compilation of the period, the *Theatrum humanae vitae*, and of Conrad Gesner of Zurich (1516–1565), a great compiler of bibliographical and natural historical material, who explicitly advocated the use of slips, notably to form an index.[35] Zwinger acknowledged using material collected by his stepfather Conrad Lycosthenes in compiling his massive *Theatrum*. Indeed, we find in the Zwinger *Nachlass* excerpts written in Lycosthenes' hand that follow the format of the printed *Theatrum* (with capitalized keywords beginning each short paragraph). Some other slips survive, too, in a much messier hand, possibly Zwinger's own (*see fig. 1*). While Zwinger's slips were all manuscript, the slips on which Gesner took notes (as glued, for example, into a three-volume folio manuscript prepared by Gesner's executor Caspar Wolf as the "Thesaurus medicinae practicae") included passages cut out from a wide range of sources: letters he received, manuscripts marked up for casting off in preparation for printing, and printed books, both new and as marked up in the printing process, notably to prepare a later edition.[36]

Aldrovandi reportedly kept his loose slips (prior to gluing) in canvas bags, one for each letter of the alphabet.[37] We do not know how either Zwinger or Gesner stored the slips before they ended up in their current form. Presumably Gesner's slips were stored under the topical headings under which they were later glued. The slips in the Zwinger manuscripts were bound into the last volume of Zwinger's letters in the nineteenth century. But some of the slips in Lycosthenes' hand refer to other slips by folio number in a "tomus," which implies that they were stored in volumes, possibly in the way that was

Slips in the hand of Conrad Lycosthenes that match the format used in his stepson Theodor Zwinger's Theatrum Humanae Vitae (1565). The few surviving slips were bound at the end of a volume of other Zwinger manuscripts (mostly letters) in the nineteenth century. Note the cross-reference on one of them "Vide tomum 4 fol 343," which suggests that the slips were originally kept in volumes or tomes. Reproduced by kind permission of the Universitätsbibliothek Basel; Frey Mscr I, 13 no. 159-63.

illustrated in print much later in Vincent Placcius's *De arte excerpendi* (1689; see fig. 2). The manuscripts at the University of Basel also include some contemporary records—of scholarships awarded to students at the university in the late sixteenth century—left in their original state. These individual sheets of paper were folded twice, forming a little bundle that was tied shut with a string and inscribed with the name of the student and the field studied. These

Slips in another hand, likely Zwinger's own, and much less legible. Note the headword for each entry in the margin (e.g., "vipera cum murena"). The numbers were added by librarians at the moment when the slips were bound into volumes. Reproduced by kind permission of the Universitätsbibliothek Basel; Frey Mscr I, 13 no. 167-71.

"Amerbach slips" (*schedae Amerbachianae*) are preserved in loose alphabetical order in a wooden oval box. Although the catalog describes the box as "old," it may postdate the formation of this archive in the sixteenth century.[38]

Both Zwinger and Gesner had the help of amanuenses, as Zwinger explained in the preface to the third edition of his *Theatrum Humanae Vitae*: "I relied for three years and more on the help only of Basilius Lucius, my very dear cousin, in copying with his faithful and elegant hand those passages which resisted the sharpness of scissors, and in gluing together things which were to be gathered together" (Zwinger1586, sig \*\*\*5r). In addition to this synchronic help, the cutting and pasting from earlier notes and publications constitutes a second form of collaboration. This diachronic collaboration was usually involuntary on the part of the author whose work was recycled in this way. Gesner made a habit of acknowledging in print those contemporaries who contributed observations and specimens, but the notes he cut up from earlier sources were generally not attributed. Many of Zwinger's excerpts include the author and possibly a title, though the source name is not necessarily the source that Zwinger actually used. The variation in these references between different editions is evidence of considerable latitude in

*Left:* An example of how to store slips in volumes, from Vincent Placcius, De arte excerpendi (1689). Reproduced by permission of Houghton Library, Harvard University.

*Below:* The sole remaining example of an earlier form of storage of the "schedae Amerbachianae" containing records of fellowships granted to students at the university in Basel. The Amerbach family was a dominant presence in Basel throughout the 16th century; these records date from the period of Basil Amerbach (1533–1591). Reproduced by kind permission of the Universitätsbibliothek Basel; Mscr C VIa 96.

choosing a source to name, particularly when the authors in question were dead. Title pages often named some people who had a hand in creating successive editions of a reference book, but these were only a small subset of those actually involved. Many editors and indexers and all the lowlier amanuenses and copyists remained, to use Shapin's memorable phrase, "invisible technicians" of text management (Shapin 1989). Seventeenth-century editions of Mirabelli's *Polyanthea* named five or six men as responsible for major developments in the work since its first edition of 1503. Similarly in the preface to his massive *Magnum theatrum*, Laurentius Beyerlinck named five different people who laid the foundation for his own work. The list culminated in his printer Antonius Hieratus, who generously provided him with a copy of Zwinger's *Theatrum* (presumably two, in fact, so as to facilitate cutting out text from both sides of each leaf) from which he describes cutting and pasting passages to form the *Magnum theatrum*.[39] In tripling its contents Beyerlinck most certainly cut and pasted liberally from other works as well. Beyerlinck acknowledged, for example, relying on a work on astronomers by Heinrich Rantzau from which he lifted material for twenty pages of his article on "astronomy, astrology."[40]

In medieval and Renaissance compilations originality of contents was never a prime goal. Compilers took credit for the selection of items and their assignment to headings, as well as for the arrangement of headings and for finding devices that facilitated use. But compilers generally took limited responsibility for the items being compiled—they promised only to compile faithfully the claims of others. This stance of ideological neutrality enabled compilers to include items with which they would not have wanted to be personally associated in print. For example, Zwinger could include Paracelsian theories, while maintaining his standing as a university professor of medicine expected to uphold Galenic teaching. Zwinger was sympathetic to Paracelsianism, but reluctant to advertise his beliefs publicly.[41]

Renaissance compilers were clearly adept at manipulating (both seeking and avoiding) authorial credit to their best advantage. The question of how authorial strategies differed in the case of the *Encyclopédie* is a complex one. On the one hand, Diderot and d'Alembert sought and acquired authorial status for their work. On the other hand, the work derives much of its authority from its identification with a "society of men of letters," many of whom remained anonymous. Some contributors called attention to their work in the book, while others sought to hide it.[42] Although the specifics of Diderot's working methods have not been studied in detail, it is likely that Diderot penned articles attributed to others and modified articles contributed by others. Some of the articles displayed great originality in argumentation and content and articulated positions easily identified with Enlightenment thinkers, but others were indebted to existing sources that were not acknowledged.[43]

In the eighteenth century, large-scale compilation posed problems that were familiar to compilers in the sixteenth century and relied on similar solutions. Samuel Johnson used slips to compose his dictionary, some of which have survived only because they were accidentally left out of the new edition for which they had been made (Reddick 1996, 4–5). In compiling the first edition of the *Encyclopædia Britannica* (3 vols., 1768–1771), William Smellie also reported cutting and pasting from existing works: "[H]e used to say jocularly, that he had made a Dictionary of Arts and Sciences with a *pair of scissors*, clipping out from various books a *quantum sufficit* of matter for the printer" (Kerr 1811, 1: 362–363 [emphases in the original], as discussed in Yeo 2001, 180). Although we do not know how widespread cutting from printed books was, the use of slips became a standard technique of lexicographers and the index card, developed in the late nineteenth century, became essential to library catalogs and scholarly research techniques. The first standardized slips to be used in library catalogs and note taking (for example by Montesquieu) were developed in the eighteenth century and they were made from playing cards. These offered a convenient place for writing since their backs were blank before the nineteenth century.[44]

Samuel Johnson noted in his preface that "a large work is difficult, because it is large." By taxing or overtaxing ordinary working methods, the composition of large works stimulated innovative strategies for stockpiling and accessing information, recycling existing notes and works, and engaging multiple contributors in collective projects. At the same time, collaborative encyclopedias and dictionaries were generally attributed to the heroic labors of named authors. It is true that one can find such attributions in the Renaissance. But John Minsheu's massive 1617 dictionary is prefaced not only by a list of all the subscribers that made the project feasible but also by an account of the academics who had carefully checked (and helped to compile) the entries.[45] In the case of the Calepino dictionary, which was printed with constant modifications and additions in 165 editions from 1502 to 1785, the attribution of each edition to "Ambrogio Calepino" (1440–1510) as compiler of the first edition served as a brand rather than an indication of authorship (Labarre 1975). In 1685 Adrien Baillet noted that so many able hands had been involved in modifying and improving Calepino's original (which Baillet called "pitiful") that "today ... there is almost nothing left by Calepino but the title and name of the book."[46]

Compilations highlight especially vividly the inadequacy of the modern conception of "authorship" to describe texts that relied on so many contributions, from multiple printed sources to generations of scribes, editors and helpers who were only occasionally named. The modern regime of attributing works to single authors has obscured the complexity of many kinds of early modern texts. A particularly radical effect of the drive to associated texts with single authors are visible in the revised *Short-Title Catalogue of Books Printed in England, Scotland, and Ireland . . 1475–1640* (Pollard et al. 1986–1991). The *Short-Title Catalogue* contains no entry at all for "Anonymous." The nearest that it comes to such a category is "*Anonymus*," which contains a mere four cross-references to entries elsewhere in the volume. Yet the majority of all these *Short-Title Catalogue* books, which are now organized under author headings, were printed anonymously. In other words, a regime of authorship that had always been invoked for particular categories of book was now generalized as the method of organizing *all* books. As with the *Short-Title Catalogue*, the reorganization of new forms of knowledge in the eighteenth century entailed the reorganization of the past as well. Indeed, "Shakespeare" became the most powerful of all authorial figures in the Enlightenment and a central figure in disputes over copyright. Yet not a single play by Shakespeare had appeared with his name on it prior to 1598. And even when his work was gathered together in 1623, genre was the principle by which the plays were organized. Genre, in emphasizing the conventions within which texts are produced, places limits on the unbounded genius of the individual author. The work of Shakespeare's eighteenth-century editors was to undo any such constraints. It now became crucial first to date each work and then to place it in the order in which the author supposedly wrote it.[47] Thus, in tracing the order of Shakespeare's plays, one was simultaneously tracing the "growth of a poet's mind" (the subtitle that Wordsworth applied to *The Prelude*).

Against this emphasis on individual genius, we can trace the continuing traditions of collaborative and anonymous authorship through the eighteenth century. As a new regime of authorship (and copyright) expanded in Europe, Benjamin Franklin actively defended plagiarism as a virtue.[48] Franklin published the longest pamphlet he ever wrote during his career as a printer in support of Samuel Hemphill, a preacher who had been accused first of religious heterodoxy and then of plagiarism. Franklin wrote that Hemphill's accusers

> endeavour to lessen [him], by representing him as a Plagiary, and say, *They are apt to think, that if he had honestly given credit to the several Authors from whom he borrowed much of what he deliver'd, it wou'd*

*have made a considerable Abatement of the Reputation he supposes he gain'd, &c.*

But which of these Gentlemen, or their Brethren, is it, that does give due Credit for what he borrows? Are they beholden to no Author, ancient or modern, for what they know, or what they preach? ... They chuse the dullest Authors to read and study, and retail the dullest Parts of those Authors to the Publick. It seems as if they search'd only for Stupidity and Nonsense.... But when Hemphill had Occasion to borrow, he gave us the best Parts of the best Writers of the Age. Thus the Difference between him and most of his Brethren, in this part of the World, is the same with that between the Bee and the Fly in the Garden. The one wanders from Flower to Flower, and for the use of others collects from the whole the most delightful Honey; while the other (of a quite different Taste) places her Happiness entirely in Filth, Corruption, and Ordure.[49]

Nowhere is Franklin closer to the long Renaissance tradition of commonplacing and collaborative writing than in his account of the bee and the fly. Both are dependent upon what they collect from others. The difference is that the fly collects "Ordure" while the bee collects pollen. Franklin "plagiarized" his account of the bee from one of his favorite writers: Plutarch. In his autobiography, Franklin wrote that he "read abundantly [in Plutarch's *Lives*], and I still think that time spent to great Advantage" (Franklin 1986, 9). In defending Hemphill, Franklin turned to the *Moralia*, in which, as we noted above, Plutarch describes how a reader should be like a bee, finding and sucking "the mildest and best honie, out of the sharpest and most eager flowers" (Plutarch 1657, 43). The bee's lesson could be broken down into three processes: gathering pollen (taking "promiscuous notes" on one's reading), storing the pollen in the cells of the honeycomb (selecting and organizing one's notes under topical headings), and producing honey (putting one's reading to use to preach sermons, write poetry, or compile almanacs).

Franklin's modern editors are clearly embarrassed by Franklin's defense of Hemphill, suggesting that he was "[p]utting on the best face he could" (Franklin 1959, 90). But this is surely not right, since Franklin returned to champion Hemphill in his autobiography, fifty-three years later. There, he gave both a more extreme version of Hemphill's plagiarism and a more extreme defense:

One of our Adversaries having heard [Hemphill] preach a Sermon that was much admired, thought he had somewhere read that Sermon before, or at least a part of it. On Search he found that Part quoted at length in one of the British Reviews, from a Discourse of Dr Foster's. The Detection gave many of our Party Disgust, who accordingly abandoned his Cause. . . . I stuck by him however, *as I rather approv'd his giving us good Sermons compos'd by others, than bad ones of his own Manufacture;* tho' the latter was the Practice of our common Teachers. He afterwards acknowledg'd to me that none of those he preach'd were his own; adding that his Memory was such as enabled him to retain and repeat any Sermon after one Reading only. (Franklin 1986, 82, emphasis added)

For Franklin, ideas were a common treasury to be shared by all. It was not imitation or even plagiarism that was the problem; it was the claim to intellectual property, a claim that justified itself by *producing* "plagiarism" (i.e., the possibility of shared knowledge) as its moral (and later, legal) antithesis. Franklin argued that the immorality lay in the fences that intellectual property erected that preserved knowledge for the rich and powerful and prevented its free circulation.

In his autobiography, Franklin extended his critique of the ownership of knowledge to an explicit rejection of patents:

Governor Thomas was so pleas'd with the Construction of [my] Stove. . . that he offer'd to give me a Patent for the sole Vending of them for a Term of Years; but I declin'd it from a Principle which has ever weigh'd with me on such Occasions, viz. *That as we enjoy great Advantages from the Inventions of Others, we should be glad of an Opportunity to serve others by any Invention of ours, and this we should do freely and generously.* (Franklin 1986, 98, emphasis in the original)

The problem for Franklin was not the circulation and reuse of a common store of knowledge; it was how to get access to that knowledge so that one could learn from it by imitation. Franklin first got "Access to better Books" (Franklin 1986, 10) as an apprentice printer, and it was from those books that he drew the materials out of which he began to compose. As a writer, like the bee that he praised, he learned how to suck the nectar from the flowers of other people's knowledge, how to store that knowledge in the cells of a honeycomb, organizing it so as to make it accessible and retrievable, and finally how to make honey by composing his own work out of "the Sense of all Ages and Nations" (Franklin 1959, 7: 530).

One narrative of the Enlightenment is that of an age of heroic authorship. But Franklin's writings stand against that narrative. In the role of Poor Richard, Franklin defended the fact that "not many of [the verses] are of my own Making":

I know as well as thee, that I am no poet born; and it is a trade I never learnt, nor indeed could learn. . . . Why then should I give my readers bad lines of my own, when good ones of other people's are so plenty? 'Tis methinks a poor excuse for the bad entertainment of guests, that the food we set before them, though coarse and ordinary, is of one's own raising, off one's own plantation, etc. when there is plenty of what is ten times better, to be had in the market. (Franklin 1745)

Whatever the contributions of Diderot, d'Alembert, and others to the making of the *Encyclopédie*, they, like Franklin, also depended on the information that was "to be had in the market," a market that had been constituted by new practices of note taking, by new finding aids, and by a new regime of authorship that denied the very foundations on which that collaborative enterprise was built.

In the long history of information management, the first early modern period (ca. 1450–1650) was especially significant in the development of new techniques and the refinement of existing ones to manage an explosion of printed matter and manuscript record keeping. In portraying their work as a radical break from the Renaissance, Enlightenment authors often obscured the indebtedness of their works to preexisting methods of compiling.

# MEDIATED ENLIGHTENMENT

## THE SYSTEM OF THE WORLD

### CLIFFORD SISKIN

When Kant answered the question, "What is Enlightenment?" in 1784, he defined it not only as a philosophical concept but also as a particular moment in history. "We do live," he insisted, in an *age of enlightenment*" (Kant 2007). The irony, for us, of Kant's confident assertion is that he made it at precisely the moment that has since come to mark the start of another age: the period we call Romantic. Kant's certainty about his own age is now a central *uncertainty* of our own: welcome to the desert of periodization.

If you are in my discipline, literary studies, and you choose the red pill—like the hero of the film *The Matrix*—the comforting everyday landscape of the *Norton Anthology*, and the scholarly societies that have colonized its periods, begin to dissolve. The editors of the recent volume *Borders of Romanticism*, for example, speculate that "Romanticism" may be out as a historical category in light of effective work in the "long eighteenth century" (Davis 2004, 9). But that would leave much evidence, not to mention career debris, behind. What we need, I argue, is a way of reconciling the evidence of discontinuity—of a break between Enlightenment and what follows—with what the analytic success of the long eighteenth century tells us: that we have been overlooking some form of continuity. I identify that form as, quite literally, a form: the genre of "system." Since we can only experience the past through the mediation of its genres, I will use system to track Enlightenment as they cross back and forth across the English/Scottish border—from Isaac Newton to Adam Smith to William Wordsworth to Walter Scott. Then we will venture into the desert—and, I hope, reappear with a new history of Enlightenment.

For students of the Enlightenment, this turn to system will not surprise. System was the formal means to Enlightenment's end: comprehensive knowledge of a world that *could* be known—of parts that formed a whole. Both the many self-described systems of the late seventeenth and eighteenth centuries, as well as the proliferation of interrelated forms, from encyclopedias to treatises, are widely recognized markers of Enlightenment aspiration.

Students of Romanticism, however, will be on less familiar terms with system, in part because standard literary histories have fixed upon a different set of terms and genres to signal and embody what William Hazlitt called "the Spirit of the Age." Hazlitt used that phrase to describe Wordsworth's "genius" as an "emanation" of that "Spirit"—a formulation that seems initially to suggest an almost effortless passivity or even ventriloquism. But if we follow his argument for just a few more sentences, we will find that Hazlitt understood that genius to be something much more concrete and quite deliberate. It is shaped by a purpose or, to put it more precisely, by a genre: Wordsworth's enterprise, Hazlitt emphasizes, was "to compound a new *system* of poetry" (Hazlitt 1886, 151–152).

Understood as system making, the "Spirit of the Age" sounds much more like the "howl[ing]" battlecry of Blake's Los in *Jerusalem*: "I must Create a System, or be enslav'd by another Mans" (Blake 1970, 151, §1.10.20). System was, I argue, as crucial to the writing of the late eighteenth and early nineteenth centuries as Blake's embattled declaration makes it sound; in fact, invocations of, and accusations regarding, system were the discursive weapons with which the period we call Romanticism configured *itself*.

Take, for example, the dividing up of writing into "schools." "With Mr. Wordsworth and his friends," complained Francis Jeffrey, "it is plain that their peculiarities of diction are things of *choice*, and not of accident. They write as they do *upon* principle and system" (Woof 2001, 185–201). As case after case followed the principle articulated in *Don Juan*—"One system eats another up" (Byron 1980–1993, 559, §14.2.5)—the discursive map of Britain was redrawn, with a "Lake School" now at one end and a "Cockney School" at another.

Many other features of that map, from generations to genres, were similarly inscribed. In system, then, lies the secret history of Romanticism—its tale of self-configuration and thus its continuities with and departures from

Enlightenment.[1] To hear it we have to follow system's fate through both periods, tracking it not just as an *idea* but as a *genre*. By recovering the history of system as something embodied—as something that mediates through its generic embodiments—we can cast off some of the confusion surrounding the Enlightenment/Romanticism divide: "[Y]ou cannot behold him," wrote Blake, "till he be reveald in his System" (Blake 1970, 191).

## The System of the World

Isaac Newton refused to reveal himself in any other form. He first published on optics in a 1672 article in the *Transactions of the Royal Society*, an effort that elicited a wide range of criticisms requiring detailed rebuttal. For Newton, that kind of debate was not healthy, for it left the knowledge he produced looking like old knowledge—the unconvincing result of deductive hypothesizing and Scholastic debate. His reaction was absolute. Newton, with only one minor exception, *never* again published anything in a journal. He was to present his major physical findings only within books—the complete and comprehensive systems of the *Opticks* and the *Principia*, forms that reduced opposing arguments from debatable differences "to error" (Bazerman 1988, 82–83, 119). Such systems talked to themselves, quieting discourse in favor of an internal conversation among parts: a singular voice of reason in a newly nonrhetorical universe.

Systems simplified. To be more precise, Newton's systems formally enacted the central enterprise of the new science: the reworking of the relationship between complexity and simplicity, between what Bacon called "things as they are" and the principles posed to explain them. This is, let me quickly add, ongoing work, as evidenced by our current turns to chaos and complexity theory, emergence, butterfly effects, and algorithmic Darwinism. The *Principia*'s grand conclusion, "The System of the World," begins with Newton's "Rules for the Study of Natural Philosophy." And the very first rule was his very own version of Ockham's razor: "No more causes of natural things should be admitted than are both true and sufficient to explain their phenomena" (Newton 1999, 794). One law for apples and trees, planets and the sun—and for one reason: "nature," insisted Newton, "is simple and does not indulge in the luxury of superfluous causes." For Newton, this meant no longer indulging in Scholasticism or turning to the supernatural. To write systems was to imitate nature. The imperative of Newtonian Enlightenment was to simplify.

## Border Crossing No. 1: Master Systems

What first drove Enlightenment across the border to Scotland was the opportunity to follow that imperative in a slightly different way. Newton set the stage by setting a limit on his own simplifying. In his introduction to "The System of the World," he revealed that he had "composed an earlier version . . . in popular form, so that it might be more widely read." But worried that some readers would "not perceive the force of the conclusions" because they "have not sufficiently grasped the principles"—and thus engage him in precisely the "lengthy disputations" he wrote systems to avoid—Newton gave up on the popular. To seal the system from dispute, he "translated the substance of the earlier version into propositions in a mathematical style, so that they may be read only by those who have first mastered the principles" (Newton 1999, 793).

For Scots such as Adam Smith, seeking modes of inclusion after the '45—the signal defeat of Jacobite hopes for Scottish independence—Newton's opting out of the popular—his exclusion of readers—gave them a chance to opt in, to, in a social sense, extend the boundaries of system under the Enlightenment banner of simplicity. Far from being just a happy meeting of great minds, a fortuitous flowering of knowledge, what we now know as the Scottish Enlightenment was a carefully planned foray into the newly expanding world of print, what today we might call—minus the cynicism—a public relations ploy.

Writing in 1755 in the *Edinburgh Review*, Smith surveyed the scene and laid out the plan.[2] At that historical moment, he admits, Scotland, "which is but just beginning to attempt figuring in the learned world, produces as yet so few works of reputation, that it is scarce possible a paper which criticises upon them chiefly, should interest the public for any considerable time" (Smith 1795, 15). For Smith, this is no cause for despair, but rather an opportunity for Scotland to carve out a special place in the newly forming system of nations generated by print—the system of the world that came to be called the Republic of Letters.

The pleasure Smith feels in English accomplishments is a window into the complexities of British national identity at midcentury: "As, since the union, we are apt to regard ourselves in some measure as the countrymen of those great men, it flattered my vanity, as a Briton, to observe the superiority of the English philosophy thus acknowledged by their rival nation" (Smith 1795, 18). But here is the Scottish twist. At the very moment of apparent identification with the English under the rubric of Britishness, Smith identifies a gap between the two categories—English and British—a gap in which something distinctly Scottish can flourish.

This opportunity arose directly out of the Newtonian retreat from the popular:

> The English seem to have employed themselves entirely in inventing, and to have disdained the more inglorious but not less useful labour of arranging and methodizing their discoveries, and of expressing them in the most *simple* and natural terms. (Smith 1795, 18–19, emphasis added)

Scotland, Smith realized, could enter the learned world by writing systems, but systems of a very particular kind: master systems that would simplify and popularize by arranging and methodizing *all* earlier systems. That is why "simple and natural" expression was *not* a polite *after*thought for Smith, David Hume, and the other writers of the Scottish Enlightenment, but a guiding *first* principle of their joint effort to fit *into* Britain and *into* the learned world. And that is why Smith's major works always included specific sections for comprehending the competition within a larger whole. Of the seven parts of his very first book, *The Theory of the Moral Sentiments* ("theory," according to Samuel Johnson, being a "system yet subsisting only in the mind"), the longest part is the final one; there we find embedded the "particular system[s]" formed out of the "different theories" (Smith 1759, 265) of his predecessors.

By *Wealth of Nations* two decades later, Smith and his cohort had succeeded in their master plan for master systems, but they quickly became victims of their own success: more writing of more systems made reconciliation into a single system less and less likely—there was simply too much system for system to master. In the last two decades of the eighteenth century, the reputation of Scotch knowledge began to wane.

## Border Crossing No. 2: Embedding System

At that precise moment, as overall levels of publication rather abruptly accelerated across Britain, a young man just across the border in England sought, like Smith had earlier, to read the market. Letters by William Wordsworth and his sister, Dorothy, repeatedly turn to what they called "pecuniary" matters. Money was to be made, but the growing market was growing more competitive, and for the Wordsworths this became an issue of genre. Even after publishing *An Evening Walk* and *Descriptive Sketches* in 1793, William spent the spring of 1794 planning to launch his literary career in earnest and in prose by starting a "monthly miscellany" on moral issues "from which some emolument might be drawn" (Wordsworth 1967, 1, 118–20). The purposeful focus on moral philosophy would give him access to an established audience expecting more Enlightenment, but William recognized that attracting its attention in an already packed periodical marketplace was a risky ploy.

The stage was thus set for Coleridge's arrival and a turn to risky business of another kind. Seeking a distinctive role in Britain's expanding print culture, together they formulated a new way "to deliver upon authority a system of philosophy," a task that Coleridge later simply referred to as "what I have been all my life doing" (Coleridge 1971, 2.177, no. 403). In a plan as deliberate as Smith's, Wordsworth and Coleridge plotted the future of Enlightenment — and did so under the same imperative that drove Newton and the Scots: "[N]ature is simple." The generic home of simplicity, however, would no longer be the conversational prose of Glasgow and Edinburgh but, as Enlightenment crossed the border once again, verse conversant with the English countryside. At the very end of a century already full of them, Wordsworth would write yet another system, but this one would be in the form of a "great" *poem*.

The burden of their first joint project, then, was to justify that generic twist: can poetry do it, and can it do it better than prose? The 1798 edition of *Lyrical Ballads, with a Few Other Poems* thus began with an advertisement that formulated the case for verse into two complementary principles. First, poetry was up to the task of Enlightenment — of philosophical enquiry into Man — because its "honourable characteristic" is that "its materials are to be found in every subject which can interest the human mind." Poetry conceived in this capacious manner could thus rival the Scottish form of Enlightenment: the "books of moral philosophy" that Wordsworth pointedly derides in two of the lyrical ballads ("Expostulation and Reply" and "The Tables Turned"). Those poems are *not* about ripping up books to roll in the grass but about choosing the right kind of books — books that do not take us from, but *give* us, nature. *Lyrical Ballads*, he claimed, was a book that "*contains* a *natural* delineation of human passions, human characters, and human incidents" (Wordsworth 1974, 1.116).

Second, poetry's delineations are more "natural" than those of prose because it teaches, just like "Nature" does, through *pleasure*. Wordsworth equated prose and poetry in all other ways in order to claim this single, salient difference: poetry's advantage over prose is that it offers more pleasure and thus can better engage more readers. But how do you measure pleasure? Wordsworth's Newtonian solution was to offer the poems themselves as "experiments" for gauging how much better poetry could be.

The readers of *Lyrical Ballads* willingly played their roles in this Enlightenment enterprise. *All* of the reviewers of the 1798 edition read the poems through the frame of the advertisement. In the short term, Wordsworth's reputation was at stake. What emerged in the long term, however, was a ongoing field of inquiry: an extended discussion of system and pleasure, of the possibilities and consequences of mixing the two. Is being systematic conducive to pleasure? How systematic can and should the measurement of pleasure be? The conversation deepened, that is, into the modern discourse of aesthetics—aesthetics transformed, as Coleridge noted with some regret, from the original eighteenth-century sense of a "science of the senses" to matters of "taste."

In *this* crossing of the border, the focus shifted from where it had been in Newton and Smith—on system itself and the comprehensive knowledge of nature that system was supposed to contain—to the vehicle for system and its more local knowledges and practices: in Wordsworth's case, poetry and the practice of aesthetics. Whereas master systems simplified by including everything in one thing, embedded systems gave us the divide-and-conquer strategy of modernity: simplification through specialization. The result was the modern disciplines. Pleasure measuring, for example, turned "literature" from the *Encyclopædia Britannica*'s inclusive, eighteenth-century sense of, simply, "learning or skill in letters" into the specialization we call English Literature.

The fate of Wordsworth's system, then, need not be reduced to a tale of personal failure,[3] unless doing so really does give you pleasure; it can be told more productively as a subplot of Enlightenment. By 1814, Wordsworth's ambitions had followed the logic of specialization: he narrowed the scope of his great "philosophical poem" to "the sensations and opinions of a *poet living in retirement*." Announcing that it was not his "intention formally to announce a system," he turned the task of "extracting the system" over to the "Reader" (Wordsworth 1974, III.6).

## Border Crossing No. 3: The System of the World Revisited

That very same year, across the border, Walter Scott abandoned poetry entirely and turned to the novel. Motivated, like Wordsworth had been, by "pecuniary matters," he, too, was playing the market—a market that Anna Barbauld had handicapped just a few years earlier: "Let me make the novels of a country," she wrote in 1810, "and let who will make the systems" (Barbauld 1810, 1: 61–62).

Far from turning *from* system, however, Scott accelerated the process Wordsworth had started: the embedding of that form *into* other forms. As Marshall McLuhan has argued, old forms become the content of new ones.

Scott put systems into history as the new touchstones of novelistic narrative. In fact, from Mark Twain's post–American Civil War point of view, that was the big problem with Scott. His twice-told reanimations of "decayed and degraded systems of government . . . did measureless harm; more real and lasting harm, perhaps, than any other individual that ever wrote" (Twain 1883, 467).

A much more favorable assessment of Scott's embedding of system had appeared much earlier in the *Edinburgh Review*:

> [W]e have, since the appearance of *Waverley*, seen the fruits of varied learning and experience displayed in that agreeable form; and we have even received from works of fiction what it would once have been thought preposterous to expect—information. . . . We have learnt, too, how greatly the sphere of the Novel may be extended, and how capable it is of becoming the vehicle almost of every species of popular knowledge. (Anon. 1832, 77)

Using philosophical terms and mechanistic images that echo back through Newton and Smith and Wordsworth, the *Review* describes the "extended" novel as a conveyor of "information": following the Enlightenment imperative to simplify, it has become a more "agreeable" and "popular" "vehicle" for more kinds of things. In fact, in the future, the *Review* speculates, the novel may come to comprehend "every" thing.[4]

This sounds like a tale Newton would have told if he was bad at maths: the novel *as* the "system of the world." If that is the story the *Review* is telling, it is certainly *not* your standard "rise of the novel"; it is the "rise of the novel" as an event *in* the history of Enlightenment. But there is a catch. The *Review* is *not* writing up *that* history: it is, in fact, helping to overwrite it by leaving out its keyword: the word "system" does not appear in this discussion of forms and vehicles of knowledge. In its absence, the persistence of Enlightenment that I have been highlighting fades from view behind a new kind of history: the kind of history that a nascent discipline begins to tell about itself—its own version of its own history.

It is time that we put these histories in historical order. Here are my guidelines for navigating the desert of periodization. First, to paraphrase 1950s science fiction, "Watch the borders!" Second, there is a reason why we have long been puzzled by what has appeared to be a palimpsest of Enlightenments: the tendency, in Julie Hayes's words, "to blur the distinction between a historically locatable phenomenon and a particular intellectual stance" (Hayes 1998, 22). My argument is that the blurring is not, at root, a dialectical or interpretative issue—these are not two sides of the same coin—but a historical one. Border watching resolves the blur. The different Enlightenments actually refer to *different* uses of the technology of writing, each deployed during a different period of time.

The "historically locatable" Enlightenment *is* historically locatable in the eighteenth century because, in the terms explained in the introduction to this volume, that event *ended* back then. One of its primary generic markers was Smith's project: the monumental efforts to contain systems within master systems that flourished in Scotland from midcentury to the 1780s. During the last two decades of the eighteenth century, that procedure gave way not just to a different "stance" but to a different procedure—to the Wordsworthian dispersing of systems into *other* forms, and the subsequent formation of specialized disciplines. It is that practice that has continued to the present day, drawing the shadow of Enlightenment over all of modernity.

Kant wrote his essay at this moment of transition, and that is the key to the problem of periodization. The year 1784 was both the close of Enlightenment *and* the onset of another event—an event that authorized periodization itself—for it was the moment that the mediations from which Enlightenment emerged started to work in a different way. By extending knowledge in new disciplinary directions, Enlightenment created the possibility of *other* histories of that age. In a sense, it invited palimpsest, change producing the new rubrics—such as the category of "Literature"—in which that change then came to be understood. By 1832—the year of the *Edinburgh Review* article—the novel finally found itself *in* something into which it *could* rise.

Romanticism, then, is the label for the tales that my discipline—literary study—tells itself about the period of time in which it became a discipline. As strange as it may sound, when understood in this fashion, it can describe more than a period *of* Literature—for it labels the moment in which that category was constructed. We do not need to bin all of the tales we have told, and we should not give up their sense of historical discontinuity for an amorphous entity called the "long eighteenth century." I am suggesting instead that we retell them within an encompassing history of mediation: a history of the forms that mediate knowledge in general and "history" in particular—in this case, the genre of system.

# ROMANTICISM, ENLIGHTENMENT, AND MEDIATION

## THE CASE OF THE INNER STRANGER

ROBERT MILES

### Introduction

The first three words of my title are as problematic as they are unavoidable. Each troubles in its own way. Like all other periodic categories, "Romantic" brackets arbitrary dates; throws a blanket of homogeneity over variety; and by seeking in this ocean of difference those features that fit its current definition, invites charges of completing an empty "hermeneutic circle." It is, unsurprisingly, a frangible term. And yet its bracketing dates encompass a distinct phase of modernity. "Enlightenment" is also a period term, but in addition it signifies an alleged congeries of events in Western history: the rise of reason, the spread of illumination, and a quickening in the long process of secularization. Where Romanticism traditionally signified widespread alterations in the styles of art,[1] Enlightenment signaled a world-changing alteration in the very bases of Western culture.

Like Romanticism, the term "Enlightenment" has been critiqued into near oblivion.[2] Among the more salient revisions, critics have pointed out that "Enlightenment," as a category, was a twentieth-century invention (in the eighteenth, insofar as it was anything, it was a process, was something you did, such as engaging in a Kantian spirit of critique; Schmidt 2006,

651, 655); that there was not one Enlightenment, but many (Sheehan 2003); and while France was a significant example of the century of light—a light that simultaneously extinguished Religion, at least officially, under the Directorate—it was also atypical insofar as doing Enlightenment, elsewhere, amounted to the revision and reform of religion, rather than a simple, secular, withering away, much less amputation (Sheehan 2003, paragraph 31). As Charles Taylor argues, the usual stories of secularization (the increasing separation of church and state; declining religion) are ajar with the facts (Taylor 2007, 2–3). While critics have been generally receptive to Isaiah Berlin's counter-argument that opponents of "reason" were as thick on the ground as its enthusiasts, they have been as skeptical of his "Counter-Enlightenment" as they have been of the systemic illumination it was meant to be countering.

But as Karen O'Brien observes, in her review of the recent, four-volume *Encyclopedia of the Enlightenment*, the term "Enlightenment" has made a comeback or refused to die:

> Yet there is broader consensus that there was a process of intellectual change worth naming as the Enlightenment, that it started as early as the mid seventeenth century, with a key role for Spinoza and the Spinozists, that theological ideas (Latitudinarianism, Arminianism, Socinianism) were central to the process, and that it is best understood as a trans-national phenomenon traceable through the history of social and print networks. (O'Brien 2005, 245)

Still, the mention of Spinoza serves to highlight the irreducible complexity of "Enlightenment." In the light of the editors' discussion of Francis Bacon (see the introduction), Enlightenment encompasses both instrumental reason (the "scientific" machine of induction) and the "idols of the Theatre, or of Systems," such as the innumerable "fantasies of reason" it famously generated. Spinoza's search for a monadic substrate to creation arguably encompasses the Enlightenment's duality of "inductive" or empiric materialism and universal system building.

"Mediation" poses a different sort of problem. All culture—all language—mediates. To put it differently, there is no such thing as the unmediated; at least, nothing we can describe in language. As such, "mediation" is analogous to "social construction." As Ian Hacking argues, the phrase "the social construction of x" only has meaning if "x" is not something that is self-evidently socially constructed (Hacking 1999). For instance, "the social construction of gender" is not a "load-bearing concept," to use Peter de Bolla's phrase, because we take it for granted that gender is so constructed (as such the phrase is more pleonasm than proposition). The "social construction of science," on the other hand, is load-bearing, as the phrase argues a case that is not self-evident, insofar as we habitually think of science as something that is neutral, objective, and in a sense, "above" the realm of the socially constructed. As the gender example also reminds us, the matter has a cultural, and therefore historical, dimension, as there have been times, or there may currently be places, where the phrase would perform linguistic work. So, too, with mediation. That is, for my present purposes, "mediation" will only signify in those cases in which mediation is not self-evident.

My essay, then, concerns an episode of mediation, one occurring in the period we habitually denominate "the Enlightenment," with repercussions on another we think of as "Romantic." In investigating my example I hope to cast some familiar problems of definition, gestured to above, in a novel and helpful light.

## The Inner Stranger

I will be considering a linguistic instance of mediation—the eighteenth-century trope of the stranger within—but shall argue that it is as material a form of mediation as the financial instruments examined by Poovey in this volume. The concept of the "inner stranger" mediates between two reifications in the realm of subjectivity, between the soul and self; or, perhaps, more accurately, the soul and the inner core of truth and authenticity found in our familiar conception of the modern, Romantic self, the unconscious, or "it" (id). The "inner stranger" (or any of its variants) is actually an unusual phrase in the eighteenth century. Perhaps its clearest expression is to be found in Edward Young's *Conjectures on Original Composition* (1759). Young's short book was, arguably, the single most influential work on original genius in the eighteenth century. As a work of literary theory, it delivered a blow for inspiration against learning, nature against erudite affectation, Shakespeare against Pope:

> Since it is plain that men may be strangers to their own abilities; and by thinking meanly of them without just cause, may possibly lose a name, perhaps, a name immortal; I would find some means to prevent these Evils. (Young 1759, 51–52)

In order to prevent them, Young recommends "two golden rules from Ethics . . . 1. Know thyself; 2dly, Reverence thyself":

> 1st. Know thyself. Of ourselves it may be said, as Martial says of a bad neighbour, Nil tam prope, proculque nobis . . . Therefore dive deep

into thy bosom; learn the depth, extent, biass, and full fort of thy mind; *contract full intimacy with the Stranger within thee*; excite, and cherish every spark of Intellectual light and heat, however smothered under former negligence, or scattered through the dull, dark mass of common thoughts; and collecting them into a body, let thy Genius rise (if a Genius thou hast) as the sun from Chaos; and if I should then say, like an Indian, worship it, (though too bold) yet should I say little more than my second rule enjoins, (viz.) Reverence thyself. (Young 1759, 53, emphasis added)

A Calvinist, Young overturns the customary meaning of the Latin tag (*Nil tam prope, proculque nobis*, "Nothing is so near us, and yet so distant"), which was used to enjoin sinners to stop pointing to their neighbors' failings, and to start worrying about their own, worms that they were. But in Young's formulation, the inner self we don't know refers not to our universal, inherently sinful nature but rather to the creative potential of every man: each of us has our own inner genius, which we might know, should we open our hearts, and look inward.

Young's formulation of a deep, creative, elusive self—a stranger—was to prove foundational for Romantic poetics, one clearly anticipating its ultimate expression as the unconscious. The very slipperiness of its phrasing encodes the historic transformation of "soul" to "self" (Nichols 1998, 10). For Young, as for those who came after, if authenticity was the highest creative virtue, the "stranger within" was the self to whom one was true, when one was being true (that is, sincere, and as a result, authentic). Similarly, creativity, the stamp of true genius, derived from the imprimatur of the authentic self—for Wordsworth and Coleridge, the hallmark that distinguished true poetry from mechanical verse. As Coleridge was to put it in his critical autobiography, knowledge of versification had reached such a pitch that any fool could rhyme in smooth numbers: it was now a purely mechanical skill, and any fool did. The true poem differed from these "counterfeits" (as Coleridge styles them), as an egg does from an egg shell (Coleridge 1983, 1: 38–39). Judged from the outside the counterfeit was identical in every respect to the true poem, the difference being that one lacked substance. For Coleridge, as for Wordsworth, substance derived from accessing the authentic—deep—self (Siskin 1988, 11–13).

The "stranger within," then, appeared to be the necessary link between "soul" and "self," a kind of intermediary linguistic bridge. For the Enlightenment, accessing the creative self was not, as it was for Milton, entirely synonymous with surrender to the Holy Ghost; but neither was it yet a matter of plumbing the depths of the individuated ego, or "self." The "stranger within" mediated the gap, as it was, at once, the true self one knew, when one knew oneself, in the Christian tradition (that is, a miserable sinner like other miserable sinners), and a new secular self that was not drenched, a priori, in universal sin, but marked by its own peculiar potentialities (that is, capacity for genius).

The trope of the inner stranger figures in two poems critics hold central to the foundation of British Romanticism, Anna Letitia Barbauld's "A Summer Evening's Meditation" and S. T. Coleridge's "Frost at Midnight."[3] As far as I can discover, the trope of the inner stranger is comparatively rare. Apart from Young, the main examples I can find, prior to Barbauld, are from the dissenting minister Isaac Watts, whose poems and hymns were edited by Barbauld's grandfather, and which she new well; apart from anything else, "A Summer Evening's Meditation" is a comparatively secular version of Watts's most famous poem, "The Adventurous Muse," with both being apostrophes to Urania (the muse of astronomy, the evening star in question). As we shall see, this dissenting, deistical aspect of the phrase's history is material to its meaning.

I shall turn to this history presently, but first I want to sketch in broad terms the significant differences between Barbauld's and Coleridge's treatment of the "stranger" trope.[4] Watts's poem is about the adventurous muse, whereas in her poem, Barbauld is the adventurous muse herself, meaning a secular version of the poetic figure who is adventurous by virtue of her appearing, as herself, in print, as a poetess who boldly ventures upon—trespasses—the male territory of first and final things, epic blank verse, and the question of genius. The poem features the author's persona lapsing into meditation as evening falls, in which, in a kind of extended ecstasy, her inner self, or "soul," is projected across the heavens in an act of imaginary interstellar travel:

> . . . is there not
> A tongue in every star that talks with man,
> And wooes him to be wise; nor wooes in vain:
> This dead of midnight is the noon of thought,
> And wisdom mounts her zenith with the stars.
> *At this still hour the self-collected soul*
> *Turns inward, and beholds a stranger there*
> *Of high descent, and more than mortal rank;*
> *An embryo GOD; a spark of fire divine,*
> Which must burn on for ages, when the sun,
> (Fair transitory creature of a day!)
> Has clos'd his golden eye, and wrapt in shades
> Forgets his wonted journey thro' the east.[5]

The central question is why Barbauld feels the necessity of an intermediary locution—a "stranger"—between "soul" and "genius" (meaning inner daemon, the older, conventional sense of genius). The "self-collected soul" is a significant equivocation. "Soul" either serves as a metonym for a universal person, in which case the phrase stands for everyman (an inclusive, egalitarian gesture crucial to the poem's politics), or it may be taken literally, in which case the "self-collected soul" refers to a particular quality of the speaker's soul—teasingly, a condition of the transported self in which the self has been "self-collected" (picked up by its own bootstraps?) such that it can revolve inward, in order to encounter yet another player in this odd psychomachia, the "stranger."

Collating Young's essay with another intertext central to the history of the rise of the Romantic conception of genius—that is, with Gray's *Elegy*—we can see the stranger refers to the "spark divine" that potentially makes us all "mute inglorious Miltons," where Milton is the presiding figure of Barbauld's poem, whom she frequently quotes.[6] The surface flow of the poem (of soul/person/everyman) moves us along in a Republican, "old Commonwealth" direction familiar to Dissenting politics, and as it does so it takes us over a kind of mise en abyme: in "the self-collected soul," is "soul" a synecdoche or metonym? The equivocation recalls the foundational dualism of Western modernity while casting it as an irreducible ambiguity. Furthermore, if "self" is a synonym for "soul" the phrase dissolves into tautological vacuity; if it isn't, what constitutes the difference, and how are "self" and "soul" to be articulated in relation to the third term in this bizarre trinity, the "stranger"?

In "Frost at Midnight" Coleridge transforms these equivocations into a narrative principle, one we retrospectively call "Gothic."[7] The poem plays with surface and depth. On the surface the poem narrates a transcendent arc. This is especially true of the final, 1834 version of the poem, which differs significantly from the "Frost at Midnight" that was first published in 1798. The final version is shorter, and in places, more concise (the versions range from 73 to 85 lines; Stillinger 1994, 52). It is also, arguably, less Gothic, as the deletions and changes generally have the effect of supporting the poem's optimistic arc.[8]

The surface transcendent arc begins with the speaker sitting alone in his cottage on a winter's night, minding his baby son, regarding a filmy piece of carbon dancing in the grate:

> Sea, and hill, and wood,
> With all the numberless goings-on of life,
> Inaudible as dreams! the thin blue flame

>Lies on my low-burnt fire, and quivers not;
>Only that film, which fluttered on the grate,
>Still flutters there, the sole unquiet thing.
>Methinks . . . (lines 8–17)

By a process of association, the fluttering carbon reminds the speaker that such films are familiarly known as "strangers" (line 26), harbingers of a visit from an "absent friend."[9] When he was a child, at school in London, and feeling lonely in the metropolis, he would look earnestly in the grate at such "strangers" "with most believing superstitious wish" ([1798], 155) as auguries of a visit of a loved one from his rural birthplace:

>So gazed I, till the soothing things I dreamt
>Lulled me to sleep, and sleep prolonged my dreams!
>And so I brooded all the following morn
>Awed by the *stern preceptor's* face, mine eye
>Fixed with mock study on my swimming book: (lines 34–38; emphasis added)

At such times, when the school door opened, he would break from his reveries, his heart leaping up, "For still I hoped to see the *stranger*'s face, / Townsman, or aunt, or sister more beloved, / My play-mate when we both were clothed alike!" (lines 41–43). Of course, no loved one did appear, the "stranger" being no more than a "superstitious wish." This failed form of prophecy is then contrasted with a successful one: the poet foretells that his son, raised in nature, "beneath the crags / Of ancient mountain, and beneath the clouds" (lines 55–56), will have his spirit moulded in such a way that he will "ask" (line 64), and asking, receive a transcendental lesson.

There are several ways of describing the poem's forward arc. The young Coleridge, whose imagination is quashed by the "stern preceptor" (line 37) and who wastes his creative energy in superstitious dreams, is contrasted with his baby son, whose imagination is to be nurtured by the "Great universal Teacher" (line 63) and whose creative energy will produce true visionary poetry; or between the Coleridge who is the subject of the poem, with his "self-watching subtilizing mind" ([1798], 155) neurotically and unproductively toying with the film in the grate, and the Coleridge who is the poem's author, who has transcended his funk to write a foundational Romantic poem, thus becoming the type of the poet his son will aspire to be. The poem is thus built on repetition and doubling, where the repeated term augurs transcendence, the moving to a higher plane.

This movement begins with the master trope unfolded in the first two lines: "The frost performs its secret ministry, / Unhelped by any wind . . ."

The trope means by virtue of an implied contrast with "The Eolian Harp," Coleridge's previous attempt at characterizing the imagination—an effort from which he was presently distancing himself. The Eolian harp, or creative mind, sings, because played upon by the wind, presumably God's breath, the root meaning of "inspiration." However, the figure had become contaminated through its association with the eighteenth-century philosopher David Hartley, whose psychological theory of mind had appealed to Coleridge, as it was grounded in a theory of providential benevolence, but he had lately rejected it, owing to its materialism and deterministic nature (Wheeler 1981, 1–16). Unlike the Eolian harp, the frost performs its secret task—rendering the world beautiful—"unhelped by any wind": it augurs, instead, a transcendental theory of creativity. In a moment of enthusiasm Coleridge had named his son "Hartley" after the philosopher; the name now haunts the poem as its central, unspoken, pivot.

The poem, that is, swivels between antithetical possibilities. Either the repetition figures transcendence, or it collapses into neurotic doubling. Either the poem moves forward from Coleridge's stern and repressive preceptor to his son's benevolent "Great universal Teacher," or the latter is a profane repetition of the former. Either his son, Hartley, is the type of the creative imagination, nurtured by Romantic nature, or the child lives out the theory of his philosophical namesake, becoming a necessary product of his environment, a mere automaton, the product of his conditioning. That possibility appears to be hinted at when Coleridge ends the poem's first version with his son "fluttering" in his mother's arms, just as the film had "fluttered" in the grate. The 1834 version of the poem terminates with frost hanging up the "eve drops" in "silent icicles" shining in the moon, whereas the first finishes with an extended simile:

> Like those, my babe! which, ere to-morrow's warmth
> Have capp'd their sharp keen points with pendulous drops,
> Will catch thine eye, and with their novelty
> Suspend thy little soul; then make thee shout,
> And stretch and flutter from thy mother's arms
> As thou wouldst fly for very eagerness. (Stillinger 1798, 157)

The common term for the literary modality built on doubling, or haunting, is "Gothic." The baby fluttering in his mother's arms might appear "Gothic" because it doubles as the film fluttering in the grate, suggesting a dangerous equivalence.

Through revision Coleridge endeavored to still the Gothic implications of the poem's first incarnation. The final version makes it clear that the isolated speaker is in a "fanciful" mood (meaning, in Coleridge's terms, an unproductive one). Regarding the dancing film in the grate, the narrator's reverie concludes:

> Methinks, its motion in this hush of nature
> Gives it dim sympathies with me who live,
> Making it a companionable form,
> Whose puny flaps and freaks the idling Spirit
> By its own moods interprets, every where
> Echo or mirror seeking of itself,
> And makes a toy of Thought. (lines 19–23)

Tilottoma Rajan's commentary makes the point: "The film on the grate, a residue of desire rather than evidence of the genius that joins the subjective to the objective world, seems to image the emptiness of the imagining consciousness. It dreams but does not produce anything, imagines and heralds a life beyond itself, but does not make it present except as an echo" (Rajan 1980, 2245). The 1798 version toys with the thought that the "stranger," the "sooty revenant" (VanWinkle 2004, 587), is an image of the "stranger within," the inner creative self. If the poet's meditative (and creative) self projects itself onto the film, because of a fanciful similarity, then the thought naturally arises that just as the self is like the film, the film is like the self—that is, just so much dancing carbon, a mysterious materiality. The point is underlined by yet another doubling, the repetition of the frost's secret ministry, of process without external motion, with the stranger on the grate (the film dances, even though the flame "quivers not" [1. 14]). In other words, even as the poem works toward a transcendental version of the creative imagination, emancipated from materiality (with the poet's hopes concentrated in the figure of Hartley, the son), the complex patterning of the poem permits a contrary reading of doubling rather than progressive repetition.

Read superficially, the poem appears to use the "stranger" in a way antithetical to Barbauld. Rather than one's deepest, most productive self, the genius within, Coleridge's "stranger" seems to figure something external: the promise of an "absent friend," as Coleridge explains in a note, or as it is in the poem itself, the appearance of his "sister more beloved," who "clothed alike" serves as his better or second self. Read Gothically—and this is especially true of the 1798 version—"Frost at Midnight" doubles its progenitor poem, Barbauld's "A Summer Evening's Meditation,"[10] by inverting it. Barbauld's poem turns on a moment of successful transcendence. The self is projected upward into eternal time and space, where it encounters its true inner self— the "stranger." Coleridge begins with a moment of failed transcendence (the "superstitious solipsism of a depressed sensibility") where the speaker turns inward and greets his own inner stranger, the dancing film, which figures the possibility that for a Coleridge struggling with, and against, materialism, is the worst of all possible worlds: one where the self is so much animated carbon, the soul a fluttering film. If this is the worst, it is balanced by the best: as a figure for prolepsis the "stranger" also promises the appearance of a better, or idealized self, either the speaker's second self (his sister) or, through the mediation of nature, a future one (his son). A key aspect of Coleridge's "stranger" is that it is both at once.

My thesis, then, is that Coleridge's stranger should be regarded as a figure for the unconscious, although the full force of this assertion will not be apparent without also assuming that Freud's elaboration of the unconscious is best regarded as itself a complex act of "secondary revision," in which a reification has been naturalized, so that it appears an unexceptional aspect of the real. The central kernel of Freud's formulation is to be found in the original German, where the unconscious is characterized as "*das Id*," the "it." The significant aspect of Coleridge's revision of Barbauld is that the inner "stranger" has become an "it," a fluttering film, that is at once internal and external (a duality Freud was to express as id / superego). And this in turn will not disclose its meaning to us until we focus not on the content of the figure (the claim: "the inner stranger is an "it"), but instead on the figure as itself an act of mediation, one performing cultural work.

To unfold how this is so I now want to turn to philosopher Charles Taylor's recent work on secularization, which will enable us to see how the "it," or "unconscious," is chiefly meaningful as an act of mediation. In *A Secular Age* Taylor takes issue with the common ways in which secularization is understood, as either the growing separation of the public and religious spheres, that is, of church and state (secularization 1), or that religion retreated before the onward march of Enlightenment (secularization 2)—in other words, the older, Whig history of triumphant reason and vanquished superstition. His concern, rather, following Heidegger and Wittgenstein, is with what he calls "background," meaning a prephilosophical understanding that conditions thought, is universal within the culture, and is invisible or "unconscious" (in the pre-Freudian sense of the word). Taylor detects a quality in the background of Western culture that he claims is unique in history, one that begins in the early modern period, that "transitions" during the age we usually refer to as the Enlightenment and that finally achieves its modern expression around the start of the nineteenth century: the time we think of as "Romantic."

The essential feature of this quality is our common expectation that we have a choice before us as to whether we locate the experience of "fullness" immanently or transcendentally; within the realm of the quotidian or in a sense of something "beyond"; in this world or in some other on a transcendental plane; in, for instance, faith in ecology or Southern Baptism. Taylor's version of a secular age is predicated not on the disappearance of religion, but on a change to our common, prereflective understanding of the "real." Taylor uses Schiller's classic terms, from his definition of Romanticism, to open up this changed "real": naïve and self-conscious. Secularity of this kind (secularization 3) arose

> with the possibility of exclusive humanism, which thus for the first time widened the range of possible options, ending the era of "naïve" religious faith. Exclusive humanism in a sense crept up on us through an intermediate form, Providential Deism. . . . Once this humanism is on the scene, the new plural, non-naïve predicament allows for multiplying the options beyond the original gamut. . . . a secular age [in this sense] is one in which the eclipse of all goals beyond human flourishing becomes conceivable; or better, it falls within the range of an imaginable life for masses of people. This is the crucial link between secularity and a self-sufficing humanism. (Taylor 2007, 20)

From the point of view of subjectivity, the major change between "the era of 'naïve' religious faith" and Western modernity is the transition from what Taylor calls a "porous" to a "buffered," self. The "naïve" or "porous" self is one unprotected from the animistic forces of the cosmos, whether good or evil, where time is understood in a nonsecular fashion, that is to say, as one in which there is simultaneity between the quotidian and the supernal. The "buffered self" understands itself to be impervious to such animistic forces. Instead, time is understood in a linear fashion, while the world is conceived as a realm of inert material (forms depleted of animistic content) subject to instrumental reason.

The buffered self is itself a form of interiority, and in this regard Taylor's analysis accords with that of Jürgen Habermas, who interprets the rise of the bourgeois public sphere, or "Republic of Letters," as a series of practices that have as their upshot the protection, and indeed nurturing, of an historically new sense of the private, that is, where "private" has lost the negative overtones of privation and gained the positive connotations we have come to associate with Romanticism, according to which individualism, interiority, and genius are closely allied. Providential Deism is important for Taylor, as it makes the transition phase palpable. For rational dissenters, such as Anna Letitia Barbauld, or her mentor, Joseph Priestley, the world possessed an inner, unfolding order—one susceptible to the penetrative powers of inductive reason—informed by a spirit of infinite benevolence, one geared toward the promotion of human flourishing ("Great universal Teacher" from "Frost at Midnight" is a remainder from such an outlook, and a direct trace leading back to Barbauld). It is the exiguous character of the supernatural in such an outlook, together with the emphasis on material human flourishing—the ostensible goal of our innate benevolence—that makes Providential Deism the obvious transition phase leading into the modern order, where "exclusive humanism" is a pervasive possibility in the Western social imaginary. Of course Providential Deism, of the kind espoused by Joseph Priestley, did not conceive of itself as a tool of a coming secular age. On the contrary, both Priestley and Barbauld were profoundly religious; hence Taylor's argument that secularization was not a simple story of progress, a Whig history, but a winding and often accidental affair.

Taylor opposes his thesis to what he calls "subtraction stories," where secularization is understood as a series of deletions, of chimeras slain by reason: "Against this kind of story, I will steadily be arguing that Western modernity, including its secularity, is the fruit of new inventions, newly constructed self-understandings and related practices, and can't be explained in terms of perennial features of human life" (Taylor 2007, 22). "The great invention of the West," he argues, "was that of an immanent order in nature, whose working could be systematically understood and explained on its own terms, leaving open the question whether this whole order had a deeper significance, and whether, if it did, we should infer a transcendent Creator beyond it" (Taylor 2007, 15). Our common, contemporary sense of the real, where the real is that which is capable of scientific verification, is, then, a principle invention supporting "secularization" as Taylor argues it.

The complex and contradictory assembly of attitudes critics habitually designate via the shorthand "sensibility" would be an example of a cultural practice that served to entrench secularization 3. Critics have often been exercised by the problems posed by the diverse ideological positions subsumed within sensibility itself, of how to reconcile, for instance, the sensibility of Rousseau and Wollstonecraft, on one side, and that of Smith and Burke, on the other.[11] From Taylor's perspective, such differences matter less than the cultural work performed by sensibility, which was to reaffirm the central tenets of Providential Deism, which was that nature, including human nature, was ordered on benevolent principles, where benevolence was understood in terms of quotidian human flourishing: as such it fitted perfectly with the demands of a polite and commercial age.

Taylor helps us to read the Enlightenment and Romanticism as different phases in the history of mediation. Using Taylor's terms one can conveniently distinguish Romanticism from Enlightenment, or at any rate, British Romantic literary culture, from Providential Deism, by saying that the former turns on nature being a site of ambiguity as to whether its meaning is transcendental or immanent (a condition of secularity 3), whereas for the latter it is axiomatic that it is both at once. Similarly, one can say that Romanticism is distinguished by a self-consciousness that simultaneously looks backward toward a state of naivety from which history has permanently deviated, and forward toward new forms of expression. Both formulations rework distinctions that are as old as Romanticism itself. But this is just to mark our point of departure, which is that in the history of secularity 3, Romanticism is less a transition stage and more a "cusp" that partakes of both at once: that is, it is a Janus-faced bridge between the earlier transitional stage (Providential Deism) and modernity (fully developed secularity 3). Thus one of the fundamental ironies of Romanticism: it is often most modern when most "nostaligic," or backward-looking.

Hence "Frost at Midnight," which sustains its reputation as a foundational Romantic poem, one belonging to an avant-garde, because it invented a conversational voice—the illusion of a man talking to other men—that was to become canonical via its influence on Wordsworth, who perfected this new poetic "system." On the one hand, it is a poem that exemplifies the cultural practice of "mediation," hence its modernity; and on the other, its poetic inspiration is to appear (by the poetic standards of the time) as a poem unmediated by poetic convention. The point is not the familiar "deconstructive" one that its pretence at being unmediated (the record of a spontaneous, inward reverie) is undermined by the impossibility of escaping poetic or rhetorical form; it is, rather, to note that the poem is fully engaged with the historic reality of mediation, as a condition of "secularity 3," a condition that makes its presence felt not least in the gestures the poem makes to a putative "naïve" time when it was possible to speak in an unmediated fashion. As Gillen D'Arcy Wood has noted, the first generation of English Romantic poets found "simulation"—the creation of virtual realities, through panoramas, billboards, or phantasmagorias—especially noxious (Wood 2001). Their response to new technologies of representation was highly reactionary, as they dreamt fondly of "unmediated writing"; but this did not stop their own poetry from working through the contradictions inherent in the very notion of an unmediated representation. "Frost at Midnight" is once again exemplary. The poem's transcendental arc promises a form of mediation where the mediation (like the secret ministry of frost) is "invisible," most notably, the mediation of nature, the great universal teacher, that mysteriously instructs, mediates, Hartley's character. Meanwhile the Gothic counternarrative locates the poem squarely in the fashionable literary modes of the London market for print.

It is through the trope of the stranger that the poem most fully engages with the historic reality of mediation in modern subjectivity as an invention and cultural practice. Simply, a self that is "buffered" is also one that is mediated. Marshall McLuhan's quip about one age's form being another's content will help in the present instance, but before I turn to the "content" in question, I want to return to my earlier point about the stranger trope as an instance of a mediating practice—a form—that performs cultural work. The earlier form in question, then, is one that belonged to what Taylor calls the "porous self." The porous self was based on a set of cultural practices in which the self and cosmos were understood to mirror each other, through analogy; what happened in the cosmos readily finds its echo, or correspondence, in the self. The self was thus, in a manner of speaking, unprotected against the malevolent forces that enjoyed a ceaseless to and fro traffic in a continuous world of "anima," apart from the prophylactics it was able to employ through prayer, magic, or luck. It is this "form" that has become the "content" of Coleridge's version of the inner stranger. Barbauld's inner stranger belongs to the logic of Providential Deism, where to revolve inward, and contact the "spark divine," was to access a realm of anima constrained by its place in a benevolently ordered universe where it served to promote human flourishing. As such, Barbauld's inner stranger, as a trope or cultural practice, passed with the waning of Providential Deism.

Critics writing about "Frost at Midnight" often seem to care about the final position the poem might be adducing, as regards the questions of transcendence or immanence, whereas the salient point is that it is, indeed, a foundational Romantic poem, and what makes it Romantic is that the poem equivocates between transcendence and immanence. Such equivocation is the least interesting aspect of it—critically speaking, it is the surface of the poem. The interesting questions concern the cultural work performed by its formal innovations. The transformation of the inner stranger, to an "it," is central to the poem's formal innovation. To recap, the old form is the porous self; the new form is a simulation of a real self, a personality, a man, as it were, talking to other men, a form of poetry that does not appear to be mediated by other poems or the traces of their formal properties: what we have since come to call "conversation" poems. The old form that has become the new content is, in Taylor's terms, the "porous self," that is, animism. Only now the permeability and anima have been displaced from outside/in, to inside/out.

The stakes are, I think, considerable, at least within the limited realm of Romantic criticism. The stranger that is simultaneously outside, objectified as an "it" (the film in the grate) and inside (what we see when we look into the interior's self's inward mirror) derives its meaning from its formal properties. A central formal quality, constituted by the poem itself, is doubleness, its Janus face. The point about the poem is not that it is really "Gothic" beneath its flowing conversational surface, but that it holds both in equipoise. Read "superficially," the poem refers to the stranger as an external object in which its meaning, as a second, or better, self, is displaced and objectified. Reading beneath the surface, that is, "Gothically," the stranger appears as an "it," a figuration of something we now call the "unconscious," meaning a realm beyond our conscious access where what is represented is what we are not (the amoral desires we repress) and what we mostly deeper are (the amoral desires that structure the foundations of our personality). Holding both readings together produces the stranger as an "it" *and* "second self," thus completing the form.

For a century literary critics have been deeply concerned with reading ghosts, doubles, and specters, a trend that has arguably accelerated. If one accepts the premise that Freudian theory is a secondary revision of a form that first appears as part of the Western "background" during the period we call Romantic (that is, not as isolated instances but as part of the fabric of the cultural imaginary), then the Freudian model of reading merely repeats, rather than illuminates, what is at issue. Likewise, reading specters as deconstructive traces replicates the phenomenon (the critical obsession with specters and doubles) rather than explains it. My argument, then, is that the critical obsession with such spectral traces is itself an expression of the survival of an older form (the animistic world of the porous self, where the self contains both what it is and is not) that has become the content of a new form, where the new form performs the cultural work of maintaining the buffered self.

If one were being highly speculative, one might say that for the Western imaginary to "move on," with the buffered self in place, it had to contain the power of an older, constitutive form, meaning the narrative modalities of the porous self. By absorbing the older forms into the new as its content, the buffered self both contained the old and drew strength from it as it developed new practices, not the least of which was the endless talk of the unconscious, where the border crossings of the porous self (between self and environment) were internalized (across the membrane of what Freud calls the "preconscious"). I put "move on" in quotation marks because, for Taylor, there is no question of teleology, or inner purpose to this: secularization 3 "happened" because of the accidental and unpredictable confluence of numerous factors. The business at hand, rather, is to know where we are. Taylor's argument, in the present instance, helps us understand the familiar contours of Romanticism in terms that explain, rather than replicate, its typical concerns.

# THE PRESENT OF ENLIGHTENMENT

## TEMPORALITY AND MEDIATION IN KANT, FOUCAULT, AND JEAN PAUL

### HELGE JORDHEIM

In his famous essay on the Enlightenment, "Qu'est-ce que les Lumières?" (What Is Enlightenment?) from 1984, Michel Foucault presents a reading of Kant's article from the *Berlinische Monatsschrift*, "Beantwortung der Frage: Was ist Aufklärung?" (An Answer to the Question: What Is Enlightenment?) from 1783. Foucault argues that the novelty of Kant's essay lies "in the reflection on 'today' as difference in history and a particular philosophical task," that is, in the reflection on the present (Foucault 1994c, 1387).[1] It is the first time, Foucault continues in another version of the essay, "we see philosophy ... problematizing its own discursive contemporaneity: a contemporaneity that it questions as an event, as an event whose meaning, value and philosophical particularity it is its task to bring out and in which it has to find both its own raison d'être and the grounds for what it says" (Foucault 1994a, 1499). In this article I will take a closer look at some of these claims, asking how we might understand the references to "'today' as difference in history" or "the discursive contemporaneity of philosophy as an event" in terms of attempts to grasp a kind of temporality or temporal experience specific to the Enlightenment—both as a historical epoch and as project, completed or not.

## Enlightenment and the Reflection on the Present

At the center of the notion of Enlightenment is a concept of time. Traditionally the predominant temporality of Enlightenment is considered to be the idea of progress, as in the Kantian notion of the *Ausgang*, the *Ausgang des Menschen aus seiner selbst verschuldeten Unmündigkeit*. In the canonical 1970 English translation by H. B. Nisbet this key phrase reads, "[M]an's emergence from his self-incurred immaturity" (Kant 1985, 54), whereas James Schmidt in a recent translation has chosen the more literal and less obviously teleological "exit" for the original German word *Ausgang* (Kant 1996a, 58). In Kant's essay this notion represents—among other things—a way of reworking Rousseau's concept of *perfectibilité*, which in the German context is gradually transformed into an idea of progress. Foucault, however, who made himself a name as a fierce critic of all kinds of teleological ideas of history, sees this differently. In his reading the dominating temporality in Kant's essay is not the utopian dream of eternal progress toward an ideal society, but the experience of the present, the "now," in response to the question of how today differs from yesterday. In this way the essay on Enlightenment sets itself off from all other works by the German philosopher:

> In his other texts on history, Kant occasionally raises questions of origin or defines the internal teleology of a historical process. In the text on *Aufklärung*, he deals with the question of contemporary reality alone. He is not seeking to understand the present on the basis of a totality or of a future achievement. He is looking for a difference: What difference does today introduce with respect to yesterday? (Foucault 1994c, 1383)

This question of "contemporary reality alone," in terms of a temporal experience of the present, unfolding in different texts on the Enlightenment, is the topic to be addressed here.

The reflection on the present, however, as a specific philosophical task of the late eighteenth century can only take place within a particular discourse—or, in Foucault's words, what philosophy is doing in this period, and especially in Kant's essay, is problematizing its own "discursive contemporaneity." Hence, to study the temporality of the present means to study the ways in which it manifests itself in discourse—in other words, the ways in which it is mediated. In Kant's text the emergence of Enlightenment is not least due to the use of new media, primarily the printed text, as a necessary precondition for the universality of reason. In considering the distribution and circulation of printed matter in late eighteenth-century Europe it becomes clear that universal reason on the one hand, and writing as a specific historical and cultural practice and product on the other, might indeed be imbued with very different temporal structures and processes. Reason and writing are not necessarily contemporaneous, in the literal sense of the word. How can Enlightenment, as a process and an activity, defend its claims to universality as long as the media technologies involved by necessity possess their own historical particularity? The historical and empirical preconditions for this question have been widely studied by scholars in the field of media and book history, such as Elizabeth Eisenstein, Robert Darnton, Roger Chartier, and Adrian Johns (Eisenstein 1983; Darnton 1979; Chartier 1992; Johns 1998). I am not going to repeat the conclusions and debates from these great works. My interest lies in analyzing the different, incongruent, and highly noncontemporaneous notions and experiences of time inherent in these categories of universality and particularity in light of the question of how Enlightenment is mediated.

## The Universal Voice

According to Reinhart Koselleck, the German historian and theorist of history, one main feature of the period between 1750 and 1850, for which he famously coined the term *Sattelzeit*, "saddle time," is the process of "temporalization [*Verzeitlichung*]," through which the social and political world, as a matrix of key concepts, develops a temporal dimension that it didn't have before (Koselleck 1972, xv). Through this process, concepts like "democracy," "progress," and "history," only to mention a few, cease to be labels for concrete empirical or theoretical phenomena and become concepts of movement, pointing toward or even anticipating an open and endless future, as a field of political battle and planning. In face of this temporalization and caught between the dreams of an idyllic past and the hopes for a utopian future, Enlightenment thinkers and writers tried to seize and define the present, as a position, a place from which it is possible to speak and to act—and, in the end, to change the world. In this way the idea of a universal and transparent present as a place of reason and communication enters into literary and philosophical discourse.

To be universal, to speak with a "universal voice," as Kant puts it in his *Critique of Judgement* (Kant 1952, 154), the Enlightenment has to communicate as if everyone and everything were present in the same moment, in the same "now." The ideal of universal communicability, as formulated by Kant, rests upon the assumption of a total simultaneity between sender and recipient, between writer and reader—or even between writer, reader, and the event that is represented. However, such a total simultaneity can never be achieved, for several reasons, but mainly because Enlightenment can only take place by means of technologies, such as writing and print, that wield their own historical particularity and thus unfold their own temporality. As a consequence, the "universal voice" imagined by Kant is reintroduced into the complex temporal structure of history.

Kant's "An Answer to the Question: What Is Enlightenment?" first published in December 1783 in the journal *Berlinische Monatsschrift*, and Foucault's "Qu'est-ce que les Lumières?" in two different versions from Paris and the United States, both printed in 1984, belong to the absolute classics of the literature on the Enlightenment—defined not as a chronological period that ended in 1789, but as a historical movement starting in the eighteenth century and continuing into the twentieth or even into the twenty-first century. In rereading these texts, I am going to make three arguments. First, I show how both texts contain an implicit or even hidden reflection on the question of mediation, or at least an opening for such a reflection, rarely commented upon in the huge secondary literature. Second, I discuss how the intersection between Enlightenment and mediation comes to the fore in the question of temporality, or more precisely, in the question of the present, of the "now," as a place of enunciation and communication. And third, I investigate how this idea of an absolute, transparent "now," of a universal communicative present, prominent in both texts, is contested by the particularity of mediation itself, by the inherent noncontemporaneity of writing—for which Jacques Derrida famously coined the term "*differance*."

My argument then links up with more recent concerns, in questioning the possibility of anchoring the project of Enlightenment in a "now" that is supposed to be the same everywhere, a cosmopolitan and even universal present. In an interesting critique of Foucault's version of Enlightenment as an "ontology of the present," the postcolonial theorist Homi K. Bhabha asks, "What if the 'distance' that constitutes the meaning of the Revolution as a sign, the *signifying lag* between event and enunciation stretches not across the Place de la Bastille or the rue des Blancs-Monteaux, but spans the temporal difference of the colonial space?" (Bhabha 1994, 244). In this intervention Bhabha first attacks the idea of a universal present by pointing at the lag between event and enunciation; then he moves on to suggest that this temporal lag can be understood in terms of a spatial, indeed geographical, distance, thus moving from a universal present to the heterogeneity of both times and spaces.

## Event, Writing, Reading: Jean Paul's *Die Unsichtbare Loge*

But before I go on to discuss these questions and texts I shall give an example of how the experience of the present, in the sense of a condition of simultaneity between events, writing, and reading, is represented in one of the widely read novels of the late eighteenth century, *Die Unsichtbare Loge* (*The Invisible Lodge*) by the German author Johannes Paul Friedrich Richter, who took the artist's name of Jean Paul in veneration of his great idol Jean-Jacques Rousseau. In *Die Unsichtbare Loge*, published in 1793—part *Bildungsroman* (novel of education), part *Staatsroman* (state novel), part novel about a secret society—the author is striving to achieve total simultaneity between the unfolding of the events of the novel, the process of describing these events in writing, and the practice of reading. The hero acts, the narrator writes, and the reader reads all at the same time, as parts of the same present.

The literary framework for this condition of simultaneity, this present, of which hero, narrator, and reader are all part, is the genre often referred to as a "discursive novel," *Diskursroman*, in which the narrator constantly seeks to explain and to control his communication with the reader, expressing his constant doubt if it is indeed possible to communicate at all (Lindner 1976, 71). As it turns out, one of the main problems of communication is the issue of writing—of addressing an absent recipient through the medium of a text or book—which is a recurring topic in all Jean Paul's novels. The way Jean Paul analyzes the relationship between event, writing, and reading has a lot in common with the analysis made by Jacques Derrida in his infamous text "Sign, Event, Context" (Derrida 1988, 1–23). However, the main problem in Jean Paul's novels is not the loss of meaning, but in fact the gain of time, the advancing time causing a lag, a time lag between event, description, and reading. The ambition of the narrator—named Jean Paul, just like the author—is to obtain total simultaneity between events, signs, and following his way of addressing the reader, reading:

> In the heat of the moment I have completely abandoned my biographical plan: I wanted to hide from the world of readers (and until now I succeeded) that all these adventures are in fact not old and that shortly the life of these persons will unfold *hand in hand simultaneously* with their own life story—But now I have lit the fuse. (Jean Paul 1981, 1: 181, emphasis added)

Lives and the description of the lives are unfolding in a parallel way, simultaneously and, as Jean Paul puts it, "hand in hand." The main predicament of the narrator, however, arises because the whole process of writing, the entire technology of the written word, constantly seems to delay his rendering of the events, the life of the hero Gustav von Falkenberg. Halfway through the novel this time lag becomes so problematic that the narrator is forced to make a deal with the reader:

> Today the reader and I start a completely new life together. To begin with we are going to figure everything out in peace and quiet. Firstly I am still lagging one year behind Gustav's life; but in eight weeks I plan to have caught up with him in writing. Already half a year ago I thought that I was going to catch up with him; but it is easier to live a life than to narrate it, especially in a stylistically successful way. (Jean Paul 1981, 1: 288)

Between the events and the process of writing there is a time lag of one year, which the narrator, however, promises to catch up with—*erschreiben*—within eight weeks. The difficulties he faces when trying to narrate Gustav's life as it unfolds are mainly due to his ambition to portray him, as he says, "in a stylistically successful way," *gut stylisiert*. Another problem, however, consists in the sheer bulk of writing, of written material he is confronted with in his capacity as a lawyer. This, he claims, has to be taken into account, when his work is being read and judged by public opinion, especially by the literary critics of the literary journal *Literatur-Zeitung*:

> Does the literary journal know about the terrible amount of work I face? One would have to have seen the food cupboard full of deeds, in which, moreover, I haven't written a word, because I just received them from the paper mill.... In the whole of Scheerau, who is the one solicitor responsible for a case, which will shortly ... end up at the Wetzlaer gate under the secession tables of the imperial court of appeals, who really knows about good style? (Jean Paul 1981, 1:. 288)

Though he didn't aspire to become a lawyer, probably no other German author of the time knew more about the time-consuming process of writing and the successive accumulation of written material than Jean Paul, who in the course of his life, in addition to writing several long novels, philosophical and pedagogical treatises, and a large number of satires, filled no less than 110 exercise books, the so-called *Exzerptenhefte*, with excerpts from works by other authors. Indeed, this both theoretical and practical knowledge of the use and the materiality of writing also must have made him aware of the temporality and the historicity of the whole process: that writing never takes place in a condition of absolute simultaneity, but unfolds in time and space due to its specific material and technological conditions.

I will return later to Jean Paul and another one of his great novels, the bestselling *Hesperus*, published in 1795, in which the single, universal present dissolves into a heterogony of spaces. My main reason for discussing the *Unsichtbare Loge*, however, is to point at the way the narrator tries to establish a completely transparent, all-encompassing, communicative present in the form of simultaneity between events, writing, and reading, as well as how this attempt fails because of the temporality, the time lag inherent in the process of writing itself. Moving on to Kant and Foucault, I am going to look at how they deal with the same question, or the same paradox—of postulating the condition of the present, of contemporaneity or simultaneity as the main temporal horizon of Enlightenment, while on the other hand relying on technologies of transfer and mediation which necessarily wield other temporal horizons and experiences. Thus, the condition of contemporaneity postulated by Foucault might become a condition of the contemporaneity of the noncontemporaneous, *die Gleichzeitigkeit des Ungleichzeitigen*, as this topos is defined in the German tradition, by Ernst Bloch and Reinhart Koselleck (Bloch 1962; Koselleck 2000).

## "What Is Enlightenment?" as a Media Event

In themselves the essays by Kant and Foucault are complex media events. Kant's essay was printed in the journal *Berliner Monatsschrift*, published by Johann Erich Biester and Friedrich Gedike, both prominent members of the so-called Mittwochsgesellschaft, a closed society, working in secret to promote the goals of the Enlightenment. Among the other members were several important German philosophers and men of letters, such as Moses Mendelssohn, Friedrich Nicolai, and Carl Suarez. Another member of the inner circle of the Mittwochsgesellschaft was the theologian and priest Johann Friedrich Zöllner, who first raised the question "What is Enlightenment?" adding that it seemed to him to be a good idea to find an answer to this question before starting to enlighten the public (Zöllner 1973, 107–116).

However, the discussion did not start with Zöllner. In September 1783, the same year as that the journal was founded, a small contribution was published, signed "E.v.K.," a pseudonym often used by the editor himself, Johann Biester, with the somewhat malicious title: "Vorschlag, die Geistlichen nicht mehr bei der Vollziehung der Ehen zu bemühen" (Zöllner 1973, 95–106). The "suggestion, not to bother the clergy with the consummation of weddings," as the title reads, but to turn the wedding into a completely civil ceremony, started an intense debate in the *Berliner Monatsschrift*, to which Zöllner contributed, about the whole idea of Enlightenment. The answers came from Kant and Mendelssohn, among others. Indeed, the complexity of Kant's essay as a media event in itself questions the idea of a transparent, communicative present. The dialogical structure of the event, going back to the suggestion by Biester, maps a time span of over a year. Moreover, the journals, genres, and institutions involved, the *Berliner Monatsschrift*, the Mittwochsgesellschaft, and different types of texts published, as well as the topics discussed, unfold different temporalities and make it difficult to think of a present that is not, in one way or another, permeated and pervaded by the communicative structures of the past and the future. The anonymity of the original publications as well as all the mechanisms of secrecy at work in the Mittwochsgesellschaft seem to unfold an indefinite, but complex temporality—at the same time pointing backward to the long tradition of secret societies and forward toward the utopian goals of the Enlightenment. Indeed—as has been documented by Enlightenment scholars such as James Schmidt and Norbert Hinske (Hinske 1981; Schmidt 1996)—the temporalities of the "What is Enlightenment? debate" could itself be the subject of an article. It was the achievement of Hinske to show how Kant's essay could not be read as an instant philosophical classic, transcending the intellectual context, but must be understood as an answer to concerns in his own time. Neither Hinske nor Schmidt, however, has pointed at the specifically temporal and media historical paradoxes haunting this text. Moreover, my concern is not with Kant alone, but with the tradition of conceptualizing the Enlightenment in general—what Schmidt has recently summed up in the title of an anthology of texts from this debate, called *What is Enlightenment? Eighteenth-Century Answers and Twentieth-Century Questions*, thus mapping out a time span of more than two hundred years.

Indeed, there can be no doubt that this question, or rather this set of questions and arguments, "spans the temporal difference of colonial space," to use Bhabha's phrase. We need only to consider the essay by Foucault, or rather the two essays published on two different continents in the same year. In 1984 two essays by Foucault with the title "Qu'est-ce que les Lumières?" were published. The only reason they were not confused was that one of them had an English title—"What Is Enlightenment?"—and appeared in in *The Foucault Reader*, edited by Paul Rabinow and published by Pantheon Books in 1984. It did not come out in French until 1993, when it appeared in *Magazine littéraire* under the title "Kant et la modernité." The other essay, however, was printed in *Magazine littéraire*, almost ten years earlier, in the May edition of 1984 with the original French title "Qu'est-ce que les Lumières?" Furthermore, in 1988 this text was translated into English and published in another Foucault reader, edited by Lawrence D. Kritzman, with the title *Politics, Philosophy, Culture*. Probably to avoid confusion, the essay got the somewhat cryptic title "The Art of Telling the Truth" (Foucault 1988). This version has had a huge impact in the English-speaking world, coining the famous Foucauldian topic of an "ontology of the present." However, both these written texts—or rather, the four of them, in two different languages—have the same oral source, the lectures Foucault gave at the College de France in 1983 on Kant's text on the *Aufklärung*. The French original in *Magazine littéraire* even gives as its source the first, introductory lecture of that year, from January 5.

This little piece of publication history, which surely could be made much more complex, illustrates how the communicative and critical present that Foucault describes in these essays expands in every possible direction and at the same time loses its transparency. The relatively simple communicative situation of the lecture, an oral presentation, in a particular place, the College de France, and at a particular time, January 5, 1983, given in French as part of a course on Kant, are totally transformed by the medium of writing into a set of multiple texts, circulating in different geographical areas, in different languages, being used in different contexts and for different purposes. Interestingly, this transformation from an oral to a written medium is also one of the main topics of the essay by Kant, which I will come to shortly. But first I will have a further look at the two texts by Foucault and how they conceptualize the relationship between mediation and the reflection on the present.

## Foucault on Philosophy and Journalism

Why, we might ask, is it so important for Foucault to redefine the temporal aspects of the Enlightenment from a utopian idea of progress to a relationship to the present? As has been noted many times, Foucault uses his reading of Kant to develop an alternative view of the Enlightenment very different from the rather critical or even defamatory picture he paints in earlier work such as *Histoire de la folie* (*Madness and Civilization*) from 1961 and *Surveiller et punir* (*Discipline and Punish*) from 1975. In both cases he wants to show how the alleged progression of humanist values, in psychiatry and law, really belonged in a completely different discursive framework, in which the goal was to produce knowledge, not to improve the living conditions of prisoners and patients. Hence, turning Enlightenment into a positive force would mean to cut it loose from the traditional temporal frameworks of teleology and continuity and reinterpreting it as a moment of rupture and discontinuity. This, I would claim, is the background for Foucault's reading of Kant: in Kant's text, Foucault claims, it is not a question of representing the present as belonging to a certain historical age (Plato), as consisting of signs pointing at something that will happen in the future (Augustine) or as the dawn of a new world (Vico). On the contrary, Kant wants to understand the present as such, independent of the past and the future.

But as Foucault moves on in his argumentation it becomes obvious that the Enlightenment—the attempt to reflect on one's own present—is defined not only negatively way as a rupture, but also positively as an attitude or even an *ethos*. By this Foucault understands "a voluntary choice made by certain people; in the end, a way of thinking and feeling; a way, too, of acting and behaving that at one and the same time marks a relation of belonging and presents itself as a task" (Foucault 1994c, 1390). But what kind of task does he have in mind? In the end the attitude or the *ethos* represented by the Enlightenment, as a fundamentally philosophical task, amounts to a form of critique, more precisely "the permanent critique of our historical being" (Foucault 1994c, 1386). Hence, to return to the question I posed above, Foucault's ambition in redefining the inherent temporal *telos* of Enlightenment—not the future, but the present—consists in constructing a specific position of historical enunciation and communication or, more specifically, an enunciative position of critique.

To understand Foucault's text we need to consider to what extent this is a text about historical enunciation, about formulating, mediating, and communicating opinion. In the American version of the essay he opens with a reference to the world of newspapers, to journalism. According to Foucault, one of the important differences between eighteenth-century and twentieth-century newspapers or journals has to do with today's newspapers already knowing the answers to every question they ask, whereas in the eighteenth century they were still curious about the answers. "What is Enlightenment?" was such a question, to which, according to Foucault, "one exactly did not know the answer" (Foucault 1994c, 1381). This link between Enlightenment and journalism, sharing the same attitude to the present, is elaborated in an article from 1979, entitled "Pour une morale de l'inconfort" and published in the French journal *Le Nouvel Observateur*, as a homage to the journalist and author Jean Daniel, one of the cofounders of this journal. Indeed, this text precedes both the other texts on Kant and the Enlightenment and thus contains Foucault's preliminary remarks on the question of the Enlightenment. To begin with he draws a parallel between Daniel's *Nouvel Observateur* and Biester's *Berlinische Monatsschrift*:

> The Prussian journal posed a fundamental question: "What just happened to us? What is this event which is nothing else than what we just said, what we just thought, and what we just did—nothing else than ourselves, that something that we have been and still are?" This singular investigation, should it be inscribed into the history of journalism or the history of philosophy? I just know that after this moment there are not many philosophies that don't ask themselves the question, "Who are we at the present time? What is this fragile moment from which our identity cannot be separated and which takes it along with it? [Qui sommes-nous à l'heure qu'il est? Quel est donc ce moment si fragile dont nous ne pouvons pas détacher notre identité et qui l'emportera avec lui?]" But, as far as I am concerned, this question is also the basis of the profession as a journalist. The wish to tell what is happening—Jean Daniel, will he contradict me?—is not primarily guided by the desire to know how something can happen, everywhere and always, but rather by the desire to find out what is hiding behind the precise, fleeting, mysterious, totally simple word: "Today." (Foucault 1994b, 783)

This passage invites us to note that many of the topics that are central to the essays on the Enlightenment appear for the first time in a discussion of the practices of journalism. Hence, from the very beginning, one could claim, Foucault's interest in the Enlightenment as an "ontology of the present" has been a way of searching for specific forms of communication and enunciation, journalistic or philosophical. According to Foucault, the common ground of modern philosophy and journalism—of Immanuel Kant and Jean Daniel—consists in their attempts to use language to conceptualize and intervene in the present. This reflection on the role of journalism and of the journalist—both in the case of the *Berliner Monatsschrift* and *Le Nouvel Observateur*—does not, however, lead to a reflection on the function of media and media technologies in themselves, on the writing, printing, and distribution of texts. On the contrary, in Foucault's texts the idea of the present as both object and context of communication remains totally abstract and transparent—as if it was still a question of "universal communicability" and a "universal voice."

## Kant on Oral and Written Communication

On closer inspection, however, there is no universal voice to be heard and no universal present to be experienced in any of these texts. On the contrary, in both cases we are faced with complex media events, unfolding in different and often contrasting temporalities, and therefore I would like to explore what kind of communicative and enunciative present appears in Kant's essay, especially in the well-known distinction he makes between the private and public use of reason. I start with Kant's claim that only very few people have succeeded "in freeing themselves from immaturity," as he puts it, "by cultivating their own minds." On the contrary, Kant continues, "there is a much better chance of an entire public enlightening itself"; it is indeed "almost inevitable, if only the public concerned is left in freedom" (Kant 1985, 54f.). Hence, the subject of Enlightenment is not an individual, but the public, *das Publikum*—analogous to what Jürgen Habermas later calls "the public sphere," also with reference to Kant (Habermas 1962, 117–131).

From this distinction between individual and public Enlightenment follows the next distinction, between the private and public use of reason (*Privatgebrauch* and *öffentlicher Gerbrauch*). However, it is never a question of "private" in the modern sense, in terms of a separate sphere in which the individual can think and talk freely with his or her closest family and friends. This modern idea of the private doesn't concern Kant at all here, simply because Enlightenment can only take place in public, when groups of people enlighten each other and themselves. Hence, the private use of reason is always already public, in a minimal, non-normative sense of the word. For Kant, however, the difference between private and public lies elsewhere: "What I term the private use of reason," he states, "is that which a person may make of it in a particular *civil* post or office with which he is entrusted" (Kant 1985, 55, emphasis in the original). The examples he gives are the military officer, the fiscal clerk, and the clergyman. By the public use of reason, on the other hand, Kant writes, "I mean that use which anyone may make of it *as a man of learning* addressing the entire *reading public*" (Kant 1985, 55, emphasis in the original). Hence, the difference between the private and public use of reason lies primarily in the different subject positions, to use a Foucauldian term, as a civil servant or as a man of learning.

But there is something else at stake here as well. For the private use of reason Kant does not specify the means of mediation, not at this point anyway, but in the case of the public use it is different. The public has suddenly become a "reading public"; hence the means of mediation or, if you like, the technologies of transfer must be writing and print. In fact, the original German expression is "*[das] ganze[] Publikum der Leserwelt*," which could be translated into something like "the global world of readers," expanding the notion of the reading public in a very specific way, to which I shall return below. However, what concerns me here is the question of mediation, of mediating Enlightenment, and the decisive, though rather implicit, shift—in Kant—from oral to written communication.

Let's first look at how Kant imagines a society where the freedom to make public use of one's reason is threatened from all sides by the different private uses:

> But I hear on all sides the cry: *Don't argue!* The officer says: Don't argue, get on parade! The tax official: Don't argue, pay! The clergyman: Don't argue, believe! (Kant 1985, 55, emphasis in the original)

If freedom is restricted in so many ways, the result, of course, will be tyranny or, in view of how Kant imagines the total control of society by the private use of reason, totalitarianism. So that his investigation into the distinction between the public and the private reads like an accusation against the enlightened, but pragmatic and rather brutal ruler of Prussia, Frederick the Great, Kant adds: "Only one ruler in the world says: '*Argue*, as much as you want and about whatever you want, *but obey!*'" (Kant 1985, 55, emphasis in the original). But what is most striking about this passage is the way it is written. For some reason and for this passage only Kant abandons his lucid, philosophical style and instead adopts a kind of literary discourse, presenting the conflict between the private and the public use of reason as a piece of theatrical drama. Every one of the three civil servants and figures of authority, the military officer, the fiscal official, and the clergyman, and in the end even the king himself, have been given specific lines, by which they address their subjects. It would be possible to claim that the dramatic lines and the repetition of the enunciative verb "says" give the entire passage a simplistic feeling, disregarding the complexity of the problem and making it stand out from the rest of Kant's analytical prose. In light of the question of mediation, however, there might be a very good reason for Kant to proceed in this way, establishing a sharp distinction not only between private and public use of reason, but also between oral and written communication. Thus, what is really illustrated by this passage, is how the private use of reason manifests itself orally, in oral discourse, by means of utterances and orders addressing the subjects—whereas the public use of reason, as we just saw, addresses "the entire world of readers" and hence must take place in writing and print. Indeed, these connections between the uses of reason and the means of mediation might have appeared as coincidental, if they had not introduced a longer passage in which Kant returns to these questions several times, discussing both the genres of speech, the ways in which they are used, and by whom.

In the examples provided by Kant for the private use of reason, mainly two rhetorical genres are evoked: the military order and the religious sermon. In some "affairs of the commonwealth [*des gemeinen Wesens*]," Kant states, "we require a certain mechanism whereby some members of the commonwealth must behave purely passively, so that they may . . . be employed by the government for public ends" (Kant 1985, 56). To organize these affairs different rhetorical genres are in use, as "mechanisms," according to Kant, among them the order and the sermon. The main common feature of these genres is that they belong to the field of oral communication. Both orders and sermons are given orally. Kant writes: "Thus it would be very harmful if an officer receiving an order from his superiors would quibble openly, while on duty, about the appropriateness or usefulness of the order in question" (Kant 1985, 55). In a later passage he turns to the example of the clergyman: "In the same way, a clergyman is bound to instruct his pupils and his congregation in accordance with the doctrines of the church he serves" (Kant 1985, 57). Hence, the use he makes of his reason "in the presence of his congregation is purely *private*, since a congregation, however large it is, is never any more than a domestic gathering." At this point Kant's understanding of the "private" in terms of a "domestic gathering" overlaps with the modern understanding. If we should proceed to ask what exactly makes the congregation a private and domestic and not a public gathering, one answer could be that the public, for Kant, is a sphere constituting itself through the use of written, not oral, communication, excluding the priestly address. On the contrary, the clergyman might very well make public use of his reason in the cases when he is "addressing the real public (i.e., the world at large) through his writings." The point here is that the probably most well-known distinction from Kant's Enlightenment essay, between the public and the private use of reason, overlaps with a distinction between oral and written communication, to the extent that Kant at one point, a bit further on in the essay, equates the concept *öffentlich*, "public," with *durch Schriften*, "through texts." However, as soon as the idea of a large number of texts circulating and being distributed in the entire world, at least theoretically, is invoked, the question arises of the technology that makes this circulation and distribution possible.

## Kant and Piracy

If we for a moment turn to the famous text on human progress by the French philosopher Antoine-Nicolas de Condorcet, "Esquisse d'un tableau historique des progres de l'esprit humain" (Sketch of a historical tableau of the progress of the human spirit; 1793–1794), we will find that his eighth period in the history of mankind is characterized by the invention of print culture, the possibility of multiplying the copies of a work indefinitely. Hence, the whole idea of "public opinion," analogous to Kant's "public use of reason," for Condorcet is linked to the invention of the printing press, stabilizing and at the same time universalizing linguistic communication—in a global context (Condorcet 1988, 188ff.). But to address a global audience *durch Schriften*, that is, by means of printed texts, which is the operative definition of "public opinion" both in Kant's essay and in Condorcet's sketch, is not without problems. Indeed, Foucault's claim that this kind of historical address and communication might be understood in terms of a reflection on the present, in the present, is contradicted by the sheer complexity, both temporally and textually, of the distribution and circulation of printed matter.

This must have been a pressing issue also for Kant, because only one year after the publication of the essay on the Enlightenment he wrote another essay entitled "Von der Unrechtmäßigkeit des Büchernachdrucks" (On the illegality of the reprinting of books). Here he brings several different and rather subtle legal arguments intending to limit the practice of piracy, of reprinting and publishing books without the permission of the author or the original publisher. To avoid this practice, Kant—to use a later phrase—wants to separate the medium from the message. "In a book as writing," he states, "the author *speaks* to his reader; and he who has printed the book, *speaks* through the copies not for himself, but completely in the name of the author" (Kant 1922, 215).[2] In the subsequent passages Kant distinguishes the book, "das stumme Werkzeug der Überbringung einer Rede des Autors ans Publikum" (the mute tool for the transmission of a speech by the author to the audience), which is the product of the publisher, from its linguistic and intellectual content, which is the rightful work of the author and which the publisher can only publish in the author's name. Obviously, the communicative structures to which Kant wants to adapt his conception of written and printed culture are taken over from the field of oral communication. The reason why he calls the book a "mute tool," he adds in a footnote, is to show the connection to as well as the difference from the sounds of speaking (Kant 1922, 215 n. 1). Thus, from a legal point of view there is no significant difference between an author speaking to his audience and the circulation of printed texts. The relationship between message and sender remains the same: as if the author was still present in the context of communication, speaking to his reader. For the same reason books cannot be put in the same legal category as other works of art. Whereas artworks can be copied, books can't—because, as Kant says, the first ones are "works," in the sense of "things existing for themselves," the others "actions" and thus "can only have their existence in a person" (Kant 1922, 221). Although there are complex legal considerations concerning the status of both publishers and pirated books, it still seems that Kant is using the idea of someone talking to an audience as a blueprint for his understanding of print culture. In this way he is able to hold on to the idea of a communicative present, of a kind of simultaneity between author and reader, which, however, do not really fit the realities of written communication. As discussed with reference to the novel by Jean Paul, writing and print, but also, as we shall see shortly in another novel by the same author, the distribution and circulation of texts causes time lags as well as duplications and divisions of temporalities, irreducible to a single, homogenous present.

For Kant, however, in the text on the illegitimacy of reprinting books there is only one aspect of the book industry that cannot be fitted directly into the model of oral communication, which is the general model of communication presented in this text: translation—because translation, he concludes, "is not the author speaking, although the thoughts might be exactly the same" (Kant 1922, 222). Again, the model for understanding is oral communication: "the author speaking." But how can an author address the entire "reading world" if his words are really lost, if they disappear as soon as they are translated? Even though it is quite possible to agree with Kant in his view of translation, the highly problematic consequences of this way of reasoning give us yet another hint that his model of oral communication cannot account for the complexity of written communication and print culture. For the same reasons the idea of a universal communicative present, a "discursive contemporaneity," to use Foucault's term, seems increasingly improbable—a remnant of a communication model that at the end of the eighteenth century is becoming obsolete.

## The Claim to Universality

The emphasis on writing and print as the conditions of possibility for making public use of reason is one element Kant and Condorcet have in common; the other is the claim to universality, to universal communication directed at the world at large, at *l'humanité* or the *Weltbürgergesellschaft*, "the cosmopolitan society." In the works by both philosophers we find the idea of a universal print culture as a vehicle of the Enlightenment in the world at large. But the question is how this idea of a global culture of writing and print relate to the idea, advocated by Foucault, that in Kant's essay on the Enlightenment we are confronted with a new notion of the present, of a self-referential "now"—*aujourd'hui*—as a philosophical task? And, furthermore, how does it fit in with Foucault's attempts to isolate the present as a place of enunciation, communication, and finally, of critique? As we have seen, in texts by Kant and Jean Paul, the idea of a universal communicative present seems to have major difficulties in coming to terms with the complex temporalities and temporal paradoxes of written communication, of writing and print. But this temporal structure is bound to become even more complex the moment we have to take seriously the claim that the reading audience or the public includes not only the European cultures of the Enlightenment, but indeed the entire world, *die Weltbürgergesellschaft* or, as Kant puts it, *das ganze Publikum der Leserwelt*, "the entire audience of the world of readers."

In spite of their appeals to a universal audience, neither Kant nor Foucault asks what it might mean to frame the project and activity of Enlightenment within a global communicative context. To Bhabha, however, this final question is the decisive one. In the article "'Race,' Time and the Revision of Modernity" he refers to the notion of modernity, found both in Kant and in Foucault and more or less equivalent to the notion of Enlightenment, as "the historical construction of a specific position of historical enunciation and address" (Bhabha 1994, 243). In this essay I have made a point of showing how this position of enunciation and communication—historically constructed at the end of the eighteenth century—is characterized by the complete absence of any temporal or spatial coordinates, invoking instead, as we have seen, a universal present. However, these canonical texts, by Kant, Foucault, and Jean Paul, can also be used to illustrate how this idea of the present, and hence, of a universal position of enunciation is deconstructed by the processes of writing, print, and distribution of texts, causing time lags and temporal shifts. Adding to the same argument and taking the consequence of historical particularity of enunciation and communication, Bhabha discusses how the exposure to the cultural differences of the colonial and the postcolonial worlds draws our attention to what he calls the "split" or "splitting" of modernity, between event and enunciation. This split, he claims, is a temporal one, a "time lag."

According to Bhabha, the goal of postcolonial criticism is to open up "an interruptive time-lag in the 'progressive' myth of modernity" (Bhabha 1994, 240). His method of opening up this time lag is to start with all the traditional ideas of contemporaneity, hence of the present, and to investigate how the "splitting" of this present is taking place—not unlike the way I have worked here. "[T]his," he continues, "makes it all the more crucial to specify the discursive and historical temporality that interrupts the enunciative 'present' in which the self-inventions of modernity take place" (Bhabha 1994, 240). As I have tried to show in this paper, one of the major forces of splitting the communicative and enunciative present of Enlightenment has been writing and print, introducing not one, but several alternative discursive and historical temporalities into the universal present of modernity. Moreover, if we want to see the world as a reading public, we will have to take into account all the different time lags interrupting and opening up the global present of modernity. This seems to be an all-important task for the Enlightenment in the twenty-first century. However, this "reflection on the present"—different from the one Foucault finds in Kant's essay, in the sense that it wants to map out the radical temporal and spatial heterogeneity inherent in the idea of the complete universal simultaneity of events, writing and reading—also took place in the eighteenth century, more precisely, in the works of Jean Paul.

## Conclusion: Jean Paul and Colonial Space

I would like to conclude by returning to Jean Paul, this time to another one of his novels, the *Hesperus oder die 45 Hundposttage* (Hesperus or the 45 dog-mail days) from 1795, which became a huge bestseller at the time, especially among the women of the nobility, who cherished the author for his sentimental style. In the guise of a sentimental novel, however, Jean Paul continues his reflections on the heterogeneous temporalities of writing and reading, against the background of the Enlightenment ideal of—and, indeed, quest for—a complete discursive simultaneity or contemporaneity. All but anticipating the postcolonial perspective, Jean Paul explores how the time lags of writing, which had already had a prominent place in the *Unsichtbare Loge*, reproduce or are reproduced by geographical distances in the global community of writers and readers. In the middle of the first chapter of the *Hesperus* we find the following passage:

> Another writer would have acted stupidly and started at once with the beginning; but I thought I should start by telling where I am staying—really at the equator; because I live on the island of *St. Johannis*, which, as you know, is situated in the East Indian waters, surrounded by the principality of *Scheerau*. (Jean Paul 1960, 506)

Apparently Jean Paul locates his narrator, who is also named Jean Paul and works as a miner, a *Berg-Hauptmann*, on an island in the East Indian waters, near the Equator, in a global geography—in "colonial space," to use Bhabha's term. However, those who have read Jean Paul's first novel, *Die Unsichtbare Loge*, will know that this geography is purely fictitious, and that both the island, the East Indian waters, and the principality of Scheerau surrounding them, are really situated somewhere in the German-speaking part of Europe. In fact, the author informs us that the islands, called "*die Molukken*," were built artificially for the commercial purpose of importing and exporting spices. Nevertheless, in spite of—or maybe even because of—the obvious artificiality of this entire geography it can very well be seen as a representation of "colonial space," the references to the East Indian waters and the spice trade serving as metonymical markers. Reading on, we soon recognize that the role of this fictitious colonial space in the novel is to be a communicative space, a space of the circulation and distribution of texts.

Sitting on the island of St. Johannis, the narrator writes the novel on the basis of letters brought to him by a stray dog, pinned to a gourd hanging around its neck—hence the name of the chapters of the novel, *Hundposttage*, "dog-mail days." His correspondent is a certain Knef (an anagram for one of the main characters of *Die Unsichtbare Loge*, named Fenk), living in the German principality of Flachsenfingen, in which the events of the novel take place and from which Knef reports. However, in the same way as in *Die Unsichtbare Loge* the chain of events making up the story has not come to an end as the narrator starts receiving the letters by "dog mail" and embarks on the writing of the story; on the contrary, the narrator Jean Paul is continuously trying to evoke a kind of simultaneity between the succession of events and the process of writing, according to a temporal structure described by the narrator in the following way:

> [B]ecause fate is still at work on this story and its development, and here he [Knef] only hands me the snout and is going to transfer to me one member after the other, the way they fall from the woodturning lathe [*Drechselbank*] of time, until we have the tail. (Jean Paul 1960, 508)

Apart from the rather peculiar canine metaphor, this evocation of simultaneity, of a communicative present, interrupted by the time lag of written communication is more or less the same as in *Die Unsichtbare Loge*—only this time the distribution and circulation of written material, the transportation of letters from the principality of Flachsenfingen to the East Indian island of St. Johannis, "spans the temporal difference of colonial space," to use Bhabha's expression. By consequence, the story cannot be written until the letters have been transported the long distance to the island, by the stray dog, and, hence, it is never able to catch up to the events taking place in the principality:

> [F]or this reason the maildog will regularly swim to and forth like a *poste aux ânes* [donkey mail], but I am not allowed to follow the dog back—and so (the correspondent concluded, signing as Knef) like a Pegasus the dog will bring me so much nutritional juice that in place of the thin forget-me-not of the almanac I will produce a thick cabbage stalk of folios. (Jean Paul 1960, 508f)[3]

Again Jean Paul is drawing our attention to the sheer bulk of written material, "a thick cabbage stalk of folios," making up the novel. As the novel proceeds, the time lag caused by the transportation by a stray dog of the written material over substantial geographical distances becomes an ever more important factor in the evolving of the plot and contributes to the complex temporal structure of the book—as in the following passage:

> The prince gave him a sincere hug; the lord returned it just as warmly and said: on October 31 (that is today, and he said it yesterday) he will seal his honorable intentions towards the prince in a way which decides more than all words. . . . I am writing this on October 31 in the morning at 10 o'clock. (Jean Paul 1960, 1228)

Thus, the narrator is not able to move beyond the time lag created by the circulation of written material in geographical space, and by consequence, the idea of a universal communicative present is dissolving into a rather opaque play of different and often conflicting temporal references—what Jean Paul aptly calls the *Drechselbank der Zeit*, "the woodturning lathe of time."

In the end the attempts made both by Kant and most intensely by Foucault to anchor the project of Enlightenment in a universal communicative present cannot escape this logic of time and mediation. Even today, in the age of the World Wide Web, mediation will always cause temporal shifts, which in turn will influence the message and ideas mediated—even the universalistic dreams of the Enlightenment.

# THE STRANGE LIGHT OF POSTCOLONIAL ENLIGHTENMENT

## MEDIATIC FORM AND PUBLICITY IN INDIA

ARVIND RAJAGOPAL

Kant defines Enlightenment, it is well known, as a people's overcoming of their self-incurred tutelage. Some restrictions are considered necessary; the measure for distinguishing between what kinds of restrictions obstruct and those that promote enlightenment are to be decided on the basis of what limits a people would choose to impose upon themselves (Kant 1997, 16). Kant's text is less a manifesto than a proposal for a compact between a prince and his subjects: obedience in return for freedom of opinion and good governance, where the latter is defined as the responsibly timed increase of liberties made available to the people. The character of this compact clearly makes it difficult to determine where the "enlightened" individual will begin and the guardian state will end, since the one is constituted through the other.

The freedoms Kant advocates are discursive freedoms; in their social roles he advocates that people function like "a cog in a machine" (Foucault 1997, 109). There is thus a tension built into Kant's program. Criticism is meant to be socially transformative, but only when the ruler allows it; meanwhile, the terms of the agreement are not in fact altered. In the West, the formation of enlightened citizens in fact occurs less through overt pedagogy than through what Foucault describes as the internalization of the protocols of government and of self-governance, of being both subject and sovereign.

Simultaneously, however, the civilizational subjugation of colonial nations produced their inhabitants as quintessentially pedagogical subjects, their colonial unfreedom translated as backwardness, and requiring to be overcome by external intervention. Anticolonial nationalism's response to this positioning was ambivalent, for example, in India colonial superiority was rejected, and the nationalist right to politics was emphatically asserted. But Indian nationalists also reproduced the view of their country as backward, as needing to catch up and achieve material progress as measured by the West.

Whereas enlightenment is understood, in its ideal form, to involve a transparent process of mediation, transparency was usually regarded as a ruse of power in colonial conditions and in any case was contradicted by colonial claims of racial superiority. Nationalists responded by asserting their own inscrutable forms of difference as the basis of their claim to sovereignty. These competing claims were adjudicated not by epistemic means, for they were designed to be incommensurable. Rather, it was through the contingencies of political struggle that superiority was asserted.

If colonial subjugation compromised the possibility of enlightened subject formation through internalization of the rules of governance, the postcolonial period both overcame some colonial limits and introduced new ones. Thus the postcolonial Indian state defined its mode of intervention in terms of national development, according to which citizens were the objects of rational planning, designed to improve material conditions. Meanwhile mass franchise and democratic elections ensured that planners and politicians would themselves become the objects of popular politics (Chatterjee 1993). What resulted was a social formation in which knowledge could not be delinked from questions of power and in which the stagecraft of state action was liable to be challenged as it had been in the colonial period.

The euphoria of decolonization, and the optimism that control over the levers of state power in India would ensure the ability to overcome the past, were significant, however. The belief in the technology of the state as a means of reshaping society was affirmed by the experience of the Soviet Union and more recently of Keynesianism and the New Deal in the United States. But in the absence of changing property relations or providing mass employment, what was the state to do? Here it was economic planning that was understood as the key to success, maximizing the use of resources for the nation as a whole. Planners understood economic production as generating capital for the private sector, while questions of distribution were deferred to the future (Gadgil 1972, 305–306). If the lopsided character of the process did not come into focus, an important reason was that the process of democratic feedback within the plans, ensured via the electoral system, was not complemented by a communication policy that acknowledged the twin objectives (or constraints) of democracy and development. Rather, there was a persistence in treating communication purely as a tool in the state's own plans, which were themselves frequently reduced to the interests of the ruling party.

Communication was an important aspect of the infrastructure of development, of course, one that grew relatively slowly at first, and later, with the establishment of television, very rapidly. In this paper I use the issue of communication as a means of highlighting the limits of the state's pedagogical efforts, and of illuminating the transition from state-led developmentalism to market-centered economic growth. I will very briefly indicate here some characteristics of postindependence developmentalism, and the period of the National Emergency of 1975–1977 that, I argue, led to a shift away from overt state pedagogy, and away from state-led development. As an activity apparently conceived as external to the developmental process and to the work of planners, communication as political propaganda and as consumer exhortation enables a symptomatic reading of the state's consensus-formation practices and illuminates the shifts across changing political configurations.

## Antipolitics? Messages to the Nation

In the heyday of the developmentalist era, communication was no mere catalyst, but was believed to be a kind of master key to human society, underlying all activities and, until the arrival of modern technology, lacking the infrastructure appropriate to its importance. Communication became a stand-in for modernization, signifying its philosophy and process and holding the promise of a positive outcome as well. Stimulating empathy by engaging those embedded in traditional society appeared to be a sure means of opening their imaginations and generating their capacity for new kinds of aspiration.[1] Well-meaning and often well-funded, many of these developmental communication initiatives were notable for their optimism that newspaper readers and radio listeners would align in favor of modernization as planners understood it. There was a persistent tendency on the part of technocrats to assume that the means of publicity would remodel themselves in accordance with state priorities. They displayed a consistently instrumental approach to communications, assuming that a one-way exchange would be adequate to their purposes. In other words, their own empathy with other modes of modernization than their own, that sometimes stared them in the face, was scarce.

From the start, few, including the first prime minister of India, Jawahar-lal Nehru, believed it would be feasible to undo or transform the publicity apparatus set up by the British. The technocratic form of government thus extended to the regulation of media, and the government's monopoly over it. For example, the first Five-Year Plan (1951–1956) stated, "[A] widespread understanding of the Plan is an essential stage in its fulfillment." The Second Plan (1956–1961) observed, "In the program for publicity, the help and co-operation of the press is being specially sought." In addition to newspapers and radio, the Films Division, the Five-Year Plan Publicity programs (later merged to form the Field Publicity Directorate), and audio-visual methods were used. The Third Plan (1961–1966) sought to "intensify" arrangements for "carrying the message of the Plan to the masses throughout the country" (Desai 1988, 6–7). Years later, one scholar noted wryly, "Plan publicity entails a two-way traffic. Planners have to know as much about public reactions as people about planning" (Desai 1988, 7).

To be sure, this was not a simple matter when such a diverse society was the target. Protocols had to be devised for the sustained, cross-class, and community forms of address that planners were fashioning, for which the only precedent was wartime British propaganda. In 1981, 76 percent of the population lived in rural areas, spread over nearly 600,000 villages, often in remote areas. Hardly a third of the population could be defined as literate at the time, where to be counted as literate it was sufficient to be able to sign one's name. There were at least fourteen major languages, to say nothing of so-called minor languages and dialects. A concerted publicity effort therefore had to include elements such as press advertising, posters, broadsheets, wall newspapers, folders, brochures, outdoor publicity media like billboards, kiosks, cinema slides, tablets, wall paintings, and transit advertising on buses and trains, broadcast media such as radio and television, and exhibition units which included exhibition vans that could be taken to village fairgrounds and markets as well as towns (Venkataraman 1983, 1). In one year, the Directorate of Advertising and Visual Publicity recorded using 402 hoardings, 6,910 kiosks, 3,740 wall paintings, 7,385 bus panels, 868 banners, 36,227 cinema slides, and 5 million bus tickets, among other devices, to publicize government programs on, for example, national integration and communal harmony, rural development, drug abuse, and untouchability (India Ministry of Broadcasting 1999, 45). In the same year, the Directorate of Field Publicity staged 50,000 film shows, 65,000 oral communications, 35,000 photo exhibitions, and 10,000 special programs such as symposia, debates, essay and elocution competitions, and healthy baby shows (India Ministry of Broadcasting 1999, 48).

With such a range of publicity vehicles and methods, planning could easily produce divergent rather than convergent understandings. Attempts to increase coordination and control were noteworthy mainly for the insight they provided on how plans faltered as they moved from the national capital to the states and to the rural areas. Illustrating and reinforcing the divide was a linguistic separation of the spheres of deliberation and discussion from those of mass publicity. Planners conducted their discussions in English, whose inaccessibility to the majority led to a more insular style of debate than would otherwise have been possible, while Indian languages were seen as conveyor belts to transmit the resultant end-products of these deliberations to citizens. The structures of miscommunication between citizens and the state thus indexed a more fundamental misrecognition of the nature of postcolonial state authority. This is an issue that came into spectacular visibility during the period of the National Emergency of 1975–1977.

## Interregnum and Miscommunication: The Failed Magic of the State

On June 26, 1975, then Prime Minister Indira Gandhi declared a national emergency, allegedly to prevent a conspiracy from undermining the progressive measures being undertaken by her. Civil rights were suspended, press censorship was imposed, and extraordinary powers of detention were assumed and activated, jailing the entire leadership of the opposition and hundreds of other dissidents and activists. The government's aim appeared to be to stop at the source all conceivable political opposition and to instead divert energies preoccupied with politics toward economic production and national unity. Thus the ubiquitous billboards and posters in towns and cities contained slogans and exhortations such as the following: "Discipline Makes the Nation Great," "The 20 Point Program Is the Nation's Charter," "Rumormongers Are the Nation's Enemies," "Efficiency Is Our Watchword," "Produce More for Prosperity," and "Less Talk, More Work."[2] The stern, admonitory character of the publicity presumed the existence of a willing and obedient citizenry; the profuse deployment of police and other repressive measures suggested the absence of such a population. Taken together, they indicated an inability to transcend the political crisis that the Emergency was meant to resolve, and they gave a hint of where at least one crucial problem might lie. In vernacular propaganda, the translation of slogans could contribute to the failure of propaganda. When the slogan "The Only Magic Is Hard Work" appeared in Marathi, for example, "only magic" was translated as *ekatz jadu*—but *jadu* in Marathi signaled deceit or trickery, and beside "hard work" was liable to confuse its reader, or indicate the communicator's own confusion (Schlesinger 1977). As well, there was perhaps an overly abstract conception of the audience of these messages, as citizens predisposed to discipline, hard work, and national pride. But as Indira Gandhi herself said, in a 1976 interview, "One thing that people outside simply can't understand [is] that India is a different country" (cited in Palmer 1977).[3] If national difference could sanction authoritarianism, it could also withdraw consent, as events unfolded.

The problem of establishing and maintaining a sovereign authority that would act in the people's name while at the same time seeking to improve the people, was an intractable one, of course. When the only judge of the rightful defense of state power for nationalist ends lay within the state itself, it was hardly surprising that from such a perspective, there was little distinction between the spontaneous generation of popular consent and the staging and simulation of consent for instrumental ends. The Shah Commission of Inquiry, instituted after the defeat of Indira Gandhi's government at the polls in 1977, in fact staged a public inquiry, unprecedented in its scope, into the corrupt machinery of the state. Begun with an inquisitorial vengeance, the inquiry ended with a series of banal and nonbinding indictments. It was perhaps an improbable exercise from the start, since the inquiry's success could compromise the authority of the successor ruling party, which relied on the same state machinery.

In retrospect, the centrality to postcolonial development of the communicative infrastructure and its representational work upset the smooth reproduction of centralized power. In many ways, the National Emergency brought home the truth of that fact, and posed the need to include the production of consent into the rituals of governance and to complement or go beyond the ceremony of elections. Ironically then, the development of a national television system, for which the foundation was laid during the Emergency, would eventually inaugurate a new visual regime in which the outlines of a postcolonial sensorium would be brought to the surface.

Important here is what we can call the banal materiality of television, which is also the source of television's power. This accrues from television's ability to knit together divergent publics through an accelerated circulation of the image and the expanded circuitry of televisual dissemination; but it also emanates from television's role in the production (and circulation) of capitalist value. Television audiences across society "tune in" to programs, their time of viewing flowing alongside but separate from the time of the image (Dienst 1994, 58–59; Weber 1996, 120). The anonymous intimacy so created is a technologically mediated sociality distinct from that of print capitalism, given the sensuous character of sound and image, as opposed to the more abstract character of print communication.

Since the growth of a technologically mediated visual regime has increasingly become a key element of commodity exchange, it is helpful, even cursorily, to indicate the character of its effects as far as television goes: television introduces a recalibration of sociality so that the connection between audiences is simultaneously rendered both abstract, as a shared mode of perception, and more palpable, as a common set of viewing experiences. There are elements of a rational-critical mode of reading present here, interfused with affective and aesthetic elements, since the codes of intimacy cannot be presumed but require to be engaged at the same time. That is, the framework of intelligibility assumed by a reader cannot relegate questions of the shared affective community within which the reader/viewer is placed in the background, as in the Habermasian model, but have to be engaged simultaneously during any rational-critical engagement with a given text.

## The Magic of Money

During the Nehruvian era Indian businesses had evolved a set of codes to translate the political consensus of developmentalism into marketing terms. What this meant in practice was a division between the premium market and the mass market, the former comprised of "people like us" (PLUS), capable of realizing their aspirations, while the latter were constrained to live a life of relative austerity. Meanwhile the "people like us," who represented the counterpart of an elite secular consensus in the political sphere, constituted a relatively small urban middle class. As the character of political consensus changed and economic liberalization gathered momentum in the 1980s, there developed a search for new sources of value within advertising, with local culture increasingly used to endow goods with symbolic distinction. If Indian advertising had evolved a set of codes to address a limited elite audience that fashioned itself as standing for the nation as a whole, these codes now had suddenly to be brought into alignment with a truly nationwide market. What would be the terms on which this genuinely mass market would be included, into what had hitherto been an elite public, and what kind of public would be constituted as a result of this engagement?

Although Indian advertising scarcely conceived of its mission in these grandiose terms, some of the burden of solving this vexing historical-political conundrum willy-nilly fell to its lot, with the failure of political elites to fulfill their own tasks. Without doubt, advertisers sought to maximize market share and to win as many new consumers as they could. They were, however, limited by their long recalcitrance in refusing to perceive the enormous plurality of consumers that had for decades lain under their noses. As well, they were constrained by their political timidity in imagining alternative modes of configuring the social that would disrupt the existing mode of distribution of capital.

Indian businesses now faced a challenge to their understanding that was more than technical. How were they going to address a greatly expanded mass market that had demonstrated its capacity for aspiration? Marketers had to learn to imagine what lower castes wanted and to overcome their own ritually sanctioned apprehension of any contact with these groups. What kind of a market or public would be constituted as a result of this engagement? Although lower casts tend to be described in triumphal terms of late, as the overdue awakening of an economic force to be reckoned with, the ways in which class is depicted in advertisements bears discussion.

Advertisements form a virtual market reflecting the real sphere of commodity exchange and are therefore instrumental to the completion of those real exchanges. Locally rooted relationships of dependence, based on caste, community, and gender, are gradually linked in generalized relations of commodity exchange, as more insular regional markets are transformed and consolidated within a more global market. In the process advertisers transcribe fragments of local knowledges within a wider orbit of intelligibility.[4]

There is a twofold character to this operation. Advertisers tend to seek appeals that are familiar and recognizable, and that avoid arousing the prejudices of their audiences, while at the same time making the case for what is in some sense new behavior, that is, a more individually oriented structure of decision making, and a more psychological rather than, say, ritual or community-centered basis for consumption. If this is only part of a much larger process of social change, ads are at any rate useful in transforming "otherwise opaque goings-on," in Erving Goffman's phrase, "into easily readable form" (Goffman 1976, 27). Advertisements constitute an archive of efforts at microecological changes in social orientation, one that critics have tended to regard in negative or neutral rather than in positive terms. Thus, much critical scholarship either assumes that ads participate in the erosion of historical meaning due to the fluidity of their signifying practices, or else perceives advertising as simply one sphere of socialization, not very different in form or substance from other kinds of socialization.[5] The first approach typically evokes an age when use-value dominated the description of things, and oscillates between nostalgia and modern-day utilitarianism.[6] The second approach is ahistorical rather than anachronistic, failing to apprehend the centrality of advertising in capitalist society. Both approaches miss the specificity of advertising as a discourse linking culture and economy, and as a set of meanings that participate in the production of value at a given conjuncture.

I will now briefly discuss an ad that was released in 2004, for the *Times of India*, certainly one of the most prominent papers in India during the last century of British rule and a firm supporter of the Raj, transformed after independence into a leading national daily.[7] But with this series of ads, the English-language paper addresses its audience in demotic Hindi, in racy and colloquial terms. Produced at the height of market deregulation and economic liberalization, the ad discussed below is a sophisticated commentary on the work of representation and on the inherent deceptivity of such work. Following a series of chance encounters involving a range of different cash transactions, it shows both the trust and the delusion in them. The ad thereby presents a moral critique of the market economy as a system indifferent to truth. The failure to achieve truth therefore reflects a human rather than a social defect, one that can be portrayed, however, with meticulously detailed camera footage used in this television ad.

The ad won an open competition conducted by the *Times* for promoting its brand. The winning advertising agency would pay the costs of production, for the privilege of having the *Times* promote their ad, in the fashion of a contemporary patron of the arts; each ad in the series is about one minute in duration, and hence more expansive than is customary, a statement about market leadership as much as an attempt to sell the brand.

This ad follows a series of transactions made with a fake 100-rupee note, the omniscience of the camera allowing the viewer to discern how the counterfeit can easily take the place of the real. The fact that it is money that is counterfeit indicates the charge exercised by the universal commodity equivalent; few who receive it look very closely at it. The physical object that is money typically is not assumed to require scrutiny. Its image, and the fact of possessing it, are usually adequate; the image is customarily taken as real and as ensuring the ability to be exchanged. Since it is the ability to be exchanged that defines money, the adequacy of the counterfeit for the purpose dramatizes the indeterminate character of the real and the power of the image as currency in itself. Told through a series of video images, the reflection that money is an image opens out onto a larger meditation on the seductions and betrayals of the sensible world, and of desire itself.

The sequence opens with the words "A Day in the Life of India" on-screen, followed by a voice-over, spoken in a high-pitched idiosyncratic tone.

The voice is not that of an authoritative narrator; rather, it implies that the speaker is something of a trickster. His words point to the story, but his tone points to himself. Even if the trickster speaks truth, there is a question mark against his views, of course.

> *Party keheta hai ki woh police wala asli hai.* [You think that policeman is a real one.]

A uniformed policeman stands on a Mumbai street. A taxi driver is making a third, and illegal, lane, driving on the wrong side of the road. He makes the characteristic pleading gestures to the alert policeman, who rebukes him (fig. 1). Both sides understand that their conversation is a negotiation over the amount of the bribe, not about the wrongdoing. The taxi driver offers his driver's license, suggesting a submissive response to the reprimand. But in fact, the reality lies behind this façade; in this case it is the bribe he is offering, but it is a fake note (figs. 2, 3).

The policeman pockets the bribe and walks off when a man bumps into him. Again we see a pleading gesture of the kind the taxi driver made to the policeman. Again, the gesture conceals something, since the man who bumps into him is a pickpocket and knows exactly what he was doing (fig. 4).

A song starts in the background here—*Rita!! Ta-ra-ta-ra. Ta-ra-ta-ra! to* the sound of trumpets. It is a cabaret song, from the 1972 film *Apna Desh* (My Country)—starring Rajesh Khanna and Mumtaz—

> *Duniya mein logon ko*
> *dhokha kabhi ho jata hein.*
> *Annkhon hi annkhon mein*
> *yaaron ka dil kho jata hai.*
>
> [In this world, every now and again
> Fools are made out of women and men.
> The eye can only see what it can see
> And friends just lose their hearts on what they see.]

The pickpocket is in a state of high excitement and runs into a girlie bar—where bar girls are pirouetting on stage. He holds the currency note between his teeth, and one of the girls gracefully retrieves it from him (figs. 5–6). The camera cuts to the dressing room, where the girl hands the note over to the madam (fig. 7), who soon hands over to her boss a stack of 100-rupee notes, with documents indicating an official transaction (fig. 8). The boss, a well-oiled gentleman, smiles and receives the notes and the documents. Now it's the boss's turn. Traveling in a state vehicle, he arrives at a fancy beauty parlor. The girls there go into a tizzy when they see him coming. The boss

Fig. 1. Policeman stops erring taxi driver. Figures are from a television ad for the *Times of India* newspaper.

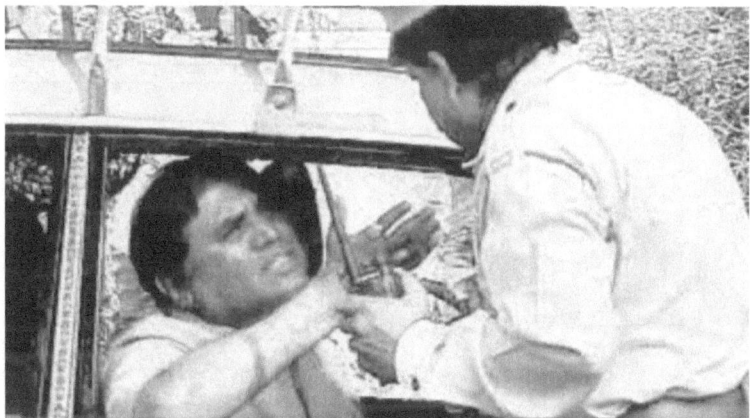

Fig. 2. Cabdriver pleads with policeman.

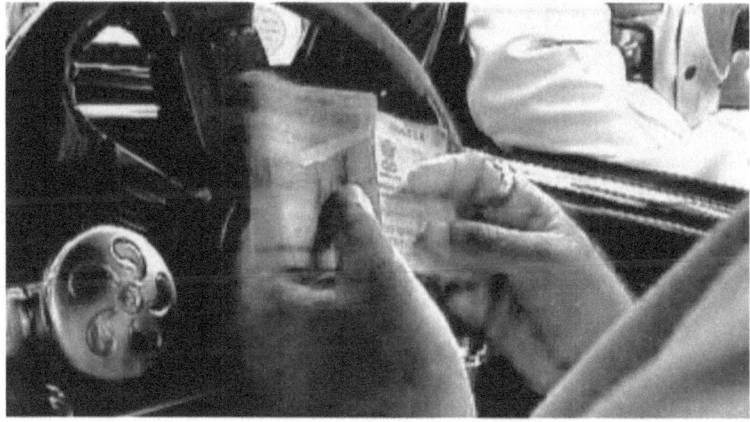

Fig. 3. Cabdriver folds a 100-rupee note into his driver's license to hand over to the policeman.

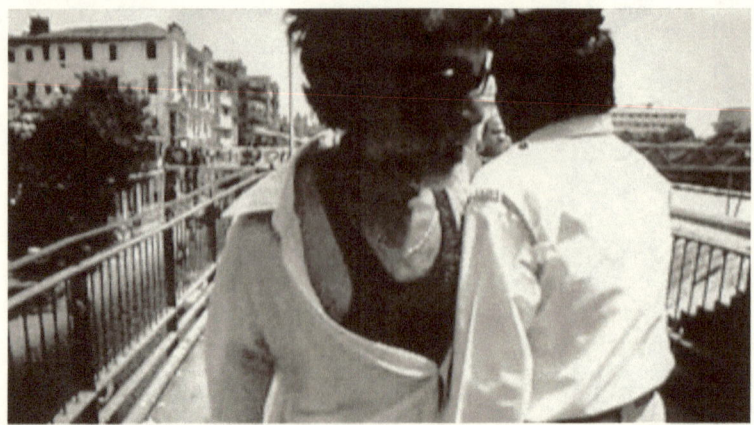

Fig. 4. A pickpocket bumps into the policeman as he departs from the cabdriver.

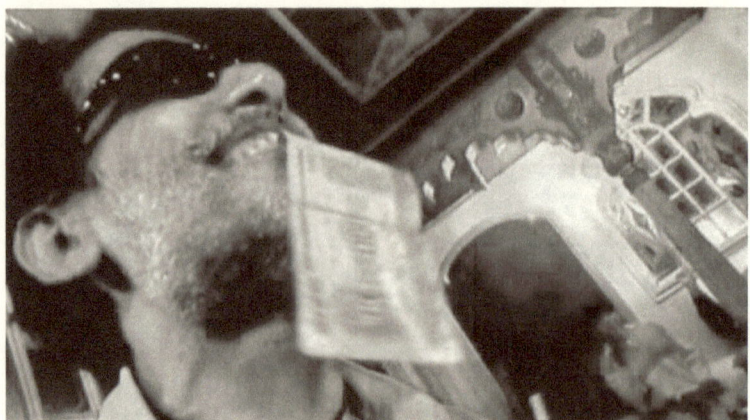

Fig. 5. Pickpocket flourishes his new 100-rupee note in a dancehall.

Fig. 6. The bar dancer accepts the 100-rupee note from the pickpocket.

Fig. 7. The bar dancer hands the note to the madam.

Fig. 8. The madam arrives to make a payment to the politician.

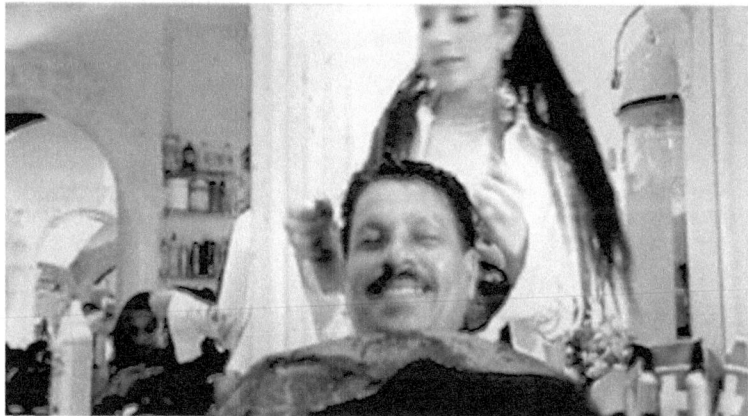

Fig. 9. The politician goes to a beauty salon, where he tips one of the girls 100 rupees.

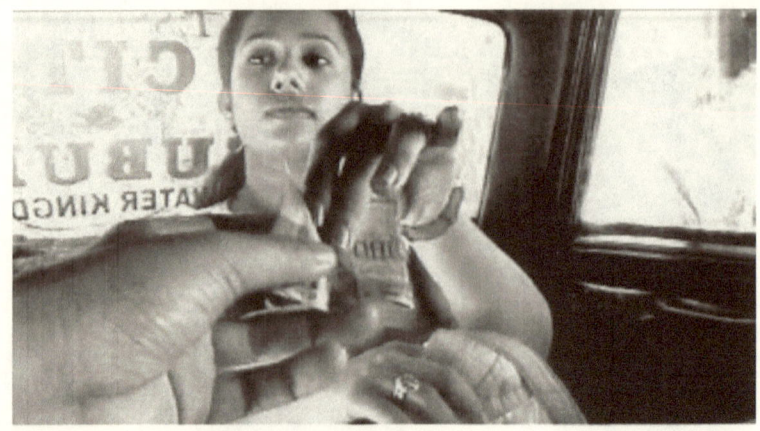

Fig. 10. Salon girl uses the money to pay for a taxi ride.

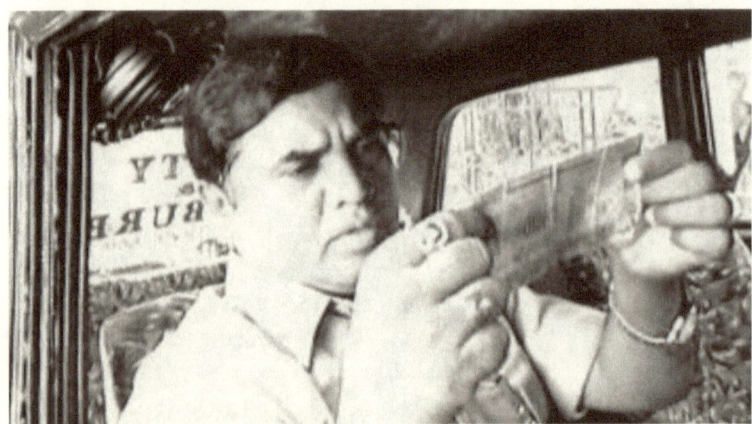

Fig. 11. Taxi driver realizes the note looks familiar.

Fig. 12. The taxi driver has made a wrong turn, and he is accosted by the same policeman once again.

is given his special treatment (fig. 9), no doubt euphemistically portrayed in the ad, and he in turn hands over payment, consisting of some 100-rupee notes, one of which reappears with one of the girls, who heads off after work in a taxi. The ride over, the girl hands over a 100-rupee note (fig. 10) and the taxi driver from the earlier sequence, declares—*Shishter, yeh note to nakli hai!* (Sister! This note is fake!; fig. 11). A policeman comes running to apprehend the taxi driver for making a wrong turn, the same policeman as before, pursuing the same offense, and is about to receive the same response (fig. 12). After a moment's reflection, the driver hands over the note, realizing that this was the same note he had handed over to the policeman earlier that day. Time has progressed and events have elapsed, but nothing has changed.

> NARRATOR VOICE-OVER: *Party kaisa aadmi hai! Jis note ne itna kaam kiya, bolta hai ki nakli hai! Pagal hai! Ehhh!*
>
> [What kind of a fellow is he. The currency note that has done so much work, he is calling fake! He's crazy!]

If the world is deceptive, we cannot be expected to treat the revelation with solemnity, since the disclosure applies to the mediator as well as the object of his lesson. Truth and falsehood, like good and evil, are intermixed; in this world their coexistence is unavoidable (Doniger 1976, 357).

> [Cut to the brand logo.]
> *The Times of India.*
> The Masthead of India.

The policeman (who may be real or fake) takes the money and walks off, in a sequence of images identical to the start of the film. Not only is the currency counterfeit, so perhaps is the incarnation of the law itself. The movement of money, like that of the narrative, is cyclical, and to assume these are progressive is to treat their fictions as fact.

"A Day in the Life of India" is what the *Times of India* claims to capture. But what does the newspaper of record do here? It makes no claims about civic virtue or serving the public interest. Its satisfaction is rather in letting viewers (who will presumably wish to be readers) witness an entire circuit of corruption, through images that the soundtrack reminds us are themselves illusions, emblems of our own desire and as illusory as the 100-rupee note that seems so real. But we are left with a conundrum. If the false works just as well as the real, for whom is the difference relevant? The ad is aimed at a public that appears postcivic and is expected to relish the unveiling of corruption that lies beneath pretensions of good government. We see here a market where the velocity of illicit circulation is such that a fake note returns to its user within a day, provoking not indignation but a detached enjoyment.

The use of the image of a rupee bill in this context deserves comment. There is tacit equation of money with the image: on the one hand, the image has implications of universal adaptability and equivalence, of an absence of affiliation, available to the highest bidder so to speak, the omniscient spectator able to track the circulation of images and so arrive at both an analytic and a synthetic conception of the sociopolitical field, just as, on the other hand, following the money elicits dynamic liaisons through which alliances were being fortified. What indigenous conceptions of vision are being drawn upon here, what native distrust of perception? In the context of an apparently naïve form of realism accompanying modern instruments of image documentation, with the democratization of access that they entail, what kind of interaction can we map here between these different modes of seeing?

The camera here of course, does not lie—or does it? We see everything, as privileged spectators, albeit in a music video MTV style of rendition. We see the *asli* (real) as well as the *naqli* (counterfeit); due to the privilege of an omniscient camera, we are actually able to tell the real from the fake. So in a sense the audio track, chiming in as it does with a time-honored piece of wisdom, is contradicted by the visual narrative. I suggest what we see here is the attempted ascendancy of a visual regime that can in fact be treated as transparent and unmediated, although also acknowledging its coexistence alongside an older oral culture that distrusts perception and relegates it to the realm of ephemera and deceit.

## Conclusion

Enlightenment is envisioned as the transfer of sovereign authority from the state to its citizens, so that, at the hypothetical end of the process (which is never reached, since the state remains a guardian state, albeit in new ways) humankind would have altogether cast off its yoke of "self-incurred tutelage." In the colonial context however, such a logic of historical lag, which relegates subjugated nations to the "waiting room" of history, was explicitly rejected by nationalist movements that instead defined history as promising themselves full subjecthood, denied only by alien aggression.

Rather than progress from abstractly conceived or juridically formulated rights to real and substantive rights, decolonization and the achievement of national sovereignty bundled the various moments that are typically understood as distinct, in gradualist accounts of European democratization (Marshall 1964). Economic, social, political—and we may add, religious, rights overlapped and were not necessarily perceived as distinct from each other, since they were acquired simultaneously (Chakrabarty 2005). Such an understanding was tacitly affirmed in the granting of universal franchise, recognizing the contribution of nonliterate masses in the achievement of national independence.

The nearly simultaneous development of communicative infrastructure and political modernity in countries like India ensures that the perceptual and the political, the affective and the rational-critical, are conjoint events with a shared genealogy, unlike their divergent histories in received accounts of the modern West. Thinking about "enlightenment" in a postcolonial context such as India shows the extent to which the problem of perception is always already a (political) question of subject formation.

In the work of advertisers we can observe some of the more sensitive attempts to introduce a modernizing pedagogy, compromised, however, by assumptions that the space of consumption was genuinely a space of self-actualization rather than acknowledging its parasitism upon the prevailing political dispensation.[8] Where overt state authority has ceded its place to the market, it is corruption that most reliably offers pedagogical instruction. And where the law itself is corrupt, it is money whose authority requires unveiling, through audio-visual technologies that claim to tell us everything. We are left with technological mediation itself, as a mode of disclosure that evokes desire, not reason, as the ground of knowledge, and thus with instruments understood elsewhere as vehicles of enlightenment but here regarded as means of mystification. Adapted to a long-standing distrust of the phenomenal world, such a view awaits enlightenment, but in the next world.

# PROLIFERATION
MEDIATION AND PRINT

# MEDIATING MEDIA PAST AND PRESENT

TOWARD A GENEALOGY OF "PRINT CULTURE" AND "ORAL TRADITION"

PAULA MCDOWELL

Origins of the "Oral-Literate Equation"

In a 1987 conference paper titled "The Oral-Literate Equation: A Formula for the Modern Mind," Eric A. Havelock looked back over his career and tried to pinpoint a moment when this formula first began to make sense to scholars. He mused, "[G]oing back twenty years, or even less, I do not think that the program of a colloquium of distinguished scholars from five countries would have carried the title 'Orality and Literacy.' To be sure, phrases like 'oral formula' and 'oral composition' in connection with Homer had come into currency at Harvard . . . after the Second World War. . . . because of the close connection of Milman Parry and Albert Lord with that university." But even then, "the application of these terms was still met with strong resistance from conservative scholars" (Havelock 1991, 11). In Milman Parry's published doctoral thesis, *L'Épithète traditionnelle dans Homère* (Paris, 1928), the "founding document of the modern Homeric oralist theory of composition," was gaining notice in the United States, and in 1951, "the oral-literate question (as it was later to become) received impetus from a very unexpected quarter when Harold Innis published *The Bias of Communication*." In 1958, Walter Ong published *Ramus: Method and the Decay of Dialogue*, "a preliminary exposure of a problem that was to bear directly upon the oral-literate equation but coming this time from the study and practice of rhetoric." Then, in 1962–1963, there appeared to be a "breakthrough":

> Within the space of less than twelve months there appeared four publications that, in retrospect, can be said to have made a joint announcement: that orality (or oralism) had to be put on the map.... These works were *The Gutenberg Galaxy* by McLuhan (1962), *Le pensée sauvage* by Lévi-Strauss (1962), an article by Jack Goody and Ian Watt entitled "The Consequences of Literacy" (1963), and finally *Preface to Plato* by myself (1963).... *Was this grouping as it occurred a pure accident or did it reflect a common and widespread response, even if an unconscious one, in France, England, the United States, and Canada, to a shared experience of a technological revolution in the means of human communication?* Radio, not to mention its immediate predecessor, the telephone, and its successor, television, was transforming the reach of the spoken, that is, of the oral, word. (Havelock 1991, 12–15, emphasis added)

In 1967, a few years after this "breakthrough," Ong himself remarked the way that a relatively sudden awareness of media shift in one generation seemed to trigger groundbreaking insights into parallel historical moments:

> Awareness of the succession of media stages and wonder about the meaning of this succession are themselves the product of the succession.... [O]nly as we have entered the electronic stage has man become aware of the profundity of differences, some of which have been before his eyes for thousands of years ... between the old oral culture and the culture initiated with writing and matured with alphabetic type.... As late as the 1930s ... the differences between speech and writing were still impossibly occluded for even the most astute scholars. (Ong 1967, 17–18)

In both Havelock's and Ong's accounts of the twentieth-century emergence of the concept of oralism and the heuristic of "orality and literacy," scholarly efforts to come to terms with the technological revolution of "electronic culture" led to a breakthrough in thinking about "orality" and "oral culture." Today, Havelock concludes, "the nouns *orality* and *oralism* are on a different footing, symbolizing conceptions that have extended far beyond Homer and the Greeks" (Havelock 1991, 11).[1]

## "Print Culture": Origins of the Term

The same years that Havelock and Ong retrospectively identified as witnessing a "breakthrough" in studies of "orality" and "oral culture," Marshall McLuhan employed the term "print culture" as one among many similar terms ("typographic era," "Gutenberg era," "mechanical era," "electric age," and so forth) in *The Gutenberg Galaxy: The Making of Typographic Man* (1962). Particularly striking is the way that McLuhan's use of "print culture" was a self-conscious extension of earlier work on orality by Parry and Lord. He begins *The Gutenberg Galaxy* with the statement:

> The present volume is in many respects complementary to *The Singer of Tales* by Albert B. Lord. Professor Lord has continued the work of Milman Parry, whose Homeric studies had led him to consider how oral and written poetry naturally followed diverse patterns and functions.

He states that he will extend this focus on difference, contrasting the "Gutenberg era" with oral, written, and electronic societies: "[T]he enterprise which Milman Parry undertook with reference to the contrasted *forms* of oral and written poetry is here extended to the *forms* of thought and the organization of experience in society and politics" (McLuhan 1962, 1, emphasis in the original). As the subtitle of his book, "The Making of Typographic Man," makes clear, McLuhan held that the introduction and spread of printing had profound implications not only for society but also for the human psyche. Five years later, in 1967, McLuhan's student, Ong, would employ the term "typographic culture" as part of an explicitly developed evolutionary model of media shift whose distinct phases include "oral culture," "scribal culture," "typographic culture," and the "electronic stage." Significantly, though, Ong's evolutionary model initially consisted of only three "stages": "in terms of communications media, cultures can be divided ... into three successive stages: (1) oral or oral-aural (2) script, which reaches critical breakthroughs with the invention first of the alphabet and then later of alphabetic moveable type, and (3) electronic" (Ong 1967, 17). Writing and print were modeled as one "stage." As late as 1971, Ong was still using the phrase "writing-and-print culture," suggesting that he did not yet see print as a distinct phase but rather as an outgrowth or extension of writing (Ong 2002, 91).

In 1979, Elizabeth L. Eisenstein's *The Printing Press as an Agent of Change: Communications and Cultural Transformations in Early-Modern Europe* launched the term "print culture" into common parlance. Today, thirty years later, it seems remarkable that Eisenstein's explanation of her use of this specific term in her eight-hundred-page work consists of a brief remark in the preface and two footnotes in the opening chapter. In the preface, she references McLuhan's work on "print culture," then states that her own subject is not the consequences of printing in general but "how printing altered *written communications within the Commonwealth of Learning*.... the term 'print culture' is used throughout this book in a special parochial Western sense: to refer to post-Gutenberg developments in the West" (Eisenstein 1979, xiv). In the two footnotes in the main body of the text, she references work by Havelock, Goody, Watt, and Ong on "the distinction between oral and literate cultures." But she emphasizes that her book focuses on another kind of difference: "despite passing reference to the work of McLuhan and Ong in Goody's introduction, the difference between scribal culture and print culture tends to be blurred by arguments which contrast alphabetic with ideographic writing and oral with written transmission but not script with print" (9, n. 16).[2] In a recent exchange with Adrian Johns, Eisenstein reiterates the original intellectual context of *The Printing Press as an Agent of Change*, again referencing the work of Walter Ong. Responding to a reviewer's charge that her use of "print culture" in *Printing Press* is "curiously metaphysical," she writes, "I had used the term quite specifically to contrast diverse procedures employed by scribes and manuscript dealers with those employed by printers—substituting 'scribal culture' and 'print culture' for the more recondite terms 'chirographic culture' and 'typographic culture,' used by Walter Ong" (Eisenstein 2002, 88).

Despite immediate and ongoing critique of Eisenstein's thesis, the term and concept of "print culture" are today evoked more than ever by book historians, literary scholars, and media theorists. In a review of *The Printing Press as an Agent of Change* that appeared almost as soon as the book was published, William Bouwsma acknowledged Eisenstein's work as a major contribution to early modern history yet accused her of taking "the printing press itself entirely out of history. For Eisenstein, print seems to be an independent force in human affairs, a cause but never a result of historical processes. She refuses to see it as a tool, brought into existence and exploited by forces outside itself" (Bouwsma 1979, 1,357). In his 1990 study of the "cultural meaning of printedness" in colonial America, Michael Warner similarly critiques what he labels the "Whig-McLuhanite model of print history"— especially the assumption that "technology has an ontological status prior to culture." In the work of McLuhan, Eisenstein, and others, he observes, "Print technology is seen as having a logic internal to itself, a logic which then exerts causative force in human affairs" (Warner 1990, xi, 5, 7, 5). Most recently, Adrian Johns has mounted a full-scale critique of Eisenstein's notion of print culture. In his view, Eisenstein's print culture "is characterized primarily in terms of certain traits that print is taken to endow on texts" (especially fixity). But at least until the nineteenth century, "Eisenstein's print culture does not exist." "Print culture" does not emerge directly from the press; instead, "the very identity of print itself has had to be *made*" (Johns 1998, 10, 19, 2).[3] Today, Eisenstein herself laments that the term print culture is "in danger of becoming a meaningless cliché." In particular, she warns, "'Eighteenth-Century Print Culture' is used as an umbrella title to cover miscellaneous topics" (Eisenstein 2002, 88, 88 n. 9). Nonetheless, despite three decades of critique and refinement of the term and concept of print culture, the proliferation of projects and institutions under the rubric of "print culture studies" seems if anything to have intensified. Witness, for instance, the title of a recent valuable collection of essays, *Agent of Change: Print Culture Studies after Elizabeth L. Eisenstein* (2007), in a series titled Studies in Print Culture and the History of the Book.[4]

## If Print Culture Had to Be Made, Who Made It? The Eighteenth Century as Turning Point

Print culture, then, did not just appear with the invention of printing. In Britain, there was a time lag of about three centuries between the introduction of printing technology and the crystallization of anything we can without major qualifications label a "print society." To make matters still more complicated, the phrase "print culture" is anachronistic for the eighteenth century. No eighteenth-century author employed this phrase (or the corollary "oral culture") for, as Raymond Williams and others have shown, the word "culture" was not used as a noun signifying "a particular way of life" until the nineteenth century: "Culture as an independent noun, an abstract process or the product of such a process, is not important before lC18 and is not common before mC19" (Williams 1985, 90, 88).[5] At the turn of the nineteenth century, "culture" took on new and important meanings, but until then, it typically meant "the 'tending of natural growth,' and then, by analogy, a process of human training" (Williams 1966, xiv). Many early eighteenth-century authors wrote extensively about the spread of print, and especially, what they took to be the alarming expansion of the press after the lapse of the Licensing Act in 1695. But authors such as Jonathan Swift and Alexander Pope represent the spread of print commerce as contributing to a decline of culture in the sense of cultivation. In the judgment of Martinus Scriblerus, Pope's fictional "learned commentator" on his mock-epic poem *The Dunciad*, "Providence ... permitted the invention of Printing as a *scourge* for the sins of the learned"—not as a superior vehicle of learning or tool for the advancement of judgment, morals, or taste (Pope 1999, 70, emphasis added). Nonetheless, while these authors do not employ the term "print culture," they do gesture—satirically—toward this concept.[6] Literary texts are a valuable—if notoriously tricky—register of contemporary awareness of media shift, and Pope, Swift, and other members of the satiric "Scriblerus Club" exhibit an intense awareness of dramatic contemporary changes happening around them having to do with printing. It is no accident that McLuhan held up *The Dunciad* as one of the "four massive myths of the Gutenberg transformation of society." "It is to *The Dunciad*," he pronounced, "that we must turn for the epic of the printed word.... For here is the explicit study of plunging of the human mind into the sludge of an unconscious engendered by the book" (McLuhan 1962, 147, 255).

The early eighteenth century was a decisive transitional period in the history of the British book trade. In 1695, the Printing or Licensing Act of 1662 was allowed to lapse for good, ending prepublication censorship and government and Stationers' Company restrictions on the number of presses, printers, and apprentices. The decades immediately following were a time of anarchic expansion: while the Printing Act had tried to limit the number of master printers in all of England to twenty-four, by 1705 there were between sixty-five and seventy printing houses in London alone (Treadwell 1980, 6).[7] Despite the efforts of the Stationers' Company to regain control of the trade—including a decade of failed attempts to renew the Licensing Act and so protect ancient guild privileges—an older, guild-based model of control was being displaced by a more openly competitive commercial model. This shift is often represented as the demise of a more "gentlemanly" culture of printing, but for the vocal printer-author Elinor James it signaled a decline in the "Art and Mistery" of an ancient craft authorized by the Crown. As James urged in one of her many broadside petitions to Parliament urging renewal of the Licensing Act, "Printing is not a Trade as other Trades are, but it is an Art and Mistery that ought... not to be made so common, as that it should be slighted and trampled under Foot."[8] For most of James's lifetime (c. 1645–1719), the London book trade was small and closely knit, but by the mid-eighteenth century, the print trade had penetrated into the provinces, and "by 1800, print issued from hundreds of presses operating in London and almost every small town in the country" (Raven 2001, 1). There is no question that printing deeply affected English life between 1450 and 1695, but in the eighteenth century, "printing began to affect the structure of social life at every level." Most important, for the eighteenth-century literary authors I will consider all too briefly next, print was "restructuring rather than merely modifying" the world of letters (Kernan 1987, 48, 9).

## Pope, Swift, and Print: *The Dunciad* and *A Tale of a Tub*

For twenty-five years after the lapse of the Licensing Act, Elinor James lamented the transformation of the ancient "Art and Mistery" of printing to a mere commercial "Trade." The early eighteenth century also saw the development of a powerful satiric construct of commercial print society. Authors such as Swift and Pope lived through a time of significant, *specific* economic and political reconfigurations of the press, and their perceptions of change are powerfully registered in texts such as *A Tale of a Tub* (partly drafted in 1696–1697; pub. 1704) and *The Dunciad* (1728–1743). While these texts are commonly read as indictments of "print culture," such readings overstate their case.[9] Neither Swift nor Pope was antiprint. Instead, what James McLaverty has observed of Pope might also be said of Swift: we need to acknowledge both "the Pope who loved print and the Pope who hated it" (McLaverty 2001, 1).[10] It was not print technology, the spread of printing, or print per se that was making these authors feel like an epochal shift had occurred. Rather, there was a sense that what we would call a "technology" was on the brink of being *used* in profoundly new ways. The distinctive self-consciousness of these authors about print and its users makes them (and the other "Scriblerians") powerful commentators on what we might call media shift. With the collapse of prepublication licensing and Stationers' Company control, there was in these authors' view "no public punishment left, but what a good Writer inflicts" (Pope 1999, 34). Printing and letters were being reduced to mere market-oriented trades without adequate moral, legal, and economic safeguards. One of Swift's key concerns in *A Tale of a Tub* is the religious and political threat of uncontrolled print: "[N]ew levies of wits, all appointed (as there is reason to fear) with pen, ink, and paper, which may at an hour's warning be drawn out into pamphlets and other offensive weapons" to attack church and state (Swift 1999, 18). Swift also satirizes modern methods for coping with the vast overproduction of knowledge—especially indexes, digests, and other tools for navigating and sorting printed books. In "A Digression in Praise of Digressions," he observes that the would-be wits "of this age have discovered a shorter and more prudent method to become *scholars* and *wits*, without the fatigue of *reading* or of *thinking*. . . . the profounder, and politer method, [is] to get a thorough insight into the *index*, by which the whole book is governed and turned, like *fishes* by the *tail*" (70).[11] In *The Dunciad*, Pope similarly satirizes "shameless, mercenary booksellers," ill-judging patrons, and the fickle, undiscerning public, but he emphasizes that Dulness affects all sectors of society. McLuhan was not unjustified in describing *The Dunciad* as a "myth . . . of the Gutenberg transformation of society," (McLuhan 1962, 147) for the way that the poem represents the reach and influence of print, especially in book 4, does come close to our modern sense of a culture as a "whole network of social relations" or "total way of life."

In later versions of Pope's poem, certain broad social changes seem to start happening almost as if by themselves. The spread of printing produces something unexpected—though not necessarily inherent in the technology. Print—or rather, new *uses* of print—are contributing to a total, hegemonic takeover of religious, political, educational, and other institutions. But it is not only human agency but also a *lack* of human action due to unawareness or indifference that is triggering these effects. For Pope, the willingness of literate gentlemen to allow themselves to be caught up in the fog of Dulness is at least as much of a problem as too many bad writers. In his reading of the *Dunciad*, Alvin Kernan ascribes to Pope the view of Marshall McLuhan that print ushers in dramatic cognitive, as well as social, shifts: "[T]he kind of mental confusion that McLuhan refers to was, in fact, Pope's central satiric subject" (Kernan 1989, 15). But Augustan poets, I suggest, are not working with abstract concepts like "print logic" or "typographic man." Pope would never have dreamed of separating the technology of printing from its users. (In fact, his satire was criticized for being too personal.) He used the word "print" chiefly as a verb, not a noun—to indicate a process, not a product.[12] It is not print per se but specific human uses of and responses to print that are the problem. Furthermore, while Pope does associate the spread of print with massive (and possibly even cognitive) shifts, it is not a direct causal relationship, nor is it an inevitable one. Pope was not a technological determinist. *The Dunciad* is at once a topical poem *and* a prophecy of a future that need not necessarily happen. It is up to humane intellectuals to scrutinize and shape the directions of a communications technology; to make what Paul Starr calls "constitutive choices" (Starr 2004, 1–7 and passim).

## The Spread of Print Commerce Triggers Heightened Reflection on Oral Communication

In the twentieth century, attempts by Parry, Lord, Ong and others to understand oral poetry and "oral culture" led to the coining of the term "print culture." In the eighteenth century, by way of contrast, attempts to theorize the implications of print triggered a distinctly new degree of self-conscious reflection on oral communication and its actual and potential threatening intersections with an unrestrained press. Augustan authors made sense of what seemed to them the new world of print commerce by linking it to familiar "vulgar" or popular oral practices. In *The Dunciad*, Pope states as the subject of his poem in brief the movement of the "Smithfield Muses" to the "ear of Kings" (Pope 1999, 97, 1: 2). Pope's great "epic of the printed word" (McLuhan 1962, 255) is filled with ears, mouths, and tongues—dangerous bodily organs of sense. In book 2, Queen Dulness commands the dunces to learn "the wond'rous pow'r of Noise." The mock heroic games held to celebrate the new King of Dulness include a noise-making contest wherein a "thousand tongues are heard in one loud din" (2: 221–268). Similarly, in *A Tale of a Tub*, Swift constructs his satire in opposition not only to the degradations of the literary marketplace (and the threat of uncontrolled print) but also particular oral practices. Throughout the eighteenth century, for instance, dissenting preachers' oral appeal to the masses was an enormous concern. Anglican authors expressed alarm that the populace was being seduced by "enthusiasts"—especially Quakers and Methodists—more cunning in the use of intonation and gesture in public speaking. As a freshly ordained clergyman, Swift knew that at this time of widespread illiteracy, tongues and ears were the chief organs of mass manipulation. In his satire of "corruptions in Religion and Learning," he foregrounds tongues and ears, as much as books and pamphlets, as powerful organs of sedition and dissent (Swift 1999, 2). Indeed, he depicts so broad a range of human vocal activities—from belching to humming to preaching to droning—that for once the impossibly broad category of "orality" seems to fit, as these practices can't easily be subsumed under any narrower label such as "speech." Swift's satire reminds us that oral communication is more than a verbal (or even vocal) phenomenon. In his satire of "the learned Aeolists," who "maintain the original cause of all things to be *wind*," he depicts a dissenting preacher swollen with inspiration:

> In this posture he disembogues whole tempests upon his auditory, as the spirit from beneath gives him utterance, which issuing *ex adytis* and *penetralibus*, is not performed without much pain and gripings. And the wind in breaking forth deals with his face as it does with that of the sea, first *blackening*, then *wrinkling*, and at last *bursting it into a foam*. (Swift 1999, 75, emphasis in original)

Similarly, in *The Dunciad*, Pope satirizes both dissenting preachers and Grub Street authors as braying assess. In the aforementioned noise-making contest, he compares the competitors ("Authors, Stationers") to "long-ear'd" asses, then compares the asses' music to the "Sound" made by the "lab'ring lungs" of "Enthusiast" preachers—most notably Methodist leader George Whitefield, who was known for his field preaching to enormous crowds

(2: 31; 247–258). Augustan authors do not satirize "print culture" and "orality." Nevertheless, in works such as *The Dunciad* and *A Tale of a Tub*, Pope and Swift reflect on and register threatening oral practices as part of their extended meditation upon the problems and possibilities of print.

## The Theological Notion of Oral Tradition

In *A Tale of a Tub* Swift satirizes not only "low" oral practices but also the high theological notion of oral tradition. In his allegory of the three brothers, pointedly named Peter, Martin, and Jack, he vehemently rejects the idea of reliable oral tradition as a dangerous Papist hoax. The 1680s saw the intensification of longstanding debates between Protestants and Catholics concerning Scripture versus tradition as a rule of faith. For Anglican authors faced with the prospect of a Catholic king, this was a question of urgent national political importance, "a major war in the history of ideas, in which big guns on both sides were employed" (Walsh 1990, 291). The official position of the Catholic church was that truth was to be found in *both* Scripture and unwritten tradition, but in the tense political context of the 1680s (and the heated environment of polemical debate generally) Catholic polemicists such as English priest John Gother intensified their arguments for the stability and reliability of oral tradition as preserved in the Church versus the uncertainty of textual transmission and interpretation. As one anonymous polemicist remarked in 1685, "of late . . . *Oral Tradition* has quite carried away *the Credit*" (anon. 1685, A4r).

Throughout the eighteenth century, Anglicans remained deeply suspicious of the proposition that any unwritten tradition preserved by the Church might be considered of equal authority to the Bible. Swift depicts the father of Peter, Martin, and Jack handing his sons his *written* will, providing each brother with an immortal coat (implicitly, the doctrine of Christianity). The will contains "full Instructions" concerning the care of these coats, and the sons observe these instructions, until one day they realize that their coats are out of style: "[T]hey went immediately to consult their father's Will, read it over and over, but not a word of the *shoulder-knot*" (a fashion trend they wish to follow). "What should they do?" (Swift 1999, 38). When they can't find passages authorizing shoulder-knots, brother Peter sets his siblings to searching the will for constituent letters (a, b, c, and so on!) that can be reshuffled into passages authorizing any new fashion he wishes to implement. At this point in the text, a footnote by Anglican William Wotton scoffs, "When the Papists cannot find anything which they want in Scripture they go to *Oral Tradition*" (Swift 1999, 39 n.). Later, another footnote (this time likely by Swift himself) also scorns the Catholic doctrine of oral tradition: "By this is meant *tradition*, allowed to have equal authority with the scripture, or rather greater" (Swift 1999, 40 n.). Later in life, Swift would revisit the question of oral tradition in *Gulliver's Travels* (1726). Book 4 depicts a society of virtuous horses, the Houhynhnms, who pass down valuable customs, learning, and letters via tradition because they have no books. But Swift never seriously entertained the possibility that any complex, valuable body of knowledge could be passed down entirely without writing, and in this way he was typical of his era. His purpose in *Gulliver's Travels* is "satiric rather than ethnographic" (Hudson 1996b, 165)[13] (these are horses, after all!) and crucially, the Houhynhnms are not Christians—and so could never be mistaken for Catholics.

### The Crystallization of an Ethnographic Concept of Oral Tradition

Throughout the eighteenth century, the dominant understanding of "oral tradition" remained theological. Around 1730, however, one increasingly sees this phrase used in an ethnographic context. In 1724, two years before *Gulliver's Travels*, Jesuit missionary Joseph François Lafitau's *Moeurs des sauvages amériquains* advanced the enlightened idea that "savages" without writing might nonetheless have a highly developed system of laws, customs, and arts preserved through oral tradition. Lafitau lived among the Iroquois near Montreal from 1712 to 1717, and his modern editors credit him with having founded comparative ethnology.[14] While he never advanced a systematic argument for "oral tradition," his grounding in Catholic theological notions of tradition may have helped him to move beyond the widespread assumption of European intellectuals that cultures without writing were lawless and barbaric. In the 1730s, classical scholars began cautiously advancing arguments for the possibility of sophisticated oral societies. The eighteenth century would see a major reevaluation of Homeric poetry: a shift from a neoclassical approach, emphasizing what was universal and timeless, to a new interest in the specific historical circumstances affecting the production of works of art. Increasingly, there was a sense that Homer's poetry belonged to a particular period of social development and that its most puzzling characteristics (such as the repetition of epithets) might be explained if the poetry was understood in its original social, political, and geographical contexts. Primitivists were developing the idea of the relativity of human societies, and in 1735, Edinburgh scholar Thomas Blackwell's *Enquiry into the Life and Writings of Homer* linked Homer's art to his "rude society" and its particular stage of development with respect to manners, language, and political and social organization. Blackwell never suggested that Homer could not read or write (this would have been a shocking proposition), but he argued that Homer owed the vigorousness of his language to his "primitive" environment. In 1769, the traveler and antiquarian Robert Wood in his *Essay on the Original Genius and Writings of Homer* (1775) explicitly suggested that Homer could not read or write.[15] His proposal was greeted with scorn by many contemporaries, but it was taken seriously by the German classicist F. A. Wolf, whose own *Prolegomena ad Homerum* (1795) would greatly influence Homeric scholarship. Eighteenth-century debates concerning Homer and oral tradition were foundational to modern oral-formulaic theory and to Milman Parry's discovery of the workings of oral-formulaic epithets in Yugoslavian epic poetry. In eighteenth-century Britain, few scholars valorized Homer's "rude and unlettered state of society" to the extent that Jean-Jacques Rousseau did in his unpublished *Essay on the Origin of Languages*, (c. 1762–1763). As Rousseau famously declared, "other poets had written; Homer alone had sung. And people have always listened in rapture to these songs, even when Europe has been overrun by barbarians who try to judge what they are incapable of experiencing" (Rousseau 1966, 24).[16] Nonetheless, classical scholars and other learned gentlemen increasingly exercised nostalgia for "rude societies" before the invention of letters. They especially lamented the decline of what Edinburgh moral philosopher Dugald Stewart would later call "the culture of memory."[17] As Wood mused, "in a rude and unlettered state of society the memory is loaded with nothing that is either useless or unintelligible; whereas modern education employs us chiefly in getting by heart, while we are young, what we forget before we are old" (Wood 1775, 260).

After about 1760, the number of British (especially Scottish) texts advancing arguments for sophisticated oral societies rose dramatically. That year, Highlander James Macpherson began publishing his phenomenally popular Ossianic poetry, claiming to have translated fragments of ancient oral poetry passed down from a third-century Highland bard chiefly by word of mouth. Macpherson was a student at Aberdeen College where Thomas Blackwell was principal; he also came under the influence of rhetorician Hugh Blair, who suggested that preliterate cultures were fertile ground for the growth of impassioned, "epic" language. Macpherson's scandalous claims for a sophisticated bardic tradition of oral poetry were notoriously debated even among his fellow Scots, but they also triggered extensive scholarly research into Celtic cultures, and the Ossian phenomenon raised the question of sophisticated oral societies to the level of a "popular" debate. By the end of the eighteenth century, we see an epochal shift in attitudes toward "oral tradition," and the crystallization of the modern secularized version of this concept.

## "Rescuing" the Oral, 1: The Elocution Movement

In their own era of print and perceived rising literacy, eighteenth-century poets, rhetoricians, antiquarians, and others began to rethink and valorize the legacy and power of the human voice (sometimes even "vulgar" voices) in new ways and to model themselves as heroic "rescuers" of valuable oral traditions they depicted as on the brink of being lost. The 1730s onward also saw the flowering of the elocution movement, as a wide variety of entrepreneurs sought to restore ancient eloquence for distinctly modern purposes. Elocutionists such as John "Orator" Henley (d. 1756) or the Irish actor-turned-elocutionist Thomas Sheridan (the father of playwright and renowned parliamentary orator Richard Brinsley Sheridan) made a new commercial opportunity out of what used to be one branch of classical rhetoric. Between 1726 and 1756, Henley operated an oratory above a meat market in the heart of working London where he lectured on elocution to socially diverse audiences. Later in the century, Sheridan lectured at a more polite level to audiences in major urban centers throughout England, Ireland, and Scotland. In their oral/physical performances, Henley, Sheridan, and other elocutionists at once touted and embodied those elements of spoken communication that cannot be fully reproduced in written language (tone, pitch, cadence, and especially, gesture). Sheridan argued that the propagation of writing, print, and even literacy had undermined public speaking skills. In his *Lectures on Elocution* (1762), he proposed that "some of our greatest men have been trying to do that with the pen, which can only be performed by the tongue" (Sheridan 1968, xii). Echoing Sheridan, Hugh Blair held that "though Writing may answer the purposes of mere instruction, yet all the great and high efforts of eloquence must be made, by means of spoken, not of written, Language" (Blair 2005, 74). The eighteenth century saw a renewed fascination with the human body as a powerful (and potentially universal) communications medium: a neglected tool that might beneficially be exploited in a variety of arenas. Elocutionists especially lamented the "decline of pulpit oratory": the cold restraint of Anglican preachers, and accordingly, the missed opportunities to engage the populace through an impassioned, physical style of preaching. At the same time, though, later eighteenth-century elocutionists such as Sheridan worked hard to distinguish their own genteel oral endeavors from the practices of groups such as the Quakers or the Methodists who were already making powerful use of the same insights. The elocutionists' arguments for the superior expressive power of oral communication might appear to challenge widespread European assumptions about the superiority of writing, but reread in the context of their own media moment, it becomes clear that Sheridan and his contemporaries, like Pope and Swift earlier in the century, were theorizing oral communication chiefly as a means of grappling with the changing institutional contexts of *print*. "The cheapness of books," Sheridan observed in 1762 with considerable ambivalence, "has made the art of . . . reading familiar to the lowest people" (Sheridan 1968, 247). Eloquence was a new tool of distinction in an increasingly literate age.

## "Rescuing" the Oral, 2: The Polite Ballad Revival and Ballad Scholarship

The eighteenth century also saw the emergence of a substantial print discourse about ballads. In commentaries in periodicals, in prefaces to collections of ballads, in essays printed in these collections, and elsewhere, a wide variety of authors commented positively and negatively upon balladry as a hybrid oral and textual practice. In Britain, ballads were closely linked to commercial printing; they were also commonly represented as associated with the "lower sort." But over the course of the century, the polite ballad revival and especially the rise of ballad scholarship would forge significantly new ways of conceptualizing ballads. In compiling his phenomenally successful anthology *Reliques of Ancient English Poetry* (1765), clergyman Thomas Percy collected his ballads from print and manuscript sources (including broadsides). But in his ambitious "Essay on the Ancient Minstrels in England," appended to the *Reliques*, he represented the "Old Heroic Ballads" in his collection as the "select remains of our ancient English bards and minstrels": "oral itinerant poet[s]" who "probably never committed [their rhymes] to writing." The descendents of these noble old bards, he speculated, were tragically displaced by "an inferior sort" of "ballad-*writers* . . . for the press" (Percy 1966, preface 1: 7; appendix 1: 348, 380). By the 1780s, one detects the crystallization of a new *confrontational* model of balladry, whereby an earlier, more "authentic" tradition of "minstrel song" is seen as having been displaced by commercial print.[18] In 1781, twenty-three-year-old John Pinkerton left his native Edinburgh for London to publish his own collection, *Scottish Tragic Ballads*. Energized by his readings of Percy and Macpherson and indebted to Blair's argument for the virtues of "oral tradition" in his "Critical Dissertation Upon the Poems of Ossian" (1763), Pinkerton prefaced his collection with a "Dissertation on the Oral Tradition of Poetry" in which he aspired to give an "account of the utility of the Oral Tradition of Poetry, in that barbarous state of society which *necessarily* precedes the invention of letters" (Pinkerton 1781, ix–xxvii, x, emphasis added). Whereas Percy had only gestured toward an evolutionary model of media shift (the idea of a shift "from" oral "to" literate society), Pinkerton explicitly modeled an inevitable development whereby one stage "necessarily" follows on (and displaces) another. The eighteenth century saw the origins of modern evolutionary models of media shift. In Pinkerton's "Dissertation," this model could not be more starkly confrontational: "In proportion as Literature advanced in the world Oral Tradition disappeared" (xv).

Percy's idealizd narrative of "oral itinerant poet[s]" contributed to later ballad editors' conviction that certain *living* practices of ballad singing were surviving traces of feudal oral traditions. Glasgow editor William Motherwell opened his own collection *Minstrelsy, Ancient and Modern* with a bold claim: "This interesting body of popular poetry, part of which, in point of antiquity, may be fairly esteemed equal, if not superior, to the most ancient of our written monuments, has owed its preservation principally to oral tradition" (Motherwell 1846, 1: 3). By comparing early eighteenth-century discussions of balladry—such as Joseph Addison's in the *Spectator*,[19] where ballads are assumed to be at once oral *and* printed—to later eighteenth- and nineteenth-century scholarly (re)constructions of "authentic" ballads, we see the eighteenth-century emergence of confrontational models of print and oral tradition. Over the course of the century, I suggest, heightened reflection on the spread of *print* contributed to a new conceptualizing of valuable ballad traditions as innately *oral*. Eighteenth-century ballad scholars forged a sharp *conceptual* (not actual) separation between "oral" and "printed" ballads. In so doing, they contributed to the later binary of "orality and literacy" that many ballad scholars are still working to undo today.[20]

At the same time, though, one cannot emphasize strongly enough that this was a highly *selected* form of "oral tradition" that was being revalued by later eighteenth- and nineteenth-century scholars. In a larger book project, I am interested in the polite "rediscovery" of oral tradition *in relation to contemporary oral practices*—especially, those "vulgar" or popular oral practices that learned gentlemen routinely condemned (for instance, lay preaching, "Billingsgate rhetoric," urban political activism, or "old wives' tales," to name only a few). In order to exercise their nostalgia for an era before print commerce, ballad collectors such as Percy had to associate "valuable" ballads with a distant past and an oral tradition that was imagined as separable from print commerce. These scholars strategically avoid any consideration of contemporary broadside ballad singing (especially topical, political, or bawdy ballads), for this still-vibrant aspect of what we might now call "popular oral culture," tainted by the marketplace and associated with social and political unrest, was not the legacy that genteel or professional scholars wished to preserve.

## Origins of Evolutionary Models of Media Shift: Conjecturing Oral Societies

In her account of "the printing press as an agent of change," Eisenstein links the spread of printing and the development of "a new and distinctly modern historical consciousness" (Eisenstein 1979, 184). With the introduction of printing, she suggests, "less effort was required to preserve and pass on what was known.... Successive generations began to pride themselves on knowing more than had their forebears.... Human history itself acquired the character of an indefinitely extended unfolding sequence" (Eisenstein 1986, 6). In the late eighteenth century, we begin to see the idea of communications technologies as part of an inevitable, unfolding sequence of human history. In sketching out developmental models of mankind, later eighteenth-century Scottish moral philosophers, especially those whom Dugald Stewart would later label conjectural historians, gestured toward modern evolutionary models of media shift. In their efforts to trace the origins of commercial society, authors such as Adam Smith in his *Lectures on Rhetoric and Belles Lettres*, Adam Ferguson in his *Essay on the History of Civil Society*, William Robertson in *A View of the Progress of Society* and *History of the Discovery and Settlement of America*, and Henry Home, Lord Kames in his *Sketches of the History of Man* confronted and coped with a paucity of records for the earliest stages of mankind. Accordingly, they worked backward from what was known, employing assumptions about Providence and human nature and developing a series of working abstractions such as "society," "the economy," and "progress."[21] Scottish intellectuals saw their nation being rapidly transformed, and they contrasted the modern commercial towns of Glasgow and Edinburgh with what seemed to be the contemporaneous survival of older forms of social organization in the Highlands.[22] Seeking to account for these differences and organize them into an explanatory framework that could be used as a tool for further investigation, they developed a new model of history, the "four-stages" theory. Stadial theory held that society naturally progressed over time through a series of phases, each corresponding to a different mode of subsistence (hunter-gatherer, pasturage, agriculture, and commerce) and each with its own characteristic institutions, economy, manners, and social arrangements. These phases were linked not only to different forms of economic organization and social and artistic development[23] but also, in some instances, to developments in the history of communications (such as the invention of letters, alphabetic writing, and especially, printing). At such moments, we come close to the idea that individual societies move inexorably forward through a succession of communications stages beginning with the development of speech. Ronald L. Meek suggests that we should see four-stages theory as "the first great theoretical embodiment" of "the notion of techno-economic determinism, and the principal of cultural evolutionism" (Meek 1976, 242).[24] While this succession of communications "stages" was most often viewed as "progress," one also sees elite nostalgia for the supposed benefits of "rude societies" without complex communications technologies. In *The Origin and Progress of Language* (6 vols., 1773-1792), James Burnett, Lord Monboddo questioned whether the invention of writing had on the whole contributed to the advancement of human knowledge (Monboddo 1773-1792, 2: 24-25). Ironically, highly literate authors such as Monboddo deployed the posited virtues of an unlettered, distant "past" to critique their own "inauthentic" historical moment of writing and print.

Across the English Channel, the fugitive Marquis de Condorcet was hurriedly drafting his *Sketch for a Historical Picture of the Progress of the Human Mind* (pub. posthumously in 1795). Like British conjectural historians, Condorcet aspired to trace the development of the human mind "as it manifests itself... from generation to generation.... Such a picture is historical, since it... is based on the observation of human societies throughout the different stages of their development" (Condorcet 1955b, 4). He divided up history into ten ages rather than four, but he too modeled the history of mankind as a continuous chain: "All peoples whose history is recorded fall somewhere between our present degree of civilization and that which we still see amongst savage tribes.... so welding an uninterrupted chain between the beginning of historical time and the century in which we live" (8). He also systematically linked various stages of human social development to developments in the technology of communications. In a move that surely anticipates what Ruth Finnegan and others have critiqued as the "Great Divide" model of orality and literacy, he represents the "before" and "after" of alphabetic writing as "two great eras of the human race" (9). With the development of the alphabet, he enthused, "all that was necessary was to know how to recognize and reproduce these very few signs, and this final step assured the progress of the human race forever" (7). But Condorcet's most triumphant stage is the period "from the invention of printing to the time when philosophy and the sciences shook off the yoke of authority" (99). For him, as for Luther, the invention of printing was an epochal event, inaugurating a new age of human history that would end priestly oppression. Condorcet self-consciously worked backward from his own historical moment, noting that he had to "conjecture the stages" due to the "scarcity of records" (8, 171). Meanwhile, Dugald Stewart was also explicitly measuring human progress in terms of various communications developments (especially the spread of printing): "[T]he means of communication afforded by the press, have, in the course of two centuries, accelerated the progress of the human mind, far beyond what the most sanguine hopes of our predecessors could have imagined."[25] Mary Poovey has suggested that one effect of the conjectural historians' "efforts to generate systematic knowledge was the production of a set of abstractions, which rapidly became the objects of these sciences" (Poovey 1998, 15). Was one such abstraction "oral society," eventually leading to the coinage of an even more influential abstraction, "oral culture"? Stewart came close to conjecturing an oral "stage" of society in terms anticipating our modern concept of oral culture when, in an ambiguous usage in which "culture" could be read either as a verb or a noun, he writes of the "culture of memory" and "the principles on which the culture of memory depends."[26]

The eighteenth century saw the emergence of a sustained discourse questioning the effects of different media forms. The dramatic proliferation of print and the specter of future mass literacy generated widespread consideration of the nature and implications of media shift. In this essay I have contributed toward a genealogy of the ideas of "print culture" and "oral tradition." I have sketched the eighteenth-century emergence of an originally negative, but increasingly positive idea of oral tradition and suggested that literate groups' ideas about oral forms and practices developed in an especially close dialectical relationship with ideas about *print* (especially print commerce). Today, a valuable and growing body of work on "oral culture" in early modern Britain by scholars such as Keith Thomas, Daniel Woolf, Adam Fox, and Alexandra Walsham routinely stresses that "literacy" did not displace "orality." Rather—in the terms of this scholarship—"literacy and orality coexisted . . . in a mutually enriching equilibrium" (Walsham 2002, 173). But where, we must ask, did this model of a division into "literacy and orality" come from in the first place? It is to the mid- and later eighteenth century, I have suggested, that we can trace the development of an "antagonistic" model of oral and literate communication, and the related development of "evolutionary" models of media shift (the idea that one media "stage" succeeds and/or displaces another).[27] "Orality," "print culture," and so on are not so much *things* as abstract concepts with interwoven histories. They are aspects of a heuristic that we employ, rather as our eighteenth-century predecessors did, in an attempt to organize and understand complex phenomena.

# MEDIATING ANTIQUARIANS IN BRITAIN, 1760–1830

THE INVENTION OF ORAL TRADITION; OR,
CLOSE READING BEFORE COLERIDGE

MAUREEN N. MCLANE

1. Preliminaries and Goads: Ballad Inquiries, "Culture,"
"Media," "Enlightenment"

"The modern study of culture begins with the study of ballads." Tom Cheesman and Sigrid Rieuwerts thus launch their preface to *Ballads into Books: The Legacies of Francis James Child* (1997).

In a footnote they remark: "The ballad has always been in and out of whatever media are in existence" (5, 16).

These two statements suggest how ballads and balladeering might be located at the conjunction of "culture" and "media." Eighteenth-century antiquarian balladeering toggles between the concept of culture and the historicity of media, between orders of knowledge and piles of data. Mediating between practice and theory, sifting through manuscripts, private letters, broadsides, books, and eventually oral recitations, English and Scottish balladeers (working circa 1760–1830) conjoined concepts and histories, emergent objects and modes of inquiry. Throughout this essay I invoke "balladeering" to suggest a loosely connected but strongly hierarchized network, encompassing everything from the singing, making, inventing, forging, collecting, transcribing, sifting, and editing to the printing of ballads.[1] I focus here on a narrow precinct of balladeering: the antiquarian traffic in ballads in the late eighteenth century, and their transmediation and codification in printed books. And here I largely restrict myself, as did eighteenth-century British balladeers, to a British domain: the full flowering of comparative balladeering had to wait for the nineteenth-century development of comparative philology and folklore studies.

Katie Trumpener suggests that the ballad collection be considered an "emergent genre" in the eighteenth century alongside (for example) the national tale (Trumpener 1997, xi). One distinguishing feature of this genre is its overwhelming investment in testimonial apparatus. That Cheesman's and Rieuwert's remarks above about ballads, culture, and media occur in a preface and a footnote within the preface is not incidental: prefaces, footnotes, appendices, dissertations (long, exploratory, quasi-historical essays), and in particular, headnotes were the textual locations of choice for eighteenth-century antiquarians devoted to balladeering inquiries. In eighteenth-century ballad collections and indeed in ballad books since, these apparently marginal spaces are central: they are where the arguments get made (or obscured), where literary histories are forged (in both senses), where antagonists are skewered or politely dismissed, friendly correspondents saluted, documents displayed.

In *Always Already New* (2006), Lisa Gitelman asks us to explore "media as historical subjects" in their full historical and historicizable complexity. Balladeering is one such subject, both for us and for the antiquarians themselves, who began a methodological inquiry into the condition and historicity of mediality.[2] One genealogy for a historical media analysis of poetry and culture lies in the eighteenth-century British ballad revival, its attendant "scandals of the ballad"—the proliferating forgeries and frauds and their exposures (here I invoke Stewart 1994, 102–131)—and related ethnopoetic phenomena such as the Ossian poems (those "fragments" and "epics" published by James Macpherson in the 1760s, purportedly the translations of the poetic corpus of a third-century Scottish Gaelic bard).[3] These episodes belong not just to literary history, folklore studies, or cultural studies but also to a historically alert media studies, for it was through these ethnopoetical controversies that British literati began to theorize—precisely through their antagonisms—the status of oral tradition alongside and against other modes of poetic mediation (e.g., multiple, simultaneous, and sometimes overlapping oral, scribal, and print modalities). Many eighteenth-century literary-cultural disputes with a decidedly culturally nationalistic turn—the Ossian controversy most famously—must be understood also as *media* controversies: arguments about mediums and mediation. Antiquarian balladeers collectively and polemically undertook a project of remediation; they also began to theorize that project. What we find in this period is not so much the "invention of tradition" (Hobsbawm and Ranger 1984) as the invention of traditional mediation.

Taking antiquarian balladeering seriously also sheds light on the conditions of producing (and obscuring) knowledge within and about what we now call the humanities. In recent years scholars have reanimated the ballad revival and the literary-historical stakes of cultural nationalism in this period, and more scholars are recognizing that a broader frame is required to consider literary production, vernacular literatures, and oral traditions together. What has been too little noted (with some striking recent exceptions) is the way these controversies consistently forced a definition of the objects in view. In other words: what was (or is) a ballad?[4] And what was (or is) "oral tradition"?[5] Despite the remarkable proliferation of ballad collections in the eighteenth century, it was by no means obvious what a ballad was. And then too, polite editors strove to excise or ignore large swaths of a vital, ongoing ballad tradition—not least street ballads, those broadsides topical and political and sometimes bawdy. The "hybrid textual and oral" status of ballads (to invoke McDowell 2006, 158) offers us a striking test case for considering both the historicity and the ideologics of representing media.

Late eighteenth-century British balladeering thus sits at a crucial juncture of media and Enlightenment: its primary figures were literary antiquarians, a species of scholar typically contrasted with Enlightenment thinkers (viz. Arnold Momigliano's seminal work,[6] and satires within the period). Yet a complex dialectic emerges between eighteenth-century "antiquarianism" and "enlightenment," as Susan Manning's and Mark Salber Phillips's work differently but pointedly suggests. Scottish Enlightenment historiography famously elaborated a "stadial theory" of history, a model summarized by Adam Smith thus: "The four stages of society are hunting, pasturage, farming, and commerce" (Smith 1997, 1: 31).[7] Despite the reputed incompatibility of antiquarian and Enlightenment research, versions of Enlightenment "stadial theory" often provided the framework for antiquarian research and musing; the proliferation of detail for which antiquarians were famous loosely coexisted with and often within these broader sociological paradigms of progressive development. And Scottish Enlightenment thinkers (Adam Smith, William Robertson, David Hume) were themselves omnivorous cultural data gatherers interested in ranging through, comparing, and systematizing all kinds of evidence, including poems, customs, linguistic data, legends, and law. The cultural rummaging so characteristic of antiquarian collecting provided Enlightenment thinkers much grist for their conceptual mills. Antiquarians must be regarded, then, as important contributors to what Hume called the "Science of Man."

Noting that ballads "may be objects of interest to the curious antiquary, and the philosophical inquirer, into the history of men and manners," the Scottish antiquarian and linguist Robert Jamieson pointed his readers in 1806 beyond antiquarian eclecticism to the historiographic discourse most prominent in Scottish intellectual circles, that of philosophical history.[8] Stadial historical periodization and plotting influenced the organization of ballad materials and profoundly informed the historical and critical dissertations and notes of many collections—from John Pinkerton's musings in 1781 on poetry as "the original language of men in the infant state of society in all countries" (Pinkerton 1781, ix–x), to Joseph Ritson's discussion of the shepherd state of society and his analogy to "the savage tribes of America" when discussing the origin and progress of "national song" (Ritson 1783, iv, ii–iii), to Walter Scott's and Robert Jamieson's description of ballads as possessing "considerable interest for the moral philosopher and general historian" (Scott 1830, 6).

Balladeering retains such "considerable interest" (viz. Scott) for a wide range of scholars (not to mention singers), though we might label ourselves otherwise—as (for example) literary historians, cultural historians, folklore scholars, ethnomusicologists, or media theorists. It is precisely because ballads are "objects of interest" (viz. Jamieson) for several disciplines that they continue to resound in contemporary scholarship; or perhaps it is more precise to say that the trans- and intermedial status of ballads liberates them from exclusively literary, or exclusively historical, or exclusively musical, or exclusively folkloric, study. In its preoccupation with mediality and its navigation of both Enlightenment historiography and antiquarian eclecticism, balladeering asks us to complicate our standard accounts of "enlightenment" and "media." I would also argue that antiquarian balladeering asks us to take another look at "close reading," for it was precisely through an agonistic, forensic close reading that antiquarians made their cases, established their authority, and bequeathed to later scholars the literary-historical paradigms, objects, and anthologies within and against which we still move.

## 2. Ballad Traffic, Ballad Books, Ballad Objects, and Citation Codes

A few basics: Major texts and personages in the ballad revival, and more broadly in the British vernacular revival, include: James Macpherson's Ossian poems (published 1760–1765, translated throughout Europe, with Edinburgh literatus Hugh Blair a major supporter and theorist); Thomas Percy's *Reliques of Ancient English Poetry* (1765), itself spurred by, and reacting to, Macpherson's Scottish vernacular sensation; Joseph Ritson's several works on English and Scottish song and balladry in the 1780s–90s; John Pinkerton's works on Scottish national song; Walter Scott's *Minstrelsy of the Scottish Border* (1802–1803, with new editions up through 1833); Robert Burns's contributions of over two hundred songs to James Johnson's song compendium, *The Scots Musical Museum* (1787–1803); and Robert Jamieson's *Popular Ballads and Songs, from Tradition, Manuscripts, and Scarce Editions* (1806). Other important early nineteenth-century figures include James Hogg and William Motherwell. Though not all were antiquarians, all engaged antiquarian balladeering.

Such a partial list only begins to give a sense of the terrain; but as the full title of Jamieson's work suggests, antiquarians by the early nineteenth century were announcing their complex processing of sources in and from several media (e.g., Jamieson's collocation of "tradition"—which in this context always meant "oral tradition"—with manuscripts, and "scarce editions" of books). Throughout the eighteenth century, antiquarians and poet-editors found themselves struggling to define ballads and to establish a balladeering provenance, typically inflected by various national, political, and aesthetic allegiances; these literati also struggled to surmount their own anti-oral prejudices (often aligned with anti-Scottish prejudice). Late eighteenth-century and early nineteenth-century ballad collections were very peculiar composite objects, coordinating everything from broadsides to manuscripts to oral recitations to other ballad books, such that their editors increasingly felt the need to theorize these heterogeneous materials and their medial condition. The whole problem of representing something like a ballad in print, moreover—its tune as well as its words, its variants, its ellipses—is one that eighteenth-century editors identified and grappled with in revealing ways. Equally telling, the late eighteenth-century problem of representing ballad informants—indeed, whether to represent them at all—forecasts the kinds of debates scholars like Johannes Fabian, Edward Said, James Clifford, and others have animated regarding twentieth-century ethnography and more broadly the representation of "others."

Antiquarians not only debated editing methods and the comparative value of sources; they displayed these debates in their appendices, prefaces, dissertations, headnotes, and footnotes. The proliferation of this authenticating, explanatory discourse was symptomatic of a crisis in the handling of source materials and more broadly of the problematic of authenticity created by the eighteenth-century ballad revival.[9] However labored, rebarbative, or *recherché* such apparatus may now seem (and in fact often seemed to the balladeers' contemporaries), this discourse was not extraneous to but rather constitutive of the ballad collection. The consolidation of this genre involved the collaborative (yet often competitive) work of numerous collectors, transcribers, annotators, correspondents, editors, printers, and publishers; it also required, at the level of representation, the formalization of various rhetorical and discursive protocols.

Antiquarian balladeers addressed the methodological problem of handling, hierarchizing, and authorizing medially disparate sources by developing a complex system of citation, a system which was for balladeers—as it is today in academic monographs and legal briefs—a kind of technology for authentication as well as remembrance. And this returns us to a phrase in my title—for the grammatical undecidability of "mediating antiquarians" points to their double function: antiquarians were both the subjects and objects of mediation, both "mediating" and "mediated." They processed source materials in many media yet were themselves processed, as their own publications—and their correspondence (typically called "communications" or "transmissions")—entered the annotative apparatus of ballad books. From Percy's 1765 *Reliques* onward, we find that—alongside notices of manuscripts, garlands, and previously published books—traces of antiquarian correspondence entered the ballad collection: for example, when Percy observes in his headnote to "Edom O'Gordon, a Scottish ballad," "We are indebted for its publication (with many other valuable things in these volumes) to Sir David Dalrymple, Bart., who gave it as it was preserved in the memory of a lady that is now dead" (Percy 1996, 140). Or, for a later example, when Walter Scott in his *Minstrelsy* hails another antiquarian correspondent in his headnote to "The Queen's Marie": "that [copy] principally used *was communicated to me*, in the most polite manner, by Mr. Kirkpatrick Sharpe, of Hoddom, to whom I am indebted for many similar favours" (Scott 1830, 171). The point I wish to stress here is that not only does antiquarian correspondence function as a mediating circuit for balladry, a transmission channel: ballad editors made the citation of such correspondence a constitutive generic element of the ballad collection.

Ballads, then, needed not authors but authenticators: bona fide sources and bona fide transmitters. A source, as Percy's note suggests, need not have a name; he or she did need, however, a pedigree and a locale, in other words, a provenance. In the course of remediation and artifactualization into printed books, the multiple collaborations that made balladeering possible thus entered specific discursive spaces and submitted to specific protocols for representing and differentiating (and, as one often discovers, suppressing or finessing) the kinds and degrees of collaboration involved.

One might instructively contrast antiquarian ballad citation—and its predilection for the headnote—with the development of the historical footnote, as illuminated in Anthony Grafton's *The Footnote: A Curious History* (1997). If the footnote becomes the major technique through which historians present their second story—that of their research apparatus and critical comparison of sources—the headnote becomes the space through which antiquarians do the same but also frame and authenticate their documents *as documents*. Antiquarians represent themselves, then, as establishing, as well as gathering, documentary collections; historians present themselves as narrators of a past critically worked up out of primary sources. Grafton concludes: "A full literary analysis of modern historical writing would have to include a rhetoric of annotation as well as some version of the existing rhetorics of narration" (233). I suggest that we regard antiquarian balladeering as a repository of such annotative "modern historical writing" as well as a form of literary-cultural spelunking.

Suffice it to say that the antiquarian balladeering headnote ultimately accommodated "oral communications" as one possible citable resource among others. Oral tradition, humble though it was, came to acquire—especially in the work of Scottish balladeers—a new and unembarrassed status both as an authenticating source and as an archival domain. More particularly, the oral-source medium, the living transmitter, acquired a special status, since he or she could serve as both an authentic medium of the ballad message and also as a putative documentary link in a chain of oral transmission.

One might call this transformation, "how oral tradition became respectable and sometimes got a name." Under the cover of "tradition," it is true, balladeers could smuggle in dubious ballad goods.[10] That "tradition" as a source was still somewhat disreputable in the 1790s, at least for English antiquarians, is indicated by Joseph Ritson, who observed in his "Historical Essay on Scotish Song" (1794) "how poetry is preserved for a succession of ages by mere tradition" (lxxxi). Yet Ritson's "mere tradition" was losing its self-evidence as a sneer. Invoked and theorized, we observe, almost exclusively in the context of Scottish traditionary poetry (even though Herder and Goethe were busily pursuing their own balladeering in Germany), "tradition" persisted as a citable source and an axis of authentication, as when Scott later wrote in his note to "Jellon Grame": "[T]his ballad is published from tradition, with some conjectural emendations. It is corrected from a copy in Mrs. Brown's MS, from which it differs in the concluding stanza" (Scott 1830, 150).

Scott's note, coordinating "tradition" with Mrs. Brown's manuscript (itself supposedly a textualization of tradition, preserved by Mrs. Brown's memory[11]), suggests a multilayered albeit highly regulated absorption and deployment of oral tradition. By 1800 oral tradition enters the printed ballad collection as an editor's competitive bid for authority over sources *and over other editors* (particularly Percy, whose *Reliques* established a kind of gold-standard); access to oral tradition served as well as an index of an editor's Scottish and ultimately British cultural capital. Scotland was infamously more "oral" than its southern neighbor, its rich and still-vital stores of song, balladry, and story oft-proclaimed. That Scottish editors might have privileged access to reciters, that they might "recollect" ballads from themselves (to use the diction of Scott, Jamieson, and other Scottish editors): this was no small incentive to admit the oral into your editing purview.

As subtle, agonistic conceptualizers of the problem of the source, source mediation, cultural transmission, orders of evidence, and mediality itself, the balladeers developed sophisticated tools for reflecting on method and handling highly differentiated material. Perhaps even more important, they created a space for arguing about these methodological issues. Long before the twentieth-century linguistic and anthropological turns in history, long before the critique of textualism and the writing/print monopoly underpinning the human sciences, balladeers were forced to become cultural historians and media theorists. Even if balladeers were often more concerned to document *that* a recitation happened than to publish its contents, they nevertheless anticipated the desire for sound recording technologies that only the wax-cylinder and gramophone recording technologies would begin to fulfill.

### 3. The Invention of Traditional Mediation

The ballad revival reveals not so much the waning (or the invention) of tradition as the waning of, and the simultaneous preoccupation with, traditional mediation. It is a truism that the ballad revival was part of a cultural revival, especially in Scotland, the zealous efforts of ballad hunters making clear to singers that their old ballads were of interest and value. Some of these singers were concerned with what printing did to, as well as with, ballads: the informant Mrs. Hogg famously rebuked Scott for having "spoilt" her ballads by printing them: "[T]hey were made for singin' and no' for readin'."[12] Regarding such medial transformations, scholars have long suggested that printing, and more profoundly writing, kills orality. The antiquarian, scholar, and forger John Pinkerton argued the same two centuries ago: "In proportion as Literature advanced in the world Oral Tradition disappeared" (Pinkerton

1781, xv). While other critics have found this announcement of the death of orality to be premature, it is true that writing and print technologies transform, in their remediations, oral *materia*; it is also true that print mediates oral materials differentially—consider that for decades, ballads made it into print (for centuries, if we think of the broadside medium), but that it was only in the late eighteenth century that testimonial documentation about reciters and traditionary lore began to appear alongside them. It may be that printed ballad collections supported the sustaining as well as the transformation of traditional singing and reciting practice, a phenomenon with which we are so familiar that the "invention of tradition" may be one definition of modernity itself.

Historians of cooking, music, sex, midwifery and any number of other human activities have long argued that print lags behind practice; historians of balladeering might argue the same. Print can, however, serve as a spur to further practice—in this case, ballad collecting. Balladeers returned to the field when confronted with competing publications or when hoping to improve their own: the practice of revising, reediting, and in some cases completely overhauling ballad collections suggests that we might best describe balladeering as a complex, multiply mediated feedback loop.

That balladeering might best be modeled as such a complex loop—with all the possibilities of self-correction and amplification such a metaphor implies—is supported by a number of developments, not least Scott's successive editions of the *Minstrelsy*, with its exfoliating apparatus, added "imitations," revisions, reshufflings, and reworkings. We might note too that some balladeers and their publishers solicited readers to send in new versions of ballads as well as any new or never-before-published finds. Appeals to native informants persisted through the nineteenth and twentieth centuries, Francis James Child not only corresponding with antiquarians and local historians in Britain but also, through the advertisements prefacing successive volumes of his *English and Scottish Popular Ballads* (1882–1898), inviting less eminent folk to send him material. Child also recommended ballad collecting closer to home, inviting American college students "to unite in an effort to collect popular ballads from oral tradition."[13] Alan Lomax's trip to Scotland in 1950, the collector lugging a new Magnecord tape machine, is only one example of the more recent historical fortunes of the medial technologizing of the endlessly revived ballad word; the digitization of the Child ballads is well underway.

Balladeering thus opens up the space for numerous historical and theoretical questions, among them: was writing indeed the universal medium in 1800, as Friedrich Kittler argues? Was it even possible to have a concept of medium in 1800?[14] The differential processing of words and also sounds, texts, and music, into ballad collections suggests that print is the best choice if we are looking for a "universal medium" circa 1800. And as Celeste Langan has brilliantly argued, print reveals itself by 1800 to be quite "recognizable *as* a medium."[15]

Ballad books are print objects that ceaselessly point beyond print and to other modes of communication—singing, reciting, speaking, saying, writing. Yet eighteenth-century ballad books neither processed nor presented other materials and media in an undifferentiated fashion: this is what we must remember when assessing such remarks as Cheesman's and Rieuwert's observations about ballads being "in and out of whatever media are in existence."

### 4. How to Close-Read in Antiquarian: Method, Scrutiny, Debate, Authority

Antiquarian balladeers developed specific, forensic protocols of close reading precisely because they were trafficking in debatable media: eighteenth-century ballad scandals eventually generated—fitfully, at first inadvertently, and not without much spilled ink—methods and criteria for assessing, arbitrating, and arguing for the authenticity, value, merits, historicity, and medial status of ballads. It is no accident that many literary antiquarians were lawyers or trained in the law.

For all the current Sturm und Drang about close reading versus distant reading (viz. Franco Moretti), versus "slow reading" (viz. Lindsay Waters of Harvard University Press, e.g., his February 2007 article, "Time for Reading," in the *Chronicle of Higher Education*), it is too little acknowledged that

1. All close reading is not the same.
2. Close-reading procedures, and rationales for them, have their own complex histories.

Antiquarian close reading shares less with *explication du texte* or mid-twentieth-century American New Criticism than with a forensic case method. (When Samuel Johnson thundered, regarding the Ossian poems, "Show us the manuscripts!" he was calling not just for ocular proof but for documents susceptible of scrutiny. He was also of course disparaging oral tradition, which could not in his view stand as an authoritative source of, or evidence for, anything, other than the degradation of Scottish culture.) Following the Ossian controversy, questions about Percy's *Reliques* (just where was *his* source text, the famous "folio manuscript," anyway?), and other ballad scandals, an aura of fraudulence haunted the balladeering venture: indeed most scholars now recognize that an authenticity problematic was constitutive of the ballad revival. Given this problematic, ballad editors seeking polite authority and a polite audience took it upon themselves to set forth their collecting and editing methods, not just ballad texts.

Consider that most formidable of antiquarian editors: Joseph Ritson. The most famously and vividly polemical of ballad editors, Ritson's several collections and dissertations on, among other things, balladry, minstrels, and national song, are chock-full of acerbic takedowns of Thomas Percy in particular, with some energy reserved for thrashing John Pinkerton, the prolific and occasionally hoaxing Scottish antiquarian based in London. What is important is not just that Ritson bashed Percy but that Ritson *made a case against* Percy. And he made his case (against, for example, Percy's "touching up" or "improving" of ballads, and against his nationalistic, aspirationally aristocratic theory of English minstrels) such that even those like Scott, who preferred Percy's genteel affiliations and taste to Ritson's lower-middle-class radical politics and stylistic venom, had to concede that Ritson had the better of the argument. And the irascible Ritson earned this often begrudging respect by avidly pursuing a form of potentially verifiable close reading, which had become de rigueur across the balladeering field.

Thus, rehearsing the controversy over the ballad "Hardyknute"—"the illegitimate offspring of Mrs. Wardlaw, by Sir John Bruce"—Ritson declared it in *Scotish Songs* (1794) "a palpable and bungling forgery," a judgment supported "from every species of evidence, intrinsic or extrinsic" (Ritson 1794, lxi). Only national prejudice, he asserts, could have prevented learned men from coming to the same conclusion:

> That a composition abounding with evident imitations of, and direct allusions to modern and familiar poetry (54), in short, that a palpable and bungling forgery, without the slightest resemblance of any thing ancient or original, should have passed, either in England or Scotland, for a genuine relique of antiquity, would appear almost incredible and miraculous, if there were not subsequent instances of a similar delusion. Why the Scotish [*sic*] literati should be more particularly addicted to literary imposition than those of any other country, might be a curious subject of investigation for their new Royal Society. (Ritson 1794, lxiii)

More important than Ritson's anti-Scottish barbs is his display of his method and evidence: number 54 above marks a footnote, in which Ritson offers his evidence:

"*Drinking the blude-reid wine.*" Stan. 5.1. 8. [i.e., Stanza 5, line 8, in "Hardyknute"]
"*Drinking the blude reid wine.*" Sir Patrick Spence.
"*Full twenty thousand* glittering *spears.*" Stan. 6.1. 3.
"*Full twenty thousand* Scottish *spears.*" Chevy Chase.

Showing how "Hardyknute" recycles lines from well-attested old ballads—"Sir Patrick Spens," "Chevy Chase"—Ritson demonstrates its derivative, and thus to him decidedly spurious, status. (In this local instance, modern scholars would not endorse his reasoning, since we now recognize that such recurring, mobile, shared lines and stanzas—formulas and "floating stanzas," in the parlance—are characteristic of oral tradition, no decisive sign *in themselves* of greater or less authenticity or antiquity. This borders on the complex issue of how to identify anachronisms, especially across media. What looks to be a *literary* anachronism may well be a sign of a completely vital and unbroken *oral transmission.*) With "Hardyknute," Ritson was right to smell something fishy: he also notes its allusions to *Paradise Lost* (lxvii), and identifies other anachronistic lapses in diction and formulation. Again, my point here is not that Ritson was right to identify "Hardyknute" as an eighteenth-century and not a medieval composition—though he was—but rather to point to the procedures through which he did so.

As Walter Scott would later say in another related context: the editor is suspicious. Here—as in Percy's previous and later Scott's extensive balladeering apparatus, or in Hugh Blair's powerful, learned defense of Macpherson's Ossian in his 1765 "Critical Dissertation"—a comparative textual criticism is practiced, displayed, and set forth for the reader to assess. An editor of vernacular poetries announces himself as assessing both evidence "extrinsic" (historical data, customary testimony, the history of a given manuscript, the testimonies of transmitters) and evidence "intrinsic" (linguistic and formal features of the text).

Ritson looked not for poetic beauties but for documentary accuracy; like the classical philologists and scholars of comparative literature, and like the eminent humanist scholars who had developed and refined such procedures long before antiquarians of the vernacular, Ritson worked hard to establish the texts of his inquiry. He resisted the temptation to fill in blanks, to emend infelicities, to "supply" what a manuscript, or the occasional reciter, failed to supply.

We recall that ballad texts were meant to serve many masters, often within the same volume: aesthetic pleasure, genteel reverie, radical insurgence, medievalizing nostalgia, national romance, a patron's fancy, the cultural capital of the editor. That these masters might be in conflict Ritson and his colleagues made plain. Ritson might despise an old ballad for its roughness (as he did the old version of "Chevy Chase"), but he would never "improve" it or smooth it out to make it accord with eighteenth-century taste; in this he was unlike Percy, and indeed much more rigorous than Scott.

Confronted with these simultaneous and sometimes competing bases for valuing (and evaluating) ballad texts, we might wonder: What does a ballad want? What does a balladeer want? It is not at all clear that a ballad invites close reading, but to show that *your* ballad was a better "edition" (as Scott put it) of a ballad than *his* ballad, you might, as a late eighteenth- or early nineteenth-century ballad editor, invite your discerning reader to compare versions, evaluate the differences, develop preferences, make judgments, and articulate the reasons for such. You, as an increasingly sophisticated balladeer, might thus invite your discerning reader to *close-read*.

Not only did balladeers close-read, then: they modeled it for, and enjoined it of, their readers. Balladeers extended such invitations in their headnotes, less often in their footnotes. Thus Scott, in the headnote to "The Duel of Wharton and Stuart" in *Minstrelsy of the Scottish Border*, wrote: "I am thus particular, that the reader may be able, if he pleases, to compare the traditional ballad with the original edition." Indeed, Scott invites readers to compare his older version of "Katharine Janfarie" in previous editions of the *Minstrelsy* with the new and improved version in his latest edition—this most current ballad "edition" improved via recitation.

Balladeers invited readers' collaborative scrutiny, then, not only to identify frauds or demonstrate forgeries, but also to make their bid for balladeering distinction. A balladeer could distinguish his ballad, and more broadly his collection, by indicating in what ways his ballad versions and balladeering vision were different from (and presumably better than) his predecessors' and rivals'. Thus Walter Scott and his antiquarian comrades relentlessly subtitled their ballads with such phrases as: "Never before printed," "For the first time published," "this more complete copy" ("Sir Patrick Spens," Scott 1830, 45).

Certainly a prosecutorial ghost never ceases to haunt balladeers' invitations to close-read. The discriminating reader might decide, for example, that as Scott himself suspects (he reports in his headnote), "Fause Foodrage" contains a line so close to the infamously scandalous ballad "Hardyknute" that "Fause Foodrage" too should be considered a modern imposition (Scott 1830, 159–160).

Balladeering scrutiny is a quasi-forensic procedure arising out of a prior, generalized, and constitutive suspicion. Such close reading aimed not to demonstrate the beauties of a poem—though these were often celebrated alongside its other merits, for example, its value as historical, ethnographic, or customary evidence. Balladeering close reading aimed instead to demonstrate the authenticity and historicity of a ballad, fragment, or poetic work, to secure it in an established chronotope, to locate it as a document before (that is, logically prior to the moment) it could be assessed as a monument—whether of art, an "early period of society," the "genius" of the people, what have you.

The skepticism of Scott, and the literary-forensic methods he inherited and refined, bears as well upon his double status as the founder of the historical novel (according to Lukács) and as the revitalizer of historical writing per se (according to Ranke). For Scott's minidiscourses on authenticity, evidence, arbitration, and judgment resemble not only legal procedures but indeed that broader following of clues within a "conjectural paradigm" that Carlo Ginzburg argues is central to the historical method itself (Ginzburg 1980, 5–36).

Through close reading, balladeers began to make their objects, and to lay out the principles for making those objects. Disputatious antiquarians brought ballad editing to a definitive threshold of scholarly enunciation and formalization. For it was by arguing about what a ballad was that the balladeers converged on what a ballad was. For it was none other than Pinkerton, target of Ritson's ire, who first proposed a formal definition of "ballad" (in *Scotish Tragic Ballads, with a Dissertation on the Oral Tradition in Poetry*, 1781). And it was Hugh Blair, eminent Edinburgh literatus and first professor of rhetoric and belles lettres at the University of Edinburgh, who invoked the concept of an "oral edition" when defending Macpherson's disputed Ossian poems (in the appendix to his "Critical Dissertation," *The Poems of Ossian*, 1765). And it was William Motherwell who developed a preliminary theory of oral composition,[16] one that anticipates in some striking ways the magisterial oral theory developed in the twentieth century by Homerists Milman Parry and Albert Lord. And it was Ritson—no lover of the Scots—who nevertheless praised "Scotish music" (*sic*), insisted that "the words and melody of a Scotish song should ever be inseparable" (Ritson 1794, i), and called for the collecting of tunes; Ritson who exposed hoaxers, trashed emenders; Ritson who vigorously advanced the forensic protocols for close-reading vernacular poetries. And it was through their disputes over what a ballad was that they came to a common sense of what a ballad was—this before the emergence of comparative philology in the nineteenth century.

In antiquarian close reading, it is true, we might discern the tracks of several dead ends, dead not because theirs were worthless pursuits but because ascendant disciplines, methods, and conceptual paradigms both subsumed and displaced their work. Yet antiquarians' work continues to flow into contemporary, still vital streams: not least *The Norton Anthology of Modern Poetry* (2006), or—via Francis James Child's compendium, *The English and Scottish Popular Ballads* (1882–1898) (itself greatly indebted to Percy, Scott, and Motherwell)—numerous "folk" and "world music" recordings.

Polemical scrutiny persisted in balladeering along other medial axes, as editors took printed *musics* as well as *verbal texts* as objects of study and debate. Thus William Stenhouse, editor and annotator of the 1853 edition of Johnson's *Scots Musical Museum*, writes in his notes to "Hap Me with Thy Pettycoat":

> The reader is here presented with the original air in its ancient purity. The copy which is inserted in Ritson's Historical Essay [on national song], is erroneous in several particulars, as will appear obvious on comparing it with the following: [Here air is inserted]
>
> The reader will, from this example, be enabled to form a pretty accurate notion respecting the intrinsic value of those modern refinements which have been made on several of the old Scottish melodies, by comparing the above air with that which is inserted in the Museum and other recent publications. (Johnson 1853, 4: 130)

Once again we see the invitation to close-read and compare, an invitation extended to what Stenhouse elsewhere calls "the musical reader" (132).[17]

Over a century would have to pass before the strict scrutinies of close reading would make equal room for the necessities of *close listening*: indeed most scholars now would find it inexcusable to exclude ballad musics from any consideration of balladry. And it is no accident that an almost exclusively textual scholarship became an even more orally alert and methodologically sophisticated scholarship once the phonograph and other recording technologies made their ethnographic and ethnopoetic impact felt. This is a history too complex to tease out here. Suffice it to say that the desire for authenticity haunting the eighteenth century persists into new media formations.

Let us be reminded, moreover, that any fantasy of a "progress of media" runs up against the inconvenient fact that changes in media neither determine nor improve ballad conceptualization; nor do twentieth-century sound-recording technologies necessarily make for more "authentic" or "accurate" "records"—this last a word encoding in its history the changing technomaterial bases for "inscribing" materials. (Scott made records with pens, pencils, and by notching wood as a mnemonic; Alan Lomax with tape; their successors with digital media.) As William Motherwell's work best showed, it was possible for at least one early nineteenth-century editor to conceive of a ballad collection grounded in recitation and oral tradition; he rejected the "collated edition" model of Scott,[18] and insisted on single recitations as integral phenomena. No splicing of stanzas or lines for him. He arrived at these commitments long before electronic sound-recording technologies might have aided his fieldwork, and long before fieldwork itself became the distinguishing professional mark of ethnographic research, or "performance" a category of analysis. This is not to say that Motherwell was a full-blown twentieth-century oralist before the fact but rather to suggest that by the early nineteenth century, oral tradition and ballad recitation had begun to find rigorous theorizers whose methods and assumptions contemporary scholars continue to endorse.

## V. Close Reading (In)Terminable? Mediating "Literature" Past and Present

The closing phrase in my title is, "or, Close Reading Before Coleridge." Here we might distinguish between the antiquarian close reading I've been mapping—its motivations and procedures—from that elaborated in Coleridge's work, or by his later heirs, for example I. A. Richards, or by twentieth-century theorists of verbal icons and well-wrought urns. To reconstruct antiquarian close reading—even to expose oneself to its texture—is to see that antiquarians oriented both to the medium and the message: to lapses in writing and print, to the arguable status of oral informants, as well as to the historical, national, and/or aesthetic meanings of balladry. One reason antiquarian close reading has another flavor than, say, new-critical exegesis, is its necessary investment in establishing and perfecting texts; another reason is that antiquarians in the main did not have to worry about the author, who continues to preoccupy literary critics no matter how often his death is announced or his intentions are bracketed under the rubric, fallacious. The special merits of a ballad or a ballad tradition might be considerable, but they were not individually authored or approached as such. Or rather, the problematic of authorship, authenticity, and authority was placed right back into what Homi Bhabha calls "the location of culture," rather than referring to the psychology or mentalité of the author.

*We know how to read texts, now let's learn how not to read them* (Moretti 2000, 57). Franco Moretti's injunction emerges as part of a turn to world-system theory among several ambitious literary and cultural historians, and has been laid out (and is the subject of illuminating debate in) the *New Left*

*Review* over the past eight or so years, as well as in signal books (Pascale Casanova's *Le République Mondiale des Lettres* [1999], Moretti's *Maps, Graphs, Trees* [2005]) that aim to transform the paradigm for conceptualizing the literary field in world literary time and space. Recent calls to dispense with close reading seem to be multiply determined: by a desire to write the final epitaph for belles-lettrism, or for late twentieth-century modes of formalist readings, whether deconstructive or not; a desire to write the epitaph for literature; an envy of the social sciences; a desire to formalize more rigorously objects of study and research methods; a desire to "produce knowledge," as Pierre Macherey encouraged literary critics to do and as many have undertaken since.[19] Yet it is striking how calls to ban close reading are almost always calls to ban *literary* close reading or, rather, to proscribe the close reading of those texts typically taught and purveyed under the rubric "literature." No one calls for, say, my copy editor at the *Chicago Tribune* to abandon close reading, or for lawyers or judges to do so, or for the savants in the computer-support office to do so, when I ask them to help me with bugs in my machine's code. It is not close reading but the *literary objects* of close reading that attract such ire, it would seem. And perhaps justly so.

But I would suggest that an inquiry into prehistories of "literary" close reading might restore to twenty-first-century literary studies a too-long-suppressed aspect: antiquarians were alive to the many simultaneous and sometimes competing bases for valuing poems and other "literary" or cultural materials. Antiquarians were unable, in the end, to autonomize the aesthetic, and that may have been one of their strengths, however much at the time it seemed a weakness (as when editors lambasted each other for their poor taste). Ballads have a way of escaping their scholars, their official editors, their collectors; they are sung or not, transmitted or not, living lives in other media alongside and sometimes interpenetrating with higher cultural concerns and genres.

A return to antiquarian balladeering reminds us, moreover, that this venture required as much an enquiry into *media* as it did into "literature": the transmedial, as well as transhistorical, nature of balladry confounded ballad editors but also encouraged them to think beyond as well as in print. At the closing of the Gutenberg era it is increasingly inexcusable to remain—what shall we say?—undermediatized (question: has anyone coined an un-ugly word for "critically versed in or alert to mediality"? that is, *able to assess the production and transmission of knowledge via specific historical media channels?*) Balladeering brings to the fore, for us as for the antiquarians, problems of conceptualization. For the question remains: what is the object of our analysis? And have we hypostasized that object? Moretti has recently argued: "Texts certainly are the real objects of literature... but they are not the right objects of knowledge for literary history" (76). I agree with this, but it is not clear in advance that literary history's objects of knowledge may be partitioned from those of other histories—media history, for one. We need graphs, maps, and trees—to invoke Franco Moretti's proposed models for a renovated literary sociology; but we also need a literary sociology alive to its convergence with other media histories and sociologies.

I am enough of a romantic and a romanticist to think that "literature"—as well as songs, videos, movies, etc.—produces feeling; that "literature" might continue to generate transpersonal, albeit fragile, affiliation; that poems (for example) are movements as well as objects; that while poems or songs might be reified into print or fixed data-streams, they are also unbound and rebound as each reader/hearer/interfacer (*sic*) interacts with them. Close reading is one intense way of moving through, along, and with a text, a way to let the text occupy the mind, even as close listening allows a song to move through the attentive listener. Casual reading, or tactical reading, or middle-distance reading: these too have their pleasures and payoffs. And "distant reading" as envisioned by Moretti has much to recommend it, not least its trans- and international vision, its intellectual vigor and scope, and its implicit challenge both to "totalize the situation" (as Marxists used to put it) and to "always historicize" (as Fredric Jameson enjoined decades ago). But to think that one could pursue distant reading without close reading seems a strikingly undialectical position (and not, I should say, Moretti's): how would one even begin to identify the "unit of analysis" that would diagnostically and comparatively cut across world-historical genres, like the novel? It was a close, not (only) a distant, reader, who identified free-indirect style; a close, not (only) a distant, reader, who specified the formal features of the ballad; a close, not (only) a distant reader, who recognized that the final "e" in Chaucer should be vocalized.[20] If varieties of twentieth-century close reading could seem in their decadent phases empty either of ideas (viz., the more rigid forms of New Criticism) or of objects (viz., the dematerializing *mise-en-abyme* effects of deconstruction), twenty-first-century close reading might restore to us a productive relation between concepts and objects, ideas and specific encounters. Close reading is a way to structure experience and to make it shareable; it is not in itself better or worse than other modes of engagement, but it remains available as a mode of engagement. Its fortunes may improve as its imagined hegemony wanes.

# MEDIATING
# LE PHILOSOPHE

DIDEROT'S STRATEGIC
SELF-REPRESENTATIONS

ANNE FASTRUP

Let me point to three major reasons why Denis Diderot, the French philosopher and art critic, may claim a central role in the discussion between the Enlightenment movement and the media. First, he was the editor of the most influential of the Enlightenment encyclopedias; second, he took an active, if not a particularly "philosophical," stand against the attacks on the *Encyclopedié* in the printed press, and third he himself was highly "media-conscious." Diderot made use of several different media, not least aesthetic media (painting and music) in order to convey his ideas on the role played by the philosopher in society, on communication, and on the relation between the fine arts and the public sphere as a (potentially divisive) social and political space.

In this essay, I examine Diderot's understanding of his own role by analyzing a marked tension in his account of the position of the philosopher in society in some of the "media" he personally favored (articles in the *Encyclopédie*, dialogues, paintings, essays in *ekphrasis*). Specifically, my argument turns on the philosopher's *participation in* and *withdrawal from* society on the one hand and the wider public debates in newspapers on the other hand. If you analyze Diderot's views of the encyclopedic effort in the light of the self-representations emerging from his dialogues and essays on art during the 1760s, a distinct tension reveals itself. In some of the more emphatic of these representations, Diderot envisions himself, and indeed the universal philosopher, as a (Romantic) dreamer contemplating social conflicts from a distance (as in *Rameau's Nephew*) or as an itinerant observer of beautiful natural scenery (in the *Salons*). I propose that the presence of this tension in Diderot (and in a number of contemporary fellow philosophers) may be viewed in relation both to the hostile reception of the *Encyclopedié* in various newspapers, magazines, and newsletters and to the general historical circumstances as witnessed by these publications, namely, the emergence of a new critical attitude in the reading public.[1] Notably, the *Encyclopedié* was itself part and parcel of the reading public, even if the encyclopedists for various reasons responded to the press with hostility.

I suggest, therefore, that we may understand the tension between participation and withdrawal as specifically related to a confrontation between the philosopher and the journalist. Addressing the public, the philosopher promotes Enlightenment via publication of knowledge, while the journalist, who likewise desires to enlighten the public, does so in a critical examination of the philosopher's message. Interestingly, both newspaper critics and encyclopedists claim to speak on behalf of the general reading public, indicting the other party as biased.

My argument falls into two parts. I begin with a general and introductory account of Diderot's (and, by implication, the encyclopedists') view of the philosopher, of journalism, and of the printed media (newspapers, periodicals, and newsletters). I follow this with a discussion of Diderot's representations of other, ideal ways of public communication in the form of a mise-en-scène: the philosopher introduces his private person into the object of his analysis in order to represent *les philosophes* in a favorable light—as noble defenders of humanity, truth, equality, and reason, while denigrating the partiality of the journalists.

## The Participation: Diderot in the *Encyclopédie*

In his article "L'Encyclopédie," Diderot informs his readers that the philosopher should collect, produce, and transmit knowledge to the people "with whom we live" and to "those who come after us," promoting virtue and happiness among humankind. In, "le Philosophe," an entry not written but edited by him, readers are assured of the philosopher's sincere love of society and his active participation in it. In both articles readers get the impression of the philosopher as a man of letters who makes his general and pedagogical knowledge available to the public, not someone who merely serves the requirements of the elite or of a particular social group. The *Encyclopedié*, as Diderot points out in "l'Encyclopédie," is written by universal man in order "to investigate, debate, and examine everything without fear or favor, irrespective of what anybody might think or feel"; narrow-mindedness and personal considerations for those "who are preoccupied only with their own small circles" would have no influence on the commitment of the *Encyclopedié* to the spread of knowledge. In particular, the encyclopedists thought it possible to raise people to a higher moral, material, and technological level through the disinterested, unprejudiced, and universal propagation of knowledge. Indeed, Diderot and his fellow philosophers saw themselves as representatives of a universal mode of thinking whose primary aim was to eliminate all forms of economic, political, and religious bias, thereby combating the negative effects of any form of partiality like fanaticism, superstition, loss of freedom, poverty, or secret dealings.

Inevitably, this ambition would clash with French society and its political and religious authorities. Diderot's perennial confrontations with different influential factions during his more than twenty years as editor and publisher of the *Encyclopédie* bears witness to this conflict and its inherent personal dangers. At the same time, his own ideas of what philosophy should be played a significant part in causing the disputes in that his universalist notions were infused with the idea that philosophy, or reason, should always be directed to society's needs. The philosopher should not remain in his chamber in splendid isolation (like Descartes in his dressing gown a century before), meditating on the principles of mathematics, physics, and other sciences. Eighteenth-century philosophers were not, philosophically speaking, rationalists or metaphysicians, but men of experience and empiricism. The object of their study was (ideally) the world that surrounded them, and they took an active part in the solution of social needs and political problems.

Thus we see a coupling of a universalist program for Enlightenment with an idea of social usefulness; the philosopher is asked to make his knowledge available for social purposes. As it turned out, this nexus resulted in a series of violent clashes with parliaments, the royal institution, and various religious parties and political factions. The ancien régime of the Enlightenment period was a society charged with conflicts and tensions that were social and economic in origin and political and ideological in nature. At the same time, the ambition to enlighten the broad public also gave rise to what we may perhaps designate a crisis of identity among the philosophers themselves, both as a group and as individuals. In fact, several of these crises were more or less directly related to the reception in the printed press of the *Encyclopédie*.

The philosopher's ideas of the dissemination of knowledge met with various kinds of resistance from state censorship as well as from sections of the privately funded printed press. Throughout the 1750s and 1760s, the printed media repeatedly voiced their disagreement with the philosophers, subjecting Diderot and his writings in the *Encyclopédie* to consistently negative, critical scrutiny. But how did Diderot represent contemporary Parisian newspapers, and how did he see his own position in the public debates?

## The Anti-philosophers

*Rameau's Nephew*, Diderot's satirical novel, is a key work for understanding both his strategic self-representation and the general attitude of the encyclopedists to the wider critical public. Diderot presumably began *Rameau's Nephew* some time in the early 1760s, shortly after the *Encyclopedié* had to go underground. As all readers are aware, the novel satirizes the so-called antiphilosophers or antiencyclopedists. However, it is often forgotten that they were really journalists and editors, gentlemen of the press, who were nicknamed *antiphilosophers* because they criticized articles on the various subjects in the *Encyclopédie*. Charles Palissot de Montenoy antiphilosophe par exellence, was closely related to the group most hostile to the encyclopedists, but he was not himself a journalist. Instead, he staged his criticism in the theater, and his fellow antiphilosophers praised him for the comedy *Les philosophes* (1757).

Thus, the antiphilosophers formed an antagonistic front within the public sphere as defined by the contemporary newspapers. The extent of the group's real influence is an unsettled question, however. Before yielding to a spontaneous inclination to side with Diderot (and with the Enlightenment, as it would seem), we should not forget that the antiencyclopedists wrote for periodicals that were subject to censorship. Indeed, the director of the press and of censorship, Guillaume-Chrétien de Lamoignon de Malesherbes on more than one occasion asked them to moderate their criticism of the *Encyclopedié*.

Some voices were even muzzled. Elie Catherine Fréon from *l'Année littéraire* received a letter from Malesherbes telling him to make friends with Diderot. He answered that it was not possible. Although controversial, the publication of the *Encyclopédie* represented an event of symbolic importance and national prestige in the eyes of people of influence within the power apparatus of the Old Regime.

However, *Rameau's Nephew* does not give the impression that Diderot regarded the antiencyclopedists as a serious threat to the political and personal security of the *philosophes*. Indeed, the antiencyclopedists primarily appear as a constant cause for annoyance. This was partly because they criticized the writings of *les philosophes*, and partly because it was feared that more powerful groups within the Old Regime would use the *Encyclopédie*'s bad press as an excuse to close it down. However that may be, let us have a look at Diderot's depiction of the antiphilosophers in *Rameau's Nephew*. The nephew himself, who frequently joins up with the antiphilosophers and their patrons, relates:

> Wolves are not more famished, tigers no more cruel. We devour like wolves when the earth has been long under snow, like tigers we tear to pieces anything succesful . . .You hear nothing but names such as Buffon, Duclos, Montesquieu, Rousseau, Voltaire, D'Alembert, Diderot, and God knows what epithets are coupled with them . . . We also have in our company the librettists of the Opéra-Comique and their actors and actresses . . . and I was forgetting the great literary critics, *L'Avant-Coureur, Les Petites-Affiches, L'Année littéraire, L'Observateur littéraire* . . . (Diderot 1966, 80, 84)

Some pages below, the nephew goes on to list the names of the editors and journalists of the reviews: Fréron (*L'Année littéraire*), Pierre Berthier (*Le Journal de Trévoux*), the Abbé de la Porte (Joseph Delaporte; *L'Observateur littéraire*), among others—all historical persons who were known for their strong reservations against the encyclopedists. The above passage from *Rameau's Nephew* depicts the antiphilosophers as they have come together at a social gathering. As it happens, their negative portrayal is all the more striking because they meet as private individuals, disregarding good manners in any form. Thanks to the disloyalty of the nephew, we are given a glimpse of how they "really are," leaving no doubt that their public appearance reflects the aggressive brutishness noticed by the nephew. This "private" animality, we learn, unmasks its hideousness in public, which is especially evident when the antiphilosophers write their negative reviews of Diderot and his fellow philosophers.

In the image of the beast of prey, *Rameau's Nephew* conveys a picture of the antiphilosophers as primitive, destructive, aliens to reason, who are unable to participate in the kind of polite conversation sought by the philosophers in their salons. In a wider perspective, the two groups are not only opposed to each other, but their antagonism is a manifestation of reason versus unreason, civilization versus barbarism, and educated conversation versus satirical misrepresentation.

Diderot's Hobbesian beast of prey may not be a fair image of the antiphilosophers or a convincing explanation of their disagreement with the *Encyclopédie*. But his animalization of the antiphilosophers gives us a full view of his dislike of the printed media and what he saw as the risks he ran in a public sphere inhabited by snarling reviewers eagerly waiting for an opportunity to strike any weaknesses or flaws, ridicule the arguments of the encyclopedists, or mock them as private individuals. Like the other encyclopedists, Diderot had a strong urge to withdraw into defensive hostility whenever a reviewer raised his critical voice.

Much could be said about the philosophers' not very philosophical reaction to criticism, but I shall mention only one aspect: their response to criticism was unfailingly emotional;[2] the philosophers considered it a personal affront to receive bad press from journalists whose intellect they despised and whose political impartiality they did not trust. The encyclopedists, we recall, invariably looked upon themselves as an intellectual and cultural elite, defenders of universal reason.

At the same time, the press relayed the encyclopedists' work in often grotesque and satirical form, distorting individual writers and misrepresenting political intentions. This, they felt, was to strike below the belt. In addition, they feared that such misrepresentations could easily ignite the latent opposition in the parliaments and at the royal court.

Diderot was unwavering in his belief in the importance of enlightening society by disseminating knowledge; at the same time he was far from happy about the social function of the printed media.[3] We have already noticed this in connection with *Rameau's Nephew*, but according to Paul Benhamou the *Encyclopédie* likewise voices very "conservative, even reactionary ... perceptions of the press"[4] and its role in society. Indeed, the encyclopedists responded to the printed media as if they were completely unaware of the close connection between their own desire for public debate in the *Encyclopédie* and the existence of a printed press that was free to review their project and discuss it on their own terms.

As a publicistic undertaking on a large scale, the *Encyclopédie* joined the newsletters, periodicals, and newspapers as part and parcel of the historical development of the public sphere throughout Europe. The encyclopedists were seemingly unaware that the boom in the volume of printed media in the first half of the century paved the way for their project's unprecedented dissemination of thought and ideas. Indeed, they appear to disregard altogether the importance of the political reforms that facilitated increased public access to knowledge as such. Thus, they failed to see what was evident to posterity, namely, that journalistic printed media and the *Encyclopédie* were both important players in the revolution we term Enlightenment.

## Two Antitheses: The Philosopher and the Journalist

Diderot's description of the printed media as subject to a Hobbesian state of war was not a single instance of satirical distortion but formed an integral part of the encyclopedists' discourse. But how does the encyclopedists' discourse on the press compare with their image of themselves as philosophers? An answer to this may be found if we compare the entries "Philosophe" and "Journaliste" in the *Encyclopédie*.

It comes as no surprise, perhaps, that the entry "Philosophe" provides a *strategic* image of the philosopher designed to disarm the political and ideological skepticism voiced against the *Encyclopédie*; the *philosopher* is depicted as a specimen of moral perfection and knowledge. In the dialectics of contrast, he is the antithesis of "the other men," "the people," and "wits"; in the rhetoric of identity, he is akin to "l'honnête homme."

In contrast to "the other men," the philosopher is keenly observant, reflective, and sensible, a man who thinks before he acts. Whereas "the wits" cannot see beyond their own narrow perspective, the philosopher has a notion of others' views as transparent as his knowledge of his own ideas. The philosopher enters freely into other people's way of thinking, and he pleases his surroundings by inspiring confidence, evoking love, and awakening feelings of friendship; thus, he suffers from no hostile intentions whatsoever. Indeed, the ability to please is due to the firm control he exercises over his passions, particularly his ambition—always a source of dangerous rivalry. Unhampered by egotism and fired by a sincere and unselfish wish to serve society, the philosopher would be the very antithesis of a despot, if ever someone saw fit to elect him king. An unblemished, enlightened prince, thinker, and "honnête homme" all in one, the philosopher is known by his reason, his will to live at peace with his fellow men, his desire to sacrifice himself for their happiness, and his unlimited awareness of what is good for the welfare of his subjects. In his person, reason, virtue, and politics form a synthesis.

Like all ideals, this image presupposes the absence of disputes and conflicting interests; or rather, the ideal implies the end of all strife. The dialectics of opposing forces, the whole foundation of disagreement and debate, cease the very moment the philosopher comes to occupy the social and political sphere as its sovereign. Hence there will be no politics, no negotiations, no exchange of different opinions . . . and no press.

By contrast, the reader will be faced with a marked change of style in the article "Journaliste," which was written by Diderot himself. The tone is sarcastic, aggressive in a petty way, admonitory, and personal. Journalists are very nearly singled out by name: thus the journalists of *Le Journal de Trévoux* are characterized as ignoramuses who do not know the first thing about chemistry, geometry, or literature. This is followed by a series of patronizing exhortations: journalists must refrain from using satire because satire betrays partiality; journalists must not be partial on any account; journalists must treat superior talents and geniuses with consideration and respect because only a fool can be an enemy of a Voltaire, a Montesquieu, a Buffon, and "some other of the same mold."[5] All of a sudden, the philosopher speaks a language of patronizing discontent. Notably, we witness the *Encyclopédie* adopting its own dissatisfied tone of voice to address the conflict-ridden society of partiality, power struggles, and private interests—conforming to the realities of politics, in short. Of course, the philosopher was a member of this society all along, even if it was his ambition to translate it into a state of postpolitical peacefulness.

The tone, the style, and the content of "Journaliste" in the *Encyclopédie* is not unusual in its description of the printed media. Under the entry "Hebdominaire" (written by Diderot), the reader is informed that such papers were food for ignoramuses and not to be taken seriously. Magazines are written for people who judge without reading, an abomination to serious-minded people who read before they pass judgment. In the entry "Journal" Diderot goes on in the same vein, stating that many newspapers in France are written by "barren minds" who are themselves incapable of writing books. Under the entry "Gazette," Marmontel, normally one of the moderates, characterizes journalists hostile to the *Encyclopédie* as

> [w]riters [who] prostitute their pen for money, favor, deceit, envy, and vices of the most unworthy kind for a gifted man.[6]

Neither is Friedrich-Melchior Grimm, the editor of *La corréspondance littéraire*, favorably inclined toward journalists, protesting that they excerpt from other people's books, denouncing such "makers of excerpts" as the most "useless in the world." However, Grimm seems oblivious to the fact that the journalists were largely responsible for making knowledge and information, previously a privilege for the educated, accessible to the wider reading public.

It is clear, then, that the encyclopedists looked upon newspapers and periodicals as a growing evil. Only a mouthpiece of political and religious interests, the journalist parasitically reiterates the laborious contributions of others. His own contribution is vanity, strife, and disagreement. According to the Diderot of *Rameau's Nephew*, journalists disgraced politics and society by reducing it to a Hobbesian state of natural war where no one, in particular not "the learned," "superior talents," or "men of genius," could feel secure. In the mouth of the journalist the voice of reason would invariably succumb to the roar of the predator.

What should the philosopher do in a situation where the public sphere has degenerated into a bloody menagerie, where his works, his role as *philosophe*, and his whole person have been torn to pieces and reduced to objects of ridicule? In a fit of pessimism some fourteen years later in *Observations d'un philosophe sur l'Instruction de Sa Majesté Impériale aux députés pour la confection des lois* (Observations of a Philosopher on the Instruction of His Imperial Majesty for Deputies for the Making of Laws; 1774), Diderot described his own era as devoid of morality and education, a cruel and cynical battleground. On more than one occasion, he chose to hit back. However, the sheer acrimony and resentment of these exchanges apparently caused a minor identity crisis in the philosopher. My guess is that Diderot felt his participation in this type of argument to be improper and beneath the dignity of a philosopher, indeed as an animalization of the debate. It is this displeasure—personal, moral, and political—as well as a growing feeling of impotence with respect to the possible improvement of "publique morals" which is behind the depiction of the philosopher Moi in the prologue to *Rameau's Nephew*:

> Come rain or shine, my custom is to go for a stroll in the Palais-Royal every afternoon at about five. I am always to be seen there alone, sitting on a seat in the Allée d'Argenson, mediating. I hold discussions with myself on politics, love, taste, or philosophy, and let my thoughts wander in complete abandon, leaving them free to follow the first wise or foolish idea that comes along, like those young rakes we see in the Allée de Foy who run after a giddy-looking little piece with a laughing face, sparkling eye and tip-tilted nose, only to leave her for another, accosting them all, but sticking to none. In my case, my thoughts are my wenches. (Diderot 1966, 33)

The philosopher, Moi, has turned his back on the public sphere as a political and social space. Neither caring one bit for it, nor indeed wishing to participate in it, he sees nothing besides vain power plays and aggressive struggles for recognition. Consequently, he withdraws from the world to observe it disinterestedly and from afar, securely ensconced in private, pleasurable, and naively frivolous fantasies. Only once a year does he pull himself together to have look at society in order to record its events. This happens when he meets with Rameau's nephew, a man both disillusioned with the world and experienced in its immorality, its cynicism, and its unending battles. They talk ... and then suddenly, in the midst of a crowd of untalented actresses, gluttonous cardinals, and inane tycoons, the ironical remarks of the nephew directs the reader's attention to hordes of aggressive and discredited journalists and newspaper editors. With hungry looks and ravenous minds they take up their vaunted seats at the tables of the rich, flattering the vanity of their host, and slandering his enemies, the encyclopedists.

Now, this image of the philosopher as a powerless, disinterested, and introverted observer of city life in *Rameau's Nephew* is not the only significant self-portraits created by Diderot during the 1760s. Diderot, it will be recalled, assigned an essentially communicative, public dimension to the philosopher's activities. However, although he viewed the public sphere through a Hobbesian prism, he neither could nor would withdraw entirely from public life. Consequently, he was all the more keen on constructing other—ideal—forms of public communication as alternatives to the "animal" way. This also induced him to create a picture of the *philosophe* that differed from what his enemies saw. To achieve this other image, Diderot chose paintings as a medium for his purposes. Or rather: he embarked on a novel form of verbal description of paintings in the *Salons*.

## The Withdrawal: Diderot *in* Painting

Diderot commenced work as an art critic at the biannual exhibitions in the Louvre in 1759, that is, at the time when the State Council had banned the further publication of the *Encyclopédie* and when the accusations against the encyclopedists for hatching a political plot reached a first peak. Diderot, always busy, was persuaded by the editor, Grimm of the *Corréspondance littéraire*, to become art critic for this small and exclusive magazine. The readership were a select group of enlightened and cultured Europeans (many were aristocrats) who besides a lively interest in literature, philosophy, and science also favored French painting, often with a mind to buy.

Diderot undertook his business in a way that was signally different from other art critics. The specifically evaluative aspects of the profession—the question of pictorial quality—are strikingly reduced in Diderot. Instead, he favors a descriptive approach. As a rule, Diderot introduces his texts in the *Salons* with a description of the picture (which was invisible to the reader, of course), subsequently followed by an account of his physical, sensual, and emotional impressions. In between description and account he would then enlarge on wider questions of epistemology and morality provoked by the paintings. A frequent item in his *Salons* would be a fictive dialogue between himself and one of his friends.

To the extent that the physical and emotional effects of the paintings on the beholder play a central role, you may say that there is a direct line from the *Salons* to Kant's *Critique of Judgment*: the aesthetic interpretation is transposed from the object—its composition and rules—to subjective experience. The transposition is incomplete, however, and it would perhaps be better to speak of a phenomenological inseparability of subjective experience and object.

The comments in which Diderot as a sentient and speaking agent, the "Diderot body," is most prominently present appear in connection with landscape painters such as Le Prince, Louthenbourg, Hubert Robert, and Joseph Vernet—the most famous of which was the so-called *Promenade Vernet* from the *Salon* of 1767 where Diderot discusses the landscape paintings of Vernet exhibited in that year. At the time of writing, Diderot was also editing *Rameau's Nephew*, and the two works are thematically related in a number of ways. In terms of genre, the *Promenade Vernet* is very much a hybrid. The *Promenade Vernet* consists of equal parts art criticism, philosophical dialogue, and personal account reconstructed as the author's imagined physical entry into the paintings. Thus, Diderot proposes to take the reader along with him on a promenade through Vernet's paintings which he, by virtue of his writing, had recast as real landscapes, where he walked about in the company of a kind, if slightly naïve, local abbot. The creation of this fiction is a trick that Diderot also makes use of in connection with other painters, and it has some novel implications for the more neutral descriptions in the other *Salons*. Bearing in mind Michael McKeon's essay in this volume, "Mediation as Primal Word: The Arts, the Sciences, and the Origins of the Aesthetic," the transformation of the painterly landscape into an empirical landscape could be construed as testifying to the idea of aesthetic effect. As pointed out by McKeon, aesthetic effect, according to the common view of the period, lies in the "empirical naturalness" of the artwork. However, in my own account of this transformation emphasis is being placed on the strategic and performative function of the fictional entry into the painted landscape in relation to Diderot's attempt to position himself in the public sphere.

According to Michael Fried's reading of the *Promenade Vernet*, the reader is invited not only to see "the painting through his (Diderot's) eyes, but also to see him as a figure in the painting" (Fried 1980, 125). The idea, then, is to actually see Diderot *inside* the painting. But what, we must ask, is the broader strategic significance of this transposition?

However fictional, Diderot's reappearance inside the painting serves to displace his readers' awareness of his physical presence outside the paintings—in the galleries at the Louvre where the public was introduced to them in the first place. The reader is asked to contemplate Diderot in Vernet's sunny picturesque scenery, in a suggestion that he may, if only for a while, forget the physical fact of the exhibition room. Thomas Crow, among others, has pointed out that the galleries in the Louvre were infused with commercial interests and saturated with aesthetic and political discussion. According to Crow (in his preface to Diderot 1995), the art criticism accompanying the biannual salons therefore rapidly began "to record in print the currents of opinion which flowed through the crowd."[7] However, since the reports of public opinion were not invariably favorable, and since they habitually linked certain paintings to specific discussions, the authorities feared that the painters' reputations would suffer and sales endangered. Late in the 1750s the "unregulated Salon writing" was deemed risky and was banned. Thus, with the increased commercialization of art, public criticism was no longer limited to narcissistic concerns but potentially posed real economic problems for the painters. Many feared adverse criticism and refused to exhibit their works at the Louvre. Moreover, they did not want to be associated with politically dangerous issues, deeming it potentially detrimental to the national intentions underlying the Academy's and the king's public display of French art. At the same time, it was unthinkable, of course, that the country's best and most popular artists would not present their works at the salons.

On entering the pictorial landscape of the *Promenade Vernet*, Diderot dissociates himself from the exhibition room and its "unregulated Salon writing." The purpose of this fiction is to convince his readers (and his many friends among the painters) that art, Diderot himself (as art critic and philosopher), and the general reading public have no connection whatsoever to the showroom and the powers that be. They stand aloof and are not caught in the triangular trap of public opinion, the artists' commercial interests, and the concerns of the art critic and philosopher for his personal reputation. Vernet and (in particular) Diderot being enmeshed in this web, the latter attempts to disentangle both the fine arts and himself from its implications (foreshadowing the idea of the autonomy of art). The implication in the *Salons*, notably in the *Promenade Vernet*, is that the fine arts, the critic, and the public join hands in a space that is ideally free from money and politics. However, in this gesture Diderot also manages to isolate the fine arts from the open debate of the very same public space he framed in the *Salons*.

Diderot introduces his *Promenade Vernet* by informing the reader that he has gone into the countryside, away from

> [the] tumultuous discussion of the new principles of the economists, the utility or the uselessness of philosophy, religion, morals, actors, ac-

tresses, goverment, the relative merits of the two kinds of music, the fine arts, literature, and other important questions. (Diderot 1995, 2: 87)

The debates referred to by Diderot take place in a wider Parisian public space, specifically in the printed media. His departure from Paris in the beginning of the *Promenade Vernet* suggests a reading where the journey to "a country close to the sea and celebrated for the beauty of its sights" constitutes an allegory of the encyclopedists' withdrawal not only from the galleries of the salons but, indeed, from the general public debate. But why, we may ask, this philosophical retreat? Is the philosopher threatened by censorship and incarceration? No, indeed, he retreats because he abhors the intolerable waste of time in the public debates, where answers are found at the bottom of an empty bottle and where the debates are committed to nothing—words, nothing but words. Thus, the journey into the country is also a liberation from the evils of civilization: "ambition, hatred, jealousy, and love, and . . . the thirst of honor and riches" (Diderot 1995, 2: 97). To Diderot, the pessimist, Paris is a place of fruitless discussion and lack of authenticity coupled with personal bias fueled by desire, ambition, and rivalry.

Stepping inside the painting, Diderot creates an allegorical image of artistic and aesthetic autonomy; in addition, *Promenade Vernet* is a fiction that also contains a hint of its own origin. As mentioned above, *Rameau's Nephew* was simultaneous with the *Promenade Vernet*; if we associate the appearance of the word *tumultuous* in the beginning of the latter work with the many occurrences of the same word in the depictions of the antiphilosophers' debates in the novel, the entry into the painted landscape looks very much like an escape into art from the interminable wrangling and partisan skirmishes of life in the city—an escape from the lies and the inevitable flattery, from the inanities of greed and gluttony, that is, an escape from the superficial absurdities of public debate. In the end, Diderot's *Promenade* is basically concerned with aesthetic experience as disinterested pleasure, coupled with a private experience of authenticity and meaning.

But what happens to art and aesthetic perception once it is translated into disinterested pleasure that includes the experience of authenticity and completion? According to Diderot, the beholder's confrontation with the painting gives rise to reflection and provokes an awareness of his mental resources and corporeal capacities.

> I was . . . nonchalantly stretched out in an armchair, allowing my mind to wander as it would, a delicious state in which the soul is unselfconsciously honest, the mind effortless, precise and fastidious, in which ideas and feelings emerge naturally, as from a favorable soil; my eyes

were fixed on an admirable landscape ... I feel ... the pleasure of knowing myself to be as good as I am, the pleasure of examining and taking delight in myself, and the still sweeter pleasure of forgetting myself: Where am I at this moment? What is all this surrounding me? I don't know, I can't say. What's lacking? Nothing. What do I want? Nothing. If there's a God, his being must be like this, taking pleasure in himself. (Diderot 1995, 2: 98)

At this stage Diderot's description of the painting has been replaced by his own bodily sensations and moral emotions. The beauty of the landscape gives way to the beholder's experience of moral beauty or perfection resulting in an undifferentiated merger of the natural beauty (of the painting) with the beholder's experience of moral perfection. The outcome is the construction of a chiastic reciprocity where natural perfection is depicted via the perfection of the beholder's emotion and vice versa. Perfection in one place generates perfection in another. But what, specifically, is the nature of the moral perfection thus magically bestowed on the human subject by the act of contemplating beautiful nature? It is quite obviously not a feeling accompanied by the moral will or the desire to act, nor indeed by a notion of what constitutes the morally valid action, the good deed. Instead, it is an emotion linked only to a feeling of autoerotic pleasure spontaneously associated with a languorous longing to share this blissful state with likeminded fellow beings—the beloved, indeed, who is fittingly addressed in the following sentence in the quotation above. Encountering nature, or rather, in his encounter with art, the philosopher recaptures a feeling of moral integrity, virtue, goodness, and happiness. He may do so because nature is not a subject and therefore cannot be possessed by passions and the will; nature may desire nothing of him and he may demand nothing of it. The alienating, demoralizing, and degenerate struggles for recognition caused by man's desire and stirred by the play of his passions is annulled in the presence of nature and art, allowing the beholder to be nothing but his very own self.

Inevitably, the moral perfection conveyed by Diderot at this point in the *Promenade Vernet* rapidly approaches a state of hedonistic passivity; seemingly, its only active and outward dimension is a spontaneous impulse to communicate and to share the various sensual and emotional benefits derived from the pleasurable details of the act of contemplation. However, just as it is not possible for Diderot to entertain any designs on nature/art or experience any desire related to it, he also has no plans with other people—his readership, in this case. He desires nothing they possess or might possibly wish. Thus, the *Promenade* displays no trace of rivalry or jealousy between

Diderot, as the guiding ego, and the world in which he moves, nor in his relationship to his readers—only generous and spontaneous communication of emotions:

> It is for my friends as well as myself that I read, reflect, write, meditate, listen, look, and feel; in their absence, my devotion relates everything to them, I dream ceaselessly of their happiness; if a beautiful phrase makes an impression on me, they know of it; if I stumble on a good deed, I resolve to tell them about it; if I have before my eyes an enchanting spectacle, without being aware of it I contemplate how I should describe it to them. I have consecrated the use of all my senses and all my faculties to them and perhaps this explains why everything in my discourse and my imagination is exaggerated and enriched; and sometimes they reproach me for this, the ungrateful wretches! (Diderot 1995, 2: 101)

The active social aspect of the moral perfection of Diderot's guiding ego may be seen in the spontaneous will—or inclination—to share his feelings with others by the act of recounting them. In other words, doing your neighbor a good turn consists in a passive and spontaneous transmission of one's private sensual experiences and emotions in an open, intimate, or transparent act of communication. In fact, we see a communicative fellowship, a public sphere—the very antithesis of the divisive, Hobbesian public space of *Rameau's Nephew*. The act of sharing experiences with others and making friends in the process liberates the *public experience* from polemics and assertion of selfhood, creating a public sphere—the republic of readers—which is ruled by an intimate community of fellow beings, a *sensus communis*.

## The Visible Physical Body

This leads me to a question that I have so far neglected: Why does the strategic construction of the autonomy and specific significance of the fine arts and the aesthetic experience take place in connection with painting as a visual medium? Why is painting (or indeed, visuality as such) especially adequate as a vehicle for the philosopher's moral perfection? I suggest that the strategic *mise-en-scène* of the philosopher in some sense stands in need of the painting's visual semiotics of nature. The visual medium of the painting is especially suited to represent the philosopher as a being raised above petty partisanship—as possessing, in fact, a specific link to universal reason and to humanity as such. In order to make this connection clear, I must make a detour to the ekphrastic aspect of Diderot's *Salons*.

To Diderot (and to many other sensually minded linguistics in the eighteenth century), writing about painting was a way to prevent the tendency in language from cutting away from the designated object (the sense impression), fluttering about in the world without direction or purpose. Now, this is precisely what takes place in the world pictured in *Rameau's Nephew*, "where words have separated from reality and have come to supplant it" as Norman Bryson phrases it in *Word and Image: French Patinting of the Ancien Régime* (Bryson 1981, 183). For if language is cut loose from reality to create a reality of its own, it can be used by anyone to say whatever he wants of whomever he pleases. As a result, lies, flattery, and other distortions of reality make inroads into the public sphere. This, according to the author of *Rameau's Nephew*, was what happened when the antiphilosophers targeted him and his friends, whether in newspapers, periodicals, pamphlets, or comedies. In other words, the separation between language and the world lays the basis for unfounded, partisan meanings—a phenomenon discussed by *I* and *He* under the heading *métier-idiotisme* ("trade idioms") in *Rameau's Nephew*. Diderot's critique of linguistic abstraction can be seen as part of the widespread septical attitude toward print culture discussed by Paula McDowell in her essay "Mediating Media Past and Present: Toward a Genealogy of 'Print Culture' and 'Oral Tradition.'" The way to combat this evil—the division of language and meaning in locally determined subjective, partisan, and professional significance—was to recover the sensory charge language had at birth. Diderot saw it as a fundamental task to translate images into language; he wrote ekphrases. As art critic he wanted to create an ekphrastic language endowed with the hieroglyphic capacity of poetic language. What happens in this language is that

> at the same time [that] the soul is moved, the imagination sees and the ears hear what is represented, and discourse ... [becomes] ... a tissue of hieroglyphs gathered one upon the other that paint what is represented.[8] (Diderot 1978, 4: 169)

The hieroglyph produces an image of the signified in the imagination, slowing down the nominalistic abstraction in both speech and writing. This, very precisely, is what Diderot desires with his ekphrastic descriptions. Thus, his descriptions achieve this goal if they succeed in creating a language entirely backed by visual fact. Diderot believes it possible to create a language that is rooted in sensibility and charged with visuality—hence also endowed with objectivity and blessed with universality. Over and above the critical objective, his criticism also served to promote ideas of language philosophy and language politics; he wanted to discover a medicine against nominalistic abstraction, which reduced language to an instrument for partisan politics and manipulation of reality. As it happens, Diderot in several places (so also in the *Promenade Vernet*) denies the possibility of such a reestablishment of language in reality. However, this does not prevent him from employing a sensually based linguistic utopia in his strategic *mise-en-scène* of the philosopher as the *passive* saviour of an increasingly hostile society. I deliberately emphasise the word *passive*, since the philosopher does not fulfil his political role through active participation or intervention in society's conflicts—nor would he probably be allowed to do so. Instead, he stands out as an example to follow, pointing to a better and more civilized future: as he says of the philosopher, he writes and thinks usefully for the future.

When Diderot invites his readers to observe him in Vernet's landscapes, he underpins the typographical and written Diderot-ego with an imagined, visual Diderot-ego. The fiction of his physical entry into the picture incarnates the written incorporeal ego in a body that walks, senses, experiences, feels, and makes gestures. In other words, the visual body is also a physical body; the textual Diderot is reproduced as a living, moving, physical being. We may ask why the philosopher is endowed with a *physical* body by Diderot? First, the physical body is everyman's body. Everybody has a physical body—therefore it is universal; second, in contradistinction to the mechanical body, the physical (or rather, the *physiological*) body may move about of its own accord, it is gifted with life, and it is not moved (or governed) by external forces. In this respect, it connotes freedom and autonomy. The body that moves, senses, and walks about perceives the world as a space of *possibilities* (it can move to a specific destination, or it may choose a different place, or a third—which is precisely what Diderot is doing and of which he is informing his readers in the *Promenade Vernet*). To the physical body the world is not an already established existing fact given to it as a social and political geometry to which the subject must adapt. Third, the physical body is invariably transparent. In virtue of the body's inherent sensuousness, which ties its many parts together into a coherent whole, there is a continually ongoing translation or communication of sense impressions from one part of the body to other parts, a process taking place beyond will and consciousness. Thus, the physical body communicates spontaneously and invariably both inside itself and outside with the world. Neither will nor consciousness is involved in this process, no intentional editing or conventionally regulated translation of sense impressions takes place. This body, therefore, can only speak the truth. It cannot lie, and it cannot flatter. Nor can it employ language as a tool to promote partisan interests or as a weapon to fight rivals and enemies. Moreover, it possesses an undeniable, corporeally based fullness of sense and meaning.

Listen to the way this bodily subject communicates:

Oh nature, how grand you are! Oh nature, how imposing, majestic, and beautiful you are! Such were the words that emerged from the depths of my soul, but how could I convey to you the variety of delicious sensations that accompanied these words as I repeated them over and over to myself? Doubtless they would have been legible on my face, they would have been discernible in the accents of my voice, alternatively weak, vehement, hesitant, and continuous. Sometimes my eyes and arms rose toward the heavens, only to fall back against my side as driven there by lassitude. I believe I shed a few tears. (Diderot 1995, 2: 115)

In several instances in the *Promenade Vernet* the expressive outburst of uncontrolled gesture and tearful visuality replaces the semiotics of conventional nominalistic signs. Because it belongs to the fundamental existent modes of the body, the semiotics of gestures and tears can never be cut loose from its sensory and corporeal origin; natural, mimetic signs can never degenerate into a system of nominalistic terms of abstract manipulation to be exploited at will. Endowed with the visual and bodily support lacking in the printed media, Diderot's ekphrastic descriptions and visual gestures unite to constitute an ideal language.

During the 1760s, Diderot increasingly transposes his philosophical activities to art (and to some extent to science), while he also attempts to cut the fine arts away from the social and political realms. At the same time, he embarks on a retreat from this space in order, paradoxically, to gain a further foothold in the public sphere. The isolation of art (and of the artist and the critic) thus brought about by Diderot sheds new light upon the emergence of modern art criticism, an event for which he is often credited. The birth of modern art criticism now turns out to be coincident with the isolation of art from the political sphere. One could say that Diderot does to art what the English Romantics Wordsworth and Coleridge did to literature (cf. Miles, Siskin) In each case a specialization of the aesthetic is taking place: the differentiation of art and politics is deeply intertwined with the formation of the notion of aesthetic autonomy. In Diderot's work, the genesis of the idea of autonomy emerges within a discursive struggle between universal and uplifting scholarship and knowledge formation, on the one hand, and the highly biased public space of newspapers, on the other.

Securely ensconced in the self-contained arena of fine arts or situated at the observational distance provided by the paintings, Diderot availed himself of a private and intimate public persona when he and his colleagues intervened in the public debates. Physical Diderot is not only a public figure, but also a private one—not in terms of private interests or subjective passions (jealousy, desire, hate, etc.) but private in a physical and universal sense. In the *Promenade Vernet* subjectivity and intimacy (e.g., the sensuousness, the gestures, and the pleasures of the body) appertain to universal man. However, we must not forget that universal humanity may only be experienced in the company of friends—among the happy few, that is.

# NOVEL KNOWLEDGE

## JUDGMENT, EXPERIENCE, EXPERIMENT

### JOHN BENDER

## I

I begin with Émile Zola's manifesto "Le Roman Expérimental" of 1880, although my own essay is concerned with the novel of the first half of the eighteenth century, and specifically with the place of the new novel of that time in the scientific revolution. Inspired by the writings of the physician Claude Bernard about contemporary medical research, Zola set forth a program for the novel, emphasizing its power to define the workings of the human machine in society. "What constitutes the experimental novel," Zola says, is "to possess a knowledge of the mechanism of the phenomena inherent in man, to show the machinery of his intellectual and sensory manifestations, under the influences of heredity and environment, such as physiology shall give them to us, and then finally to exhibit man living in social conditions produced by himself, which he modifies daily, and in the heart of which he himself experiences a continual transformation." Paraphrasing Bernard, Zola declares that "experiment is but provoked observation." He goes on to insist that "all experimental reasoning is based on doubt, for the experimentalist should have no preconceived idea, in the face of nature, and should always retain his liberty of thought. He simply accepts the phenomena that are produced, when they are proved" (Zola 1964, 20–21 and 3). Zola's novelist was heir to Sir Francis Bacon's skeptical natural philosopher.

It is something of a reach from Zola back to a Daniel Defoe, Henry Fielding, or Samuel Richardson. But the line of skeptical, experimental inquiry bridges across time from the earlier period to its later and exaggerated form in the positivist program of naturalist fiction—a program underpinned by Zola's insistence upon empirical observation governed by doubt. The long strand of invasive, fact-obsessed, even indecent realism was more obvious to the nineteenth-century American Oliver Wendell Holmes than it may be for us today. His critique of Henry David Thoreau linked *Robinson Crusoe* to *Walden*, and both in turn to Zola—that master "scavenger" with a "slop-pail"—as a "story of Nature in undress as only one who had hidden in her bedroom could have told it." Holmes explicitly understood the link of realism to scientific inquiry: "Happy were it for the world if M. Zola and his tribe would stop even there; but when they cross the borders of science into its infected districts, leaving behind them the reserve and delicacy which the genuine scientific observer never forgets to carry with him, they disgust even those to whom the worst scenes they describe are too wretchedly familiar" (Gougeon 1994, 111–114). Holmes traced the realist lineage from *Robinson Crusoe*, to *Walden*, to the poems of Walt Whitman, to the novels of Zola. The connection of Thoreau to scientific inquiry may seem surprising, yet he does reject received knowledge and insists from the early pages of *Walden* on the validity of experience based in experiment. "How could youths better learn to live," he says, "than by at once trying the experiment of living" (Thoreau 1959, 41).[1] In Holmes's frame of reference, a statement like this participated in the dangerous social values he associated with extreme realism.

In a reversal of the usual scientific expectations, Zola insisted that the novel is equal or superior to medical science. Like the physician, the novelist can engage in structured observation and description. But above all, the novelist can employ the experimental method to reveal the inner workings of living beings interacting in society, whereas analytic medicine has to deal with individuals, and largely with dead ones at that. Zola insists that the element of imagination no longer should find a place in the novelist's profession. In doing so, he merges novelistic fiction with the natural sciences and philosophy. He shares this proximity with earlier novelists and continues their ambition to communicate complex findings to their audiences. William Godwin in *Caleb Williams*, for instance, aimed to bring his own "refined and abstract" rationalist analysis of "Things as They Are" to "persons whom books of philosophy and science are never likely to reach." The title

"Things as They Are" lets readers know that he wants to teach "a valuable lesson, without subtracting from . . . interest and passion" (Godwin 1970, 1). Here, as with Fielding's insistence in *Tom Jones* upon the "probable" as the proper realm of action for the novel, the explicit purpose is to open wider experience to a large public by, as Fielding says, "showing many persons and things which may possibly have never fallen within the knowledge of great part of his readers" (Fielding 1996, 352). Early critics often suggested that readers might best remain free of enlightenment.

My beginning with Zola throws into relief likenesses and differences between knowledge systems, including the novel, that are separated by two hundred years and more. The novel of the first half of the eighteenth century was indeed a novel of experiment, but not precisely in Zola's sense or with his explicitly programmatic demands. For Zola, doubt was a tool of inquiry. In the earlier period doubt more often had remained an implicit epistemological stance. Yet, as I consider here, the earlier novel did also participate in the aspirations and uncertainties about knowledge, experience, and experiment pervasive during the scientific revolution of which it was a part.

## II

The place of the novel in the cross currents of experimental natural philosophy is the chief concern of this essay. My title reflects the central terms and ideas that I will be exploring, "judgment," "experience," and "experiment." These terms link into a broad range of concerns about the relationship of novelistic fictions in the eighteenth century to hypothesis and knowledge making. Novels often were criticized in the eighteenth century because they were licentious or excessively absorptive: their fictional diversion of readers from work, education, or constructive social exchange appeared to be a threat. But perhaps novels were both attractive and criticized because they were sites of experiment issuing into surrogate experience. Perhaps they produced not too much knowledge about vice but too many thought experiments and, with them, too great an expansion of experience and, with it, a potentially dangerous capacity for independent judgment.

The clergyman who instructs the heroine Arabella toward the end of *The Female Quixote* by Charlotte Lennox enters on both sides of the debate when he says, on the one hand, that the "Power of Prognostication, may, by Reading and Conversation, be extended beyond our own Knowledge: and the great Use of Books, is that of participating without Labour or Hazard [in] the experience of others." On the other hand, he narrows the range of valid fiction to that of the empiricist novel when he attacks the kind of romance that disfigures the whole Appearance of the World, and represents every Thing in a Form different from that which Experience has shewn. It is the Fault of the best Fictions, that they teach young Minds to expect strange Adventures and sudden Vicissitudes, and therefore encourage them often to trust to Chance. A long life may be passed without a single Occurrence that can cause much Surprize, or produce any unexpected Consequence... the Order of the World is so established, that all human Affairs proceed in a regular Method, and very little Opportunity is left for Sallies or Hazard, for Assault or Rescue; but the Brave and the Coward, the Sprightly and the Dull, suffer themselves to the carried alike down the Stream of Custom.

Given the close connection between experiment and experience in the thought of the time, novels seem to have been feared because their experiments produced a surplus of experience. This same chapter of *The Female Quixote* contains a ringing endorsement of the newly defined novel of experience: "Truth is not always injured by Fiction. An admirable Writer of our own Time, has found the Way to convey the most solid Instructions, the noblest Sentiments, and the most exalted Piety, in the pleasing Dress of a Novel" (Lennox 1989, 372, 379, 377).[2] The reference to Richardson and a quotation from Samuel Johnson in the same paragraph solidly place Lennox in the latest line of thought about the new novel as a mode of fiction that dwells in the realm of fact.

## III

At one level, this essay has to be an exercise in the history of concepts—*Begriffsgeschichte*—for research on this subject is served by understanding its central terms and the semantic fields they inhabit. These terms have meanings in English and French that resonate together in the context of thought about the novel. This is the level at which I began originally to project this inquiry.

English "judgment" and French "jugement" line up rather closely in senses like "to render judgment juridically" or "to form an opinion," and, after John Locke and David Hume, also "the human faculty that judges and compares ideas." French carries important additional senses that can shade over all but invisibly into English. I have in mind both Claude Adrien Helvétius's "To feel is to judge" ("Sentir est juger"), which appears in the context of his discussion of powerful imaginative or artistic imagery, and also, in parallel, the dictionary sense in French of "to understand in one's mind—to figure forth in the mind, to imagine." Here, the French meaning of "jugement" supplements English significantly with meanings that might be summed up with words like "apprehend" or even "conceive."[3]

English "experience" and French "expérience" line up with one another but also explicitly diverge: for the French term "expérience" means "experiment" as well as "experience." Even in English, the words "experience" and "experiment" intertwine so richly, as in Hume's discussions of judgment and probability in his *Treatise of Human Nature*, that they become elements in one conceptual domain. For instance, "we consider, that tho' we are here suppos'd to have only one experiment of a particular effect, yet we have many millions to convince us of this principle; that like objects, plac'd in like circumstances, will always produce like effects.... The connexion of ideas is not habitual after one experiment; but this connexion is comprehended under another principle, that is habitual.... In all cases we transfer our experience to instances, of which we have no experience, either expressly or tacitly, either directly or indirectly" (Hume 1978, 105).[4] The domain is semantically continuous in French. It is divided in English but can flow easily with a contiguity approaching the continuous.

The word "expériment" also exists in French, of course, and with meanings that align with English. But French offers a fascinating extension of the word. For a person can be "expérimenté," meaning "one who has benefited empirically from experience" in both of its French senses. I am suggesting here that novel readers in the eighteenth century became "expérimenté." This is the condition that Thoreau defined in *Walden* when he ranged, like Crusoe, within the domain of experience governed by experiment.[5]

At another level of concern, as I have tracked these terms through dictionaries, novels, and philosophical texts, it has become clear that they bear on the large question at the heart of this essay: what kind of knowledge did novels make? And for whom? Or, perhaps more precisely, one might ask this: in the context of eighteenth-century thought, how can one characterize the knowledge novels were thought to produce?

Let us pause to ask what "knowledge" meant during the period. The answer is that knowledge forms had undergone profound change during the seventeenth century and continued to be under exacting scrutiny across the eighteenth. Broadly speaking, knowledge, which had been shaped by Aristotelian ideas for centuries before, was no longer an armature of accepted generalizations from which classifications, observations, and understanding of particulars could be derived. Interestingly, these generalizations were earlier called "experience," which in that older frame was considered to be of a general and received character, not the historical, situational, or personally specific information we now assign to the word. In the new paradigm, by contrast, experience was profuse, anecdotal, and scattered. Knowledge increasingly was formed when general principles were determined through controlled analysis of particulars as they emerged from the planned and specialized form of experience called the experiment. Knowledge became contextual, specific, and historical.

I am relying here on Peter Dear's book *Discipline and Experience*, where he declares that "a new kind of experience had become available to European philosophers: the experiment." He continues,

> At the beginning of the seventeenth century, a scientific "experience" was not an "experiment" in the sense of a historically reported experiential event. Instead, it was a statement about the world that, although known to be true thanks to the senses, did not rest on a historically specifiable instance—it was a statement such as "Heavy bodies fall" or "The sun rises in the east." Singular, unusual events were of course noticed and reported, but they were not, by definition, revealing of how nature behaves.

Dear might be placing Bacon's ideas in context when he continues,

> The new scientific experience of the seventeenth century was characterized by the singular historical event experiment, which acted as a surrogate for universal experience. The latter had routinely been regarded as the proper grounding for philosophically legitimate knowledge-statements about nature; the advent of event experiments was a practical response within the mixed mathematical science to a confrontation between such Aristotelian methodological demands and the practical exigencies of making knowledge that would be acceptable to all relevant judges. (Dear 1995, 12–13, 246)[6]

Dear does not quote Bacon's words in *The Advancement of Learning* but might well have noted Bacon's early designation of experiment as planned experience:

> There remains simple experience which, if taken as it comes, is called accident; if sought for, experiment. But this kind of experience is no better than a broom without its band, as the saying is—a mere groping, as of men in the dark, that feel all round them for the chance of finding their way, when they had much better wait for daylight, or light a candle, and then go. But the true method of experience, on the contrary, first lights the candle, and then by means of the candle shows the way; commencing as it does with experience duly ordered and digested, not bungling or erratic, and from it educing axioms, and from established

axioms again new experiments; even as it was not without order and method that the divine word operated on the created mass.[7]

Bacon expounded the institutional form of his ideal in the account of the methodical experiments conducted in Salomon's house in *The New Atlantis*, passages that often are taken to describe the basic ideals of the modern scientific method. That he turned to narrative fiction, albeit in a form traditional since Sir Thomas More's *Utopia*, signals the organic connection between his ideas and emergent new genres of storytelling.

## IV

This new approach to knowledge raised any number of issues, and while we may in retrospect imagine the scientific revolution as a focal point, experimentalists of the time explored a huge range of procedures and formations and raged with debates about method that presented internal and external challenges to the emergent epistemology. Indeed, I would insist that questions about method and the nature of knowledge are intrinsic to modernity as it takes form during the seventeenth and eighteenth centuries. I am identifying the new novel of the eighteenth century as one of the strands in these debates and as one of the modes of experimentation. Indeed, in my view, the implicit ambitions of the new novel parallel those Hume voiced for a new human science in the introduction to *A Treatise of Human Nature*:

> Moral philosophy has . . . this peculiar disadvantage, which is not found in natural, that in collecting its experiments, it cannot make them purposely, with premeditation. . . . We must therefore glean up our experiments in this science from a cautious observation of human life, and take them as they appear in the common course of the world, by men's behaviour in company, in affairs, and in their pleasures. Where experiments of this kind are judiciously collected and compared, we may hope to establish on them a science which will not be inferior in certainty, and will be much superior in utility to any other of human comprehension. (Hume 1978, xix)

*Tom Jones* cannot but come to mind as a prime novelistic exhibit in this Humean frame of reference. Can the novel overcome the disadvantages of Hume's new science of the human?

Fielding's continual presence in *Tom Jones*, especially in the opening chapters of each book, points to the work's organization of the scattered experience of the characters into the focused and methodical order of experiment. *Tom Jones* explicitly puts its leading character into the laboratory and asks readers to observe his behavior side-by-side with the narrator. The theme is clear, for instance, when Mr. Allworthy refuses to allow Thwackum to continue a whipping that, "possibly fell little short of the torture with which confessions are in some countries extorted from criminals," in order to break young Tom's stalwart unwillingness to implicate Allworthy's gamekeeper in an episode of poaching: "But Mr. Allworthy absolutely refused to consent to the experiment. He said the boy had suffered enough already for concealing the truth, even if he was guilty, seeing that he could have no motive but a mistaken point of honour" (Fielding 1996, 107). Mr. Allworthy draws the line at this experiment with a human subject, one verging on torture.

The fictional flexibility of the novel as a genre opens a range of experimental possibilities that Hume does not consider when he writes, again in his introduction, "When I am at a loss to know the effects of one body upon another in any situation, I need only put them in that situation, and observe what results from it. But should I endeavour to clear up after the same manner any doubt in moral philosophy, by placing myself in the same case with that which I consider, 'tis evident this reflection and premeditation would so disturb the operation of my natural principles, as must render it impossible to form any just conclusion from the phaenomenon" (Hume 1978, xix). As Fielding's narrative experiment unfolds, his introductions encourage readers to become moral philosophers and active critical enquirers under his guidance. Readers must constantly judge evidence, probability, and the chain of cause and effect as he pushes them toward the inductive method of moral philosophy.

Concurrently, the very existence of a narrative frame and the internal logic of the plot, so strongly emphasized by Fielding as a clockwork device, guarantee that such induction will uncover patterns of cause and effect that underlie the action. Fielding, one might say, builds a novel on the very defect that Hume had identified in Newtonian induction: that its conclusions are prefigured in its very premises and methodological rules. The very circular character of induction so devastatingly criticized by Hume meshes in *Tom Jones* with a plot literally mapped across England in a circular pattern of error and return.

The halts, starts, and erroneous trials in *Tom Jones* call to mind the many false starts and failed attempts in Robert Boyle's published experiments. Boyle's form of presentation was structured, as Steven Shapin and Simon Schaffer show in *Leviathan and the Air-Pump*, to project a rhetorical formation that they name the "virtual witness" to the experiments—a witness who authenticates Boyle's findings for readers who, by definition, participate at a distance. This virtual witnessing parallels surrogate observation in novels by witnesses who stand in for readers or who, as with the narrator of *Tom Jones*, set the very terms of observation (Shapin and Schaffer 1985, chaps. 2 and 6).[8]

And so, with this framework from Hume and Fielding in view, among the many interrelated questions germane to our consideration of the novel in this essay, and among the many circulating at the time, three strike me as central to inquiry about the place of the novel during the period.

The first, as I have been arguing, is that of surrogate witnessing. This is the practice in early modern science of placing a single experiment at the foundation of a generalizing inductive process even though this unique experiment could not have been witnessed by the wide audience required for assent to newly defined general principles, or indeed witnessed by anyone or any but a very small group present at the experimental site. What Robert Hooke called the *instantia crusis* and Sir Isaac Newton the *experimentum crusis* demands that we place our trust in accounts of the historical experience of others and use their accounts to extend our own experience to the point of assent—despite the potential for deceit or fictionalization.

The second question has to do with the contrived nature of these experiments. The methodological move was away from a Scholastic, formally mediated observation of a nature that was imagined as a book to be read, and toward experimental contrivances involving precision-manufactured devices like the telescope, the microscope, the refined glass prism, or the finely blown glass–globed air pump. Artificiality and contrivance all raised the specter of fictionality and trust. As knowledge became extrinsic rather than intrinsic, the concurrent insistence on replicability that was, for instance, so much a part of the reception of Newton's *Opticks*, emerged as a response to this specter. Replicability makes possible a literal witnessing by further limited observers but did not eliminate the benefits of virtual witnessing as produced linguistically.[9]

My third question has to do with the challenge of moving from the unique historical particularity and contrivance of the *experimentum crusis* to truths of general validity. Baconian induction became, in Newton's hands, the device to resolve this challenge. Newton's "Rules of Reasoning in Philosophy" aimed to codify the method. The last of the four rules, added to the *Principia* in 1726, directly addressed the standing of inductive findings as knowledge: "In experimental philosophy we are to look upon propositions collected by general induction from phaenomena as accurately or very nearly true, notwithstanding any contrary hypotheses that may be imagined, till such time as other phaenomena occur, by which they may either be made more accurate, or liable to exceptions."[10] Hume, who originally aimed to follow Newton's example in his *Treatise*, delimited induction much more sharply. He found that induction, for all of its theoretical and practical benefits, crumbled under skeptical scrutiny, and lost its epistemological stability because it was at ground a device for filling in the gap between empirical, factually based sensory observation and mental constructs dependent on human memory and mental fictions of causality. For Hume, these fictions enabled provisional findings to be made and worked to stabilize our perception of the real but they did not certify knowledge. I consider here that the manifest fictions of the new novel could work, paradoxically, to guarantee induction by framing it within tightly controlled narrative structures. Thomas Reid's reassertion of Newtonian induction under the banner of his common-sense philosophy did not close the gap Hume had opened in his treatment of the problem of induction, and the so-called "problem of induction" remains an active philosophical topic even now.

My claim in this essay, at its core, then, is quite simple: that the early novel figures in specific ways in the discursive network now called the scientific revolution, and that our understanding of the novel as a genre is expanded by viewing it as a system that puts into play the three basic issues I have identified.

V

The early novel in its many permutations, including works by Defoe, Richardson and Fielding, depended crucially upon devices associated with surrogate observation of the kind described by Shapin and Schaffer under the heading "virtual witnessing." Let us recall here that these devices are largely those of a historically specific sort of verbal rhetoric. The novel depends fundamentally on a rhetoric that allows, even demands, that readers add to their stock of knowledge through assent to the truth of absent experience. Defoe early experimented with rhetoric of this kind in *A True Relation of the Apparition of Mrs. Veal* (1706), a story of visitation from the dead that is attested in the manner of an affidavit with minute evidentiary particulars certified by a gentleman justice of the peace of Maidstone, Kent: "This relation is matter of fact, and attended with such circumstances as may induce any reasonable man to believe it." It ends with an assertion that might seem like a prefiguration of Hume through a glass darkly: "This thing has very much affected me, and I am as well satisfied as I am of the best grounded matter of fact. And why should we dispute mater of fact because we cannot solve things of which we can have no certain or demonstrative notions, seems strange to me" (Defoe 1977, 294–301).[11] The powerful frame of narration here works to certify the evidence and points to its factuality by simulating the effect not only of a legal document but also of a scientific report. Bacon's unbound broom of experience is shaped into an account resembling that of an *experimentum crusis*.

Richardson's definition of the precisely balanced mental posture he hoped for in readers of Clarissa's fictional letters remarkably mirrors Newton's fourth rule, albeit from the inversely parallel realm of the novel:

> I could wish that the *Air* of Genuineness had been kept up, tho' I want not the letters to be *thought* genuine; only so far kept up, I mean, as they would not prefatically be owned *not* to be genuine: and this for fear of weakening their Influence where any of them are aimed to be exemplary; as well as to avoid hurting that kind of Historical Faith which Fiction itself is generally read with, tho we know it to be Fiction. (Richardson to William Warburton, 19 April 1748 in Richardson 1964, 85)

In other words, Richardson wants readers to be poised on a skeptical knife edge between acceptance of his novelistic letters as real and awareness that they are fictions. Catherine Gallagher embraces the term "ironic credulity" to account for this posture in fiction more broadly (Gallagher 2006).[12]

In parallel to my second question about contrivance in experiments, the novel also contrives situations—often extreme and counterintuitive—that transform fictional experience into decisive experiments in the course of their action. A contrivance of this kind is what Arabella's clergyman instructor notes in *The Female Quixote*. Indeed, Arabella's own awakening to reality comes after a contrivance, within the plot of the novel, of what she takes to be a life-threatening attack on her. And, in tandem with my third question about the standing of the unique event, the quasi-inductive leap from particulars to general principles that Defoe, Richardson, and Fielding aspired to actuate in readers of their novels operates in these books through the causal sequences we call narratives. In a reverse system, cause and effect frame induction and even stand in for it rather than being its outcome. The precise operation of machinery contrived by the novelist—as Fielding continually informs his readers—replaces the clockmaker God's precision. Novels of this kind suspend the limitations of induction for their duration.

## VI

Modern theory of the novel includes a concept that assists my thinking in this essay. It is Ian Watt's term "realism of assessment" as he applied it to the novel—especially the novels of Henry Fielding and Jane Austen. Realism of assessment, in the context of Watt's central category of "realism of presentation," means something like judgment founded on experiment and experience. The experience in question for Watt is that of the represented narrator, or so it seems to me, though of course such assessment has the reader as its audience (Watt 1959, 256–257 and 288–297).

Assessment is at the heart of both Locke's and Hume's accounts of judgment but for them this judgment does not attain the status of knowledge. Locke observes of this limit that, "I must apply my self to *Experience;* as far as that reaches, I may have certain Knowledge, but not father." He continues, "I deny not, but a Man accustomed to rational and regular Experiments shall be able to see farther into the Nature of Bodies, and guess righter at their yet unknown Properties, than one, that is a Stranger to them: But yet, as I have said, this is but Judgment and Opinion, not Knowledge and Certainty" (Locke 1975, 645). Hume asserts that "since it is not from knowledge or any scientific reasoning that we derive the opinion of the necessity of a cause to every new production, that opinion must necessarily arise from observation and experience." And he goes on to insist that, "'Tis therefore by experience only that we can infer the existence of one object from that of another. The nature of experience is this" (Hume 1978, 82 and 87). Clarissa claims as much when she writes to Miss Howe—herself impersonating an elderly lady giving advice to a younger mother:

> Nothing but experience can give us a strong and efficacious conviction... and when we would inculcate the fruits of *that* upon the minds of those we love, who have not lived long enough to find those fruits, and would hope that our *advice* should have as much force upon *them* as *experience* has upon *us;* and which, perhaps *our* parents' advice had not upon *ourselves* at our daughters' time of life; should we not proceed by patient reasoning and gentleness, that we may not harden where we would convince? (Richardson 1982, 4: 295–296)

We should not be deceived by Richardson's post-facto moralistic explications of *Clarissa* or by his pietism, for he appears to have been quite attuned to the problematics with which I am concerned here.

Robinson Crusoe illustrates the theory of experiment-based experience when he describes his acquisition of knowledge about the strategy of planting crops:

> The rainy season, and the dry season, began now to appear regular to me, and I learn'd to divide them so, as to provide for them accordingly. But I bought all by experience before I had it; and this I am going to relate, was one of the most discouraging experiments that I made at all:

> I have mention'd that I had sav'd the few ears of barley and rice which I had so surprisingly found spring up, as I thought, of themselves, and believe there were about thirty stalks of rice, and about twenty of barley; and now I thought it a proper time to sow it after the rains, the sun being in its *southern* position going from me.
>
> Accordingly I dug up a Piece of Ground, as well as I could with my wooden spade, and dividing it into two parts, I sow'd my grain; but as I was sowing, it casually occur'd to my thoughts, that I would not sow it all at first, because I did not know when was the proper time for it; so I sow'd about two thirds of the seed, leaving about a handful of each.

Crusoe forms his judgment through ongoing experimental assessment based on observation and probability. He makes a prudential decision founded on experience, and he emerges with knowledge as Hume later will characterize it. His repertory of knowledge grows across the action, developing into a virtuoso expertise, not just in natural processes but, as Zola says, in the capacity "to exhibit man living in social conditions produced by himself, which he modifies daily, and in the heart of which he himself experiences a continual transformation." Significant here is the reach of Crusoe's experience across time, for the concept of experience would mean little without memory of the past and projection into the future. The reach of remembered experience as history is crucial when, a few pages before his story about the crops, Crusoe recounts having found abundant fruit, especially grapes, in his island's highland woods: "I was exceeding glad of them; but I was warn'd by my experience to eat sparingly of them, remembering, that when I was ashore in *Barbary*, the eating of Grapes kill'd several of our *English* Men who were slaves there, by throwing them into fluxes and fevers" (Defoe 2001, 83–84 and 79–80).[13] With expertise gained by experience at Crusoe's command, he is able to stage the episode toward the end of his island stay in which he entraps the mutineers. His expertise now comprehends not only experience and its special variant, experiment, but also the power to make the narrative fictions with which he lures his prey (Bender 1987, 55–56).

What other approach might Defoe have written for Crusoe to take as a character? It is hard to imagine Crusoe as a master of received knowledge and deduction rather than of sense observation and induction, but we may speculate that he could have employed the opposite of his experiential experimentalism, which was called "theory" in his own time. Clarissa's own Lovelace, for instance, declares of one Miss Rawlins that she is, "an agreeable young Lady enough; but not beautiful. She has sense, and would be thought *to know the world*, as it is called; but, for her knowledge, is more indebted to *theory* than *experience*. A mere whipped-syllabub knowledge this, Jack, that always fails the person who trusts to it, when it should hold to do her service.... But, for Miss Rawlins, if I can add *experience* to her *theory*, what an accomplished person will she be!" (Richardson 1982, 3: 216) Although Lovelace gives the idea of experience a salacious twist here, he is operating within the epistemology of his day. Did *Clarissa* protect the Miss Rawlinses of the world by expanding their experience? Richardson seems sincerely to have believed that it would.

Jonathan Swift's Gulliver has experiment forced upon him, and vows that it confirms both what he has heard and his own past experience when confronted with a gigantic domestic cat in the phantasmatically huge realm of Brobdignaag:

> I heard a Noise behind me like that of a Dozen Stocking-Weavers at work; and turning my Head, I found it proceeded from the Purring of this Animal, who seemed to be three Times larger than an Ox, as I computed by the View of her Head, and one of her Paws.... The Fierceness of this Creature's Countenance altogether discomposed me; although I stood... above fifty Foot off.... But it happened there was no Danger; for the Cat took not the least Notice of me when my Master placed me within three Yards of her. And as I have been always told, and found true by Experience in my Travels, that flying, or discovering Fear before a fierce Animal, is a certain Way to make it pursue or attack you; so I resolved in this dangerous Juncture to shew no Manner of Concern. I walked with Intrepidity five or six Times before the very Head of the Cat, and came within half a Yard of her; whereupon she drew her self back, as if she were more afraid of me. (Swift 2005, 81–82)[14]

Gulliver's senses deceive him into thinking about stocking weavers but his experience, and what he has been told, secure his safety despite the doubtful analogy between wild and domestic animals. Crusoe's assessments based on experience are confirmed by experiment, and Gulliver's prove at least in part to be. But their actions do not both constitute realism of assessment in Watt's sense. Rather, the narrations in which the two appear as characters frame their assessments in ways that produce quite diverse effects. The implicit ironic asides of Swift's narration, as it presents Gulliver's alternate cowering and swaggering, guide the reader to a specific stance. And one wonders in Swift how integral Gulliver's narration is supposed to be when it is possible that the metaphor of the stocking weavers may be a retrospective ornament on the hero's part. Close readers also may question Gulliver's judgment if they recall the episode when huge Brobdignaagian field workers bear down on him and he decrees that everyone knows animals to be more savage the larger they are. This is precisely the opposite of what he could have observed in Lilliput where he himself is a gentle giant and the Lilliputians are, on the whole, vicious.

Swift's critique of scientific inquiry run amuck in book 3 of *Gulliver's Travels* could seem to diminish the probability that his narratives in the other books would intersect with the rhetoric of the scientific revolution. But his satire of excess in that one book does not rule out what one might call "normal science" in the others—books that are often treated as part of the history of the new novel. Swift's generic choice of the travel story as the armature of his accounts also worked in the 1720s, after the enormous impact of *Robinson Crusoe*, to embed devices of the empiricist novel in his narrative. Even as he satirizes such narratives, he was swept into their technical vortex. Another dimension of *Gulliver's Travels* that may seem to cut against any association of it with the new novel is the element of fantasy as the core of each book's action. Yet, fantastic stories are not necessarily incompatible with the narrative techniques of realism, as the linguistic practices of the Gothic novel reveal in Horace Walpole's *Castle of Otranto* and its heirs. Indeed, many works in the canon of the nineteenth-century British and American novel have powerful Gothic aspects and yet are narrated in the modes of realism (Bender 1998, 16–18; Bender 2009).

Swift's ironic signposts, which become so massive in book 3 of *Gulliver's Travels* that they move away from implication and indirect statement to manifesto, define possible responses. The much more neutral presentation of Crusoe by Defoe opens the potential for readers to make judgments of their own—that is, to the weighing of evidence, experience, and experiment in order to arrive at judgments of the kind characteristic of Fielding's or Austen's "realism of assessment."

## VII

Realism of assessment implicitly includes the consideration of probability. Locke devoted an entire chapter to the topic in book 4 of his *Essay concerning Human Understanding*. Knowledge being, in his account, "nothing but the perception of connexion and agreement, or disagreement and repugnancy of any of our ideas," probability "is nothing but the appearance of such an Agreement, or Disagreement, by the intervention of Proofs, whose connexion is not constant and immutable, or at least is not perceived to be so, but is, or appears for the most part to be so, and is enough to induce the Mind to *judge* the Proposition to be true, or false, rather than the contrary." He continues, "*Probability* is likeliness to be true, the very notation of the Word signifying such a Proposition, for which there be Arguments or Proofs, to make it pass or to be received for true. The entertainment the Mind gives this sort of Propositions, is called *Belief, Assent,* or *Opinion*" (Locke 1975, 525 and 654–655).[15] In such a context, as Peter Dear notes, citing Ian Hacking, the "probable" means "worthy of approbation" rather than simply "likely" (Dear 1995, 23). We should not hurry, then, to bring the modernist rise of mathematical probabilities too quickly into the picture in thinking about novelistic knowledge during the first half of the century or even later.

Although many speculations about probabilistic understanding in moral, ethical, and judicial affairs were undertaken in the eighteenth century, and the Marquis de Condorcet, for instance, tried to apply mathematical probabilistic thinking to aspects of society including judicial practice, the sense that the calculus of probability might govern practical human decisions was not widespread.[16] Even in the realm of games of chance, where Edmund Hoyle's work was very broadly disseminated beginning in the 1740s and 1750s, the practical effects were few.[17] Insurance brokers and annuity writers, for instance, were slow to bring into practice the findings of mathematicians—even findings that were specifically about the field of business (Gigerenzer 1989, chap. 1). In addition, and in general harmony with Locke's approach to probability, which includes an element of intuition, the very modern assumption that the rational, probabilistic projection of circumstance is at odds with common sense does not reflect eighteenth-century practice, in which, according to Lorraine Daston, the mathematicians studying probability actively sought to align their findings with those of commonsense reasoning—even sometimes adjusting their math to conform to common sense (Gigerenzer 1989, chap. 1).

*The Female Quixote* is the novelistic *locus classicus* defining the kind of judgment that Watt calls "realism of assessment" and that he assigns to narrators. This novel also includes a debate on the issues of concern here. At the end of this work, as noted earlier, the clergyman who appears in order to set the heroine, Arabella, to rights and to correct her uncritical belief in fantastical romance fictions, asserts that, "When the sailor in certain latitudes sees the clouds rise, experience bids him expect a storm. When any monarch levies armies, his neighbors prepare to repel any invasion." And then, "The only Excellence of Falsehood... is its Resemblance to Truth; as therefore any Narrative is more liable to be confuted by its Inconsistency with known Fact, it is a greater Distance from the Perfection of Fiction; for there can be no Difficulty in framing a Tale, if we are left at Liberty to invert all history and Nature for our own Conveniency" (Lennox 1989, 372 and 378). The good divine is functioning as a hybrid of narrator and character when he works Arabella through a series of empirical tests of her faith in romance. He is, from the point of view I take here, framing a distinction, on the one hand, between fictions that enhance the powers of readers as they form the probabilistic judgments with which they must make their way through he world, and on the other hand, fictions that diminish these powers or, at worst, foster delusion. He is framing a method for using experience to distinguish between fiction and reality. For this purpose, the broad expansion of experience that the empiricist novel made possible functioned as knowledge.

Do the fictions that the Divine implicitly endorses—the ones we now call "realist" novels—actually make knowledge for readers? Or for science? Certainly, they can provide templates for practical reason or judgment based in experiment, experience, and—to invoke that French sense of "jugement"—intuitive apprehension of the world. As John Richetti says of Locke's *Essay*, "Within the dramatizations of Book II at least, 'reality' itself is an ultimate hypothesis, an extrapolation from the data experience provides" (Richetti 1983, 89).[18]

I would suggest in closing that novelistic knowledge resides not only in the new novel's expansion of experience but also in the genre's staging of the act of assessment as ongoing probabilistic judgment. And is this knowledge? Let us recall, as I give Hume the last word in this essay, that his arguments come down to this astonishing finding—one that in itself could be described as a theory of the novel:

> We must . . . in every reasoning form a new judgment, as a check or controul on our first judgment or belief; and must enlarge our view to comprehend a kind of history of all the instances, wherein our understanding has deceiv'd us, compar'd with those, wherein its testimony was just and true. Our reason must be consider'd as a kind of cause, of which truth is the natural effect; but such-a-one as by the irruption of other causes, and by the inconstancy of our mental powers, may frequently be prevented. By this means all knowledge degenerates into probability; and this probability is greater or less, according to our experience of the veracity or deceitfulness of our understanding, and according to the simplicity or intricacy of the question. (Hume 1978, 180)

Perhaps this is the best we can do, useful as the discipline of what we now call the scientific method has proven to be. But the new novel of Hume's own time was experimenting with methods to improve the odds.

# THE PIRATICAL ENLIGHTENMENT

ADRIAN JOHNS

The term *Enlightenment* carries connotations of a certain kind of information dispersal. The association is with illumination itself—of light spreading equally in all directions from a central source. The image is a powerful one, but it was not universally invoked in the eighteenth century itself, and when it was, it was attended by problems and contradictions. Those problems and contradictions become apparent as soon as practical questions are posed about enlightening as a process. What were the means, motors, and routes by which "light" actually spread? What obstacles did it face? In reality, the transfer from place to place of texts, ideas, practices, and the like was scarcely amenable to such a simple model. As this book shows in detail, mediation was an essential and complex constituent of the process itself. The consequential point, however, was not that the model was wrong, but that the gaps between it and the mundane experiences of those involved—authors, readers, booksellers, printers, and censors—provoked movements for change. If the practice of communication was not lightlike, they asked, then what radical transformation to institutions, practices, and beliefs might make it so? Toward the end of the eighteenth century, many countries and colonies saw sustained and passionate debates around this question. They articulated and turned on issues of epistemology, political economy, and ethics. This chapter is about how some of those debates proceeded, especially in the German lands, such that they gave rise to a broad-based concept of "creativity" of which we, for good and ill, are the inheritors.

## Piracy and the Trajectories of Enlightenment

The kind of ubiquity that accompanied certain Enlightenment works and ideas is not one with which we are nowadays very familiar. We are used to living in a world where the system of publishing operates according to more or less common standards; internationalized copyright laws are, among other things, the projection of those standards into the legal sphere. In general, we have something of a hub-and-spoke system, with works published from central locations—London, New York, Frankfurt, Paris. (At least, this was true until very recently: digital technology and networked print-on-demand systems are now changing the game once again.) Industry and capital have fostered a regime that does, after the fact, more or less accord with the model of enlightened dissemination. In the eighteenth century, things were very different. Printing was a local craft, addressing local and regional markets. Its legal, conventional, and moral institutions were local, too. Printed ideas attained ubiquity not only by distribution from major centers, but also by tension and competition between them and a more numerous set of reprinters. The reprinters were relays, if you will, en route between publisher and reader. The more the competition, the greater the ubiquity.

That distinction separates our own perceptions quite radically from those of readers in the early modern Republic of Letters. We tend to think of the great cultural upheavals of that epoch in terms of arguments disseminating in raylike fashion from central sources, especially Paris and, a little later, Edinburgh. But what actually happened was far more *mediated* than that. John Locke's works, for example, emerged first from London but were reprinted in Dublin, Glasgow, Amsterdam, The Hague, Rotterdam, Geneva, Brussels, Paris, Leipzig, Uppsala, Jena, Mannheim, Milan, Naples, Stockholm (by order of the Swedish Riksdag, no less), and, ultimately, Boston (Attig 1985; Yolton 1998). Jean-Jacques Rousseau's *Nouvelle Héloïse*, appearing first in Paris, was soon reproduced in "Amsterdam" (actually London), Geneva, Lausanne, Neuchâtel, Basle, Leipzig, and Brussels (McEachern 1993). Montesquieu's work, again first published in Paris, reappeared in all the same countries. Voltaire's appeared initially, sometimes, in Geneva, only to be reprinted in Paris and London. In Berlin, Friedrich Nicolai attempted to reprint all the best English literary works (Selwyn 2000, 31–32). Goethe's *Sorrows of Young Werther*, probably the most sensational single publishing phenomenon of the century, achieved that status by virtue of appearing in some thirty different editions, many of them in translation, and almost all unauthorized (Blanning 2002, 251–252). In each case the reprinters acted independently—or at least, they seemed to. And that is not even to venture into the fascinating but shadowy world of the "radical" Enlightenment, in which tracts circulated in manuscript or in editions with false imprints—the world of "Spinozisme," of John Toland, and of the Illuminati.[1]

When readers invoked concepts like diffusion, dissemination, or, for that matter, Enlightenment to describe this, they were therefore adopting metaphors whose relation to what actually happened could never be straightforward. Insofar as Enlightenment existed at all, this was its foundation and its manifestation. From vast multivolume enterprises (the *Encyclopédie*) to small, fugitive castaways (scientific papers and newspaper stories), every conceivable kind of knowledge spread across the Continent and beyond in *this* way, through multiple reappropriations, generally unauthorized and often denounced. Cultural dispersion operated as a kind of chain reaction. Or rather, to use a more apposite image, it resembled not an orrery (representing the model of central illumination) but the kind of firework that amazed eighteenth-century observers by producing successive staggered bursts across the sky. An initial edition from one location would find its way to a place of reprinting, which would generate a thousand new copies; one of those would then spark another explosion of copies from another reprint center; and so on. Cascades of reprints carried ideas across Europe. When Italian readers encountered Locke, they were much less likely to be viewing Locke's own words than those words as translated into Italian from a French rendering manufactured in the Netherlands. This was the everyday nature of the book. No piracy, we might say, no Enlightenment (Darnton 2003, 3–29).[2]

But it was not as simple as that. For the most part, reprinting was not technically "piracy." That is, it was not illicit. The defining characteristic of licit reprinting was that it was a cross-border phenomenon. Printers in Swiss cantons reproduced the editions of the Paris book guild; those in the Low Countries reprinted French, German, and English titles; and booksellers in Edinburgh, Glasgow, and Dublin commissioned reprints of London works. In Vienna, most notoriously of all, the imperial court munificently supported the huge reprinting empire of Johannes Thomas Edler von Trattner. There was no legal basis whatsoever for literary "property" to forbid such activities. Moreover, mercantilist economic doctrines suggested that domestic reprinting was to be *preferred*, as an article of national policy, to the importing of books from abroad. In consequence, it was perfectly possible—indeed, probable—for a given volume to be either legitimate or piratical depending on where a reader happened to encounter it. Piracy was an attribute of the politics of space. So, therefore, was Enlightenment.

It followed that the most fertile sites of reprinting were places with indistinct borders—places whose political autonomy was ambiguous. One of these was Scotland, only subsumed into a "United Kingdom" in 1707 and retaining a largely discrete legal system. Another was Ireland, a separate kingdom with its own parliament but a shared monarch. The German states had a similarly metaphysical status vis à vis the Holy Roman Empire, as did the papal enclave of Avignon vis à vis France for much of the period. In each case, as a result, participants in clashes over reprinting ended up articulating rival understandings of nationhood itself. Irish reprinters portrayed their reproductions of Richardson as national projects; Scotland's urged Edinburgh readers to buy their reprints in order to preserve Scottish culture from English predations.

One can identify broadly three kinds of polity in which reprinting became controversial in such high terms: centralized monarchies, colonies, and composite states. The first of these was exemplified by France, where authorial property was conjoined to royal power by a complex system of censorship and *privilèges* designed to restrain rival publishers in the provinces and neighboring realms without quite forcing them into outright smuggling. The second was exemplified by America, where manufacturing was discouraged on mercantilist grounds. Reprinting in Philadelphia and Boston therefore was an act of defiance, especially in the hands of a Paineite like Robert Bell, the ex-Scottish, ex-Dublin reprinter par excellence. Eventually it would become an act of nation-building. And the third kind was exemplified by Scotland, Ireland, or best of all, the German lands. The roughly three hundred German states both were and were not autonomous, and reprinting across their borders was ubiquitous. As a result, the "public sphere" there differed significantly from that in France or Britain. Much of this essay will deal with the peculiarities to which this composite polity of print gave rise.

Each of these locations produced its own practice, ideology, and even epistemology of what we may loosely call piracy. Their debates were about shaping futures as much as about making the best of the present. Each therefore charted a different—often profoundly different—trajectory of Enlightenment. For example, debates over authorship, literary property, and piracy advanced various ideals of public debate itself.[3] The public sphere depended on the credibility of a representation of print as something like Adam Smith's "great mercantile republic" of commerce: an ideal system of circulation enjoying "perfect liberty" (Smith 1976a, 1: 443, 2: 606). It was of paramount importance that the creation, circulation, and commerce of printed works be accepted as nondistorting processes. But just as no nation embraced free trade to Smith's ideal extent, so none had a book trade that was innocent of regulations, bylaws, cartels, and craft customs. The equivalents of duties and bounties pervaded the Republic of Letters. As works moved through this space, being reprinted and reedited as they went, the fidelity of editions was sustained as well as imperiled by complex interplays of regulation and competition, constraint and enterprise. Exactly how this took place in particular polities affected the nature and reputation of public reason in each of them. The arguments of Diderot and Condorcet, which have been restored to view recently by Carla Hesse and Roger Chartier, are cases in point (Hesse 1990; Chartier 1991, 47–66).

Metropolitan booksellers (*publishers* did not yet exist as a clear and distinct kind) almost always affected to deplore the reprinting enterprise—when it was practiced by others. They denounced it as a sin against the order, the very nature, of print. It endangered the fragile economy of credit on which the manufacture and distribution of substantial works depended. Their own capital typically resided in a small range of steady-selling titles, and they claimed that only by keeping these secure could they take risks on the production of new and worthy books. Their ideal was a trade of relatively compact groups of established operators, sharing principles of civility on the basis of which they could extend credit to each other across distances. Distinctions certainly existed—most obviously, Britain and France had no counterpart to the German practice of bartering sheets at fairs—but there was no room at all for radical volatility. They thus claimed that reprinting posed a threat to both the production of literature and the identity of the literature that was produced. What *was* the *Nouvelle Héloïse* if every locale was producing its own version? How could public reason coalesce around it?

Reprinters had a robust answer to that challenge. They said that reprinting actually secured public reason. Not only did it spread more works more widely, but it bolstered textual fidelity, for competition weeded out inaccuracies more effectively than the printing press alone ever could. After all, they competed to be the most faithful. What changes they did introduce, they claimed, were improvements. In addition, they stood for liberty against monopoly, and for province against metropole. If illumination were really supposed to spread across a neutral field, only they upheld that neutrality. After the middle of the eighteenth century such arguments began to be made consistently in many European centers of reprinting: Edinburgh, Neuchâtel, Vienna, Dublin, even Philadelphia.

The problem for the reprinters was that there was not just one case to be made for their practice, but two—and they were mutually exclusive. The first was in line with mercantilist principles. It emphasized the virtues of replacing imported manufactures with home production. There was no reason why this principle should apply any less to printed books than it did to textiles or corn. This was the axiom that the Austrian empress upheld in earnest by bankrolling Trattner, and counterparts could be found in many German states and statelets up to and including Prussia. On this account, pirates were vanguards of national economic prowess. And the argument meshed neatly with state concerns for culture—for education, orthodoxy, and political allegiance. Local production meant that content could be more effectively policed.

The alternative pro-piracy case was, by contrast, robustly antimercantilist and anticensorship. From midcentury onward, some advocates of laissez-faire began to argue that literary property—that mysterious and novel concept championed by the metropolitan booksellers—was just another restraint imposed on a market that ought to be as free as possible. It was, they declared, at once absolutist, monopolistic, iniquitous to the public good, and philosophically absurd. It amounted to the imposition of tariffs on ideas themselves. And it militated against provincial and international operations that would otherwise furnish literary goods cheaper, more faithfully, and more plentifully. On this account, pirates were exemplars of free trade—indeed, of freedom in general. Needless to say, while the first kind of argument tended to hold good in metropolitan centers like Vienna, this second sprang from upstart founts of Enlightenment like Edinburgh, Dublin, and Philadelphia. But both, it is worth emphasizing, were not merely economic arguments. They were economic, political, social, and epistemological all at once. Their subject was the basic infrastructure of culture.

Arguments about piracy thus raged across Europe and beyond, in law courts, coffeehouses, theaters, bookshops, palaces, and studies. They appeared in correspondence, learned journals, and the pages of newspapers. And as the age of revolution began, they gave rise to convictions that would endure far beyond the eighteenth century. The most important of them was that of "rights." In 1700, almost nobody spoke in any sustained way of authorial rights. By 1750, many writers did. Interestingly, this discourse of rights was tried out in various centers at much the same time, but with divergent results. In Britain, for example, "copyrights" were endorsed, but not as perpetual, natural axioms arising from authors' labors or selves. They ended up being not *properties* as such, but something more like routinized patents. In prerevolutionary France, on the other hand, authorial rights were rejected by the Crown because they implied an encroachment on prerogative, and literary titles remained gifts of royal "grace" until 1789—at which point they disappeared altogether. In the Germanys they took on yet another form, becoming associated with Kantian principles and the idealist convictions of *Naturphilosophie*. Because of the one-and-many political character of that region, debates about reprinting and Enlightenment took on perhaps their highest form there.

### Reprinting, Sensation, and the Physiology of Genius

In the German lands the problems and opportunities of reprinting across territorial boundaries multiplied vastly. Hundreds of states of widely varying size and power sprawled across the region, with no central metropolis. To cope with this the book trade developed customs, in particular those of fairs and barter, with no counterpart in France or Britain. (Or in America, although in the early nineteenth century Mathew Carey would try with partial success to introduce German-style fairs there.) Yet this situation, in which the position of authors was especially weak, eventually produced a Romantic conception of authorship itself that was higher than anything in contemporary Britain or France. This conception emerged from what was to become *Naturphilosophie*—the Romantic merger of nature and the self that dominated German learning by the end of the century.[4] Expressed though it was in the language of high idealism, its implications affected the most mundane writing, publishing, and reading practices. Modern concepts of *creativity* and *intellectual property* both owe a large debt to the concepts of *Naturphilosophie*.

The question of how each of the three-hundred-odd German states related to the Empire was almost metaphysical. Each jurisdiction, including the emperor's, had the ability to grant privileges, but none was obliged to honor those of its neighbors. In theory, imperial privileges overrode such territorial divisions, but they were difficult to obtain and their enforcement was patchy. At the same time, each jurisdiction was also intent on pursuing the mercantilist imperative to encourage domestic manufactures. Many therefore supported printing establishments devoted to "piracy" (variously *Büchernachdruck, falschen Nachdruck*, or *Raubdruck*). The best-known instance was the firm of Johannes Thomas Edler von Trattner, in the imperial capital of Vienna itself. Trattner prospered with the full, enthusiastic, and explicit backing of the imperial court for his unauthorized reprints of works originating throughout Germany and central Europe. He maintained not only a printing house and a publishing operation, but a bindery, type foundry, and paper mill; the bookseller Friedrich Nicolai visited his premises and could not but be impressed. But lesser Trattners could be found in many other states. Frederick II of Prussia, for example, maintained candidly that regimes like his encouraged reprinting, and one Berlin bookseller in particular, Joachim Pauli, was well known for it. In the largely Roman Catholic south, moreover, ministries supported local reprinting for what might be termed ideological reasons as well as economic ones. They were keen to counter the importation of Protestant schoolbooks and other materials that might affect popular culture. Christian Friedrich Schwan thus warned that "probably no printer has ever benefited more from the imperial privileges than the pirates of Karlsruhe and Reutlingen" (Selwyn 2000, 220). And even Protestants to the north were sometimes ambivalent about this, so firmly did they believe that more print meant more Enlightenment.

The trade came together at regular fairs, the most important of which occurred in Leipzig and Frankfurt. There, publishing booksellers from across the Empire would convene to do business, discuss affairs, and socialize, maintaining the bonds on which their Republic of Letters depended. Printed works were carted in from across the Empire, bartered, and then distributed again to bookshops to be sold retail. Booksellers called this bartering the *Tauschsystem*. At its core was a simple protocol of exchange, a sheet of one book being swapped for a sheet of another. The practice minimized the problems of providing credit across long distances and diverse jurisdictions. But it also meant that the writers of books essentially acted as providers of a commodity—printed pages. There was no institutionalized recognition of differences in quality in what they provided. And authors, in fact, were typically remunerated by honoraria, not by royalties or anything approaching a proportionate purchase price for a literary property.

Leipzig and Frankfurt were also the closest the trade came to moral centers. Privileges were routinely registered with commissions there, and hearings regularly held at both to prevent the culture of the book from descending into what was feared as a "war of all against all" (Selwyn 2002, 15, 88ff, 185–186, 189, 219–229, 234, 236). Booksellers wanted to believe in this communal virtue. Nicolai in particular tried repeatedly to base a moral economy of the trade on it. He thus declaimed against Dutch booksellers for violating trade civilities in his novel *Sebaldus Nothanker*. The Dutch, he charged, claimed rights in books that did not yet exist, plotted to seize others' journals, and upheld the "cardinal principle" that "other people had no business owning anything that might be useful to [them]." But Nicolai also distrusted top-down administrative solutions, feeling that community came before rules. For that reason he declined to participate in Philipp Erasmus Reich's 1764 *Buchhandlungsgesellschaft* (society of booksellers), an initiative formed expressly to counter reprinting (Selwyn 2002, 15–19, 70, 99–101, 116).

Practitioners of *Büchernachdruck* were not shy about defending their practice. They discomfited their opponents by forthrightly laying claim to the ideals of Enlightenment. Reprinting undercut monopolies; it made knowledge available at lower prices, across wider regions, to more readers. Enlightenment *required* it. A book was not an "ideal" thing, but an object of manufacture like any other, so it should be treated the same way. Concepts like literary property were at best "useless" (Krause, quoted in Woodmansee 1994, 50). These arguments all bore similarities to counterparts advanced in France and Britain. But here they came backed by state governments, and above all by the imperial court itself. In the German lands, it was the *defenders* of literary property who lacked a political base.

In this environment few learned writers could live by authorship.[5] That was a major reason why Enlightenment, *Aufklärung*, needed the patronage of a Frederick the Great: its authors had to be supported either by patronage or by the holding of official positions. And periodicals, not books, were its central vehicles, more than two thousand being launched in the generation after 1765. They classified the public into discrete segments based in particular topics: chemistry, medicine, philology, and so on (Broman 2002, 225–238). In this sense, Condorcet's vision of an authorless public realm was becoming fact in Germany when he articulated it futilely in France.[6] Yet readers were voracious, encouraging the perpetual hope that authorship might be made into a vocation. An epidemic of "reading mania" (*Leseseuche*) broke out across Germany after midcentury, the principal symptom of which was a breathless desire to experience sensations through the reading of novels. The best-known vector was Goethe's *Sorrows of Young Werther*; stories proliferated about readers committing suicide in emulation of its young hero. Rampant pirating actuated readers by spreading the work across Europe. Some even claim that this "mania" heralded a "reading revolution."[7] It certainly provoked a transformation in what reading was understood to be. It now took effect as the central process in *Bildung*—the formation or cultivation of the self. This concept emphasized the reader's sympathetic engagement with the work, in conscious opposition to what was often derided as the sterility of encyclopedism.

In 1764, Leipzig's booksellers abruptly abandoned the *Tauschsystem* and demanded payment in cash. This collapse of the barter system had profound consequences. By reversing the status of the page as a commodity, it gave rise to a commerce of print in which content itself took on financial meaning—that is, one in which authorship acquired value. It was thus the major spark that ignited a debate about authorship destined to be bitter, prolonged, and profound. The protagonists in that debate were not only the leading booksellers of the time, but its major authors, too—authors including Lessing, Kant, Fichte, Hegel, Feuerbach, and Schopenhauer. Piracy alone did not cause the heightened conception of the creative author, for such protagonists were also concerned about issues like linguistic culture, education, and the troublesome authority of the public (Redekop 2000, 45–46). But piracy was the occasion for its articulation. As such, it helped to shape the understanding of authorship that in fact emerged—and those of culture, education, and the public as well.

As Martha Woodmansee has demonstrated, poet Friedrich Klopstock inaugurated the conflict in 1772 when he launched his so-called *Deutsche Gelehrtenrepublik*, or "German Republic of Letters." This was a plan to allow authors to take "property" of their works by bypassing booksellers and publishing them directly to subscribers. In common with similar schemes in England and France, it was not a great success—such projects never were. Still, the plan triggered extensive debates on the claims of authors to some kind of property in their writings. Gotthold Lessing thus defended the moral legitimacy of authorship as a livelihood, in a proposal for reorganizing the trade begun in 1772 but never finished. Jean Paul contributed "Seven last words, or, postscripts against pirating." Christoph Wieland struggled to define "the mercantile relationship between writer and publisher." And Lichtenberg too could be found in the lists. Dozens of separate papers flowed from the presses, many of them soon to be reprinted in a volume devoted to the battle. The furor even gave rise to stage plays. One called *The Pirates* was performed in Leipzig itself, while another appeared in Prague as *This Is the Way a Writer Takes Revenge on Treacherous Pirates*.[8] It would take a book in its own right to trace the connections that these many combatants drew between reprinting, authorship, and Romantic and idealist philosophies. Here it is possible to do no more than hint at some of the more consequential of them.

We can start with an assertion that the very foundations of human creativity lay in a reprinting process. The prime perpetrator of this notion—a kind of piratical descendent of the old Aristotelian sealing-wax account of sensation—was Johann Gottfried Herder, who developed it in the context of contributing to a debate about education and aesthetics. Herder meant to provide an alternative to the then fashionable language of "genius," which enjoyed a tremendous vogue in Germany during the years of the age of genius, or *Geniezeit* (1760–1775). Genius was in one guise an import from England, and specifically from the furor surrounding Hogarth's campaign against imitative connoisseurship.[9] But in another it could, I suspect, be traced back to the craft traditions of early modern German artisans and alchemists that Pamela Smith has highlighted.[10] Either way, invoked as the motor of "invention," genius was supposedly the power by which new discoveries and original works came about. Anything produced in its absence was by definition not original but "servile imitation" (Gerard 1774, 9). Genius was thus a principle of originality itself—the very principle that underpinned the progress that recent generations had seen in natural philosophy and industry. As Alexander Gerard put it, in an essay published in the year that *Donaldson vs. Becket* destroyed perpetual literary property in Britain but written two decades earlier, understanding genius must now be central to any "science of human nature" (Gerard 1774, 1–2). And the program to achieve that understanding directly implicated two major areas of culture: education (the formation of the self) and literary property (the sustenance of the self in commercial society).

The operation of genius could certainly be described in terms of faculty psychology and Lockean epistemology. But more often writers portrayed it in very different terms. It was active and organic. As Gerard put it, genius bore "a greater resemblance to *nature* in its operations, than to the less perfect energies of *art*" (Gerard 1774, 63). An original work, Edward Young agreed, was "of a *vegetable* nature; it arises spontaneously from the vital root of Genius; it *grows*, it is not *made*" (Young 1759, 8). This implied that a work must include some component peculiar to its individual creator, as the spring or soil from which it had grown. Advocates of a science of genius therefore decried imitation as unnatural: it was "servile," or merely "a sort of *Manufacture*." Emulating others' works could "by no process of poetical chymistry" generate real originality. The point was that contemporary education practice did indeed rest on emulation, especially of the classics; so the science of genius demanded sweeping changes in pedagogy. It thus became a fulcrum around which turned some of the most important cultural debates of the time. Nature created us as individuals, as Young poignantly put it; but after enduring schoolwork "we die *Copies*" (Young 1759, 24).[11]

The other major implication arose most clearly with the few individuals who were now said to *be* geniuses. These individuals apparently experienced an excess of the power. "A man of Genius" was "a kind of different being from the rest of his species" (Duff 1770, 339–340, 363–365). He displayed "peculiar manners" and might well seem unsociable (Duff 1770, 159–160, 176–177, 265). Such a person was liable to pour forth all kinds of extravagant ideas; hence it was that authors like Edmund Burke associated genius with revolutionary fanaticism. The broader point was that in the world of commercial print "the life of a man of Genius, like that of a Christian, is for the most part a state of warfare" (Gerard 1774, 421–422). For someone who was unworldly by nature, the only way of surviving this warfare was by clinging to property. Ideally, counseled Young, "his words will stand distinguished, his the sole Property of them"—"which Property alone can confer the noble title of an *Author*" (Young 1759, 30).

In a strange way, Herder's view of genius found expression as an indirect result of his experiencing for himself these vicissitudes of print. One of his earliest ventures into authorship was an anonymous volume that included an implied slur against one Christian Klotz, a scholar and poet who exalted the imitation of the Latin classics (one enemy called him an "Allemannic freebooter"). Unfortunately for Herder, or so the story goes, Klotz's agents surreptitiously obtained sheets for his second edition from the printing house, and an acolyte promptly appropriated them to reveal Herder's authorship and retaliate against the young philosopher by deploying unauthorized excerpts in a set of *Letters about the Public*. Herder, dismayed, first suppressed his own book, then abruptly fled for Marseille. In this way an all-too-typical piece of printing-house shenanigans led him to his first personal experience of French literary culture. And, as is well known, he swiftly rejected it as sharing with Klotz's neoclassicism a fatal imitative quality. Herder decried it as a form of living "on the ruins" of earlier authorship. "Their taste for encyclopedias, dictionaries, anthologies, and digests," he declared—sweeping up French Enlightenment scholarship tout court —"advertises their lack of original works" (Clark 1955, 59–99). The understanding of creative originality that he formulated in response would become a weapon in the pirate wars.

Herder's view of creative authorship was grounded in his vitalist natural philosophy. His was a natural world both populated with countless unique things and yet constituting an organic whole. In place of encyclopedism, he advocated a science that would apprehend "each individual thing" in that whole as unique in itself. He saw the very material of the universe as active, thanks to the operation of vital powers (*Kräfte*). These forces operated constantly to sustain the phenomena of life and change, but they acted in different ways depending on location. That was why people from one part of the earth would wither if moved to a different culture, just as plants withered when moved to a new climate (something, not incidentally, that contemporary British and French colonialists were actually attempting to do on a large scale).[12] And *Kraft* was also what underpinned the unity and individualism of mind. Reason was an application of it (Barnard 1965, 35–36, 41–42). Although he had read the British literature on genius, therefore, Herder was impatient with its cruder individualist aspects. He saw genius as the natural character of any individual, as developed through experiences that were collective and cultural. Thus Vaucanson, the famed maker of automata, had apparently aroused his own genius while watching a clock. On this account, nature was as fertile in geniuses as it was in trees, and every human being was a genius "in his place, in his work, for his vocation." Everyone was a potential author. But Herder's view also directed attention to the ways in which genius could in fact be "cultivated." He held that an original work *grew* within an author by means of the operation of *Kraft*. Its shoots then sprang forth apparently spontaneously from a reservoir of "inner ether." Klopstock's work thus possessed for him a unique quality akin to the individuality that nature inscribed in organisms. He even likened *King Lear* to a shrub.[13]

Herder made clear the extent of his organicism in a prize essay that he drafted for the Berlin Academy in 1775; it was published three years later as "On the Cognition and Sensation of the Human Soul." The essay seized upon the botanist and physician Albrecht Haller's theory of "irritation"—a small, inexplicable expansion and contraction of a muscle when stimulated—to suggest how art and knowledge arose. Knowledge came from sensations, in his account, but in a manner very different from Lockean empiricism. Sensations themselves were multitudes of events similar to irritations. The endless flow of such events that impinged on all of us gave rise to the various histories of individuals, of cultures, and even of life itself. Literary origination was therefore but one aspect of a natural phenomenon that also explained physical reproduction and maturation. Indeed, the archetype for it was sexual procreation itself. Herder defined this as a process in which two bodies, excited by massive irritations, combined to produce a "reprint" (*Abdruck*) of themselves. Philosophers tended to shy away from recognizing the commonalty of this with other forms of creativity, he insinuated, because they were embarrassed that the wellsprings of intellectual acts lay "under the diaphragm."[14] But for him the status of reproduction and creation as forms of reprinting was all-important.

Herder's notion of the reprint had three principal connotations. The first was that sensation was active, not passive as in a Lockean scheme; it involved the individual reaching out and imprinting nature with his "impress." The character of one's impress would reflect one's linguistic culture as well as one's individual self, and one's sense-based knowledge would thus reflect both too. This meant that initiatives to imitate classical culture, for example, were not only ill-advised but futile, because those cultures really were *other*, and hence inimitable. Second, as a "reprint" (*Abdruck* again), a work of art or intellect would indeed reproduce one's *self*. It could not have been produced by any other person, any more than a child could have been. Uniqueness of authorship rested in this. And, third, an artistic or literary work was not a static entity, but was dynamic. It was like speech, not statuary. It partook of a continuous flow of *Kraft* that energized public discourse.[15] And these connotations shaped how to approach the nature, use, and regulation of printed objects. Herder maintained that although cognition and sensation truly lived only "*in action*," Germany's institutions were rendering them static. Printed poems were corpselike. Commercial print was even worse, because it demanded that the author cordon off discrete parts of the self. (Herder became a patron saint of the *Sturm und Drang* movement that defied this compartmentalization.) What he recommended was a sustained project to redirect print itself. He urged that readers appropriate the medium to explore the "manner of origination" of all authors—what they owed to the past, how they related to the present, and how the future attempted to imitate them. "A history of authors that was executed in accordance with this conception," he exclaimed: "what a work it would be!"

Writing at the very apex of the reading mania—*Werther* had been published only a year earlier—Herder further made a point of proclaiming how much books could *not* do. When Aristotle's works went to the Arabs, he announced, Aristotle in a sense became Muslim; when the pope's went to China, the pontiff became a Confucian. Reading was another deployment of *Kraft*, and was thus very powerful. So how should this activity be carried out? The key was once again to recognize that every book was in essence a reprint—a reprint of the author's "soul." The more accurate the "print," therefore, the more foreign a book *must* seem to a skillful reader. A book was "a riddle without a solution," "a coin without a marginal inscription." And reading was an exquisite exercise in incommensurability. What enabled the act to proceed at all was the principle of the author. "One knows the author," Herder noted in 1755, "and he becomes the key." To read "in the spirit of the author" was to apprehend the author's unique physiology of sensation. Only when one succeeded in doing this could one really "understand" a work—which in Herder's terms meant to "feel it from its root up to the shoot." He called this "*living reading*," and declared that it amounted to a "divination into the author's soul." This, he concluded, was "the deepest means of education [*Bildung*]."[16]

By the mid-1780s, Herder had developed this into a fully fledged vitalist vision of Enlightenment through education and reading. The "seed" of each person would grow according to where it was "planted" and how it was "cultivated." All such cultivation was imitative in a peculiar organic meaning of the term, "as in the digestion of food," but would produce originality in the end. Teachers would "seed sprouts with germinating reason," eventually producing "new blossoms and fruit." And a radical reshaping of the public would emerge as a result.[17] Gone would be the cosmopolitan public without borders. Herder instead maintained that each linguistic culture generated its own "property." Each *Volk* manifested its own originality and its own progress. Each would prosper by the flow of *Kraft*, as long as it was not impeded by censorship or by institutions of imitation (universities, for example).[18]

These were radical views, and they were by no means universally accepted. Yet in their broad outlines—the organicism, the vitalism, the stress on originality, the focus on both authorship and reading—Herder did set the tone for what followed. Nor was this necessarily indicative of an incipient Romantic reaction; vitalism and organicism were far more prevalent doctrines in the Enlightenment itself than has tended to be acknowledged (Reill 2005, 121–128). Kant provides the most prominent and influential example of how such doctrines could be put to use, in both his teasing out of the relations between originality, judgment, and genius, and his pronouncements on print and the public sphere.

## Reprinting as Ventriloquism

The problem of the incommensurability of reading provides one entrance into this subject. Kant, like Herder, refused to subject creative genius to rules, and even famously denied that science was a province of geniuses because its works *could be* produced by following algorithms. Nonetheless, he also insisted that authorship have a rulelike aspect—a "mechanism," as he put it—because otherwise it would be unassimilable. There would be no standards by which works could be judged, and no way of communicating their purposes. Or, as he put it elsewhere, genius might be like a forest, but "art is like a garden" (Kant 2005, 487, 503, 516–517, 523). Three things played into this. First, genius's "primary characteristic" was indeed originality, as everyone agreed; it was a talent for producing something for which there was no existing rule. And, second, genius itself was unique to the individual. An artist's genius "cannot be communicated," Kant insisted. But, third, its products must also be "exemplary": that is, they must serve as *models* for others or as bases for future rules. How could this happen? In two ways. The first, rarer, way was for some future genius to be excited to *emulation*. Properly speaking, this was not imitation at all. The future genius was instead "awakened to the feeling of his own originality." Far more common was the second way, in which a work became foundational to a "school" based in rulebound imitative pedagogy. This, Kant thought, was broadly acceptable, but it could easily degenerate into mere "aping," when students copied slavishly. "Mannerism" was an instance of this, in which students tried to imitate the appearance of originality itself.

Kant was engaged here in rethinking the very nature of three fundamental cultural activities: origination, reading (or emulation), and communication. His arguments tied concepts of originality and copying to the very bases of Enlightenment. We can see as much in his famous discussion of the nature of Enlightenment itself that appeared in 1785.[19] Kant's essay received enormous attention, then and later; it has been treated in recent years as an authoritative description of the public sphere itself. It portrayed that sphere as composed of a vast population of readers of periodicals, whose duty as constituents was to practice thinking for themselves. The results of this activity were to be displayed through print to the same borderless realm (without the linguistic rifts that Herder identified). Kant insisted on the illegitimacy of censorship to control this realm. He did, however, allow that the state could restrict citizens acting in their capacities as bureaucrats, military officers, clergymen, and so on. In that capacity a subject exercised what he termed "private" reason. Only in withdrawal from one's professional post, therefore, perhaps in a secluded study, could one address oneself to the borderless realm and exercise "public" reason. Public reason was produced in (what we would call) private. In public, an author spoke "in his own person." The interaction of such public utterances would manifest a general maturation, and it was this process that Kant identified as Enlightenment.

This disquisition is, as just noted, very famous indeed. What is almost always forgotten is that shortly after it appeared, Kant took up his pen again to write a related argument that addressed similar themes. This second paper is nowadays almost completely unknown; yet it took up and extended the claims of the Enlightenment essay. And it reminds us that Kant himself was thoroughly proficient in the mundane practices of authorship, reading, and publishing on which any kind of public sphere depended (even if he was not, as Nicolai mischievously insinuated, a bookseller's hack). It was entitled "On the Wrongfulness of the Unauthorized Publication of Books," and it appeared in the same journal, the *Berlinische Monatsschrift* (Kant 1996b, 23–35).[20] We do not know the occasion of its composition, but it very possibly arose from the same group of "Friends of the Enlightenment" that inspired the more renowned essay. At any rate, it adopted the argument of that essay as its tacit premise.

The question implicitly addressed in Kant's second essay arose directly from the conclusion of the first, that public reason was a matter of each author writing "in his own person." What if the mediating agents of print appropriated that person—as, in a piratical world, they often did? Kant argued that a bookseller who undertook to produce an edition had an obligation to do so, and to do so faithfully. This fidelity was made possible in practice by the provision of exclusive rights. Yet, he conceded, decades of attempts to outlaw reprinting by adducing some kind of property had failed. They would always fail, Kant now maintained, because the author's property, if it existed at all, was in a basic sense inalienable—that was the inescapable inference from all theories of creative genius. In any case, no purchaser would ever accept liability for his or her copy becoming the basis for a reprint, so a real property right would simply kill publishing. Instead, Kant returned to his idea that a true author exercised a freedom to speak in his own person. He reasserted this principle, remarking that a book was not merely a passive container of meaning, but a vehicle for a dynamic process of communication. The publisher was properly comparable to an "instrument" for this process—something like a speaking trumpet. It followed that what was wrong with unauthorized reprinting had nothing to do with property at all, but that it was a form of ventriloquism. The pirate hijacked another person's voice. Worse, piracy obligated authors—it made them answerable for meanings transmitted without their consent. In short, it violated the principle of speaking in one's own name. It was this violation of the author's *identity* that made piracy unacceptable: it was this that made it potentially fatal to the very idea of a public sphere, and hence to Enlightenment. And Kant would later reiterate the same point in his *Metaphysics of Morals*, this time under the revealingly broad question, What is a book? (Kant 1996c, 437–438).

In sum, Kant's objection to reprinting was that it threatened to make Enlightenment impossible. His notion of Enlightenment depended on authors exercising public reason. They relied on the mediation of an estate of booksellers to achieve this (and the booksellers in turn, Kant acknowledged, depended on the mediation of a third group, the printers). Reprinting imperiled this ideal because it mixed authorship with mediation. Middlemen became, as it were, pseudoauthors. This eliminated the space in which subjects could reliably act as real authors. To Kant, the fact that reprinting dispersed learning more widely, cheaply, and accessibly—the principal defense of pirates at the time—was true but beside the point. It would no longer be *public*, because authors would no longer be *private*. And, after all, those remarks about being obligated by pirates were no mere conceit. Authors in Kant's day were in fact legally responsible for what they said—and for what they were now made to say by the pirates. Under the reactionary Frederick William II, censorship was once again in the ascent. For authors to be rendered vulnerable by "speech" over which they had no oversight was thus a very consequential matter indeed. Not least, it was consequential for Kant himself, whose own work fell afoul of the police at just this point.

There is something resonant about Kant's objection to reprinting as a form of ventriloquism. It appeared at the high point of a period that had seen mimetic automata multiply across the Continent. From Neuchâtel — that great center of reprinting — the Jacquet-Droz brothers had sent forth machines to the great capitals of Europe that could play music, draw, and write. Amazed audiences witnessed their feats and wondered how far they embodied knowledge of what human processes really were. Was man really, as La Mettrie had notoriously claimed, a machine? And when a child-android seemed to pause as it wrote, wondering if it had got the spelling and syntax right, who was doing the thinking? As Romantic philosophies of self and soul emerged and derided what they saw as the dry encyclopedism of the Enlightenment, so the uncanny potential of such machines became the focus of extended attention. E. T. A. Hoffmann's sandman is only the best-known example. Mesmeric practitioners deployed and exploited similar conceptions in taking control of the bodies of their subjects. At just this moment, to insist on the primacy of an authorial reasoning voice was a gesture of fairly specific meaning. The fate of Enlightenment, apparently, had much in common with the meaning of that *frisson* punters felt when they saw the junction of autonomy and automaton in a coffeehouse show.[21]

## The Invention of Creativity

Johann Gottlieb Fichte was at first so much a Kant disciple that his maiden book was widely assumed to be by Kant himself. But the two had parted ways by the time their respective papers on piracy appeared. Where Herder was concerned about creative culture, and Kant about public reason, Fichte insisted that a response to piracy must rest on an analysis of the nature of the book itself. His "Proof of the Illegality of Reprinting," begun in 1791 and published in 1793, furnished that analysis.

Fichte claimed not only that a book had an ideal or intellectual (*geistig*) aspect as well as a corporeal one — this much was a commonplace — but that the *geistig* component itself might be resolved into "material" ideas and their expression, or "form." The buyer of a book certainly purchased the corporeal object — again a conventional observation. According to Fichte he or she also bought the knowledge it contained, at least insofar as it could be shared by a reader. What a buyer did *not* purchase, however, in Fichte's view, was the form in which that knowledge was expressed. To do so would be logically impossible, because the form an author gave to the knowledge in a work depended on the self producing that knowledge. This was where the incommensurability of genius over which Herder and Kant puzzled really took effect. To truly make a work's expression one's own, Fichte reasoned, a reader would have to express it again—and the result would inevitably be a new expression, reflecting that reader's own individuality. Nobody could "appropriate" the thoughts of an author "without thereby altering their form." This provided for Fichte a rationale and a substrate for a strong concept of literary property, based on the bond between the self and the "form" of an idea expressed in a book.[22]

Herder, Kant, and Fichte, along with the countless other writers and booksellers who stuck their heads over the parapet, defined a field of possible responses to unauthorized reprinting. What was at stake began with the physiology of originality—Novalis, Oken, Ritter, Schelling, and Humboldt were at just this point exploring the interaction of individual and world by making themselves into subjects in some remarkably painful electrical experiments. And from there the debate proceeded through authorship and the nature of the book, to the constitution of publics and the culture of Enlightenment. And as the old systems broke down in the Napoleonic years, so these became the grounds on which an order of print might be reconstructed. Prussia became the first state to incorporate an explicit commitment against reprinting in its state law as early as 1794. In 1810, alongside the adoption of the Napoleonic Code, a German state, Baden, recognized authorship as creating a property right. Within the trade, a group formed at Potsdam revived plans to use the Leipzig fair to enforce a universal system. And in 1813, Ludwig Feuerbach wrote the relevant section of a new Bavarian penal code that largely adopted the terms set by Kant and Fichte. The subsequent defeat of Napoleon therefore coincided with a moment when all seemed possible, and the prominent publisher Johann Cotta traveled to the Congress of Vienna in person to try to negotiate a Germany-wide copyright law as part of the postwar order. The playwright August von Kotzebue issued a manifesto; Goethe agitated for it, as did Wilhelm von Humboldt. Metternich himself, cornered by Cotta in Vienna, at first promised help, and vouchsafed regret at Austria's previous record of patronizing piracy. But still it came to nothing. A Viennese publisher pirated Kotzebue's manifesto, adding a polemical refutation; and Metternich murmured evasively that he had no authority over internal Austrian matters. Before long the emperor had personally intervened to reject "English principles."[23] Not until the mid-nineteenth century would common legislation for Germany come to pass. Still, when it did, it inherited the convictions of the Romantics.

Romantic theories of authorship, deployed as they were in debates about piracy, fostered something deeper and more important than any one law. They provoked a revaluation of creation—invention, discovery, originality—as the raison d'être of intellectual and cultural work. In education, teachers were exhorted to convey not rules or systems, but the process of original discovery. Perhaps most emphatically, Schelling insisted in 1802 that pedagogy be devoted to conveying something "whose inner essence can be grasped only by a kindred genius through a rediscovery in the literal sense." Such Romantic convictions were to be entrenched in such fundamental institutions as the modern research university. Science would become an enterprise defined by its production of discoveries.[24] The very concept of creativity (*Kreativität*) had its roots here. Unknown in English before the nineteenth century, it seems to have been adopted out of the German in the context of Coleridge's idealist critiques of contemporary expertise and technical culture. Along with those strange species the "scientist" and the "creative artist" (not to mention the concept of Enlightenment itself), it then proliferated in mid- to late-nineteenth-century writings (Schmidt 2003, 421–443). In that context, it seems likely that it partook of the desire by figures like David Brewster and Charles Babbage to devise some single underlying principle to underpin what had hitherto been distinct legal and cultural entities— copyrights, patents, and trademarks. Fighting a rearguard action against industrialists who wanted the law of patents abolished, Brewster and his allies tried to establish such a principle in order to affirm the great stakes of such a policy. They would make abolition more threatening by insisting that if patents disappeared, so must copyrights. The entity they adopted to make this case was one they christened *intellectual property*. Only after midcentury does that entity begin to exist as a major area of law, with subdivisions for industry, law, designs, and so on.[25] What was "creativity," then? It was the principle, descended from an organicism that had in practice always been central to Enlightenment, which made intellectual property not only possible but necessary. We are still struggling to free ourselves from the consequences.

# EFFECTS
EMERGENT PRACTICES

# *FINANCING ENLIGHTENMENT, PART ONE*

MONEY MATTERS

MARY POOVEY

Why should we think about money when we think about "Mediating Enlightenment"?[1] Assuming that neither Ian Baucom (below) nor I will be able to tell you exactly who financed the Enlightenment (which we cannot), and assuming that the Enlightenment primarily involved new assumptions about knowledge (which it did), how will adding money change the current understandings of the Enlightenment? In these brief introductory remarks, I want to name five ways of understanding money that might make us rethink the Enlightenment. Then I will offer two very brief historical accounts: one summarizes the condition of (English) money during the Enlightenment, and the second chronicles some of the stages by which money lost its own history, as part of a more general cultural process of mystification or erasure. In concluding part 1 of this paper, I will suggest that some version of this erasure is intrinsic to Enlightenment, both past and present, as one of the conditions of its possibility.

## Why Money Matters

In modern commercial societies, money is understood to serve numerous functions. Among these, economists often highlight money's abilities to facilitate exchange, to store value, and to permit international commerce and internal record keeping. Instead of emphasizing these functions, however, I want first to list five ways of thinking about money that more obviously link it to our topic.

1. Money mediates value. As a form of *mediation*, money reminds us that *representation* is not the only function of signifying systems. As a form of mediation, money also reminds us that the medium in which transfer occurs always affects whatever it carries. When sound passes through water, it is slightly altered; when you pay for a new camera with a credit card, cost can be altered, too—as you will discover if you don't pay your monthly balance in full.
2. Money is a technology of transfer. In the case of money, technology matters. When a monetary instrument is handwritten, as most early credit paper was, it is susceptible to alteration and fraud. When it is partially or wholly printed, a monetary instrument becomes more secure, but forgery is still possible, especially if the counterfeiters perfect their own technologies—their own note presses, for example. There is an even more literal sense in which money and transfer are connected: in the days before paper monetary instruments (letters of credit, bills of exchange) were widely accepted, travelers had to carry the gold and silver they needed with them. As you can imagine, this made travel both burdensome and dangerous, for gold was heavy and bait for highwaymen.
3. Money consists of various genres. While we do not often think of money as consisting of genres, we all know that it assumes numerous forms, which have many of the features of genres: each kind has formal features, which are ranked in a hierarchy of importance and which interrelate with other features (the image on a coin can be the same as or a variant of the image on a paper note). When we think of the genres of money, these come to mind: coins; an enormous variety of paper forms, which are all instruments of credit; and (now) digital signals, some of which (financial derivatives) are not (yet) permanently recorded or regulated by national governments. For all kinds of reasons, the genre in which your money appears makes a difference in what you can do with it, its exchange value, and its currency. When the new state of Virginia tried to use tobacco leaves as money, for example, citizens discovered that their savings did not travel, the leaves were a poor store of value, and other people would rather smoke their money than accept it.
4. Money is mysterious. As the titles of early British monetary pamphlets

remind us, representative money has long been considered difficult to understand and sometimes sinister. In 1676, for example, one writer tried to expose "The Mystery of the New Fashioned Goldsmiths," only to reveal that he couldn't quite grasp how these early bankers managed to make money from the gold with which merchants entrusted them. I will suggest below that the mystification that surrounds many monetary genres is simultaneously a source of money's (imaginative and actual) power and necessary to its ability to perform its various functions.

5. Money can carry violence—across geographical space, across class and race divisions, and even across time. In some of its forms (speculative capital), in fact, money seems inextricably linked to violence (on this, see part 2 of this essay, written by Baucom).

## A Brief History of England's Money

To explain why it is so easy (and so essential) to forget that money has a history, I first need to provide a few details of the history some of us may have forgotten. I will restrict my remarks to England, which is the monetary system whose history I detail more extensively in *Genres of the Credit Economy* (Poovey 2008). In the last decades of the seventeenth century, several kinds of monetary instruments circulated in England. There were gold and silver coins, of course, but the vast majority of coins had lost much of the precious metal they supposedly contained through ordinary wear or criminal clipping and sweating. In an international cash flow known as Gresham's law, bad money always drove out good, and as a consequence, Britons did not have enough quality coins to conduct ordinary business. The government tried to rectify this situation in 1695 with a general recoinage, but by the middle of the eighteenth century, the nation's coins were once again worn, clipped, and in seriously short supply.

It was partly to supplement the chronically inadequate supply of coins that various forms of credit paper were introduced. Some of these were private innovations, but the chronic need for funds on the part of the English government meant that the Crown, and then Parliament, were forced to devise special financial instruments, which, ideally, would operate on a national, not simply local, scale. Thus, beginning sometime in the early seventeenth century, private businessmen called goldsmiths began issuing receipts for the gold merchants deposited with them; these sometimes took the form of "running notes," which were negotiable by endorsement. When England was defeated by the Dutch in the 1660s, Parliament began to demand more regular accounting, and this led to lenders being given government receipts for their loans; these were also negotiable to a limited extent. Such "gilt-edged" securities were soon joined by other forms of national credit paper: Treasury Orders (1667–1671); annuities, which were the first long-term investment instruments (1677); shares in the National Debt (from 1692), which initiated long-term borrowing secured by a permanently funded debt; and promissory notes issued by the Bank of England, which was founded in 1694 to manage the Debt. In addition to such state-issued paper, Britons living in the late seventeenth century and the entirety of the eighteenth would have been able to use any combination of the following forms of privately issued credit paper: bills of exchange (both inland and foreign), notes issued by country banks (from about 1750), promissory notes (generally handwritten), checks (also handwritten, although these were eventually partly and later fully printed), and a bewildering variety of tradesmen's tokens, which were issued for use in areas that lacked a bank or other regular source of money.

At least three things follow from this monetary situation, which obtained for the entire period we now call the Enlightenment. The first is that money was, for the most part, extremely local. Apart from foreign bills of exchange and letters of credit (which were invented to facilitate travel), most monetary genres did not retain their value over even short distances. Bank of England notes, for example, were generally not accepted beyond a twenty-mile radius of London; checks had to be returned to the bank of issue within two days of receipt; and notes issued by a country bank were good only in the immediate neighborhood of the bank. This meant that most individuals had no means to pay for their own travel and that, in order to expand their horizons, their businesses, or their purchases, they had to develop some relationship to someone who could provide money (or credit) and make it travel.

Second, the Enlightenment monetary situation made money expensive. Because almost all forms of money represented credit (that is, indebtedness), getting money to spend or invest involved paying some kind of interest. This could take the form of the "discount" issuers of bills of exchange charged up front, the fees charged by banks for their services, or the interest that nearly every monetary form included for the time the bill circulated before falling due. The high cost of money tended to exacerbate already extreme differences in the ability of different groups to benefit from money, as well as to heighten prejudices against those who profited most: a shrewd tradesman could parlay the steep fees he paid in interest for enormous returns on money cannily invested (or on the goods he bought for resale); a landowner who invested only in "improvements" could grow impoverished as inflation and falling rents made his estate too expensive to keep; and nearly everyone grew suspicious of bankers, who seemed mysteriously to profit in good times and bad.

Third, the complex Enlightenment monetary situation exacerbated other kinds of social inequities and gaps in knowledge, which persisted even beyond the eighteenth century. By this I mean to extend the implications of what William St. Clair (2004) has taught us: because luxury goods (like books) were expensive and because money was local and expensive too, the individuals who could participate in the Enlightenment represented only a small percentage of Britain's overall population. But I also want to extend this point by stressing, as Deborah Valenze (2006) has recently done, that, partly because money was hard to come by, especially in the first decades of the eighteenth century, a coin or a paper note could carry meanings for some Britons that had little to do with its function as a medium of exchange. In the 1710s, someone not versed in the ways of trade might bend a coin to neutralize its devilish power, for example; in the 1770s, someone who considered Bank notes signs of prestige might endorse each note that passed through his hands (even though this was not necessary) as a way of flouting his sheer proximity to money. Because money could carry multiple meanings in the period, and because some monetary instruments continued to do so, each one was susceptible to numerous interpretations by various groups that viewed money differently. Effacing these multiple connotations proved an essential part of the social process by which various monetary genres were gradually stripped of their differences from each other and money as a whole was purged of its history as multiple genres.

## Effacing the History of Money

I can give only a rudimentary sketch here of the erasure of money's generic history. Let me note at the outset that nearly everyone who has written about money pays lip service to its history; many cite the Kings of Lydia, who first struck coins, or the Solonic Reform of Athenian currency in the sixth century B.C.; some wax even more eloquent about its lineage, as did John Maynard Keynes in 1930: "Its origins are lost in the mists when the ice was melting," Keynes rhapsodized, "and may well stretch back into the paradisaic intervals in human history of the interglacial periods, when the weather was delightful and the mind free to be fertile of new ideas" (Keynes 1950, 13). The kind of erasure I have in mind involves not just these allusions to a history "lost in the mists" (which is really not a history but a way to universalize the monetary function), but also denials that money consists of different kinds (genres). To deny that money assumes different generic forms is to forget important facts about monetary history—that different genres have had different relations to the functions that money performs; that different monetary forms relate differently to other cultural artifacts; and that some kinds of money were once amenable to politicization. These denials are most obvious in our own day, for the increasingly abstract forms that money now takes (with derivatives approaching the zero degree of abstraction) tend to make writers view all money as abstract—that is, as mattering only insofar as one views it in the abstract. Privileging abstraction over historical accounts of difference, I suggest, is one of the forms of mystification that characterizes all Enlightenment "knowledge."

Here I will just offer a series of snapshots, which move chronologically back in time, to show how a few writers have depicted (or effaced) money's many historical forms. I will begin with Hannah Arendt, *Origins of Totalitarianism*, originally published in 1950, was only incidentally concerned with money, of course, but her passing reference to monetary forms is symptomatic of a certain kind of post–World War II history. According to Arendt, imperialism began in 1884 in the scramble for Africa; this international competition for resources and high returns made visible what she calls the "inherent law" of the capitalist system: capital always seeks to grow through geographical expansion. In her account, it was not nations that led the scramble for Africa but private businessmen and investors, who, having made too much money, now wanted to find safe outlets for it.

> Imperialist expansion had been touched off by a curious kind of economic crisis, the overproduction of capital and the emergence of "superfluous" money, the result of oversaving, which could no longer find productive investment within the national borders. For the first time, investment of power did not pave the way for investment of money, but export of power followed meekly in the train of exported money, since uncontrollable investments in distant countries threatened to transform large strata of society into gamblers, to change the whole capitalist economy from a system of production into a system of financial speculation, and to replace the profits of production with profits in commissions.... The first consequence of power export was that the state's instruments of violence, the police and the army, which in the framework of the nation ... were controlled by other national institutions, were separated from this body and promoted to the position of national representatives in uncivilized or weak countries. Here, in backward regions ... the bourgeoisie's empty desire to have money beget money as men beget men [was realized]... Money could finally beget money be-

cause power ... could appropriate wealth. Only when exported money succeeded in stimulating the export of power could it accomplish its owner's designs. Only the unlimited accumulation of power could bring about the unlimited assimilation of capital. (Arendt 1971, 135, 136–137)

No longer routed through production—and, equally important for my argument, no longer routed through the instruments that facilitated international investment—money simply becomes "capital," an abstraction that is both "lawful" and vested with almost supernatural agency.

Without disputing Arendt's main points, let's think for a moment about how different this account would look if it were differently scaled. After all, no nineteenth-century "imperialist" could have taken his "capital" to an "uncivilized" country in the form in which his "oversaving" was stored at home. Cecil Rhodes did not simply arrive in Africa with a checkbook or a wallet filled with pound notes and start exchanging paper for lumps of gold. Rhodes presumably worked through his agents, including a merchant bank, which, presumably again, either already had or had to establish a relationship with money men already located in Africa. No matter what their race, these individuals—who served as the interface between the imperialists and the colonized—had to establish more local relations—with chiefs of various tribes, which had their own form of money and their own social customs. At critical points along this complex network of relationships and transit, exchanges would have taken place that were simultaneously monetary and social; in each of these, some individuals would have charged a fee or extracted a modicum of prestige for services performed. Some of the individuals who would have benefited in this way would have been native Africans, for Africans as a group were not altogether passive victims, nor were they all "colonized" in the same way. At this level of detail, we would be able to see that every exchange is also a social relationship with different implications for the individuals involved. "Power" would still be involved, of course, but this would no longer look monolithic; nor would all the agents in the story be abstractions ("exported money," "unlimited accumulation of power"; Ogborn [2007] uses this kind of scale to restore to various written documents the importance they had in the East India Company's initial forays into the Subcontinent).

Now to a different example, which demonstrates another consequence of abstraction. In this example, abstraction is not simply produced by the large scale of description; instead, it is a function of the writer's having isolated function from the specific instruments that perform this function (differently). This example comes from Keynes's *Treatise on Money* (1930). Unlike

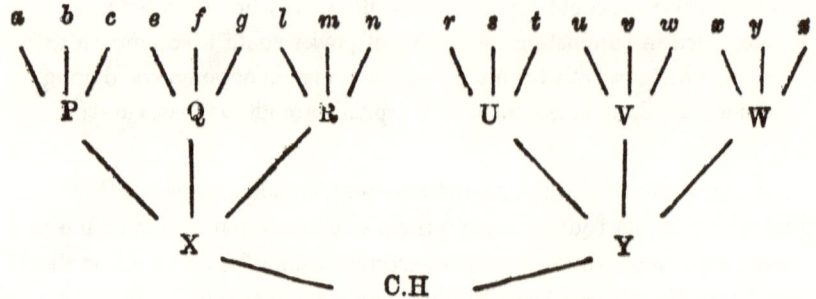

Diagram from John Maynard Keynes, *Treatise on Money* (1930).

Arendt, Keynes was primarily interested in money; unlike Arendt again, he was also fully aware that money assumed different forms. When he mapped these forms as a "genealogical tree," however, monetary instruments and their histories disappeared in favor of ahistorical monetary functions.

I won't explain all of these terms in Keynes's diagram, nor will I rehearse the specific argument he was making (which primarily involved "managed money" and the velocity of circulation). For my purposes, what matters is how easily this abstraction from the specific instrument to the monetary type (which is itself derived from function) allows Keynes to move to another level of abstraction, one that is quasi-mathematical in nature. Thus, at the end of book 1, his narrative account, which has already incorporated diagrams, begins to borrow formal features from a representational system common not to historical narrative but to mathematics and philosophy. Here is a brief example: "It is evident from the above that the proportion, $K^n$, of the average level of business-deposits to the volume of business transactions may be quite different from $K^d$, the proportion of the income-deposits to the income transactions. Also it is likely both to vary differently and to be much more variable, some estimates as to the magnitude of $K^n$, or rather of its inverse $V^n$ will be given in Volume II" (Keynes 1950, 48–49).

Despite Keynes's explicit references to the history of money and his acknowledgment that money has generic kinds, his decision to define these kinds by function ultimately moves his analysis out of the historical register and into the universalized register of mathematics and philosophy. By generating mathematical formulae, he was able to make generalizations about how nations managed money; in doing this, of course, he began to overlook the differences among kinds of money, for they no longer mattered to him.

Now let's take another step back in time, to a moment at which these differences in kind did matter but the allure of abstraction was already clear.

The example I'll use is W. Stanley Jevons's 1875 volume called *Money and the Mechanism of Exchange*, which the political economist presented as an "elementary grammar" for practitioners of the "moral and political sciences" (Jevons 1908, vi). Jevons was acutely aware that money assumed different forms; in addition to several chapters on coins and international money, he included discussions of four kinds of promissory notes, four kinds of credit documents, and two kinds of checks. Each of these discussions addresses the relative advantages and disadvantages of the monetary genre, its relationship to other kinds of money, and its ability to perform three of the important functions of money. Near the end of this book, in his discussion of England's book credit and banking system, Jevons reveals that what has looked like a survey of monetary kinds is actually a teleological narrative, which moves toward what Jevons considered a kind of "perfection." The terminus of this narrative is the national clearing system, a set of relationships among banks that caused all of the checks and bills used anywhere in the United Kingdom to flow, through a system of twenty-six agency banks, to a single place, a "room of moderate dimensions," located in the London Clearing House (Jevons 1908, 263). Like Keynes, Jevons used a diagram to describe this system of banks (see fig. 2), but when he turned his attention to the all-important activity in the little room, he reverted to a detailed narrative.

> The Clearing House is a plain oblong room, with rows of desks in compartments round three sides, and down the middle. A small office for the two superintendents stands at one end. Each bank sends as many clerks to the House as may be requisite for the rapid completion of the work, and some banks have as many as six clerks. The cheques and bills

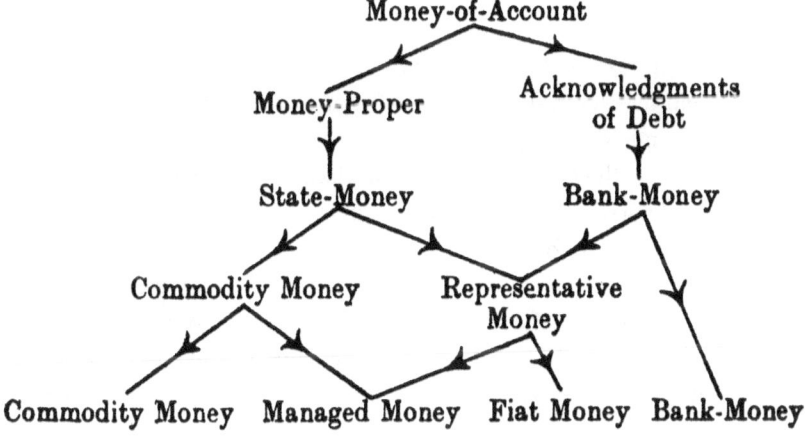

Diagram from W. Stanley Jevons, *Money and the Mechanism of Exchange* (1908).

to be presented by any one clearing banker, say the Alliance Bank, upon any other clearing banker, are entered at home in the "Out-clearing book," and are then sorted into twenty-five parcels, one of which is to be presented on each of the other clearing banks. On reaching the Clearing House, these parcels are distributed round the room to the desks of the clerks representing the several paying banks, who immediately begin to enter them in the "In-clearing books" in columns bearing at the head the name of the presenting bank.... At the end of the day the clerks of the Alliance Bank are able to add up the whole of the claims which have been made upon them by the other twenty-five banks, and they learn from the out-clearing book the amount of the claims which the Alliance Bank is making on other banks. The difference is the balance which the Alliance Bank has either to pay or receive as the case may be. These balances being communicated to the superintendents of the House are by them inserted in a kind of balance sheet....

The advantages of the system are evidently of enormous magnitude. All the larger payments are made with a minimum of risk, loss of time, trouble, or use of the precious metals. While the cheque representing a payment is traveling about the country, the money which it is transferring is reposing in the vaults of some bank, or rather, not being needed in the operation at all, is lent or sent out of the country, so that its interest is saved.... The security with which the payments are effected is also an element of importance.... Through the agency of banks, whether by crossed cheques or credit notes, the largest payments may be made with almost absolute immunity from risk. The cheques, bills, and other documents transferred in the clearing house are, as a general rule, so crossed or endorsed as to be of no value to any one but the legal owners, and in any case are regarded by thieves as "duffer," with which they dare not meddle. (Jevons 1908, 266–267, 284)

Jevons's enthusiasm for this system is palpable: He clearly admired both its detail and its overall function, which was to transform valuable monetary instruments (cheques, bills) into both book entries (mere writing) and "duffer" (the worthless signs of someone else's monetary transactions). In the backward narrative I am constructing, Jevons's little book stands at the critical turning point, for he knew that the different forms money assumed mattered (Bank of England notes could not be cleared in this manner), yet he also longed for a system that could abstract value from those instruments so that the actual "money" they represented (the Bank of England notes but, beyond them, gold) could "repose" in a vault or go traveling the world. Jevons wanted a "perfect" system of monetary representation that would match the "perfect" system of banking, in other words (Jevons 1908, 260); in this perfected system, writing (book entries) would presumably function as money, and nothing whose value could be purloined would ever change hands.

Now let's take another step back, this time to the first decade of the nineteenth century. In a series of letters written from Newgate Prison, William Cobbett, the radical gadfly of William Pitt's tenure as prime minister, took full measure of the different monetary genres that confronted his contemporaries. With Britain at war with France, gold and silver were in short supply, but paper money was everywhere. Some of this paper was issued by the Bank of England, presumably against the security of its gold reserve; some of it was issued by country banks, which, in 1810, would have been private companies with no more than six shareholders to guarantee the bank's notes. To Cobbett, however, all such paper was equally worthless, mere "dirty rags" (Cobbett 1828, 19) intended to swindle the poor. In fact, Cobbett considered Bank of England paper, like the National Debt, a diabolical scheme designed to seduce workers into pernicious belief in England's "funding system." Here is Cobbett on the origin of Bank of England notes:

> The Act of Parliament . . . points out the manner in which the Bank Company shall carry on their trade . . . allowing them, amongst other things, to trade in gold and silver, bills of exchange, and other things, under certain restrictions; but, as to what are called *bank-notes*, the Company was not empowered to issue any such, in any other way, or upon any other footing, than merely as *promissory notes*, for the amount of which, in the coin of the country, they were liable to be sued and arrested. Having, however, a greater credit than any other individuals, or company of individuals, the Bank Company issued notes to a greater amount; and, which was something new in England, they were made payable, not to any *particular person*, or his *order*, and not at any *particular time*; but to the *bearer*, and on *demand*. These characteristics, which distinguished the promissory notes of the Bank of England from all other promissory notes, gave the people greater confidence in them; and, as the Bank Company were always ready to pay the notes in Gold and Silver, when presented for payment, the notes became, in time, to be looked on as being as good as gold and silver. Hence came our country sayings:—"*As good as the Bank*"; "*As solid as the Bank*"; and the like. Yet, the Bank was, as we have seen, merely a company of mortal men, formed into an association of traders; and their notes nothing more than written promises to pay the bearer so much money in gold or silver. (Cobbett 1828, 8)

While Cobbett could remember this history, and while he was always suspicious of the blind confidence his contemporaries reposed in the Bank, the rage he expressed in *Paper against Gold* was provoked by a specific event: the extraordinary measure Parliament took in 1797, when it suspended the Bank's promise to redeem its notes with gold. Although Cobbett would not have used these terms, the Restriction Act, which remained in force until 1821, removed the British pound from the gold standard and rendered this paper "fiat money"—money backed by nothing but a government's decree. The U.S. dollar is fiat money, as is nearly every other form of modern money, but this no longer bothers us because most of us trust our government. In the first decades of the nineteenth century, by contrast, fiat money was extremely alarming to many Britons—not least because the two revolutions that had so recently damaged Britain (the rebellion of the American colonies and the French Revolution) were both financed by fiat money. In the wake of the Restriction, and partly because of Cobbett's extremely influential pamphlet, paper money became an intensely political issue, for it was associated with a government that some assumed was stealing the nation's money to finance a war they hated and feared.

I am sure you are beginning to see the point of this historical exercise, but let me just give you one more example. In 1755, a landowner named Lord Elibank published a little pamphlet entitled "Essay on Paper-Money and Banking" in his collection, *Essays on the Public Debt*. Unlike Cobbett's *Paper against Gold*, which was published in a cheap edition that reached tens of thousands of Britons, Elibank's pamphlet was neither cheap nor widely read. It was no doubt intended for other, like-minded landowners who might be in or have influence over Parliament. Elibank's express reason for writing was his concern over the midcentury "scarcity of gold and silver money," the "decay of trade and manufactures," and "the increase of luxury, and expence, of living" (Elibank 1993, 213). In the course of the pamphlet, he identifies the cause of this "misery": "the currency of PAPER-MONEY or BANK-NOTES, which by increasing the quantity, has sunk the intrinsic value of our money, and introduced all the real inconveniences of plenty of money, without the smallest advantage to any individual but the bankers themselves" (Elibank 1993, 214).

For Elibank, the differences among kinds of monetary instruments was both visible and critically important: "an imaginary money of paper" had begun to replace "real money" (gold), and by means of the "fiction" of this "imaginary money," the "real money" was flowing to an interested few, the bankers (Elibank 1993, 215, 217). Dreading the "evil consequences of this implicit faith, this unlimited trust, this lethargic carelessness of [his] countrymen," Elibank called upon the "landed gentlemen, farmers, and manufacturers" to refuse all paper money, demand and give only gold and silver, and so restore the nation to prosperity (Elibank 1993, 219). Like David Hume, Elibank's more famous monetary skeptic, this Enlightenment nobleman detested the very quality that made this particular monetary instrument so attractive to later theorists (like Jevons)—paper's ability to take the place of gold and thus to abstract value from its material ground and embodiment.

## The Importance of Forgetting

In order for any representative money to perform most of the functions that modern money is expected to serve, the people who use it have to forget about the various forms money takes. By extension, the ability of any monetary genre to mediate and transfer value depends upon money's losing its history *as* differentiated genres, for if we were to remember that genre once mattered, then we would be tempted to mistake particular genres or particular instances of a genre (particular dollar bills) for their abstract function—which is the only thing that *should* matter in an Enlightened world. Some such erasure—some such process of mystification—is necessary to every Enlightenment project, for, insofar as the epistemological claim of the Enlightenment is "that the World is a System whose parts can be known" (Siskin and Warner, "Description of Conference"), then the materiality and historical specificity of the instruments by which those parts are revealed must vanish as the whole gradually takes the place of its parts. Restoring to money its history as a set of genres reminds us that both value and knowledge are always mediated by instruments, whose idiosyncratic functions can exceed or even impede the abstract function they also perform. At the very least, this should be a cautionary reminder of the price we (unthinkingly) pay for the (undeniable) benefits of knowledge that effaces the conditions of its own production.

# *FINANCING ENLIGHTENMENT, PART TWO*

EXTRAORDINARY EXPENDITURE

IAN BAUCOM

Mary Poovey's essay "Financing Enlightenment, Part One," offers a reverse chronology of some of the stages through which money loses its history, isolating five moments: the 1950 publication of Hannah Arendt's *Origins of Totalitarianism* and—moving backward—the publication in 1930 of John Maynard Keynes's *Treatise on Money*, in 1875 of W. Stanley Jevon's *Money*, in 1810 of William Cobbett's *Paper against Gold*, and in 1755 of Lord Elibank's "Essay on Paper Money and Banking." I want to begin by leaping yet one further century back, to 1660, in which year Jan Van Riebeeck, the founding commander of the Dutch East India Company's fort and provisioning settlement at the Cape of Good Hope, sent a lengthy letter to the Council of Seventeen (the Company's board of governors in Holland) providing his first comprehensive financial account of the flow of money in and out of his station at the southern tip of Africa. I'd like to start with that 1660 piece of accounting in part because it is a Cape text (although as I will also be suggesting, it should simultaneously be read as an Atlantic and Indian Ocean document) and as such casts some light both on Arendt's *Origins of Totalitarianism* and on Poovey's reading of Arendt, but also because it is a 1660 text, or, more precisely, a 1652–1660 text (the dates covered by Van Riebeeck from the establishment of the settlement in 1652 to the year of his writing), and because that mid-seventeenth century decade is crucial to the fuller argument I will make. In brief, that argument suggests that we add another to Poovey's list of several of money's functions (it is a universal equivalent, which facilitates exchange; a store of value, which allows people to amass wealth; and a unit of account, which permits international commerce and internal record keeping): money is a carrier of law that, in expanding the ambits of the law, expands the boundaries of law-sanctioned violence.

The decade of the 1650s is pertinent to that argument because it is, I believe, during this span of years, in texts as apparently disparate as Jan Van Riebeeck's balance sheet, Thomas Hobbes's *Leviathan* (1651), and Richard Zouch's *Exposition of Fecial Law and Procedure, or of Law Between Nations* (1651) that we can begin to see money, law, and violence assuming a distinctly modern form of interentanglement. The argument is, in turn, pertinent to a volume on Enlightenment mediation because, as I understand it, it is in an Enlightenment discourse on law (particularly international law) that this nexus of law/money/violence assumes formal philosophical sanction and elevation to the level of a global imperative or universal rule (through the work, however surprisingly, of a text such as Kant's *Metaphysics of Morals*). And that Kantian text is, finally, pertinent to this volume's moment because what Kant inherits in this text—explicitly from Hobbes and implicitly from a Hobbesian moment that Zouch and Van Riebeeck helped to fashion—is something we have recently been asked to inherit again, this time as an unabashedly conjoined theory and practice of international law, global war, and (speculative) capital set forth (and set to work) in the Bush Administration's "National Security Strateg[ies]" of the United States and in a series of key security studies texts that have informed those strategies, texts which explicitly position themselves (and the United States) in a Hobbesian-Kantian line of descent (as aspirational global "Leviathan" and guarantor of "perpetual peace"), texts whose most significant exemplars include Robert Kagan's amply discussed "Paradise and Power" and Thomas P. Barnett's somewhat less-known but equally influential *The Pentagon's New Map*.

In that last text—a result of Barnett's work as director of the New Rules Set project, a collaborative venture jointly organized by the Wall Street investment firm Cantor Fitzgerald and the Naval War College—the law- (and violence-) carrying function of money coheres, spectacularly but I believe unsurprisingly, in a neo-Enlightenment project of imperial war and, cohering so, lends a distinct urgency to Poovey's injunction that we return to money its history: a history that I want to suggest we can trace both by attending to what she calls the varying and evolving "genres" of money and by establishing something like a periodizing account of those genres as they rise, fall, and rise again. In the account I am sketching, a history of money might be periodized in relation to three moments (the mid-seventeenth, late eighteenth, and late twentieth–early twenty-first centuries) in which the speculative genres of money (and related instruments of credit and finance capital) repeatedly predominate and repeatedly carry with them a recurring order of law and violence (whether in proto-, high-, or re-Enlightenment form).

To venture a critique of the Enlightenment (and its pre- and posthistories) in these terms is, however, to risk both the impulse toward abstraction (via, among other procedures, an amplification of argumentative scale) that Poovey so convincingly links to that "process of mystification" "necessary" to the Enlightenment project itself. Indeed, to follow her argument one step further, it is to risk extending, in the guise of critique, a project that in seeking to grasp the "'world [as] . . . a system whose parts can be known" causes "the materiality and historical specificity of the instruments by which those parts are revealed . . . [to] . . . vanish, as the whole gradually takes the place of its parts." And because I take the weight and the twinned epistemological and methodological dilemma of that critique quite seriously, I want now to shift scale, to set aside the speculative whole of my argument, and take up one of its starting parts: Van Riebeeck's 1652–1660 balance sheet.

The Dutch East India Company's "fortified refreshment station" at the Cape of Good Hope was established in 1652, four years after the signing of the Treaty of Westphalia and (given the coincident 1651 publications of Thomas Hobbes's *Leviathan* and Richard Zouch's *Exposition*) one year after the advent of what Carl Schmitt has identified as the textual *annus mirabilis* of the *Jus Publicum Europaeum*: the legal and political system through which, with their wars of religion settled, the Continental state powers were able to establish a globe-encompassing juridical order; a "nomos of the earth" predicated on the dual regulation of war within the European state system and the legally sanctioned extension/suspension of the law-of-war in the juridically "free" and empty spaces "beyond the line" of the Continent's shores; an order predicated in effect and in law on a distinction contemporary legal and political theorists were able to draw between a Continental state system that, in its relation to itself, had entered into a state of "civil society" and an extra-European world languishing in a Hobbesian "state of nature" (Schmitt 2003, 93 and ff).

Instructed by the Dutch East India Company's Lords Seventeen to establish a provisioning station at one outpost of this legally "empty" world beyond Europe's "amity lines," a station whose fruit and vegetable gardens and cattle pens could be counted on to supply both the outward and return fleets traveling to and from Batavia with a sufficient supply of food at the midpoint of their Atlantic- and Indian-ocean voyages, Van Riebeeck arrived at the Cape equipped with both a knowledge of that post-Westphalian law-of-war through which he could extend a claim to title over the territories under his command, and a fund of "cash" with which to establish the Company's outpost. Almost a decade was to pass between Van Riebeeck's landing at the Cape and his explicit recourse to the law of war whose representative, as commander of a European-chartered company's provisioning settlement in Africa, he unembarrassedly understood himself to be. The money he set to use immediately.

Where that first fund of cash came from, Van Riebeeck nowhere considers in the multiple letters he sent to the Lords Seventeen detailing his actions and, scrupulously (though, until the 1660 balance sheet, not comprehensively) accounting for his every expenditure and intake. Financial histories of the period, and of the Company, give a fairly clear sense, however, of how that initial allotment would have become available. The commodity trade in goods from the "Indies" would have provided, in abundance, funds from which the Company could have drawn to establish its Cape outpost. But fundamental to that oceans-spanning trade, as Giovanni Arrighi among others has detailed, was the Company's emergence as a joint-stock corporation within a Dutch market in speculative capital: a market that by the mid-seventeenth century had become, Arrighi argues, the global headquarter of finance capital, its dominant "space of flows" (Arrighi 1994). Converted from some combination of stock coupons and commodity sales into the cash that the company issued to Van Riebeeck to establish the Cape of Good Hope settlement, that initial treasury was multiply reconverted by him into a set of local instruments. Van Riebeeck established a credit system at the Cape (through which he managed the payment of his garrison's salaries); imported cloth (from Europe), copper chains (from China), and glass beads (from Japan) for use as barter items in the purchase of cattle from the indigenes of the Cape; inaugurated a further import of cowries (from Sri Lanka) on discovering that this "shell-money" was used by the inhabitants of the slave coast of Africa with whom he also wished to establish trade relations; created a system of "board money" by which to account for the meals eaten by his men; and generally experimented with any instrument of money that came available.

All these local forms and instruments through which Van Riebeeck's treasury expressed its buying, selling, lending, bartering, and wage-paying capacities vanish, however, when reexpressed (by means of a first-order abstraction) as a list of numbers in the "loss" and "profit" columns of his 1660 balance sheet.

Van Riebeeck's 1652–1660 balance sheet.

| | | Loss | Profit |
|---|---|---|---|
| | | | 1660. 19th March. |
| 1652. | Expenditure on loans, or advances to the men on account, equivalent to their monthly wages | £3,082 19 12 | |
| | Donations | 10 0 12 | |
| | Extraordinary expenditure | 133 4 0 | |
| | Expenditure of merchandise | 41 14 0 | |
| | Provisions | 54 15 10 | |
| | Total of general expenditure during 1652 | £3,325 4 2 | |
| | And profits | 578 7 5 | |
| | Or a deficit of | | £2746 16 13 |
| 1653. | Expenditure on loans, &c. | £6,751 6 14 | |
| | Provisions | 2,151 11 0 | |
| | Extraordinary expenditure | 488 16 4 | |
| | Munitions of war | 15 0 0 | |
| | Cooks' utensils | 3 0 0 | |
| | Materials | 136 18 12 | |
| | Sundry | 48 0 0 | |
| | Total expenditure | £8,364 12 14 | |
| | Profits | 2,656 7 9 | |
| | Or a deficit of | | 5,708 5 5 |
| 1654. | Expenditure on loans, &c. | £6,770 11 12 | |
| | Ammunition | 27 10 0 | |
| | Provisions | 2,674 12 8 | |
| | Extraordinary expenses | 792 18 14 | |
| | Materials | 795 0 10 | |
| | Knives used | 36 0 0 | |
| | Barber's (surgeon's) shop | 350 0 0 | |
| | Writing material | 19 10 0 | |
| | Yarn used (guaren) | 22 10 4 | |
| | Cooks' utensils | 61 18 0 | |
| | Butlers' do. | 39 13 13 | |
| | Total of expenditure | £10,804 3 4 | |
| | Profits | 377 9 7 | |
| | Or a deficit of | | 9,916 13 13 |
| 1655. | Loans, &c. | £6,024 10 12 | |
| | Extraordinary expenses | 4,137 15 5 | |
| | Provisions | 2,066 17 0 | |
| | Surgeon's shop | 709 12 12 | |
| | Total of general expenditure | £12,938 16 3 | |
| | Profits | 3,382 3 10 | |
| | Or a deficit of | | 9,556 11 9 |
| 1656. | Loans, &c. | £11,360 17 6 | |
| | Board money for the officials | 1,456 6 2 | |
| | Provisions for the men (guaren) | 2,461 8 3 | |
| | Extraordinary expenditure | 529 4 8 | |
| | Materials used | 6 18 0 | |
| | Cooks' utensils | 51 19 0 | |
| | Butlers' do. | 26 0 0 | |
| | Ammunition | 98 10 0 | |
| | Office furniture | 669 12 12 | |
| | Surgeon's shop | 373 12 4 | |
| | The Robbejesjes | | |
| | Total of expenditure | £10,167 10 4 | |
| | Profits | 4,190 16 5 | |
| | Deficiency | | 14,066 13 15 |

| | | | | |
|---|---|---|---|---|
| 1657. | Loans, &c. | £1,969 0 12 | | |
| | Board money | 1,574 10 0 | | |
| | Provisions | 1,780 16 0 | | |
| | Extraordinary expenditure | 1,677 10 12 | | |
| | Materials | 810 14 4 | | |
| | Cooks' utensils | 60 10 0 | | |
| | Butlers' do. | 71 19 0 | | |
| | Equipments | 45 0 0 | | |
| | Ammunition | 100 10 0 | | |
| | Office furniture | 41 14 0 | | |
| | Robbejesjes | | | |
| | Total of general expenditure | £17,905 6 8 | | |
| | Profits | 8,890 4 10 | | |
| | Deficiency | | 9,016 1 14 | |
| 1658. | Loans, &c. | £9,153 2 6 | | |
| | Ordinary rations or board money | 1,306 9 0 | | |
| | Provisions, inclusive of those for the slaves | 3,619 0 5 | | |
| | Extraordinary expenses | 2,698 31 0 | | |
| | Materials | 858 7 0 | | |
| | Equipments | 29 0 0 | | |
| | Ammunition | 61 19 0 | | |
| | Cooks' utensils | 45 0 0 | | |
| | Butlers' do. | 35 2 0 | | |
| | Office furniture | 96 0 6 | | |
| | Total of expenditure | £18,203 1 3 | | |
| | Profits | 21,306 8 10 | | |
| | Surplus | | | £3,103 7 |
| 1659. | Loans, &c. | £9,500 10 4 | | |
| | Ordinary rations | 2,860 16 6 | | |
| | Wages and salaries | 678 16 0 | | |
| | Provisions for all, slaves included | 4,741 10 12 | | |
| | Extraordinary expenditure | 4,151 14 8 | | |
| | Materials | 782 13 6 | | |
| | Equipments | 57 3 1 | | |
| | Ammunition | 67 1 8 | | |
| | Cooks' utensils | 6 3 8 | | |
| | Butlers' do. | 6 5 0 | | |
| | Masons' tools | 63 0 6 | | |
| | Malt refuse? (Bastel werck) | 63 15 0 | | |
| | Damaged stockings | 118 0 0 | | |
| | Office accessories | 308 17 12 | | |
| | Hospital | 404 0 0 | | |
| | Iron | | | |
| | Total expenditure | £24,246 7 10 | | |
| | Profits | 16,125 13 11 | | |
| | Deficiency | | | 4 £8,103 7 |
| | Grand total | £61,033 17 4 | | |
| | Deduct from this the surplus of 1658 | 3,103 7 7 | | |
| | | £57,930 9 3 | | |

And there will still be a deficiency of

The first thing to note about this balance sheet is that without this capacity of money to abstract itself, through an accounting procedure, as such a list of losses and profits, Van Riebeeck could not long have continued doing business at the Cape. In each of his first six years as commander, Van Riebeeck's station ran significant deficits: ranging from an initial net loss of 2,746 guilders in 1652 to a particularly bleak deficit of 14,966 guilders in 1656. That the settlement could continue to operate was due to the fact that Van Riebeeck's ledger was but one of a vast number of such accounting books littered all around the Indian, Atlantic, and European outposts of the Company; that those books, by equivalently abstracting an endless variety of instruments of payment and intake into a common numerical form, could set their various flows of money into conversation with one another; that a loss in one corner of the Company's empire could be debited against a credit at another; that through this apparently simple first-order accounting abstraction, the Company's circum-oceanic and trans-Continental flows of money could be managed, controlled, and directed. The local credit economy that Van Riebeeck established for his garrison was, in brief, but one small part of the vast internal and external credit market that allowed the Company to exist. Outfitted with "cash," Van Riebeeck could operate not on the exclusive basis of that cash but because his enterprise was part of a semiglobal credit economy, one through which a speculative revolution originating in Amsterdam could reexpress itself around the world. Without that credit network, Van Riebeeck's settlement would have folded and the Company itself would have collapsed.

But cash and credit (and before either of those, the Dutch stock market) were not enough to enable Commander Van Riebeeck's settlement to survive. He required, also, law: an elementary form of contract law, at one level, to which he could appeal to render binding his exchanges of beads, cloth, and copper for the cattle of the Cape's indigenous inhabitants but also, and more crucially, a law of war to justify his willingness to punish these *Hottentoos* and *Caapmen* when he found them in violation of their contracts and, prior to that, to legitimate his power of command over the lives both of his garrison and the Africans on whose land he had settled.

As I have suggested above, the law necessary to Van Riebeeck should not be regarded as parallel to the money (whether in cash or credit forms) he required, but as something the money forms flowing through his treasury "carried" intrinsically with them. The example of contract law conveys, fairly apparently, this money-carrying-function of law: for without a law of contract to bind exchanges money cannot function and, relatedly, where money is, contract law must follow (or coincidentally appear). But the law

I primarily have in mind is another order of law that money, on its network of travels around the globe, carries with it: international law, particularly, in the moments of finance capital's high generic dominance, the international law of war. To the extent that money, as a convertible unit of account, renders possible exchange across national markets and so renders possible one of the fundamental practices of the international (international commerce), the international law that money carries is again a version of contract law. But as I hope to demonstrate by returning once more to Van Riebeeck's balance sheet, the law it carries is also (most crucially at the moments in which, over the course of the past three-and-a-half centuries, speculative capital has claimed a global or semi-global hegemony) an international law of war and, so, a law of violence.

In making that argument I am, in part, following on the suggestion Hannah Arendt develops in the chapter of *The Origins of Totalitarianism* to which Poovey referred above. In that chapter, "The Political Emancipation of the Bourgeosie," Arendt reads imperialism as providing a twin solution to a crisis intrinsic to the modern European state as it unfolds itself in Hobbesian form. The Hobbesian state, Arendt argues,

> sprang from the theoretically indisputable proposition that a never-ending accumulation of property must be based on a never-ending accumulation of power. The philosophical correlative of the inherent instability of a community founded on power is the image of an endless process of history which, in order to be consistent with the constant growth of power, inexorably catches up with individuals, peoples, and finally all mankind. The limitless process of capital accumulation needs the political structure of so "unlimited a Power" that it can protect growing property by constantly growing more powerful ... When the accumulation of capital had reached its natural, national limits, the bourgeoisie understood that only with an "expansion is everything" ideology and only with a corresponding power-accumulating process, would it be possible to set the old motor into motion again. (Arendt 1968, 143–144)

As capital accumulates within the Hobbesian state, to put things another way, so too must power. Or, to rephrase things yet again, the core logic of the "Commonwealth," in Arendt's reading, is one predicated on a dialectical interaction of the never-ending accumulation of power and capital. To revise a Marxian formula, the logic of the modern state might thus be expressed as M-V-M' or V-M-V' (rather than Marx's M-C-M'—money-capital-money *plus*) where M continues to stand for money but V denotes violence. The founding monopoly on legitimate, law-sanctioned violence through which the commonwealth is established, thus creates the conditions for the accumulation of money, which, as it continues to accumulate, necessitates an intensification of the state's capacity for violence (V-M-V': violence-money-violence *plus*). A further extension of this formula: as money accumulates, so too must the over-awing violence of a sovereign power expand, which then enables a yet further accumulation of money (M-V-M': money-violence-money *plus*). Locked in a never-ending cycle of the overaccumulation of money and violence (whose full sequence runs violence-money-violence *plus*-money *plus*-violence *plus plus*-money *plus plus*, ad infinitum), the commonwealth however, inevitably runs up against its national boundaries, which, Arendt argues, money is the first to overleap but which the power-accumulating-machine then also trespasses as it extends its monopoly on legitimate violence into the zones captured by money. As imperialism thereby "solves" for the national state the twin, and periodically recurrent, problems of the overaccumulation of money and violence, money, in the terms I have been using, thus serially carries the violence of an "over-awing" power with it onto the spaces of the imperial world: not anarchically, but in law—"a direct emanation," as Arendt has it, "from the monopoly power of the state" (Arendt 1968, 141).

Such, at least, is the general formula I have in mind (and from which I am drawing the overarching money/law/violence periodizing framework of my argument). In returning to see how that formula might find itself expressed in Van Riebeeck's balance sheet some immediate problems, however, present themselves. The law-sanctioned violence of the Hobbesian state is one directed *toward that state's citizens* (those who can be said to have consented to exchange the insecurity of the "state of nature" for the security of life within the commonwealth), and that power of violence, obviously enough, is one accumulating within a *sovereign state*. Neither of these conditions was apposite to Van Riebeeck's settlement, where, as the representative not of a sovereign state but of a chartered company, the subjects of his command were not citizens but the employees of the Company and the native inhabitants of the Cape. If the money flowing through his station was to carry, in law, an over-awing power of violence with it, then that law could not be the civil (or constitutional) law of a state but of another legal order: one which would permit Van Riebeeck to arrogate to the Company the over-awing properties of a sovereign state (or to treat the interests of one as isomorphic with the interests of the other) *and* to extend over a body of noncitizens (indeed, and most crucially, over a body of individuals living, putatively, in a state of nature) a legally sanctioned power of violence independent of their expression of consent or entry into the state form. As I have indicated, that law existed (and continues to exist) in the form of an international law of war whose modern origins trace to the late sixteenth and early seventeenth centuries: a body of law that had been designed, in significant part, for situations just such as those in which Van Riebeeck found himself; a body of law that found its post-Westphalian moment of arrival in Richard Zouch's 1651 *Exposition* and which, having found expression in that text and a set of "humanist" legal writings that preceded it, has continued to articulate the violence-and-money-entangled international law of our own moment and of the speculative Enlightenment period that lies between our present and Van Riebeeck's contemporaneity.

Where does that repeating law find itself expressed in Van Riebeeck's ledger? In a sense, both nowhere and everywhere; as the invisible but always present force animating the very existence of that accounting sheet and authorizing all of Van Riebeeck's activities at the Cape. More particularly still, however, it finds itself recorded in the sum tally Van Riebeeck provided for his "extraordinary expenditure" for the year 1659. As Van Riebeeck had reported in an earlier section of his March 19, 1660, letter, 1659 had been an entirely eventful year, one in which he and his garrison had become embroiled in a war against the *Hottentoos* and *Caapmen* living in the area around the Company's settlement. Van Riebeeck's chief antagonist in this conflict was a man named Doman, formerly his chief interpreter, who had now installed himself "as Captain-General over the warriors that had congregated together from the Caapmen and tobacco thieves" (Van Riebeeck 1897a 134). Summoned together by Doman, these "beach rangers and brigands," Van Riebeeck reported, "attack[ed] us suddenly... on all sides" (Van Riebeeck 1897a 135). "The tables," he continued, "were accordingly quickly and completely turned against us, and everything of which we had been able to give such favorable accounts in our last letters appeared to be going to ruin... [B]eing so short of men, we did not know whither to turn, or how to defend ourselves in this sudden predatory war" (Van Riebeeck 1897a 135).

Van Riebeeck did not long remain indecisive. He issued a proclamation giving "full permission" to "everyone to seize or shoot them [the Caapmen] wherever they are found," (Van Riebeeck 1897b, 21) and issued a bounty of 100 guilders for Doman if captured "alive" and "50 guilders if dead" (Van Riebeeck 1897b, 22). For the capture of any of "the rest of these robbers," the Commander offered the further reward of "20 guilders each if alive and 10 if dead. Half price for women and children" (Van Riebeeck 1897b*l*, 22). Unconvinced that those steps alone would have the desired effect of "impressing" his foes "with a proper panic" (Van Riebeeck 1897b, 21), Van Riebeeck also requisitioned a company of soldiers from a Company ship anchored in the bay, complemented these troops with members of his own garrison and a militia raised from the "free" Dutch farmers in the surrounding vicinity and, having captured a "Hottentoo of the tobacco thieves" and "by means of threats and otherwise" forced from him the location of Doman's encampment, dispatched a combined force of 150 men on an "expedition for the destruction of our enemies" (Van Riebeeck 1897b, 52, 53).

The expedition accomplished little of its stated objective. Doman was quickly discovered but he escaped capture and Van Riebeeck's troops found themselves trailing a fleeing enemy whom they could not force to fight in a standing battle. A fortnight later, however, Van Riebeeck finally received welcome news. A detachment of men under the command of Corporal Elias Giers had discovered a "Hottentoo" "camp, consisting of three reed huts, in which were 13 male adults and about as many women and children" (Van Riebeeck 1897b, 61). Corporal Giers attempted to take the inhabitants of the camp captive with the idea of claiming the reward for them. But when they began to flee, "our men," as Van Riebeeck noted in his journal, "not desir[ing] to have a fruitless journey... fired at them, capturing their chief Captain... and killing two others," and they destroyed the three huts and "everything they contained" (Van Riebeeck 1897b, 61). The prisoner Corporal Giers had taken presented a problem, however. He was too old to easily accompany the Corporal and his men back to the Governor's Fort at the Cape, where the reward could be claimed for his capture. So Giers cut off his upper lip and brought that to Van Riebeeck as evidence.

In concluding his account of this "war" (whose expenses, including the bounty paid on the lip of Corporal Giers's prisoner, Van Riebeeck appears, quite aptly, to have accounted for in his record of "extraordinary expenditure" for the year) the Commander explained to the Lords Seventeen the utter legality of all the steps he had taken in licensing and rewarding such slaughter: "in consequence of the war made against us they had completely forfeited their rights and ... we were not inclined to restore them, as the country had become the property of the Company by the sword and the rights of war" (Van Riebeeck 1897a 166).

What rights-canceling "rights of war," one might ask, did Van Riebeeck have in mind, and was he legally correct to claim them? In the event, he was. Or at least, arguably so. First, by the doctrine of "reprisals" which, according to the existing law of war, enabled the delegation of the punitive rights (and *in situ* personality) of a sovereign state to a private entity, such as the Company and its representatives. Second, by the productive vagueness in the definition of sovereign personhood provided by Hugo Grotius (former legal counsel to the Company, author of the seminal 1625 volume, *The Rights of War and Peace* and, with Alberico Gentili, one of the two primary sources for Zouch's *Exposition*): a definition that in designating as sovereign "that power . . . whose actions are not subject to the control of any other power" (Grotius 1901, book 1, 62) reads uncannily like Schmitt's theory of sovereignty avant la lettre and, given the licensed monopoly supplied to the Dutch East Company by the Estates-General of the Netherlands, could certainly be claimed by Van Riebeeck as applying to him as the Company's representative at the Cape. Most crucially however (with this twin grounding of his appeal to sovereign personality in place), Van Riebeeck's claim to possess a law-sanctioned power of violence found authentication in the global "right of punishment" on which Grotius and a fellow company of late-Renaissance humanist jurists had staked their claim to have defined for the European powers global jurisdiction over the "law of nature" (which meant in practice, jurisdiction over any territory beyond the boundaries of the European state system). As Grotius quite unambiguously put it: "[T]hose who are possessed of a sovereign power have a right to exact punishment not only for injuries affecting immediately themselves or their own subjects, but for gross violations of the law of nature and of nations, done to other states and subjects. . . . Upon this principle there can be no hesitation in pronouncing all wars to be just, that are made upon pirates, general robbers, and enemies of the human race. . . . [It is] a right resulting entirely from the law of nature" (Grotius 1901, book 2, 247).

Key to this assertion was not only the contention that any individual "sovereign power" possessed global jurisdiction over the "law of nature" but the question of what precisely might constitute a punishable "violation of the law of nature." Grotius's answer is contained in the elaboration he provides to the general "principle" he is insisting on. Primary among the grossest violations of the law of nature are piracy and general robbery, though why either should constitute not simply a civil crime but an affront to the law of nature is not yet clear, so, in a subsequent portion of his text, Grotius explains his reasoning by drawing a distinction not, as one might expect, between the types of *action* committed by pirates and robbers and those acts consistent with the law of nature but between the *forms of social organization* characteristic of the state, on one hand, and piracy on the other: "A state, though it may commit some act of aggression, or injustice, does not thereby lose its political capacity, *nor can a band of pirates or robbers ever become a state* . . . For with the latter the commission of crime is the sole bond of union" (Grotius 1901, book 3, 315, emphasis added). The pirate or the general robber,

Grotius argues, violates the law of nature not in consequence of any discrete act of theft or violence but by a prior and continuing refusal to enter into the political, law-and-contract–bound community of a commonwealth. To refuse the bond of union provided by the European state form is to violate the law of nature, to become an enemy of the human race, and so, in Grotius's opinion, to forfeit all rights and become subject to sovereign punishment. Or, to put things in terms directly relevant to Van Riebeeck's actions: purely by virtue of their apparent form of social organization, by virtue of appearing to him in the guise of "brigands" or "beach rangers," the "Caapmen" and "Hottentoos" could be said to be living in violation of that *law* of nature that demanded that they abandon the *state of nature* and consent to their sovereign governance, and so (*quite apart from and prior to any act of belligerence on their part*) had "forfeited their rights," and rendered themselves punishable.

Nor is this opinion exclusive to Grotius and his fellow humanist jurists—it is central to Hobbes's own understanding of the complex interplay between the "state" and the "law" of nature, organizational, in fact, to his account of the ways in which the fundamental legal obligation of those living within the otherwise lawless anarchy of the state of nature is that they abandon that condition and enter into life within the state. Precisely because the first "right" of nature (which affirms "the liberty every man hath . . . for the preservation of his own nature") exists in irreconcilable tension with the warlike *condition* of the state of nature in which no man can guarantee his own preservation, the first "law" of nature is that man must abandon the insecurity of the war of all against all and enter into the protection of a commonwealth under the sovereign command of an over-awing power. In mirroring Hobbes's arguments, Grotius and his fellow humanists were not, therefore, so much inventing a law of nature that they held pirates, robbers, brigands and other "such men" to be violating as asserting its pertinence to not only the philosophical but also the juridical domain, rendering violations of this law explicitly, legally, actionable, defining the failure to belong to a recognizable sovereign state as an offense punishable under the twinned laws of nature and war. And while the generic examples Grotius cites of these stateless "enemies of the human race" are those of the pirate and the robber, the historical example provided by Van Riebeeck's actions at the Cape suggest that the real enemies subject to this universally asserted right of punishment were the indigenous peoples of the expanding, formal and informal European empires.

One problem, however, remained. For in affirming the right of punishment on which Van Riebeeck can be seen to have been relying, Grotius had put himself in a paradoxical position. Where in one section of his text he explicitly endorses the right of a sovereign power to wage war against precisely the type of foe the Commander represented himself to be confronting ("robbers," "brigands," and "beach-rangers," as he variously calls them), elsewhere in his text Grotius seems to insist upon the precise opposite:

> To what kind of war such an appellation ["just"] most duly belongs will be best understood by considering the definition, which the Roman Lawyers have given of a PUBLIC or NATIONAL enemy. "Those, *says Pomponius*, are PUBLIC and LAWFUL ENEMIES, with whose STATE our own is engaged in war: but enemies of every other description, come under the denomination of pirates and robbers . . . So that by the opinion of the Roman Lawyers it is evident, that no war is considered lawful, regular, and formal, except that which is begun and carried on by the sovereign power of each country. (Grotius 1901, 3: 314–315)

Grotius was not alone among the humanist jurists from whom the modern law of war derives in arguing thus. "War," Gentili had previously insisted in his 1588 *De Iure Belli*, "derives its name from the fact that there is a contest for victory between two equal parties, and for that reason it was first called *duellem*, 'a contest of two'. . . In the same way we have *perduellem*, 'war,' *duelles* and *perduelles*, 'enemies,' whom we now call *hostes* . . . . In fact, *hostire* means 'to make equal' . . . therefore *hostis* is a person with whom war is waged and who is the equal of his opponent." Thus, he concluded, any definition of war as "'armed force against a foreign prince or people,' is shown to be incorrect by the fact that it applies the term 'war' also to the violence of private individuals and of brigands" (Gentili 1933, 2: 12).

Licensed by the right of punishment to wage war against pirates, robbers, and brigands "wherever they are found," while restricted from identifying "war" against "such men" as "war" in any just and proper sense, the humanist law of war thus found itself at an apparent impasse, one motivated by the twin, but conflicting, historical pressures to which Grotius, Gentili, and their intellectual companions were responding. For if the impulse to define war as a contest between formally equal sovereign counterparts had been motivated by the need to resolve Europe's otherwise irresolvable wars of religion, and if the humanist key to solving that puzzle had been, as Schmitt and others have argued, to have derived, from the sovereign equality of belligerent state actors, the concept of the "just enemy" (*justus hostis*) with whom a peace treaty could be concluded, the historical moment in which that legal puzzle was solved was also one in which the Continental powers were embarking on an intensified global round of empire building and imperial war making against an array of "peoples" whom they were distinctly disinclined to recognize as sovereign, much less equal, much less just (Schmitt 2003, 153 and ff). To balance the twin imperatives of crafting a law of war that would strengthen the sovereignty of European states without necessitating a recognition of the sovereignty of the extra-European peoples on whom they were waging war, a second key figure was thus required, one to set alongside but as a negative double to the "hostis," one, that is, to set *within* the law of war as legally *outside* the law of war: the figure of the "unjust enemy," against whom one could legally wage war, but to whom, as Van Riebeeck had contended, the rights of war did not apply.

It was in finally and formally codifying this figure that Zouch's *Exposition* was to prove so vital. Returning to both Grotius's and Gentili's writings and to a body of Roman law that, in concert with natural law theory, had provided a common foundation to their work, Zouch teased out from Roman legal thought, particularly from Cicero's speeches and writings and, more specifically still, from Cicero's *Philipics*, full warrant for the legal enshrinement of this "unjust enemy." For in that series of speeches denouncing Mark Antony and asserting for the Roman people the right to make war against this "bandit" and his "villainous band of brigands," while simultaneously denying that this stateless man deserved any reciprocal recognition as a legitimate foe, Cicero had identified the very legal figure the humanists were searching for: a nonsovereign enemy against whom a sovereign state could go to war while excepting that enemy from the rights and protections stipulated by the laws of war (Cicero 1986, 145). Hence, as Zouch's strategic references to Grotius's and Gentili's writings makes evident, the regularity with which each of the major humanist legal thinkers of the period cites and recites an identical single passage from the *Philipics*. Grotius cites it. Gentili cites it at the close of a lengthy chapter on the unprotected place of "brigands" in the law of war, and Zouche, Gentili's successor as professor of law at Oxford, then cites it again in what might be the clearest exposition of the uses to which a Ciceronian theory of Roman law was put in resolving the legal paradox confronting the humanists.

Concluding a section of the *Exposition* in which he distinguishes between the two types of "enemies" with whom a state might find itself at war, "some of whom are of a worse and others of a better condition," Zouche identifies the latter as "lawful enemies . . . to whom are due all the rights of war" and then, quoting Cicero, clarifies who such a lawful enemy might be: "[O]ne who has a State, Senate, Treasury, citizens consenting and agreeing and some method of making peace" (Zouche 1902, 37–38). Against these licit, protected foes, he posed all those other enemies "of the worse condition . . . [those] to whom the laws of war do not apply"—"robbers," "brigands," "pirates," or as his group name for this second type of belligerent, this less and worse than an enemy, "inimici," those who are "inimical"—and inimical in a particular sense: inimical by virtue of failing to possess a state, senate, and treasury (Zouche 1902, 37–38); inimical, as Grotius elsewhere makes clear, by virtue of having violated Hobbes's first "law of nature"; inimical by virtue of having refused to abandon the insecurity of the state of nature for the wealth of life under the over-awing power of a sovereign state; inimical, in Hobbes's terms, by virtue of not having abandoned a condition in which "there is no place for industry . . . no culture of the earth, no navigation, no use of the commodities that might be imported by sea, no commodious building. . . . no arts, no letters, no society, and which is worst of all, continual fear and danger of violent death, and the life of man, solitary, poor, nasty, brutish and short." Life, "solitary, poor, nasty, brutish, and short," may be the most famous items of this litany of scandals, but as the preceding elements of Hobbes's charge sheet make clear and as the humanist jurists of the late sixteenth and early seventeenth century chose, by criminalizing, to emphasize, the true outrage of the unjust enemy was to exist outside the state form, and, by existing so, to refuse, in exchange for subordination to the ever accumulating power of the commonwealth, to enter into a life of ever accumulating industry, cultivation, and commodity exchange, life under the dual, reciprocal sovereignty of state and treasury, violence and money.

If Jan Van Riebeeck could find in his adversaries, in the "brigands and robbers" with whom he reported himself to be at war, a company of "unjust enemies" whose "rights" he understood himself to possess legal title to declare "forfeit," then he is not the last to have thought or done so. Nor, indeed, were his actions exceptional to his moment. They were, I am arguing, generic, and generically exemplary of the moment of overaccumulating finance capital he inhabited, a moment in which, as it leaps the boundaries of the national, finance capital (in all its local instruments) carries a law of war-making sovereign violence with it. My prior recourse to Giovanni Arrighi's account of modern capital's long cycles of accumulation and my effort to provide a reading, through Hannah Arendt, of an enduring, recurring, accumulating cycle of money- and law-carried violence suggest that the next historical moment in which finance capital (in its relentless quests for new markets) assumes generic global or semiglobal dominance would again be a moment in which the question of the unjust enemy (the question of one falling under the globally sovereign power of money but living outside the civil or constitutional law of the national state), would repeat itself as a crucial issue for international law. After the 1650s, Arrighi argues, the next moment of finance capital's dominance is the period of the late eighteenth century, the period we more commonly know as the Enlightenment. And it is no accident, I am arguing, that the central philosophical text of Enlightenment international law, Kant's *Metaphysics of Morals*, finds itself triply haunted: by the ghost of Hobbes, the shadow of global financial flows, and most signally, by the reappearing specter of inimical life.

As Kant puts it in a startling passage of the *Metaphysics*: "The rights of a state against an *unjust enemy* are unlimited in quantity or degree" (Kant 1970, 170). This rather startling statement, from the section "International Right" in the *Metaphysics*, provides the sole exception to Kant's general understanding of the grounds and limits of the state's "right to make war" against its enemies, and is immediately followed by his attempt to define who this "unjust enemy" might be: "But what can the expression 'an unjust enemy' mean in relation to the concepts of international rights. . . ? It must mean someone whose publicly expressed will, whether expressed in word or in deed, displays a maxim which would make peace among nations impossible and would lead to a perpetual state of nature if it were made into a general rule. Under this heading would come violations of public contracts, which can be assumed to affect the interests of all nations" (Kant 1970, 170). Who, then, is Kant's "unjust enemy"? One, like Zouch's *inimicus*, who is unwilling to enter into a contract with sovereignty or its institutional forms; one, in more explicitly Hobbesian terms, who is unwilling to abide by the public contract on which the commonwealth is founded: the contractual exchange of the fear of death for the promise of security, contractual legality, and financial reward. Against such an enemy, Kant determines, the rights of the state are unlimited.

It is only fair to note that in the subsequent portion of his text (on "Cosmopolitan Right"), Kant can be seen to attempt to limit the implications of what he has just licensed (by means of an extended meditation that touches directly, perhaps surprisingly but entirely aptly, on the ways in which his theory of law might apply to "the Hottentots" of the Cape), while nevertheless, I believe, yet more intimately bundling together, within a now universal theory of "right," the global flows of money and the international law of war. "Cosmopolitan Right," as Kant makes clear in these pages of the *Metaphysics*, fundamentally implies a global right to commerce, and while it is necessary to enshrine that right in law, to do so, he acknowledges, is to risk (and perhaps to endorse) a global right to violence in defense of that law.

Kant's thoughts on this "right" and the violence it invites are, in their mix of clarity and torturous self-hesitation, worth citing at length:

[A]ll nations are *originally* members of a community of the land. But this is not a *legal community* of possession (*communio*) and utilization of the land, nor a community of ownership. It is a community of reciprocal action (*commercium*), which is physically possible, and each member of it accordingly has constant relations with all the others. Each may *offer* to have commerce with the rest, and they all have a right to make such overtures without being treated by foreigners as enemies. This right, in so far as it affords the prospect that all nations may unite for the purpose of creating certain universal laws to regulate the intercourse they may have with one another, may be termed *cosmopolitan* (*ius cosmopoliticum*).

... With the art of navigation, [the oceans] constitute the greatest natural incentive to international commerce, and the greater the number of neighbouring coastlines there are ... the livelier this commerce will be. Yet these visits to foreign shores ... can also occasion evil and violence in one part of the globe with ensuing repercussions which are felt everywhere else. But although such abuses are possible, they do not deprive the world's citizens of the right to *attempt* to enter into a community with everyone else and to *visit* all regions of the earth with this intention.

... [O]ne might ask whether a nation may establish a *settlement alongside another nation* (*accolatus*) in newly discovered regions, or whether it may take possession of land in the vicinity of a nation which has already settled in the same area, even without the latter's consent. The answer is that the right to do so is incontestable ... But if the nations involved are pastoral or hunting peoples (like the Hottentots, the Tunguses, and most native American nations) who rely upon large tracts of wasteland for their sustenance, settlements should not be established by violence, but only by treaty... Nevertheless, there are plausible enough arguments for the use of violence on the grounds that it is in the best interest of the world as a whole ... But all these supposedly good intentions cannot wash away the stain of injustice from the means which are used to implement them. Yet one might object that the whole world would perhaps still be in a lawless condition if men had any such compunction about using violence when they first created a law-governed state. But this can as little annul the above condition of right as can the plea of political revolutionaries that the people are entitled to reform constitutions by force if they become corrupt. (Kant 1970, 172–173)

In summary terms, Kant's fundamental argument is that a global right to commerce is not only irrefutable but foundational to the emergence of an international (indeed "universal") legal order. Moreover, he contends, this cosmopolitan right to commerce and this universal international law extend (via a right to settlement and regardless of indigenous "consent") into those regions of the earth inhabited by peoples ("like the Hottentots") living in a "lawless condition." It is on this point, though, that he runs into difficulties. For while it is also his argument that these "lawless" people should only be made to enter into a universal cosmopolitanism "by treaty," it is a condition of their lawlessness that they are incapable of regarding treaties as instruments possessing binding contractual force. Hence, simultaneous to his proposition that while international law (and cosmopolitan right) should be extended by treaty rather than by violence, his contention that the "consent" of the lawless is not, in fact, necessary (indeed, in a strictly legal and philosophical sense, it is impossible). Hence also, Kant's ensuing, troubled set of arguments and counter-arguments against and for the use of violence in subordinating such lawless people to law (in the interest of extending the operating spheres of global commerce). At last, Kant finds himself at an impasse. Clearly wishing to express both a moral repugnance for (and refusal of) violence as a means of establishing, globally, the condition of cosmopolitan right, and at the same time compelled, by the Hobbesian logic of his own arguments, to acknowledge violence as the only copula between "a lawless condition" and "a law-governed state," he seems at once to wish to deny and to find no way to avoid entertaining the efficacy of a recourse to what more recent theoretical discourse calls constituting violence.

And while, in the last sentence I have cited, Kant can find a way to reject such constituting violence in the national arena (on the grounds that, however corrupt, constituted power can at least be said already to exist within the national state), all his express moral qualms cannot allow him to explain how global commerce, international law, and cosmopolitan right can come into existence without it. It is his good fortune that he doesn't have to provide that explanation here. For he has, in fact, done so earlier in his text, in his discussion of the "unjust enemy," which comes to his aid and solves his dilemma in much the same fashion that that figure had solved the dilemmas of Kant's mid-seventeenth-century intellectual predecessors. For precisely to the extent that "lawless people" (like the Hottentots) can be said to be living in a state of nature, living, that is, in a condition of the stateless, a-commercial, a-contractual "war of all against all," they can be said (as a pure fact of their apparent form of social organization and their exteriority to the realm of "public contract") to represent "a threat to the freedom" "of all nations" to pursue their cosmopolitan right. Accordingly, in this situation, and this situation only, Kant's text endorses a recourse to constituting violence or, as he puts it, affirms that against such "unjust enemies" "all nations" have the right to "unite" and "make them to accept a new constitution" (Kant 1970, 170).

If those final words seem uncannily pertinent to our own moment, then, in closing, I want very briefly to consider how that Kantian formula (or, more accurately, that Kantian reformulation of a mid-seventeenth-century Hobbesian law of war) is not merely apposite but crucial to that global theory and project of war with whose consequences we are still living; crucial to a global "security" discourse that in providing theoretical license for such war, claims philosophical dignity for itself by claiming direct lineal descent from Hobbes and Kant. By way of example, let me return to the text published by Thomas P. M. Barnett following his period as director of the Naval War College and Cantor Fitzgerald's collaborative "New Rules Sets Project," a text that brings to the present the cyclical history of money, law, and war I have been tracing.

The centerpiece of Barnett's argument is a map that was published, with a short accompanying essay, in the March 2003 issue of *Esquire* magazine under the title "The Pentagon's New Map." (Lest his readers miss the urgent historical pertinence of that map, Barnett's opening sentences read: "Let me tell you why military engagement with Saddam Hussein's regime in Baghdad is not only necessary and inevitable, but good ... a historical tipping point ... the moment when Washington takes real ownership of strategic security in the age of globalization.") Subsequently expanded and published in book form, Barnett's article has a fairly straightforward argument: the contemporary world is divisible in two, though not in the terms that Samuel Huntington divides it. Instead of being antagonistically counterposed on civilizational lines, the two worlds of the global present, Barnett argues, split off from one another as zones of security and insecurity: zones in which stable, state-governed polities have realized Kant's "dream of perpetual peace" and zones in which stateless, rogue-state, or failed-state polities are condemned to Hobbes's "state of nature." Isomorphic to this political distinction, Barnett's argument continues, is an economic distinction: in the global security zone, flows of capital and energy proceed unimpeded; in the zone of insecurity, finance capital is absent, energy is frequently abundant as a natural resource but unavailable to industry, and financial contracts are radically unenforceable where they can be said to exist at all. The security zone, in short, is characterized by stable state structures, the thick presence of political and economic "rule sets," and its concomitant integration into networks of global capital (particularly global finance capital); the insecurity zone is characterized by the absence of all three: states, rules, and investment capital. From these arguments, Barnett draws his fundamental conclusion: the boundary between the zones of security and insecurity (or, as he ultimately identifies it, between the territories of the "Functioning Core" and the "Non-Integrating Gap"), between the regions of capital flow and the dearth of capital, between the world that has achieved the "dream of Immanuel Kant's perpetual peace" and the world living in a Hobbesian state of nature, is not simply a new name for the borderline between the "developed" and "underdeveloped" worlds (Barnett 2004, 161). It is, instead, the new borderland of global war, the conflict zone along whose curving global line the wars of the twenty-first century will and should be fought: not defensively, but preemptively, in order to "shrink the gap" or, as he puts it, to move the territories within this insecurity zone "from Hobbes to Kant" (Barnett 2004, 166). That task, he finally insists, should not, however, be left to the U.S. military alone. Rather, the project of global war in the twenty-first century must become the shared project of the Pentagon and the finance capital industry working in combination as a new "global Leviathan" to secure for the planet as a whole a Kantian "perpetual peace" whose unfolding moment of arrival will be marked, and measured, by the cross-planetary extension of political, legal, and economic "rule sets."

The key argument central to the mid-seventeenth-century law of war, and central again, in overtly Hobbesian terms, to Kant's own theory of international and cosmopolitan right, thus returns as key to Barnett's new map of capital, law, and war. In response to the appearance of a people living in a putatively real state of nature on the boundaries and beyond the outposts of stable nation-states and the circulating flow of capital—people living in that "lawless condition in which man is a wolf to man (*homo homini lupus*)," the condition of human life, one of perpetual war of all against all, and the pursuit of commerce impossible in the absence of an over-awing, law-and-contract–securing power—sovereign power can again extend itself as a constituting power, and in so extending itself extend the flow of global capital *and* the law-carrying-function of money. As I have been suggesting, this return is not accidental but exemplary: exemplary of the form taken by international law when it is carried, by the flows of commerce, beyond the boundary of an ordering system of sovereign states in one of those moments of speculative capital that bracket either end of Arrighi's cycles of capital accumulation. Nor, to make one last point, is it an accident that at this moment, once again, the figure of the *inimicus* should return (now in the guise of the "unprivileged belligerent" or "unlawful enemy," one who now, as then, is lawfully unlawful by failing to belong to a recognized state entity); not an accident that at the repeating center of the cyclically recurrent, pre-, high-, and re-Enlightenment history of money I have been sketching, we should again find a figure whose rights are "forfeit," another in the long line of "Caapmen," "Hottentoos," "brigands," "*inimici*," "unjust enemies," and "unprivileged belligerents" who for the past three-and-a-half centuries have been made to be part of a world it is one of our tasks to make known—though not, to quote Poovey one last time, only as a world in which the function of these "parts" is "to vanish, as the whole gradually takes [their] place."

# "THE HORRIFYING TIES, FROM WHICH THE PUBLIC ORDER ORIGINATES"

THE POLICE IN SCHILLER AND MERCIER

BERNHARD SIEGERT

I

The way one comprehends the meaning of the conference title "Mediating Enlightenment" depends on the philosophical presumptions that determine how we conceive the logic of the relationship between the notions "media" and "Enlightenment." Thus, I presume, many people read the conference title "Mediating Enlightenment" as a circumscription of what has been called "the Public" by Reinhart Koselleck or Jürgen Habermas. According to Koselleck, Enlightenment has been mediated from the very beginning, since it had been coupled with the development of the public sphere. "The Enlightenment begins its triumphant success in as much as it extends the private inner sphere into the public" (Koselleck 1973, 41). Thus one would have to subsume media under the notion of "the Public"; mediating Enlightenment would then mean the same as "to produce public" or "to make something public." The media of the eighteenth century that mediate Enlightenment would then be first of all the journals, intelligence papers (*Intelligenzblatt*), and the political, literary, and scholarly correspondences that oscillate between the private and the public sphere, the national theaters, the parlor, and especially the secret societies and their complex use of postal services and letters.

What one is used to calling Enlightenment is the process by which the private opinions of the citizens are turned into law by virtue of an inborne capacity for publicity. "The public sphere and the private sphere are so far from excluding each other that on the contrary the one is created by the other" (Koselleck 1973, 44). The secret space and the public space presuppose each other: the public is the "medium" (Koselleck 1973, 44)[1] through which private opinions, intentions, and judgments of good taste (*Geschmacksurteile*) will always be moral law, because private opinion is first of all constituted by its capacity for publicity. Thus, the assumption, corroboration, and citation of an opposition between state and society is the ritual by which bourgeois society describes and rationalizes itself—even until the professional moralists today.

Therefore the confrontation of a moral authority of the citizens and a political authority of the state occurred first of all by virtue of a third authority—the media of the public. However, the public's media render themselves invisible inasmuch as they appear as a mirror of public opinion, one that disappears while bourgeois society constitutes itself through this mirror first of all according to the rules of narcissism and Lacan's mirror stage.[2] Marshall McLuhan, Jacques Lacan, and Jean Baudrillard converge on this point: Mass media—while practicing their moral censorship over reality—do not represent society; instead, the mass media and society have always been intertwined and constitute each other by means of a narcissistic relationship of identification across a constitutive split that they both aspire to make disappear.

This teleology of the media, that they are bound to become completely absorbed by the notion of "the Public," leads inevitably to the theoretical consequence that media are not part of the sphere of the state and governmental knowledge, but instead are assigned solely to the sphere of society. According to Werner Sombart and Jürgen Habermas, a "postal service," for instance, only existed after the "regular opportunity for the letter transport was opened to the public" (Habermas 1984, 30). By this argument a connection between the history of the two-hundred-year-old institution of the postal service as an imperial or state-run institution and the institution for the transportation of private communications are denied categorically. Therefore, the interface between communication and state power, the Cabinet noir, or black cabinet, where agents opened and read private mail, can be seen only as an agent of negativity (which suppresses and prohibits communication) instead of an agent that produces communication and power. Corresponding to this notion of the Public is a notion of the Individual (or *society*), which is opposed to power (the absolutist sovereign). In modernity, therefore, critical potential is assigned to art in general and literature and theater in particular. The beautiful stands (since Schiller) on the side of freedom; the state and art have to be conceived as opponents a priori, which relate to each other as law does to critique.

There are three critical interventions that one can make against this more than two-hundred-year-old myth of media history. First, the teleology, which defines the purpose of media as the production of the public and thus the creation of a moral judgment as a third law underpinning power beneath natural law and civil law, dissolves as soon as one relinquishes the arbitrary assumption of an opposition between society and state or between individual and power. "Thus the individual," wrote Foucault in contrast to bourgeois historiography, "is not the opponent of power, it is instead one of its first effects" (Foucault 1999, 39).

Second, the history of knowledge about the state suggests that one should abandon the theory that Enlightenment arose out of the struggle of society against the absolutist state. In the seventeenth century, beneath the philosophical theories of natural law and the social contract (*contrat social*) there appeared a different understanding of the fundaments of the state. This new understanding was no longer concerned with legal relations but with passions, interests, and manners of behavior, no longer concerned with political representation but with the regulation of medical, social, urban, and economic milieus, it was no longer concerned with the question of political founding but with the problem of administrative control (Vogl 2000, 602). The political was no longer part of the courtly representation of the sovereign, but instead projected itself as a field of relationships that provoked regulative forms of power below and distinct from the sphere of law. Thus there arose a political economy, a population policy, a health policy, a governmental policy, and so on. Thereby specialized governmental knowledge was produced that was given the title "Police" [German, *Polizey*], and referred to the empirical totality of the physical and moral life of the state.

This kind of governmental knowledge refers to a network of relations between the people and things, as well as between people themselves:

> That means, the things a government has to take care of are the people, but the people in their relations, their involvements with the things that constitute their wealth, resources, and subsistence . . . people in their relation to these other things that are their manners, habits, customs, their ways of acting or thinking. (Foucault 1989, 100)[3]

To govern became an art that presupposed some kind of factual knowledge requiring the media of a "data mining service" of the police (*Erkennungs-*

*dienst*): a knowledge about the forces of the state, the soil, the climate, the raw materials, the state of the mechanical arts, financial traffic, but first of all about the population, its number, its state of health, its mortality, its fertility, its moral state, its productivity. The complex relationship between all these factors was part of the "Police" in the eighteenth century.

A third intervention when discussing the history of media involves the fact that philosophers of the Enlightenment like Friedrich Schiller knew—and maybe that is the reason for his current relevance—that buried in the notion of Enlightenment is a meaning deeply connected to the Police. In fact, *Aufklärung* (Enlightenment) has in the German language also a military meaning, as well as a meaning related to police activities. One *reconnoitres*—as a cavalry scout—some ground, or one *solves*—as a detective—a crime. Both verbs are translated into German as *aufklären*.

Schiller focused on the logic of disrupted transitions in his plays and in his historiographical and editorial projects: he was obsessed by *coup d'états*, conspiracies, revolts, and intrigues. Schiller was so interested in César Vichard de Saint-Réal's story *Conspiracy of the Spaniards against Venice in 1618* that he edited it in the German language. In Saint-Réal's famous reconstruction of this conspiracy, everything amounts to the question of how one can possibly control chance. Under the sign of chance the historical enters the very center of power. The Marqués of Bedmar, ambassador to Venice, "one of the most powerful geniuses and one of the most dangerous spirits Spain has ever produced," gains his wisdom from historical studies.

> He compared the affairs, which those [the historiographs] described, with those, which happened in his own time. He observed accurately the differences and the resemblances of the affairs and how the differences changed the circumstances in which they resembled each other. He used to judge the outcome of an enterprise as soon as he knew the plan and its basis. When he found out in the following that he did not guess it right, he went back to the source of his mistake and tried to discover what had deceived him. (de Saint-Réal 1990, 13)

The goal of this experimenting with history is to eliminate chance. As soon as one discovers the reasons for the unforeseen, chance is no longer chance. Therefore "data mining" capacities and media are needed to uncover the laws behind those events that seem to occur by chance. Politics, defined in the *Political Testament* of the Prussian king Frederick the Great, is the art "to read the future" (quoted in Schneider 1994, 327);[4] both the conspirator, who wishes to overthrow the established order, and the police, who wish to maintain the order, face the challenge of rendering the future of the state predictable (Vogl 2000, 607). The secret society of conspirators, in which the freemason Lessing already recognized the essence of Enlightenment, is prefigured by the secret police. Enlightenment and the secret, Koselleck wrote, enter the stage as historical twins (Koselleck 1973, 4). Both conspirators and police lieutenants operate in seclusion, both are oriented toward the connection and regulation of arbitrary events. Everywhere—whether in the domains of medicine, trade, public morals, or domestic security—it is assumed that the state is an institution that provides against accidents and disruption.

## II

Schiller's early reflections on the playhouse as a moral institution resonated with programs of police science, which designed the theater as an institution for social control. Thus in the writings of the Viennese cameralist Joseph von Sonnenfels the elements of enlightened theater poetics—mixed characters, identification between spectator and stage, transfer of emotions, contract of illusion—were explicitly appreciated as appropriate ways to realize the police's control function (Vogl 2000, 619). But in the years around 1800 it is not the theater as an institution appropriated by the police that interested Schiller. He was now concerned with police aesthetics in a much more fundamental way: The question was whether the very possibility of modern theater was not determined by the specific cognitive capability of the police. These reflections formed the context of schemes for a crime drama that Schiller planned to call "The Police" ("Die Polizey").[5] Insofar as these were schemes for a play designed to stage the conditions of the possibility of theater itself, one could call it "meta-theater."

> The scene of the drama is set in the metropolis of Paris in the era of Louis XIV. The action starts in the audience hall of the police lieutenant, who is debriefing his clerks and talks at length about the different branches of police business in all the quarters of the large capital. The spectator sees himself placed in the midst of the enormous city and sees at the same time the moving wheels of the big machine . . . A huge amount of activity has to be processed so the spectator is not confused by the manifoldness of the actions and the multitude of characters. There has to be some guiding thread that connects everybody, the characters have to be linked together among themselves or by the superintendence [*Aufsicht*] of the police, and in the end everything must be solved mutually in the hall of the police lieutenant. (Schiller 1982, 12: 91)

The prototype of Schiller's police lieutenant was the famous and notorious d'Argenson, who was appointed lieutenant general de police de la ville de Paris in 1697. Schiller had found a similar description of the audience in Fontenelle's "Eloge de Monsieur d'Argenson" of 1740.[6] Although Fontenelle compared the regularity of the order, which is established by the police, with the regularity of the celestial bodies (Fontenelle 1740, 144), the foundations of this order are not the incommutable laws of Kepler, but a secret network of channels of communication and manipulation.

> The penetration through subterranean channels into the interior of families to observe unconfessed secrets; to be present everywhere without being seen (*être present par tout sans être vû*); to move and to arrest an immense and tumultous diversity; to be the always moving and nearly unknown soul of this huge body, *voilà*, these are the functions of the police magistrate in general. (Fontenelle 1740, 2: 144)

Governmental knowledge of the business of the public, in both the empirical diversity of all single factors and their complex interplay, becomes a problem of representation. The historical drama has left the tragic stage of major operations of kings and statesmen where politics was situated between the divine laws and sovereign power or between the first and the second body of the king. History is leaving the domain of tragedy as well as the domain of comedy: neither tragic entanglements nor comedian intricacies will do justice to the nature of a connection that is neither formed by some miraculous accident nor by fateful revenge, but that first of all establishes a problem of cognition that concerns the unity of place and the unity of the action. While the unity of place is shifted from the stage to the invisible network of channels (which Fontenelle described), the problem of the unity of action turns into a question of transcendental aesthetics. The problem of Kantian *comprehensio aesthetica* amounts to the very task of the police, namely, "to grasp [*überblicken*] the secret links between the manifold events" (Schiller 1982, 12.91).

"The true unity is the police [*Die eigentliche Einheit ist die Polizey*]" (Schiller 1982, 12. 91). If one understands the notion of unity here in its Kantian and therefore transcendental meaning—which is quite natural in the case of Schiller, who was a dedicated follower of Kant—then Schiller has taken a step that in principle reorients the whole question of the media and the public. This decisive step separates the question of the media from the classical theory of the public and relocates it in the context of the transcendental epistemological question about what constitutes the objects of our experience and knowledge. Past and present are mingled into each other: how we think about media in the present has much to do with the trends that were set by thinking of media in the past, and whether we are able to "enlighten" the blind spots of our thinking of media. The moment Schiller transferred the transcendental capability of imagination and reason so as to synthesize the manifold one into the police, the police became a medium. The police constitute the unity of scenes and stories inside transcendental aesthetics.

> The question arises, *how* several independent actions, which are finally linked together in a common *denouement* [i.e., to undo a knot], can be introduced in the exposition and continued without causing too much confusion? (Schiller 1982, 105, emphasis added)

"Confusion" is the key notion of this transcendental aesthetics, whose central institution is the power of imagination (*Einbildungskraft*) which is, for Schelling, always the power of making into one [*Ineinsbildungskraft*]. That the police, in Schiller, comprise the true unity, means that the police take over the function of Kantian synthesis.

> ... [T]he notion of connection carries with itself not only the notions of the manifold and the synthesis of the same, but also the notion of the unity of the same. Connection is the imagination of the synthetic unity of the manifold. (Kant 2001, 135 [B 130–131])

Kant calls this unity the "transcendental unity of self-consciousness" or the "I think." In Schiller its name is "the police": "The true unity is the police." The police occupy as an empirical institution the business of the transcendental—with its means of cognition/detection, investigation/*Aufklärung*, and intervention. Therefore in "The true unity is the police" Schiller is using the ontological "is" instead of a constructivist "is brought about" or "is observed by." The police not only *causes* connection, history, narration, and regularity as the transcendental reason for the unity of the manifold, it *is* in itself this connection and therefore constitutes the very being-object of objects. It constitutes history as history, the state as state, and objects as objects. The place of the simple and empty "I think," which one has always to presuppose where the powers of imagination and reason have constituted a connection among the diversity of the manifold, is occupied by the police office. Schiller "transcendentalizes" d'Argenson.

## III

While the police appear as a transcendental subject, which constitutes the basis of all representations of connections, the police appear also as an origin of the literary. It is not by chance that Schiller chose Paris at the times of Louis XIV as the scene of his play. Schiller was prompted to start his metatheatrical experiment by his reading of Louis-Sébastien Mercier's *Tableau de Paris*, which was published between 1782 and 1788 in twelve volumes. Once again Schiller met here the character of the police lieutenant, who appears in Mercier as a hypothetical teacher of the philosopher:

> If the magistrate [of the police] lets the philosopher know everything he knows, everything he learns, everything he sees, and lets him take part in certain secret things about which only he is informed, there would be nothing more worthy to see and more instructing under the quill of the philosopher . . . But the magistrate is like the big father confessor: he understands all and reports nothing. (Mercier 1782–1788, 1: 207)

The police lieutenant governs not by force but by means of secret manipulations and secret knowledge: "The police lieutenant has become an important secretary. He has a secret and miraculous influence; he knows so many things" (Mercier 1782–1788, 1: 201). In Mercier's *Tableau* the police lieutenant occupies not a central perspective (which would have corresponded to the box of the prince in baroque theater architecture). Instead, one finds chapters distributed over all the volumes, in which members of the different service trades of the city are presented as secret servants of the police. In principle all the little rogues and cheaters, the servants, the tarts, the *filles d'opéra*, the night watchman, the letter carriers or lantern carriers could be "Hommes de Police" (Mercier 2000, 105):

> An uninterrupted correspondence between the magistrate and his employees or representatives causes perfect knowledge of everything that happens, and one prevents disorder as much as one punishes it. The investigations, information, and proof come together in a center where everything is united, which is important for public security. (Mercier 1782–1788, 1: 199)

"Such is the universal instrument used in Paris to absorb secrets, and it is this [instrument] that determines the political actions of the ministers much more often than one can imagine" (Mercier 1782–1788, 1: 186).

Every sort of clothing is a kind of costume, every costume is some sort of camouflage of a spy.

> Every individual of the regime has a special uniform that he changes into every day. Nothing is so quick and so astonishing as these powers of metamorphosis. The one who carries a rapier in the morning, takes up a Geneva band in the evening; one moment he plays a peaceful legal

eagle with long hair, the next a ruffian with the rapier at his hip; the next day he plays a man of finance who carries a stick with a golden knob . . . he changes his physiognomy as fast as his clothes . . . he is just eyes, just ears, just legs. (Mercier 1782–1788, 1: 185)

The theater play has left its original institution, where it imitated onstage an idealized reality. Play and reality mingle and mix into each other on the stage of the city. Private individuals and police operatives become indistinguishable. Society and the state not only not oppose each other, society is the production of the state, when the police and its media are operating always already behind the communications through which society constitutes itself. The screen and the scene is one. Mimesis turns into mimicry, the simulacrum turns into travesty; the space of the traffic of private opinions and the space of surveillance of the police become indistinguishable. This general travesty Schiller planned to make the dramatic principle of his play: "It [the police] shows itself in its true colors in the beginning and in the end; in the course of the play it acts all the time but under disguise and in quietness. The officials and the chief of the police have to be involved in the story as private persons, too."[7]

The public and the police are inseparable: together they constitute reality. In this point Mercier is ruthlessly clear: "These are the horrifying ties," he wrote, "from which public order originates. . . . Such is the admirable order made, which governs Paris" (Mercier 1782–1788, 1: 192 f.) If the media space of the public is not opposed to the secret channels of the police, then in consequence the police comprise the essential nucleus not only of transcendental aesthetics but of literature, too.

> Someone has published a small brochure: *la petite Poste dévalisée* [the plundered penny-Post]. These letters are fictions, but if it were allowed out of pure curiosity to open the mail boxes on the street and read a day's worth of correspondence, my God! what strange and interesting things one could then read! The certainty that these letters were written for one person alone, that the soul has freely poured itself out, would form unique contrasts and a unique reading: never would the fantasy of an author be able to produce anything comparable to that: the greatest distress, the misfortune, the misery, the love, the jealousy, the arrogance, would deliver different piquant pictures, and since nobody could doubt the truth, there would be much interest. How much pleasure to see the naked style of a businessman, or of the Marquis, the courtesan, the young girls in love, the regular customer of the parish, the borrower, the hypocrite of all classes! (Mercier 1782–1788, 3: 342 f.)

Such a fantasy is not a singular case. The idea that the institution of the Cabinet noir would be the only true institution of literature can be found, for instance, in a letter to Frederick II of Prussia by his friend Voltaire dated from 1776.

> This time the honest servants of the post, which . . . open the letters that are on the way to Germany . . ., were more desiring than usual to teach themselves or to see for passing the time what a great king might have the mercy to write to a poor, sad philosopher and what the philosopher is answering to the great king. One has to admit, Sire, that these servants of the post are indeed and in the full sense of the word men of letters (*gens de lettres*), and ones who desire to collect the beautiful.[8]

In Samuel Richardson's *Pamela*, the reader, who is allowed to read letters replete with the erotic temptations and troubles afflicting the soul of the virtuous Pamela, finds himself mirrored by Mr. B.\*\*\*, her "wicked master," who has, as the narrator lets the reader know, intercepted all her letters.

> It is also to be observed, that the messenger of her letters to her father, who so often pretended business that way, was an implement in his master's hands, and employed by him for that purpose; and who always gave her letters first to him, and his master used to open and to read them, and then send them on; by which means, as he hints to her . . . he was no stranger to what she wrote. (Richardson 1971, 89)

If Jacques Lacan was right that a letter always reaches its destination (Lacan 1966, 41), then one can conclude that Pamela's unconscious has always destined her letters to address Mr. B. Thus by means of a subtle strategy aristocracy is initiated into the secrets of a soul instead of having fun with a beautiful body. Acts of and with bodies are systematically replaced by acts of reading and thereby turn into files of the heart. When acts are replaced by files, the diplomacy of seduction or the foreign policy of bodies (which is still ruling in Choderlos de Laclos's *Liaisons dangereuses*) is replaced by the domestic policy of bourgeois morality. The war of the sexes, following Nietzsche, is replaced by the police action, which "enlightens" the aristocrats of the ancien régime by the use of the postal service.

The book mentioned by Mercier, *La Petite-Poste Dévalisée*, was published in Paris in 1767. Its anonymous author was, as we know today, one Jean-Baptiste Artaud. Artaud's fantasy, however, was less fictional as he himself might have probably known. The Petite-Poste, an institution created after the model of the London penny Post, was established in 1759 in Paris by Claude Humbert Piarron de Chamousset, the chief of the Paris audit division. In the beginning, however, the Parisian society met the new medium of communication with distrust and fear. "The main objection one raises against the establishment of the Petite-Poste," wrote an employee of the *Journal officiel*,

> is the fear that it would only encourage the anonymous letter ... One felt fear in thinking that the anger, the rancors, the jealousies, would be tempted by the always open letter boxes, to carry confusion and argument into the parlors, to disturb the boudoirs, the chambers of the mind, these sweet intellectual business affairs, which are sometimes held together only by very fragile ties. (Quoted in de Rothschild 1880, 140)

While *la société* feared that the Petite-Poste could be used to destroy the delicate and tender ties that held the Parisian society together, its founder Chamousset knew that it was in fact an instrument of the police serving the maintenance of public order, since all the letters transmitted by the Petite-Poste were basically surveilled by the Cabinet noir, whose chief Jannel thus was the nonfictional model for the reader dreamed of by Mercier. Chamousset referred to the idea that the police's aim for control was made much easier by the Petite-Poste and that the institute could help to find suspects who operate only inside Paris (Vaillé 1950, 166). According to Walter Benjamin, the *Petite Poste* is a machine to increase the traces, which are supplied for the reading enthusiasm of the police (Benjamin 1983, 1: 297–298). Balzac would make this point absolutely clear in *Modeste Mignon*.

Treason is the *causa finalis* of the secret. Thus in Schiller the minister of the police appears (as in Mercier before) as the secularized manifestation of the father confessor. "The minister of the police knows, like the father confessor, all the weaknesses of many families and needs like the former highest confidentiality. A situation often occurs where someone is astonished and terrified by the omniscience of the latter" (Schiller 1982, 12: 95). That the knowledge of the police is a secularized form of divine omniscience is supported by the image that Schiller attributed to the police when he compared it with the "all-penetrating eye" (which was at the same time the emblem of the illuminati and decorates today the one-dollar bill; Schiller 1982, 12: 96). "Police" was the term for a secular power able to mobilize knowledge of the most intimate desires of the heart. Thanks to the police, the intimate space was extended into the literary public and, at least in the fantasies of Mercier, without having to encounter the paradoxes of the actor. Inasmuch as the police produce the perfect example of the authentic, it is the secret center of Enlightenment itself.

# THE PREACHER'S FOOTING

## MICHAEL WARNER

My topic in this essay is the media culture of evangelical preaching. In the context of this volume that topic will raise an obvious question: what has evangelicalism to do with enlightenment? To many, the intuitive answer is nothing: evangelicalism was if anything an antithesis, a direct reaction against the Enlightenment. In this essay I will proceed on the basis of a very different view: far from being simply a reaction against an already congealed "Enlightenment," eighteenth-century evangelical practices came into being through many of the same media and norms of discourse. What we now call evangelicalism can be seen as the transformation of older strains of pietism by public-sphere forms. Were these better understood, we might be less puzzled by the alliance of deists and evangelicals that, at the end of the century, gave us disestablishment. Indeed, it is not clear that enlightenment and evangelical religion were recognizable to contemporaries as opposing forces—at least in the colonial Anglophone world. We might see them as such only because of later, contingent developments in the nineteenth and twentieth centuries.

Both "evangelicalism" and "Enlightenment" represent deeply engrained habits of thought that spring naturally to most modern scholars. These concepts ensure that our historical narratives will organize themselves around the confrontation between religion and the secular. But in recent years intensive critical debate has questioned many of the standard ways of understanding this opposition and has given us new reason to reexamine this history, its periodizations, and its teleological assumptions.[1] I do not propose to argue this view in detail in this essay; the problem is too complex, and I take up parts of it elsewhere.[2]

Given the focus of this volume on mediation, I will concentrate instead on the widely held view that evangelical religion and Enlightenment were defined by different media. Many indeed seem tempted to equate print with secular rationality, in contrast to the orality of popular affective religion.[3] The problem with this view is not just that print culture was important to evangelicals, nor that oratory was part of the public sphere; that much is now widely acknowledged. The problem is rather the difficulty of analyzing how media such as print and preaching are themselves mediated. I will suggest that some very highly charged and conflicted conceptions of discourse—crucial to evangelical and to political publics alike—cut across the print/orality opposition that has transfixed so many scholars in recent years. To that end I will be looking at the discursive forms of eighteenth-century preaching, with special attention to what Ervin Goffman called "footing." This concept, though long neglected by literary scholars and historians, does much to specify what is entailed by a medium in use, and attention to it will help move beyond the seductive but false clarity of "orality" and "print culture."

Thirty years ago, Harry Stout published what proved to be an influential essay on the political importance of evangelicalism. Titled "Religion, Communications, and the Ideological Origins of the American Revolution," it argued that although there was little doctrinal or conceptual continuity between the evangelical revivals of the eighteenth century and the Revolution, nevertheless there was an important connection in the social history of language. Stout's argument rested on two main claims: first, that before the revivals there were few contexts if any in which colonists met each other regularly as strangers in a framework of voluntary association, and therefore that the revivals helped to erode norms of localism and forge a new kind of mass awareness; second, that they did this not by means of print wars and political pamphlets (Stout's title echoes that of Bernard Bailyn's *Ideological Origins of the American Revolution* in order to point up the interpretive contrast between his view and Bailyn's) but by moving beyond the restrictive literacy of "elite typographical culture." Evangelical preachers, he thought, appealed to the common sort in the demotic voice of popular orality. "Un-like print, which is essentially passive, reflective, and learned, sound is active, immediate, and spontaneously compelling in its demand for a response" (Stout 1998, 94).[4] Thus the preachers reached the people in a way that the pamphleteers never could, and created a leveling form of address with what Stout took to be obviously democratic implications.

The first of Stout's major points here—that evangelicalism was able to regiment new environments of stranger sociability in a way that "disregarded social position and local setting" (93)—is, I will argue, an important insight that still needs further analysis. But we can only properly understand it by abandoning his contrast between print and orality. Ultimately I believe that the concepts themselves are incoherent.[5] Be that as it may, his view of the revivals as essentially oral has been bluntly contradicted by recent scholarship. Frank Lambert especially has urged an exactly contradictory interpretation: that the evangelical revivals were the direct result of new *print-based* modes of organization. George Whitefield's success as an itinerant preacher rested on more than charisma; he employed advance publicity agents who promoted his tours through advertisements, circular letters, and stories planted in local newspapers. To an unprecedented degree, he published his own sermons, journals, and letters. He orchestrated controversy, making sure that his tours would become media events of a familiarly modern sort. Between 1737 and 1745, Lambert calculates, more than three hundred Whitefield imprints were issued, in such numbers as to represent one publication for every twenty people in Britain and the colonies combined. The revivals themselves were understood in a framework that quickly became genericized because of the exchange and publication of revival narratives. And as other scholars have pointed out, these strategies worked in part because the transatlantic world of evangelicals was already knit together in a web of correspondence and printed exchange.[6]

Obviously it is not very helpful to explain the revivals in one moment as a democratizing turn toward orality and in the next moment as an innovative form of print-based publicity. Both readings pick up on important features of the evangelical movement. But both lead quickly to misconceptions insofar as they are rooted in the assumption that orality and print are separate, exclusive media environments. We will need a different framework of analysis to understand how evangelical religion was mediated.

A useful beginning is a term of art that appears in the work of Erving Goffman: footing. In the essays collected as *Forms of Talk* in 1981, and in "Footing" especially, Goffman showed that the key to analyzing spoken interaction lay in discriminating the play of relationships between persons and discourse that are concealed by such folk concepts as *speaker* and *hearer*. Decomposing these categories, Goffman showed that the mere fact of speaking tells us little about how the speaking person is related to the spoken language: he or she might the mere "animator" of speech that is attributed directly or indirectly to one or more authors or principals. She might be reading or reciting text, and that text might have some other form of existence, either in speech or in writing. Alternatively, she might be performing "fresh talk." As people speak they also signal in various ways how they are related to their speech, and this has implications for how one might understand both *what* they say and who they are. If while reading this lecture I look up and ad lib a comment, it suggests that I want you to think of me as responsive to the occasion, present in a wider range of my social self than the author of the paper. Goffman calls this a shift of footing.

Hearers, meanwhile, are not just face-to-face interlocutors. They might be ratified or unratified participants, with various possibilities of byplay, inattention, overhearing, eavesdropping, back-channel participation, turn taking, among other things. They might be aware of each other or not. And audiences, as Goffman notes, have a way of hearing that is peculiar to them. Moreover these relationships of footing, in addition to being subject to frequent change, can also be quotatively or modally embedded, laminated, or bracketed, to use Goffman's terms, creating extremely complex repertoires of involvement. *Footing* indicates the modes of relationship constantly being performed and construed as a necessary byproduct of rendering language intelligible.

It is in this light that I wish to consider the struggles over the nature of preaching spread across the Atlantic rim in the late 1730s and early 1740s. From Scotland to Georgia to St. Thomas, passionate disputes arose: who is authorized to preach? where? in what relationship of the preacher to his language and to his audience? how should this audience be composed in physical and institutional space? how should one hear or read, with what effect, with what kind of response? how often and with what awareness of preaching elsewhere? It is no exaggeration to say that during the revivals one of the principal subjects of evangelical preaching was preaching itself. And these disputes, which are explicit, tell us something about the implicit operations of footing in preaching and in sermon audition.

A good example is the most famous sermon by the Presbyterian preacher Gilbert Tennent, *The Danger of an Unconverted Ministry* (Tennent 1742). (The sermon, interestingly, was not just preached; it became famous because it was also printed, and by none other than Benjamin Franklin.) Tennent lays out an evangelical understanding of the preacher's relation to his speech as the necessary condition for an outcome of conversion. In the language of the day, this was a call for "experimental" preaching: a conversionist discourse taking the preacher's own spirit-filled experience as the basis of a prophetic rather than merely pastoral address. The exponents of this tradition believed that they were following the ancient example of the Puritan preachers going back to Thomas Cartwright. But their prophetic conception of preaching was quickly perceived as a threat to the culture built around a more pastoral understanding of preaching; and in fact a breakup of the synod followed.

The same threat was succinctly stated, in a different but related context, in *The Testimony of the President, Professors, Tutors and Hebrew Instructor of Harvard College in Cambridge, against the Reverend Mr. George Whitefield, and his Conduct*, a pamphlet laying out the objections against the emergent evangelical movement. The problem was "the Manner of his Preaching; and this in Two respects, both as an *Extempore* and as an *Itinerant* Preacher" (Holyoke 1744, 12). The crux of the issue, though obviously charged with theological significance, is here stated as a matter of textual and spatial form.

What was the objection to Whitefield's extemporizing? It was not, as modern critics have been tempted to think, the demotic appeal of something now called "orality"; in fact the Harvard testimony complains extensively of Whitefield's use of print, and in particular, his published journal. Extempore preaching, they thought, weakened the necessity of a clerical office set apart through learning and intramural communication. The preference for learned, composed, and memorized sermons encoded a thick set of norms about preacherly speech and the relationships that constituted it. Extempore preaching, according to the Harvard critique, also reinforced another Whitefield departure, the doctrine of an "inner assurance" of salvation; the two together seemed to imply too close a link between audition to Whitefield's sermons and the experience of conversion itself. The subjectivity at stake in hearing sermons was also perceived to be at issue.

This conflict lay very much within the Reformed tradition and was all the more intense because both sides saw themselves as exponents of the Reformed movement. Both sides understood the situation of preaching and sermon audition in contrast to the established practices of Anglican parish preaching. Modern readers might find it hard to understand the intensity of feeling mobilized over Tennent's and Whitefield's practice, but the older, established view of the preacher's footing is, if anything, even more strange.

Consider, for example, the work titled *Certain Sermons* but also known as the *Book of Homilies*, first disseminated to the English churches in 1547 but repeatedly issued thereafter with some significant changes. In one way the many imprints of this work look quite familiar: printed texts, with titles and a table of contents and other marks of clear segmentation and replicability. But in other ways these are quite strange: they name no author, though

Thomas Cranmer played a large role in the first version; the texts change substantially without comment in later editions; and their publication in print is oriented not to private, silent reading, but to repeated public enunciation by the preachers of the realm. Originality is quite the opposite of the point: the sermons were mandated to be read and reread in cycles, and were issued in connection with official efforts to license preachers. Thus the standardization, dissemination, and replication of the texts allowed the gap between the (unnamed, corporate) author and the multiple, dispersed animators of the text to be understood as a sign of authority. Elizabethan editions carried a preface explaining that such centralization was needful because "all they which are appointed Ministers, have not the gift of Preaching sufficiently to instruct the People."[7]

Solomon Stoddard, a key figure in the evangelical tradition before Tennent and Whitefield, had this text in mind in his 1723 sermon *The Defects of Preachers Reproved*, in which he denounces the reading of sermons:

> It was ordered in *England* in the Days of King *Edward* the Sixth, *That Ministers should Read Printed Homilies in Publick:* And there was great necessity of it, for there was not One in Ten, that were able to make Sermons. But it has been the manner of worthy men both here and in other Places, to deliver their Sermons without their Notes. (Stoddard 1724, 23–24)

Note that originality is not Stoddard's main concern—though it is certainly significant that printed sermons became, after the Elizabethan period, the most consistently *authorized* of all publications, in an age marked by anonymous and pseudonymous writing, and for reasons that lie very obliquely against our histories of authorship and intellectual property.

Be that as it may, the oralization of a prescripted text evidently means something very different for Stoddard than it did for those who produced and reproduced the *Book of Homilies*. Like almost all the New England and middle-colony preachers of the colonial period, Stoddard invokes a spiritistic conception of the preacher's speech that does not preclude the use of script—indeed, preachers in this tradition are equally distrustful of extempore improvisation—but understands the difference between the inscribing author and the performing speaker as indicating ideally a more than human animation. "Sermons when Read are not delivered with Authority and in an affecting way. . . . it is far more Profitable to Preach in the Demonstration of the Spirit, than with the enticing Words of mans wisdom" (24–25).

Stoddard's argument is not new; since the late sixteenth century there had been a tradition of Reformed complaints about read sermons, answered by defenses in which the complaint is misrecognized. In *A Discourse of Profiting by Sermons* (1683), for example, Bishop Patrick had answered what he thought to be the dissenting complaint about reading sermons. Patrick took the dissenters to be desiring a more emphatic and entertaining enunciation. But Stoddard's later language is to the point here: what was demanded was not the "enticing Words of mans wisdom" but preaching "in the Demonstration of the Spirit"—a personally exigent submission of the preacher to his speech, which precedes and inhabits him superpersonally. This is why Whitefield publicly declared that Tillotson—the iconic figure of the literary sermon—had no more knowledge of saving grace "than Mahomet" (quoted in Stout 1991, 101).

Cotton Mather spells out the process of sermon making in his *Manuductio ad Ministerium* in a way that emphasizes this split between the preacher as author and the preacher as animator of his own speech, with the gap between these being spiritistically conceived. After recommending a long shelf of reference works such as the *Commonplace Book to the Holy Bible* and the *Biblioteca Sacra,* he describes the process of oralization:

> And when you have dispatched a *Paragraph* of a Sermon, I wish it might be a frequent Practice with you, To make a *Pause* upon it; and *get your Sermon by Heart,* I mean, get your *Heart suitably touched* with what you have prepared, before you go any further, and cast into the *Mould* of the *Sanctifying Truths,* by such *Confessions* and such *Petitions,* as you may *Dart* up to Heaven upon them. At least, let this be done, in your *Perusing* of your *Whole Sermon* before your Preaching of it. Some celebrated Preachers have piously declared, *They never durst preach a Sermon to others, till they have got some good by it themselves.* To *feel* what you *speak,* how wondrously will it qualify you to be a *Lively Speaker!* (Mather 1726, 103)

Two things bear emphasizing about this passage, given the vogue of the concept of orality. The first is that this idea of the preacher as a lively speaker is entirely enabled by script. Sermonizing practice in the Reformed tradition enfolds many layers of script mediation: it required clergy specially qualified by the learning needed to navigate scriptures, theological literature, notebooks, manuscripts, and the self-inscription of memory. Printers produced all manner of finding aids and reference works for sermon production.[8] Puritans especially understood preaching as derivative of the scripture on which it is nominally a commentary, and although eighteenth-century Puritan preachers were less and less likely to preach sermon series organized as systematic expositions of books of scripture, they maintained the scriptural point of departure long after the essayistically topical sermon had become the norm among Anglicans.

The second is that when Mather describes the advantages of oral performance, what he emphasizes is a complex footing that is exactly the opposite of an expressive identity. Authoritative speech is that in which the preacher is himself submissive; in the Puritan tradition this has partly to do with the scripting and memorization process; partly with local turns of rhetoric; partly with the sabbatarian rhythms and ritual staging of performance. The preacher is a speaker only after he is a reader, a writer, a reader again, a memorizer, a sensitive registrant of existential demands laid upon him by the speech of which he is the vehicle. He must perform, in speaking, the burdens of his office rather than the spontaneous expressivity of his person.

The same Reformed tradition relied heavily on the formal division of its text/doctrine/application apparatus, along with the outline form of *eighthly*s and *twelfthly*s, to imply a normative shape to sermon audition. These devices enabled congregational note taking, just as they enabled preacherly memorization. With the congregation, as with the preacher himself, sermon-going often involved inscription.[9] Comenius noted during his visit in England in the early 1640s that "a large number of the men and youth copy out sermons with their pens," and this practice clearly carried over to the colonies (quoted in Ben-Chaim 1998, 277–278). As George Selement observed long ago, "if the taking of copious notes had not been part of the New England Way, works by many pastors would have never been published" (Selement 1980, 237–238).[10]

Whether they took notes or not, churchgoers were for their part routinely advised to hear in a special way. There is little scholarship on the audition culture of sermon going, though preachers themselves wrote copiously on the topic. (Examples include Thomas Shepherd and Jonathan Mayhew, as well as Whitefield himself.[11]) The consistent themes are a rigorous demand of personal, private hearing, with no attention to those gathered in the meetinghouse, and an application of the words of the preacher to oneself as though addressed by God to one's soul. As Tennent asked: "What are, or ought to be, the Ends of Hearing, but the Getting of Grace?" (Heimert and Miller 1967, 90). The privatization of hearing, despite the public ritual character of audition, had been neatly captured by Henry Smith (d. 1591) in the sixteenth century: "to preach simply is not to preach rudely, nor unlearnedly, nor confusedly, but to preach plainly and perspicuously, that the simplest man may understand what is taught, as if he did hear his name." Jonathan Parsons echoed this tradition in the revivals when he testified that "he could not forget the Sermon, especially that Part of it which was to backward Christians; and tho' he tho't, or endeavour'd to think, that it was a censorious Discourse, yet, as he told me afterwards, it never left him until he was made to see that he was the very Man to whose Case it was suited above any Sermon that ever he had heard" (Heimert and Miller 1967, 197). Edwards also said, "When any minister preached, the business of every one was to listen and attend to what he said, and apply it to his own heart" (284). Now to some degree this idea of sermon audition as the repression of any awareness of copresent auditors is preacherly ideology, to be sure. But it is also built into the spatialization, architecture, and facing relationships of preaching before the revivals. A congregation sits collectively but hears privately.

Whitefield's way of combining extempore preaching and prolific publication both deepened this Reformed idea of spiritistic preaching and broke with the footing relationships of pastoral office. To understand this shift fully, however, we need to consider it in relation to yet another contemporary phenomenon with which it is dialectically engaged: the literary sermon. Established preachers in England, by contrast, had mostly shifted over to an essayistic form in the Restoration, and they did so amid a culture that understood preaching as an essentially persuasive art.

>   Sermons, like Plays, some please us at the Ear,
>   But never will a serious Reading bear:
>   Some in the Closet edify enough,
>   That from the Pulpit seem'd but sorry Stuff.

So writes Robert Dodsley, the footman turned poet and playwright, in *The Art of Preaching, in Imitation of Horace's Art of Poetry* (Dodsley 1739). Dodsley's title gives the idea of comparative evaluation of sermons a pedigree in pagan poetics, of all things. At the time of this poem's appearance in 1738, Dodsley had just used the gains from his successful play, *The Toy-Shop*, to capitalize his venture into bookselling and publishing. (He later brought out Akenside, Collins, Gray, and many others.) So it is not entirely surprising that his critical project rests on the circulation of vendible printed sermons:

>   Morals please some, and others Points of Faith;
>   But he's the Man, he's the admir'd Divine,
>   In whose Discourses Truth and Virtue join:
>   These are the Sermons which will ever live,
>   By these our *Tonsons* and our *Knaptons* thrive;
>   How such are read, and prais'd, and how they sell,
>   Let *Barrow's*, *Clarke's* and *Butler's* Sermons tell. (16)

Sermons have become the objects of sale, criticism, and canonization all at once, by a condensation that goes without comment in the literary marketplace of London in the 1730s. Dodsley associates the possibility of critical appreciation particularly with the printed sermon, but not exclusively so. Audition, too, is criticism:

> For should your Manner differ from your Theme,
> Or on quite different Subjects be the same,
> Despis'd and laugh'd at, you must travel down,
> And hide such Talents in some Country Town. (9–10)

The implication, for which there is ample evidence beyond this poem, is that churchgoers, given the close proximity of different churches in London, compared preachers and rated them; preachers who could not keep their attention were in effect forced to the provinces, where parishioners presumably had no choice. To understand the conventions by which the sermon is imagined as a literary text, then, we would need to look beyond the distinction between written text and spoken delivery, inquiring instead into the place of sermons in the book trade; the cultural geography of parish, city, and crowd; Anglican ecclesiology, etc. London was unusual as a place to hear sermons: preachers hoping for preferment hopped about from pulpit to pulpit, hoping to impress by an occasional sermon, or a weekday lecture, or a pulpit exchange. Londoners, in marked contrast to colonists and provincials, could regularly hear sermons by preachers with whom they had no ongoing relationship. Franklin tells us that he practiced this kind of circulating audition when he was in London in the 1720s.[12]

What I have so far avoided disclosing about the Dodsley poem is that, saturated as it seems to be with the special attitudes of an Anglican print culture in London, it was also printed in the colonies at the very onset of the revivals, by none other than Benjamin Franklin. He issued the poem three times: in 1739 and again in 1741 as a stand-alone pamphlet, and in 1744 in the *American Magazine*. Franklin in these years was working the revivals for everything they were worth. He befriended Whitefield and Tennent, publishing Whitefield in numerous editions, and in fact printed on both sides of the controversies as long as they lasted. If anyone had an interest in promoting a genericized conception of sermons as textual commodities, it was Benjamin Franklin.

Franklin's decision to publish the Dodsley poem at this juncture was something of an intervention in the preaching disputes. It reflects both his experience with urban audition and his assimilation of the metadiscursive norms of free thought, already strongly suggested by his polemical involvement in an earlier controversy: the affair of Samuel Hemphill, remembered in Franklin's autobiography as the plagiarizing preacher.

Almost all literary-critical studies of sermons take the same point of departure as Dodsley: a genericized consideration of the sermon text as extricable from the situation of its preaching for the purposes of comparison with other performances with which it is considered analogous. This procedure is hardly neutral. It creates a new object—the sermon—with a new metadiscursive regimentation that includes new criteria of evaluation. Manifestly ethical criteria of appropriateness to situation are replaced by criteria of skillfulness in performance—criteria that carry ethical weight for the evaluator but bracket those of the performer's situation.[13] I do not wish to be understood as complaining that the sermon is decontextualized when it is considered as a literary text; the act of comparison is itself a context, and one that presupposes some set of devices for treating sermons as having a unity and purposiveness apart from their preaching. So there is no question here of relating text to context, as we used to say; the very act of textualization is a kind of contextualization. The question I want to ask is how such procedures transform the social footing and ethical problematics of discourse.

While most of the genres that literary criticism treats in this way have a long history of being practiced for this kind of evaluation, such that their genericization can be taken for granted, the sermon is manifestly a borderline case. Some traditions of preaching—especially the one mapped by Dodsley—are better adapted to it than others. It was a relatively small leap for Dodsley, and before him for Addison, to treat Tillotson as a literary composer whose sermons could be read in privacy and evaluated in relation to, say, Francis Atterbury's. To perform the same operation in the case of colonial American preaching, however, requires a more radical recontextualization. The colonies were more like the British provinces than like London. Neither the material nor the ideological conditions presupposed by Dodsley obtained there. (There are many social reasons for this: the unusually long tenure of preachers; no lectureships; federal theology and its pastoralism.) The works of the preachers named by Tillotson and Barrow would have been available in the colonies—as was Dodsley's poem—but colonial preachers had neither the mobile, densely urban publics of London nor the commodity trade in sermon collections that Dodsley takes for granted.

The social conditions that might have allowed comparative audition of different preachers were deliberately avoided, with only a few exceptions such as the Thursday lecture sermons in Boston. As several historians have observed, the whole relation of preaching was conceptualized with a density of ethicalized address that militated against the possibility of preaching to strangers—at least until the revivals of the late 1730s, when the Reformed tradition suddenly found itself destabilized.

One of the most interesting texts from that moment is *Some Thoughts concerning the Present Revival of Religion in New-England*, by Jonathan Edwards, published in 1742. From the first sentence, Edwards confronts an apparent discrepancy between the public-sphere norms of print discourse and the authoritarian discourse of clergymen. Obviously his proximate target here is Old Light critics of the revival; it is they, and not ministers in general, who have presumed too much. But Edwards does not identify his enemies in terms of their doctrinal commitments; he condemns the discourse norms of monological authority:

> In the ensuing treatise, I condemn ministers' assuming, or taking too much upon them, and appearing as though they supposed that they were the persons to whom it especially belonged to dictate, direct and determine; but perhaps shall be thought to be very guilty of it myself: and some when they read this treatise, may be ready to say that I condemn this in others, that I may have the monopoly of it. (Edwards 1972, 4.291)

It is an unfamiliar stance in which to find the man who did so much to prop up clerical authority and whose own congregation would depose him for excessive zeal in that endeavor only eight years later. Here he not unreasonably anticipates that the complaint of monological authoritarianism will be lodged against him in turn.

In parrying that complaint, Edwards goes on to give a classic expression of the public-sphere norms that he associates with print:

> In a free nation, such liberty of the press is allowed, that every author takes leave without offense, freely to speak his opinion concerning the management of public affairs, and the duty of the legislature, and those that are at the head of the administration, though vastly his superiors. (Edward 1972, 291)

So also with respect to the revivals and the disputes over religious norms: "private persons may speak their minds without arrogance" (292).

Notice that Edwards worries here about the ethics of status in speech: who can speak "without arrogance" to those who are "vastly his superiors"? Later in the same work he asks the same question specifically about preaching. I do not think it merely tactical that Edwards argues this way. Tactical it is, to be sure: the contrasting images he gives of discursive legitimacy are to some degree merely political (Old Lights presume to dictate; I merely offer my opinion). The difference is also largely generic: one can assume a liberty in a treatise that hearers of sermons do not have. Writers often adopt a different posture of authority in printed controversy than they do elsewhere.

For whatever reason, Edwards here registers, as an inescapable fact, the changing environment of public discourse in general; and he comes remarkably close to undermining the model of authoritative discourse of which preaching is the sacred instance. As he well knew, there *was* a powerful movement in his day toward imagining a form of religiosity totally consistent with the idea that "private persons may speak their minds without arrogance": it was called free-thought.

Naturally, whatever Edwards has to say about Old Light authoritarianism, he does not mean to delegitimate clerical authority or preaching in general; nor to elevate, in the manner of freethought, *the superior truth value of impersonal circulating discourse.* That he takes up language with this evident tendency is an indication of the deep challenge facing him in this treatise. *Some Thoughts concerning the Present Revival of Religion* is an attempt to theorize a then emergent mode of evangelical Christian practice, though Edwards is at some pains to deny that it contains anything new. The norms and understanding of preaching were, however, undergoing a profound dialectical adjustment to public-sphere forms, including the sort of print controversy in which Edwards was engaged. Sermons *were* in circulation in a transatlantic circuit in which they mingled with a deist theology that was largely about circulation. In Edwards's language we sense some overlay of different footings.

Edwards at a later moment in *Some Thoughts concerning the Present Revival of Religion in New-England* offers an extensive thought experiment that shows the breadth of the question. It appears in a discussion of lay exhorting in part 4. This is a topic, he notes, about which "there has been abundance of disputing, jangling, and contention" (483). Edwards embraces, as he had done in a related passage of part 3, the ideal of lay people both exuberantly conversing and exhorting one another. The question then becomes how to tell the difference between talking, which anyone can do, and preaching, distinctive of clerical office.

> The two ways of teaching and exhorting, the one of which ought ordinarily to be left to ministers, and the other of which may and ought to be practiced by the people, may be expressed by those two names of *preaching* and *exhorting* in a way of Christian conversation. But then a great deal of difficulty and controversy arises to determine what is preaching and what is Christian conversation. (485)

Edwards first asserts that the distinction is about authority: "The common people in exhorting one another ought not to clothe themselves with the like authority with that which is proper for ministers" (484). But what does authority mean here? Does the repeated metaphor of *clothing* oneself in authority mean that it is a stylistic, or rhetorical, device? In that case what determines its legitimacy? In answer, Edwards appeals to the standard ministerial ideology: ministers speak not *in propria persona* but as "the ambassadors or messengers of Christ . . . speaking in Christ's stead, and as having a message from him"—a constantly reiterated theme in clerical rhetoric, especially in ordination sermons. (Note, in Goffman's terms, the footing issues of animator and principal that it entails.) Edwards clearly thinks it doesn't solve the problem, because he goes on to imagine a number of ambiguous situations, including some where ordinary people—even women!—can legitimately speak in the presence of "their superiors" and expect solemn attention:

> If something very extraordinary happens to persons, or if they are in extraordinary circumstances: as if a person be struck with lightning in the midst of a great company, or if he lies a dying, it appears to none any violation of modesty for him to speak freely before those that are much his superiors. I have seen some women and children in such circumstances, on religious accounts, that it has appeared to me no more a transgressing the laws of humility and modesty for them to speak freely, let who will be present, than if they were dying. (486)

Edwards's whole treatise is attentive in this way to gradations of station, office, gender, generation, and rank; because he attributes a divine rightness to norms of modesty and deference, it takes special, "extraordinary" circumstances to justify a socially indiscriminate address—"let who will be present." Yet the matter of the gospel clearly counts for Edwards as such an "extraordinary" circumstance of existential urgency, so that it is "no more a transgressing the laws of humility and modesty." The personal exigency of speaking paradoxically legitimates a socially unmarked address.

The logic of the passage would seem to be either authorizing a priesthood of all believers in a way that would deprive ministers of a special right to preach or preaching of a special status among the genres of speech and writing. In order to forestall such Quakerish inferences, he sketches out a kind of ethnography of the preaching situation:

> But then may a man be said to set up himself as a public teacher, when he in a set speech, of design, directs himself to a multitude, either in the meetinghouse or elsewhere, as looking that they should compose themselves to attend to what he has to say; and much more when this is a contrived and premeditated thing, without anything like a constraint, by any extraordinary sense or affection that he is then under; and more still, when meetings are appointed on purpose to hear lay persons ex-

hort, and they take it as their business to be speakers, while they expect that others should come, and compose themselves, and attend as hearers ... this has the appearance of authoritative teaching. (486)

Each of the features that Edwards lists, which determine whether something is preaching or merely exhorting, was destabilized in the revivals. Is a sermon "a set speech"? Or is it a continuous stream of talk? Is it speech "of design," or wholly extempore? Is it "directed to a multitude," or can it take place on a small scale, as in a private house? Under what circumstances can one "expect that others should come, and compose themselves, and attend as hearers"? Edwards's treatise tries to sketch out what was then understood as a moderate position, preserving the distinctiveness of clerical office and the sermon as the privileged form of public worship, while also carving out some legitimacy for the new understanding in which the existential urgency of conversionistic preaching is itself sufficient warrant for public address regardless of status or context.

Many of the expectations of the revivals faded into disappointment soon after the publication of *Some Thoughts,* and scholars have increasingly come to see that the idea of a "Great Awakening" has made them seem more of a turning point than they were. This midcentury reinsertion of preaching into a temporal and spatial field of circulation among strangers did not mean the sudden realization of modern denominationalist evangelicalism. But toward the end of the eighteenth century, this newer understanding of the preacher's footing became more prevalent, achieving dominance in the nineteenth century—though this story, full of complexities of its own, is beyond my topic here.

There had long been a tension in Protestant preaching about the degree to which preachers are meant to address nonmembers, and the Puritan tradition sometimes—as with John Robinson of the Leyden church—eschewed conversionistic address altogether.[14] But by the early nineteenth century, in many quarters a conversionistic address to strangers came to be the ideological image of preaching per se. The prophetic and conversionist address to strangers, outside of the embedding framework of ongoing pastoral relationship, had social implications as well. Preaching so understood constitutes its audience ad hoc, and requires that the preacher legitimate his claim to preach primarily through the performance of prophetic urgency. In so doing it helped instantiate a social imaginary of denominationalism; churches oriented themselves less to stable local populations that could theoretically be encompassed under a single congregation for life, saturating the local public space of intellectual and moral authority, and began instead to orient themselves to transitory movements of strangers who would attach themselves to the congregation as a form of voluntary association.

In this framework, by which evangelical preaching eventually codified its understanding of public space, the aspiration to the national church was abandoned, partly because the new conception enabled a prophetic solicitation of numberless potential converts at a time when a numberless audience—a mass—was also coming to be central to the social imaginary. But the evangelical call to this public also had tensions that have never been resolved: the churchgoing public was construed simultaneously as a Christian nation and as the unredeemed mass from which converts must be called. We might even say that in addressing a world of strangers prophetically, evangelical preaching helped to produce the field of the secular—though it was also by then generally committed to a Christian nationalism in which that field would be denied.

# *MEDIATION AS PRIMAL WORD*

## THE ARTS, THE SCIENCES, AND THE ORIGINS OF THE AESTHETIC

MICHAEL MCKEON

Although inquiry into the nature of beauty is as old as Plato, it has become a commonplace that the idea of the aesthetic emerged during the seventeenth and eighteenth centuries and is therefore a modern phenomenon. What distinguishes the idea of the aesthetic from earlier thought about beauty and the beautiful is first of all the premise that all such thought may be subsumed under a general category—the "aesthetic"—that has reference to the entire range of the arts and that constitutes an autonomous discipline, a separate field of experience and study. The guiding principle by which the aesthetic was separated out in this fashion is epistemological. The aesthetic coheres as a body of knowledge when its status as a mode of knowledge becomes the central focus of inquiry. Judging by the word itself, "aesthetics" (from the Greek *aisthétikos*, "sensitive") and the empirical sciences have always been closely associated. Alexander Gottlieb Baumgarten coined the term in 1735 to designate "a science of how things are to be known by means of the senses," a definition he later refined to "the science of sensitive cognition."[1] Baumgarten's word became the standard one for designating an interest

---

A version of this essay originally appeared in *Eighteenth-Century Novel* 6–7 (2009): 197–259. Reprinted with permission of AMS Press, Inc. All rights reserved.

that already was preoccupying people in Germany, France, and England, a concern not, as traditionally, with the nature of the beautiful object but with the singular way we know it: with our perception of, our somatic response to, and our subjective attitude toward, aspects of experience that we deem aesthetic.[2]

Yet if the idea of the aesthetic was thus formulated as a subcategory of empirical epistemology, customary modern usage instead tends to construe aesthetic experience over against empirical or "scientific" knowledge; and this oppositional tendency also is rooted in eighteenth-century developments. For the well-known Renaissance efforts to conceive the arts as a distinctive sort of activity bore substantial fruit only in the late seventeenth-century Quarrel between the Ancients and the Moderns, which posited the division between the humanistic arts and the empiricist sciences that was to become a defining feature of modern culture.[3] My aim in this essay is to suggest the coherence of this seeming contradiction. That is, the effort to define the integrity and autonomy of aesthetic response and aesthetic judgment—of the epistemology and psychology of the art experience—took place not in opposition to, but in explicit emulation of, a normative model of empirical and scientific cognition. It was by imitating the emergent method and value system of the natural sciences that the arts learned their own distinctive, aesthetic mode of being. After all, like science poetry takes "nature" as its object of study. And yet this modeling process would not have been possible had not seventeenth-century thought already separated out "the arts" from "the sciences," conceiving them as discourses sufficiently independent of each other to posit a conception of the former as entering into an imitative or derivative relationship with the latter. Moreover, although this division may look like the modern habit of dividing the aesthetic from the empirical, I will argue that the Enlightenment opposition has a dialectical subtlety that the modern one has lost.

This conference aims to reflect on a category—"mediation"—that common usage construes as "connection," "conciliation," or "communication." But to mediate, from the Latin *mediare*, also means to "intervene" or to "divide in the middle." I treat "mediation" here as one of those "primal words" whose "antithetical sense" Sigmund Freud, building on the work of the philologist Karl Abel, finds not only in ancient languages but also in the archaic language of the dream-work.[4] My interest in the aesthetic concerns not language and psychology but, more broadly, history and culture—specifically, the notion that modernity in the West emerges in a two-part process in which separation is the highly proximate precondition for conflation. The separation out of science from the arts is one of a number of conceptual developments that might be adduced to substantiate this approach to the emergence of the modern. By the same token, the comparison of the past with the present is inconceivable in the absence of the preceding division between antiquity and modernity that coalesced in the Renaissance and was solidified in the seventeenth century.

## Ancients and Moderns, Arts and Sciences

The late seventeenth-century Quarrel of the Ancients and the Moderns marks the final stage in a momentous diachronic separation out of two historical periods, a division whose origins lie in the earliest decades of the Renaissance. Why did the Quarrel also occasion the division between the arts and the sciences, the equally momentous first stage in a synchronic separation out of two fundamental modes of knowledge and practice? Ancients versus Moderns entailed arts versus sciences because the more closely moderns examined the grounds for claiming the superiority of either period over the other, the clearer it became that any claim to superiority turned on which kind of knowledge was under consideration. On the one hand, by the first years of the seventeenth century enough evidence had accumulated to show that in matters of what we call science and contemporaries called "natural" or "the new philosophy," Aristotle in particular had gotten much of it wrong. On the other hand, the excellence of Homer and Aeschylus, Virgil and Horace persisted over time in a way that seemed impervious to the sort of standard by which Aristotle confidently could be criticized. This was a standard of empirical demonstrability that dictated an inductive method of inquiry that, in the words of Francis Bacon, "derives axioms from the senses and particulars, rising by a gradual and unbroken ascent, . . . opening and laying out . . . a road for the human understanding direct from the sense, by a course of experiment orderly conducted and well built up . . ." (Bacon 1905, 261, 280, 267). But in Bacon's program, point of origin is no more important than departure from it, for "the greatest hindrance and aberration of the human understanding proceeds from the dulness, incompetency, and deceptions of the senses" (Bacon 1905, 261, 280, 267).

By the later decades of the seventeenth century, Baconian method was being adapted experimentally across a range of endeavors, and with it the premise that probable belief and knowledge are a function of sense experience. What about the arts? One of the reasons it can be hard to tell what contemporaries thought on this issue is that precisely because the separation of the arts and the sciences was in process at this time, those terms could be used both to discriminate between modes of knowledge and, more traditionally, to describe, like *scientia*, the general category of knowledge as such. In his own usage Bacon had made no consistent distinction between "the sciences" and "the arts." Indeed, he might describe the "gradual and unbroken ascent" of inductive progress yet associate it, as a practical rather than a theoretical mode, with the "arts" rather than the "sciences": "[W]hat is founded on nature grows and increases; while what is founded on opinion varies but increases not." Today "the sciences stand where they did [two thousand years ago] and remain almost in the same condition; receiving no noticeable increase, but on the contrary, thriving most under their first founder, and then declining. Whereas in the mechanical arts, which are founded on nature and the light of experience, we see the contrary happen, for these (as long as they are popular) are continually thriving and growing" (Bacon 1905, 277). And for a while *scientia* continued most often to designate simply knowledge as such.

When John Dryden inquired into the nature of drama fifty years after Bacon wrote, he had one of his speakers, Lisideius, define a play as a "just and lively image of human nature." In response to this another speaker, Crites, praised what he referred to as the "arts and sciences" of recent decades for their remarkable success in capturing nature. "It has been observed of arts and sciences that in one and the same century they have arriv'd to great perfection . . . Is it not evident in these last hundred years (when the study of philosophy has been the business of all the virtuosi in Christendom) that almost a new nature has been revealed to us? that more errors of the school have been detected, more useful experiments in philosophy have been made, more noble secrets in optics, medicine, anatomy, astronomy discovered, than in all those credulous and doting ages from Aristotle to us? so true it is, that nothing spreads more fast than science, when rightly and generally cultivated" (Dryden 1962, 1: 25, 26). Although his terminology is to our eyes ambiguous, Crites's point is that "poesy," unlike "philosophy," has been ill-cultivated by the moderns. His antagonist Eugenius sustains this terminological ambiguity regarding the "arts" and "sciences" in arguing that by Crites's own logic, their common grounding in nature makes modern poetry the equal of modern philosophy: "I deny not what you urge of arts and sciences, that they have flourished in some ages more than others; but your instance in philosophy makes for me: for if natural causes be more known now than in the time of Aristotle, because more studied, it follows that poesy and other arts may, with the same pains, arrive still nearer to perfection" (Dryden 1962, 1: 32). But if Eugenius wins this particular battle, his recourse to the esteemed but opaque category "nature" signals that the war itself has been lost; for the question concerns not, strictly speaking, the kind of object but the kind of knowledge we are able to have of it. In Bernard de Fontenelle we read, twenty years later, the clearest recognition of this basic principle:

> [I]f the moderns are to be able to improve continually on the ancients, the fields in which they are working must be of a kind which allows progress. Eloquence and poetry [*la poésie*] require only a certain number of rather narrow ideas as compared with other arts, and they depend for their effect primarily upon the liveliness of the imagination. Now mankind could easily amass in a few centuries a small number of ideas, and liveliness of imagination has no need of a long sequence of experiences nor of many rules before it reaches the furthest perfection of which it is capable. But science [*la physique*], medicine, mathematics, are composed of numberless ideas and depend upon precision of thought which improves with extreme slowness, and is always improving. (Fontenelle 1970, 362)[5]

Fontenelle's notion of a kind of knowledge that "allows progress" because it slowly "improves" over time requires "a long sequence of experiences" the logic of whose ordering is determined by a "precision of thought" that successively derives "rules" from each experience to determine what the next one should be. This is the language of careful deliberation and temporal self-consciousness we associate with scientific experiment, which Fontenelle's contemporaries already were laboring to formulate. The members of the Royal Society, Thomas Sprat wrote in 1667,

> have endeavour'd, to separate the Knowledge of *Nature*, from the Colours of *Rhetorick*, the Devices of *Fancy*, or the delightful Deceit of *Fables*.... They have tried to put it into a Condition of perpetual Increasing; by settling an inviolable Correspondence between the Hand and the Brain. They have studied, to make it not only an Enterprise of one Season, or of some lucky Opportunity; but a Business of Time; a steady, a lasting, a popular, an uninterrupted Work.... Those, to whom the Conduct of the *Experiment* is committed, ... after they have perform'd the *Trial*, ... bring all the *History* of its *Process* back again to the *Test*. Then comes in the second great Work of the *Assembly*; which is to *judge* and *resolve* upon the Matter of *Fact*. In this part of their Imployment, they us'd to take an exact View of the Repetition of the whole Course of the *Experiment*; here they observ'd all the *Chances*, and the *Regularities* of the Proceeding; what *Nature* does willingly, what constrain'd; what with its own Power, what by the succours of Art. (Sprat 1722, 62–63, 99)

And in the words of Robert Hooke, master experimentalist of the Royal Society,

> [i]n the making of all kind of Observations or Experiments there ought to be a huge deal of Circumspection, to take notice of every the least perceivable Circumstance that seems to be significant either in the promoting or hindering, or any ways influencing the Effect. And to this end, ... it were very desirable that both Observations and Experiments should be divers times repeated, and that at several Seasons and with several Circumstances, both of the Mind and of Persons, Time, Place, Instruments and Materials.... [These are the] ways by which Nature may be trac'd, by which we may be able to find out the material Efficient and Instrumental Causes of divers Effects, not too far removed beyond the reach of our Senses. (Hooke 1971, 61–62)

Experiment is only a methodical exploitation of experience, which, gained through sense perception, is in John Locke's vastly influential empiricist epistemology the sole source of knowledge. But if we would know nature we must separate it from the art that inevitably clouds its perception and description, which is to say from the punctual and local conditions of its knowing: not simply Sprat's "rhetoric," "fancy," and "fables" but all those "artificial" factors that might complicate or confuse our engagement with "the matter of fact" in itself. In modern terms, experiment treats these sensible conditions of knowing as variables that can be controlled for by methods of quantification.

## Controlling for Time, Place, and Persons: Drama

It is not hard to see why drama was the first of the genres on which was focused the ambition to elevate the arts to the status of quasi-scientific knowledge. For one thing, the theater was still the most popular and active of the arts. Even more important for our purposes, unlike printed literature, plays combine language with physical, material performance, and this makes their relationship to the naturalness of sensible experience a good deal more immediate than literature's can be. But as we have seen, proximity to the senses did not in itself ensure proximity to nature, and many contemporaries were attentive not to the promise entailed in the dramatic imitation of science but to the dangers of science imitating the dramatic distortions of nature. Some described the Royal Society's experiments as though they were popular entertainments akin to juggling acts, magic shows, and displays of prestidigitation.[6] Perhaps the most striking testimony to this sort of skepticism is to be found in the century-long preoccupation with the similarities between the theater and the laboratory. This preoccupation was most acute and suggestive when it actually took dramatic form. The analogy between the spaces of the theater and the laboratory, and between the ambitions of those who worked in them, were self-consciously thematized and satirized in a number of plays, most notably Ben Jonson's *The Alchemist* (1610), Dryden and William Davenant's revision of Shakespeare's *The Tempest* (1667), George Villiers, Duke of Buckingham's *The Rehearsal* (1671), and Thomas Shadwell's *The Virtuoso* (1676). Although theatrical performance by no means eluded critique in these plays, their broad impulse was to use the ancient practice of dramatic representation to hold an unflattering light to the work of a novel practice that imitated the apparatus of dramatic art even as it sought to eschew all associations with artistic framing. Brought to the dramatic stage, not only the laboratory but also the entire technology of experimental instrumentation became a mirror of theatrical technology and its arts of illusion. So for awhile natural philosophy's quest for nature was metonymically incorporated within a dramatic practice that itself was learning to emulate the epistemology of experiment.

Nonetheless the opposite influence—the potential of experimental method in science as a model for drama—was very powerful. The development of scientific method depended on two basic insights: first, that the knowledge of nature must proceed through sense experience; second, that the knowledge of nature must be distanced from the multiple and variable circumstances of time, place, and person under which it is impressed upon the senses. The earliest attempts to practice scientific method in drama, dazzled by the sensible nature of theatrical performance, tended to overvalue the sheer immediacy of sense experience and to undervalue the need to control for it. The neoclassical doctrine of the three unities concerned the three dimensions of time, place, and action that pertain to dramatic representation, and it was really only the first two that became controversial (most commentators agreed both that the unity of action was important and that Aristotle clearly had affirmed it). Like scientific experiment, the doctrine capitalized on quantitative measure. If a play is to be credible to its spectators, the amount of time and the extent of space undertaken to perform it should be quantitatively as close as possible to the duration and the locale that are represented within that play. That is, representation aspires toward the literalistic illusion of spatio-temporal presence. What underlay the doctrine of the two unities was the issue of dramatic credibility, and the ensuing debate soon rose to this more general level. How close must dramatic representation be to the actual presence of nature for its audience to "believe" it?

Returning to Dryden's *Essay*, Crites deplores the noncorrespondence between the object and the circumstances of representation in drama because the spectator's "fancy" will find it "unnatural" (45). Lisideius expands the point: "For what is more ridiculous than to represent an army with a drum and five men behind it, . . . or to see a duel fought, and one slain with two or three thrusts of the foils, which we know are so blunted that we might give a man an hour to kill another in good earnest with them[?]" (65). The success of the new philosophy in establishing a standard of demonstrative truth based on the evidence of the senses had given the idea of the natural an unprecedented concreteness and authority. The effect of this establishment is the ambition to discover how the arts as well as the sciences can be shown to excel by the emergent standards of empiricist epistemology. Not that artistic excellence has lost its traditional connection to beauty. But the empirical naturalness of art, and the credibility of that naturalness, have become an essential precondition for the achievement of excellence in art. Dryden discloses two different paths to this end. The first is the doctrine of the two unities; the second he expresses in Neander's dissent from the notion that staged fighting is ridiculous because it is unbelievable: "For why may not our imagination as well suffer itself to be deluded with the probability of it as with any other thing in the play? For my part, I can with as great ease persuade myself that the blows which are struck are given in good earnest, as I can that they who strike them are kings or princes" (75).

Although it is not immediately evident in Neander's words, the new standard of empirical truth is as important to the development of this latter argument as it is to the more obviously empiricist doctrine of the two unities. Joseph Addison made this clear by bringing the arts and the sciences into a common framework that defined their comparative proximity to and distance from the realm of the senses. The three mental faculties at work in his analysis are the senses, the imagination, and the understanding. According to Addison, "[t]he Pleasures of the Imagination, taken in their full Extent, are not so gross as those of Sense, nor so refined as those of the Understanding." That is, the imagination mediates between the senses and the understanding. Its pleasures are less "grossly" actual than those of the senses because it takes an imaginative distance on sensible experience, and they are less abstractedly "refined" than those of the understanding because its distance from the senses is not as great. But if they are less refined because they are more embedded in the realm of the senses, the pleasures of the imagination are not so difficult to obtain as those of the understanding, which transforms the actuality of sensible experience into the pure abstraction of concepts. By contrast, the work of the imagination turns actuality into virtuality, mental images that still bear the visual likeness of the objects they replace. True, the pleasures of the understanding are finally "more preferable" than those of the imagination "because they are founded on some new Knowledge or

Improvement in the Mind of Man," reasons that recall the norms of demonstrable truth and incremental progress Bacon had stressed. But although less refined, the pleasures of the imagination have their own proper virtues, and they are "as great and as transporting as the other. A beautiful Prospect delights the Soul, as much as a Demonstration," and such views "are more obvious, and more easie to be acquired," and "do not require such a Bent of Thought as is necessary to our more serious Employments," which demand "too violent a Labour of the Brain." So the imagination produces the pastoral pleasures of leisure, not labor, a point Addison makes also by describing the other end of the process, the way the imagination refines the senses: "A Man of a Polite Imagination, is let into a great many Pleasures that the Vulgar are not capable of receiving.... He meets with a secret Refreshment in a Description, and often feels a greater Satisfaction in the Prospect of Fields and Meadows, than another does in the Possession. It gives him, indeed, a kind of Property in every thing he sees, and makes the most rude uncultivated Parts of Nature administer to his Pleasures."[7]

For present purposes, the most illuminating aspect of Addison's discussion is the precision with which he analyzes the kind of distance that's involved in the movement from sense impressions to imaginative figures without proceeding further to the full detachment of abstract ideas. In Addison's argument, imaginative distantiation has four stages. The first is the special capacity of sight, among the other senses, to sustain the powerful impact of sensible experience while detached from it in time and space—or as Addison puts it, the way sight "converses with its Objects at the greatest Distance, and continues longest in Action without being tired or satiated with its proper Enjoyments." The second is the imagination's ability to exploit this distantiating power of vision by creating detached, virtual versions of its sensible actuality. Third, Addison distinguishes between the "Primary" and "Secondary" pleasures of the imagination, that is, between those that on the one hand "entirely proceed from such Objects as are before our Eyes," and on the other hand those that "flow from the Ideas of visible Objects, when the Objects are not actually before the Eye, but are called up into our Memories" (Addison and Steele 1965, no. 411 [June 21, 1712]). As by this point we would expect, Addison values the secondary over the primary pleasures of the imagination because the images we have of objects that are absent from our eyes are yet more detached than the images that are directly produced by vision. These secondary images are the product of "representation," and in their greater detachment they also take in the primary images from which they are derived. "Representation," Addison writes, is an "Action of the Mind, which compares the Ideas arising from the Original Objects, with the ideas we receive from the Statue, Picture, Description, or Sound that represents them." The key here is the pleasure involved in the self-conscious act of comparing one sort of image with another. And it is the heightening of the pleasure of comparison that is the basis for the fourth and final stage of imaginative distantiation. As the preceding passage suggests, there are several media of artistic representation, principally sculpture, painting, literate description, and sound. Of these, the imagery produced by language "runs yet further" than do the plastic arts "from the things it represents," and written language allows us, through the act of reading, to compare primary and secondary images most attentively and mindfully (Addison and Steele 1965, no. 416 [June 27, 1712]). This is "a new Principle of Pleasure, which is nothing else but the Action of the Mind, which *compares* the Ideas that arise from Words, with the Ideas that arise from the Objects themselves" (Addison and Steele 1965, no. 418 [June 30, 1712]). The pleasures of imaginative reading are thus four times removed: sight from the other senses, the imagination from sight, the representational from the visual imagination, and description from the other media of representation.

By comparing and contrasting the imagination and the understanding in this way, Addison goes far toward meeting the challenge to the arts posed by the Quarrel of the Ancients and Moderns and its incipient separation out of the arts and the sciences. The challenge is met by theorizing the imagination as an aesthetic and therefore an empirical faculty, based in sense experience but abstracted from it in a fashion and to a degree different from the abstraction peculiar to the understanding. Like the understanding, the imagination is produced by sense impressions. Unlike the understanding, its detachment from the senses stops as it were halfway, producing an epistemological effect that has less cognitive power but, because of its relative proximity to the senses, a greater representational force. This analysis allows Addison to restate Neander's defense of drama in a more positive register. Not only is a close approximation to actual time and place unneeded to maintain the belief of the dramatic spectator; it is detrimental to the kind of knowledge that is proper to drama. Immediate sense experience is as likely as not to lead to "Vice," "Folly," and the "Criminal" (Addison and Steele 1965, no. 411 [June 21, 1712]). The imaginative mediation of sense experience possesses its own system of refinement that filters out the brute materiality of the senses and thereby improves upon their emotional heft.

Like Dryden, Addison demonstrates this with the example of drama—although it is notable that what he has in mind is for the most part not the experience of watching the performance of a play but the experience of reading it. Returning to Aristotle's famous argument that pity and fear are the emotions proper to tragedy, Addison wonders why "such Passions as are very unpleasant at all other times" give us such pleasure in "description." His answer is that dramatic representation provides us both a physical and a psychological distance from the temporal and spatial actuality that prevail in more immediate sense experience. "When we look on such hideous Objects, we are not a little pleased to think we are in no Danger of them. We consider them at the same time, as Dreadful and Harmless; so that the more frightful Appearance they make, the greater is the Pleasure we receive from the Sense of our own Safety.... It is for the same Reason that we are delighted with the reflecting upon Dangers that are past, or in looking on a Precipice at a distance, which would fill us with a different kind of Horrour, if we saw it hanging over our Heads.... This is, however, such a kind of Pleasure as we are not capable of receiving, when we see a Person actually lying under... Torture...; because in this Case, the Object presses too close upon our Senses, and bears so hard upon us, that it does not give us time or leisure to reflect on our selves" (Addison and Steele 1965, no. 418 [June 30, 1712]).

We are so accustomed to reading Edmund Burke's influential early treatise through the lens of post-Romantic theories of sublime inexpressibility and infinitude that we are in some danger of overlooking the scope of the debate into which it entered. This was to a great extent Addison's debate. Burke begins the *Philosophical Enquiry* (1757) with the empiricist and inductive aim to perform "a diligent examination of our passions in our own breasts" (Burke 1958, 1). Further from the passions he'll move to the body that excites those passions, thence to the properties of objects that influence the body, and finally to the laws of nature that determine this influence. Insisting that "Longinus's" categories of the sublime and the beautiful must be separated out from one another, Burke also discloses their basic similarity. This similarity consists in the fact that both are relative passions that arise not in the immediate presence of bodily sensation but at a certain temporal and spatial remove from it. Thus our feeling for the beautiful arises as the passion of love for an object rather than lust, but of love mixed "with an idea at the same time of having irretrievably lost" that object (Burke 1958, 51). This temporal distance from the loved object is also a spatial detachment from it similar to the relatively disinterested pleasure that Addison, Berkeley, and Shaftesbury find in the "prospect" rather than the "possession" of a landscape. Thus Burke distinguishes love, "that satisfaction that arises to the mind upon contemplating any thing beautiful, of whatsoever nature it may be, from desire or lust; which is an energy of the mind, that hurries us on to the possession of certain objects, that do not affect us as they are beautiful, but by means altogether different" (Burke 1958, 91).

As with the beautiful, so, more famously, with the sublime. In terms of the temporal dimension, the passion of the sublime becomes available to us in a relationship with painful sensation, but only in the "ceasing or diminution," the "removal or moderation" of pain, as the present moment is increasingly distanced from a painful past (Burke 1958, 35). To describe the spatial register of the sublime in general terms, Burke echoes Addison: "When danger or pain press too nearly [elsewhere "too close"], they are incapable of giving any delight, and are simply terrible; but at certain distances, and with certain modifications, they may be, and they are delightful" (Burke 1958, 40, 46). Burke also has recourse to the Aristotelian example of the terror produced by the dramatic experience of tragedy; but for him the distance necessary for the delight of the sublime to be felt is minimal compared to Addison's: "I am convinced we have a degree of delight, and that no small one, in the real misfortunes and pains of others; . . . [and] I imagine we shall be much mistaken if we attribute any considerable part of our satisfaction in tragedy to a consideration that tragedy is a deceit, and its representations no realities. The nearer it approaches the reality, and the further it removes us from all ideas of fiction, the more perfect is its power. But be its power of what kind it will, it never approaches to what it represents. Chuse a day on which to represent the most sublime and affecting tragedy we have; . . . let it be reported that a state criminal of high rank is on the point of being executed in the adjoining square; in a moment the emptiness of the theatre would demonstrate the comparative weakness of the imitative arts" (Burke 1958, 45, 47). In other words, the only sort of sensible experience that precludes the delight of sublimity is that which directly impinges on one's own body, making one not a spectator at all but a suffering actor or agent.

So for Burke the range of aesthetic experience is a great deal broader than it is for Addison. But for Addison the crux of the matter is not simply that we know the difference between dramatic representation and actuality. It is also the subliminal comparison and contrast we make between our own actual state in the theater or the library and the virtual representation we watch or read there, whereby we feel a given object to be, as Addison says, both "Dreadful and Harmless." The opportunity provided by artistic experience to feel these emotions simultaneously sharpens our sense of the nature of the relationship between the sort of distance entailed in the epistemology of the understanding or scientific cognition and the sort of distance entailed in artistic experience. If the understanding requires a strict division between the subject and the object of knowledge, the imagination requires a differential interplay between them. But in both cases, the empiricist divisibility of subject and object is the premise on which both the understanding and the imagination operate, since the sense of imaginative interplay depends on a prior sense of division. This is a psychological state whose textual counterpart is the signature mark of the aesthetic attitude, the reflexive relationship between form and content (a point to which I will return). I don't mean to suggest that writers like Addison invented the doubled experience of the aesthetic attitude, the relative distance it takes on sense impressions. Rather, they named and described in explicit terms a state of mind that, we may assume, in some fashion always has characterized the reception of artistic performance. No doubt the rise of aesthetic theory in this period is greatly overdetermined. My point is that one of its most important efficient causes is the unprecedented authority of empirical epistemology, not as a negative norm that the aesthetic was defined against but as a constitutively positive standard of cognition.

This may be seen in the stance taken by Edward Young on the Quarrel of the Ancients and Moderns and the separation of the arts and the sciences it precipitated. "[T]hese are as the root, and composition [i.e., literature], as the flower; and as the root spreads, and thrives, shall the flower fail?" (Young 1759, 75). The problem with modern literary composition is that unlike the sciences, which aim at originality, literature contents itself with imitating the ancients: imitation "deprives the liberal and politer arts of an advantage which the mechanic enjoy: In these, men are ever endeavouring to go beyond their Predecessors; in the former, to follow them. ... [H]ence while arts Mechanic are in perpetual progress, and increase, the Liberal are in retrogradation, and decay" (Young 1759, 41). Over the long term, even literary enthusiasts will agree that the language of incremental "increase" and epistemological "progress" are suitable to the sciences in a way that never can apply to the arts. But Young's manifesto strikingly suggests that the Romantic call for expressive originality over mere imitation, for the lamp over the mirror, is also an empiricist call to imitate the sciences.

In summary, natural philosophy controls for the variables of time and place through the technology of the laboratory and experimental repetition, and it thereby generalizes from the sensible experience of nature to its abstract universal character. Drama controls for time and place through the multiple techniques of representation, refining the disparate passions of experience into emotions that are universally pleasurable. Drama gives us not essential concepts of nature with which to affect it, but comparable images of nature—the visual and the literate, the actuality of ourselves and the virtuality of characters—with which to know nature as a human setting. The distance the understanding takes on the world enables a belief that is justified because it is a general constant derived from, and exclusive of, all variable particulars (although during the first century of science there were many who were highly skeptical about scientific method and its results). The lesser distance taken by the imagination on staged or read events enables the mixed sort of belief that is peculiar to reflexivity and situated between particulars and the general, between content and form, a state of mind that is both involved and detached, one that allows us to consider "hideous Objects" as both "Dreadful and Harmless."

## Controlling for Time, Place, and Persons: The Novel

I've argued so far that in its emulation of scientific experiment, the dramatic aesthetic developed in two stages. The first stage is the naive empiricism of the two unities and the confidence they express in the transparency of sense impressions. The second stage evolved from the first as the view that like scientific method, the imagination abstracts from the level of sense impressions far enough to exceed the illusion of nature's concrete presence, but not so far as to sacrifice, as scientific experiment does, nature's figurative image—or rather, its double image. For the greatest pleasure of the imagination depends on its reflexivity, one's consciousness of the fact of representation, the knowledge that what one experiences is both "nature"—the sensible object itself—and "art"—the process by which we experience it. So dramatic epistemology both embraces and suspends the scientific axiom that the knower must be methodically detached from the known. We both believe in and disbelieve the actuality of what is represented; we identify with the characters even as we remain convinced of our own identities.

Now, the dramatic ideal of the two unities entails a principle of decorum that consists in establishing in the spectator an illusion of immediacy or spatiotemporal presence. Even if this illusion is possible when a play is performed, it would seem to be impossible when it is read. What might be the rough equivalent, for literate narrative, of the illusion of presence in performed drama? Elsewhere I have called the first, or naive empiricist, stage in this narrative development "the claim to historicity" (McKeon 1987, 45–47), because it amounts to the pretence that the fictional characters and events one reads about have an actual existence, a pretence that in its own way also asserts the immediacy of the experience it presents. We might say that the claim to historicity does the next best thing, promising a representation so faithful, even "transparent" in its use of linguistic arts, that it opens a window onto the truth of nature. But in time, once the naive claim to historicity had been outmoded, critics would discover that the literate arts themselves have a singular capacity to absorb the reader through a process of psychological identification that requires not a transparency but an obliquity effect, which produces that ocular blankness we recognize in others in the act of reading as a kind of interior perception.

The claim to historicity is the most definitive formal marker of the early novel as it emerged out of older narrative genres. Its essence can be found often enough in the title pages and prefaces of these transitional narratives, and I will not belabor the examples. Aphra Behn calls *Oroonoko* (1688) and *The Fair Jilt* (1696) "true histories" (Behn 1998, 3, 74). The title page of Daniel Defoe's *Robinson Crusoe* (1719), which was published anonymously, contains the words "*Written by Himself*" (Defoe 1998, iii, emphasis in the original]). In the preface to *The Fair Hebrew* (1729) Eliza Haywood writes that "I have not inserted one Incident which was not related to me by a Person nearly concerned in the Family of that unfortunate Gentleman" (Haywood 1729, A2r–B1v). And throughout the first edition of *Pamela* (1740), Samuel Richardson represents himself as "the Editor" of these letters (Richardson 2001, 3, 4, 92, 98, 498). These formal testimonies to the authenticity of the narratives that contain them show the influence of empirical, even experimental, method not only in the fundamental assertion of the actuality of the subjects of the text but also in the effort to conceive the text itself as a determinate object (or, as in the case of epistolary novels, objects) that has been found in an identifiable location and therefore can be verified as having an objective existence—not necessarily objectivity but objecthood. Even quantitative criteria, like the repetition of scientific experiments, have a kind of parallel in the multiple citations of eyewitnesses to different parts of the novelistic plot. True, the text remains an artifactual rather than a strictly "factual" entity like a natural specimen; but it is crucially represented as the artifice not of an imaginative author but of one or more actual persons who have used language for the more basic and practical purposes of record keeping or information exchange.

Even in this first stage of its epistemological development, the signature reflexivity of the novel ensures that formal techniques of experimental abstraction like these will have their equivalent on the level of content. The enumeration of time, place, and quantity is everywhere in the early novel, from the nautical measurements pertaining to Robinson's voyages to the minute date keeping in his journal to the record keeping of finances and livestock that punctuates his daily life on and off the island. This sort of detail has an obvious relation to the Royal Society's authorization of quantitative measure in natural histories and sea voyages, but we can also see some basic plots of the early novel as narrative representations of scientific experiment. I am thinking especially of plots in which the discovery of terra incognita, the unknown land, plays a central role. Literal travel plots like these often dovetailed with the idea of the State of Nature that Hobbes and Locke used to counter traditional doctrines of political sovereignty based on divine donation or inheritance. In his *Second Treatise of Government* (1690), Locke conducted a thought experiment whose work involved not stripping away variables to reveal a natural constant, but positing a constant, the State of Nature, at the outset and watching legitimate government—in effect, the variable confirmed by nature—emerge over time. This may suggest one difference between the experimental procedures initiated by laboratory and literary hypothesis: the former works back from what is empirically given to its underlying foundations, whereas the latter works forward from what is imaginatively given to its empirical implications. But Locke also buttressed his hypothesis with empirical evidence of what the State of Nature must have been like in the distant European past. Referring not to the English colonists but to native inhabitants, Locke, echoing the book of Genesis, wrote: "[I]n the beginning all the World was *America*" (Locke 1967, 319). For him and others, the discovery of the New World offered something like a scientific laboratory in reverse, where people might be observed living in their stripped-down form, in the absence of custom, cultural convention, and ideological presupposition.

One of the levels on which *Robinson Crusoe* can be seen to proceed like an experimental hypothesis is the political. Shipwreck a man on a desert island—at one point Robinson actually describes it as "a mere state of nature" (Defoe 1998, 118)—thereby isolating him from all social variables. How does government come into being? Early on and alone with his animals, Robinson abstracts enough from his sense impressions to imagine himself "Prince and Lord of the whole Island; I had the Lives of all my Subjects at my absolute Command. I could hang, give Liberty, and take it away, and no Rebels among all my Subjects" (Defoe 1998, 148). And as the island is slowly populated, Robinson transforms the virtual image of absolute power into actuality: "My island was now peopled," he writes, shortly before he leaves it. "How like a King I look'd.... My people were perfectly subjected: I was absolute Lord and Law-giver ... we had but three Subjects, and they were of three different Religions.... However, I allow'd a Liberty of Conscience throughout my Dominions" (Defoe 1998, 241). And before he returns to England, Robinson deals wisely and justly with a rebellion against his newly established authority. So the laboratory of the desert island helps Defoe imagine how a political culture of enlightened monarchy might be justified as a natural development from the virtuality of solitary imaginings to the actuality of society.

But there are ways of thinking about *Robinson Crusoe* as an experimental narrative that seem closer to the model of scientific hypothesis, which begins with an actual object and subjects it to multiple tests that reduce it to an invariant natural form. Take an Englishman whose ungodly nature has been corrupted by the vicious practices of capitalist accumulation and exchange. Since these vices are social, remove that man from the economic corruptions of society by placing him in a state of nature where he has no one on whom to practice his vices: "I had nothing to covet," writes Robinson; "for I had all that I was now capable of enjoying . . . There were no Rivals. I had no Competitor, none to dispute Sovereignty or Command with me. I might have rais'd Ship Loadings of Corn; but I had no use for it" (Defoe 1998, 128). Subject this man to a religious conversion (the word "experiment" had an important religious meaning at this time) that enables him to see that his apparent solitude is really the society of God, that God has made "up to me, the Deficiencies of my Solitary State, and the want of Humane Society by his Presence" (Defoe 1998, 112). Can the vicious capitalist, once stripped of his artful depravity, obtain the natural virtue of a good Christian? In this scenario, the final stage of Defoe's experiment requires that Robinson return to human society so that we can see if his vices return as soon as the opportunity to exercise them does, a question that all readers are obliged to confront.

Where scientists build upon their observations of sense data through techniques of quantification, narrative builds upon observation by telling stories about human crises that turn what had seemed the constants of everyday life into an ambiguous compound of constants and variables, what is necessary and "natural" and what is contingent and dispensable. Broadly speaking, the novel genre came into being in order to engage the multitude of collective crises—political, religious, social, economic, familial, sexual—that arose in the seventeenth and eighteenth centuries, and often enough these early narratives can be read fruitfully on the model of the experiment. That is, the work of the novelistic plot in this case is to elaborate a sample of experience broad and diverse enough to provide multiple testing grounds for plausibly separating out natural constants from artificial or customary variables. Richardson's *Pamela* opens soon after Pamela's mistress, who has treated her indulgently as though she were herself a gentlewoman, suddenly dies. But Pamela is a servant girl, and the death of her mistress means that the socially artificial circumstances under which Pamela has been bred are no longer there to support her. She is metaphorically shipwrecked: How will she behave toward, how will she be taken by, others? What is "natural" to her? Behind this question lies the social crisis that had been building for the previous two centuries. Aristocratic tradition held that birth equals worth, that inner virtue is grounded in the naturalness of noble blood. As social mobility became more common, the injustice of this ideology was increasingly recognized and challenged. The tacit truth that birth equals worth became a social—and literary—convention ripe for experimental testing. Mr. B., Pamela's new master, assumes that she is naturally available to be sexually seduced. And in the end, his failure to corrupt Pamela also may be read as the isolation of a natural constant beyond all social variables, the successful revelation that virtue is her irreducible nature.

But it is useful to see that the "shipwreck" with which *Pamela* opens and that dictates the first half of its plot is only the first of several. Crucial to Pamela's eventual triumph is her imprisonment in the Lincolnshire house, which Mr. B. engineers in order to have his way with her more easily, but which ironically sequesters her from her customary work so as to make her not just an occasional letter writer but (in his words) a brilliantly persuasive "Novel" writer (Richardson 2001, 232) whose extended narrative transforms Mr. B. from aristocratic libertinage into a suitor of her hand. So the fact that Pamela is experimentally "beached" at Lincolnshire ensures that her virtuous nature will be not only revealed but rewarded by an upwardly mobile marriage whose social meaning is that birth has nothing to do with worth. But a final shipwreck is yet in store for Pamela because Mr. B.'s proud sister refuses to accept the marriage, seeing Pamela as a social interloper who has polluted the purity of the family line and threatening her with force if she will not serve her at table. In Richardson's words, Pamela is once again a "Prisoner" (Richardson 2001, 384, 386); and although Lady Davers is soon reconciled with both Pamela and her brother, the disturbing episode raises questions of social injustice that Richardson may not have anticipated. Before their marriage, Pamela was vulnerable because she was doubly subordinate, as a servant and as a woman; but the novel's intense focus on social conflict early on made gender and sexual subordination relatively latent if not invisible. When Pamela's status rises through marriage, however, she becomes (as most readers are troubled to note) if anything more deferential to Mr. B., and this is because she has entered into the most ancient institution of inequality, marriage. The episode with Lady Davers catalyzes our sense that there is a vital experiment that has not been and never will be performed in this novel—the experiment that would test if the truth of nature may reside beyond sex, in the simplicity and equality of a gender-neutral *human* nature.

I have been suggesting that it is helpful to see the literary influence of scientific method at those crucial moments in the plots of early novels that seem to evoke the aura of the state of nature, whose force, not necessarily political in implication, is to throw "things as they are" into question by asking, is this natural or cultural? The way novelistic plots control for variables is not (like scientific experiment) methodically inductive, nor is the history of the novel (like the history of science) one of measurably progressive improvement, either in the artistic success of the genre or in the evolution of the values it represents over time. Nor would we expect this to be so, since the difference between the arts and the sciences bequeathed to us by the Quarrel of the Ancients and the Moderns is (to simplify) the difference between quality and quantity, between the representation of nature and the abstracted recovery of its effective presence. I have argued that the epistemological development of the drama moves from the naive empiricism of the two unities, which takes the artistic or imaginative mediation of nature to be roughly comparable to that of scientific understanding, to a model of representation that consists in taking a relatively greater distance on nature that permits a reflexive contemplation of the comparison between the sensible object and the imaginative image. If the novel begins with the naive claim to historicity as late seventeenth-century drama does with the two unities, how can we describe the aesthetic stage of thinking to which the novel aesthetic evolves?

The breakthrough in the development of the narrative aesthetic, or "realism," was less closely rationalized than that of the dramatic, but its breakthrough, too, made the notion of artistic "experiment" more fruitful in application to novelistic representation than the claim to historicity had done. Broadly speaking, the early novelists, impressed like their contemporaries by the evident truth value of empirical factuality, tended to rationalize the claim to historicity on the grounds that their readers would be more likely to take to heart the moral and religious teachings of their stories if they believed the exemplary figures they read about had an actual existence. And Defoe in particular struggled throughout his career with the problems involved in claiming the historicity of his fictional characters. These were primarily ethical problems—how can the cause of virtue be served by the vice of falsehood?—but also epistemological. Shortly after *Robinson Crusoe* appeared, Defoe conceded that "nothing is more common than to have two Men tell the same Story quite differing one from another, yet both of them Eye-witnesses to the Fact related," and the novels he published after his first one are obscure and evasive about the claim to historicity they continue halfheartedly to make (Defoe 1998, 113). Similarly, despite Richardson's claim in *Pamela*, when its second edition came out three months after the first he was at best careless about preserving the fiction of Pamela's actual existence. Why Richardson's change of heart?

There are a number of answers to this question. What I'd like to emphasize right now is how the change seems to be implicated in, and to grow out of, the very logic of what it leaves behind, the claim to historicity. We can see this happening on the level of plot or content even before Richardson abandons the formal role of editor in the second edition of *Pamela*. Although Mr. B.'s feelings have been softening gradually, until he reads the long and absorbing narrative that Pamela is obliged to produce in her isolation, he sees her as a "romancer"—that is, at best deceptive and at worst a liar. But he is so deeply moved by Pamela's account of the suffering he has caused her—"[Y]ou have touch'd me sensibly with your mournful Relation"—that his literalistic empiricism of the senses gives way to a standard of imaginative identification. Not that he strictly believes now the factuality of all she's written about him; rather, he has become receptive to a different standard of truth. So when Pamela says of the writings he is about to read, "[A]ll that they contain you know, as well as I," he replies: "But I don't know . . . the Light you put Things in" (Richardson 2001, 241, 239). For the reformed Mr. B., Pamela's writings no longer contain simply a representation of what happened that may be factually false; they also contain the emotional truth of the representation itself. And Mr. B.'s aesthetic reflexivity is reinforced by the way his sympathetic mode of reading provides us actual readers with a model for the aesthetic approach we too might take to the putatively "factual" narrative we are reading. A century later, "realism" came to designate the specifically narrative mode of the aesthetic, and what it designates is not "the real" but something that we are pleased to read as though it were real, a story that is not history but historylike, faithful not to this or that event but to the kinds of experience we tend to have. At this level, it doesn't matter if Mr. B. or Pamela ever had a real existence. And in this sense, novels are experiments that capture the experience of the senses not by reproducing it in all its particularity but by controlling for the variables of time, place, and persons so as to reveal, as Robert Hooke phrased it about laboratory experiments, "the ways by which Nature may be trac'd, . . . not too far removed beyond the reach of our Senses" (Hooke 1971, 62). But the realist experiment removes us a good deal less far from the senses than the laboratory does. By having us confront the world that language reflects with the way it reflects it, realism achieves the superior emotional pleasure of imaginative identification that results from a subtly oblique detachment, one that is neither sensible identity nor abstract idea but virtual figuration. To put this another way, if literary content is the world that language reflects and literary form is the way language reflects that world, the signature mark of realism is reflexivity, the thematization of form as content.

Among the many things that Henry Fielding disliked about *Pamela* was its claim to historicity, and in *Shamela* (1741) he mercilessly and hilariously parodied Richardson's efforts to persuade us not only that its plot had really happened but that, through the immediacy of the epistolary mode, it was somehow happening before our very eyes. A year later Fielding abandoned parody in order to write, in *Joseph Andrews* (1742), a positive alternative to *Pamela*. Besides *Don Quixote* (1605, 1615), *Joseph Andrews* is probably the most reflexive novel that had thus far been written—that is, that most draws attention to its own process of representation in the very act of doing it. In the preface to its third volume Fielding also composed the first full account of realism, which, after the brief heyday of the claim to historicity, now became the definitive formal doctrine of the novel genre. So far from denying the relationship between historical factuality and the novel, however, Fielding calls *Joseph Andrews* a biography, and he pointedly asserts the superiority of its fidelity to fact over the naive empiricism of those books we commonly call "histories." Most important for our purposes, he explicitly connects the breakthrough in novelistic realism that he is now in the process of achieving with the recent breakthrough in the dramatic aesthetic. Perhaps in part because he has just turned from playwriting to novel writing, Fielding frames his argument about narrative in allusion to the dramatic doctrine of the two unities. Those who call themselves historians, Fielding writes, might better be termed "Topographers or Chorographers," because their chief concern is to record the facts of place and time as accurately as they can. What they ignore, Fielding continues, is the unity of action, or in his terms "the Actions and Characters of Men": "Now with us Biographers the Case is different, the Facts we deliver may be relied on, tho' we often mistake the Age and Country wherein they happened" (Fielding 1999, bk. 3, ch. 1, 162). This is in the spirit of the reformed reader Mr. B., who learns to read Pamela for the pleasing correspondence between her self-representation, and herself in the light *he* knows it. The crucial implication—for us if less so for Mr. B.—is that the truth of novels is relative not to a singular actuality but to many instances of it, a point Fielding makes acutely about his own realism: "I question not but several of my Readers will know the Lawyer in the Stage-Coach, the Moment they hear his Voice. . . . I describe not Men, but Manners, not an Individual, but a Species. Perhaps it will be answered, Are not the Characters then taken from Life? To which I answer in the Affirmative; nay, I believe I might aver, that I have writ little more than I have seen. The Lawyer is not only alive, but hath been so these 4000 Years" (Fielding 1999, bk. 3, ch. 1, 164). Yet Fielding is no more oblivious here of the truth of "history" than Hooke is of the truth of nature. Fielding uses the words "fact" and "seen" with a self-conscious amusement that aims not to subvert their empirical reference but to extend it beyond the scope required for sensibly observed and physically actual entities.

In *Tristram Shandy* (1759–1767), Laurence Sterne picks up Fielding's aesthetic reflexivity and runs with it so far as totally to subsume the pleasures of the senses within those of the imagination and content within form—or so it might seem. It is probably more accurate to say that Sterne, more rigorously and intricately even than Fielding, adapts representational reflexivity to the genre of the novel. And like Fielding he does this by alluding to the dramatic controversies about the two unities. So when Tristram supposes the reader will accuse him of violating "the unity . . . of time" (Sterne 1965, bk. 2, ch. 8, 79), we are made to understand that the change in medium from drama to narrative transforms the disparity between the actual, empirical time of representation and the virtual time that is represented. For as Tristram insists, the time taken to represent *Tristram Shandy* is an indeterminate interplay of *two* temporalities, the period of writing and the period of reading. And since he works so hard to represent this interplay with accuracy and precision, it becomes the major portion of the representation itself, thematizing form as content and leaving no room for at least half of what Sterne's title page announces will be the substance of this novel, *The Life and Opinions of Tristram Shandy, Gentleman*. In fact we do get Sterne's "Life" as well as his opinions. But the content or plot of *Tristram Shandy* is so implicated within its mode of narration that it takes some labor on the reader's part to see that Sterne's form and content are mirror images of each other. The form of *Tristram Shandy* might justly be summarized as the failure of the narrative line, owing to the triangulating entanglement of virtual or represented time and the two modes of actual temporality, writing and reading time. But the content of the novel is the failure of the Shandy family line—that is, its failure to reproduce itself owing to Tristram's overdetermined infertility, whose implacable narration also helps explain the linear infertility of Sterne's plot. The story is incomplete because it is a story about incompletion. But on another level, *Tristram Shandy* is more complete than any novel had been, because in experimentally treating as a "natural" constant what others have tended to treat as expendable variables—namely, the mental activity of narrator and readers—it represents in unprecedentedly comprehensive terms its own process of representation.

This is once again the phenomenon of reflexivity. We may be tempted to take it as strictly negative, a parody of naive empiricism that reduces it to absurdity, but no less than Fielding Sterne is also clearing the ground for a positive view of novelistic realism. In fact, he is a rigorous Lockean empiricist not only in jest but also in earnest, as he claims at one point to his reader: "Pray, Sir, in all the reading which you have ever read, did you ever read such a book as *Locke*'s Essay upon the Human Understanding? . . . It is a history.—A history! of who? what? where? when? Don't hurry yourself.—It is a history-book, Sir, ... of what passes in a man's own mind" (Sterne 1965, bk. 2, ch. 2, 66). In the second sentence of his *Essay concerning Human Understanding* (1690) Locke announces his ambition in just these terms: "The Understanding, like the Eye, whilst it makes us see, and perceive all other Things, takes no notice of it self: And it requires Art and Pains to set it at a distance, and make it its own Object" (Locke 1975, bk. 1, ch. 1, 43). This is the "Labour of the Brain" Addison refers to in contrasting the pleasures of the understanding with those of the imagination, and Locke is in no doubt regarding the difficulty of his enterprise, in which the cardinal principle of understanding, the division of the subject from the object of knowledge, would seem to come up against the reflexive interplay entailed in making the understanding "its own Object." Sterne has great fun explicating Locke's warning against the association of ideas and his affirmation of the division of wit from judgment by showing how focusing on one of these faculties alone cannot fail "to put one in mind of the want of the other" (Sterne 1965, bk. 3, ch. 20, 149). But in this Sterne only imitates the associative fun Locke has in explaining his insight that the association of ideas is a "sort of Madness." For the insight came to him, Locke writes, when, "enquiring a little by the bye into the Nature of Madness, I found it to spring from the very same Root, and to depend on the very same Cause we are here speaking of. This consideration of the thing it self, at a time when I thought not the least on the Subject which I am now treating of, suggested it to me" (Locke 1975, bk. 2, ch. 33, 395).

In refining Locke's principles, his greatest successor in empiricist epistemology, David Hume, also situated the origins of this philosophy within the larger context of the Quarrel of the Ancients and Moderns and the separation out of the arts from the sciences, which both men's philosophical efforts aimed in part to overcome:

> 'Tis no astonishing reflection to consider, that the application of experimental philosophy to moral subjects should come after that to natural at the distance of above a whole century; since we find in fact, that there was about the same interval betwixt the origins of these sciences; and that reckoning from THALES to SOCRATES, the space of time is nearly equal to that betwixt my Lord BACON[8] and some late philosophers in England, who have begun to put the science of man on a new footing, and have engaged the attention, and excited the curiosity of the public.... For to me it seems evident, that the essence of the mind being equally unknown to us with that of external bodies, it must be equally impossible to form any notion of its powers and qualities otherwise than

from careful and exact experiments ... [W]e cannot go beyond experience ... [But] Moral philosophy has, indeed, this peculiar disadvantage, which is not found in natural, that in collecting its experiments, it cannot make them purposely, with premeditation, and after such a manner as to satisfy itself concerning every particular difficulty which may arise. When I am at a loss to know the effects of one body upon another in any situation, I need only put them in that situation, and observe what results from it. But should I endeavour to clear up after the same manner any doubt in moral philosophy, by placing myself in the same case with that which I consider, 'tis evident this reflection and premeditation would so disturb the operation of my natural principles, as must render it impossible to form any just conclusion from the phaenomenon. (Hume 1978, xvi–xvii, xviii–xix)

In the empiricism of philosophical inquiry, reflexivity is a problem because it threatens to compromise the degree of distance required by the understanding to disembed the nature of the thing itself as an abstract and general idea, in this case the human mind and its operations. In the empiricism of aesthetics, however, reflexivity marks the crucially lesser distance that the imagination takes on its object, signifying that what is being represented is not only the nature of the thing but also, as figuration rather than full abstraction, the formal process of its representation.

The publication of *Tristram Shandy* marks as well as any other event the point at which in the wake of the Quarrel of the Ancients and the Moderns, literature learned to practice and perfect its modern self-understanding as a distinctive mode of empirical knowledge. A century earlier, Sprat had described the work of laboratory experimenters in terms that also describe the work of *Tristram Shandy*: "[A]fter they have perform'd the *Trial*" they "bring all the *History* of its *Process* back again to the *Test* ... , observ[ing] all the *Chances*, and the *Regularities* of the Proceeding; what *Nature* does willingly, what constrain'd; what with its own Power, what by the succours of Art." Central to literature, as to science, is the experimental trial, the history of whose process is brought back again to the test. What distinguishes them is what becomes of that history in each kind of experiment. Scientific experiment abstracts from experiential data an understanding of nature that has the probability of universal sensible application, an understanding in which the data themselves, an indispensable means of reaching this point, now play no part. In the lesser abstraction achieved by the literary text, the history of the process by which experiment abstracts from experiential data a probable figuration of human nature persists as part of the end product. In the aesthetic attitude, that is, the arts discovered a mode of experiment whose aim is an empirical removal from sensible actuality to imaginative virtuality that bears with it the evidence of that removal. Time, place, and person, to some degree disembedded from experience, persist in the literary text as a formal or figurative residue. In Sprat's terms, the record of the "trial" or "test" remains in the text itself at the level of form, internalizing within the experimental results a comparative record of how those results came to be. In this sense, the literary text is itself an experiment as the end of scientific experiment never can be. The empirical nature of science is most importantly confirmed in the wake of experiment, in the applicability to sensible actuality of the concepts it has derived from experiment. The empirical nature of literature is most importantly confirmed by the formality and figurative thickness of its texts, which is the history of an experimental mediation between sensible actuality and imaginative virtuality. Therefore the literary end-product of experiment itself has the character of an experiment.

## Qualitative and Quantitative Value

Thus far I have been describing the efforts of contemporaries to conceive the aesthetic as an empirical mode of knowledge with respect to the kind of response we have to literary works and the kind of belief we invest in them. To this end I have been speaking primarily about the formal strategies of literary works (but also, more briefly, about the way their plots are constructed as though they were experiments). There was also, however, the question of how we judge the value of literary works.

In his preface to *The Plays of William Shakespeare* (1765), Samuel Johnson made what is perhaps the definitive contribution to the first topic, the debate about dramatic response and belief:

> The necessity of observing the unities of time and place arises from the supposed necessity of making the drama credible. [But] [i]t is false, that any representation is mistaken for reality; that any dramatic fable in its materiality was ever credible, or, for a single moment, was ever credited.... Delusion, if delusion be admitted, has no certain limitation... The truth is, that the spectators are always in their senses, and know, from the first act to the last, that the stage is only a stage, and that the players are only players.... It will be asked, how the drama moves, if it is not credited. It is credited with all the credit due to a drama. It is credited, whenever it moves, as a just picture of a real original ... If there be any fallacy, it is not that we fancy the players, but that we fancy ourselves unhappy for a moment ... The delight of tragedy proceeds from our consciousness of fiction; if we thought murders and treasons real, they

would please no more. Imitations produce pain or pleasure, not because they are mistaken for realities, but because they bring realities to mind.[9]

However, Johnson also raises the question of value, and he does so within the implicit context of the Quarrel of the Ancients and Moderns and in terms that recall the evaluative criteria evinced in the previous century by proponents of scientific method: "To works," Johnson writes, "of which the excellence is not absolute and definite, but gradual and comparative; to works not raised upon principles demonstrative and scientifick, but appealing wholly to observation and experience, no other test can be applied than length of duration and continuance of esteem. What mankind have long possessed they have often examined and compared, and if they persist to value the possession, it is because frequent comparisons have confirmed opinion in its favour" (59–60). Johnson seeks what might be called the closest equivalent for works of art, to the standard of judgment available for works of science, and he discovers it in the quantifiability of which both empirical and aesthetic experience is susceptible. But the comparison of qualitatively different objects cannot in itself yield a standard of aesthetic value because differences in quality are by definition incomparable. What is needed is a mechanism of quantification, a standard by which qualitatively different works can be rendered comparable, and Johnson finds this standard in the test of time. Shakespeare "has long outlived his century, the term commonly fixed as the test of literary merit [see Horace, *Epistles*, 2.i. 39]. Whatever advantages he might once derive from personal allusions, local customs, or temporary opinions, have for many years been lost. . . . [H]is works support no opinion with arguments, nor supply any faction with invectives; they can neither indulge vanity nor gratify malignity, but are read without any other reason than the desire of pleasure, and are therefore praised only as pleasure is obtained" (Johnson 1968, 61).

In Johnson's analysis, the test of time enables judgments of aesthetic value because it entails a generalizing abstraction from the variables—the personal, the local, and the temporary; competition, friendship, enmity, opinion, faction, vanity, malignity—that constituted the experiential context in which Shakespeare's plays first were written, viewed, and read. The test of time is like a scientific experiment that controls for variables and isolates what is constant—abstract pleasure—not by means of a laboratory apparatus but by a version of experimental repetition, the winnowing effect of the winds of time, a temporal version of the scientific principle of repeatability that Hooke formulates when he observes that "it were very desirable that both Observations and Experiments should be divers times repeated, and that at several Seasons and with several Circumstances, both of the Mind and of Persons, Time, Place, Instruments and Materials" (Hooke 1971, 61). Johnson concludes these prefatory reflections with the famous statement that in the present context reminds us that the means by which the positive judgment of Shakespeare's aesthetic value is made are the same as those by which his plays make their aesthetic claim on our imaginations: "Nothing can please many, and please long, but just representations of general nature" (Johnson 1968, 61). Lest this pronouncement seem (as it too often has) to celebrate transcendence of particularity alone as the aesthetic norm, Johnson soon after complements it with the praise that "the dialogue of this authour is often so evidently determined by the incident which produces it, and is pursued with so much ease and simplicity, that it seems scarcely to claim the merit of fiction, but to have been gleaned by diligent selection out of common conversation, and common occurrences" (Johnson 1968, 63). Like inductive method, aesthetic method entails a dialectical reciprocity between the particular and the general according to which neither can prevail in the absence of the other.

The problem of value preoccupied Enlightenment thinkers across a broad range of phenomena. In the modern world, aesthetic value is commonly understood to be antithetical to—divided or "mediated" from—the quantifying standard not only of empirical materialism but specifically of commodity exchange on the economic market. My preceding argument suggests instead that aesthetic value and exchange value, connected or "mediated" by the power and success of empirical epistemology, may be quantifying versions of each other. Twelve years after Johnson's preface appeared, Adam Smith's *An Inquiry into the Nature and Causes of the Wealth of Nations* (1776) laid out the theory of exchange value with unprecedented clarity and force. In its capacity to turn objects of consumption and use into objects of circulation and exchange (or commodities), the market translates qualitative difference into quantitative comparability and equivalence. The "real measure" of exchange value, "the real price of all commodities," is the "quantity of labour we exchange for what is supposed at the time to contain the value of an equal quantity.... But though labour be the real measure of the exchangeable value of all commodities, it is not that by which their value is commonly estimated," a result that is achieved, "not by any accurate measure, but by the higgling and bargaining of the market, according to that sort of rough equality which, though not exact, is sufficient for carrying on the business of common life" (Smith 1981, 46, 47–48, 49). Unlike the test of time, commodity exchange works in a basically synchronic rather than in a diachronic dimension, but like the test of time it deracinates the object or experience from its particular and local uses so as to isolate it in the purity of its sharability, which in both cases is the fundamental standard of value: in the case of the commodity, its monetary value; in the case of the artwork, its abstract pleasure.

The aesthetic and the market were being theorized and put into practice during the same period, and contemporaries were aware of these similarities (to some degree perhaps because artworks were among the commodities that circulated on the market). No one else made this connection with the proleptic perspicuity of Alexander Pope. In *Peri Bathous: Of the Art of Sinking in Poetry* (1727) Pope parodied *Peri Hupsous*, "Longinus's" ancient text on the art of the sublime, in the broadly mock-heroic spirit of a critique of modern poetry measured against the normative standards of the ancient. Much of the satire occurs at the linguistic level of unintentionally bathetic tropes and figures of speech, but it is grounded in an attack on the modern institutionalization and mechanization of poetic production and consumption that puts quantity at a premium. Expanding on the well-known Horatian dictum, Pope's speaker remarks that "if the Intent of all Poetry be to divert and instruct, certainly that Kind which diverts and instructs the greatest Number, is to be preferr'd" (Pope 1965, ch. 2, 45, 46, ch. 4, 49). *Peri Bathous* is also anticipatorily parodic of Johnson's test of time, whereby we judge poetic achievement according to how far pure "pleasure is obtained" from generations of consumers. Of "our wiser authors" Pope remarks that "[t]heir true design is profit or gain; in order to acquire which, 'tis necessary to procure applause, by administring pleasure to the reader"—(Pope 1965, ch. 2, 45, 46, ch. 4, 49) thus "the universal applause daily given to the admirable entertainments of harlequins and magicians on our stage." Johnson's mechanism for quantifying Shakespeare's dramatic value is the winnowing effect of temporality, "length of duration and continuance of esteem." Pope's is a more opportunistic project in the spatial amplification of theaters and the financial profit to be derived from the multiplication of theatrical consumers.

What Pope understood at the very origins of the aesthetic is that if it aspires to the virtual and transcendent status of the supersensible, it is equally rooted in the immanence of brute sense experience. And if—to alter the figure but not its import—the signature of the aesthetic attitude is a reflexivity of form and content, art is equally a mode of knowing by reflecting the world, and one that parallels, at a lesser degree of abstraction, scientific epistemology. This understanding defines the eighteenth-century view of the aesthetic imagination as analogous not only to experimental method but also to the circulation and exchange of commodities. All three of these Enlightenment developments, so indispensable to modern thought, are a function of "mediation" in its "primal" sense: that is, as both separation and conflation. That the aesthetic soon lost its dialectical relation to both transcendence and immanence, the general and the particular, the virtual and the actual, can be seen in the way mainstream modern thought soon abandoned the intuition of an analogical linkage between the aesthetic imagination, science, and the market economy, reinforcing a fundamental separation between the arts on the one hand and the (physical and social) sciences on the other. Efforts to overcome this monolithic division, which have flourished at a number of points in our modern present, are ill-fated so long as they either define themselves against the Enlightenment past, whose exclusive investment in separation is a modern projection, or model themselves on a premodern past, whose tacit conception of distinct categories as nonetheless inseparable is intrinsically at odds with the explicit aim to conflate categories that exist as such only by virtue of their separability. This dialectical relationship is the inheritance that modernity was bequeathed by the Enlightenment, which despite strenuous efforts to bury it has never really died.

# NOTES

### CLIFFORD SISKIN AND WILLIAM WARNER, "INTRODUCTION"

1. Bacon 2000, 7. We have used two different translations of Bacon (1994 and 2000) to help us best capture what we understand to be the meaning and force of his arguments.
2. For the most comprehensive treatment of this conversation in Germany, see Schmidt 1996, 1–11, 49–52. In a 2007 lecture available on his Web site, Schmidt argues that ignorance of that conversation has led to two basic ways of "Misunderstanding the Question: 'What is Enlightenment?'" The first reads Kant's essay as if it was a response to a request for a characterization of a period, and the second reads it as a "jumping off point for an evaluation of the degree to which the aspirations of his age might still have a claim on us" (4–5). Our introduction maps out an alternative that identifies Kant's claim as philosophical, not historical, and that turns back to Bacon rather than forward into claims about modernity.
3. We quote from Lewis White Beck's translation of "Was ist Aufklärung," originally published in *Foundations of the Metaphysics of Morals*, but now conveniently reprinted together with Foucault's lectures on Kant and Enlightenment in Foucault, *The Politics of Truth*, 2007. Hereafter cited as Kant 2007, emphasis in the original.
4. Asking how we "know knowledge" thus became for Foucault the "bold move that one must make" (2007, 80) to join his own late twentieth-century project to recast history as "genealogy." That effort became known, of course, for the next move: Foucault's strategy of moving boldly against the "human" as the subject and object of traditional histories. Deporting the question of the "self" itself into critique, he described Kant's Enlightenment both "negatively" and "positively." What it is not is "humanism." Since "the humanistic thematic is in itself too supple, too diverse, too inconsistent to serve as an axis for reflection," we must not confuse, he argued, "the theme of humanism with the question of the Enlightenment." What that question

became, in Kant's hands, was just such an axis, an axis for "reflecting upon limits" through a "critique of what we are saying, thinking, and doing" (111–113). Crucially for Foucault, however, this "critical ontology of ourselves" is not finally about ourselves (118). For us, as opposed to Kant, it has congealed into a "philosophical attitude" that "has to be translated into the labor of diverse inquiries"—inquiries that have "their methodological coherence in the at once archaeological and genealogical study of practices" (118, emphasis added). Although the specific kinds of inquiries Foucault called for were new, the project itself—advocating new forms of knowledge derived from a new methodology—was not. It is an obvious echo of Bacon's induction-based "renewal," one that is amplified even further by chronological coincidence. Bacon, the Great Verulam, began his hybrid career in knowledge and politics exactly four hundred years before Foucault's ended, having been elected to Parliament in 1584, two years after completing his law degree.

5. For the changing historical meanings of "mediation" and related terms, see the essays by Eliassen and Jacobsen and Guillory in this volume.
6. Guillory sees Bacon as "hesitat[ing] on the threshold" between "our concept of medium" in regard to "communication" and an "earlier semantic complex" of "means" and "imitation."
7. See Foucault's disdainful dismissal of taking Enlightenment to be "a mere episode in the history of ideas" (Foucault 2007, 93).
8. For an earlier attempt by Siskin and Warner to situate the study of Enlightenment in relation to what has been called the digital mutation, please see the site for the "Digital Retroaction" conference given at the University of California, Santa Barbara, in October, 2004. http://dc-mrg.english.ucsb.edu/conference/D_Retro/conference.html.
9. We are here referring, of course, to what Julie Hayes calls the "historically locatable" Enlightenment rather than the transhistorical Homer-to-Hitler varieties (Hayes 1998).
10. Deborah Harkness highlights the importance of "print culture" to Bacon and to his legacy, but casts it negatively as a product of his avoiding the "labor-intensive" work of science and a desire to value the work of gentlemen over "humble practitioners" (Harkness 2007, 250–253).
11. There is no absolute logic of mediation at work here. Unlike the natural and conjectural histories of the eighteenth century or more current but still Whig histories of science and technology, the history of mediation is not bound to a teleology of progress or to any other tale that it *must* ztell. Instead, it facilitates the kinds of pattern recognition we need to make sense of things without imposing patterns on everything or reducing everything to the same pattern.
12. Print can be best described as becoming dominant within a changing hierarchy of mediating technologies—in the same way that literary genres do at particular historical moments. Its position is not only a matter of more but of how its features function within the other kinds. The power of satire in early eighteenth-century Britain, for example, is indexed both by the number of satires published and by the incorporation of satiric features in other forms—thus Alexander Pope's "Epistle to

Arbuthnot" taking shape as a satiric letter. For a discussion of this aspect of genre theory, see Siskin 1988, 9–14.

13. Our point is that mediation as we use it here can happen in many ways: yes, through the various forms of media, but also through tool use, associational practices, genre formation, the development of concepts, the use of protocols, etc. Although a history of mediation can give us access to the way change happens, it is not a normative ideal. The history of mediation does not necessarily describe progress toward a greater or better world. It is the unruly plurality of mediation(s) that makes our use of the term very different than that found in the philosophy of Hegel. There, mediation (*Vermittlung*) is embedded in the process of the dialectic, by which two terms enter into a dynamic exchange and produce a new and more comprehensive term. So, for example, when Hegel turns to the Enlightenment in the final chapter of *The Philosophy of History*, the new science is said to produce a reconciliation of nature, now grasped through its rational laws, and human consciousness, so that, through a "Reason" that comprehends both man and nature, "man finds himself at home in [nature], and that only passes for truth in which he finds himself at home . . . The recognition of the validity of these laws was designated by the term Elarcissement (*Aufklärung*)." In this volume, Michael McKeon's essay bears the closest connection to a Hegelian usage of dialectic as mediation— but without the imperative of progress. At the end of this introduction, we gesture vicariously through Geof Bowker toward the more philosophical implications of mediation—not as dialectic but as an "ontological priority" (Hegel 1956, 440, 441).

14. We hope it is clear, in this introduction and throughout the volume, that "ideas" have not been left by the wayside. Instead, we are pointing here to the problem of constructing a history of ideas unmediated by genre, technology, etc.

15. Enlightenment was also successful in the basic way that "events" can be said to be successful. As "one possible outcome of doing something"—in this case, as an outcome of mediation—the event of Enlightenment became a condition of possibility for subsequent events. This "outcome" definition of "event" is important to the study of probability. See Siegel and Shim 2005.

16. Berhard Siegert offers this formulation of the principle that subtends the postal system in Siegert 1999, 9.

17. We have used the conventional translation of this phrase, though, the French word "gens" is gender neutral.

18. According to John Nichols's monumental *Literary Anecdotes*, Shaw was "among the most eminent and extensively useful of those writers to whom the English Reader is indebted" (Nichols 1815, 764). He was joint editor with Chambers of the editions of Boerhaave's *Chemistry*. See Nichols 1815.

19. The change we are identifying conforms to what we now call "emergence." For connections between emergence and the proliferation of print, see Siskin 2005, 819–823.

20. E-mail correspondence between the authors, John Bender, and Dan Edelstein, 30 April, 2007. The quotation from Fontenelle is "Il s'est répandu depuis un temps un esprit philosophique presque tout nouveau, une lumière qui n'avoit guères éclairé nos Ancêtres" [For some time, an almost entirely new philosophical mindset has

spread, a light which had hardly illuminated our Ancestors)]. The quotation from Dubos is "les lumieres que l'esprit philosophique a répanduës sur notre siecle" [The illumination which the philosophical mind has spread over our century].

21. Useful recent overviews of studies of Enlightenment may be found in *The Enlightenment* (Outram 1995/2005) and *The Case for Enlightenment* (Robertson 2005), as well as the three collections discussed in this introduction (Clark, Golinski, Shaffer, 1999; Knott and Taylor 2005; Carey and Festa 2009). In the overviews of Enlightenment studies offered in these five books, there are discussions of (by our count) thirty-four different books published since 1995 which contribute to a redefinition of Enlightenment. These synthetic overviews document the shift from pioneering intellectual history (the thought of the *philosophe*) to an emphasis on social practices (like reading), to an emphasis on national strains of Enlightenment (like the Scottish Enlightenment), as well as a tendency toward pluralizing Enlightenment until it loses any coherence. In *The Case for Enlightenment*, Robertson notes that the low repute that had befallen the Enlightenment by the 1980s and 1990s may have incited a very diverse set of scholars to challenge arguments that make Enlightenment the convenient "straight man" of every progressive critique, whether it was staged from the right (in the wake of Edmund Burke) or left (in the wake of Max Horkheimer and Theodor Adorno). Most recent scholars of the eighteenth century refuse the "blackmail" of Enlightenment that Foucault attributed to this position (see above).

22. The work of Charles W. J. Withers in *Placing the Enlightenment* (2007) points to geography as another direction to take in mapping the mutations and proliferations of mediation as conditions of possibility for Enlightenment. In that book, "the idea of geography as an active agency—as practices carried out by people in and over spaces," becomes part of the practice of Enlightenment: a way "contemporaries came to terms with the extent and content of the terraqueous globe—the earth—as home" (15). This approach entails understanding geography as capacious—the mapping of the places and spaces of Enlightenment as an occurrence, as a way of conducting practical exploration of the earth, and as an emerging discipline of knowledge.

JOHN GUILLORY, "ENLIGHTENING MEDIATION"

1. Howell 1971, 548–549, argues that Adam Smith's *Lectures on Rhetoric and Belles Lettres* (written in 1748–1749, but not published until the twentieth century) systematizes a turn in British rhetoric from persuasion to communication.

2. The construction of rhetorical speech as irremediably tainted by the possibility of lying is very much an antirhetorical position. It is also the "semiotic" view, as Umberto Eco affirms without moralization when he calls semiotics a "theory of the lie" in Eco 1979, 6–8.

3. Locke's conventionalism is in a line that linguists trace to Aristotle, in the opening of the *De Interpretatione* (also referenced by Bacon in the passage quoted above): "Now spoken sounds are symbols of affections in the soul, and written marks symbols of spoken sounds. And just as written marks are not the same for all men,

neither are spoken sounds" (Aristotle 1984, 1: 25). This passage is often loosely cited as representing a theory of "communication," which it seems to me it does not. In addition to the fact that Aristotle asserts a naturally corresponding relation between "affections" and "things," which is the relation that Locke attempts to clarify rather than assume, he is most interested in the *De Interpretatione* with determining how propositions (not words) can be true or false statements about the world. This is the concern he begins to address immediately after the famous paragraph and in the remainder of this text: "Just as some thoughts in the soul are neither true nor false while some are necessarily one or the other, so also with spoken sounds." As usual in antiquity, the interest is in the adequacy of language to the world, or the "truth," with the success or failure of communication a secondary consideration. Nevertheless conventionalism such as Locke defines it (i.e., differently from Aristotle) lays the groundwork for the elaboration of the communication function in modern discourse.

4. On this point, see Aarsleff 1982, 72.

5. Williams 1976, 204, also picks out these two quotations from the *OED*'s list. It would be difficult to say, without considerable further research, just how common these uses are. On the basis of my own reading in the early modern period, my guess is that the sense of mediation in the theological and political contexts are vastly more common, and that the connection of mediation with books, either manuscript or print, is rare.

6. See the important comment in Hegel 1969, 68: "there is nothing, nothing in heaven, or in nature or in mind or anywhere else which does not equally contain both immediacy and mediation." The theme of mediation figures largely in the *Science of Logic*.

7. Hegel's dialectic of mediation is peculiar in that it does not start with two terms but only one, as in his unfolding of *being* in the terms *nothing* and *becoming*.

8. A significant exception is Schleiermacher, *Hermeneutics and Criticism*, which defines speech as "the mediation [*Vermittlung*] of the communal nature of thought," and also "mediation of thought for the individual" (Schleiermacher 1998, 7). Schleiermacher consistently sets hermeneutics in the larger context of communication but does not pursue further elaboration of the mediation concept.

9. For an interesting discussion of Peirce's theory in its more global implications, see Parmentier 1985, 23–48. Parmentier notes that Peirce was relatively uninterested in the physical medium of communication, a point of significant difference with twentieth-century communications theory (Parmentier 1985, 33).

10. See Aristotle, *Poetics* 1447a, where he writes that the modes of imitation "differ from one another in three ways, either in their means, or in their objects, or in the manner of their imitations." The translation is from Aristotle 1984, 2: 2316. Other translators (e.g., S. H. Butcher, *Aristotle's Theory of Poetry and Fine Art* [New York: Dover Publications, 1951], 7), give "medium" here for "means." Gérard Genette, *The Architexte: An Introduction*, explicates this phrase as meaning "literally 'in what?'"—meaning "the sense of one's expressing oneself 'in gestures' or 'in words,' 'in Greek' or 'in English,' 'in prose' or 'in verse,' 'in pentameter' or 'in trimeter,' etc."

(Genette 1992, 12). Aristotle dimly grasps "medium" here, but as inclusive of both what we would call medium and other aspects of language use, such as form or genre. The *Poetics* is concerned after this passage entirely with "objects" and "manners" of imitation; the question of means/medium is dropped altogether. For more extensive commentary on this passage of the *Poetics*, see the edition of Aristotle 1987, 68.

11. The most surprising common use of the word *medium* in the period, however, is (3): "A person believed to be in contact with the spirits of the dead and to communicate between the living and the dead." The puzzle of nineteenth-century spiritualism, which we need only acknowledge briefly here, has been greatly illuminated by historians of technology, who have shown convincingly that such spiritualism is a shadow cast by communications technology itself, a wonderful joke of history confirmed by the tenacity with which the spiritualists sought to use modern technology to capture the voices and images of the dead. For a good discussion of the connection between spiritualism and ideas about communication, see Peters 1999, 89–108.

12. Derrida's objections to Saussure in *Of Grammatology* (Derrida 1974, 29–55) retain its primal deconstructive force, subordinated however to a philosophical agenda that is irrelevant to the concern of this essay. In making the case for writing, Derrida of course wants to claim that all language is, in the special sense of his argument, writing, whereas what I would like to remind us of is the fact of writing as a medium, different from other media and possessing its peculiar effectivity by virtue of that difference.

13. The essay was first delivered in 1958 and published in 1960. Claude E. Shannon published "The Mathematical Theory of Communication" in 1948. It was republished as a book, Claude E. Shannon and Warren Weaver, *The Mathematical Theory of Communication* (Shannon and Weaver 1963). Most of our current notions about the mechanics of communication can be found in Shannon's work, including of course the analysis of the "channel."

14. One might mention Friedrich Kittler in this context, not because his work is by any conceivable measure naïve, but rather because he succeeds in grafting a sophisticated postmodernism onto the premise of technological determinism by way of a certain version of materialism shared by both.

15. Thompson 1995. Thompson gives an account of three types of interaction, (1) face-to-face, (2) mediated interaction, and (3) mediated quasi-interaction. The second refers to interactions such as telephonic, mail, email etc. The third refers to more one-sided seeming interactions initiated by media forms that require no direct response to the maker of the content. These would include novels, most television and film, and many other forms of "entertainment," high or low.

16. With the recession of High Theory, the concept of representation has come to dominate cultural analysis once again, and the challenge to representation by the concept of mediation may be said thus far to have failed. One might cite here the flagship journal of New Historicism, *Representations*, which symptomatically catapulted the concept of representation back to the top of theoretical argot.

### WILLIAM WARNER, "TRANSMITTING LIBERTY"

1. For example, modern scholarship has refuted the long held assumption of the "propaganda school" that Samuel Adams favored, and plotted for, independence from Britain from the earliest years of the imperial crisis (Maier 1976; O'Toole 1976).
2. Such a way of analyzing the American Revolution traverses heterogeneous objects and the disciplines that privilege those objects: the material means of communication practices (communication and technology studies), group organizations (sociology), rhetorical analysis (literary studies), history of ideas (intellectual history), and the narrative of events (political history).
3. Here are few examples of this general trend in recent scholarship: from literary studies of the early period: the collection edited by Neil Rhodes, *The Renaissance Computer: Knowledge Technology in the First Age of Print* (London: Routlege, 2000); and William Warner's *Licensing Entertainment: the Elevation of Novel Reading in Britain, 1684–1750* (1998); from literary studies of new media and science fiction, Katherine Hayles's influential *How We Became Posthuman* (Chicago: University of Chicago Press, 1999); from a political economy of books and copyright, William St. Clair's *The Reading Nation in the Romantic Period* (2004); from media history, Paul Star, *The Creation of the Media: The Political Origins of Modern Communications* (2004); from film and new media studies, Lev Manovich, *The Language of New Media* (2000); from political science, Bruce Bimber, *Information and American Democracy: Technology in the Evolution of Political Power* (Cambridge: Cambridge University Press, 2003); from legal studies, Lawrence Lessig, *Code and Other Laws of the Internet* (2000) and *Free Culture: How Big Media Uses Technology and the law to Lock Down Culture and Control Creativity* (New York: Penguin, 2005); and from early American history, the collection edited by Alfred D. Chandler Jr. and James W. Cortada, *A Nation Transformed by Information: How Information Has Shaped the United States from Colonial Times to the Present* (2000).
4. *American Heritage Dictionary* (New York: Random House, 2009).
5. For this broader application of the concept of the interface, see Johnson 1999. For the concept of a "cultural interface" I am indebted to Lev Manovich's discussion in Manovich 2000, chapter 5. For examples of the utopian longings stirred by interface design, one can contrast Samuel Adams's letters touting the power of the committee of correspondence to other Whigs (Arthur Lee; Richard Henry Lee and Charles Thomson) with David Sarnoff's promotion of radio broadcasting in the early decades of the twentieth century and the "sell" for the networked computer found in Bill Gates's *The Road Ahead* (1995), or the Netscape first annual report (1996).
6. Alex Galloway (2004) offers this suggestive interpretation of protocols: "Protocol is a technique for achieving voluntary regulation within a contingent environment" (7). Galloway's study suggests the many different ways in which voluntary as well as embedded protocols influence the form and content of communication.

### LISA GITELMAN, "MODES AND CODES"

1. This chapter is part of an ongoing project and has already benefited from generous readings by Pat Johnston, P. J. Brownlee, and William Warner. I am grateful for their suggestions.

2. Peters 2006, 142, quoting Samuel Thomas Soemmering of 1809.
3. Switching is the subject of Bernhard Siegert's *Passage des Digitalen* (2003), cited in Peters 2006, 138 and passim. Eliassen and Jacobsen are responding to Crary 1990.
4. Samuel F. B. Morse Papers at the Library of Congress, 1791–1919, Manuscript Division, Library of Congress, Washington, D.C http://memory.loc.gov/ammem/sfbmhtml/sfbmhome.html 10 October 2001 (accessed August 2006).
5. See "Building the Digital Collection," which indicates that "long items were often folded and filmed in segments," so that the contractor who digitized them "reunited the segments to recreate the entire item." http://memory.loc.gov/ammem/sfbmhtml/sfbmbuilding.html (accessed September 2006).
6. http://memory.loc.gov/ammem/mcchtml/corhome.html (accessed August 2006). One could say simply that Words and Deeds is a *digital* collection whereas the Morse Papers is a *digitized* one, were it not for dates on the LOC site that suggest Words and Deeds preceded Morse on-line.
7. Other nations have other "first" telegrams and other inventors of telegraphy.
8. See Thompson 1947, 24.
9. Morse to Vail, May 1, 1844, with addendum of May 2, 1844, box 1A, Vail Telegraph Collection, Smithsonian Institution Archive.
10. Morse, draft caveat, 3 October 1837, Morse Papers 6: 373–378.
11. The painting is part of the collection of the Terra Foundation for American Art.
12. As in other examples of this genre (the gallery picture or *Kunstkammer*), the painter "of necessity 'rehung' the works and in some cases altered their relative sizes" as part of his composition. Tatham 1981, 38–40, esp. 40.
13. See the pencil study of "1226 Louvre Titian," diary of December 1829–February 1830, Morse Papers, http://memory.loc.gov/mss/mmorse/059/059002/0038.jpg.
14. See Staiti 1989, 175–206, quotations from 205, 191. On copying at the Louvre, where rules were instituted later to regulate the practice, see McClellan 1994.
15. Morse to Sidney, 18 January 1832, Samuel F. B. Morse Papers at the Library of Congress, 1791–1919, Manuscript Division, Library of Congress, Washington, D.C.
16. Johnston 2006, 46–47. Morse 1983, 58–59. Morse delivered his lectures in the spring of 1826 but continued to revise them until at least 1840.
17. Staiti 1989, 191; followed in Johnston 2006, 43.
18. Morse to J. F. Cooper 6 September 1832. Papers of Samuel Morse, typescript. Art conservator Felicity Campbell helped me think through Morse's painting process.
19. Cooper's Rembrandt by Morse was *The Angel Leaving Tobias*, which the two friends referred to as "'the steamboat,' a name coined by Mrs. Cooper who likened the apparent motion of the angel's wings to that of the sidewheels [sic] of a steamer." It appears in *The Gallery* at the lower left, reduced in proportion to Teniers's *The Knife Grinder*, so that the two paintings could hang symmetrically behind an ensemble meant to be the Cooper family (Tatham 1981, 40, 44).
20. The Terra Foundation for American Art possesses *Francis I, Study for "The Gallery of the Louvre,"* a copy after Titian, but the location of Cooper's Rembrandt is unknown. Titian's *Francis I, Study for "The Gallery of the Louvre"* (Terra Foundation for American Art); see http://www.terraamericanart.org (accessed November 2006); the copy is 8"×10" and inscribed on its reverse, "To C.R. Leslie, Esq., RA/

from his old friend/Sam. F.B. Morse, P.N.A/Copy of Titian's Francis 1st/New York/ April 1834."
21. Patent 1,647 (20 June 1840), "Telegraph Signs." United States Patent and Trademark Office, http://www.uspto.gov.
22. 11 October 1837 and 24 October 1837, Morse to Vail; Vail Telegraph Collection Box 1A.
23. Undated ink holograph, Morse Papers 6:404.
24. Morse and Vail had terrible trouble keeping the pencil sharpened and ready, so they tried a pen equipped with a reservoir of ink, but that tended to clog up or dry out, and they finally settled upon a simple steel point, which made "an impression upon the paper, not to be mistaken" (Vail 1845, 19).
25. "Grooved railway" is from Morse's patent 1,647 of 1840 and its two reissues.
26. This point is made by Bracha 2005, 458; http://www.obracha.net, accessed September 2006.
27. 56 U.S. 113. See Bracha 2005, chap. 4, for a full discussion of the case and its implications.
28. *Morse et al. v. O'Reilly et al. CCD Ky 1848*; 17 Fed Cas. 871.
29. Vail 1845, 23, 21–22. Vail even had a small set of type cast so that he could include a printed "Specimen of the Telegraphic Language" in his *Description of the American Electro Magnetic Telegraph* (1845). Vail corresponded with F. Lucas of Baltimore about having "points and dashes" cast as type from special matrices, 50 cents per pound; Vail 20 May 1845, Vail Telegraph Collection, box 4.
30. Morse to Vail, 29 May 1844, Vail Telegraph Collection, box 1A.
31. My discussion of the alphabet has been informed by Crain 2000.
32. *Argument of B. R. Curtis, Esq. of Boston, in the Case of Francis O. J. Smith, Complain't vs. Hugh Downing and Als., Respon'ts, in the circuit court of the U.S., Massachusetts District, Hon. Levi Woodbury, Judge Presiding, for an infringement of the letters patent of Samuel F. B. Morse, for the electro magnetic telegraph, June 25 and 26, 1850* (Portland [MA], 1850), 51.
33. *Argument of St. Geo. T. Campbell, Esq. delivered December 1852 before the Supreme Court of the United States, in support of the validity of Morse's Patents for the Electro-Magnetic Telegraph* (Philadelphia 1853), 24; *Argument of George Gifford, Esq. of New York, Delivered in December 1852 at Washington, before the Supreme Court of the United States, in the Case of Henry O'Reilly et al., Appellants, vs. Samuel F.B. Morse, F.O.J. Smith et al., Appellees. Being an appeal from a decision of the U.S. Circuit Court for the district of Kentucky in favor of Prof. Morse's Patents for 'The American Electro-Magnetic Telegraph'* (New York: Wm. C. Bryant & Co., 1853), 23–24.
34. Both from *Telegraph Cases decided in the Courts of America, Great Britain, and Ireland* 1873, 169, 458; emphasis added.

ANN BLAIR AND PETER STALLYBRASS,
"MEDIATING INFORMATION, 1450–1800"

1. See Kwakkel 2003. In England, which was certainly well behind the time, paper was rarely used in the making of books at the beginning of the fifteenth century. But more than half of all English books were made of paper by the end of the century.

2. The first use of "chapter and verse" given by the *Oxford English Dictionary* (*OED*) is 1628, but the phrase was in use in Europe by the end of the sixteenth century. See Saenger 1996, 237–301, 255. See also Smith 1988 and Rouse and Rouse 1991.
3. We use "information," "knowledge" and "data" following the distinctions articulated in Brown and Duguid 2000, 118–120 and Nunberg 1996.
4. This word count is based on Beauvais 1964: 8226 columns at 70 lines per column and 8 words per line.
5. Word count for Nani Mirabelli 1503 based on: 339 folios, 4 columns per folio, 53 lines per column and 6 words per line; for edition of 1620: 2987 columns, 75 lines per column and 12 words per line.
6. Word count for Zwinger 1565: 1428 pages, 2 columns and 70 full lines per page on average, 9 words per line = 1,800,000; Zwinger 1586: 4373 pages, 2 columns and 80 lines per page, 9 words per line = 6,300,000; Beyerlinck 1631: 7468 pages, 2 columns and 77 lines per page, 9 words per line = 10 million.
7. Available on line at http://mdz10.bib-bvb.de/~zedler/zedler2007/index.html. The *Universallexicon* comprised 125,142 columns according to Quedenbaum 1977, 300; I have estimated 8 words per line and 67 lines per column, for a total word count of 67,076,112.
8. I am grateful to Matthew Loy for a word count of the *Encyclopédie* from the facsimile edition (Diderot et al. 1966), based on estimates of two columns per page, 74 lines per column and 9 words per line. Important precursors for books illustrated on a large scale included botanical books. The Plantin Press in Antwerp assembled more that 3,700 woodblocks of plants by the end of the sixteenth century. White 1993 and Voet 1972, 194–252.
9. Vogel 1999, 186. For a detailed analysis of how a preacher stockpiled notes and used them for composing sermons, see Kimnach 1992.
10. For an entry into the literature on medieval *reportationes*, see Bériou 1989; and Hamesse 1986. More generally on early modern notes from oral events see Blair 2008.
11. These include diplomatic correspondence as studied in Dover 2007 or the large surviving correspondence of the Paston family, 1422–1509, in Davis et al., 2004.
12. By the end of the fourteenth century, "paper was four to eight times cheaper than parchment" (Kwakkel 2003, 243). On the explosion of new paper mills during the first decades of printing, see Weiss 1983, 62–69. The role of printing in stimulating paper production is made explicit in De Hamel 1992, 16.
13. Pliny the Younger 1969, I, 176–177 (III.v).
14. Self-improvement was another of Drake's motives, see Sharpe 2000, 89.
15. An attempted purchase of the notes of the German legal scholar Hermann Conring (1606–1681) is reported in Placcius 1689, 185. Books annotated by famous scholars like Joseph Scaliger were also especially sought after; see Scaliger 1977, 4–5. After the death of Carl Linnaeus, Jr., in 1783, a wide variety of people, including Catherine the Great of Russia, King Gustav of Sweden, and botanists in Denmark, Holland, France, Switzerland and Sweden, tried to purchase his father's herbarium, consisting of about 19,000 dried and mounted plants together with his notes on them. Joseph Banks persuaded James Edward Smith to purchase the herbarium, together

with Linnaeus's library and other collections, for £900. See Wulf 2008, 222–223; on this corpus of notes now at the Linnean Society of London, see Müller-Wille and Scharf 2009.

16. We are grateful to Chris Kyle and Jason Peacey for sharing their unpublished work, including Kyle's "Pen, Pencil, Paper, Print: Political Note-taking in Early Stuart England," presented at the History of Material Texts seminar, University of Pennsylvania, March 19, 2007, and Peacey's "Print Ephemera and Political Culture in Seventeenth-Century England," presented at the same seminar on October 7, 2005. See also Mendle 2006 and Henderson 2001.

17. "A Note of goods the Governor took away from divers persons out of the Alfandige," Foster 1900. See also Foster 1896–1902, 4: 81–82.

18. On erasable writing tables, see Stallybrass et al. 2004; Stallybrass 2006; and Stallybrass 2007.

19. Jan Gossart, *Portrait of a Merchant*, Washington, D.C., National Gallery of Art. There is another version of this painting in the John G. Johnson Collection, Philadelphia Museum of Art. See Friedländer et al. 1972, plates 57 and 56. See also Hand and Wolff 1986, 103–107.

20. These erasable notebooks with woodcuts of coins and multiplication tables were printed from Frank Adams's 1577 [?] tables to Oliver Ridge's in 1628 [?]. Given the fragmentary state of many copies, the number of editions that survive in only one copy, and the disappearance rate of all such small books, it is probable that not only most copies but also most *editions* have been lost. John Barnard notes that "the most forcible way to emphasize the high loss rates among short, small-format publications is that the primer, printed in tens of thousands year by year from 1660 to 1700, is now represented by only a single copy in a single library" (Barnard 1999, 150).

21. William Wotton to Evelyn, letter dated Aug. 8, 1699, British Library Evelyn Collection MS 3.3.112, as quoted in Hunter 1998, 123. See also Locke's comment about the publication of Boyle's *General History of the Air*: "I have read them [Boyle's papers] all over very carefully, numbered them according to the titles they belong to and laid them in that order, as best I could, according to the state they are in . . . but yet for all this they are not in a condition to be sent to the printer." Locke to Boyle, letter dated Oct. 21 1691, in *The Correspondence of John Locke*, as quoted in Yeo 2004, 3.

22. Boyle's "indigested" notes are the antithesis of properly ordered notes, which are repeatedly described as "digested." Samuel Hartlib, for instance, emphasizes the importance of "digesting the marrow" of a book in his account of "ordered reading" (or "concinnation"). The reading techniques that Hartlib recommends include the "Pellian and Reineran analytical reading," the "Ordered doctrinal reading of Streso," "Brooks's Method of construing," the "Marginal reading of Dury (or 'methodus duaraeus')" and "Brinsley's Army of Analytical Questions." Hartlib was particularly impressed by Thomas Harrison's "compleatest Art . . . of *excerpendi*." "Hartlib described the technology thus: 'Hee aimes by it to gather 1) All the Authors 2) their Notions or Axiomes 3) their whole discourses. . . The ground of it [is] a passe port with as much paper vpon it as you please. Vpon it there bee slices of paper put on which can bee removed and transposed as one pleases which carries a world of con-

veniences in it.' The result was 'an incredibly easy compend[ium] for quotations,' that Hartlib praised for its 'Compertibility' since it offered 'Mobility to transpose your notions where you will to put in to find presently.' Harrison proposed a system of cross-referencing ('allegations by ciphers') and hoped to complete 'a special logick for the art of collecting'" (Greengrass 2002, 312–313; see also Malcolm 2004).

23. On transposition, see Hunter and Davis 1996, 227.
24. See, for example, the prefaces to the indexes in Zwinger 1586 in which he explains the difficulties posed by synonyms and the diversity of proper names; see also Gesner 1548, 19v: "It is often unpleasant to always go to the index to look for something." "Indicem semper quaerendi causa adire, saepe molestum est." See Blair 2000 and Blair forthcoming, chap. 3.
25. "In illis voluminibus id plerumque minime invenies, quod maxime quaesieris" [In these volumes most often you find least what you seek the most]. Drexel 1638, 139–140; see also 73–74.
26. In his copy of Lodovico Domenichi's *Facetie* (1571), Folger MS H.a.2, Gabriel Harvey wrote: "Enioy the souerain repetition of your most excellent notes. Quotidie lege, lege; sed repete, repete, repete [Daily read, read; but also repeat, repeat, repeat]" (f. 36r).
27. Malebranche, for example, criticized the sciences of memory as a hindrance to clear thinking and a cause of arrogance: "But those sciences relying on memory confuse the mind, upset clear ideas and furnish it with many probabilities of all sorts of subjects, which are our reward for not knowing how to distinguish, examine and see. . . . Sciences relying on memory also naturally inspire pride, for the souls gets inflated and swelled up, so to speak, by the multitude of facts with which the head is filled." Malebranche 1993, II.X.13, 196. Discussed in Grell 2000, 63. But Hooke described a similar observation as proverbial: "[H]ow usual tis for one of these to be defective where the other prevails, may be sufficiently evident from the almost proverbial saying that good wits have ill memories . . . man's memory seems very shallow and infirm and so is very prone to forget circumstances besides it cannot very well propound all it does remember, to be examine'd in order before others and some things with more vehemence and greater concern, and accordingly the understanding is more apt to be sway'd to this or that hand according as it is more affect or presst by this or that instance, and is very liable to oversee some considerable passages, or to neglect them; and thus very apt to be seduced in pronouncing positively for this or that opinion." As quoted in Mulligan 1992. On the shifting valuation of memory, see Yeo 2007 and Yeo 2004.
28. For Melanchthon's account of note taking, we are indebted to Francis Goyet's unpublished essay on *Hamlet* and the commonplace tradition and to Warkentin 2005.
29. We are indebted to the notes of and to conversations with Brooke Palmieri on Pastorius.
30. A precursor to the filing system that Gossart depicts is the legal filing system in medieval England. Leaves of parchment were being filed together with linen thread from at least the twelfth century, and files of English statutes were produced commercially for private consumption by the thirteenth century. See Skemer 1995. Don

Skemer notes that "[a]rchivists have all but ignored the history of the book, while manuscript specialists and codicologists have been wont to exclude archival material (even those in book form) from their purview, though documents account for the vast bulk of writing during five millennia of recorded history" (193).

31. We are deeply indebted to Heather Wolfe's unpublished work on filing systems, some of which was presented as "Note-taking and Filing" at the Renaissance Society of America, Cambridge University, 7 April 2005. For another example of such filing systems, see a file of mid-seventeenth-century tax records in the Public Record Office, London, SP 28/296.

32. "A Bill of money expended by me Henry Linch for necessaries &c for the Comittee at Cambden howse Dec 21th 1643," Public Record Office (PRO), SP 28/212; "An Accompt of what hath been deliver'd for His Majestys Service, To the Clerk of the Hon.ble House of Commons," Folger, MS Add 911. We are indebted to Heather Wolfe for the latter reference.

33. For some suggestive discussions of these movements which have yet to be studied closely, see Zedelmaier 2004, 203; and te Heesen 2005.

34. For some descriptions, see for example, Aldrovandi 1907, listing among his manuscripts: index on burial ritual; catalog of similitudes from the book of similitudes of John of St Giminiano; "index of the *Theatrum vitae humanae* formed with the usual slips glued in alphabetical order on the pages, most of them in the hand of Aldrovandi" (31), Latin proverbs, vernacular proverbs (29), lexicon on crowns (27), Pandechion epistenomicon (103), index of the places where various natural things are born (105), catalog of images of herbs (105).

35. See Gesner 1548, ff. 19r ff (trans., Wellisch 1981).

36. On Gesner's compilation techniques, see Blair 2010, chap. 4.

37. See Tugnoli Pattaro 1977, 15.

38. Steinmann 1987, 20. For some attention to the history of archiving in early modern Europe, see Vismann 2000; and Blair and Milligan 2007.

39. Beyerlinck 1631, proscenium, sig. e2r–e3v. For a later book made entirely from cutting and pasting previous printed books, see Thomas Jefferson's "demystification" of Christianity, *The Life and Morals of Jesus of Nazareth*. Jefferson composed his quadrilingual anti-transcendental "life" from passages clipped out of six copies of the New Testament: two copies of a London 1794 Greek-Latin edition; two copies of a 1802 French edition, printed in Paris; and two copies of an 1804 English edition, printed in Philadelphia. As Jefferson made clear when purchasing his French copies, "a single [copy], or two of different editions would not answer to my purpose" (Jefferson 1982, 30; see also Goodspeed 1947).

40. Beyerlinck 1631, A564. A long section (to A575) is announced: "Catalog of the emperors, kings and illustrious men who exercised astrology, gathered especially from the work of Henricus Ranzovius" and on A575 the following section (to A586) is entitled "warning concerning astrological predictions, from the same work." Beyerlinck referred here quite precisely to Henricus Ranzovius, *Catalogus imperatorum regum et virorum illustrium qui artem Astrologicam amarunt, exercuerunt et ornarunt* (1584).

41. For a nuanced discussion of Zwinger's attitude toward Paracelsus, see Gilly 1977, 57-137, Gilly 1978, 125-223, and Gilly 2002, 253-273.
42. The preface announced that authors would be identified by a letter at the end of each article keyed to a list of contributors and that unsigned articles were authored by Diderot and starred ones edited by him, but this was not consistently put into practice even in the first volume. In later volumes, especially after the book was forbidden in France in 1759, authors identified themselves less frequently, though some continued to do so. Diderot acknowledged too that some authors never allowed themselves to be identified—one of these (possibly d'Holbach) noted that he could only partake of a "collective existence in the Republic of Letters." For an analysis of this difficult question that has attracted considerable scholarship, see Schwab 1969, 244.
43. For example, many of the plates were copied from those made by the Académie des Sciences as part of a survey of trades begun in the seventeenth century and never completed. See Pinault 1991, 355-367.
44. For a history of the use of cards and card catalogs, see Krajewski 2002; also Shackleton 1961, 181.
45. See Minsheu 1617 and Bodleian Library 1983, 32n. 3: Minsheu "brought his dictionary to Oxford, where it was thoroughly checked by his company of 'strangers' and scholars of the University, so that the latter judged it worthy of publication."
46. "The Calepino was nothing at first; it was a pitiable work when it came out of the hands of Ambrogio Calepino. Nonetheless there were skilled people who, seeing that one could make something good from his project, did the work of cleaning it up, of putting it in order and of augmenting it to the point where we see it today. So that there is almost nothing left but the title and the name of the author that come from Calepino." (Baillet 1685, vol. 1, avertissement au lecteur, sig. eiijr-v.)
47. See De Grazia 1991.
48. Our account of Franklin and intellectual property is largely drawn from Green 2006.
49. *A Defence of the Rev. Mr. Hemphill's Observations; Or, an Answer to the Vindication of the Reverend Commission* (Philadelphia: Benjamin Franklin, 1735) in Franklin 1959, 96-97.

### CLIFFORD SISKIN, "MEDIATED ENLIGHTENMENT"

1. For a full recasting of the Romantic period in terms of system, see Siskin 2009.
2. The opening the Scots capitalized on was the kind of opening that appears when a society that produces a new technology becomes saturated by it. In Britain's case in the eighteenth century, a society with print became a print culture, reconfiguring along fault lines both abstract and literal. The fault line of national identity materialized for Smith as open shelf space in a newly public library, and he literally filled it.
3. For a rethinking of Wordsworth's entire career in terms of his connection to Enlightenment, see Siskin 2006.
4. The interrelations between the novel and system through the long eighteenth century are traced in Siskin 2001.

ROBERT MILES, "ROMANTICISM, ENLIGHTENMENT, AND MEDIATION"
1. Thus René Wellek's influential definition of the subject of Romanticism: "Imagination for the view of poetry, nature for the view of the world, and symbol and myth for poetic style" (cited in McGann 1992, 735).
2. For a recent reflection, see O'Brien 2005, 243–245.
3. For example, see Wordsworth 1993 and Thompson 1997, 427.
4. For an extended comparison of the two poems, see Miles 2008, chapter 5.
5. http://www.rc.umd.edu/editions/contemps/barbauld/poems1773/meditation.html.
6. For the role of Milton in Barbauld's poem, see Miles 2008.
7. For a reading of *Frost at Midnight* as a Gothic poem, see Hogle 1998, 283–292.
8. I shall compare the first and final versions, as the changes conveniently highlight the major themes of my reading. All quotations are from the varorium edition of the poem found in Stillinger 1994, 154–157. Unqualified line references are to the final, 1834 version. Stillinger does not give line references for the 1798 variants; accordingly, page numbers are used.
9. In a footnote attached to the 1798 and 1812 versions of the poem Coleridge explains that "[i]n all parts of the kingdom these films are called *strangers*, and supposed to portend the arrival of some absent friend" (Stillinger 1994, 154).
10. Wordsworth 1993, n.p.
11. For a study of the diverse ideological positions encoded within sensibility, see Jones 1993.

HELGE JORDHEIM, "THE PRESENT OF ENLIGHTENMENT"
1. For my translations of both Foucault's "Qu'est-ce que les Lumières" texts, I have consulted the English versions in Foucault 1988 and Foucault 1994d.
2. "In einem Buche als Schrift *redet* der Autor zu seinem Leser; und der, welcher sie gedruckt hat, *redet* durch seine Exemplare nicht für sich selbst, sondern ganz und gar in Namen des Verfassers."
3. "[D]aher werde der briefliche Spitz regelmäßig weg- und anschwimmen wie eine poste aux ânes, aber nachschiffen dürfe ich den Briefträger nicht—und so (schließet der Korrespondent, der sich *Knef* unterzeichnet) werde mir der Hund wie ein Pegasus so viel Nahrungsaft zutragen, daß ich statt des dünnen Vergißmeinnichts eines Almanachs einen dicken Kohlstrunk von Folianten in die Höhe zöge."

ARVIND RAJAGOPAL, "ENLIGHTENMENT IN INDIA"
1. The argument about promoting empathy via communication was influentially formulated in Lerner 1958. For a recent reformulation of this argument, see Appadurai 1996.
2. See the discussion in Schlesinger 1977, 633–634.
3. The interview was broadcast over American educational television on September 21, 1976.
4. See, in this connection, Goffman 1976, 22.
5. For an example that approximates the first kind of approach, see Williamson 1978. Williamson concedes that ads work by fostering a process of identification, bypassing any analytical criticism that may be made of ads. Nevertheless, she returns

again and again to criticize the endless chain of equivalences set up by advertising, assuming that communication based in nonmarket structures are liable to be more rooted and historically accurate. For an example of the second kind of approach, see Goffman 1976.

6. Adorno expressed his criticism of such an approach thus: "[T]he mere concept of use-value by no means suffices for a critique of the commodity character, but only leads back to a stage prior to the division of labor." Adorno to Benjamin, letter dated 2 August 1935 (Adorno et al. 2007, 114). Goffman for his part observes, parenthetically, "It is rather wrong, alas, to say that only advertisers advertise. Indeed, even those concerned to oppose commercial versions of the world must pictorialize their arguments through images which are selected according to much the same principles as those employed by the enemy" (Goffman 1976, 27).

7. Of the top ten newspapers in India, only one is English, namely, the *Times of India*—and although it is smaller by far in circulation than Malayalam papers like *Manorama*, or Hindi papers like *Dainik Bhaskar* and *Jagran*, its revenues are by far the highest, signaling the buying power of the English-language readership as well as the cultural predilection of advertisers to spend disproportionately on this audience segment.

8. It may be argued that the Indian film industry has addressed and resolved the questions of the depiction of desire and fulfillment and thus represents a fully developed public culture in post-Independence India, but this is not necessarily correct. Social conflicts as depicted in film narratives are invariably resolved by a mode of external intervention, either of the law or of the local or family patriarch, and often in an alliance of the two. The actual contradictions within relationships may therefore be depicted without necessarily carrying them through to their own internal resolution. In advertisements, by contrast, such a device is unsatisfactory, since the narrative must culminate in a latent or patent message of commodity consumption. The entire sequence of the ad has to build up to this conclusion, whereas the film's worth is not so dependent on its ending. Some process of working through actually existing relationships is therefore unavoidable in ads.

### PAULA MCDOWELL, "MEDIATING MEDIA PAST AND PRESENT"

1. Havelock and other theorists of what Ong calls "primary oral cultures (cultures with no knowledge at all of writing)" employ the concept of "orality" in a specific sense that needs to be distinguished from the vague usage in common parlance today. Nonetheless, it should be noted that the term "orality" is not a modern coinage but dates back to at least 1666, where it was used in a theological context as part of a vigorous ongoing debate concerning scripture versus "oral tradition" as the rule of faith (discussed below).
2. See also 9 n. 18.
3. For a more recent commentary, see Johns 2002, 106–125.
4. Baron, Lindquist, and Shevlin, eds. 2007. This volume contains essays by Ann Blair, Roger Chartier, Peter Stallybrass, and myself, among others.
5. See also Williams 1966; Kroeber and Kluckhohn 1952; and Siskin 1998, 72–74.

6. For an important reminder that the crystallization of a concept may predate the use of any particular word or phrase, see Peter de Bolla's essay in this volume.
7. I explore some of the implications of the lapse of the Licensing Act in *The Women of Grub Street* (McDowell 1998). See also Feather 1988 and Astbury 1978.
8. James, *To the Honourable House of Commons. Gentlemen, Since You have been pleased to lay such a heavy Tax upon Paper*, n.d. (c. 1696–1698), reprinted in James 2005, 96–97. James was the grandmother of Jacob Ilive (discussed by Adrian Johns in this volume).
9. See, for instance, Kernan's reading of Pope through the lens of McLuhan in Kernan 1989, 8–16.
10. See also Foxon 1991.
11. On early modern scholars' methods for information management, see the essay by Ann Blair and Peter Stallybrass in this volume.
12. See, for instance, *An Epistle from Mr. Pope, to Dr. Arbuthnot* (London, 1734), in which Pope repeatedly uses the word "print," but only as a verb.
13. I have also benefited here from Hudson 1996a "'O Divinum Scripturae Beneficium!'"
14. Lafitau, ed. Fenton and Moore, 1974–1977, 1: lxxxvi. Lafitau's work was originally published as *Moeurs des sauvages amériquains, comparées aux moeurs des premiers temps*.
15. Significantly, Wood's essay was first published privately in 1767 and 1769 as *An Essay on the Original Genius of Homer* [no place of publication given on title page]. Only after his death in 1771 was the title changed to *An Essay on the Original Genius and Writings of Homer* (London, 1775), my emphasis.
16. Rousseau also briefly speculates that Homer might have been unable to write.
17. Stewart, *Elements of the Philosophy of the Human Mind*, Part 1 [1792], reprinted in Hamilton, ed., *Works* (1854–1860), 2: 391.
18. I argue this in detail in "'The Art of Printing Was Fatal'" (McDowell 2010) and "'The Manufacture and Lingua-facture of *Ballad-Making*'" (McDowell 2006). See also Maureen McLane's essay in this volume.
19. See Addison, *Spectator* 70 (21 May 1711), 74 (25 May 1711), and 85 (7 June 1711).
20. For recent attempts to undo this binary, see Fumerton and Guerrini forthcoming; Perry 2006 on "Ballads and Songs in the Long Eighteenth Century"; McLane's essay in the present volume; and McDowell 2006.
21. See Poovey 1998, especially 15.
22. Johannes Fabian suggests that the "denial of coevalness" of actually coexisting peoples is a "constitutive phenomenon" of the modern discipline of anthropology, a discipline whose origins he traces to this period (Matti Bunzl, foreword to Fabian 2003, x–xi).
23. See, for instance, Blair's "Critical Dissertation on the Poems of Ossian," where he explicitly links the characteristics of Ossian's oral poetry to his "very remote aera": "there are four great stages through which men successively pass in the progress of society. The first and earliest is the life of hunters; pasturage succeeds to this, as the ideas of property begin to take root; next agriculture; and lastly, commerce. Throughout Ossian's poems, we plainly find ourselves in the first of these periods of society" (reprinted in Macpherson 1996, 345–408; 353).

24. See also McLane 2006, which shows how James Beattie's poem "The Minstrel; or, The Progress of Genius" adapts stadial theory to theorize the evolution of poetry since "rude ages."
25. Stewart, *Life . . . of Adam Smith* [1793], reprinted in Hamilton, ed., *Works* (1854–1860), 10: 54.
26. Stewart, *Elements of the Philosophy of the Human Mind*, Part 1 [1792], reprinted in Hamilton, ed., *Works* (1854–1860), 2: 391.
27. For a concise critique of the "stages" model of media shift, see Love 2003, 45–64.

MAUREEN N. MCLANE, "MEDIATING ANTIQUARIANS IN BRITAIN, 1760–1830"

1. My discussion here and throughout the first half of this essay draws upon McLane 2008, especially chapters 2 and 3.
2. On "mediality" as "the general condition within with, under certain circumstances, something like 'poetry' or 'literature' can take shape," see David E. Wellbery's foreword to Kittler 1995, xiii. To Wellbery's "poetry" and "literature," we might add "balladeering," "literary history," or "cultural nationalism," all of which took shape within the circumstances of late eighteenth-century print.
3. One can't help but give short shrift here to the full nuances, historical, inter/national, and theoretical, of Ossian, debates over Ossian, and "Ossianism," but regarding the current state of scholarly discussion, it is perhaps most economical to quote Fiona Stafford: "*The Poems of Ossian* look less and less like the quaint hoax of a few decades ago" (Stafford 1996, xviii). For revitalized discussion in folklore as well as literary studies, see Porter 2001. See, too, Manning 2007, 517–540.
4. For a trenchant analysis of the problem of defining a "ballad," see Dugaw 2006, 97–113. Dugaw notes that most scholars adopt a fairly standard distinction between "traditional" and "broadside" ballads; yet these distinctions will not always hold and were themselves artifacts of eighteenth-century balladeers' polemical classifications and their "new confrontational model of balladry" (150), as Paula McDowell strikingly argues in McDowell 2006, 149–176.
5. See especially Paula McDowell's essay in this volume; and Nicholas Hudson's several works, including Hudson 2002, 240–255.
6. On the range of historical writing and method in the eighteenth century, and on the methodological debates between *érudits* and *philosophes* (loosely approximating the split between antiquarians and philosophical historians in Scotland), see Momigliano 1966, 1–39.
7. Quoted in Andrew Skinner's (1997) introduction.
8. "Note to Child Maurice" in Jamieson 1806, 3.
9. On source mediation, see Groom 1999; for example, his introduction, 7, and 191. On the problematic of authenticity, see, for example, Stewart 1994.
10. See, for example, Pinkerton 1781, featuring several poems "now first published from tradition," which within five years he conceded were his own. For his confession and retraction, see Pinkerton 1786, cxxviii, cxxix.
11. On Mrs. Brown, a famous "polite" informant for Scott, Jamieson, and indirectly for later compilers like Child, see Walter Scott's 1802 introduction to Scott 1830, 37.

12. In a famous and possibly invented passage in her son James Hogg's *Memoirs*, much quoted in the literature since: see Armstrong 1997, 249.
13. See Child 1881. That college students were asked to collect ballads from Irish Americans suggests the continuing class stratifications in balladeering as well as its ethnic turn in the United States.
14. See Kevis Goodman's trenchant discussion of "medium," etc., in Goodman 2004, 77–78.
15. See Langan 2001, 49–70: "[T]he medium of print becomes recognizable *as* a medium (contra Kittler) by its attempt to 'deliver' audiovisual information" (70). A "universal medium" does not mean a *monolithic* or *monotechnological* medium, however: there were and are many technical ways to enter the kingdom (or republic?) of print.
16. See Motherwell 1827, introduction. On Motherwell's theoretical contribution, see Brown 1996, 175–189.
17. Extended "inquiries" and sharp-eyed and eared scrutiny also ultimately revealed the author of one of the popular eighteenth-century settings of the old air known as "The Flowers of the Forest." Stenhouse wrote with satisfaction: "Miss Elliot's ballad was published anonymously about the year 1755. From its close and happy imitation of ancient manners, it was by many considered as a genuine production of some old but long-forgotten minstrel. It did not, however, deceive the eagle eye of Burns. 'This fine ballad,' says he, 'is an even more palpable imitation than *Hardyknute*. The *manners* are indeed old, but the language is of yesterday. Its author must very soon be discovered.'—*Reliques*. It was so" (Johnson 1853, 4: 66). Here we see the tracks of a communal detection, Burns's natively informed instinctive suspicion followed up and confirmed by sedulous antiquaries (and fellow Scots), among them Walter Scott.
18. For Scott's concept of a "collated edition," see, for example, his note to "Dowie Dens of Yarrow": "I found it easy to collect a variety of copies; but very difficult to select from them such a collated edition, as might, in any degree, suit the taste of these more light and giddy-paced times" (Scott 1830, 147). Scott did not seek to publish a single version of a ballad; he believed in the comparative scrutiny of copies, when possible, and exercised a rather free, if informed, editorial hand—much to the consternation of later ballad collectors and compilers (e.g., Child and James Kinsley, editor of the 1969 *Oxford Book of Ballads*).
19. Macherey explicitly calls for a critical science which would produce, rather than assume, an object of knowledge. Literary criticism emerges, in his account, as a kind of knowledge which should produce its object, literature. See Macherey 1978, 7.
20. This insight into Chaucerian pronunciation came from none other than Francis James Child (see his "Observations on the Language of Chaucer" [Child 1863]). Child was, among other things, the first professor of literature at Harvard, a medievalist, and the editor of the magisterial *English and Scottish Popular Ballads* (Boston: Houghton Mifflin, 1882–1898): a diagnostic conjunction of research interests.

## ANNE FASTRUP, "MEDIATING *LE PHILOSOPHE*"

1. As we know there was neither freedom of the press nor freedom of speech in the Old Regime. The printed public was subject to censorship.
2. P. N. Furbank sums up the reaction of the philosophers to bad press in this way: "It cannot be said that, as a body, the philosophes were very philosophical in the face of criticism. They were inclined to put it down to unprincipled malice and would react very testily, each in his own way: Voltaire with gleeful vengefulness, Diderot with self-righteous indignation and d'Alembert with petulant haughtiness. Nor were they squeamish in the means they resorted to suppress it. For d'Alembert, though, criticism was more than an annoyance: it was an outrage to all civilised values, and he could see no reason why he should put up with it" (Secker and Warburg 1992, 169).
3. Here I am relying on the very negative representation of journalism and the printed press in the *Encyclopédie*; and Benhamou 1986; Shaw 1966; and finally Gary Bruce Rodgers, who describes Diderot's attitude to the press as being increasingly paranoid, hostile, and defensive. See Rodgers 1973, 75.
4. Benhamou 1986, 410.
5. *Encyclopédie* (Stuttgart-Bad Cannstart 1967, Friedrich Frommann Verlag), 8, 898.
6. "Ecrivains [qui] prostituaient leurs plumes à l'argent, à la faveur, au mensonge, à l'envie et aux vices les plus indignes d'une homme bien né," *Encyclopédie*, vol 13, p. 502.
7. Denis Diderot, *Diderot on Art*, vol. 1, *The Salon of 1765 and Notes on Painting*, ed. and trans. John Goodman, intro. by Thomas Crow (New Haven: Yale University Press, 1995), pp. x–xi.
8. "les choses sont dites et représentées tout à la fois; que dans le même temps que l'entendement les saisit, l'âme en est émue, l'imagination les voit, et l'oreille les entend" (*Lettre sur les sourds et muets*).

## JOHN BENDER, "NOVEL KNOWLEDGE"

1. The episodes in *Walden* titled "Economy" and "The Bean-Field" specifically recall Crusoe's experiments with crops.
2. Lennox was in direct correspondence with Richardson and Johnson during the composition of the novel. The claim that Johnson may have written the final chapter, from which these quotations are drawn, is skeptically addressed by Margaret Doody in the appendix to Lennox 1989, 419–428. On the standing of fiction as a mode of inquiry leading to fact or truth, see Bender 1998.
3. Dictionary citations come from the various editions of the *Dictionnaire de l'Académie Française* contained in the ARTFL database (http://humanities.uchicago.edu/orgs/ARTFL/). English citations are from the *Oxford English Dictionary Online* (http://dictionary.oed.com/entrance.dtl).
4. I have dropped Hume's italics. See the analytical index in Hume 1978 under "experience," "experiment," "knowledge," "judgement," and "probability."
5. For instances of Thoreau's many uses of "experiment" and "experience," see, for instance, *Walden* (Thoreau 1959), 1, 6, 41, 44–45, 52, 135, 171, 251.
6. Bacon is taken as background in Dear's book and receives light treatment because the focus is on developments across the seventeenth century.

7. Sir Francis Bacon, *The Advancement of Learning*, 72. Located in the database found at http://etext.library.adelaide.edu.au/b/bacon/francis/.
8. On factuality, see also Poovey 1998 and Daston 2005, 11–24.
9. Attempts at replication raised their own specters because the literal replication of the equipment that produced the original findings was dependent on highly skilled professionals. On the central role of technical glassmaking to Newton's success in his optical experiments, see Schaffer 1989.
10. The "Rules of Reasoning" is discussed by McMullin 1967 and by Westfall 1991, 801.
11. The authorship of this piece has not generally been disputed, nor is Defoe's authorship necessary to my argument. For doubts about Defoe's authorship, see Starr 2003. For a rebuttal, see Walton 2007.
12. Gallagher, in turn, cites Martinez-Bonati 1980.
13. The citations may also be found by searching "experience" in *Robinson Crusoe* at http://collections.chadwyck.com.
14. The citations may also be found by searching "experience" in *Gulliver's Travels* at http://collections.chadwyck.com.
15. I have dropped some of Locke's italics.
16. On Condorcet, see Gigerenzer 1989, 17. See also Condorcet 1955b.
17. See Molesworth 2004.
18. John Richetti read an early draft of this essay and suggested the idea, noted earlier, that Gulliver is inconsistent in his judgments.

ADRIAN JOHNS, "THE PIRATICAL ENLIGHTENMENT"

1. Israel 2001, esp. 275–294, 684–703; Champion 2003, 45–68; Jacob 1981, 182–208.
2. For Enlightenment fireworks, see Werrett 2007a; 2007b, 325–347.
3. The source of modern theories on this subject is, of course, Jürgen Habermas's *The Structural Transformation of the Public Sphere: An Inquiry into a Category of Bourgeois Society* (Habermas 1989). There is now a very large literature on it. Good introductions to the British, French, and German literature are Brewer 1995, 1–21; Chartier 1991; and Redekop 2000. For an introduction, see Blanning 2002, 103–182; and for theoretical perspectives, extending well beyond the eighteenth century, Warner 2002.
4. The standard discussion of this topic is Woodmansee 1994, 35–55. Woodmansee is currently writing a book that will give the definitive account of these debates. The best brief introduction to *Naturphilosophie* in English is Jardine 1996, 230–245. The best introduction to book piracy in Germany in this period is Wittmann 2004, presented at the conference The History of Books and Intellectual History, Princeton University, 2004, http://www.princeton.edu/csb/conferences/december_2004/papers/Wittman_Paper.doc.
5. Meusel 1778; Ward 1974, 84–91.
6. Redekop 2000, esp. 31–32, 37–39; Woodmansee 1994, 11–34, esp. 27–29; 40–41.
7. Wittmann 1999, 284–312, esp. 295–301; Blanning 2002, 136–144, 158–159; Ward 1974, 59–91; Cook 1993, 25–63.
8. Lessing 1970–1979, 5: 781–787, esp. 5: 784; Goethe 1981, 9: 517–518; Graff 1981, 7.1: 191–588; Woodmansee 1994, 48; Unseld 1996, 27–28, 75–79.

9. For a sampling of sources, see Ashfield and de Bolla 1996.
10. Smith 2004; see also Abrams 1953, 57–59; Kind 1906, 14–58; Steinke 1917, 17–40; and Cunningham and Jardine 1990, 1–9.
11. Duff 1770, 341; Duff 1767, 169–170, 275, 281; Redekop 2000, 218–220; Schaffer 1990, 82–98. For Richardson's editorial comments in the composition of the *Conjectures* see Pettit 1971, 479–492; and on the circulation and reception, 495–504.
12. Berlin 1998, 393; for the French projects, see Spary 2000, e.g., 88–98.
13. Herder 2002, 205–206; Abrams 1953, 204–205; Blanning 2002, 244.
14. Herder 2002, 193–194, 196; Richards 2002, 222–225. Herder also associated the creative power of genius with "mating," resulting in a spontaneity that was not characteristic of ordered thought: Schick 1971, 81–87.
15. Forster 2002, ix, 217; Berlin 1998, 418.
16. Herder 2002, 172–173, 217–219 and n35; Berlin 1998, 385–386.
17. Redekop 2000, 168–220, esp. 187–189. Herder's "Do we still have the Public and Fatherland of the Ancients?" was composed in 1765 and republished three decades later in his *Briefe zur Beförderung der Humanität*.
18. Barnard 1965, 77–78; Berlin 1998, 359–435, esp. 395; Vopa 1995, 5–24, esp. 17; Redekop 2000, 205, 239.
19. Schmidt 1996.
20. This was one of Kant's first pieces to be translated into English, in 1798, along with the Enlightenment essay and several others. The translation referred to unauthorized reprinters as "counterfeiters" and made new reference to "copyright." See Kant 1798, 1: 225–239. See also Selwyn 2000, 21.
21. These speculations are inspired by the rich literature on the uncanny but also by an emerging discussion of automata. Sources include Schaffer 1999, 126–165; Chapuis and Droz 1958; Chapuis and Gelis 1928; Riskin 2004, 99–133; and Winter 1998.
22. Fichte 1964, 409–426 (orig. May 1793); Woodmansee 1994, 52.
23. Jardine 1996; Richards 2002, e.g., 159–166; Woodmansee 1994, 52–53; Moran 1990, 117–134.
24. See Guillory 2002, 19–43, esp. 26–28.
25. Sherman and Bently 1999.

MARY POOVEY, "FINANCING ENLIGHTENMENT, PART ONE"

1. NOTE BY MARY POOVEY AND IAN BAUCOM: Ah, collaboration! It seems like such a wonderful idea, with ideas passing back and forth in scintillating conversation, words tumbling from one person's syntax into the other's, as both writers become cleverer together. In the fall of 2006, when Mary was briefly teaching at Duke, where Ian was department chair, collaboration also momentarily seemed possible. It was this possibility—as well as the reward it promised—that inspired the pages that follow. In practice, however, and despite the undeniable advantages digital communications now give us, it proved impossible for us to engage in an ongoing exchange of ideas and writing. In the end, Ian and Mary managed one long, face-to-face conversation in a coffeehouse in Durham and one brief telephone conversation; then Mary wrote her half of the essay and sent it to Ian, who wrote his half, out of the research he had been doing as much as in response to Mary's part. We

next talked just before our presentation at the Mediating Enlightenment conference, in the kind of telegraphic staccato mandated by plane delays and the press of other obligations. We preface our contribution, in this two-part essay sharing a common title, with these remarks to underscore one of the main points each of us makes in these pages: when subjected to the crucible of everyday habits and demands, abstract ideas often turn out to be less than the sum of their parts. Or, more to the point, ideas formulated at the level of abstraction can cover over or distort features that more detailed analysis can make visible. In the case of our contribution to this volume, the abstraction we wanted to complicate by this only slightly more detailed account of our work is "collaboration": in one sense, we did collaborate; but, in another, our separate institutional, professional, and familial obligations made our fantasy version of collaboration impossible. In the case of the pages that follow, the abstractions we want to interrogate include those that assimilate a range of monetary forms into "money," a variety of colonial activities into the numbers in a company ledger, and bodies (or parts of bodies) into proof that violence belongs to a "just war." Mary's emphasis falls on the monetary side of this tally sheet, Ian on the juridical; but both of us want to ask readers to consider the extent to which "enlightenment"—not to mention "the Enlightenment"—typically turns on effacing a level of detail so as to make a(nother) level of abstraction clear.

BERNHARD SIEGERT, "'THE HORRIFYING TIES, FROM WHICH THE PUBLIC ORDER ORIGINATES'"

1. Koselleck explicitly described the public (*Öffentlichkeit*) as a "medium" of private opinions in which these prove to be laws.
2. Jacques Lacan, "The *Mirror Stage* as Formative of the Function of the I as Revealed in Psychoanalytic Theory" (1949) in Lacan 1966.
3. "C'est-à-dire que ces choses dont le gouvernement doit prendre la charge, ce sont les hommes, mais dans leurs rapports, leurs liens, leurs intrications avec choses que sont les richesses, les ressources, les subsistances ... ce sont les hommes dans leurs rapports avec ces autres choses que sont les costumes, les habitudes, les manières de faire ou de penser ..." (Foucault 1989, 100).
4. "La politique est l'art de lire dans l'avenir" (quoted in Schneider 1994, 327).
5. "Die Polizey" was first mentioned in 1799 by Schiller as a play he intended to write.
6. See Fontenelle 1740, 2: 146 f.
7. Schiller 2004, 3: 190.
8. Voltaire to Friedrich II, letter dated November 14, 1776, in Frederick II, King of Prussia, *Friedrich des Zweiten von Preussen hinterlassene Werke* (1789), 14: 316.

MICHAEL WARNER, "THE PREACHER'S FOOTING"

1. The debates I have in mind are too extensive to be summarized easily, but essential works include Bhargava 1998, Asad 2003, Scott and Hirschkind 2006, Taylor 2007, Warner, VanAntwerpen, and Calhoun 2010, and Masuzawa 2005.
2. The present essay is part of a larger project that is slated to be published by the University of Pennsylvania press under the title *The Evangelical Public Sphere*; that book will lay out this argument in more detail.

3. To my dismay, I have sometimes seen my own work cited to support this view. Important recent works in this vein include Gustafson 2000, Gustafson 2008, Looby 1996, and Loughran 2007.
4. Bailyn's book had been published in 1967.
5. Stout, like Gustafson and others to whom the concept of orality is important, seems not to have noticed that his use of the term is so different from the understanding proposed by Walter Ong that Ong cannot be cited as a precedent; and no theoretical justification for the new usage was worked out. Ong famously distinguished between primary orality, found only in societies without writing, and secondary orality, in which writing is practiced by elites but does not touch large segments of the society (Ong 1982). Neither of these apply to modern state societies, which are so thoroughly structured around literate institutions and imaginaries that no one, no matter how illiterate, is untouched by the ideologies of script. In such contexts, one can speak at best of tertiary orality. But what would justify the assumption that all contexts of speaking and hearing have a common significance in such a society? The term "orality" generally signals an a priori commitment to that view rather than an argument for it.
6. See Lambert 1999, Hall 1994, and O'Brien 1994.
7. The 1547 edition is titled *Certayne sermons, or homelies appoynted by the kynges Maiestie, to be declared and redde, by all persones, vicars, or curates, euery Sondaye in their churches, where they haue cure*. Its preface decries the "idolatrie" that has resulted from "diversitie of preachyng" and prescribes itself as a remedy. "Finally, that all Curates, of what learnynge soever they be may have some Godly and fruitful lessons in a readines, to reade and declare unto their parishioners, for their edifying instruction, and comforte . . . his Majestie commaundeth and streyghtely chargeth, all Persones, Vicares, Curates, and all other, havyng spirituall cure, every Sondaye in the yere, at high Masse, when the people be moste gathered together to reade and declare to their parishioners playnly, and distinctely, in suche ordre, as they stande in the boke, (excepte any Sermon bee Preached) and then for that cause onely, and for none other, the reading of the sayde Homelie, to be differred unto the nexte Sondaye folowyng. And when the foresayde boke of Homelies is redde over, the kynges Maiesties pleasure is, that the same bee repeted, and redde agayn, in suche lyke sorte, as was before prescribed, unto suche tyme, as hys graces pleasure, shall further be knowen in thys behalfe" (A3–4). By the time of the 1582 edition, printed by Christopher Barker, the preface has been changed to make explicit the complaint that "all they which are appointed Ministers, have not the gift of preaching sufficiently to instruct the people, which is committed unto them" (*Certaine sermons* 1582, A2).
8. As the scriptoria had earlier. Useful studies of the media involved in medieval preaching include D'Avray 1985 and Rouse 1979.
9. This is the subject of a book in progress by Meredith Neuman of Clark University.
10. It seems to me that evidence of this shorthand culture declines sharply after the first quarter of the eighteenth century, and it would be interesting to know if that trend correlates with evangelicalism.
11. Thomas Shepard's sermon "Of Ineffectual Hearing of the Word" is available in Warner 1999.

12. J. A. Leo Lemay speculates on the preachers Franklin might have heard in Lemay 2005.
13. See the very important analysis of this phenomenon in Ford 2002.
14. On this subject, see Hall 1972.

MICHAEL MCKEON, "MEDIATION AS PRIMAL WORD"

1. See Alexander Gottlieb Baumgarten, *Meditationes philosophicae de nonnullis ad poema pertinentibus* (1735), secs. cxv–cxvi; *Aesthetica* (1750), sec. 1. See the discussion and translations in Guyer 2004, 15.
2. For an account of this shift from an object- to a subject-oriented interest in beauty, see Stolnitz 1961, 185–204.
3. See generally Kristeller 1965, 163–227.
4. Freud 1957, 11: 155–161.
5. See Fontenelle, "Digression sur les anciens et les modernes" (1688), in Fontenelle 1955, 166. The "Digression" first appeared in Fontenelle's *Poésies pastorales* (1688). The significance of the Quarrel for the modern division between the arts and the sciences, as well as for the emergence of the idea of the aesthetic, receives excellent treatment by Patey 1997, 32–71. As in the case of the "Scientific Revolution," the oppositional categorization of the "arts" and the "sciences" was far less definitive, even by the end of the eighteenth century, than historical hindsight might presume. For a more detailed and less tidy account of this development, see Spadafora 1990, chap. 2.
6. See Shanahan 2008, 2002. This paragraph is indebted to Shanahan's work.
7. Addison and Steele 1965, no. 411 (June 21, 1712). Compare George Berkeley: "[I]t is usual with me to consider my self, as having a natural Property in every Object that administers Pleasure to me. . . . By these Principles I am possessed of half a dozen of the finest Seats in *England*, which in the Eye of the Law belong to certain of my Acquaintance," Berkeley 1982, *Guardian*, no. 49, May 7, 1713. The third Earl of Shaftesbury's principle of disinterestedness, according to which virtue, truth, and beauty are their own reward, has a similar application. "[T]aken with the Beauty of the Ocean," Shaftesbury writes, "and seeking how to command it," the Doge of Venice goes "in Nuptial Ceremony . . . to wed the *Gulf*" so as to call it "properly *my own*." Yet in that action he "has less *Possession* than the poor *Shepherd*, who from a hanging Rock, or Point of some high Promontory, stretch'd at his ease, forgets his feeding flock, while he admires *her Beauty*." Shaftesbury points the moral by remarking how "absurd" would be he who, viewing a beautiful landscape, "shou'd for the *Enjoyment* of the Prospect, require the *Property* or *Possession* of the Land" (Shaftesbury 1711, 2: pt. 3, sec. 2, 396–397).
8. "Mr. *Locke*, my Lord *Shaftsbury*, Dr. *Mandeville*, Mr. *Hutchinson*, Dr. *Butler*, &c." (Hume's note).
9. Johnson 1968, 76–78. Johnson's commonsensical critique does not do justice, perhaps, to the reflexive or doubled state of mind that other commentators have noted. After all, to affirm that the spectators are "always in their senses" lacks the necessary precision if the real question is the degree to which they are in their senses.

# REFERENCES

Aarsleff, Hans. 1982. *From Locke to Saussure: Essays on the Study of Language and Intellectual History.* Minneapolis: University of Minnesota Press.

Abrams, M. H. 1953. *The Mirror and the Lamp: Romantic Theory and the Critical Tradition.* New York: Oxford University Press.

Adams, Frank. 1577? *Writing Tables, with a Necessarie Calendar for xxv Yeares.* London: Frank Adams.

Adams, John. 1989. *Papers of John Adams.* Ed. Gregg L. Lint. Vol. 8, March 1779–February 1780. Cambridge, Massachusetts: The Belknap Press of Harvard University Press.

———. 1996. *Papers of John Adams.* Ed. Gregg L. Lint. Vol. 9, March 1780–July 1780. Cambridge, Massachusetts: The Belknap Press of Harvard University Press.

Adams, Samuel. 1904–1908. *The Writings of Samuel Adams.* 4 vols. Ed. Harry Alonzo Cushing. New York: Putnam.

Addison, Joseph, and Richard Steele. 1965. *The Spectator.* 5 vols. Ed. Donald Frederic Bond. Oxford: Clarendon Press.

Agamben, Giorgio. 2005. *State of Exception.* Chicago: University of Chicago Press.

Aldrovandi, Ulisse, et al. 1907. *Catalogo dei Manoscritti di Ulisse Aldrovandi.* Ed. Lodovico Frati, with Alessandro Ghigi and Albano Sorbelli. Bologna: N. Zanichelli.

Allen, Charles, ed. 1873. *Telegraph Cases Decided in the Courts of America, Great Britain, and Ireland.* New York: Hurd and Houghton.

Anon. 1685. *An Enquiry: Whether Oral Tradition or the Sacred Writings, Be the Safest Conservatory and Conveyance of Divine Truths, Down from Their Original Delivery, through All Succeeding Ages in Two Parts.* London: Printed for Robert Clavel.

Anon. 1832. "Review of the Waverly Novels and Tales of My Landlord." *Edinburgh Review,* January: 61–79.

Anon. 1837. "Electro-Magnetic Telegraph." *Journal of the Franklin Institute,* 20: 323–325.

Appadurai, Arjun. 1996. *Modernity at Large: Cultural Dimensions of Globalization.* Public Worlds. Minneapolis: University of Minnesota Press.

Arendt, Hannah. 1968. *The Origins of Totalitarianism.* New ed. New York: Harcourt, Brace & World.

———. 1971. *The Origins of Totalitarianism.* 2d enl. ed. New York: Meridian Books.

———. 2000. *The Portable Hannah Arendt.* Ed. P. R. Baehr. Viking Portable Library. New York: Penguin Books.

Asad, Talal. 2003. *Formations of the Secular: Christianity, Islam, Modernity.* Stanford: Stanford University Press.

Austin, J. L. 1976. *How to Do Things with Words,* Oxford: Oxford University Press.

Aristotle. 1984. *The Complete Works of Aristotle: The Revised Oxford Translation.* 2 vols. Ed. Jonathan Barnes. Bollingen Series. Princeton: Princeton University Press.

———. 1987. *Poetics I; with, the Tractatus Coislinianus; A Hypothitical Reconstruction of Poetics Ii; the Fragments of the on Poets.* Ed. Richard Janko. Hackett Classics. Indianapolis: Hackett Pub. Co..

Arrighi, Giovanni. 1994. *The Long Twentieth Century: Money, Power, and the Origins of Our Times.* London; New York: Verso.

ARTFL. "Dictionnaire de l'Académie Française." http://humanities.uchicago.edu/orgs/ARTFL/.

Ashfield, Andrew, and Peter De Bolla. 1996. *The Sublime: A Reader in British Eighteenth-Century Aesthetic Theory.* Cambridge: Cambridge University Press.

Astbury, Raymond. 1978. "The Renewal of the Licensing Act in 1693 and its Lapse in 1695." *Library* 5th ser., 33: 296–322.

Attig, John C. 1985. *The Works of John Locke: A Comprehensive Bibliography from the Seventeenth Century to the Present.* Bibliographies and Indexes in Philosophy. Westport: Greenwood Press.

Babbage, Charles. 1837. *The Ninth Bridgewater Treatise. A Fragment.* London: J. Murray.

Bacon, Sir Francis. 1905. *New Organon* [1620]. *The Philosophical Works of Francis Bacon.* Ed. Robert L. Ellis and James Spedding, rev. ed. John M. Robertson. London: Routledge.

———. 1994. *Novum Organon with Other Parts of The Great Instauration.* Trans. and ed. P. Urbach and J. Gibson. Chicago: Open Court.

———. 1996. *Francis Bacon.* Ed. Brian Vickers. Oxford: Oxford University Press.

———. 2000. *The New Organon.* Edited by L. Jardine and M. Silverthorne. Cambridge Texts in the History of Philosophy. Cambridge: Cambridge University Press.

———. N.d. http://etext.library.adelaide.edu.au/b/bacon/francis/.

Bacon, Francis, and Peter Shaw. 1773. *The Philosophical Works of Francis Bacon.* 3 vols. London: Printed for J. J. and P. Knapton, D. Midwinter and A. Ward, A. Bettesworth and C. Hitch . . . . [and 8 others].

Baillet, Adrien. 1685. *Jugemens des sçavans sur les principaux ouvrages des auteurs.* Paris: Antoine Dezallier.

Baker, Keith Michael. 1990. *Inventing the French Revolution: Essays on French Political Culture in the Eighteenth Century.* Ideas in Context. Cambridge: Cambridge University Press.

Balzac, Honoré de. 1977. *Modeste Mignon.* Zurich.

Barbauld, Anna Laetitia. 1810. *The British Novelists; with an Essay; and Prefaces, Biographical and Critical*. London: F.C. and J. Rivington.

Barnard, F. M. 1965. *Herder's Social and Political Thought; from Enlightenment to Nationalism*. Oxford: Clarendon Press.

Barnard, John. 1999. "Bibliographical Note. The Survival and Loss Rates of Psalms, Abcs, Psalters and Primers from the Stationers' Stock, 1660–1700." *Library* 21, no. 2: 148–150.

Barnett, Thomas P. M. 2003. "The Pentagon's New Map." *Esquire*.

———. 2004. *The Pentagon's New Map: War and Peace in the Twenty-First Century*. New York: G. P. Putnam's Sons.

Baron, Sabrina Alcorn, Eric N. Lindquist, and Eleanor F. Shevlin, eds. 2007. *Agent of Change: Print Culture Studies after Elizabeth L. Eisenstein*. Studies in Print Culture and the History of the Book. Amherst: University of Massachusetts Press; in association with The Center for the Book, Library of Congress.

Baumgarten, Alexander Gottlieb. 1735. *Meditationes philosophicae de nonnullis ad poema pertinentibus / Philosophische Betrachtungen über einige Bedingungen des Gedichtes*. Parallel Latin and German texts ed. Heinz Paetzold. Hamburg: Felix Meiner, 1983.

———. 1750. *Aesthetica*. Frankfurt an der Oder, 1750–1758. Reprint, Hildesheim: Georg Olms, 1961.

Bazerman, Charles. 1988. *Shaping Written Knowledge: The Genre and Activity of the Experimental Article in Science*. Rhetoric of the Human Sciences. Madison: University of Wisconsin Press.

Beauvais, Vincent of. 1964. *Bibliotheca Mundi*. Graz: Akademische Druck- und Verlagsanstalt.

Behn, Aphra. 1998. *Oroonoko, and Other Writings*. Ed. Paul Salzman. World's Classics. Oxford: Oxford University Press.

Ben-Chaim, Michael. 1998. "Doctrine and Use: Newton's 'Gift of Preaching.'" *History of Science* 36: 269–298.

Bender, John. 1987. *Imagining the Penitentiary: Fiction and the Architecture of Mind in Eighteenth-Century England*. Chicago: University of Chicago Press.

———. 1998. "Enlightenment Fiction and the Scientific Hypothesis." *Representations* 61: 6–28.

———. 2009. "The Novel as Modern Myth." In *Defoe's Footprints: Essays in Honor of Maximillian E. Novak*, ed. Robert M. Maniquis and Carl Fisher. Toronto: University of Toronto Press.

Benhamou, Paul. 1986. "The Periodical Press in the *Encyclopedie*." *French Review* 59, no. 3: 410–417.

Beniger, James R. 1986. *The Control Revolution: Technological and Economic Origins of the Information Society*. Cambridge: Harvard University Press.

Benjamin, Walter. 1983. *Das Passagen-Werk*. Vol. 1. Ed. Rolf Tiedemann. Frankfurt am Main: Suhrkamp.

Bensaude-Vincent, B. 1989. "Lavoisier: Une révolution scientifique." In *Éléments d'histoire des science*. Ed. M. Serres, 363–386. Paris: Bordas.

Berkeley, George. 1982. *Guardian* no. 49. *The Guardian*. Ed. John Calhoun Stephens. Lexington, Kentucky: University Press of Kentucky.

Berlin, Isaiah, Henry Hardy, and Roger Hausheer. 1998. *The Proper Study of Mankind: An Anthology of Essays.* 1st Farrar, Straus and Giroux ed. New York: Farrar, Straus and Giroux.

Bériou, Nicole. 1989. "La réportation des sermons Parisiens à la fin du XIIIe siècle." *Medioevo e Rinascimento* 3: 87–123.

Bernays, Edward L. 1923. *Crystallizing Public Opinion.* New York: Boni and Liveright.

Beyerlinck, Laurentius. 1631. "Magnum Theatrum Humanae Vitae." Cologne: Hieratus.

Bhabha, Homi K. 1994. *The Location of Culture.* London: Routledge.

Bhargava, Rajeev, ed. 1998. *Secularism and Its Critics.* Delhi: Oxford University Press.

Blackwell, Thomas. 1735. *Enquiry into the Life and Writings of Homer.* London.

Blainey, Geoffrey. 1966. *The Tyranny of Distance; How Distance Shaped Australia's History.* Melbourne: Sun Books.

Blair, Ann. 2000. "Annotating and Indexing Natural Philosophy." *Books and the Sciences in History*, ed. Marina Frasca-Spada and Nick Jardine, 69–89. Cambridge: Cambridge University Press.

———. 2008. "Textbooks and Methods of Note-Taking in Early Modern Europe." *Scholarly Knowledge: The Transmission of Social Practice in Academic Textbooks, 1450–1650.* Ed. Anja-Silvia Goeing. Geneva: Droz.

———. Forthcoming. *Too Much to Know: Managing Scholarly Information before the Modern Age.* New Haven: Yale University Press.

Blair, Ann, and Jennifer Milligan, eds. 2007. "Toward a Cultural History of Archives." Special issue of *Archival Science* 7, no. 4.

Blair, Hugh. 2005. *Lectures on Rhetoric and Belles Lettres* [rev. ed., 1785]. Ed. Linda Ferreira-Buckley and S. Michael Halloran. Carbondale: Southern Illinois University Press.

Blake, William. 1970. *The Poetry and Prose of William Blake.* Ed. David V. Erdman with commentary by Harold Bloom. New York: Doubleday.

Blanning, T. C. 2002. *The Culture of Power and the Power of Culture: Old Regime Europe, 1660–1789.* Oxford: Oxford University Press.

Bloch, Ernst, et al. 2007. *Aesthetics and Politics.* Radical Thinkers. London: Verso.

Bloch, Ernst. 1962. *Erbschaft dieser Zeit.* His Gesamtausgabe. Erweiterte Ausg. [Frankfurt am Main]: Suhrkamp.

Bodleian Library and Gwen Hampshire. 1983. *The Bodleian Library Account Book, 1613–1646.* Oxford Bibliographical Society Publications, n.s., 21. Oxford: Oxford Bibliographical Society.

Bolz, Norbert W. 1993. *Am Ende Der Gutenberg-Galaxis: Die Neuen Kommunikationsverhältnisse.* Munich: Fink Verlag.

Boston Committee of Correspondence. 1772. *The Votes and Proceedings of the Town of Boston in Town Meeting Assembled, According to Law.* Boston: Edes & Gill.

Bouwsma, William. 1979. "Review of Eisenstein, *The Printing Press as an Agent of Change.*" *American Historical Review* 84: 1356–1357.

Bouza, Fernando. 1999. "Communication, Knowledge, and Memory in Early Modern Spain." Ed. Sonia López and Agnew Michael. Philadelphia: University of Pennsylvania Press.

Bracha Oren. 2005. "Owning Ideas: A History of Anglo-American Intellectual Property." SJD diss., Harvard Law School, 2005.

Brand, Stewart. 1999. *The Clock of the Long Now: Time and Responsibility*. 1st ed. New York: Basic Books.

Brewer, J. 1995. "This, That and the Other: Public, Social and Private in the Seventeenth and Eighteenth Centuries." *Shifting the Boundaries: Transformation of the Languages of Public and Private in the Eighteenth* Century, ed. D. Castiglione Sharpe, 1-21. Exeter: University of Exeter Press.

Brewer, John, and Roy Porter. 1993. *Consumption and the World of Goods*. London: Routledge.

Bridenbaugh, Carl. 1962. *Mitre and Sceptre; Transatlantic Faiths, Ideas, Personalities, and Politics, 1689-1775*. New York: Oxford University Press.

Broman, Thomas. 2000. "Periodical Literature." *Books and the Sciences in History*. Ed. M. Frasca-Spada Jardine, 225-238. Cambridge: Cambridge University Press.

Brown, John Seely, and Paul Duguid. 2002. *The Social Life of Information*. Boston: Harvard Business School Press.

Brown, Mary Ellen. 1996. "The Mechanism of the Ancient Ballad: William Motherwell's Explanation." *Oral Tradition* 11: 175-189.

Brown, Richard D. 1970. *Revolutionary Politics in Massachusetts; the Boston Committee of Correspondence and the Towns, 1772-1774*. Cambridge: Harvard University Press.

Bryson, Norman. 1981. *Word and Image: French Painting of the Ancien Régime*. Cambridge: Cambridge University Press.

*Building the Digital Collection*. 2001. http://memory.loc.gov/ammem/sfbmhtml/sfbm building.html.

Burke, Edmund. 1958. *A Philosophical Enquiry into the Origin of Our Ideas of the Sublime and Beautiful*. Edited with an Introduction and Notes by J. T. Boulton. Ed. James Thompson Boulton. Routledge & Kegan Paul: London.

Butcher, S. H. 1951. *Aristotle's Theory of Poetry and Fine Art*. New York: Dover Publications.

Byron, George Gordon Lord Byron. 1980. *The Complete Poetical Works*. 7 vols. Ed. Jerome J. McGann, and Barry Weller. Oxford English Texts. Oxford: Clarendon Press.

Campbell, George. 1853. *Argument of St. Geo. T. Campbell, Esq. delivered December 1852 before the Supreme Court of the United States, in support of the validity of Morse's Patents for the Electro-Magnetic Telegraph*. Philadelphia, 1853.

———. 1992. *The Philosophy of Rhetoric*. American Linguistics, 1700-1900. Delmar: Scholars' Facsimiles & Reprints.

Carey, Daniel, and Lynn M. Festa. 2009. *The Postcolonial Enlightenment: Eighteenth-Century Colonialism and Postcolonial Theory*. Oxford: Oxford University Press.

Cassirer, Ernst. 1979. *The Philosophy of the Enlightenment*. Princeton: Princeton University Press.

*Certaine sermons: appointed by the Queenes Maiestie, to be declared and read, by all parsons, vicars, and curates, euery Sunday and holy day in their churches: and by her graces aduice perused and ouerseene, for the better vnderstanding of the simple people*. 1582. London.

*Certayne sermons, or homilies appoynted by the kynges Maiestie, to be declared and redde, by all persones, vicars, or curates, euery Sondaye in their churches, where they haue cure.* 1547. London.

Chakrabarty, Dipesh. 2005. "Legacies of Bandung: Decolonisation and the Politics of Culture." *Economic and Political Weekly*, November 12, 412–418.

Chambers, Ephraim. 1728. *Cyclopædia; or, An Universal Dictionary of Arts and Sciences.* 2 vols. London: Printed for J. and J. Knapton [and 18 others].

Champion, Justin. 2003. *Republican Learning: John Toland and the Crisis of Christian Culture, 1696–1722.* Politics, Culture, and Society in Early Modern Britain. Manchester: Manchester University Press.

Chandler, Alfred Dupont, and James W. Cortada. 2000. *A Nation Transformed by Information: How Information Has Shaped the United States from Colonial Times to the Present.* New York: Oxford University Press.

Chapuis, Alfred, and Edmond Droz. 1958. *Automata; a Historical and Technological Study.* Neuchâtel.

Chapuis, A. and E. Gélis. 1928. *Le monde des Automates.* 2 vols. Paris: E. Gélis.

Chartier, Roger. 1991. *The Cultural Origins of the French Revolution.* Bicentennial Reflections on the French Revolution. Durham: Duke University Press.

———. 1992. *L'ordre des livres. Lecteurs, auteurs, bibliothèques en Europe entre XIVe et XVIIIe siècle.*

Chatterjee, Partha. 1993. *Nationalist Thought and the Colonial World: A Derivative Discourse.* Minnesota: University of Minnesota Press.

Cheesman, Tom, and Sigrid Rieuwerts. 1997. *Ballads into Books: The Legacies of Francis James Child.* Bern: Peter Lang.

Child, Francis James. 1863. "Observations on the Language of Chaucer (based on Wright's Edition of the *Canterbury Tales*, Harleian MS No. 7334." *Memoirs of the American Academy of Arts and Sciences* n.s., 8, no. 2: 445–502.

———. 1881. *Invitation to Unite in an Effort to Collect Popular Ballads from Oral Tradition; Addressed Particularly to Students in Colleges.* Cambridge.

———. 1882–1898. *English and Scottish Popular Ballads.* 10 vols. Boston: Houghton Mifflin.

Cicero. *Philipics.* 1986. Ed. and trans. D. R. Shackleton Bailey. Chapel Hill: University of North Carolina Press.

Clanchy, M. T. 1993. *From Memory to Written Record: England, 1066–1307.* 2d ed. Oxford: Blackwell.

Clark, Robert Thomas. 1955. *Herder; His Life and Thought.* Berkeley: University of California Press.

Clark, William, Jan Golinski, and Simon Schaffer, eds. 1999. *The Sciences in Enlightened Europe.* Chicago: University of Chicago Press.

Clifford, James. 1988. "On Ethnographic Authority." *The Predicament of Culture: Twentieth-Century Ethnography, Literature, and Art.* Cambridge: Harvard University Press.

Cobbett, William, and Bank of England. 1828. *Paper against Gold, or, the History and Mystery of the Bank of England, of the Debt, of the Stocks, of the Sinking Fund, and of All the Other Tricks and Contrivances, Carried on by the Means of Paper Money*. Printed and published by W. Cobbett.

Coleridge, Samuel Taylor. 1969. *The Collected Works of Samuel Taylor Coleridge*. Bollingen Series. [London], [Princeton]: Routledge and K. Paul; Princeton University Press.

———. 1971–2001. *The Collected Works of Samuel Taylor Coleridge*. 16 vols. Edited by Kathleen Coburn. Bollingen Series. Princeton and London: Princeton University Press; Routledge.

———. 1983. *Biographia Literaria; or, Biographical Sketches of My Literary Life and Opinions, II*. Vol. 7 *The Collected Works of Samuel Taylor Coleridge*. Ed. James Engell and W. Jackson Bate. London: Routledge and Kegan Paul.

Condillac, Etienne Bonnot de. 1984 [1754]. *Traité des Sensations*. 1st ed. Paris: Fayard.

Condorcet, Antoine-Nicolas de. 1955a. *Sketch for a Historical Picture of the Progress of the Human Mind*. Trans. June Barraclough. Westport, Connecticut: Hyperion Press.

———. 1955b [1795; orig. French 1793]. *Sketch for a Historical Picture of the Progress of the Human Mind*. Trans. June Barraclough, with an intro. by Stuart Hampshire. London: Weidenfeld and Nicolson.

———. 1988. *Esquisse d'un tableau historique des progrès de l'esprit humain suivi de Fragment sur l'Atlantide*. Paris.

Congar, Yves. 1980. "*In dulcedine societatis quaerere veritatem*: Notes sur le travail en équipe chez St Albert et chez les prêcheurs au XIIIe siècle." *Albertus Magnus, Doctor universalis: 1280 / 1980*. Ed. G. Meyer and A Zimmermann. Mainz: Matthias-Grünewald-Verlag.

Cook, Roger F. 199. *The Demise of the Author: Autonomy and the German Writer, 1770–1848*. Studies in Modern German Literature. New York: P. Lang.

Cowan, Brian William. 2005. *The Social Life of Coffee: The Emergence of the British Coffeehouse*. New Haven [Conn.]: Yale University Press.

Crain, Patricia. 2000. *The Story of A: The Alphabetization of America from the New England Primer to the Scarlet Letter*. Stanford: Stanford University Press.

Crary, Jonathan. 1990. *Techniques of the Observer: On Vision and Modernity in the Nineteenth Century*. Cambridge: MIT Press.

Cunningham, A., and N. Jardine. 1990. "The Age of Reflexion." *Romanticism and the Sciences*. Ed. A. Cunningham and N. Jardine, 1–9. Cambridge: Cambridge University Press.

Curtis, B. R. 1850. *Argument of B. R. Curtis, Esq. of Boston, in the Case of Francis O.J. Smith, Complain't vs. Hugh Downing and Als., Respon'ts, in the circuit court of the U.S., Massachusetts District, Hon. Levi Woodbury, Judge Presiding, for an infringement of the letters patent of Samuel F.B. Morse, for the electro magnetic telegraph, June 25 and 26, 1850*. Portland [MA].

Décultot, Elisabeth. 2003. Introduction. *Lire, copier, écrire: Les bibliothèques manuscrites et leurs usages au XVIIIe siècle*. Paris: CNRS.

Darnton, Robert. 1970. *The Business of Enlightenment: A Publishing History of the Encyclopédie, 1775–1800*. Cambridge: Belknap Press.

———. 2003. "The Science of Piracy: A Crucial Ingredient in Eighteenth-Century Publishing." *Studies in Voltaire and the Eighteenth Century* 12: 3–29.

Daston, Lorraine. 2005. "Description by Omission: Nature Enlightened and Obscured." *Regimes of Description: In the Archive of the Eighteenth Century.* Ed. John Bender Marrinan and Michael. Stanford: Stanford University Press.

David, Paul A. 1985. *Computer and Dynamo: The Modern Productivity Paradox in a Not-Too-Distant Mirror.* Stanford: Center for Economic Policy Research, Stanford University.

Davis, Leith, Ian Duncan, and Janet Sorensen. 2004. *Scotland and the Borders of Romanticism.* Cambridge: Cambridge University Press.

Davis, Norman, et al. 2004–2005. *Paston Letters and Papers of the Fifteenth Century.* 3 vols. Oxford: Oxford University Press.

D'Avray, D. L. 1985. *The Preaching of the Friars: Sermons Diffused from Paris before 1300.* Oxford: Oxford University Press.

De Grazia, Margreta. 1991. *Shakespeare Verbatim: The Reproduction of Authenticity and the 1790 Apparatus.* Oxford: Clarendon Press.

De Hamel, Christopher, and British Museum. 1992. *Scribes and Illuminators.* Medieval Craftsmen. Toronto: University of Toronto Press.

De Saint-Réal, César Vichard. 1990. *Die Verschwörung der Spanier gegen Venedig 1618.* Trans. Peter Weiß. Vienna and Leipzig.

Dear, Peter Robert. 1995. *Discipline and Experience: The Mathematical Way in the Scientific Revolution.* Science and Its Conceptual Foundations. Chicago: University of Chicago Press.

———. 1998. "A Mechanical Microcosm: Bodily Passions, Good Manners, and Cartesian Mechanism." *Science Incarnate. Historical Embodiments of Natural Knowledge.* Ed. Christopher Lawrence and Steven Shapin. Chicago: University of Chicago Press.

Debray, Régis. 1994. *Manifestes médiologiques.* Gallimard.

———. 2000. *Transmitting Culture.* European Perspectives. New York: Columbia University Press.

———. 2004. *Transmitting Culture.* European Perspectives. New York: Columbia University Press.

Defoe, Daniel. 1720. *Serious Reflections During the Life and Surprising Adventures of Robinson Crusoe: With His Vision of the Angelick World.* London: Printed for W. Taylor.

———. 1977. *Robinson Crusoe: And Other Writings.* Ed. James Runcieman Sutherland. The Gotham Library of the New York University Press. New York: New York University Press.

———. 1998. *The Life and Strange Surprizing Adventures of Robinson Crusoe of York, Mariner: Who Lived Eight and Twenty Years, All Alone in an Un-Inhabited Island on the Coast of America, near the Mouth of the Great River of Oroonoque, Having Been Cast on Shore by Shipwreck, Wherein All the Men Perished but Himself with an Account How He Was at Last as Strangely Deliver'd by Pyrates, Written by Himself.* Ed. J. Donald Crowley. Oxford: Oxford World's Classics.

———. 2001. *Robinson Crusoe.* Ed. John J. Richetti. Penguin Classics. London: Penguin Books.

Derrida, Jacques. 1974. *Of Grammatology.* Trans. Gayatri Chakravorty Spivak. 1st American ed. Baltimore: Johns Hopkins University Press.

---. 1988. *Limited Inc.* Evanston: Northwestern University Press.
---. 1995. *Mal d'archive: Une impression freudienne.* Incises. Paris: Galilee.
Desai, M. V. 1988. "Giving a Voice to the People." *Mass Media in India.* New Delhi: Government of India, Ministry of Information and Broadcasting.
Descartes, René. 1996a [1637]. *Dioptrics. Œuvres.* Paris: Vrin.
---. 1996b [1629–1633]. *Le Monde, ou Traite de la lumière. Œuvres.* Paris: Vrin.
Diderot, Denis. 1966. *Rameau's Nephew, and D'Alembert's Dream.* Penguin Classics. Harmondsworth: Penguin.
---. 1978."Lettre sur les sourds et muets." In vol. 4, *Oeuvres Complètes de Diderot.* Paris: Hermann
---. 1995. *Diderot on Art.* 2 vols. Ed. John Goodman. New Haven: Yale University Press.
Diderot, Denis and Jean Le Rond d Alembert. 1966. *Encyclopédie ou Dictionnaire Raisonné des Sciences, des Arts et des Métiers.* Nouvelle impression en facsimilé de la première édition de 1751–1780 ed. 35 vols. Stuttgart-Bad Cannstatt: Frommann.
Diderot, Denis, and John Goodman. 1995. *Diderot on Art.* 2 vols. New Haven: Yale University Press.
Dienst, Richard. 1994. *Still Life in Real Time: Theory after Television.* Post-Contemporary Interventions. Durham: Duke University Press.
Dodsley, Robert. 1739. *The Art of Preaching, in Imitation of Horace's Art of Poetry.* Philadelphia.
Domenichi, Lodovico. 1571. *Facetie, Motti, et Burli di Diversi Signori et Persone Private.* Venice: Appresso Andrea Muschio.
Dondaine, Antoine. 1956. *Secrétaires de Saint Thomas.* Editores Operum Sancti Thomae De Aquino. Rome: S. Tommaso.
Doniger, Wendy. 1976. *The Origins of Evil in Hindu Mythology.* Hermeneutics, Studies in the History of Religions, 6. Berkeley: University of California Press.
Dover, Paul. 2007. "Deciphering the Diplomatic Archives of Fifteenth-Century Italy." *Archival Science* 7, no. 4: 297–316.
Drexel SJ, Jeremias. 1638. *Aurifodina artium et scientiarum omnium; excerpendi sollertia, omnibus litterarum amantibus monstrata,* Antwerp: vidua Ioannis Cnobbari.
Dryden, John. 1962. *Of Dramatic Poesy, and Other Critical Essays.* Ed. George Watson. 2 vols. Everyman's Library. London and New York: J. M. Dent; Dutton.
Dubos, Jean-Baptiste. 1733. *Réflexions critiques sur la poésie et sur la peinture.* Paris: P-J Mariette.
Duff, William. 1767. *An Essay on Original Genius: And Its Various Modes of Exertion in Philosophy and the Fine Arts, Particularly in Poetry.* London: Printed for Edward and Charles Dilly in the Poultry, near the Mansion-House.
---. 1770. "Critical Observations on the Writings of the Most Celebrated Original Geniuses in Poetry Being a Sequel to the Essay on Original Genius. By W. Duff, A.M." [n.p.]: Printed for T. Becket, and P. A. de Hondt.
Dugaw, Dianne. 2006. "On the 'Darling Songs' of Poets, Scholars, and Singers: An Introduction." *Eighteenth Century: Theory and Interpretation* 47, nos. 2–3 (Summer/Fall): 97–113.

Eco, Umberto. 1979. *A Theory of Semiotics*. Advances in Semiotics. Bloomington: Indiana University Press.

Edwards, Jonathan. 1972. "Some Thoughts concerning the Present Revival of Religion in New-England (Boston, 1742)." *The Works of Jonathan Edwards*. Ed. C. C. Goen. New Haven: Yale University Press.

Eisenstein, Elizabeth L. 1979. *The Printing Press as an Agent of Change: Communications and Cultural Transformations in Early-Modern Europe*. Cambridge: Cambridge University Press, 1979.

———. 1983. *The Printing Revolution in Early Modern Europe*. Cambridge: Cambridge University Press, 1983.

———. 1986. *Print Culture and Enlightenment Thought*. Hanes Lecture. [Chapel Hill]: Hanes Foundation, Rare Book Collection/University Library, University of North Carolina at Chapel Hill.

———. 2002. "An Unacknowledged Revolution Revisited." *American Historical Review* 107, no. 1: 87–105.

Eliade, M. 1969. *Le mythe de l'eternel retour; archetypes et repetition*. Paris: Gallimard.

Elibank, Lord. 1993. "Essay on Paper Money and Banking (1755)." In *History of Banking*, ed. Forest H. Capie, 212–220. London: William Pickering.

Fabian, Johannes. 2003. *Time and the Other: How Anthropology Makes Its Object*. New York: Columbia University Press.

Feather, John. 1988. *A History of British Publishing*. London: Routledge.

Fichte, J. G. 1964. "Beweis der Unrechtmässigkeit des Büchernachdrucks." *Fichte, Gesamtausgabe*, vol. 1.1, *Werke, 1791–1794*. Stuttgart-Bad Canstadt: Friedrich Frommann, 1964.

Fielding, Henry. 1996. *Tom Jones*. Ed. John Bender and Simon Stern. The World's Classics. Oxford: Oxford University Press.

Fielding, Henry. 1999. *Joseph Andrews and Shamela*. Ed. Douglas Brooks-Davies and Thomas Keymer. Oxford World's Classics. Oxford: Oxford University Press.

Fielding, Henry, et al. 1993. *The Correspondence of Henry and Sarah Fielding*. Oxford and New York: Clarendon Press; Oxford University Press.

Finnegan, Ruth H. 1992. *Oral Poetry: Its Nature, Significance, and Social Context*. 1st Midland Book ed. Bloomington: Indiana University Press.

Fontenelle, Bernard Le Bovier de. 1740. *Éloges des Académiciens avec l'histoire de l'Académie Royale des Sciences en 1699*. Vol. 2. La Haye: I. vander Kloot.

———. 1955. "Digression sur les anciens et les modernes" (1688). *Entretiens sur la pluralité des mondes. Digression sur les anciens et les modernes*. Ed. Robert Shackleton. Oxford: Clarendon Press.

———. 1970. "A Digression on the Ancients and Moderns." Trans. John Hughes (with revisions). In *The Continental Model: Selected French Critical Essays of the Seventeenth Century, in English Translation*. Eds. Scott Elledge Schier and Donald. Ithaca: Cornell University Press.

———. 1998. *Réponse à l' évêque de Luçon [1732]*. [n.p.]: Éditions Bibliopolis.

Ford, Andrew. 2002. *The Origins of Criticism: Literary Culture and Poetic Theory in Classical Greece*. Princeton: Princeton University Press.

Forster, M. N. 2002. Introduction. *J. G. Von Herder, Philosophical Writings*. Ed. M. N. Forster. Cambridge: Cambridge University Press.

Foster, Sir William. 1896–1902. *Letters Received by the East India Company from Its Servants in the East: Transcribed from the 'Original Correspondence' Series of the India Office Records*. London: Sampson Low, Marston and Co.

———. 1900. "A Note of Goods the Governor Took Away from Divers Persons out of the Alfandige." *Letters Received by the East India Company from Its Servants in the East*, vol. 4, *1616*. Ed. William Foster. London: Sampson Low, Marston & Co.

Foucault, Michel. 1970. *The Order of Things: An Archaeology of the Human Sciences*. World of Man. London: Tavistock Publications.

———. 1977. *Discipline and Punish: The Birth of the Prison*. Hammondsworth: Penguin.

———. 1988. *Politics, Philosophy, Culture. Interviews and Other Writings, 1977–1984*. Edited with an intro. by Lawrence D. Kritzman. New York: Routledge.

———. 1989. "La gouvernementalité." *Magazine littéraire* 269 (Sept.): 97–103.

———. 1994a. "Qu'est-ce que les Lumières?" *Dits et Écrits: 1954–1988. Vol. 2, 1976–1988*, 1498–1507. Paris: Éditions Gallimard. [First published in *Magazine littéraire* 207/1984; English version in Foucault 1988.]

———. 1994b. "Pour une moral de l'inconfort". *Dits et Écrits: 1954–1988. Vol. 2, 1976–1988*, 783–787. Paris: Éditions Gallimard.

———. 1994c. "Qu'est-ce que les Lumières?" *Dits et Écrits: 1954–1988. Vol. 2, 1976–1988*, 1381–1397. Paris: Éditions Gallimard. [First published in Foucault 1984.]

———. 1994d. "What Is Enlightenment?" *The Foucault Reader*. Ed. Paul Rabinow. New York: Pantheon Books, 32–50.

———. 1997. *The Politics of Truth*. Ed Sylvere Lotringer. Trans. Lysa Hochroth and Catherine Porter. Los Angeles: Semotext(e).

———. 1999. *In Verteidigung der Gesellschaft. Vorlesungen am Collège de France (1975–76)*. Ed. Michaela Ott. Frankfurt: Suhrkamp, 1999.

———. 2007. *The Politics of Truth*. Ed. Sylvere Lotringer Trans.Lysa Hochroth. New York: Semiotext(e).

Fox, Adam, and Daniel Woolf, eds. 2002. *The Spoken Word: Oral Culture in Britain, 1500–1850*. Manchester: Manchester University Press.

Foxon, David F. 1991. *Pope and the Early Eighteenth-Century Book Trade*. Lyell Lectures, 1975–1976. Revised and edited by James McLaverty. Oxford: Clarendon Press.

Franklin, Benjamin. 1745. "Poor Richard for 1746." Philadelphia: Benjamin Franklin.

———. 1959. *The Papers of Benjamin Franklin*. Vol. 2, January 1, 1735 through December 31 1744. Ed. Leonard W. Labaree, Whitfield J. Bell Jr., Helen C. Boatfield, and Helene H. Fineman. New Haven: Yale University Press.

———. 1976. *The Papers of Benjamin Franklin*. Vol. 20. Ed. William B. Willcox. New Haven: Yale University Press.

———. 1986. *Benjamin Franklin's Autobiography: An Authoritative Text, Backgrounds, Criticism*. 1st ed. Ed. Paul M. Zall and J. A. Leo Lemay. A Norton Critical Edition. New York: Norton.

Freud, Sigmund. 1957. "The Antithetical Meaning of Primal Words" [1910]. *The Standard Edition of the Complete Psychological Works of Sigmund Freud*. Vol. 11, 155–161. Ed. James Strachey. London: Hogarth Press, 1957.

Fried, Michael. 1980. *Absorption and Theatricality: Painting and Beholder in the Age of Diderot*. Berkeley: University of California Press.

Friedel, Robert D. 2007. *A Culture of Improvement: Technology and the Western Millennium*. Cambridge: MIT Press.

Friedländer, Max J., Henri Pauwels, and Sadja Jacob Herzog. 1972. *Jan Gossart and Bernart Van Orley*. Books That Matter. New York: Praeger.

Frederick II, King of Prussia. 1789. [. *Friedrich des Zweiten von Preussen hinterlassene Werke*. Vol. 14. Aus dem Französischen übersetzt. Berlin: Voss und Sohn, Decker und Sohn.

Fumerton, Patricia, and Anita Guerrini. 2010. *British Ballads and Broadsides, 1550–1800*. Aldershot:Ashgate Press.

Furbank, Philip Nicholas. 1992. *Diderot: A Critical Biography*. London: Secker & Warburg.

Gadgil, D. R. 1972. *Planning and Economic Policy in India*. Rev. and enl. ed. Gokhale Institute Studies. Poona: Gokhale Institute of Politics and Economics; distributed by Orient Longman, Bombay.

Gallagher, Catherine. 2006. "The Rise of Fictionality." In *The Novel*, vol. 1, *History, Geography and Culture*, ed. Franco Moretti, 336–363. Princeton: Princeton University Press.

Galloway, Alexander R. 2004. *Protocol: How Control Exists after Decentralization*. Leonardo. Cambridge: MIT Press.

Gassendi, Pierre. 1970. *The mirrour of true nobility and gentility being the life of the renowned Nicolaus Claudius Fabricius lord of Peiresk, senator of the parliament at Aix*. Englished by W. Rand. London: printed by J Streater for Humphrey Moseley, 1657. Reprinted in Pierre Gassendi, *Peiresc and His Books*. Boston: David Godine.

Gates, Bill, Nathan Myhrvold, and Peter Rinearson. 1995. *The Road Ahead*. New York: Viking.

Geary, Patrick J. 1994. *Phantoms of Remembrance: Memory and Oblivion at the End of the First Millennium*. Princeton: Princeton University Press.

Genette, Gérard. 1992. *The Architext: An Introduction*. Quantum Books. Berkeley: University of California Press.

Gentili, Alberico, et al. 1933. *De Iure Belli Libri Tres*. The Classics of International Law. Oxford: Clarendon Press; H. Milford.

Gerard, Alexander. 1744. *An Essay on Genius. By Alexander Gerard, D.D.* Edinburgh: Printed for W. Strahan; T. Cadell; and W. Creech.

Gesner, Conrad. 1548. *Pandectae*. Zurich: Froschauer.

———. 1551. *Historia Animalium*. Zurich: Froschauer.

Gifford, George. 1853. *Argument of George Gifford, Esq. of New York, Delivered in December 1852 at Washington, before the Supreme Court of the United States, in the Case of Henry O'Reilly et al., Appellants, vs. Samuel F.B. Morse, F.O.J. Smith et al., Appellees. Being an appeal from a decision of the U.S. Circuit Court for the district of Kentucky in favor of Prof. Morse's Patents for 'The American Electro-Magnetic Telegraph.'* (New York: Wm. C. Bryant & Co, 1853).

Gigerenzer, Gerd. 1989. *The Empire of Chance: How Probability Changed Science and Everyday Life*. Ideas in Context. Cambridge: Cambridge University Press.

Gilly, Carlos. 1977–1978. "Zwischen Erfahrung Und Spekulation: Theodor Zwinger

Und Die Religiöse Und Kulturelle Krise Seiner Zeit." *Basler Zeitschrift für Geschichte und Alterumskunde* 77–78: 57–137, 25–223.

———. 2002. "Theodor Zwinger's Theatrum Humanae Vitae: From Natural Anthropology to the 'Novum Organum' of Sciences." *Magia, alchimia, scienza dal '400 al '700: l'influsso di Ermete Trismegisto = Magic, Alchemy and Science 15th–18th Centuries: The Influence of Hermes Trismegistus*. 2 vols. Ed. Carlos Gilly and Cis van Heertum. Florence: Centro Di.

Ginzburg, Carlo. 1980. "Morelli, Freud and Sherlock Holmes: Clues and Scientific Method." Introduction by Anna Davin. *History Workshop* 9: 5–36.

Gitelman, Lisa. 2006. *Always Already New: Media, History and the Data of Culture*. Cambridge: MIT Press.

Godwin, William. 1970. *Caleb Williams*. Ed. David McCracken. Oxford English Novels. London: Oxford University Press.

Goethe, Johann Wolfgang von. 1981. *Werke*. 14 vols. Munich: C. H. Beck.

Goffman, Erving. 1976. *Gender Advertisements*. Harper Colophon Books. 1st Harper Colophon ed. New York: Harper & Row.

———. 1981. *Forms of Talk*. University of Pennsylvania Publications in Conduct and Communication. Philadelphia: University of Pennsylvania Press.

Goodman, Dena. 1994. *The Republic of Letters: A Cultural History of the French Enlightenment*. Ithaca: Cornell University Press.

Goodman, Kevis. 2004. *Georgic Modernity and British Romanticism: Poetry and the Mediation of History*. Cambridge Studies in Romanticism. Cambridge: Cambridge University Press.

Goodspeed, Edgar J. 1947. "Thomas Jefferson and the Bible." *Harvard Theological Review* 40, no. 1: 71–76.

Goody, Jack, and Ian Watt. 1968. "The Consequences of Literacy." *Literacy in Traditional Societies*, ed. Jack Goody, 27–68. Cambridge: Cambridge University Press.

Gopinatha Rao, T. A., and Kalyan Kumar Dasgupta. 1971. *Elements of Hindu Iconography*. 2d ed. Varanasi: Indological Book House.

Gougeon, Len. 1994. "Holmes's Emerson and the Conservative Critique of Realism." *South Atlantic Review* 59, no. 1: 107–125.

Graff, E. M. 1981. "Versuch einer einleuchtenden Darstellung des Eigenthums und der Eigenthumsrechte des Schriftstellers und Verlegers und ihrer gegenseitigen Rechte und Verbindlichkeiten." *Quellen zur Geschichte des Buchwesens*, ed. R. Wittmann, 191–588. Munich: Kraus.

Grafton, Anthony. 1997. *The Footnote: A Curious History*. Cambridge: Harvard University Press.

Green, James N., and Peter Stallybrass. 2006. *Benjamin Franklin, Printer and Writer*. New Castle, Delaware: Oak Knoll.

Greengrass, M. 2002. "Samuel Hartlib and the Commonwealth of Learning." *The Cambridge History of the Book in Britain*, vol. 4, 1557–1695, ed. John Barnard and F. D. McKenzie, 304–322. Cambridge: Cambridge University Press.

Grell, Chantal. 2000. *Histoire Intellectuelle et Culturelle de la France au Grand Siècle, 1654–1715*. Paris: Nathan.

Groom, Nick. 1999. *The Making of Percy's Reliques*. Oxford English Monographs. Oxford: Oxford University Press.

Grotius, Hugo, and A. C. Campbell. 1901. *The Rights of War and Peace; Including the Law of Nature and of Nations*. Deluxe ed. Washington: M. W. Dunne.

Guillory, John. 1993. *Cultural Capital: The Problem of Literary Canon Formation*. Chicago: University of Chicago Press.

———. 2002. "Literary Study and the Modern System of the Disciplines." *Disciplinarity at the Fin De Siècle*, ed. A. Anderson Valente, 19–43. Princeton: Princeton University Press.

Gustafson, Sandra. 2000. *Eloquence Is Power: Oratory and Performance in Early America*. Chapel Hill: University of North Carolina Press.

———. 2008. "American Literature and the Public Sphere." *American Literary History* 20, no. 3 (Fall): 465–478.

Guyer, Paul. 2004. "The Origins of Modern Aesthetics: 1711–35." *The Blackwell Guide to Aesthetics*, ed. Peter Kivy. Oxford: Blackwell.

Hénaff, M. 2002. *Le Prix de la Vérité*. Paris: Seuil.

Habermas, Jürgen. 1962. *Strukturwandel der Öffentlichkeit. Untersuchungen zu einer Kategorie der bürgerlichen Gesellschaft*. Neuwied: Luchterhand.

———. 1984. *Strukturwandel der Öffentlichkeit. Untersuchungen zu einer Kategorie der bürgerlichen Gesellschaft*. 16th ed. Darmstadt: Luchterhand.

———. 1989. *The Structural Transformation of the Public Sphere: An Inquiry into a Category of Bourgeois Society*. [Cambridge]: Polity Press.

Hacking, Ian. 1999. *The Social Construction of What?* Cambridge: Harvard University Press.

Hall, David. 1972. *The Faithful Shepherd: A History of the New England Ministry in the Seventeenth Century*. Chapel Hill: University of North Carolina Press.

Hall, Marie Boas. 1987. "Boyle's Method of Work: Promoting His Corpuscular Philosophy." *Notes and Records of the Royal Society of London* 41, no. 2: 111–143.

Hall, Timothy D. 1994. *Contested Boundaries: Itinerancy and the Reshaping of the Colonial American World*. Durham: Duke University Press.

Hamesse, Jacqueline. 1986. "Reportatio Et Transmission De Textes." *The Editing of Theological and Philosophical Texts from the Middle Ages*, ed. Monika Asztalos, 11–34. Stockholm: Almquist and Wiksell International.

Hand, John Oliver, and Martha Wolff. 1986. *Early Netherlandish Painting*. The Collections of the National Gallery of Art: Systematic Catalogue. Washington and [New York]: National Gallery of Art; Cambridge University Press.

Haraway, Donna Jeanne. 1991. *Simians, Cyborgs, and Women: The Reinvention of Nature*. New York: Routledge.

Harkness, Deborah E. 2007. *The Jewel House: Elizabethan London and the Scientific Revolution*. New Haven: Yale University Press.

Havelock, Eric A. 1963. *Preface to Plato*. Cambridge, Mass.: Belknap; Harvard University Press.

———. 1991. "The Oral-Literate Equation: A Formula for the Modern Mind." In *Literacy and Orality*, ed. David R. Olson and Nancy Torrance, 11–27. Cambridge: Cambridge University Press.

Hayes, Julie C. 1998. "Fictions of Enlightenment: Sontag, Süskind, Norfolk, Kurzweil." In *Questioning History: The Postmodern Turn to the Eighteenth* Century, ed. Greg Clingham, 21–36. Lewisburg: Bucknell University Press.
Haywood, Eliza. 1729. *The Fair Hebrew; or, A True, but Secret History of Two Jewish Ladies Who Lately Resided in London.* London: Printed for J. Brindley.
Hazlitt, William. 1886. *The Spirit of the Age; or, Contemporary Portraits.* Ed. William Carew Hazlitt. 4th ed. London: G. Bell & Sons.
Hegel, Georg Wilhelm Friedrich. 1956. *The Philosophy of History.* New York: Dover Publications.
———. 1969. *Hegel's Science of Logic.* Muirhead Library of Philosophy. London, New York: G. Allen; Humanities Press.
Heimert, Alan, and Perry Miller. 1967. *The Great Awakening: Documents Illustrating the Crisis and Its Consequences.* The American Heritage Series, 34. Indianapolis: Bobbs-Merrill.
Henderson, Frances. 2001. "Reading, and Writing, the Text of the Putney Debates." In *The Putney Debates of 1647: The Army, the Levellers and the English* State, ed. Michael Mendle, 36–50. Cambridge: Cambridge University Press.
Herder, Johann Gottfried. 1994. "Vom Erkennen Und Empfinden Der Menschlichen Seele." *Werke.* Vol. 4. Frankfurt am Main: Deutscher Klassiker Verlag.
Hesse, Carla. 1990. "Enlightenment Epistemology and the Laws of Authorship in Revolutionary France, 1777–1793." *Representations* 30: 109–37.
Hinske, Norbert. 1981. *Was ist Aufklärung? Beiträge aus der Berlinischen Monatsschrift.* Ed. Norbert Hinske and Michael Albrecht. Darmstadt: Wissenschaftliche Buchgesellschaft.Hobbes, Thomas. 1991. *Leviathan.* Ed. Richard Tuck Cambridge Texts in the History of Political Thought. Cambridge: Cambridge University Press.
Hobsbawm, Eric. 1984. "Introduction: Inventing Traditions." In *The Invention of Tradition*, ed. Eric Hobsbawm and Terence Ranger, 1–14. Cambridge: Cambridge University Press.
Hobsbawm, E. J., and T. O. Ranger. 1984. *The Invention of Tradition.* Past and Present Publications. 1st paperback ed. Cambridge: Cambridge University Press.
Hogle, Jerrold E. 1998. "The Gothic Ghost as Counterfeit and Its Haunting of Romanticism: The Case of 'Frost at Midnight.'" *European Romantic Review* 9, no. 2: 283–292.
Holyoke, Edward. 1744. *The Testimony of the President, Professors, Tutors, and Hebrew Instructor of Harvard College in Cambridge against the Reverend Mr. George Whitefield and His Conduct.* Boston: Printed and sold by T. Fleet.
Hooke, Robert. 1971. "A General Scheme, or Idea of the Present State of Natural Philosophy." *The Posthumous Works of Robert Hooke.* Ed. Theodore M. Brown. London: Cass.
Horkheimer, Max and Theodor W. Adorno. 1969 [1947]. *Dialectic of Enlightenment.* Trans. by John Cummings. New York: Continuum.
Howell, Wilbur Samuel. 1971. *Eighteenth-Century British Logic and Rhetoric.* Princeton: Princeton University Press.
Hudson, Nicholas. 1994. *Writing and European Thought, 1600–1830.* New York: Cambridge University Press.
———. 1996a. "'O Divinum Scripturae Beneficium!' Swift's Satire of Writing and Its

Intellectual Context." In *The Age of Johnson: A Scholarly Annual*, ed. Paul Korshin, vol. 7: 343–363. New York: AMS Press.

———. 1996b. "'Oral Tradition': The Evolution of an Eighteenth-Century Concept." In *Tradition in Transition: Women Writers, Marginal Texts, and the Eighteenth-Century Canon*, ed. Alvaro Ribeiro, S.J., and James G. Basker, 161–176. Oxford: Clarendon Press.

———. 2002. "Constructing Oral Tradition: The Origins of the Concept in Enlightenment Intellectual Culture." In *The Spoken Word: Oral Culture in Britain, 1500–1850*, ed. Adam Fox and Daniel Woolf, 240–255. Manchester: Manchester University Press.

Hume, David. 1978. *A Treatise of Human Nature*. Ed. Lewis Amherst Selby-Bigge and P. H. Nidditch. 2nd ed. Oxford and New York: Clarendon Press.

———. 1985. *Essays: Moral, Political, and Literary*. Ed. Eugene F. Miller. Indianapolis: LibertyClassics.

Hunter, Michael Cyril William. 1998. *Archives of the Scientific Revolution: The Formation and Exchange of Ideas in Seventeenth-Century Europe*. Woodbridge: Boydell Press, 1998.

Hunter, Michael, and Edward B. Davis. 1996. "The Making of Robert Boyle's 'Free Enquiry into the Vulgarly Receiv'd Notion of Nature' (1686)." *Early Science and Medicine* 1, no. 2: 204–271.

India Ministry of Broadcasting, Research, Information, and Reference Division. 1999. *Mass Media in India, 1998–99*. New Delhi: Publications Division, Ministry of Information and Broadcasting, Government of India.

Innis, Harold Adams. 1951. *The Bias of Communication*. Toronto: University of Toronto Press.

Israel, Jonathan Irvine. 2001. *Radical Enlightenment: Philosophy and the Making of Modernity, 1650–1750*. New York: Oxford University Press.

Israel, Paul. 1992. *From Machine Shop to Industrial Laboratory: Telegraphy and the Changing Context of American Invention, 1830–1920*. Johns Hopkins Studies in the History of Technology. Baltimore: Johns Hopkins University Press.

Jacob, Margaret C. 1981. *The Radical Enlightenment: Pantheists, Freemasons and Republicans*. Early Modern Europe Today. London; Boston: Allen & Unwin.

Jakobson, Roman. 1981. "Linguistics and Poetics." *Roman Jakobson, Selected Writings*. The Hague: Mouton.

James, Elinor. 2005. *Elinor James: Essential Works*. Ed. Paula McDowell. The Early Modern Englishwoman, series 2: Printed Writings, 1641–1700; part 3, vol. 11. Aldershot: Ashgate, 2005.

Jamieson, Robert. 1806. *Popular Ballads and Songs, from Tradition, Manuscripts, and Scarce Editions*. Edinburgh and London: Constable; John Murray.

Jardine, N. 1996. "Naturphilosophie and the Kingdoms of Nature." In *Cultures of Natural History*, ed. J. A. Secord N. Jardine and E. C. Spary, 230–245. Cambridge: Cambridge University Press.

Jefferson, Thomas. 1982. *Jefferson's Extracts from the Gospels: "The Philosophy of Jesus" And "The Life and Morals of Jesus."* Ed. Dickinson W. Adams and Ruth W. Lester. The Papers of Thomas Jefferson, 2nd ser. Princeton: Princeton University Press.

Jevons, W. Stanley. 1908. *Money and the Mechanism of Exchange*. London: Kegan Paul, Trench, Trubner & Co.

Jean Paul. 1960. *Werke*. Erster Band. Ed. Norbert Miller. Munich: Carl Hanser Verlag.

———. 1981. *Die Unsichtbare Loge: Eine Biographie*. Munich: Edition Text + Kritik.

John, Richard R. 1995. *Spreading the News: The American Postal System from Franklin to Morse*. Cambridge: Harvard University Press.

Johns, Adrian. 1998. *The Nature of the Book: Print and Knowledge in the Making*. Chicago: University of Chicago Press.

———. 2002. "How to Acknowledge a Revolution." *American Historical Review* 107, no. 1: 106–125.

Johnson, James, ed. 1853. *The Scots Musical Museum; Consisting of Upwards of Six Hundred Songs, with Proper Basses for the Pianoforte*. 4 vols. With copious notes and illustrations of the lyric poetry and music of Scotland by the late William Stenhouse. Edinburgh: William Blackwood & Sons.

Johnson, Steven. 1999. *Interface Culture: How New Technology Transforms the Way We Create and Communicate*. New York: Basic Books.

Johnson, Samuel. 1968. "Preface" to *The Plays of William Shakespeare*. Yale Edition of the Works of Samuel Johnson. Ed. Arthur Sherbo. New Haven: Yale University Press.

Johnston, Patricia. 2006. "Samuel F.B. Morse's *Gallery of the Louvre*: Social Tensions in an Ideal World." In *Seeing High and Low: Representing Social Conflict in American Visual Culture*, ed. Patricia Johnston, 42–65. Berkeley: University of California Press.

Jones, C. B. 1993. *Radical Sensibility: Lectures and Ideas in the 1790s*. London: Routledge.

Kant, Immanuel. 1798. *Essays and Treatises on Moral, Political, and Various Philosophical Subjects*. 2 vols. Trans. J. Richardson. London: J. Richardson.

———. 1922. " Von der Unrechtmäßigkeit des Büchernachdruck." *Schriften von 1783–1788*. Berlin.

———. 1952. *The Critique of Judgement*. Ed. James Creed Meredith. Oxford: Clarendon Press.

———. 1976. *Kritik der reinen Vernunft*. Ed. Wilhelm Weischedel. 2nd ed. Frankfurt am Main: Suhrkamp Verlag.

———. 1985. "An Answer to the Question, What Is Enlightenment?" Trans. H. B. Nisbet. *Kant's Political Writings*. Ed. Hans Reiss, 54–60. Cambridge: Cambridge University Press.

———. 1996a. "An Answer to the Question: What Is Enlightenment? (1784)". Trans. James Schmidt. *What Is Enlightenment. Eighteenth-Century Answers and Twentieth-Century Quenstions*. Ed. by James Schmidt, 58–64. Berkeley: University of California Press.

———. 1996b. "On the Wrongfulness of Unauthorized Publication of Books." *Practical Philosophy*. Ed. M. J. Gregor Wood, 23–35. Cambridge: Cambridge University Press.

———. 1996c. "Metaphysics of Morals." *Practical Philosophy*. Ed. M. J. Gregor Wood, 353–604. Cambridge: Cambridge University Press.

———. 1997. "Was ist Aufklärung?" *The Politics of Truth*. Ed. Sylvère Lotringer Hochroth and Lysa. New York: Semiotext(e).

———. 2005. *Notes and Fragments.* Ed. Paul Guyer. Cambridge Edition of the Works of Immanuel Kant. Cambridge: Cambridge University Press.

———. 2007. "Was Ist Aufklarung?" *The Politics of Truth.* Ed. Sylvere Lotringer Hochroth and Lysa. New York: Semiotext(e).

Kernan, Alvin B. 1989. *Samuel Johnson and the Impact of Print.* Princeton: Princeton University Press.

Kerr, Robert. 1811. *Memoirs of the Life, Writings, & Correspondence of William Smellie, Late Printer in Edinburgh, Secretary and Superintendent of Natural History to the Society of Scotish Antiquaries.* Edinburgh: J. Anderson.

Keynes, John Maynard. 1950. *A Treatise on Money.* London: Macmillan.

Kimnach, Wilson. 1992. "Introduction to Jonathan Edwards." *Sermons and Discourses, 1720–1723.* New Haven: Yale University Press.

Kind, John Louis. 1906. "Edward Young in Germany; Historical Surveys, Influence Upon German Literature, Bibliography." Ph.D. diss., Columbia University.

Kittler, Friedrich A. 1990. *Discourse Networks 1800/1900.* Ed. and forward. David E. Wellbery. Stanford: Stanford University Press.

———. 1995. "Aufschreibesysteme 1800/1900." Munich: Wilhelm Fink.

———. 2002. "Optische Medien: Berliner Vorlesung." Berlin: Merve Verlag.

Knott, Sarah, and Barbara Taylor. 2005. *Women, Gender and Enlightenment.* Houndmills; New York: Palgrave Macmillan.

Koselleck, Reinhart. 1972. "Einleitung." *Geschichtliche Grundbegriffe. Historisches Lexikon Zur Politisch-Sozialen Sprache in Deutschland.* Herausgegeben Von Otto Brunner, Werner Conze, and Reinhart Koselleck, xii–xxvii. Band 1. Stuttgart: Klett-Cotta.

———. 1973. "Kritik und Krise. Eine Studie zur Pathogenese der bürgerlichen Welt." Frankfurt am Main: Suhrkamp Verlag.

———. 2000. "Zeitschichten. Studien Zur Historik." *Mit einem Beitrag von Hans-Georg Gadamer.* Frankfurt am Main: Suhrkamp, 9–16.

Krajewski, Markus. 2002. *Zettelwirtschaft: Die Geburt der Kartei aus dem Geist der Bibliothek.* Berlin: Kulturverlag Kadmos.

Kramnick, Isaac. 1995. *The Portable Enlightenment Reader.* Viking Portable Library. New York: Penguin Books.

Krause, J. S. 1783. "Über den Büchernachdruck." *Deutsches Museum* (May).

Kristeller, Paul Oskar. 1965. "The Modern System of the Arts." *Renaissance Thought II: Papers on Humanism and the Arts,* 163–227. New York: Harper.

Kroeber, A. L., and Clyde Kluckhohn. 1952. *Culture: A Critical Review of Concepts and Definitions.* New York: Vintage Books.

Kurke, Leslie. 1999. *Coins, Bodies, Games, and Gold: The Politics of Meaning in Archaic Greece.* Princeton: Princeton University Press.

Kwakkel, Erik. 2003. "A New Type of Book for a New Type of Reader: The Emergence of Paper in Vernacular Book Production." *Library* 7th ser., 4: 219–248.

Labarre, Albert. 1975. *Bibliographie Du Dictionarium D'ambrogio Calepino: (1502–1779).* Bibliotheca Bibliographica Aureliana. Baden-Baden: Koerner.

Lacan, Jacques. 1966. *Écrits.* Le Champ Freudien. Paris: Éditions du Seuil.

Lafitau, Joseph-François. 1974–1977. *Customs of the American Indians Compared with the Customs of Primitive Times* [1724]. Edited and translated William N. Fenton and Elizabeth L. Moore. 2 vols. Toronto: Champlain Society.

Lambert, Frank. 2001. *Inventing the "Great Awakening."* Princeton: Princeton University Press.

Langan, Celeste. 2001. "Understanding Media in 1805: Audiovisual Hallucination in the Lay of the Last Minstrel." *Studies in Romanticism* 40, no. 1: 49–70.

Latour, Bruno. 1987. *Science in Action: How to Follow Scientists and Engineers through Society.* Cambridge.: Harvard University Press.

———. 1990. "Drawing Things Together." *Representation in Scientific Practice*. 1st MIT Press ed. Ed. Michael Lynch and Steve Woolgar. Cambridge: MIT Press.

———. 1991. *We Have Never Been Modern.* Cambridge: Harvard University Press.

———. 1993. *We Have Never Been Modern.* Cambridge: Harvard University Press.

———. 1999. *Pandora's Hope: Essays on the Reality of Science Studies.* Cambridge: Harvard University Press.

Latour, Bruno, and Steve Woolgar. 1979. *Laboratory Life: The Social Construction of Scientific Facts.* Beverly Hills: Sage Publications.

Laugero, Greg. 1995. "Infrastructures of Enlightenment: Road-Making, the Public Sphere, and the Emergence of Literature." *Eighteenth-Century Studies* 29, no. 1.

La Vopa, Anthony J. 1995. "Herder's Publikum: Language, Print, and Sociability in Eighteenth-Century Germany." *Eighteenth-Century Studies* 29, no. 1: 5–24.

Lee, Richard Henry, 1970. *The Letters of Richard Henry Lee.* Vol. 1. Ed. James Curtis Ballagh. New York: Da Capo Press.

Lemay, J. A. Leo. 2005. *Life of Benjamin Franklin.* Vol. 1. Philadelphia: University of Pennsylvania Press.

Leibniz, G. W. 1962. *Mathematische Schriften.* 7 vols. Ed. C. I. Gerhardt. Berlin then Halle, 1849–63; reprint, Hildesheim: Olms.

Lennox, Charlotte. 1989. *The Female Quixote,.* Ed. Margaret Dalziel with an intro. by Margaret Anne Doody. Oxford: Oxford University Press.

Lerner, Daniel. 1958. *The Passing of Traditional Society: Modernizing the Middle East.* Glencoe: Free Press.

Lessig, Lawrence. 2000. *Code and Other Laws of Cyberspace.* New York: Basic Books.

Lessing, G. E. 1970–1979. "Leben Und Leben Lassen." *Werke.* 8 vols. Munich: Carl Hanser.

Lévi-Strauss, Claude. 1962. *La Pensée Sauvage.* Paris: Librairie Plon.

Lindner, Burkhardt. 1976. *Jean Paul: Scheiternde Aufklärung und Autorrolle.* 1. Aufl. ed. Darmstadt: Agora Verlag.

Linnaeus, Carl. 2003. *Iter Lapponcium, Lappländska Resan 1732, I Dagboken.* Ed. Hellblom et al. Umeå: Kungl. Skytteanska Samfundet.

Locke, John. 1967. "Second Treatise of Government." *Two Treatises of Government.* 2d ed. Cambridge: Cambridge University Press.

———. 1975. *An Essay concerning Human Understanding.* Ed. P. H. Nidditch. Oxford: Clarendon Press.

———. 1990. *An Essay concerning Human Understanding.* Ed. P. H. Nidditch. Oxford: Clarendon Press.

———. 1995. *An Essay concerning Human Understanding*. Great Books in Philosophy. Amherst: Prometheus Books.

———. 2001. *An Essay concerning Human Understanding*. Batoche Books.

Looby, Christopher. 1996. *Voicing America: Language, Literary Form, and the Origins of the United States*. Chicago: University of Chicago Press.

Loughran, Trish. 2007. *The Republic in Print: Print Culture in the Age of U.S. Nation Building*. New York: Columbia University Press.

Love, Harold. 2003. "Early Modern Print Culture: Assessing the Models." *Parergon: Journal of the Australian and New Zealand Association for Medieval and Early Modern Studies* 20, no. 1: 45–64.

Macherey, Pierre. 1978. *A Theory of Literary Production*. London: Routledge & Kegan Paul.

Macpherson, James. 1996. *The Poems of Ossian and Related Works*. Ed. Howard Gaskill. Edinburgh: Edinburgh University Press.

Maïer, Ida. 1965. *Les Manuscrits d'ange Politien. Catalogue Descriptif.* Travaux d'humanisme et Renaissance. Geneva: Droz.

Maier, Pauline. 1976. "Coming to Terms with Samuel Adams." *American Historical Review* 81, no. 1: 12–37.

Malcolm, Noel. 2004. "Thomas Harrison and His 'Ark of studies': An Episode in the History of the Organization of Knowledge." *Seventeenth Century* 19: 196–232.

Malebranche, Nicolas. 1993. *Treatise on Ethics* [1684]. Translated by Craig Walton. Dordrecht: Kluwer Academic Publishers.

Mandeville, Bernard. 1988. *The Fable of the Bees, or, Private Vices, Publick Benefits*. 2 vols. Ed. F. B. Kaye. Indianapolis: Liberty Classics.

Manley, Delariviere. 1999. *The Adventures of Rivella*. Broadview Literary Texts. Ed. Katherine Zelinsky. Peterborough: Broadview Press.

Manning, Susan. 2007. "Henry Mackenzie's Report on Ossian: Cultural Authority in Transition." *Modern Language Quarterly: A Journal of Literary History* 68, no. 4: 517–539.

Manovich, Lev. 2000. *The Language of New Media*. Cambridge: MIT Press.

Marshall, T. H. 1964. *Class, Citizenship, and Social Development; Essays*. 1st ed. Garden City: Doubleday.

Martinez-Bonati, Felix. 1980. "The Act of Writing Fiction." *New Literary History: A Journal of Theory and Interpretation* 11, no. 3: 425–434.

Masuzawa, Tomoko. 2005. *The Invention of World Religions*. Chicago, University of Chicago Press.

Mather, Cotton. 1726. *Manuductio Ad Ministerium: Directions for a Candidate of the Ministry: Wherein, First, a Right Foundation Is Laid for His Future Improvements, and, Then, Rules Are Offered for Such a Management of His Academical & Preparatory Studies, and Thereupon for Such a Conduct after His Appearance in the World as May Render a Skilful and Usful Minister of the Gospel*. Boston: Printed for Thomas Hancock and sold at his shop.

Mattelart, Armand. 1996. *The Invention of Communication*. Minneapolis: University of Minnesota Press.

Mayr, Otto. 1986. *Authority, Liberty, and Automatic Machinery in Early Modern Europe*.

Johns Hopkins Studies in the History of Technology. Baltimore: Johns Hopkins University Press.

McEachern, Jo-Ann E. 1993. *Bibliography of the Writings of Jean-Jacques Rousseau to 1800: Julie, ou La Nouvelle Héloïse.* Vol. 1. Oxford: Voltaire Foundation.

McClellan, Andrew. 1994. *Inventing the Louvre: Art, Politics, and the Origins of the Modern Museum in Eighteenth-Century Paris.* Cambridge: Cambridge University Press.

McDowell, Paula. 1998. *The Women of Grub Street: Press, Politics, and Gender in the London Literary Marketplace, 1678–1730.* Oxford: Clarendon Press.

———. 2006. "'The Manufacture and Lingua-facture of *Ballad-Making*': Broadside Ballads in Long Eighteenth-Century Ballad Discourse." *Eighteenth Century: Theory and Interpretation* 47, nos. 2–3: 151–178.

———. 2010. "'The Art of Printing Was Fatal': Print Culture and the Idea of Oral Tradition in Eighteenth-Century Ballad Discourse." In *British Ballads and Broadsides, 1550–1800*, ed. Patricia Fumerton and Anita Guerrini. Aldershot: Ashgate Press.

McGann, Jerome. 1992. "Reviews and Retrospects: Rethinking Romanticism." *ELH* 59, no. 3: 735–754.

McKeon, Michael. 1987. *The Origins of the English Novel, 1600–1740.* Baltimore: Johns Hopkins University Press.

McLane, Maureen N. 2006. "Dating Orality, Thinking Balladry: Of Milkmaids and Minstrels in 1771." *Eighteenth Century: Theory and Interpretation* 47, nos. 2–3: 131–49, 332.

———. 2008. *Balladeering, Minstrelsy, and the Making of British Romantic Poetry.* New York: Cambridge University Press.

McLaverty, J. 2001. *Pope, Print, and Meaning.* Oxford: Oxford University Press.

McLuhan, Marshall. 1962. *The Gutenberg Galaxy: The Making of Typographic Man.* Toronto: University of Toronto Press.

———. 2001. *Understanding Media.* 2d ed. London: Routledge.

McMullin, Ernan. 1967. "Empiricism and the Scientific Revolution." In *Art, Science, and History in the Renaissance*, ed. Charles Southward Singleton. Baltimore: Johns Hopkins Press.

Mead, Sidney Earl. 1963. *The Lively Experiment: The Shaping of Christianity in America.* New York: Harper & Row.

Meek, Ronald L. 1976. *Social Science and the Ignoble Savage.* Cambridge: Cambridge University Press.

Meinel, Christoph. 1995. "Enyzkolpädie der Welt Und Verzettelung des Wissens: Aporien der Empirie bei Joachim Jungius." In *Enzyklopädien der frühen Neuzeit: Beiträge zu ihrer Erforschung*, ed. Franz M. Eybl, 162–187. Tübingen: M. Niemeyer.

Mendle, Michael. 2006. "The 'Prints' of the Trials: The Nexus of Politics, Religion, Law and Information in Late Seventeenth-Century England." In *Fear, Exclusion and Revolution: Roger Morrice and Britain in the 1680s*, ed. Jason Mc Elligott, 123–137. Aldershot: Ashgate.

Mercier, Louis-Sebastien. 1782. *Tableau De Paris.* New ed. 12 vols. Amsterdam.

———. 2000. "Pariser Nahaufnahmen—Tableau de Paris." Trans. by Wolfgang Tschöke. Frankfurt am Main: Eichborn.

Meusel, J. G. 1778. *Das Gelehrte Teutschland*. Meyersche Buchhandlung.
Miles, Robert. 2008. *Romantic Misfits*. Houndmills: Palgrave Macmillan.
Mill, John Stuart. 1973. *Dissertations and Discussions; Political, Philosophical, and Historical*. New York: Haskell House Publishers.
Miller, Perry. 1965. *The Life of the Mind in America, from the Revolution to the Civil War*. 1st ed. New York: Harcourt.
Minsheu, John, et al. 1617. *Ductor in Linguas, The Guide into Tongues*. Londini: Apud Ioannem Browne.
Molesworth, Jesse Marti. 2004. "Against All Odds: The Sway of Chance in Eighteenth-Century Britain." *Dissertation Abstracts International, Section A: The Humanities and Social Sciences* 64, no. 9: 3307.
Momigliano, Arnaldo. 1966. "Ancient History and the Antiquarian." In *Studies in Historiography*, ed. Arnaldo Momigliano, 1–39. London: Weidenfeld and Nicolson.
Monboddo, James Burnett. 1773–1792. *Origin and Progress of Language*. 6 vols. Edinburgh: Printed for J. Balfour and T. Cadell.
Moran, Daniel. 1990. *Toward the Century of Words: Johann Cotta and the Politics of the Public Realm in Germany, 1795–1832*. Berkeley: University of California Press.
Moretti, Franco. 2000. "Conjectures on World Literature." *New Left Review* 1: 57.
———. 2003. "Graphs, Maps, Trees: Abstract Models for Literary History—1." *New Left Review* 24: 67–93.
Morse, Samuel F. B. 1973. *Samuel F. B. Morse; His Letters and Journals*. Ed. Edward Lind Morse. New York: Da Capo Press.
———. 1983. *Lectures on the Affinity of Painting with the Other Fine Arts*. Ed. Nicolai Cikovsky. Columbia: University of Missouri Press.
———. 2001. "Samuel F. B. Morse Papers at the Library of Congress, 1791–1919." August. http://memory.loc.gov/ammem/sfbmhtml/sfbmhome.html.
*Morse et al. v. O'Reilly et al.* 17 Fed. Cas. 871. CCD Ky 1848.
Motherwell, William. 1846. *Minstrelsy, Ancient and Modern* [1827]. 2 vols. Boston: W. D. Ticknor & Co.
Müller-Wille, Staffan, and Sara Scharf. 2009. "Indexing Nature: Carl Linnaeus (1707–78) and His Fact-Gathering Strategies." Working Papers on the Nature of Evidence: How Well Do "Facts" Travel? no 36/08, London School of Economics.
Mulligan, Lotte. 1992. "Robert Hooke's 'Memoranda': Memory and Natural History." *Annals of Science* 49: 47–61.
Nani Mirabelli, Domenico. 1503. *Polyanthea*. Savona: Da Silva.
———. 1620. *Polyanthea*. Lyon: Ravaud.
Naudé, Gabriel. 1963. *Advis Pour Dresser une Bibliothèque* [1628]. Reprint, Leipzig: VEB.
Newton, Isaac, I. Bernard Cohen, and Anne Miller Whitman. 1999. *The Principia: Mathematical Principles of Natural Philosophy*. Berkeley: University of California Press.
Nichols, Ashton. 1998. *The Revolutionary "I": Wordsworth and the Politics of Self-Presentation*. Romanticism in Perspective. New York: St. Martin's Press.
Nichols, John. 1815. *Literary Anecdotes of the Eighteenth Century*. London: Printed for the author, by Nichols, son, and Bentley.
Nunberg, Geoffrey. 1996. "Farewell to the Information Age." In *The Future of the Book*, ed. Geoffrey Nunberg, 103–138. Berkeley: University of California Press.

O'Brien, Karen. 2005. "World-Changing Ideas." *History Workshop Journal* 59: 243–245.
O'Brien, Susan. 1994. "Eighteenth-Century Publishing Networks in the First Years of Transatlantic Evangelicalism." In *Evangelicalism: Comparative Studies of Popular Protestantism in North America, the British Isles, and Beyond, 1700–1990*, ed. Mark Noll et al. New York: Oxford University Press.
Ogborn, Miles. 2007. *Indian Ink: Script and Print in the Making of the English East India Company*. Chicago: University of Chicago Press.
O'Hara, James G. 1998. "'A Chaos of Jottings That I Do Not Have the Leisure to Arrange and Mark with Their Headings': Leibniz's Manuscript Papers and Their Repository." In *Archives of the Scientific Revolution: The Formation and Exchange of Ideas in Seventeenth-century Europe*, ed. Michael Cyril William Hunter, 159–170. Woodbridge: Boydell Press.
Oliver, Peter. 1961. *Origin and Progress of the American Rebellion; a Tory View*. Huntington Library Publications. San Marino: Huntington Library.
Ong, Walter J. 1967. *The Presence of the Word: Some Prolegomena for Cultural and Religious History*. Terry Lectures. New Haven: Yale University Press.
———. 1982. *Orality and Literacy: The Technologizing of the Word*. London; New York: Methuen.
———. 2002. "An Interview with Walter J. Ong Conducted by George Riemer." In *An Ong Reader: Challenges for Further Inquiry*, ed. Thomas J. Farrell and Paul A. Soukup, 79–109. Hampton Press Communication Series/Media Ecology. Cresskill: Hampton Press.
———. 2004. *Ramus, Method, and the Decay of Dialogue: From the Art of Discourse to the Art of Reason*. Chicago: University of Chicago Press.
O'Toole, James M. 1976. "The Historical Interpretations of Samuel Adams." *New England Quarterly: A Historical Review of New England Life and Letters* 49, no. 1: 82–96.
Outram, Dorinda. 2005. *The Enlightenment*. 2d ed. Cambridge: Cambridge University Press.
Packer, Jeremy, and Craig Robertson. 2006. *Thinking with James Carey: Essays on Communications, Transportation, History*. Intersections in Communications and Culture. New York: Peter Lang.
Palmer, Norman D. 1977. "India in 1976: The Politics of Depolticization." *Asian Survey* 17, no. 2: 160–180.
Parmentier, Richard J. 1985. "'Signs' Place in Medias Res: Peirce's Concept of Semiotic Mediation." In *Semiotic Mediation: Sociocultural and Psychological* Perspectives, ed. Elizabeth Mertz and Richard J. Parmentier. Orlando: Academic Press.
Parry, Milman. 1928. *L'Épithète traditionnelle dans Homère*. In *The Making of Homeric Verse: The Collected Papers of Milman Parry*, ed. Adam Parry, 1–190. Oxford: Oxford University Press, 1971.
Pastorius, Francis Daniel. [1696]. *His Hive, Melliotrophium Alvear or, Rusca Apium, Begun Anno Do[Mi]Ni or, in the Year of Christian Account 1696*. MS Codex 726, Department of Special Collections, Van Pelt Library, University of Pennsylvania, Philadelphia.
Patey, Douglas Lane. "Ancients and Moderns." In *The Cambridge History of Literary*

*Criticism*, vol. 4, *The Eighteenth Century*, ed. H. B. Nisbet and Claude Rawson, 32–71. Cambridge: Cambridge University Press.

Peirce, Charles S. 1931–1935, 1958. *Collected Papers of Charles Sanders Peirce*. Ed. Charles Hartshorne and Paul Weiss. Cambridge: Harvard University Press.

Pepys, Samuel. 1972. *The Diary of Samuel Pepys*. Ed. Robert Latham and William Matthews. Vol. 7. Berkeley: University of California Press.

Percy, Thomas, ed. 1996. *Reliques of Ancient English Poetry, Consisting of Old Heroic Ballads, Songs, and Other Pieces of Our Earlier Poets, Together with Some Few of Later Date* [3 vols., 1765]. Ed. Henry B. Wheatley, 1886; reprint, New York: Dover.

Perry, Ruth, ed. 2006. "Ballads and Songs in the Eighteenth Century." Special issue, *Eighteenth Century: Theory and Interpretation* 47, nos. 2–3.

Peters, John Durham. 1999. *Speaking into the Air: A History of the Idea of Communication*. Chicago: University of Chicago Press.

———. 2006. "Technology and Ideology: The Case of the Telegraph Revisited." In *Communications, Transportation, History: Rethinking the Legacy of James Carey*, ed. Jeremy Packer and Craig Robertson. New York: Peter Lang.

Pinault, Madeleine. 1991. "Sur Le Planches de L'encyclopédie." In *L'Encyclopédisme: actes du colloque de Caen, 12-16 janvier 1987*, ed. Annie Becq, 355–367. Paris: Aux Amateurs de livres: Diffusion, Klincksieck.

Pinkerton, John. 1781. *Scottish Tragic Ballads*. London: J. Nichols.

———. 1786. *Ancient Scotish Poems, Never before in Print*. 2 vols. London and Edinburgh.

Pittock, Murray. 1997. *Inventing and Resisting Britain: Cultural Identities in Britain and Ireland, 1685–1789*. British Studies Series. New York: St. Martin's Press.

Placcius, Vincent. 1689. *De Arte Excerpendi*. Stockholm and Hamburg: Gottfried Liebezeit.

Pliny the Younger. 1969. *Letters and Panegyricus*. Trans. Betty Radice. 2 vols. Cambridge, MA: Harvard University Press.

Plutarch. 1657. "How a Yoong Man Ought to Heare Poets, and How He May Take Profit by Reading Poemes." Trans. Philemon Holland. *The Morals*. London: J. Kirton.

Pollard, Alfred W., et al. 1986–1991. *A Short-Title Catalogue of Books Printed in England, Scotland, & Ireland and of English Books Printed Abroad, 1475–1640*. London: Bibliographical Society.

Poovey, Mary. 1998. *A History of the Modern Fact: Problems of Knowledge in the Sciences of Wealth and Society*. Chicago: University of Chicago Press.

———. 2008. *Genres of the Credit Economy: Mediating Value in Eighteenth- and Nineteenth-Century Britain*. Chicago: University of Chicago Press.

Pope, Alexander. 1963. *The Twickenham Edition of the Poems of Alexander Pope*. 3rd ed. Ed. John Butt et al. London: Routledge.

———. 1965. *Peri Bathous: Of the Art of Sinking in Poetry. Literary Criticism of Alexander Pope*. Ed. Bertrand A. Goldgar. Lincoln: University of Nebraska Press.

———. 1999. *The Dunciad in Four Books* [1743]. Ed. Valerie Rumbold. Longman Annotated Texts. New York: Longman/Pearson Education.

Porter, James, ed. 2001. "James Macpherson and the Ossian Epic Debate." Special issue, *Journal of American Folklore* 114 (Fall).

Pratt, Mary Louise. 1986. "Fieldwork in Common Places." In *Writing Culture: The Poetics and Politics of Ethnography: A School of American Research Advanced Seminar*, ed. James Clifford and George E. Marcus. Berkeley: University of California Press, 1986.

Preda, Alex. 2006. "Socio-Technical Agency in Financial Markets: The Case of the Stock Ticker." *Social Studies of Science* 36, no. 5: 753–782.

Quedenbaum, Gerd. 1977. *Der Verleger Und Buchhändler Johann Heinrich Zedler, 1706–1751: E. Buchunternehmer in D. Zwängen Seiner Zeit: E. Beitr. Zur Geschichte D. Dt. Buchhandels Im 18. Jh.* Hildesheim: Olms.

Rajan, Tilottama. 1980. *Dark Interpreter: The Discourse of Romanticism*. Ithaca: Cornell University Press.

Ranzovius, Henricus. 1584. *Catalogus Imperatorum Regum Et Virorum Illustrium Qui Artem Astrologicam Amarunt, Exercuerunt Et Ornarunt*. Leipzig: Georgius Defner.

Raven, James. 2001. "The Book Trades." In *Books and Their Readers in Eighteenth-century England: New Essays*, ed. Isabel Rivers, 1–34. London: Leicester University Press.

Raymond, Joad. 2006. Introduction. *News Networks in Seventeenth-century Britain and Europe*. Ed. Joad Raymond. London.

Reddick, Allen Hilliard. 1996. *The Making of Johnson's Dictionary, 1746–1773*. Cambridge Studies in Publishing and Printing History. Rev. ed. Cambridge: Cambridge University Press.

Redekop, Benjamin W. 2000. *Enlightenment and Community: Lessing, Abbt, Herder and the Quest for a German Public*. Mcgill-Queen's Studies in the History of Ideas. Montreal: McGill-Queen's University Press.

Reill, Peter Hanns. 2005. *Vitalizing Nature in the Enlightenment*. Berkeley: University of California Press.

Reiss, Hans, ed. 1970. *Kant's Political Writings*. Cambridge: [s.n.].

Richards, Robert J. 2002. *The Romantic Conception of Life: Science and Philosophy in the Age of Goethe*. Science and Its Conceptual Foundations. Chicago: University of Chicago Press.

Richardson, Samuel. 1964. *Selected Letters of Samuel Richardson*. Ed. John Carroll. Oxford: Oxford University Press.

———. 1971. *Pamela* or, Virtue Rewarded. Ed. T.C. Duncan Eaves and Ben D. Kimpel. Boston: Houghton Mifflin Co.

——— 1982. *Clarissa; or, The History of a Young Lady*. 4 vols. Ed. John Butt. London: J. M. Dent.

———. 2001. *Pamela or Virtue Rewarded*. Ed. Tom Keymer and Alice Wakely. Oxford: Oxford University Press.

Richetti, John J. 1983. *Philosophical Writing: Locke, Berkeley, Hume*. Cambridge: Harvard University Press.

Ridge, Oliver. 1628? *Writing Tables, with a Calendar for xxiii Yeeres*. London: the Company of Stationers.

Riebeeck, Jan van. 1897a. "Precis of the Archives of the Cape of Good Hope: Letters Dispatched from the Cape, 1652–1662." Ed. H. C. V. Leibbrandt. Cape Town: W. A. Richards & Sons.

———. 1897b. "Precis of the Archives of the Cape of Good Hope: Riebeeck's Journal, January 1659–May 1662." Ed. H. C. V. Leibbrandt. Cape Town: W. A. Richards & Sons.

Riskin, J. 2004. "The Defecating Duck; or, The Ambiguous Origins of Artificial Life." In *Things*, ed. B. Brown, 99–133. Chicago: University of Chicago Press.

Ritson, Joseph. 1783. "A Historical Essay on the Origin and Progress of National Song." *A Select Collection of English Songs*. 3 vols. London: Printed for J. Johnson.

———. 1794. "Historical Essay on Scotish Song." *Scotish Song in Two Volumes*. London: Printed for J. Johnson.

Robertson, John. 2005. *The Case for the Enlightenment: Scotland and Naples 1680–1760*. Cambridge: Cambridge University Press.

Rodgers, Gary Bruce. 1973. *Diderot and the Eighteenth-Century French Press*. Banbury: Voltaire Foundation.

Rothschild, Arthur de. 1980. *Histoire de la Poste aux Lettres et du Timbre-Poste depuis leurs Origines jusqu'a Nos Jours*. Geneva.

Rouse, Mary A., and Richard H. Rouse. 1991. *Authentic Witnesses: Approaches to Medieval Texts and Manuscripts*. Publications in Medieval Studies. Notre Dame: University of Notre Dame Press.

Rouse, Richard and Mary Rouse. 1974. "The Verbal Concordance to the Scriptures." *Archivum Fratrum Praedicatorum* 44: 5–30.

———. 1979. *Preachers, Florilegia and Sermons: Studies on the Manipulus florum of Thomas of Ireland*. Toronto: Pontifical Institute of Mediaeval Studies.

Rousseau, Jean-Jacques. 1966. *Essay on the Origin of Languages* [c. 1762–1763]. Reprinted in Jean-Jacques Rousseau and Gottfried Herder, *Two Essays on the Origin of Language*. Ed. and trans. John H. Moran and Alexander Gode. Chicago: University of Chicago Press.

Ryerson, Richard Alan. 1978. *The Revolution Is Now Begun: The Radical Committees of Philadelphia, 1765–1776*. Philadelphia: University of Pennsylvania Press.

Saenger, Paul. 1996. "The Impact of the Early Printed Page on the History of Reading." *Bulletin du Bibliophile* 2: 237–301.

Saussure, Ferdinand de. 1973. *Course in General Linguistics*. Trans. Roy Harris. La Salle, IL: Open Court.

Scaliger, Joseph Juste. 1977. *The Auction Catalogue of the Library of J. J. Scaliger*. Catalogi Redivivi. Facsimile ed. Utrecht: H & S Publishers.

Schaffer, Simon. 1989. "Glass Works: Newton's Prisms and the Uses of Experiment." *The Uses of Experiment: Studies in the Natural Sciences*, ed. David Gooding, T. J. Pinch and Simon Schaffer. Cambridge: Cambridge University Press.

———. 1990. "Genius in Romantic Natural Philosophy." In *Romanticism and the Sciences*, ed. Andrew Cunningham and Nicholas Jardine, 82–98. Cambridge: Cambridge University Press.

———. 1999. "Enlightened Automata." *The Sciences in Enlightened Europe*, ed. William Clark, Jan Golinski, and Simon Schaffer. Chicago: University of Chicago Press.

Schick, Edgar B. 1971. *Metaphorical Organicism in Herder's Early Works; a Study of the Relation of Herder's Literary Idiom to His World-View*. De Proprietatibus Litterarum. Series Practica. The Hague: Mouton.

Schiller, Friedrich. 1982. "Die Polizey." *Schiller's Werke, Nationalausgabe*, vol. 12, *Dramatische Fragmente*. Weimar: Böhlaus.

———. 2004. *Fragmente, Übersetzungen, Bearbeitungen*. Ed. Jörg Robert and Albert Meier. Munich: Hanser.

Schleiermacher, Friedrich. 1998. *Hermeneutics and Criticism and Other Writings*. Ed. Andrew Bowie. Cambridge Texts in the History of Philosophy. Cambridge: Cambridge University Press.

Schlesinger, Lee I. 1997. "The Emergency in an Indian Village." *Asian Survey* 17, no. 7: 633–634.

Schmidt, James. 1996. *What Is Enlightenment?: Eighteenth-Century Answers and Twentieth-Century Questions*. Philosophical Traditions. Berkeley: University of California Press, 1996.

———. 2003. "Inventing the Enlightenment: Anti-Jacobins, British Hegelians, and the Oxford English Dictionary." *Journal of the History of Ideas* 64, no. 3: 421–443.

———. 2006. "What Enlightenment Was, What It Might Still Be, and Why Kant May Have Been Right after All." *American Behavioral Scientist* 49, no. 5: 421–443.

———. 2007. "Misunderstanding the Question: 'What Is Enlightenment?'" http://people.bu.edu/jschmidt/Havens.pdf.

Schmitt, Carl, and G. L. Ulmen. 2003. *The Nomos of the Earth in the International Law of the Jus Publicum Europaeum*. New York: Telos Press.

Schneider, Manfred. 1994. "Die Erfindung der Zukunft des Staates. Friedrich II. und das Calcul." *Gutenberg und die neue Welt*. Eds. Horst Wenzel, Friedrich A. Kittler and Manfred Schneider. Munich: W. Fink.

Schwab, Richard N. 1969. "The Diderot Problem, the Starred Articles and the Question of Attribution in the Encyclopedie." *Eighteenth-Century Studies* 2: 240–285, 370–438.

Scott, David, and Charles Hirschkind, eds. 2006. *Powers of the Secular Modern: Talal Asad and His Interlocutors*. Stanford: Stanford University Press.

Scott, Walter. 1830. *The Poetical Works of Walter Scott, Bart. Together with the Minstrelsy of the Scottish Border*. Magnum Opus edition. New York: Leavitt and Allen, 1830.

Seaver, Paul S. 1970. *The Puritan Lectureships; the Politics of Religious Dissent, 1560–1662*. Stanford: Stanford University Press.

Selement, George. 1980. "Publication and the Puritan Minister." *William and Mary Quarterly* 37, no. 2: 219–241.

Selwyn, Pamela Eve. 2000. *Everyday Life in the German Book Trade: Friedrich Nicolai as Bookseller and Publisher in the Age of Enlightenment, 1750–1810*. Penn State Series in the History of the Book. University Park: Pennsylvania State University Press.

Severs, Jan. 1527. *Calengier*. Antwerp: Jan Severs.

Sergeant, John. 1666. *Letter of Thanks from the Author of Sure-Footing To his Answerer Mr. J. T.* Paris:.

Sewel, William. 1708. *A Large Dictionary, English and Dutch*. Amsterdam: Steven Swart.

Shackleton, Robert. 1961. *Montesquieu; a Critical Biography*. London: Oxford University Press.

Shaftesbury, Anthony Ashley Cooper. 1711. *Characteristicks of Men, Manners, Opinions, Times. In Three Volumes*, vol. 1.1, *A Letter concerning Enthusiasm*. Vol. 2.3, *The Moralists; a Philosophical Rhapsody* [London]: [printed by John Darby].

Shanahan, John Henry. 2008. "Ben Jonson's Alchemist and Early Modern Laboratory Space." *Journal for Early Modern Cultural Studies* 8, no. 1: 35–66.

———. 2009. "Theatrical Space and Scientific Space in Thomas Shadwell's *Virtuoso*," *SEL*, 49, no. 3: 549–571.

Shannon, Claude Elwood, and Warren Weaver. 1963. *The Mathematical Theory of Communication*. Urbana: University of Illinois Press.

Shapin, Steven. 1989. "The Invisible Technician." *American Scientist* 77: 554–563.

Shapin, Steven, and Simon Schaffer. 1985. *Leviathan and the Air-Pump: Hobbes, Boyle, and the Experimental Life: Including a Translation of Thomas Hobbes, Dialogus Physicus De Natura Aeris by Simon Schaffer*. Princeton: Princeton University Press.

Sharpe, Kevin. 2000. *Reading Revolutions: The Politics of Reading in Early Modern England*. New Haven: Yale University Press.

Shaws, Edward P. 1966. *Problems and Policies of Malesherbes as Directeur De La Librarie in France (1750–1763)*. State University of New York.

Sheehan, Jonathan. 2003. "Enlightenment, Religion, and the Enigma of Secularization: A Review Essay." *American Historical Review* 108, no. 4: 1061–1080.

Sheridan, Thomas. 1968. *A Course of Lectures on Elocution* [1762]. New York: B. Blom.

Sherman, Brad, and Lionel Bently. 1999. *The Making of Modern Intellectual Property Law: The British Experience, 1760–1911*. Cambridge Studies in Intellectual Property Rights. Cambridge: Cambridge University Press.

Shulte-Sasse, Jochen. 2001. "Medium." *Ästhetische Grundbegriffe (ÄGB): historisches Wörterbuch in sieben Bänden*. 7 vols. Ed. Karlheinz Barck and Martin Fontius. Stuttgart: Metzler.

Siegel, Joel G., and Jae K. Shim. 2005. *Dictionary of Accounting Terms*. 4th ed. Hauppauge: Barron's.

Siegert, Bernhard. 1999. *Relays: Literature as an Epoch of the Postal System*. Writing Science. Stanford: Stanford University Press.

——— 2003. *Passage des Digitalen: Zeichenpraktiken der neuzeitlichen Wissenschaften 1500–1900*. Berlin: Brinkmann & Bose.

Silverman, Kenneth. 2003. *Lightning Man: The Accursed Life of Samuel F.B. Morse*. 1st ed. New York: Alfred A. Knopf.

Simmons, R. C., and P. D. G. Thomas. 1985. *Proceedings and Debates of the British Parliaments Respecting North America*, vol. 4, January to May 1774. White Plains: Kraus International Publications.

Simon, Julia. 1995. *Mass Enlightenment: Critical Studies in Rousseau and Diderot*. Suny Series in Social and Political Thought. Albany: State University of New York Press.

Siskin, Clifford. 1988. *The Historicity of Romantic Discourse*. New York: Oxford University Press.

———. 1998. *The Work of Writing: Literature and Social Change in Britain, 1700–1830*. Baltimore: Johns Hopkins University Press.

———. 2001. "Novels and Systems." *Novel* 34, no. 2 (Spring): 202–215.

———. 2005. "More Is Different: Literary Change in the Mid- and Late Eighteenth Century." In *The Cambridge History of English Literature, 1660–1780*, ed. John J. Richetti, 795–823. Cambridge: Cambridge University Press.

———. 2006. "William Wordsworth." *The Oxford Encyclopedia of British Literature*, ed. David Kastan, 5: 326–334. Oxford: Oxford University Press.

———. 2009. "The Problem of Periodization: Enlightenment, Romanticism, and the Fate of System." *The Cambridge History of English Romantic Literature*, ed. James Chandler, 101–126. Cambridge: Cambridge University Press.

Siskin, Clifford and Warner, William B. 2004. "Digital Retroaction: A Research Digital Symposium." http://dc-mrg.english.ucsb.edu/conference/D_Retro/conference.html.

———. 2007. *Description of Conference*. Mediating Enlightenment: Past and Present. April 15–17. http://www.mediatingenlightenment.com.

Skemer, Don C. 1995. "From Archives to the Book Trade: Private Statute Rolls in England, 1285–1307." *Journal of the Society of Archivist* 16, no. 2: 193–206.

Skinner, Andrew. 1997. Introduction. *The Wealth of Nations*. Vol. 1. Ed. Adam Smith: Hammondsworth, 1997.

Skydsgaard, Jens Erik. 1968. *Varro the Scholar: Studies in the First Book of Varro's De Re Rustica*. Analecta Romana Instituti Danici. Supplementum. Copenhagen: E. Munksgaard.

Smith, Adam. 1967. "Essays on Philosophical Subjects" [1795]. *The Early Writings of Adam Smith*. Ed. Ralph J. Lindgren. New York: Augustus M. Kelley.

———. 1976a. *An Inquiry into the Nature and Causes of the Wealth of Nations*. Chicago: University of Chicago Press.

———. 1976b. *The Theory of Moral Sentiments* [1759]. Vol. 1. Ed. D. D. Raphael and A. L. Macfie. Glasgow Edition of the Works and Correspondence of Adam Smith. Oxford: Clarendon Press.

———. 1981. *The Wealth of Nations*. The Glasgow Edition of the Works and Correspondence of Adam Smith. Ed. R. H. Campbell, A. S. Skinner, and W. B. Todd. Indianapolis: Liberty Fund.

———. 1997. *The Wealth of Nations*. 2 vols. New York: Penguin Classic.

Smith, Margaret M. 1988. "Printed Foliation: Forerunner to Printed Page-Numbers?" *Gutenberg-Jahrbuch* 63 (1988): 54–70.

Smith, Pamela H. 2004. *The Body of the Artisan: Art and Experience in the Scientific Revolution*. Chicago: University of Chicago Press.

Spadafora, David. 1990. *The Idea of Progress in Eighteenth-Century Britain*. New Haven: Yale University Press.

Spary, E. C. 2000. *Utopia's Garden: French Natural History from Old Regime to Revolution*. Chicago: University of Chicago Press.

Sprat, Thomas. 1722. *The History of the Royal Society of London, for the Improving of Natural Knowledge*. 3d ed. London: Printed for S. Chapman.

St. Clair, William. 2004. *The Reading Nation in the Romantic Period*. Cambridge: Cambridge University Press.

Stafford, Fiona. 1996. Introduction. *The Poems of Ossian and Related Works*. Ed. Howard Gaskill. Edinburgh: Edinburgh University Press.

Stagl, Justin. 1980. "Die Apodemik Oder 'Reisekunst' Als Methodik Der Sozialforschung Vom. Humanismus Bis Zur Aufklärung." *Statistik und Staatsbeschreibung in der Neuzeit, vornehmlich im 16.–18. Jahrhundert. Bericht für ein interdisziplinäres Symposion.* Eds. Mohammed Rassem and Justin Stagl. Munich: Schöningh.

Staiti, Paul J., and Samuel Finley Breese Morse. 1989. *Samuel F.B. Morse.* Cambridge Monographs on American Artists. Cambridge: Cambridge University Press.

Stallybrass, Peter. 2006. "Benjamin Franklin: Printed Corrections and Erasable Writing." *Proceedings of the American Philosophical Society* 150, no. 44: 553–567.

———. 2007. "Erasable Notebooks and Writing Technologies, 1500–1900." *Gazette of the Grolier Club* n.s. 58: 5–44.

Stallybrass, Peter, et al. 2004. "Hamlet's Tables and the Technologies of Writing in Renaissance England." *Shakespeare Quarterly* 55, no. 4: 379–419.

Starr, George. 2003. "Why Defoe Probably Did Not Write the Apparition of Mrs. Veal." *Eighteenth-Century Fiction* 15, nos. 3–4: 421–450.

Starr, Paul. 2004. *The Creation of the Media: The Political Origins of Modern Communications.* New York: Basic Books.

Steinke, Martin William, ed. 1917. *Edward Young's "Conjectures on Original Composition" in England and Germany.* Americana Germanica, n.s., 28. New York: F. C. Stechert Co.

Steinmann, Martin. 1987. *Die Handschriften Des Universitätsbibliothek Basel.* 2d ed. Basel: Bibliothek.

Stephens, John Calhoun, Richard Steele, and Joseph Addison. 1982. *The Guardian.* Lexington: University Press of Kentucky.

Sterne, Laurence. 1965. *The Life and Opinions of Tristram Shandy, Gentleman.* Ed. Ian P. Watt. Boston: Houghton Mifflin.

Stewart, Dugald. 1792. *Elements of the Philosophy of the Human Mind*, Part 1. London: Printed for A. Strahan, and T. Cadell 1792.

———. 1854–1860. *The Collected Works of Dugald Stewart.* 11 vols. Ed. William Hamilton. Edinburgh: T. Constable and Co.

Stewart, Susan. 1994. "Scandals of the Ballad." *Crimes of Writing: Problems in the Containment of Representation.* 1st paperback ed. Durham: Duke University Press, 1994.

Stillinger, Jack. 1994. *Coleridge and Textual Instability: The Multiple Versions of the Major Poems.* New York: Oxford University Press.

Stoddard, Solomon. 1724. *The Defects of Preachers Reproved.* New London: Printed and sold by T. Green.

Stolnitz, Jerome. 1961. "'Beauty': Some Stages in the History of an Idea." *Journal of the History of Ideas* 22: 185–204.

Stout, Harry S. 1991. *Divine Dramatist: George Whitefield and the Rise of Modern Evangelicalism.* Grand Rapids: Eerdmans.

———. 1998. "Religion, Communications, and the Ideological Origins of the American Revolution." *Religion in American History: A Reader*, ed. Jon Butler and Harry S. Stout, 88–128. New York: Oxford University Press.

Strachan, Michael, et al. 1971. *The East India Company Journals of Captain William Keeling and Master Thomas Bonner, 1615–1617.* Minneapolis: University of Minnesota Press.

Swift, Jonathan. 1999. *A Tale of a Tub and Other Works.* Eds. Angus Ross and David Woolley. Oxford: Oxford University Press.

———. 2005. *Gulliver's Travels*. Ed. Claude Rawson. Oxford: Oxford University Press.
Swift, Jonathan, and Robert DeMaria. 2001. *Gulliver's Travels*. Penguin Classics. London: Penguin Books.
Tatham, David. 1981. "Samuel F. B. Morse's Gallery of the Louvre: The Figures in the Foreground." *American Art Journal* 13: 38–48.
Taylor, Charles. 2007. *A Secular Age*. Cambridge: Belknap Press.
te Heesen, Anke. 2005. "Accounting for the Natural World: Double-Entry Bookkeeping in the Field." *Colonial Botany: Science, Commerce, and Politics in the Early Modern World*, ed. Londa L. Schiebinger and Claudia Swan, 237–251. Philadelphia: University of Pennsylvania Press.
Tennent, Gilbert, and American Imprint Collection. 1742. *The Danger of an Unconverted Ministry: Considered in a Sermon on Mark Vi, 34*. Boston: Printed and sold by Rogers and Fowle.
Thompson, John B. 1995. *The Media and Modernity: A Social Theory of the Media*. Stanford: Stanford Univeristy Press.
Thompson, Judith. 1997. "An Autumnal Blast, a Killing Frost: Coleridge's Poetic Conversation with John Thelwall." *Studies in Romanticism* 36, no. 3: 427–456.
Thompson, Robert Luther. 1947. *Wiring a Continent: The History of the Telegraph Industry in the United States, 1832–1866*. Princeton: Princeton University Press.
Thomson, Charles. 1878. *Collections of the New-York Historical Society*. New York: Publication Fund Series.
Thoreau, Henry David. 1959. *Walden or Life in the Woods*. Ed. Norma Holmes Pearson. New York: Reinehart.
Tort, Patrick. 1989. *La Raison Classificatoire: Quinze Études*. Paris: Aubier.
Treadwell, Michael. 1980. "London Printers and Printing Houses in 1705." *Publishing History* 7: 5–44.
Trevor-Roper, Hugh. 1983. "The Invention of Tradition: The Highland Tradition of Scotland." In *The Invention of Tradition*, ed. E. J. Hobsbawm and T. O. Ranger, 15–41. Cambridge: Cambridge University Press.
Trumpener, Katie. 1997. *Bardic Nationalism: The Romantic Novel and the British Empire*. Princeton: Princeton University Press.
Tugnoli Pattaro, Sandra, and Ulisse Aldrovandi. 1977. *La Formazione Scientifica e Il Discorso Naturale di Ulisse Aldrovandi*. Quaderni Di Storia E Filosofia Della Scienza. Trento: Unicoop.
Turnèbe, Adrien. 1581. "*Adversariorum Tomi Iii*." Basel: Thomas Guarinus.
Twain, Mark. 1883. *Life on the Mississippi*. Boston: J. R. Osgood and Company.
Unseld, Siegfried. 1996. *Goethe and His Publishers*. Chicago: University of Chicago Press.
Vail, Alfred, and YA Pamphlet Collection. 1845. *Description of the American Electro Magnetic Telegraph: Now in Operation between the Cities of Washington and Baltimore. Illustrated by Fourteen Wood Engravings*. Washington: Printed by J. & G. S. Gideon.
Vaillé, Eugene. 1950. *Le Cabinet Noir*. Paris: Presses universitaires de France, 1950.
Valenze, Deborah M. 2006. *The Social Life of Money in the English Past*. New York: Cambridge University Press.

VanWinkle, Matthew. 2004. "Fluttering on the Grate: Revision in 'Frost at Midnight.'" *Studies in Romanticism* 43, no. 4 (2004): 583–598.

Venkataraman, G. 1983. "Reaching the Millions through Davp." *Mass Media in India, 1981–83*. New Delhi: Goverment of India, Ministry of Information and Broadcasting.

Veyne, Paul. 1971. *Comment on Écrit L'histoire, Essai D'épistómologie*. Paris: Éditions du Seuil.

Vismann, Cornelia. 2000. *Akten. Medientechnik und Recht*. Frankfurt; Fischer Taschenbuch.

Voet, Léon. 1972. *The Golden Compasses. A History and Evaluation of the Printing and Publishing Activities of the Officina Plantiniana at Antwerp*. Vol. 2. Amsterdam: Van Gendt and Co.

Vogel, Sabine. 1999. *Kulturtransfer in der Frühen Neuzeit. Die Vorworte der Lyoner Drucke des 16. Jahrhunderts*. Tübingen: Mohr Siebeck.

Vogl, Joseph. 2000. "Staatsbegehren. Zur Epoche der Polizey." *Deutsche Vierteljahrsschrift für Literaturwissenschaft und Geistesgeschichte* 74: 600–626.

Waldron, Arthur. 1990. *The Great Wall of China: From History to Myth*. Cambridge Studies in Chinese History, Literature, and Institutions. Cambridge: Cambridge University Press.

Walsh, Marcus. 1990. "Text, 'Text,' and Swift's A Tale of a Tub." *The Modern Language Review* 85, no. 2: 290–303.

Walsham, Alexandra. 2002. "Reformed Folklore? Cautionary Tales and Oral Tradition in Early Modern England." In *The Spoken Word: Oral Culture in Britain, 1500–1850*, ed. Adam Fox and D. R. Woolf, 173–195. Manchester: Manchester University Press; distributed exclusively in the U.S. by Palgrave.

Walton, James. 2007. "On the Attribution of 'Mrs. Veal.'" *Notes and Queries* 54: 60–62.

Ward, Albert. 1974. *Book Production, Fiction and the German Reading Public, 1740–1800*. Oxford: Clarendon Press.

Warkentin, Germaine. 2005. "Humanism in Hard Times: The Second Earl of Leicester." In *Challenging Humanism: Essays in Honor of Dominic Baker-Smith*, ed. Dominic Baker-Smith, A. J. Hoenselaars, and Arthur F. Kinney, 229–253. Newark: University of Delaware Press.

Warner, Michael. 1990. *The Letters of the Republic: Publication and the Public Sphere in Eighteenth-Century America*. Cambridge: Harvard University Press.

———. 1999. *American Sermons: The Pilgrims to Martin Luther King* New York: Library of America.

———. 2002. *Publics and Counterpublics*. New York: Zone Books.

Warner, Michael, et al., eds. 2010. *Varieties of Secularism in a Secular Age*. Cambridge: Harvard University Press.

Warner, William B. 1998. *Licensing Entertainment: The Elevation of Novel Reading in Britain, 1684–1750*. Berkeley: University of California Press.

———. 2005. "Communicating Liberty: The Newspapers of the British Empire as a Matrix for the American Revolution." *English Literary History* 72, no. 2: 339–361.

———. 2007. "Networking and Broadcasting in Crisis; or, How Do We Own Computable Culture?" In *Media Ownership: Research and* Regulation, ed. Ronald E. Rice. Hampton Press.

Warren, Mercy Otis. 1989. *History of the Rise, Progress, and Termination of the American Revolution: Interspersed with Biographical, Political, and Moral Observations*. Ed. Lester H. Cohen. Indianapolis: Liberty Classics.

Watt, Ian P. 1959. *The Rise of the Novel: Studies in Defoe, Richardson, and Fielding*. Berkeley: University of California Press.

Waters, Lindsay. 2007. "Time for Reading." *Chronicle of Higher Education* 53 (23) (9 February): B6–B8.

Weber, Samuel. 1996. "Television: Set and Screen." In *Mass Mediauras: Form, Technics, Media*, ed. Samuel Weber and Alan Cholodenko. Stanford: Stanford University Press, 1996.

Webster, Noah, et al. 1828. *An American Dictionary of the English Language: Intended to Exhibit, I. The Origin, Affinities and Primary Signification of English Words as Far as They Have Been Ascertained, Ii. The Genuine Orthography and Pronunciation of Words, According to General Usage or to Just Principles of Analogy, Iii. Accurate and Discriminating Definitions, with Numerous Authorities and Illustrations: To Which Is Prefixed, an Introductory Dissertation on the Origin, History, and Connection of the Languages of Western Asia and of Europe, and a Concise Grammar of the English Language*. 2 vols. New York: S. Converse.

Weiss, Wisso. *Zeittafel Zur Papiergeschichte*. Leipzig: Fachbuchverlag, 1983.

Wellisch, Hans H. 1981. "How to Make an Index—Sixteenth-century Style: Conrad Gessner on Indexes and Catalogs." *International Classifications* 8: 10–15.

Werrett, Simon. 2007a. "Explosive Affinities: Pyrotechnic Knowledge in Early Modern Europe." In *Making Knowledge in Early Modern Europe: Practices, Objects, and Texts, 1400–1800*, ed. Pamela H. Smith and Benjamin Schmidt. Chicago: University of Chicago Press.

———. 2007b. "From the Grand Whim to the Gasworks: Philosophical Fireworks in Georgian England." In *The Mindful Hand: Inquiry and Invention from the Late Renaissance to Early Industrialisation*, ed. Lissa Roberts, Simon Schaffer, and Peter Dear, 325–347. Amsterdam: Koninkliijke Nederlandse Akademie van Wetenschappen.

Westfall, Richard S. 1980. *Never at Rest: A Biography of Isaac Newton*. Cambridge: Cambridge University Press.

Wheeler, Kathleen M. 1981. "The Struggle with Associationism." *The Creative Mind in Coleridge's Poetry*. London: Heinemann.

White, Helena. 1993. "The Botanical Works of R. Dodoens, C. Clusius and M. Lobelius." *Botany in the Low Countries, End of the 15th century–ca. 1650: Plantin-Moretus Museum exhibition*, ed. W. de Backer, et al, 33–37. Antwerp: City of Antwerp: Plantin-Moretus Museum, Stedelijk Prentenkabinet (Municipal Printroom).

Wilkins, John. 1694. *Mercury; or, The Secret and Swift Messenger. Shewing, How a Man May with Privacy and Speed Communicate His Thoughts to a Friend at Any Distance*. 2d ed. London: Printed for Richard Baldwin.

———. 2002. *An Essay towards a Real Character, and a Philosophical Language*. Bristol: Thoemmes Press.

Williams, Raymond. 1966. *Culture and Society, 1780–1950* New York: Harper & Row.

———. 1976. *Keywords: A Vocabulary of Culture and Society.* New York: Oxford University Press.

———. 1977. *Marxism and Literature.* Marxist Introductions. Oxford: Oxford University Press.

———. 1985. *Keywords: A Vocabulary of Culture and Society.* New York: Oxford University Press.

Williams, Stephen. 1754–1755. *Diary, 1754–1755.* MSS C 2497. R. Stanton Avery Special Collections Department, New England Historic Genealogical Society.

Williamson, Judith. 1978. *Decoding Advertisements: Ideology and Meaning in Advertising.* Ideas in Progress. London: Boyars: Distributed by Calder and Boyars.

Wills, Garry. 1979. *Inventing America: Jefferson's Declaration of Independence.* New York: Vintage Books.

Winter, Alison. 1998. *Mesmerized: Powers of Mind in Victorian Britain.* Chicago: University of Chicago Press.

Withers, Charles W. J. 2007. *Placing the Enlightenment: Thinking Geographically about the Age of Reason.* Chicago: University of Chicago Press.

Wittmann, Reinhard. 1999. "Was There a Reading Revolution as the End of the Eighteenth Century." Trans. L. G. Cochrane. In *A History of Reading in the* West, ed. Guglielmo Cavallo, Roger Chartier and Lydia G. Cochrane, 284–312. Cambridge: Polity Press.

———. 2004. "Highwaymen or Heroes of Enlightenment? Viennese and South German Pirates and the German Market." Unpublished paper presented "The History of Books and Intellectual History," conference at Princeton University. Available online at http://www.princeton.edu/csb/conferences/december_2004/papers/Wittman_Paper.doc.

Wood, Gillen D'Arcy. 2001. *The Shock of the Real: Romanticism and Visual Culture, 1760–1860.* 1st ed. New York: Palgrave.

Wood, Robert. 1775. *An Essay on the Original Genius and Writings of Homer.* London.

Woodmansee, Martha. 1994. *The Author, Art, and the Market: Rereading the History of Aesthetics.* New York: Columbia University Press.

Woof, Robert. 2001. *William Wordsworth: The Critical Heritage.* Critical Heritage Series. Vol. 1. London; New York: Routledge.

Wordsworth, Jonathan. 1993. Introduction. *Poems 1792.* Oxford: Woodstock.

Wordsworth, William. 1974. *The Prose Works of William Wordsworth.* 3 vols. Ed. W. J. B. Owen and Jane Worthington Smyser. Oxford: Clarendon Press.

Wordsworth, William, and Dorothy Wordsworth. 1967. *The Letters of Wiliam and Dorothy Wordsworth: The Early Years, 1787–1805.* 2 vols. Ed. Ernest De Sélincourt and Chester L. Shaver. Oxford: Oxford University Press.

Wroth, Lawrence C. 1965. *The Colonial Printer.* New York: Dover.

Wulf, Andrea. 2008. *The Brother Gardeners: Botany, Empire and the Birth of an Obsession.* London: William Heinemann.

Yeo, Richard R. 2001. *Encyclopaedic Visions: Scientific Dictionaries and Enlightenment Culture.* Cambridge: Cambridge University Press.

———. 2004. "John Locke's 'New Method' of Commonplacing: Managing Memory and Information." *Eighteenth-Century Thought* 2: 1–38.

———. 2007. "Between Memory and Paperbooks: Baconianism and Natural History in Seveneeth-Century England." *History of Science* 45: 1–46.

Yolton, Jean S. 1998. *John Locke: A Descriptive Bibliography.* Bristol: Thoemmes Press.

Young, Edward. 1759a. *Conjectures on Original Composition.* Dublin: for P. Wilson.

———. 1759b. *Conjectures on Original Composition. In a Letter to the Author of Sir Charles Grandison.* London: A. Millar and R. and J. Dodsley.

———. 1971. *The Correspondence of Edward Young, 1683–1765.* Ed. Henry Pettit. Oxford: Clarendon Press.

Zedelmaier, Helmut. 2004. "Facilitas Inveniendi. Zur Pragmatik Alphabetischer Buchregister." *Wissenssicherung, Wissensordnung und Wissenverarbeitung: das europäische Modell der Enzyklopädien*, ed. Theo Stammen and Wolfgang Weber, 191–203. Berlin: Akademie Verlag.

Zola, Émile. 1964. *The Experimental Novel, and Other Essays.* New York: Haskell House.

Zöllner, Johan Friedrich. 1973. "Ist es rathsam, das Ehebündniß nicht ferner durch die Religion zu sancieren." *Was ist Aufklärung? Beiträge aus der Berlinischen Monatsschrift*, ed. Norbert Hinske and Michael Albrecht, 107–116. Darmstadt: Wissenschaftliche Buchgesellschaft.

Zouche, Richard. 1902. *An Exposition of Fecial Law and Procedure, or of Law between Nations, and Questions concerning the Same.* Trans. J. L. Brierly: Carnegie Institute.

Zwinger, Theodor. 1565. *Theatrum Vitae Humanae.*Basel: Oporinus and Froben brothers.

———. 1586. *Theatrum Humane Vitae.* Basel: Eusebius Episcopius.

# CONTRIBUTORS

IAN BAUCOM is professor of English and director of the Franklin Humanities Institute at Duke University and author of *Out of Place: Englishness, Empire and the Locations of Identity* and *Specters of the Atlantic: Finance Capital, Slavery, and the Philosophy of History.*

JOHN BENDER is the Jean G. and Morris M. Doyle Professor in Interdisciplinary Studies at Stanford University and director of the Stanford Humanities Institute. He is the author of *Imagining the Penitentiary: Fiction and the Architecture of Mind in Eighteenth-Century England.* He is coauthor, with Michael Marrinan, of *The Culture of Diagram.*

ANN BLAIR is the Henry Charles Lea Professor of History at Harvard University and author of *The Theater of Nature: Jean Bodin and Renaissance Science* and *Too Much To Know: Managing Scholarly Information Before the Modern Age.*

PETER DE BOLLA is professor of cultural history and aesthetics at the University of Cambridge, where he is also a fellow of King's College and author of *The Education of the Eye: Painting, Landscape and Architecture in Eighteenth-Century Britain* and *Art Matters.*

KNUT OVE ELIASSEN is professor of comparative literature and Scandinavian studies at the Norwegian University of Science and Technology, Trondheim. He has written on technology and literature, French philosophy and on the eighteeenth-century European novel.

ANNE FASTRUP is associate professor of arts and cultural studies at the University of Copenhagen and has written on Rousseau, Diderot, and Cervantes.

LISA GITELMAN is associate professor of English and of media, culture, and communication at New York University, and the author of *Scripts, Grooves, and Writing Machines: Representing Technology in the Edison Era* and *Always Already New: Media, History, and the Data of Culture.*

JOHN GUILLORY is Silver Professor of English at New York University and the author of *Culture Capital: The Problem of Literary Canon Formation.*

YNGVE SANDHEI JACOBSEN was senior researcher in comparative literature and Scandinavian studies at the Norwegian University of Science and Technology, Trondheim. He wrote on literature and science, technology and media.

ADRIAN JOHNS is professor of history at the University of Chicago and author of *The Nature of the Book: Print and Knowledge in the Making* and *Piracy: The Intellectual Property Wars from Gutenberg to Gates.*

HELGE JORDHEIM is senior researcher in German studies at the University of Oslo and academic director of the interdisciplinary research program KULTRANS. He is the author of *Der Staatsroman im Werk Wielands und Jean Pauls.*

PAULA MCDOWELL is associate professor of English at New York University and the author of *The Women of Grub Street: Press, Politics, and Gender in the London Literary Marketplace 1678-1730* and the editor of *Elinor James: Printed Writings.*

MICHAEL MCKEON is Board of Governors Professor of Literature at Rutgers University and author of *The Origins of the English Novel, 1600-1740* and *The Secret History of Domesticity: Public, Private, and the Division of Knowledge.*

MAUREEN MCLANE is associate professor of English at New York University and author of *Romanticism and the Human Sciences: Poetry, Population and the Discourse of the Species* and *Balladry, Minstrelsy, and the Making of British Romantic Poetry.*

ROBERT MILES is chair of the English department at the University of Victoria and author of *Gothic Writing, 1750–1820: A Genealogy* and *Romantic Misfits.*

MARY POOVEY is founder of the Institute for the History of the Production of Knowledge and the Samuel Rudin University Professor of the Humanities at New York University. She is the author of *A History of the Modern Fact: Problems of Knowledge in the Sciences of Wealth and Society* and *Genres of the Credit Economy: Mediating Value in Eighteenth- and Nineteenth-Century Britain.*

ARVIND RAJAGOPAL is professor of media studies, sociology, and social and cultural analysis at New York University and the author of *Politics after Television: Hindu Nationalism and the Reshaping of the Public in India* and editor of *The Indian Public Sphere: Readings in Media History.*

BERNHARD SIEGERT is Gerd Bucerius Professor of the History and Theory of Cultural Technologies at the Bauhaus University of Weimar and director of the International Research Institute for Cultural Technologies and Media Philosophy. He is the author of *Relays: Literature as an Epoch of the Postal System* and *Passagiere und Papiere.*

CLIFFORD SISKIN is the Henry W. and Alfred A. Berg Professor of English at New York University and director of the Re:Enlightenment Project at New York University and the New York Public Library. He is the author of *The Historicity of Romantic Discourse* and *The Work of Writing: Literature and Social Change in Britain, 1700–1830.*

PETER STALLYBRASS is the Walter H. and Leonore C. Annenberg Professor in the Humanities at the University of Pennsylvania and coauthor, with Allon White, of *The Politics and Poetics of Transgression* and, with Ann Rosalind Jones, of *Renaissance Clothing and the Materials of Memory*.

MICHAEL WARNER is the Seymour H. Knox Professor of English, professor of American studies, and chair of the English Department at Yale University. He is the author of *Publics and Counterpublics* and *The Letters of the Republic: Publication and the Public Sphere in Eighteenth-Century America*.

WILLIAM WARNER is professor of English the University of California, Santa Barbara and was the founder and director of the Digital Cultures Project. He is the author of *Reading Clarissa: The Struggles of Interpretation* and *Licensing Entertainment: The Elevation of Novel Reading in Britain, 1684–1750*.

# INDEX

*Page numbers in italic refer to illustrations.*

Abel, Karl, 385
academic specialization, 170
actor-network, 116–18
Adams, Frank, 423n20
Adams, John, 107, 108
Adams, Samuel, 107, 108, 115, 419n5
Addison, Joseph, 13, 32, 243, 378; and aesthetic attitude, 395–96; and arts and sciences, 391–96; imagination versus understanding, 406; and imaginative distantiation, 392–93, 394
Adorno, Theodor, 428n6
advertising, 10, 57; and changes in social orientation, 216; critical scholarship on, 216–17; as discourse linking culture and economy, 217. *See also* Indian advertising
Aeschylus, 386
aesthetic attitude: Addison and, 395–96; and reflexivity of form and content, 397, 403, 405, 407–8, 411
aesthetic autonomy, 276–77, 282
aesthetics: as body of knowledge, 384; and commodity exchange, 410–11;
dramatic, 397, 404; emergence of, 32; and the empirical sciences, 32, 384–85, 408; Enlightenment theory of, 127; modern usage, 170, 385; narrative, 402–3; "police," 361–65; and reflexivity, 407; transcendental, 362, 363, 365; transposition from object to subjective experience, 275
aesthetic value: and exchange value, 410; quantification of, 409–10
*aether*, 65
Agamben, Giorgio, 117
*Agents of Change: Print Culture Studies after Elizabeth L. Eisenstein*, 233
Albrecht VII, Cardinal Duke, 12
Aldrovandi, Ulisse, 154
Alembert, Jean le Rond d', 158, 163, 432n2
alphabetical index, 141, 149, 150
*Alrehande Minuten*, 152
*Alrehande Missiven*, 152
amanuenses, 156, 158
Amerbach, Basil, *157*
"Amerbach slips," *156*

479

American Revolution: and history of mediation, 25, 100–119; and transmission of liberty, 103, 105. *See also* Boston Committee of Correspondence
Ancient vs Modern Quarrel, and division between arts and sciences, 385, 386–89, 393
Anglican Church, suspicion of unwritten tradition, 238
animism, 186, 187
*l'Année littéraire*, 268, 269
anthropology, 85
antiphilosophers, 268–70
antiquarian collectors, 249–50; as mediators and inventors of oral tradition, 28. *See also* balladeering
Antonius Hieratus, 158
Aquinas, Thomas, 142
Arendt, Hannah: *Origins of Totalitarianism*, 328–29, 336, 342–43, 350
Aristotle, 5, 40, 56, 61, 386; concept of senses, 66; *De Anima*, 72; *De Interpretatione*, 416n3; *Poetics*, 56, 417n10; on tragedy, 393
Arrighi, Giovanni, 338, 350–51, 355
art, commercialization of, 276
Artaud, Jean-Baptiste, 366
art criticism, modern, and isolation of art from political sphere, 282
articulation, 82
arts and sciences, dialectical relation between, 385, 386–89, 391–96, 412
Asad, Talal, 435n1
Asiatic Society, 13
associational practices, 12, 15, 16, 18–19, 22, 107–11, 116, 333, 369, 383, 415n13; Royal Society, 18; voluntary associations, 13
Atterbury, Francis, 378
Attig, John C., 302
Austen, Jane, 294
Austin, J. L., 113
authorship: collaborative, 153–63; debates over, 304, 306–7, 309–10; Herder's view of creative, 312–14; Kant on, 317; recognized as property right in Baden, 319; Romantic theories of, 307, 310, 319–20
automata, 76–79, 312–13, 318

Babbage, Charles, 10, 66, 320
Bacon, Francis, 1, 166; *The Advancement of Learning*, 48, 57; call for "Great Renewal," 2, 6; critique of Scholasticism, 10; on current state of knowledge, 2; "delay" between Bacon and start of Enlightenment, 11, 12, 17, 25; experiment as planned experience, 289–90; *Great Instauration: The New Organon*, 3–5; and induction, 5, 292, 386–87, 413n4; versus Kant, 2–4, 20; on necessity of tools, 4–5, 6, 7; pairing of knowledge and power, 5; *Philosophical Works*, Shaw edition, 17–18; and power of print, 10; *Of the Proficiencie and Advancement of Learning*, 40–41; and reform of knowledge, 13, 18, 20; relation between language and thought, 41; use of word "mediation," 6, 41; use of word "medium," 6, 65, 414n6; and utility of writing for transfer of thoughts, 41
Baden, 319
Baillet, Adrien, 159, 426n46
Bailyn, Bernard: *Ideological Origins of the American Revolution*, 369–70
Baker, Keith, 22, 23, 104
balladeering, 242–44; authentication, 252–53; ballad collections, 248, 249, 251, 252, 254, 262; ballad scandals, 256–57; and binary of orality and literacy, 243; citation system, 252–53; close reading, modeling of for readers, 259, 261; close reading, protocols of for showing authenticity, 256–62; comparative textual criticism, 258; confrontational models of, 242; at conjunction of culture and media, 247–50; controversy over ballad "Hardyknute," 257–58; and dialectic

between eighteenth-century antiquarianism and enlightenment, 249–50; discourse on methodological issues, 254; as enquiry into media, 263; headnotes, 253; multiply mediated feedback loop, 255; printed musics as well as verbal texts as objects of study, 261; subtitling of ballads, 259
ballad informants, 251
ballad revival, 242–44, 248–49, 250–51
ballads, 28; problem of representing in print, 251; Scottish, 253; shared lines and stanzas, 258; street broadsides, 243–44, 249
*Ballads into Books: The Legacies of Francis James Child* (Cheesman and Rieuwerts), 247, 248
Balzac, Honoré de: *Modeste Mignon*, 367
banking system, 14
Bank of England, 14
Barbauld, Anna Letitia, 27, 170, 184, 186; "A Summer Evening's Meditation," 177–78, 181; and "stranger" trope, 177
Barlow, John Perry, 103
Barnard, F. M., 312
Barnard, John, 423n20, 434n18
Barnett, Thomas P.: *The Pentagon's New Map*, 337, 354–55
Barrow, Isaac, 378
Basilius Lucius, 156
Baucom, Ian: "Financing Enlightenment, Part Two: Extraordinary Expenditure," 30, 323
Baudrillard, Jean, 358
Baumgarten, Alexander Gottlieb, 384
Bazerman, Charles, 166
beautiful and sublime, 394–95
Beauvais, Vincent of, 153, 422n4
Beauvais, Vincent of: *Speculum maius*, 141
Bedmar, Marqués of, 360
*begriffsgeschichte*, 287

Behn, Aphra, 398
Bell, Robert, 304
Ben-Chaim, Michael, 375
Bender, John, 296, 298, 415n20, 432n2; "Novel Knowledge: Judgment, Experience, Experiment," 29, 32
Benhamou, Paul, 270
Beniger, James, 66
Benjamin, Walter, 367; "Theses on the Philosophy of History," 77
Berkeley, George, 70, 437n7; *An Essay towards a New Theory of Vision*, 73
Berlin, Isaiah, 174
*Berlinische Monatsschrift*, 2, 189, 192, 195–96, 198, 199, 316
Bernard, Claude, 284
Bernays, Edward L.: *Crystallizing Public Opinion*, 57
Berthier, Pierre, 268
Beyerlinck, Laurentius, 141, 158, 422n6, 425n40
Bhabha, Homi K., 192, 196, 262; "'Race,' Time and the Revision of Modernity", 205
Bhargava, Rajeev, 435n1
biblical concordances, 154
Biester, Johann Erich, 195, 196
*Bildung*, 309, 314
Black Panthers, 103
Blackwell, Thomas: *Enquiry into the Life and Writings of Homer*, 239–40
Blair, Ann: "Mediating Information, 1450–1800," 10, 26, 429n11
Blair, Hugh, 240, 241, 251; concept of "oral edition," 260; "Critical Dissertation Upon the Poems of Ossian," 242, 258, 260, 429n23
Blake, William: *Jerusalem*, 165, 166
Blanning, T. C., 303, 433n3
blind man, topos of in seventeenth- and eighteenth-century epistemology, 69
Bloch, Ernst, 195
Bonner, Thomas, 146
booksellers: denunciation of reprinting, 305; fairs and barter, 307

book trade: regulation of, 305. *See also* reprinting
Borges, Jorge Luis, Chinese encyclopedia, 80
Boston Committee of Correspondence, 25; as agency for conducting revolution, 105–6; and colonial-actor network, 116–18; as communications interface, 107–11; exploitation of eighteenth-century media, 106–7; protocols, 111–14; rewriting of petition as declaration, 111–14
Boston pamphlet. *See The Votes and Proceedings of the Town of Boston* (Edes and Gill)
Boston Port Bill, 105
Bouwsma, William, 232
Bouza, Fernando, 144
Bowker, Geof, 32–33
Boyle, Robert, 149, 291–92, 423n21, 423n22
Bradford, William, 144
Braille, 67
Brewster, David, 320
Bridenbaugh, Carl, 108
British American newspapers, 106–7
British Postal Bill of 1710, 12
broadside ballad singing, 243–44, 249
Broman, Thomas, 309
Brown, Mrs. (informant), 253–54, 430n11
Brown, Richard D., 106, 108
Bryon, George Gordon: *Don Juan*, 165
Bryson, Norman: *Word and Image: French Painting of the Ancien Régime*, 280
*Buchhandlungsgesellschaft* (society of booksellers), 308–9
Burke, Edmund, 22, 184, 311; *Philosophical Enquiry*, 394–95
Burnett, James: *The Origin and Progress of Language*, 245
Burns, Robert, 251, 431n17
Bush, G. W., Administration's "National Security Strategies," 337

Cabinet noir, 358, 366, 367
Calepino, Ambrogio, dictionary, 159, 426n46
Campbell, George: *The Philosophy of Rhetoric*, 50–51
Cape of Good Hope, 30
capitalism, imperialism and inherent law of, 328–29
cardinal mediations, 12–15, 16
Carey, Daniel, 21, 416n21
Carey, James, 124
Carey, Matthew, 307
Cartwright, Thomas, 372
Casanova, Pascale: *Le République Mondiale des Lettres*, 263
Cassirer, Ernst, 77
Castells, Manuel, 61
Catholic Church, doctrine of oral tradition, 238–39
*Cato's Letters*, 13
Cave, Edward, 15
censorship, 315, 316, 317; in French publishing, 304; moral, of mass media, 358; of *philosophes*, 268; prepublication, in Britain, 234; of press in India, 213
Chakrabarty, Dipesh, 225
Chambers, Ephraim: *Cyclopedia*, 15, 16–17
Chamousset, Claude Humbert Piarron de, 366, 367
chance, 360
Chandler, Alfred D., 110
change: Bacon's hierarchy of, 6; and collections of notes, 141; of concepts, 87; and Enlightenment, 11, 174, 191, 288; in knowledge, 288–89; in language, and demise of rhetoric, 39; and mediation, 5, 11, 20, 172; from naive religiosity to modernity, 183; from petition to declaration, 112; printing press and, 244, 245–46; in readers, 13
channel, 59
Chapuis, Alfred, 77
Charles I, 12

Charles II, 12, 115
Chartier, Roger, 23, 86, 191, 305, 428n4, 433n3
Chatterjee, Partha, 210
Chaucer, Geoffrey: *Treatise on the Astrolabe*, 53
Cheesman, Tom, 247, 248
Child, Francis James: *English and Scottish Popular Ballads*, 255, 261, 431n20
Cicero: *Philipics*, 349
cinematography, 66
Clanchy, M. T., 33
clarity, norm of, 50, 51
Clark, Robert Thomas, 312
Clark, William, 21, 416n21
classification, 82
Clifford, James, 251
clock, metaphor of, 76
close listening, 261, 264
close reading, 250, 264; balladeering protocols of, 256–62; calls to ban, 262–63; versus distant reading, 256
clubs, 13, 234, 235
Cobbett, William: *Paper Against Gold*, 333–34
code, 51
coffeehouses, 12
coins, 324
Coleridge, Samuel Taylor, 170, 427n9; and authentic self, 175; critiques of contemporary culture, 320; "The Eolian Harp," 180; "Frost at Midnight," 27, 177, 178–82; and future of Enlightenment, 169; and "stranger" trope, 177, 182
collaborative composition, methods of, 153–63
colonial space, 206, 207, 210
Comenius, John Amos, 375
commerce, cosmopolitan right to, 352–53
"committee speak," 112
communication, 4; as challenge to rhetoric, 40; and empathy, 427n1; and linguistics, 58; meaning in premodern English, 43; meaning of in *Oxford English Dictionary (OED)*, 43, 44; oral, model of, 203–4; versus persuasion, 39; protocol, 110; in sense of speech or discourse with oneself, 42, 43; six constituents of, 59; and state power, 358; technology, 47, 66; versus transmission, 103–4. *See also* oral communication; oral tradition; writing
communication studies, 55
communication theory, 56
compilations, 140–48; anonymous contributors, 158–59, 160; collaborative composition, 153–63; finding devices, 148–53; and inadequacy of modern concept of authorship, 159–60; use of slips of paper, 154–55, 159
computer: and human perception, 66; metamorphosis, 10; networked, and issues of copyright, privacy and access, 110
computer culture, meaning of interface in, 110–11
concept: changes, 87; definition of, 88; epistemological architecture of, 89; load-bearing, 91–97, 174–75; and relation to words, 59; temporal contingency, 100–101; use of word within humanities, 88–89
conceptual referentiality, 67
Condillac, Etienne Bonnot de: and automation of cognition, 75–76; consciousness as after-effect of perception, 71; definition of touch, 73; humanoid statue and urge to know, 78–79; information as result of operations beginning with sensation, 72, 75; knowledge as product of abstractions leading to habits and general ideas, 75; mechanistic ontology, 76; *Traité des Sensations*, 71–76
Condorcet, Nicolas de, 39, 41, 305; *L'Esquisse d'un tableau historique des progrès de l'esprit humain* (Sketch for a Historical Picture of the Progress of the Human Mind), 38, 202; mathe-

Condorcet, Nicolas de (*continued*)
matical probabilistic thinking, 299;
printing as undermining the art of
persuasion, 38, 245–46; *Sketch for a
Historical Picture of the Progress of
the Human Mind*, 245; universal print
culture as vehicle of Enlightenment,
204–5; vision of authorless public
realm, 309
Congar, Yves, 154
conjectural historians, 244, 245, 246
"The Consequences of Literacy" (Goody
and Watt), 230
contrived experiment, 29, 292, 294
conversation poems, 187
Cooper, James Fennimore, 128
Cooper, William, 111, 420n19
copyright, 14–15, 29; and networked
computer, 110
*La correspondance littéraire*, 272, 274
Cortada, James W., 110
cosmopolitan right of commerce, 351–53,
355; cosmopolitan universalism, 30;
present, 192; public, 314; society, 204
Cotta, Johann, 319
Cowan, Brian William, 12
Crain, Patricia, 421n31
Cranmer, Thomas, 373
Crary, Jonathan, 68, 81, 85, 420n3; shift
from classical to modern model of
perception, 65–66; *Techniques of the
Observer*, 65
creativity, 302; and authentic self, 175;
and genius, 176; invention of, 318–20;
and *Naturphilosophie*, 307; and reprinting process, 310
credit, 324, 325–26; "gilt-edged securities,"
326; "running notes," 325
*Critical Review*, 15
critique: ideology, 7, 62; and Kant, 3
Crow, Thomas, 276
cultural dispersion, 303
cultural nationalism, 249
culture of memory, 240, 246
*Cyclopedia* (Chambers), 15, 16–17

Daniel, Jean, 198
Darnton, Robert, 23, 191, 303
Daston, Lorraine, 88, 299
data mining, 359–60
Davenant, William, revision of Shake-
speare's *The Tempest*, 390
Davidson, Donald, 88
Davis, Edward B., 149
Davis, Leith, 164, 422n11
Dear, Peter, 70, 299, 432n6; *Discipline
and Experience*, 289
De Bolla, Peter, 174; "Mediation and the
Division of Labor," 7, 24
Debray, Régis, 67, 103–4
declaration: of Boston Committee of
Correspondence, 111–14; popular,
new genre of, 119
deconstruction, 264
Décultot, Elisabeth, 150
Defoe, Daniel, 13, 285, 294; problems of
historicity, 402; *Robinson Crusoe*, 32,
295–96, 298, 398, 399–400; *A True
Relation of the Apparition of Mrs.
Veal*, 293–94
Delaporte, Joseph, 268
delay, between Bacon and start of Enlightenment, 11, 12, 17, 25
Derrida, Jacques, 55, 58, 192; "Sign,
Event, Context," 193; and writing,
418n12
Desai, M. V., 212
Descartes, René, 76; *Dioptrics*, 69–70,
73; *Discourse on the Method*, 77; *Le
Monde, ou Traité de la lumière*, 70;
similarities between visual and tactile
perception of world, 69–70; on "the
animal machine," 77
*Deutsche Gelehrtenrepublik*, 310
dialectic: of arts and sciences, 385, 386–
89, 391–96, 412; between eighteenth-
century antiquarianism and enlightenment, 249–50; of mediation, 53–56,
413n13, 415n13, 417n6, 417n7; of oral
tradition and print, 28, 246; of Scholasticism, 5

Diderot, Denis, 70, 305, 432n2; aesthetic interpretation transposed from object to subjective experience, 275; as art critic, 274–79; attitude toward press, 432n2, 432n3; confrontations with political and religious factions, 267; critique of linguistic abstraction, 280; description of era as devoid of morality and education, 273; and ekphrastic language, 280–82; *Encyclopédie* article "Androïde," 78; *Encyclopédie* article "Hebdominaire," 272; *Encyclopédie* article "Journaliste," 271–72; *Encyclopédie* project, 16, 20, 28–29, 158, 163, 266–68, 426n42; imagined physical entry into paintings, 275–79; *Jacques le fataliste et son maître*, 78; *Philosophical Thoughts*, 78; *Promenade Vernet*, 275–79; *Rameau's Nephew*, 268–70, 272–74, 277, 280; on role of philosopher, 266–67, 281; *Salons*, 274–75, 279; tension between participation in and withdrawal from society, 265–66; transfer of philosophical activities to art, 282; universalist program for Enlightenment with idea of social usefulness, 267

Dienst, Richard, 214

Digges, Thomas, 107

digital images, 121, 122

digital media, 19, 261, 302

digital mutation, 414n8

digital retroaction, 110

disciplinarity and disciplines, 21, 26, 33, 164, 170–72, 284; aesthetic as autonomous discipline, 384; and analysis of American Revolution, 419n2; cultural, domination by language paradigm, 60; cultural, undertheorization of concept of mediation, 60; development of linguistics as discipline, 57; discipline of anthropology, and "denial of coevalness" of coexisting peoples, 429n22; discipline of scientific method, 300; geography as emerging discipline, 416n22; historical disciplines, and word "concept," 88; interest in ballads across discipline, 250; mediation between and across disciplines, 88; notion of mediation between disciplines, 89; and rise of printing, 28

discursive novel (*Diskursroman*), 193

disestablishment, 367

dissemination, 37

dissenting preachers, oral appeal to masses, 237–38

distance: of communication, 7, 46, 48, 50; between event and enunciation, 192, 206–8; and possibility of media, 62; writing as technology for overcoming, 48

distantiation, imaginative, 392–93, 394, 395

distant reading, 256, 264

division of labor, 24; and concept of counting separate from material counted, 100; as load-bearing concept, 91, 93; and modern concept of economy, 100; as preconceptual, 95; throughout antiquity, 98

Dodsley, Robert: *The Art of Preaching, in Imitation of Horace's Art of Poetry*, 376–78; *The Toy-Shop*, 376

Dominicans, compilations, 154

*Donaldson vs. Becket*, 311

Dondaine, Antoine, 142

Doniger, Wendy, 223

doubling, 180, 181, 187

Douglass, Frederick, 103

Drake, William, 142, 143

drama: doctrine of two unities, 390–91, 397, 402; and elevation of arts to status of quasiscientific knowledge, 389–97; new standard of empirical truth, 390–91, 397, 402; techniques of representation, 396

Drexel, Jeremias, 143, 148–49, 150

Droz, Edmund, 77

Dryden, John: *Of Dramatic Poesy, and Other Critical Essays*, 387–88, 390–91; revision of Shakespeare's *The Tempest*, 390
Dubos, Jean-Baptiste, 19
Dugaw, Dianne, 430n4
Dutch East India Company, 30, 329; Council of Seventeen, 336; "fortified refreshment station" at Cape of Good Hope, 338–39; as joint-stock corporation, 338; licensed monopoly, 346. *See also* Van Riebeeck, Jan

Eco, Umberto, 55, 416n2
Edelstein, Dan, 19
Edes, Benjamin, 108
education, and emulation, 311
Edwards, Jonathan, 376; *Some Thoughts concerning the Present Revival of Religion in New England*, 379–82
Eisenstein, Elizabeth, 191; *The Printing Press as an Agent of Change: Communications and Cultural Transformations in Early-Modern Europe*, 231–33, 244
electronic communication, 10, 19, 120–25, 230, 231, 262
Eliassen, Knut Ove: "Where were the media before the media? Mediating the world at the time of Condillac and Linnaeus," 1, 6, 24
Elibank, Lord: "Essay on Paper-Money and Banking," 334–35, 336
Elliott, Jacob, 115
Ellsworth, Annie, 122
elocution movement, 241–42
e-mail, 62
embedded systems, 168–70
emergence, 166, 415n19
empiricist novel, 290–98, 299–300, 407
emulation, 311, 315. *See also* imitation
*Encyclopædia Britannica*, 159
*Encyclopedia of the Enlightenment*, 174
encyclopedias, 142
*Encyclopédie*, 16, 22, 26, 150; authorial credit, 158; banned from further publication, 274; entries for "Philosophe," "Journaliste," and "Gazete," 271–74, 432n3; and historical development of public sphere, 270; hostile reception of, 266, 267–68, 270; symbolic importance to national prestige, 268
English East India Company, 146
English Parliament, *arcana imperii* of, 144–45
ENIAC, 10
Enlightenment: aesthetic mediations, 384–412; cardinal mediations, 12–15, 16; and change, 11, 174, 191, 288; Coleridge on future of, 169; and concept of division of labor, 87–101; critiques of, 173–74; delay between Bacon and start of, 9, 11, 12, 17, 25; dialectic between eighteenth-century antiquarianism and, 249–50; Diderot's universalist program for, 267; and differing uses of technology of writing, 172; distinctiveness of this volume's approach to, 22; and early modern information technologies, 139–63; and erasure of history of money, 323–35; as event in history of mediation, 1–12, 18–20, 20, 22–23, 26, 29, 37, 185; as experiment in mediation, 102–18; Foucault's view of, 7, 8, 118, 189, 192, 196–99, 204; in France, 174; and gender, science, and the postcolonial, 21–22; and Habermas' shift in study of, 22, 23; Herder's vitalist vision of, 314–15; historically locatable, 172; Kant's essay on, 4, 7, 164, 172, 189, 192, 209, 316; and knowledge strategies of the self, 173–88; and law/money/violence nexus, 336–56; and "media shift," 229–46; and mediation of Boston Committee of Correspondence, 105–18; mediation of novelistic knowledge, 284–300; and mediation of oral and print cultures, 247–64; mediations in communication, 37–

63; mediations in religious practices, 368–83; as period and as thematic designation, 8, 190; and piracy, 301–20; and point of saturation, 11, 19–21; in postcolonial India, 210–25; and post-Enlightenment media, 64–86, 120–35; "radical," 303; role of *les philosophes* in, 265–83; Scottish, 167–68, 249; self-ending, 11, 20; and state role in policing communications media, 357–67; and systems, 164–72; temporality, 190–91; and universal communicative present, 189–208; universal print culture as vehicle of, 204–5

*episteme*, 5

epistemology: of the aesthetic, 384–85, 396; classical, 82; of concept, 89; of division of labor, 92–101; and doubt, 286; dramatic, 397, 402; empirical, 32, 284–90, 389, 390, 391, 396, 406, 410; of the Enlightenment, 335; of mediation, 86; narrative, 398; of piracy, 304, 306; and taxonomy, 75; topos of blind man, 69; of what constitutes objects of experience and knowledge, 362

*esprit de système*, 76

"esprit philosophique," 18–19

evangelicalism, 368

evangelical preaching, 31; adjustment to public-sphere norms, 380, 383; Anglican parish preaching, 372; authoritative discourse model, 379, 380; *Certain Sermons* (Book of Homilies), 372–73, 436n7; conversionistic, 382–83; experimental, 371–72; preacher's footing, 369, 370–71, 381; preaching as subject of, 371–72; privatization of hearing, 375–76; Puritan, 374–75; spiritualized conception of, 373; split between preacher as author and as animator of speech, 374; versus talking, 380–82. *See also* literary sermon

evangelical reformed tradition, 372; complaints about reading of sermons, 373–74; congregational note taking, 375; sermonizing practice in, 31, 374, 375

evangelical revivals, 30, 31, 369, 382

event, 64, 77, 82, 268; American Revolution as, 102–5; description, and reading, 191–93; distance between event and enunciation, 192, 205, 206–8; ending of Enlightenment as, 171–73; Enlightenment as event in history of mediation, 1–12, 11, 18–20, 22–23, 26, 29, 37, 185, 199; experiments as, 289; media event, 77, 86, 104, 195–97; philosophy as, 189; and study of probability, 415n15; "What Is Enlightenment?" as media event, 195–97

exchange value, 410–11

exclusive humanism, 183, 184

*Expedition* (merchant ship), 146

experience: earlier meanings of, 288; English and French meanings of, 288; experiment-based, 294–98, 389; new paradigm of, 288–89

experiment, 289; contrived, 29, 292, 294; French extension of meaning of, 288; in literature, 398, 407–8; methodical exploitation of experience, 389; as model for drama, 390; and natural philosophy, 32, 286; with new methods for storing, retrieving, and disseminating information, 139; novel and, 284–86, 290; as planned experience, 289–90; Robert Boyle's, 291–93; Royal society's, 289; scientific, 388

*experimentum crusis*, 292, 294

Fabian, Johannes, 251, 429n22

Fastrup, Anne: "Mediating *le philosophe*—Diderot's Strategic Self-representations," 28

Ferguson, Adam: *Essay on the History of Civil Society*, 244

Festa, Lynn M., 21, 416n21

Feuerbach, Ludwig, 319

Fichte, Johann Gottlieb: "Proof of the Illegality of Reprinting," 318–19

Fielding, Henry, 285, 294; and doctrine of two unities, 404; *Joseph Andrews*, 404; *Shamela*, 403–4; *Tom Jones*, 286, 290–91
filing systems, 152–53, 424n30
film, 212
finance. *See* money
finding devices: alphabetical index, 141, 149, 150; and the decline of memory, 148–53; list of headings, 150
Finnegan, Ruth, 245
First Continental Congress, 105, 114
Fitzgerald, Cantor: "New Rules Sets Project," 354
Fleet, John, 108
Fleet, Thomas, 108
florilegia, 142, 150
Fontenelle, Bernard le Bovier de, 19, 361–62, 388; "Eloge de Monsieur d'Argenson, 362
footing: preacher's, 369, 370–71, 381; shift of, 371; of speaker and listener, 31
Ford, Andrew, 437n13
forgetting, 104, 335
form, 7, 56, 74–75, 164, 170–71, 186, 318–19
form and content, reflexivity of, 397, 403, 405, 407–8, 411
formats, extending reach of print and speech, 12
Foucault, Michel, 3, 7, 9, 27, 68, 76, 82, 85, 359, 414n7, 416n21, 435n3; and concepts, 88; and "discursive contemporaneity," 204; and enlightened citizens in West, 209; Enlightenment as current event, 7; Enlightenment as "ontology of the present," 192; Enlightenment as philosophical question, 8; *Histoire de la folie* (Madness and Civilization), 197; on Kant's view of Enlightenment, 190; *The Order of Things*, 65, 75, 80, 82, 86; on philosophy and journalism, 197–99; "Pour une morale de l'inconfort," 198–99; present as place of communication, 204; project to cast history as genealogy, 413n4; "Qu'est-ce que les Lumières?" (What Is Enlightenment?), 118, 189, 192, 196–99, 204; *Surveiller et punir* (Discipline and Punish), 197; and taxonomies, 75
*The Foucault Reader* (Rabinow), 196
"four-stages" theory. *See* stadial theory of history
Fox, Adam, 246
France: censorship in publishing, 304; encyclopedic system making, 20; Enlightenment, 174
Frankenstein syndrome, 8
Frankfurt book fairs, 308
Frankfurt school, 8–9, 30
franking, 106–7
Franklin, Benjamin, 371, 377; defense of plagiarism, 160–63; "Preface to the Declaration of the Boston Town Meeting," 113
Frederick II of Prussia, 2, 8, 308, 366
Frederick the Great, 201, 309, 360
Frederick William II, 317
Freemasons, 13
Frege, Gottlob, 55, 88
Fréon, Elie Catherine, 268, 269
Freud, Sigmund: "primal words," 385; and unconscious, 182
Fried, Michael, on *Promenade Vernet*, 275
Friedel, Robert, 120
Friends of Truth, Germany, 19
Furbank, P. N., 432n2

Gadgil, D. R., 210
Gallagher, Catherine, 294
gallery picture (*Kunstkammer*), 420n12
Galloway, Alex, 419n6
Galloway, Joseph, 114
Gandhi, Indira, 213, 214
Gassendi, Pierre, 143, 149
Gedike, Friedrich, 195
General Post Office (GPO), 12
Genette, Génette, 417n10

genius, science of, 310–13; Kant on, 315–16
genre: ballad collection as, 248, 252; declaration, popular, 106, 119; discursive novel, 193; extension of reach of print and speech, 12; limits of organization by, 160; of money, 30, 324, 335, 338; novel, 291, 293, 400, 404, 405; of "system," 19–20, 26, 164, 166, 172
Gentili, Alberico, 346; *De Jure Belli*, 348, 349
*Gentleman's Magazine*, 15
Gerard, Alexander, 311
German Republic of Letters, 310
Germany: age of genius (*Geniezeit*), 310–12; *Bildung*, 309, 314; debate about authorship, 309–10; reading mania, 309
Gesner, Conrad, 143, 154, 156
Giddens, Anthony, 61
Gigerenzer, Gerd, 299
Gill, Thomas, 108
Gitelman, Lisa: *Always Already New*, 248; "Modes and Codes: Morse and the Question of Electronic Writing," 10, 25–26
global theory and project of war, 354
glossary, 18
Goddard, William, 144
Godwin, William: *Caleb Williams*, 285–86
Goethe, Johann Wolfgang von, 253; and copyright law, 319; *Sorrows of Young Werther*, 302, 309
Goffman, Erving, 31, 428n6; "footing," 369, 370–71, 381; *Forms of Talk*, 370–71
goldsmiths, 325
Golinski, Jan, 21, 416n21
Goodman, Dena, 22
Goodman, Kevis, 431n14
Goody, Jack, 230, 232
Gordon, Thomas, 13
Gossart, Jan, 146–48, 152, 423n19
Gother, John, 238
Gothicism, 178, 180, 298

Gougeon, Len, 285
Grafton, Anthony: *The Footnote: A Curious History*, 253
gramophone recording technology, 67, 254
Gray, Thomas: *Elegy Written in a Country Churchyard*, 178
Great Awakening, 382
"Great Divide" model of orality and literacy, 243, 245
Great Telegraph Case, 132–35
Green, James N., 426n48
Greengrass, M., 424n22
Grell, Chantal, 424n27
Gresham's law, 325
Grimm, Friedrich-Melchior, 272, 274
Grotius, Hugo: *The Rights of War and Peace*, 30, 346–48, 349
Grub Street authors, 237
Guilllory, John, 414n5, 414n6; "Enlightening Mediation," 7, 24
Gustafson, Sandra, 436n3, 436n5

Habermas, Jürgen, 22, 23, 31, 183, 200, 357, 358, 433n3
Hacking, Ian, 88, 174, 299
Hall, Marie Boas, 149
Haller, Albrecht, theory of irritation, 313
Haraway, Donna Jeanne, 110
Harkness, Deborah, 414n10
Harrison, Thomas, 423n22
Hartley, David, 180
Hartlib, Samuel, 423n22
Havelock, Eric: "The Oral-Literate Equation: A Formula for the Modern Mind," 229–30, 232, 428n1
Hayes, Julie, 171, 414n9
Haywood, Eliza: *The Fair Hebrew*, 398
Hazlitt, William, 165
Hegel, Georg Wilhelm Friedrich: dialectic of mediation, 53–56, 415n13, 417n6, 417n7; *The Philosophy of History*, 415n13; *Science of Logic*, 417n6; use of *Vermittlung*, 53–54
Heimert, Alan, 375, 376

Helvétius, Claude Adrien, 287
Hemphill, Samuel, 160–62, 377
Henley, John, 241; *Oratory Transactions*, 15
Herder, Johann Gottfried, 85, 253, 310; concept of medium, 68–69; "living reading," 314; "On the Cognition and Sensation of the Human Soul," 313; on reprinting, 313–14; view of creative authorship, 312–13; view of genius, 312–13; vitalist vision of Enlightenment through education and reading, 314–15; *Vom Erkennen und Empfinden der menschlichen Seele* (On the Cognition and Sensation of the Human Soul), 68–69
Hesse, Carla, 305
Hewer, Will, 145
Hinske, Norbert, 196
historicity: of ballads, 256, 260; claim to, and drama, 397, 402; claim to, and early novel, 398, 402, 403–4; of concepts, 87; of media, 64–65, 67, 247, 248; of writing, 194
history: of ideas, 19, 238, 415n14, 419n2; media, 11; stadial theory of, 244–45, 249, 250, 430n24
history of mediation, 24–26, 414n11; and American Revolution, 25, 100–119; Enlightenment as event in, 1–12, 22, 23, 185; versus history of ideas, 8–11, 19; history of mediation, 415n13; versus media history and media theory, 11
Hobbes, Thomas: communication as rational discourse with oneself, 42, 43; derogation of print and letters, 42; *Leviathan*, 30, 41–43, 337, 338; and state, 342, 343; state of nature, 347, 354, 355, 399
Hobsbawm, E. J., 249
Hoffman, E. T. A.: "Der Sandmann," 85, 318
Hogarth, William, 310
Hogg, James, 251

Hogle, Jerrold, 427n7
Holmes, Oliver Wendell, 285
Home, Henry: *Sketches of the History of Man*, 244
Homer, 386; Odysseus as embodiment of "instrumental reason," 9; and oral tradition, 239–40
Hooke, Robert, 292, 388–89, 403, 409, 410, 424n27
Horace, 2, 3, 386
Horkheimer, Max, 9, 416n21
Howell, Wilbur Samuel, 416n1
Hoyle, Edmund, 299
Hudson, Nicholas, 239, 429n13
humanism, 197, 258, 413n4
humanist jurists, 344, 347, 348, 349, 350
human perception, new understanding of with advent of biology and psychology, 65
Humboldt, Wilhelm von, 319
Hume, David, 32, 70, 88, 95–96, 168, 249, 250, 287; on judgment, 295, 300; on Newtonian induction, 291, 293; and Quarrel of Ancients and Moderns, 406–7; *Treatise of Human Nature*, 288, 290, 291, 293
Hunter, Michael, 142
Hussein, Saddam, 354
Hutchinson, Thomas, 113

Illuminati, 303
illumination, 301
imagination: as aesthetic and empirical faculty, 393, 411, 412; distantiation, 392–93, 394, 395; power of, 363; reflexivity of, 397; and understanding, 391, 393, 406
imaginative reading, 393
imitation, 313; Enlightenment distinction between mechanical and intellectual, 127–29; and science of genius, 311, 312; *vs.* emulation, 315
imperialism: and inherent law of capitalism, 328–29; and money/law/violence cycle, 30, 343–54

improvement, 16
index card, 159
Indian advertising, 215–24; limitation of class perceptions, 216; *Times of India* advertisements, 217–24
Indian Independence, 27
Indian state, postcolonial: development of national television system, 214–15; Directorate of Advertising and Visual Publicity, 212; Directorate of Field Publicity, 212; Five-Year Plan Publicity programs, 212; miscommunication, 213–15; national development, 210–11; National Emergency of 1975–1977, 211, 213; nationalists, 210; near-simultaneous development of communicative infrastructure and political modernity, 225; publicity program, 212–13; regulation of media, 212; Second Five-Year Plan, 212; Shad Commission of Inquiry, 214; Third Plan, 212; treatment of communication as tool in state's plans, 211
indices, alphabetical, 149, 150
inductive reason, 6, 29, 184; Bacon and, 5, 292; Hume and, 291, 293; Newton and, 26, 292–93; in *Tom Jones* (Fielding), 290–91
"info lust," 143
information: body as junction for flows of, 81; conveyance of through communication, 44; electronic, 121, 124; flows, 67, 68; gathering and storing of by state, 144; management of, 148–53, 159, 163; overload, 151; processing, 66; as result of operations beginning with sensation, 72, 75; secret, 48; single-channel, 75; stockpiling of, 26, 139–48; transmission and communication of, 12, 24, 65, 85, 139, 301
information theory, 55, 59, 61
infrastructure, enabling transmission and communication of information, 12
inner stranger: mediation between soul and self, 175–88; trope of in Wordsworth's "Frost at Midnight," 186
Innis, Harold: *The Bias of Communication*, 55, 229
institution: state as, 361; theater as moral, 361; universities, 315, 320
intellectual clubs, 13
intellectual imitation, 127, 128–29
intellectual property, concept of, 162; as area of law after mid-eighteenth century, 320; and *Naturphilosophie*, 307
intelligence papers (*Intelligenzblatt*), 357
interface, 110; Boston Committee of Correspondence as, 107–11; meaning of in computer culture, 110–11; textual, 124; as zone of social possibility, 111, 419n5
intuition, 299, 300
iPhone, 10
irritation, theory of, 313
Israel, Jonathan, 78
Israel, Paul, 125

Jacobsen, Yngve: "Where were the media before the media? Mediating the world at the time of Condillac and Linnaeus," 6, 24
Jacourt, Louis de, 16
Jacquet-Droz, Henri-Louis, 77, 318
Jacquet-Droz, Pierre, 77, 318
Jakobson, Roman, 55, 57; "Linguistics and Poetics," 59–60; and poetic function, 59–60; six constituents of communication, 59
James, Elinor, 234
James, King, 18
Jameson, Fredric, 264
Jamieson, Robert, 250, 254; *Popular Ballads and Songs, from Tradition, Manuscripts, and Scare Editions*, 251
Jardine, N., 433n4
Jean Paul, 310; *Die Unsichtbare Loge*, 193–95, 204, 206, 207; *Hesperus oder die 45 Hundposttage* (Hesperus or the 45 dog-mail days), 195, 206–8; ideal of universal communicability, 204

Jeffrey, Francis, 165
Jevons, W. Stanley: *Money and the Mechanism of Exchange*, 331–33, 336
Johns, Adrian: "The Piratical Enlightenment," 29, 191, 232
Johnson, James: *The Scots Musical Museum*, 251, 261
Johnson, Samuel, 32; on Ossian poems, 256; *The Plays of William Shakespeare*, 408–9; on "theory," 168; use of slips to compose dictionary, 159; and value, 409–10, 411
Johnston, Patricia, 126, 128
Jones, William, 13
Jordheim, Helge: "The Present of Enlightenment: Temporality and Mediation in Kant, Foucault, and Jean Paul," 27
journals, ships, 146
*Le Journal de Trévoux*, 268, 272
judgment, English and French meanings of, 287–88, 300
Jungius, Joachim, 142, 143
*Jus Publicum Europaeum, annus mirabilis*, 338
just enemy (*justus hostis*), 348

Kagan, Robert: "Paradise and Power," 337
Kant, Immanuel, 2, 88; on authorship and Enlightenment, 317; versus Bacon, 2–4, 20; "Beantwortung der Frage: Was ist Aufklärung?" (An Answer to the Question: What Is Enlightenment?), 4, 7, 164, 172, 189, 192, 209, 316; call for general enlightenment, 2, 3, 20; call of the "self," 7; on censorship, 316; on creative genius, 315–16; *Critique of Judgment*, 191, 275; description of public sphere, 316; and discursive freedoms, 209; distinction between public and private use of reason, 200–202, 316; dream of perpetual peace, 354, 355; and mathematical sublime, 93; *Metaphysics of Morals*, 30, 317, 337, 351–53; model of oral communication, 203–4; notion of *Ausgang*, 190; "On the Wrongfulness of the Unauthorized Publication of Books, 316–18; on oral and written communication, 199–202; and piracy, 202–4; reprinting as ventriloquism, 317–18; on rights of state against unjust enemy, 351, 353–54; theory of international and cosmopolitan right, 351–54; and universal communicability, 191, 204; universal print culture as vehicle of Enlightenment, 204–5; use of phrase "*Sapere aude!*" 3, 19; user manual for Enlightenment, 3; "Von der Unrechtmäßigkeit des Büchernachdrucks" (On the illegality of the reprinting of books), 203–4; "What Is Enlightenment?" as media event, 195–97
"Kant et la modernité," *Magazine littéraire*, 196
Kempelen, Vargas, 77
Kernan, Alvin, 234, 236, 429n9
Keynes, John Maynard, 327; *Treatise on Money*, 329–30, 336
Keynesianism, 210
Kittler, Friedrich, 81, 85, 255, 418n14; *Optische Medien*, 66, 68
Klopstock, Friedrich, 310, 313
Klotz, Christian, 312
Knott, Sarah: *Women, Gender and the Enlightenment*, 21–22, 416n21
knowledge: access to, 14–15, 16; aesthetics as body of, 384; Bacon's call for "Great Renewal," 2, 6, 13, 20; change in during seventeenth century, 288–89; and *Encyclopédie*, 20, 267, 270; intuitive, 71; and mediation, 6, 8, 20, 32, 335; new paradigm as contextual, specific, and historical, 289–90; and print, 28, 29, 37–38; produced by novel, 286, 288–89, 300; questions about method and the nature of in modernity, 290; and sensations, 313; and system, 165, 170, 171, 172; transmission of, 40–52. *See also* information

Koselleck, Reinhart, 88, 191, 195, 357, 358, 361, 435n1
Kotzebue, August von, 319
*Kräfte* (vital powers), 312–13, 314, 315
Kramnick, Isaac, 16
Krause, J. S., 309
Kritzman, Lawrence D., 197
Kwakkel, Erik, 421n1, 422n12
Kyle, Chris, 144, 423n16

Labarre, Albert, 159
Lacan, Jacques, 358, 366
Laclos, Choderlos de: *Liaisons dangereuses*, 366
Lafitau, Joseph François: *Moeurs des sauvages amériquains*, 239
La Mettrie, Julien Offray de, 70; *L'Homme-machine*, 76; *The Natural History of the Soul*, 76; utopian rationalism, 76
Langan, Celeste, 256, 431n15
language: change in, and demise of rhetoric, 39–40; ekphrastic, 280–82; epic, 240; and footing, 371, 380; imagery produced by, 393; and mediation, 174; as medium of thought, 41, 50, 58–59; and memory, 42; of poetry, 51, 52; universal projects of, 46–47, 49
*La Petite-Poste Dévalisée*, 366
Latour, Bruno, 110; aversion to the modern, 65; *Pandora's Hope*, 64; semantic "abyss," 67; on work of the scientist, 82–83
law: Roman, 349
"lawless condition," 353
law/money/violence nexus, 30, 343–54
law of nature, violation of by those living outside of sovereign union, 346–50
law of war, 344, 355; carried by money, 342, 351; and concept of unjust enemy, 348–54; doctrine of reprisals, 345; extension of in extra-European spaces, 338; and global jurisdiction over law of nature, 346–50

Lee, Arthur, 117
Lee, Richard Henry, 117, 118, 419n5
Leibniz, G. W., 70, 75; *Monadology*, 78; notes, 149
Leipzig book fairs, 308, 319
Lemay, J. A., 437n12
Lennox, Charlotte: *The Female Quixote*, 286–87, 294, 299–300, 432n2
*Le Nouvel Observateur*, 198, 199
Le Prince, 275
Lerner, Daniel, 427n1
Lessig, Lawrence, 110
Lessing, Gotthold, 310, 361
letters, collections of, 142
*Leviathan and the Air-Pump* (Shapin and Schaffer), 291–92
Lévi-Strauss, Claude, 55; *Le pensée sauvage*, 230
liberty, tree of, 114–16
Licensing Act of 1662, 14, 234, 235
light waves, seventeenth century concept of transmission, 65
limited-term copyright, 14
Lincoln, Abraham, 103
Lindner, Burkhardt, 193
linguistics: and communication, 58; development of discipline of, 57
Linnaeus, Carl, 24, 75, 422n15; body as junction for flows of information, 81; economic limitations, 84; *Flora Lapponica*, 82; *Flora Uplandica*, 82; instruments of representation, 82; *Iter Lapponicum*, 79–85; measurement and classification, 82; and mobility, 83; *Systema Naturae*, 82; use of rod as instrument, 80, 81
literary sermon, 374, 376–83
load-bearing concept, 174–75; division of labor as, 91–97
Locke, John, 32, 287; *An Essay concerning Human Understanding*, 44; communication in social rather than physical sense, 44; conflation of speech and words, 44; conventionalist semiotics, 44–45; desire to communicate

Locke, John (*continued*)
without words, 45–46; empiricist epistemology, 389; *Essay concerning Human Understanding*, 70, 298–99, 406; on judgment, 295; "Memorandum on Licensing," 14; and perception as property of mind, 71; on probability, 298–99; *Second Treatise of Government*, 399; words as medium of thought, 50
logarithms, 69
Lomax, Alan, 255, 261
*London Gazette*, 12
long eighteenth century: and ballads, 429n20; mediations during, 22; relations of novel and system, 426n4; versus Romanticism, 164, 172
Looby, Christopher, 436n3
Lord, Albert, 229; oral theory, 260; *The Singer of Tales*, 231
Loughran, Trish, 436n3
Louvre, 276
"lumière, 19
Lycosthenes, Conrad, note slips in the hand of, 155

Macherey, Pierre, 263, 431n19
machine: and division of manufacture, 93–94; man versus, 4
Macpherson, James, Ossian poems, 240, 248, 250–51, 260, 430n3
magazines, as storehouses of previously printed materials, 15
*Magnum theatrum humanae vitae* (Beyerlinck), 141, 158
Maïer, Ida, 142, 419n1
Malcolm, Noel, 424n22
Malebranche, Nicolas, 424n27
Malesherbes, Guillaume-Chrétien de Lamoignon, 268
Mallarmé, Stephane, 51
Mandeville, Bernard de: and division of time, 100; *Fable of the Bees*, 97–99; and government regulation of production and commerce, 98; notion of division of manufacture, 98–99; and self-interest, 97–98
Mannerism, 315
Manning, Susan, 249
Manovich, Lev, 419n3, 419n5
man versus machine, 4
Marmontel, Jean-François, 272
Marshall, T. H., 224
mass literacy, 246
mass media, 65; moral censorship over reality, 358
master systems, 167–68
materialist psychology, 71
materiality, 181, 335, 338, 393; of the history of media, 67; of television, 214; of writing, 47, 194
mathematical sublime, 93
Mather, Cotton: *Manuductio ad Ministerium*, 374, 375
Mattelart, Armand, 76
Mayhew, Jonathan, 375
Mayr, Otto, 77
McDonough, John, 122
McDowell, Paula, 15, 249, xii; "Mediating Media Past and Present: Toward a Genealogy of 'Print Culture' and Oral Tradition," 28, 280, 430n5; "The Art of Printing Was Fatal," 429n18; "The Manufacture and Lingua-facture of *Ballad-Making*," 429n18, 429n20, 430n4; *The Women of Grub Street*, 429n7
McEachern, Jo-Ann E., 302
McGann, Jerome, 427n1
McKeon, Michael: "Mediation as Primal Word: The Arts, the Sciences, and the Origins of the Aesthetic," 29, 31–32, 275, 397, 415n13
McLane, Maureen: "Mediating Antiquarians in Britain, 1760–1830: The Invention of the Oral Tradition," 28, 429n18, 429n20, 430n24
McLaverty, James, 235

McLuhan, Marshall, 110, 170, 186, 358; on *The Dunciad*, 234, 235–36; *The Gutenberg Galaxy: The Making of Typographic Man*, 231; use of term "print culture," 230–31
means, and medium, 40–52
mechanical imitation, 127, 128–29
media: of artistic representation, 393; balladeering at conjunction of culture and, 247–50; digital, 19, 261, 302; and distance, 62; of eighteenth century, 357; and end of epistemology of mediation of eighteenth century, 86; historicity of, 64–65, 67, 247, 248; mass, 65, 358; and modernity, 67; and moral judgment, 359; new technology of, 25; print, and mediation as process arising from proliferation of media, 39, 414n12, 415n13; in study of earlier cultures, 65; as term to describe former arts, 57
media anthropology, 86
media ecology, 68
media event, 195–97
media history, 11
media shift, evolutionary models of, 28, 243, 244–46
media theory, 7, 11
mediation: antiquarian collectors as subjects and objects of, 252; Bacon's use of word, 6, 41; cardinal, 12–15, 16; and change, 5, 11, 20, 172; as concept in history, 24–26, 414n11; dialectic of, 53–56, 413n13, 415n13, 417n6, 417n7; and eighteenth-century literary-cultural disputes, 248; Enlightenment and Romanticism as different phases in history of, 185; Enlightenment as event in history of, 1–12, 20, 22, 23, 185; epistemology of, 86; historical hierarchy of, 11; history of, 24–26, 414n11; history of, and American Revolution, 25, 100–119; interaction over time, 10–11; "invisible," 186; and knowledge, 6, 8, 20, 32, 335; and language, 174; in Marxian and sociological theory, 54; and media, 61–63; and medium, 52–56; ontological priority of, 32, 33, 415n13; pre-media, 68–70; proliferating, 11, 15–19; and representation, 56–61; required for division of manufacturing process, 91; as result of shared discourse, 89; semiotic, 54–56; in sense of abstract process, 52–53; in sense of construction of picture of the mind in relation to the world, 53; in sense of dispute resolution, 52; as social construction, 174; between soul and self, 175–88; technological and the human, 10; and temporal shifts, 208; unconscious as act of, 182; as work done by tools, 5
medium: Bacon's use of, 6, 414n6; Herder's concept of, 68–69; light, and notion of, 37; and means, 40–52; and mediation, 52–56; mutation in concept of, 57; new conceptual analysis of in form of communication theory, 56; pre-nineteenth-century concept of, 65; print, and concept of medium of communication, 39
Meek, Ronald L., 245
Meinel, Christoph, 142, 143
Melanchthon, Philip, *151*–52
memory: and complexity, 72; culture of, 240, 246; decline of, and finding devices, 148–53; and language, 42; loss of, and reference works, 150–51; and money, 30; sciences of, 424n27
Mendelssohn, Moses, 2, 195
merchants' filing systems, 152–53
Mercier, Louis-Sébastien: *Tableau de Paris*, 31, 364, 365, 366, 367
mesmerism, 318
method: for Bacon, 5; inductive, 291; and the nature of knowledge, 290; scientific, 390

Metternich, Klemens Wenzel, Prince von, 319

Miles, Robert, 282, 427n4, 427n5; "Romanticism, Enlightenment and Mediation: the case of the inner stranger," 26–27

Mill, John Stuart: defining of poetry by comparison to oratory, 51; poetry written in disregard of communication, 52; "Thoughts on Poetry and Its Varieties, 51

Miller, Perry, 123–24, 128, 375, 376

Milton, John, 178

Minsheu, John, 159

Mirabelli, Domenico Nani, 141, 158

Mittwochsgesellschaft, 195, 196

modernity: and media, 67; questions about method and the nature of knowledge, 290; "splitting" of between event and enunciation, 205; state and art as opponents, 358–59

Molyneux's problem, 70, 74

Momigliano, Arnoldo, 249, 430n6

money: as "capital," 329; as carrier of law and law-sanctioned violence, 325, 337, 341–42; effacement of history of, 327–35; "fiat money," 334; genres of, 30, 324, 338; history of, periodized, 338; history of in England, 325–27; as mediator of value, 324; in modern commercial societies, 323–25; mystery of, 324–25; privilege of abstraction over historical accounts of, 328–35; as technology of transfer, 324. *See also* credit

Montenoy, Charles Palissot de: *Les philosophes*, 268

*Monthly Review*, 15

moral philosophy, 169, 290, 291, 407

More, Thomas: *Utopia*, 290

Moretti, Franco, 256, 262, 263–64; *Maps, Graphs, Trees*, 263

Morse, Samuel F. B., 120; anti-Catholicism, 126–27; dictionary, 130–31; *The Gallery of the Louvre*, 125–29, 420n19; and Great Telegraph Case, 132–35; "Key to the Pictures," *127*, 130; numerical signification, 130; original idea for telegraph, 129–30; 1837 patent caveat, 129, *130*; prototype of telegram machine, *126*; system of signs, 132; telegraphy, 25–26, 120–25, 129–35

Motherwell, William, 251, 261–62; *Minstrelsy, Ancient and Modern*, 243; theory of oral composition, 260

moveable type, 10

Napier, John, 69

Napoleonic Code, 319

nationalism, 210, 224

national tale, 248

naturalist fiction, 285

natural law, 359

natural philosophy, 13, 29, 32, 166, 286, 311, 312, 390, 396; experimental, 32, 286; Herder's vitalism, 312

Naudé, Gabriel, 143

Nehru, Jawahar-lal, 27, 211–12

networked computer, and issues of copyright, privacy and access, 110

Neuchâtel, 317

*The New Atlantis*, 290

New Criticism, 256, 264

New Deal, 210

*New Left Review*, 262–63

newspapers, 12–13, 106, 107

Newton, Isaac, 13; *experimentum crusis*, 292; induction, 26, 292–93; *Opticks*, 292; *Principia*, 166, 292; retreat from the popular, 167, 168; "Rules of Reasoning in Philosophy," 292; "The System of the World," 166–68

Nichols, Ashton, 176

Nicolai, Friedrich, 195, 302, 307, 316; *Sebaldus Nothanker*, 308

Nietzsche, Friedrich, 366

Nisbet, H. B., 190

notes, personal, collections of, 141–48; for common good of international Republic of Letters, 143; and "info lust," 143; as method of working out

personal values, 143; prime goal, 158; and printing, 142; ships' journals, 146; in shorthand, 145–46; slips in Zwinger's hand, *156*; slips stored in volumes, *157*; use of slips of paper, 154–55
Novalis, 319
novel: claim to historicity, 398; contrived situations, 294; controlling for time, space, and persons, 397–412; empiricist, 290–98; Gothic, 298; knowledge produced by, 288, 300; narrative aesthetic, development of, 402; "realism of assessment," 294–98, 300; realist, 403; reflexivity, 398; role in experimental natural philosophy, 286–87, 290, 400; surrogate observation, 292, 293; as system, 171; travel plots, 399

O'Brien, Karen, 174
*L'Observateur littéraire*, 268
Ockham's razor, 166
Ogborn, Miles, 329
O'Hara, James G., 149
Oliver, Peter: *Origin and Progress of the American Rebellion*, 105
Ong, Walter, 230, 232, 236; primary oral cultures, 428n1, 436n5; *Ramus: Method and the Decay of Dialogue*, 229; use of term "typographic culture," 231; writing and print modeled as one media, 231
ontological priority of mediation, 32, 33, 415n13
oral, rescuing: ballad revival, 242–44; elocution movement, 241–42
oral communication: increased emphasis on with spread of print, 236–38; model of, 203–4
oral culture, 246; primary, 428n1, 436n5
oral-formulaic theory, 240
orality and literacy, "Great Divide" model of, 243, 245, 246; origins of, 229–30
oral tradition: and appearance of anachronisms, 258; as authenticating source and archival domain, 253; eighteenth-century concept of, 28; ethnographic concept of, 239–40; in the printed ballad collection, 254; theological concept of, 238–39
oratory, pulpit, 237–38, 241
organicism, 314, 315, 320
organization: of the Bible, 139; of *Encyclopédie*, 20; of experience, 231; of genre, 160; of information, 153; of manufacturing process, 91; social, 346, 347, 353
orrery, 303
Ossian poems, 240, 248, 250–51, 260, 430n3
Outram, Dorinda, 416n21
*Oxford English Dictionary* (*OED*), and meaning of "communication," 43, 44
*Oxford Gazette*, 12

Paine, Thomas, 22
Palmer, Norman D., 214
pamphlets, eighteenth-century, anonymous and pseudonymous publication, 107
paper, 142, 421n1
paradox of access, 19
Parmentier, Richard J., 417n9
Parry, Milman: *L'Épithète traditionnelle dans Homère*, 229; and oral-formulaic workings, 240; oral theory, 260
Parsons, Jonathan, 375
party political papers, 13
Pasteur, Louis, 64, 82
Pastorius, Francis: *Francis Daniel Pastorius, His Alphabetical Hive of More than two thousand Honey-combs Begun in the year 1696*, 152
patents, Franklin's rejection of, 162
Patrick, Bishop: *A Discourse of Profiting by Sermons*, 374
Pauli, Joachim, 308
Peacey, Jason, 144, 423n16
pedagogy, 320; imitative, 315; and science of genius debate, 311

Peirce, Charles Sanders, 53, 417n9; concept of representation, 55–56; definition of sign, 55; and semiotic mediation, 54–56
Peiresc, Nicolas Fabri, 143–44, 149
Pepys, Samuel, 145
Percy, Thomas, 257; "Essay on the Ancient Minstrels in England," 242; idealized narrative of oral poet, 243; *Reliques of Ancient English Poetry*, 242, 251, 252, 254, 256
periodicals, 13; magazines as storehouses of previously printed materials, 15; newspapers, 12–13, 106–7
periodization, 172
persuasion, 24, 37, 38, 39, 40
Peters, John Durham, 65, 120, 124
Petite-Poste, 366–67
Petty, William: *Political Arithmetic*, 98
phatic utterance, 59, 60
Philadelphia Committee of Correspondence, 113
Philip II, 144
Philip IV, 144
Phillips, Mark Salber, 249
*les philosophes*: discourse on the press, 271–72; promotion of Enlightenment through publication of knowledge, 266; response to criticism, 270, 432n2
*Philosophical Works* (Bacon), Shaw edition, 17–18
philosophy: moral, 169, 290, 291, 407; natural, 13, 29, 32, 166, 286, 311, 312, 390, 396
photography, 66
Pinkerton, John, 250, 254, 257; formal definition of "ballad," 260; *Scottish Tragic Ballads, with a Dissertation on the Oral Tradition in Poetry*, 242–43, 260; works on Scottish national song, 251
piracy. *See* reprinting (piracy)
*Pirates, The*, 310
plagiarism, Franklin's defense of, 160–63
Plato, 40

Pliny, 143
Plutarch: comparison of good reader to bee, 151; *Moralia*, 161
police: data mining service of, 359–60; as origin of literary, 363–64; as transcendental subject, 363
police chief, 31
political parties, 13
*Politics, Philosophy, Culture* (Kritzman), 197
Poliziano, Angelo, 142
Pollard, Alfred W., 160
*Polyanthea* (Mirabelli), 141, 158
Poovey, Mary, 29–30, 246, 336, 337, 338, 356; "Financing Enlightenment," 14, 29–30; *Genres of the Credit Economy*, 325
Pope, Alexander: *The Dunciad*, 233, 234, 235–36, 237–38; *Peri Bathous: Of the Art of Sinking in Poetry*, 411
popular declaration, new genre of, 119
popular sovereignty, 115
*Portrait of a Merchant* (Gossart), 146–48, 147, 152
postal principle, 14
postal service, 12, 358, 366
postcolonial. *See* Indian state, postcolonial
postcolonial criticism, 205
*Postcolonial Enlightenment* (Carey and Festa), 21
poststructuralism, 55
power: of imagination, 363; knowledge and, 5; of print, 10
preacher's footing, 369, 370–71, 381
Price, Richard, 22
Priestley, Joseph, 184
print culture, 246; eighteenth century as turning point, 233–35; origins of term, 230–33, 236
printed forms, 144
printed matter, complexity of distribution and circulation of, 203, 204
printing: back formation of the "oral," 15; and concept of language use for com-

munication rather than persuasion, 39; effect on social life beginning in eighteenth century, 234, 236; in eighteenth century, 302; and mediation arising from proliferation of media, 39, 414n12, 415n13; mediation of oral materials, 254–56; and pluralized concept of medium as "media," 39; spread of, and increased emphasis on oral communication, 236–38, 243; and stockpiling of personal notes, 142; as universal medium in 1800, 256
print media, proliferation in quantity and kinds of, 28
print technology, 10
probability, 298–300
proliferating mediations, 11, 15–19
*Promenade Vernet* (Diderot), 275–79, 281; aesthetic experience as disinterested pleasure, 277; allegory of philosopher's withdrawal from public debate, 277; Diderot's imagined physical entry into paintings, 275–79, 281; isolation of art from public space, 276; philosopher's feeling of moral integrity and virtue, 278–79; subjectivity and intimacy of universal man, 283
proposition, 82
protocols, 419n6; Boston Committee of Correspondence, 111–14; of close reading in balladeering, 256–62; communication, 110; enabling constraints, 14–15
Providential Deism, 183, 184–85, 186
Prussia, commitment against reprinting, 319
public credit, 14
public houses, 12
publicity program, of Indian state, 212–13
public opinion, 202–3
public relations, 57
public sphere, 200, 357; development of, 270; Diderot and, 265, 275, 279, 280, 282; Kant's description of, 316; and private sphere, 183, 357–58
public sphere studies, 23
publishing, modern system of, 302
puppets, 77–78
Puritans, and preaching, 374–75
Pygmalion, 78

Quedenbaum, Gerd, 422n7
Quesnay, François, 75
*Qwœrenda*, 84

Rabinow, Paul, 196
Rajagopal, Arvind: "Enlightenment in India," 10, 27
Rajan, Tilottoma, 181
Rancière, Jacques, 94
Rantzau, Heinrich, 158
Ranzovius, Henricus, 425n40
Raven, James, 234
Raymond, Joad, 68
readers, change in, 13
reading, 10, 393
realism: formal doctrine of the novel, 402, 404; link to scientific inquiry, 285
"realism of assessment," 294–98, 299
reason, private use of, manifested orally, 201–2
reason, public use of, mediated by writing and print, 200, 201, 204
Reddick, Allen Hilliard, 159
Redekop, Benjamin W., 310
Reed, Joseph, 118
reference works: and loss of memory, 150–51; need for finding devices, 149; notes, 141
reflexivity: in empiricism of philosophy, 407; of Fielding's *Joseph Andrews*, 404; of form and content, 397, 403, 405, 407–8, 411; of the imagination, 397; of the novel, 398; self-reflexivity, 3
regime of copyright, 14–15
Reich, Philipp Erasmus, *Buchhandlungsgesellschaft* (society of booksellers), 308–9

Reid, Thomas, 293
Reill, Peter Hanns, 315
Renaissance writers: collections of letters, 142; collections of personal notes, 141, 143; interest in code, 48
renewal, problem of, 5
*reportationes*, 141
representation, 7, 41, 418n16; Addison on, 392–93; dominance of in Western thought, 56; and signification, 62
reprinting (piracy), 29, 302–7; in America, 304; bartering (*Tauschsystem*), 308; book fairs, 308; cross-border phenomenon, 303; defense of, 305–6, 307–8, 309; Fichte on, 318–19; in France, 304; in German states, 304, 307–15; Herder's notion of, 313–14, 319; Kant on, 202–4, 317, 319; and mercantilism, 303, 306, 307; in Prussia, 319; in Scotland and Ireland, 304; as ventriloquism, 315–18. See also authorship
Republic of Letters, 143, 183
restricted copyright, 29
*Review of the State of the British Nation*, 13
revolution, 119
Reynolds, Joshua, 127, 129
rhetoric, 40; demise of, 38–39; semiotic view of, 416n2
Rhodes, Cecil, 329
Richards, I. A., 262
Richardson, Samuel, 285; *Clarissa*, 294, 295, 296, 366; *Pamela*, 32, 398, 400–401, 402, 403
Richetti, John J., 300, 433n18
Ridge, Oliver, 423n20
Rieuwerts, Sigrid, 247, 248
Ritson, Joseph, 250, 251, 257; close reading of ballads, 257, 258–59; controversy over ballad "Hardyknute," 257–58; "Historical Essay on Scotish Song," 253, 257; praise of Scottish music, 260
Ritter, Heinrich, 319

Robert, Hubert, 275
Robertson, William, 249; *History of the Discovery and Settlement of America*, 244; *A View of the Progress of Society*, 244
Robinson, John, 416n21
Rodgers, Gary Bruce, 432n3
Roman law, 349
Romanticism, 8, 19, 51, 427n1; arbitrary dating of, 164, 173; as bridge between Providential Deism and modernity, 185; call for expressive originality over imitation, 396; and concept of inner stranger, 173–88; versus Enlightenment, 164–66, 172; versus long eighteenth century, 164, 172; and system, 165–72, 426n1; theories of authorship, 307, 310, 319–20; and virtual realities, 185–86
Rouse, Mary A., 154
Rouse, Richard H., 154
Rousseau, Jean-Jacques, 184, 193; concept of *perfectibilité*, 190; *Essay on the Origin of Languages*, 240; *Nouvelle Héloïse*, 302
Royal Mail service, 12
Royal Scientific Society, Sweden, 83
Royal Society, 13, 17, 22; authorization of quantitative measure in natural histories and sea voyages, 398; new associational practices, 18
Ryerson, Richard Alan, 114

Sacra Congregatio de propaganda fide, 68
Said, Edward, 251
Saint-Réal, César Vichard: *Conspiracy of the Spaniards against Venice in 1618*, 360
"Sapere aude!" 2, 3, 19
Sapir, Edward, 59
saturation, 11, 19–21
Saussure, Ferdinand de: *Course in General Linguistics*, 58; model of communication, 57; theory of signification, 58, 59

Scaliger, Joseph Juste, 422n15
Schaffer, Simon, 21, 291–92, 293, 416n21
Schelling, Friedrich Wilhelm Joseph, 319, 320
Schiller, Friedrich, 31, 183; "The Police" ("Die Polizey"), 360–67
Schleiermacher, Friedrich: *Hermeneutics and Criticism*, 417n8
Schlesinger, Lee I., 214
Schmidt, James, 8, 118, 173, 190, 196, 320, 413n2
Schmitt, Carl, 117, 338, 346, 348, 349
Schneider, Manfred, 360, 435n4
Scholasticism, 5, 166, 292
"schools," division of writing into, 165
Schulte-Sasse, Jochen, 68
Schwan, Christian Friedrich, 308
science, post-positivist concept of, 21
*Sciences in Enlightened Europe, The* (Clark, Golinski, and Shaffer), 21
scientific corresponding societies, 13
scientific method, 390
Scott, Walter, 26, 170–72, 250, 253, 254, 257, 258; embedding of system into other forms, 170–71; literary-forensic methods, 260, 431n17, 431n18; *Minstrelsy of the Scottish Border*, 251, 252, 255, 259; records, 261
Scottish Enlightenment, 167–68, 249
"Scriblerus Club," 234, 235
secret police, 361
secret societies, 13, 196, 357, 361
secularization, 174, 182 85
Selement, George, 375
self, 26–27; and inner stranger, 175–88; Kant and, 2, 7; knowledge strategies of, 26; writing as expression of, 29
Selwyn, Pamela Eve, 302, 308
semiotics, 44–45, 54–56, 57, 416n2
Seneca Falls Declaration of Women's Rights, 103
sensation, and knowledge, 313
sensibility, 184
sermon. *See* evangelical preaching; literary sermon

Shadwell, Thomas: *The Virtuoso*, 390
Shakespeare, William, plays organized by genre, 160
Shanahan, John Henry, 437n6
Shannon, Claude, 59; "The Mathematical Theory of Communication," 418n13
Shapin, Steven, 158, 291–92, 293
Sharpe, Kevin, 142, 143
Shaw, Peter, 17–18, 415n18
Sheehan, Jonathan, 174
Shepherd, Thomas, 375
Sheridan, Richard Brinsley, 241
Sheridan, Thomas: *British Education*, 15; *Lectures on Elocution*, 241, 242
shorthand, 145–46
*Short-Title Catalogue of Books Printed in England, Scotland, and Ireland . . . 1475–1640*, 160
Sidney, Robert, 143
Siegert, Bernhard: "'The Horrifying Ties, from which the Public Order Originates': The Police in Schiller and Mercier," 30–31, 415n16, 420n3
signification, 58, 62; numerical, 130
Silverman, Kenneth, 123, 132
Simmons, R. C., 117
simplicity, 166–71
simplification through specialization, 170
simultaneity, and temporality, 193–95, 196, 206
Siskin, Clifford, 110; and genre of "system," 19–20, 26; "Mediated Enlightenment: The System of the World," 26
Skemer, Don, 425n30
Skinner, Quentin, 88, 89
Skydsgaard, Jens Erik, 150
Smellie, William, 159
Smith, Adam, 184, 304; *An Inquiry into the Nature and Causes of the Wealth of Nations*, 24; and division of labor, 24, 90–97; and improvement through mediation, 20; *Lectures on Rhetoric and Belles Lettres*, 244, 416n1; and master systems, 167–68, 172; notion

Smith, Adam (*continued*)
of excess or surplus, 96; and Scottish Enlightenment, 26, 167–68; stadial theory of history, 249; theory of exchange value, 96, 97; *The Theory of Moral Sentiments*, 168; *The Wealth of Nations*, 90–97, 168
Smith, Henry, 375
Smith, Pamela, 311
social contract (*contrat social*), 359
Society for the Friends of Truth, 3
Sombart, Werner, 358
Sonnenfels, Joseph von, 361
Soviet Union, 210
Spanish inquisition, recording of trials on printed blanks, 144
*Spectator, The*, 13, 243
*Speculum maius*, 154
Spinoza, Baruch, 78, 174
"Spirit of the Age," 165
Sprat, Thomas, 388, 389, 407, 408
St. Clair, William, 110, 327, 419n3
stadial theory of history, 244–45, 249, 250, 430n24
Stafford, Fiona, 430n3
Staiti, Paul, 125, 126, 128
Stallybrass, Peter, 423n18, 428n4, 429n11; "Mediating Information, 1450–1800," 10, 26
Starr, Paul, 25, 110, 236
state: and art, 358–59; guardian, 209, 210–14, 224; Hobbesian, 342, 343, 347; as institution, 361; right to make war, 351, 353–54
state institutions, role in gathering and storing of information, 144
Stationer's Company, 14, 234
Statute of Anne, 14
Steele, Richard, 13
Stenhouse, William, 261, 431n17
stereoscope, 66
Sterne, Laurence: and doctrine of two unities, 405; reflexivity, 405; *Tristram Shandy*, 405–7
Stewart, Dugald, 240, 244, 246

Stewart, Susan, 248
Stillinger, Jack, 178, 180, 427n8, 427n9
Stoddard, Solomon: *The Defects of Preachers Reproved*, 373
Stout, Harry, 374; "Religion, Communications, and the Ideological Origins of the American Revolution," 369–70, 436n5
Strachen, Michael, 146
street ballads, 249
structuralism, 55
*Sturm und Drang* movement, 314
stylistic norm, 50, 52
Suarez, Carl, 195
subject: antiquarian collectors as subjects and objects of mediation, 252; of Enlightenment, 200; and object, division of, 53–54, 69, 395, 406; police as transcendental, 363
sublime and beautiful, 394–95
subtraction stories, 184
surrogate witnessing, 29, 292
Swift, Jonathan, 233; critique of scientific inquiry, 298; *Gulliver's Travels*, 239, 297–98; on oral practices and mass manipulation, 237; *A Tale of a Tub*, 235–36, 237, 238–39
switching, 121
system, 164–65; embedding, 168–70; and history of Romanticism, 165–72, 426n1; in late eighteenth- and early nineteenth-century writing, 165; master systems, 167–68; new genre of, 19–20, 26; of the world, 166–68, 170–72
systems theory, 55

"table books," 146–48
Tatham, David, 420n12, 420n19
taxonomy, 75
Taylor, Barbara: *Women, Gender and the Enlightenment*, 21–22, 416n21
Taylor, Charles, 27, 174; *A Secular Age*, 182–85
*technê*, 5
technodeterminism, 10

technology: communication, 47, 66; gramophone recording, 67, 254; media, 25; money as, 324; for overcoming distance, 48; print, 10; wax-cylinder, 254; writing as, 48, 172
telegraphy, 10, 25–26, 66, 67, 120–25; first telegram, 123, 124; and restabilization of modern subject, 121; semiotic entity, 135; and writing, 124–25, 133–35
television, role in production of capitalist value, 214–15
temporality: of Enlightenment, 190–91; of "What is Enlightenment?" debate, 195–96
Tennent, Gilbert, 375, 377; *The Danger of an Unconverted Ministry*, 371–72
text-messaging, 62
textual interface, 124
theater: as institution of social control, 361, 365; and laboratory, 389–90
*Theatrum humanae vitae* (Zwinger), 141, 154
*This Is the Way a Writer Takes Revenge on Treacherous Pirates*, 310
Thomas, Keith, 246
Thompson, John B., 61, 418n15
Thoreau, Henry David: *Walden*, 285, 288, 432n1
Tillotson, John, 374, 378
time, saving of, 94–95
*Times of India* advertisements, as moral critique of market economy, 217–24, 219 22, 428n7
Toland, John, 303
*Tom Jones* (Fielding), 286, 290–91
tools: Bacon on necessity of, 4–5, 6, 7; finding aids, 148–53; mediation as work done by, 5, 16
totalitarianism, 201
touch, transformation of perception from passive receptivity to activity, 73
traditional mediation, invention of, 254–56
tragedy, 395
transcendental aesthetics, 362, 363, 365

translation, 204
transmission, 37, 62; versus communication, 103–4
Trattner, Johannes Thomas Edler, 303, 306, 307
Treadwell, Michael, 234
Treaty of Westphalia, 338
tree of liberty, 114–16
Trenchard, John, 13
trigonometry, 69
Trumpener, Kate, 248
Turnèbe, Adrien, 143
Twain, Mark, 171
typewriter, 67

unconscious, as act of mediation, 182
universal communicative present, 191–92; interruption by time lag of written communication, 207–8
Universal encirclement, 16
universality, 204–6
universal language theorists, 46, 48
*Universal-Lexicon* (Zedler), 141
University of Basel, contemporary records, 155
unjust enemy, 344–45, 348–54
Urania, 177
U.S. national security agencies, post 9/11, 30

Vail, Alfred, 123, 131–32, 133, 134, 135, 421n29
Valenze, Deborah, 327
value: mediation by instruments, 324, 335; qualitative and quantitative, 408–12
Van Riebeeck, Jan, 30; accounting to Lords Seventeen, 336–46; 1652–1660 balance sheet, *340*; establishment of credit system at the Cape, 339; extension of properties of sovereign state over noncitizens, 343–44, 346; "extraordinary expenditure" for year 1659, 344–45; station deficits, 341; war with unjust enemies, 344–45, 350

VanWinkle, Matthew, 181
Vaucanson, Jacques de, 77, 78, 312–13
Venkataraman, G., 212
ventriloquism, reprinting (piracy) as, 315–18
*Vermittlung*, 53
Vernet, Joseph, 275, 276
Villiers, George: *The Rehearsal*, 390
Vincent Placcius: *De arte excerpendi*, 155
violence, and money and law, 30, 343–54
Virgil, 386
virtual realities, English Romantic poets, 185–86
virtual witnessing, 291–92, 293
vitalism, 312–15
Vogl, Joseph, 359, 361
Voltaire, 70, 302, 366, 432n2
voluntary associations, 13–14
*The Votes and Proceedings of the Town of Boston* (Edes and Gill), 108–9, 111–14; articulation of liberty with popular sovereignty, 114–16; rewriting of petition as declaration, 111–14; and space for performance of political opinion, 113
Vygotsky, Lev, 59

Walpole, Horace: *Castle of Otranto*, 298
Walpole, Horatio, 18
Walsh, Marcus, 238
Walsham, Alexandra, 246
Walton, James, 433n11
war, law of, 338, 342, 344, 345, 348–54, 355
Warkentin, Germaine, 143, 424n28
Warner, Michael, 22; "The Preacher's Footing," 31, 232
Warner, William, 1, 414n8, 419n1, 419n3; "Transmitting Liberty: The Boston Committee of Correspondence's Revolutionary Experiments in Enlightenment Mediation," 1, 25
Warren, Mercy Otis: *History of the Rise and Progress and Termination of the American Revolution*, 105
Waters, Lindsay, 256

Watt, Ian, 230, 232, 294, 297, 299
Watt, James, 128, 132
Watts, Isaac: "The Adventurous Muse," 177
wax-cylinder technology, 254
Weaver, Warren, 418n13
Whig Kit Kat club, 13
Whigs, and transmission of liberty, 103–5
Whitefield, George, 237, 370, 372, 374, 376, 377
Whorf, Benjamin Lee, 59
Wieland, Christoph, 310
Wilkins, John, 46–50; and code, 48–50; *Essay towards a Real Character and Philosophical Language*, 47, 49; *Mercury, the Secret and Swift Messenger*, 48, 49–50; writing as medium of speech, 50; writing as technology for overcoming distance, 48
Williams, Raymond, 54, 61–62, 233, 417n5
Williamson, Judith, 427n5
Wills, Garry, 104
Withers, Charles W. J.: *Placing the Enlightenment*, 416n22
Wittgenstein, Ludwig, 59, 88
Wittmann, Reinhard, 433n4
Wolf, Caspar, 154
Wolf, F. A.: *Prolegomena ad Homerum*, 240
Wolfe, Heather, 153
Wolff, Christian, 70
Wollstonecraft, Mary, 22, 184
*Women, Gender and the Enlightenment* (Knott and Taylor), 21
Wood, Gillen D'Arcy, 185
Wood, Robert: *Essay on the Original Genius and Writings of Homer*, 240
Woodmansee, Martha, 309, 310, 433n4
Woof, Robert, 165
Woolf, Daniel, 246
Wordsworth, William, 26; on advantage of poetry over prose, 169; *An Evening*

*Walk*, 168; and authentic self, 175; *Descriptive Sketches*, 168; and dispersing of systems into other systems, 170, 172; "Expostulation and Reply," 169; "Frost at Midnight," 185–87; *Lyrical Ballads, with a Few Other Poems*, 169–70; and moral philosophy, 169; new poetic system, 185; "The Tables Turned," 169
world-system theory, 262–63
Wotton, William, 238
writing, 10, 13; as expression of self, 29; historicity of, 194; interruption of universal communication present, 207–8; materiality of, 47, 194; as mediator for public use of reason, 200, 201, 204; as medium of speech, 50; system of in late eighteenth- and early nineteenth-century, 165; as a technology, 48, 172; as technology for overcoming distance, 48; and telegraphy, 124–25, 133–35
"writing tables," 146–48
Wroth, Lawrence C., 144
Wulf, Andrea, 423n15

Yeo, Richard R., 159, 423n21, 424n27
Yolton, Jean S., 302
Young, Edward, 26–27, 175–88, 311, 312; *Conjectures on Original Composition*, 175–76; on Quarrel of Ancients and Moderns, 396

Zedelmaier, Helmut, 425n33
Zedler, Johann, 141
Zola, Émile, 295; "Le Roman Expérimental," 284–85
Zöllner, Friedrich, 195
Zouch, Richard: *Exposition of Fecial Law and Procedure, or of Law Between Nations*, 30, 337, 338, 346, 349–50
Zwinger, Theodor, 141, 424n24; and attribution of notes, 156, 158; *Theatrum humanae vitae*, 154, 155, 156, 158

www.ingramcontent.com/pod-product-compliance
Lightning Source LLC
Chambersburg PA
CBHW021230300426
44111CB00007B/488